Tolley's Discrimination in Employment Handbook

by

members of the Employment Department, *Baker & McKenzie LLP*

and

members of *Blackstone Chambers*

edited by Sarah Gregory LLB (Hons), solicitor, and Ellen Temperton BA (Hons), solicitor, partners, Baker & McKenzie LLP

with a foreword by Lord Lester of Herne Hill QC

LexisNexis®
Tolley

Members of the LexisNexis Group worldwide

United Kingdom	LexisNexis Butterworths, a Division of Reed Elsevier (UK) Ltd, Halsbury House, 35 Chancery Lane, London, WC2A 1EL, and London House, 20–22 East London Street, Edinburgh EH7 4BQ
Argentina	LexisNexis Argentina, Buenos Aires
Australia	LexisNexis Butterworths, Chatswood, New South Wales
Austria	LexisNexis Verlag ARD Orac GmbH & Co KG, Vienna
Benelux	LexisNexis Benelux, Amsterdam
Canada	LexisNexis Canada, Markham, Ontario
Chile	LexisNexis Chile Ltda, Santiago
China	LexisNexis China, Beijing and Shanghai
France	LexisNexis SA, Paris
Germany	LexisNexis Deutschland GmbH, Munster
Hong Kong	LexisNexis Hong Kong, Hong Kong
India	LexisNexis India, New Delhi
Italy	Giuffrè Editore, Milan
Japan	LexisNexis Japan, Tokyo
Malaysia	Malayan Law Journal Sdn Bhd, Kuala Lumpur
Mexico	LexisNexis Mexico, Mexico
New Zealand	LexisNexis NZ Ltd, Wellington
Poland	Wydawnictwo Prawnicze LexisNexis Sp, Warsaw
Singapore	LexisNexis Singapore, Singapore
South Africa	LexisNexis Butterworths, Durban
USA	LexisNexis, Dayton, Ohio

© Reed Elsevier (UK) Ltd 2008

Published by LexisNexis Butterworths

A CIP Catalogue record for this book is available from the British Library.

ISBN: 978 0 7545 3171 5

Typeset by Letterpart Ltd, Reigate, Surrey

Printed and bound in Great Britain by Antony Rowe Ltd, Chippenham, Wilts

Visit LexisNexis Butterworths at www.lexisnexis.co.uk

List of contributors

Members of Baker & McKenzie LLP

Virginia Allen BA (Hons), solicitor – Sex Discrimination (8)

Jastine Barrett LLM, BA (Hons) – Race Discrimination (6)

Alex Bird LLB (Hons), LLM, solicitor – Sexual Orientation (9)

Claire Bowles LLB (Hons), solicitor – Sex Discrimination (8)

Allison Brown BA (Hons), solicitor – Disability Discrimination (3)

Katherine Coleman BA (Hons), solicitor – Sex Discrimination (8)

Lily Collyer BA (Hons), solicitor – Gender Reassignment (4)

Victoria Costella LLB (Hons), solicitor – Race Discrimination (6)

Tessa Cranfield BA (Hons) (Oxon), solicitor – Common Concepts (1)

Eugenia Dunn BA (Hons), solicitor – Fixed-term and Part-time Workers (10)

Daniel Ellis BA (Hons) (Oxon), solicitor – Gender Reassignment (4)

Chris Garrett LLB (Hons), solicitor – Disability Discrimination (3)

Paul Harrison BA (Hons) (Oxon), solicitor – Age Discrimination (2)

Sarah Hickling BA (Hons), solicitor – Common Concepts: (2)

Tom Kerr Williams BA (Hons) (Oxon), solicitor – Race Discrimination (6)

Eleanor Kewish LLB (Hons), solicitor – Race Discrimination (6)

Colin Leckey MA (Oxon), solicitor – Equal Pay (11)

Marina Murray BA (Hons), solicitor – Common Concepts (1), Religion and Belief (7)

Ana-Maria Norbury MA (Cantab), solicitor – Sex Discrimination (8)

Stephen Ratcliffe MA (Cantab), solicitor – Equal Pay (11)

Mark Rose BA (Hons), DipLaw, solicitor – Sexual Orientation (9), Fixed-term and Part-time Workers (10)

Khurram Shamsee LLB (Hons) (London), solicitor – Age Discrimination (2)

Grant Spooner LLB (Hons), solicitor – Sex Discrimination (8)

Andrew Sutton, BA (Hons), solicitor – Disability Discrimination (3)

Julia Wilson MA, LLB (Hons), solicitor – Common Concepts (1)

Members of Blackstone Chambers

Emma Dixon, BA (Hons) (Cantab), barrister – Disability Discrimination (3)

Paul Goulding QC MA (Oxon), BCL (Oxon), barrister – Age Discrimination (2)

List of contributors

Ivan Hare, LLB (Hons) (London), BCL (Oxon), LLM (Harvard), MA (Cantab), barrister – Race Discrimination (6)

Beverley Lang QC MA (Oxon), barrister – Sex Discrimination (8)

Jane Mulcahy, BA (Hons) London, barrister – Fixed-term and Part-time Workers (10)

Naina Patel, BA (Hons) (Oxon), DipLaw, MPP (Harvard), barrister – Marital Status (5), Religion and Belief (7)

David Pievsky, BA (Hons), MPhil, barrister – Marital Status (5), Sexual Orientation (9)

Tom Richards, BA (Hons), DipLaw, barrister – Age Discrimination (2)

James Segan, BA (Hons) (Oxon), barrister – Common Concepts: Partnerships, Trade organisations, Vocational training providers, Qualifying bodies, Personal liability, and Comparators (1), Gender Reassignment (4)

Iain Steele, MA (Cantab), BCL (Oxon), barrister – Equal Pay (11)

Claire Weir, BA (Hons) (Cantab), LLM (Harvard), barrister – Common Concepts: Burden of Proof (1)

Sarah Wilkinson, BA (Hons) (Oxon), DPhil (Oxon), MA (Oxon), barrister – Common Concepts: Remedies, Sanctions and Enforcement (1)

Foreword
by Lord Lester

Lord Lester of Herne Hill QC is a practising barrister at Blackstone Chambers and a Liberal Democrat peer. He introduced a Civil Partnership Bill and an Equality Bill in the House of Lords. As Special Adviser to the Home Secretary (Roy Jenkins) between 1974 and 1976, he developed policy on what became the Sex Discrimination Act 1975 and the Race Relations Act 1976. The author is grateful to Kate Beattie, Parliamentary Legal Officer at the Odysseus Trust, for her help in preparing this chapter.

This is a pivotal moment for discrimination law in the UK for three main reasons. First, Parliament has extended protection against discrimination on the grounds of age (*Employment Equality (Age) Regulations 2006 (SI 2006/1031)*), sexual orientation (*Equality Act (Sexual Orientation) Regulations 2007 (SI 2007/1263)*; *Equality Act (Sexual Orientation) Regulations (Northern Ireland) 2006 (SI 2006/439)*) and religion and belief (*Equality Act 2006, Part 2*). Second, the Equality and Human Rights Commission (EHRC) replaces the existing equality agencies in Britain and will work towards the elimination of discrimination on these grounds as well as on grounds of sex, race and disability (as well as protecting and promoting a culture of respect for human rights). Third, the Government has moved closer to developing a Single Equality Act to harmonise, simplify and modernise equality law. These three developments represent an important opportunity to build on the UK's history of equality protection by creating an effective, efficient and equitable regulatory framework which gives redress to individuals and also tackles entrenched discriminatory practices and procedures.

Current state of discrimination in the UK

Despite the long history of anti-discrimination legislation in the UK, persistent inequalities and unfair discrimination remain. The Government announced a review of the causes of discrimination in February 2005 to provide an understanding of the long-term and underlying causes of disadvantage that need to be addressed by public policy. In February 2007, the Equalities Review, chaired by Trevor Phillips, recently appointed to chair the EHRC, issued its final report, *Fairness and Freedom: The Final Report of the Equalities Review*. It found that, while significant progress has been made towards eliminating discrimination and inequality, there are areas of persistent inequality which call for a new approach. The Review found that it will take until 2085 for the gender pay gap to be closed and until 2105 to close the gap in ethnic employment (p 24). The Commons Select Committee on Communities and Local Government has recently echoed these concerns (House of Commons Communities and Local Government Committee, *Equality*, Sixth Report of Session 2006–07, HC 468), and the findings on equal pay were reinforced by the Equal Opportunities Commission (EOC) in *The Gender Agenda – The Unfinished Revolution* (July 2007), which reported that the injustice of unequal pay for women continues, despite nearly 30 years of equal pay legislation (see also EOC Scotland, *Completing the Revolution*, July 2007).

The *Equality Act 2006* ('*EqA 2006*') established the EHRC, enshrined protection against discrimination on grounds of religion and belief in areas outside employment and occupation, allowed for regulations prohibiting discrimination on grounds of sexual orientation, and created a public sector duty to promote gender equality. (The establishment of the EHRC is considered in more detail below.) Regulations have been made under the *EqA 2006* prohibiting discrimination on grounds of sexual orientation in the provision of goods, facilities and services, education, housing and public functions, for both Great Britain and Northern Ireland. The public sector gender duty came into force in April 2007 and requires public authorities in England, Scotland and Wales to promote gender equality and eliminate sex discrimination. From 1 October 2006, it became unlawful to discriminate on the grounds of age in employment, following the passage of the *Employment Equality (Age) Regulations 2006* to implement the EU *Framework Directive on Equal Treatment in Employment and Occupation*.

Single Equality Act

These recent legislative developments add to the vast array of separate discrimination and equality measures in the UK and have reinforced calls for reform of discrimination law as a whole. The Government heeded these calls by establishing the Discrimination Law Review, which was twinned with the Equalities Review and charged with addressing long-held concerns about flaws in the current anti-discrimination legislative framework. Originally scheduled to report in summer 2006, the consultation paper – *Discrimination Law Review: A Framework for Fairness: Proposals for a Single Equality Bill for Great Britain* – was finally published in June 2007. It is expected that a draft Single Equality Bill may emerge in 2008.

There was some regret that the EHRC had been established before a Single Equality Act, as the new body will have to administer the existing array of discrimination legislation in advance of any new reforming Act. The EHRC will be hampered in tackling discrimination until, in place of the tangled and incoherent mess of existing equality laws, we have a comprehensive, coherent, and user-friendly Single Equality Act.

Current legislation suffers from various problems: there are differing degrees of protection for different groups, key terms are defined differently in different legislative measures, and potential remedies for unlawful discrimination vary. There are also differences between the private and public sector, most notably that positive equality duties apply only to public authorities and not to large private providers.

The goal of effective equality legislation is to eliminate unlawful discrimination and to promote equality regardless of sex, race, colour, ethnic or national origin, religion or belief, disability, age, sexual orientation, or other status. A Single Equality Act needs to contain clear, consistent and easily intelligible standards which state the whole of the law, including EU law implementation, as far as possible. The Act needs to set out an effective, efficient and equitable regulatory framework, aimed at encouraging personal responsibility and self-generating efforts to promote equality. The system of monitoring needs to be targeted and not based on a mechanical approach of the creation of mounds of paper which are collected but unused in practice. Individuals should be free to seek redress for the harm they have suffered as a result of unlawful discrimination, through procedures which are fair, inexpensive and expeditious, and the remedies should be effective.

There are several other key points which must be followed if we are to achieve effective equality legislation. There must be no levelling down of existing protection. There must be effective individual remedies and scope for real and effective measures of enforcement. There must be less emphasis on bureaucratic procedures, and more emphasis on practical outcomes. The *Discrimination Law Review* represents a welcome opportunity to incorporate new ideas and new thinking: it must be a genuine review, and not merely patch together the existing web of discrimination laws into a consolidating statute. To achieve what is called for will require firm political leadership and technical know-how, driven by a powerful ministerial team. The fact that ministerial responsibility is still split across so many government departments will make the task more difficult.

The groundwork for a Single Equality Act has already been done, in the wide-ranging and ground-breaking report of the Independent Review of the Enforcement of UK Anti-Discrimination Legislation, *Equality: A New Framework*, by Professor Sir Robert Hepple QC, Mary Coussey, and Tufyal Choudhury, published in July 2000 ('the *Hepple Report*'). It led to my Private Member's Single Equality Bill which was passed by the House of Lords in 2003, only to die in the Commons for lack of government support.

The *Hepple Report* contained new ideas which should inform the current review. It recommended effective action to tackle pay inequity, including a duty on employers to conduct workforce reviews. It focused on government contracts and state aid: where there is persistent non-compliance with tribunal orders, companies should be ineligible for government contracts. The Report also focused on positive action and positive duties, and considered the merits of a general duty to promote equality of opportunity on all public bodies.

The Equality and Human Rights Commission

The EHRC, created by the *EqA 2006*, came into operation in October 2007. The EHRC brings together the three existing British equality commissions –

the Equal Opportunities Commission (EOC), the Disability Rights Commission (DRC), and the Commission for Racial Equality (CRE) – and is the first statutory body in Great Britain charged with the protection and promotion of human rights. (The Northern Ireland Human Rights Commission, in existence since March 1999, was created by the *Northern Ireland Act 1998, s 68*, in compliance with a commitment made by the UK Government in the Belfast (Good Friday) Agreement of 10 April 1998.)

The EHRC is a non-departmental public body. In order to ensure the EHRC's independence and accountability, the *EqA 2006* requires the Secretary of State to have regard to the desirability of ensuring that the EHRC is under as few constraints as reasonably possible in determining its activities, timetables and priorities (*EqA 2006, Sch 1, Part 4, para 42(3)*). While the Secretary of State has the power to issue a direction to the EHRC to produce a Code of Practice, this may only be used in relation to additional or new statutes or regulations included within the EHRC's remit. The *EqA 2006* provides that the EHRC must have funding which is 'reasonably sufficient' for the purpose of enabling it to perform its functions (*Sch 1, Part 3, para 38*), and the Government has set an annual operational budget of £70 million. This is more than the combined budgets of the existing commissions, but the EHRC will add human rights and new discrimination strands to its remit. The Commission's headquarters will be in Manchester, but it will need a strong presence in London to enhance its influence on government policy and decision-making.

The *EqA 2006* sets out a general duty for the EHRC, which covers both equality and human rights. Under *EqA 2006, s 3* the EHRC must exercise its functions with a view to encouraging and supporting the development of a society in which:

- people's ability to achieve their potential is not limited by prejudice or discrimination;

- there is respect for and protection of each individual's human rights;

- there is respect for the dignity and worth of each individual;

- each individual has an equal opportunity to participate in society; and

- there is mutual respect between groups based on understanding and valuing diversity and on shared respect for equality and human rights.

The EHRC has additional specific statutory duties relating to equality and diversity (*EqA 2006, s 8*), human rights (*s 9*), and good relations between different groups in society (*s 10*). A Single Equality Act will need to mirror this approach and include a statement of interpretative principles in order to help those applying the legislation to promote its purposes.

The EHRC has a range of powers including, but not limited to:

- monitoring the law and advising government about the effectiveness of equality and human rights enactments and about the likely effect of a proposed change of law (*s 11*);

- monitoring progress towards the development of a society characterised by the protection of human rights and equality (*s 12*);

- providing information and advice, education and training, and the conduct of research (*s 13*);

- issuing of codes of practice (*ss 14–15*);

- conducting inquiries into any matter relating to its duties (*s 16*);

- conducting investigations and applying for injunctions to prevent breaches of equality law (*ss 20–26*);

- providing legal assistance to individuals (*ss 28–29*); and

- bringing and intervening in judicial review proceedings (*s 30*).

In general terms, the EHRC has acquired the same powers as the existing equality commissions, with some important additions. The EHRC's powers to issue Codes of Practice are wider than those of the existing equality commissions, and the EHRC has additional powers to conduct inquiries. Its powers of inquiry have significant potential, as the EHRC may consider matters which involve different strands of equality, and wider issues of human rights: this cross-strand approach was not available to the existing commissions, which were limited in scope by their governing Acts to deal only with particular grounds of discrimination. It is to be hoped that the EHRC and, ultimately, a Single Equality Act will facilitate a more sophisticated approach to the problem of multiple discrimination. The proposals in the *Discrimination Law Review* consultation paper for an integrated public sector duty to promote equality are a step in the right direction, so long as this does not weaken the requirements that public bodies take steps to achieve equality outcomes. The *Discrimination Law Review* (paragraphs 7.31–7.34) also contemplates allowing people to bring fully combined multiple claims if they have suffered discrimination on a number of different grounds.

The EHRC has the power to institute or intervene in legal proceedings, whether for judicial review or otherwise, if it appears to the EHRC that the proceedings are relevant to a matter in connection with which the EHRC has a function. Initially the power to apply for judicial review was resisted by the Government in relation to the human rights functions of the EHRC, in spite of the history of effective use of judicial review by the CRE and the EOC and existing safeguards against the abuse of judicial review. However, following strong pressure from the Parliamentary Joint Committee on Human Rights and others, the *EqA 2006* was amended in the House of Lords to allow for this. The power of the EHRC to bring judicial review is essential because it will enable the EHRC to continue and extend the significant work of the existing equality commissions in this respect, which has proved to be cost effective and proportionate.

The EHRC is also able to assist an individual who is, or may become, party to legal proceedings under existing equality enactments and regulations (namely the *Equal Pay Act 1970*; the *Sex Discrimination Act 1975*; the *Race Relations Act 1976*; the *Disability Discrimination Act 1995*; Part 2 of the Equality Bill on religious discrimination, the *Employment Equality* (*Sexual Orientation*) *Regulations 2003* (*SI 2003/1661*) and the *Employment Equality* (*Religion or Belief*) *Regulations 2003* (*SI 2003/1660*), as defined in *EqA 2006, s 33*) or Community law relating to equality (*EqA 2006, s 28(12)*). Assistance may include the provision of legal advice, legal representation, facilities for the settlement of a dispute, or any other form of assistance.

It is vital that the new EHRC pursues strategic law enforcement, including test cases and focused investigations. The EHRC must not repeat the mistakes of the former Commissions, which were reluctant to use their strategic law-enforcement powers effectively. When the *Race Relations Act 1976* was being prepared, it was envisaged that the CRE would be a powerful public authority with strong powers and a major strategic role in enforcing the law in the public interest, by carrying out investigations, issuing non-discrimination notices, and bringing proceedings to prevent persistent discrimination. Unfortunately, during the subsequent 30 years, the CRE has not given a high priority to strategic law enforcement to tackle entrenched patterns of racial discrimination and accumulated disadvantages. The EOC has also been reluctant to use the full range of its strategic powers. The EHRC will need to make strategic law enforcement a main priority, having recourse not only to British courts but also to the European Court of Justice, where EC equality law gives greater scope than domestic legislation or case law.

Much will depend upon the knowledge and skill of discrimination lawyers in translating the relevant legal principles and rules into practical reality, not only in the interests of their clients but in the wider public interest. The detailed chapters which follow are designed to provide guidance for legal practitioners and public and private bodies affected by this important and changing area of law.

Anthony Lester QC

Contents

Foreword   *v*
Table of Statutes   xv
Table of Statutory Instruments   xxv
Table of EU Legislative Material   *xxxiii*
Table of Cases   xxxv
Abbreviations   lxvii

1 Common Concepts   1
   Introduction   1
   Common concepts   3
   Direct discrimination   21
   Comparators   27
   Indirect discrimination   34
   Harassment   44
   Victimisation   54
   Exceptions   60
   Burden of proof   64
   Genuine occupational requirements/genuine occupational qualifications 71
   Positive action   74
   Vicarious liability   78
   Sanctions, remedies and enforcement   81
   Questionnaires   86
2 Age Discrimination   89
   Legislative background   89
   The meaning of age discrimination and harassment   91
   Discrimination in employment   100
   Discrimination in recruitment   115
   Discrimination during employment   118
   Discrimination on termination of employment   122
   Discrimination following the end of employment   142
   Validity of discriminatory terms   142
   Enforcement   143
3 Disability Discrimination   145
   Introduction   145
   Scope   147
   Meaning of disability and disabled person   149
   Practical issues relating to the definition of disability 163
   Other unlawful acts   193
   In practice   195
   Enforcement   210
   No contracting out   213

Contents

4 Gender Reassignment   215
    Overview   215
    Discrimination on the grounds of gender reassignment
    (similarities/differences to sex discrimination)   217
    Key areas for dispute   219
    Genuine occupational qualifications   219
    Enforcement and remedies   220
    Guidance for employers   220
    Other sources   225

5 Marital Status and Civil Partnership   227
    Introduction   227
    Direct discrimination: less favourable treatment on grounds of marital
    status/civil partnership   229
    Indirect discrimination against married persons/civil partners   230
    Further indications of discrimination: stereotyping   230
    The harassment problem   230
    Statutory exceptions   231
    Comparative jurisprudence   232

6 Race Discrimination   233
    Legal sources and guidance material   233
    Race and racial grounds   234
    Types of race discrimination   236
    Indirect discrimination   244
    Victimisation   250
    Harassment   252
    Other unlawful acts   260
    Exceptions, defences and non-employees covered by the employment
    provisions   264
    Non-employees and non-employers covered by the employment provisions
    of RRA 1976   268
    The CRE and EHRC   270
    Institutional racism and the positive duty   271

7 Religion and Belief   273
    Introduction   273
    The 2003 Regulations   274
    Practical considerations   280

8 Sex Discrimination   287
    Introduction   287
    Sex discrimination   291
    Discrimination on the grounds of pregnancy and maternity   313
    Pregnancy and maternity rights   320
    Maternity leave and pay   326
    Other family rights   341
    Flexible working   351

Contents

9 Sexual Orientation 357
Overview 357
Definition of 'sexual orientation' 357
Direct discrimination 358
Indirect discrimination 359
Victimisation 360
Harassment 361
Unlawful discrimination 362
Genuine occupational requirement 363
Other exceptions 364
Miscellaneous 365
Enforcement and remedies 366
Goods and services 366
10 Fixed-term and Part-time Workers 367
Fixed-term employees 367
Part-time workers 378
11 Equal Pay 389
Introduction 389
Overview of the statutory framework 389
The key issues 391
Who can bring an equal pay claim? 392
The comparator 394
What can be compared? 401
How is the comparison conducted? 402
When can a difference in pay be justified? 403
Remedies 415
Practicalities 416
Index *423*

Table of Statutes

Paragraph references printed in **bold** type indicate where the Statute is set out in part or in full.

**Access to Medical Records
Act 1988**
s 3(1) 3.106
4(1) 3.106
5(1) 3.106
(2)(a), (b) 3.106

Children Act 1989
s 3 .... 8.122, 8.131

**Children and Young Persons
Act 1933**
s 18(1) 2.17

Civil Partnership Act 2004 .... 9.18
s 1 .... 5.3
251 .... 5.3

Companies Act 1985
s 293 .... 2.17

Companies Act 2006
s 157(1) 2.17

Continental Shelf Act 1964 .... 6.50
s 1(7) 3.110

Crime and Disorder Act 1998
s 32(1)(b) 6.36

**Criminal Justice and Public Order
Act 1994** 1.53, 6.35

Data Protection Act 1998 ...... 3.98, 4.11,
7.18
s 35 .... 11.41
Sch 3 .... 3.96, 3.106

**Disability Discrimination
Act 1995** 1.2, 1.5, 1.7, 1.95, 1.96,
1.101, 1.107, 1.125,
2.9, 2.28, 3.2, 3.4,
3.13, 3.24, 3.25,
3.36, 3.37, 3.41,
3.43, 3.49, 3.55,
3.66, 3.85, 3.98,
3.109, 4.4, 4.11,
8.148
Pt I (ss 1–3) 3.125

Armed Forces Act 2006
s 334 .... 11.7

British Nationality Act 1948 .... 6.6

Disability Discrimination Act 1995 –
contd
s 1(1) 3.7, 3.11, 3.14, 3.15, 3.16,
3.18, 3.19, 3.20, 3.26
(2) 3.12
2(1) 3.12
3(3) 3.18
(b) 3.118
3A(1) 3.40, 3.44, 3.57, 3.59, 3.60
(a) 1.31
(b) 3.42
(2) 3.40, 3.42, 3.44, 3.58, 3.67,
3.70, 3.84
(3) 3.42, 3.44, 3.57, 3.65
(4) 3.40, 3.42, 3.44, 3.46, 3.57,
3.58
(5) 1.27, 1.30, 1.31, 1.34, 3.40,
3.42, 3.44, 3.45,
3.48, 3.50, 3.57, 3.58
(6) 3.65, 3.67, 3.68
3B **1.48**, 1.50
(1), (2) 3.86
Pt II (ss 4–18) 3.3, 3.7, 3.8, 3.10,
3.89, 3.110, 3.111,
3.113, 3.114, 3.115
s 4 .... 1.65, 3.8, 3.9, 3.110
(1) 1.9, 1.11
(a), (b) 3.97
(c) 3.97, 3.100
(d) 3.99
(2) 1.9, 3.115
(a) 3.101
(b)–(c) 3.101, 3.113
(d) 3.86, 3.101, 3.113
(3) 1.11
(4) 1.68, 3.115
4A 1.106, 3.8, 3.40, 3.42, 3.58,
3.68, 3.69, 3.81,
3.84, 3.112, 3.113
(1) 3.70, 3.82

Table of Statutes

Disability Discrimination Act 1995 –
contd

s 4a(1) (a) 3.42
   (2) 3.71, 3.72
   (3) 3.73
 4B 1.10, 3.8
   (1), (2) 3.112
   (4), (5) 3.70, 3.112
   (6), (7) 3.112
   (8) 3.110
   (9) 3.112
 4C 1.19, 3.8
   (3)(a)–(c) 3.113
   (4)(a), (b) 3.113
 4D 1.19, 3.8, 3.113
 4E 1.19, 3.8, 3.70, 3.113
 4F 1.19, 3.8
   (2)(d)–(f) 3.113
 4G 3.8, 3.42, 3.113
 4H 3.8, 3.42, 3.70, 3.113
 4I–4K 3.8, 3.42, 3.113
 5 .... 1.65
   (1) 3.40
    (b) 3.42
   (2) 3.40
    (b) 3.42, 3.84
   (3) 3.42
   (4) 3.42, 3.84
 6 .... 1.65, 3.40
   (1)(a) 3.42, 3.74
   (2) 3.42
   (11) 3.42, 3.113
 6A 3.8, 3.113
   (1), (2) 1.12
 6B 1.12, 3.8
   (4) 3.113
 6C 3.8, 3.113
   (1) 1.12
 7 .... 1.65, 3.110
 7A 3.8
   (4) 1.20, 3.113
 7B 3.8, 3.113
 7C 3.8
   (4) 3.113
 7D 3.8, 3.113
 12 .... 3.112
 13 .... 3.8, 3.113
   (1)–(3) 1.13
 14 .... 3.8, 3.113
 14A 3.8, 3.113
   (1)(a) 1.15
   (3) 3.42, 3.113
   (5) 3.113
 14B 3.8, 3.113

Disability Discrimination Act 1995 –
contd

s 14b (1)(a) 3.42
 14C 1.14, 3.8
   (4) 3.113
   (5) 3.10, 3.110
 14D 3.8, 3.110, 3.113
 15 .... 3.113
 15A 3.8, 3.113
 15B 3.8
   (3) 3.113
 15C 3.8, 3.113
 16A 1.25, 3.42
   (4)–(6) 3.108
 16B 1.9, 3.89
   (1), (2) 3.89
   (2A), (2B) 1.11, 3.89
   (4) 1.11, 3.89
 16C 1.26, 3.90
 17(1)(c) 3.17
 17A 3.117, 3.119
   (1) 3.116
    (a) 1.15
   (1C) 1.89
   (2) 1.115
    (b) 1.117
   (3) 1.117
   (5) 1.117
 18(2) 3.22
 18A 3.75
 18B(1) 3.83
   (2) 3.78
    (j) 3.79
   (3) 3.75
   (6) 3.70
 18C 1.74
   (1) 3.115
 18D 1.50
   (1) 3.48, 3.69
   (2) 3.42, 3.74, 3.75, 3.86
Pt III (ss 19–28) 1.23, 3.71, 3.72,
                    3.115
s 19 .... 1.14
 21 .... 3.72
 21A 1.26
 21E 3.72
 25 .... 3.120
   (8) 3.119
 49A 3.96
 49D 3.96
 53A 1.4
   (8A) 3.6
 55 .... 1.56, 1.65
   (1) 3.88, 9.12

Disability Discrimination Act 1995 –
contd
s 55 (2)(a)(i)–(iii) 3.88
56 .... 3.122
  (2) 1.126
  (3)(a), (b) 1.126
57 .... 1.13, 1.26, 1.117
  (1) 3.92
  (2) 1.21, 3.93
  (3)–(5) 3.94
58 .... 1.110
  (1) 1.21, 1.117, 3.91, 3.93
  (2) 1.21, 1.26, 1.114, 3.92, 3.93
  (5) 1.13, 1.111, 3.91
59 .... 1.69, 3.42, 3.46
  (1) 3.56, 3.111
  (2A) 3.111
  (3) 1.67, 3.111
64 .... 1.16
  (2) 3.113
  (7) 1.18, 1.73, 3.10, 3.110
64A 3.113
65 .... 1.16
66 .... 3.113
68 .... 1.24, 3.16
  (1) 3.9, 3.110, 3.113
  (2)–(2C) 3.110
  (2D)(a), (b) 3.110
  (3)–(4A) 3.110
Sch 1
  para 1(1) 3.22
       2 .... 3.32
         (1) 3.33, 3.34
         (2) 3.35
       3 .... 3.19
         (1) 3.28
       4(1) 3.17, 3.23, 3.26
       5 .... 3.34
       6(1) 3.27, 3.54
         (2) 3.54
         (3) 3.27
       6A 3.19
         (1), (2) 3.32
       7 .... 3.16
       8(1) 3.31, 3.32
         (b) 3.30
Sch 2
  para 5(1) 3.12
       (2) 3.35
Sch 3
  para 3 .... 3.118
       (2) 1.23
Sch 3A
  para 1(2) 3.125

Disability Discrimination Act 1995 –
contd
Sch 3A – *contd*
  para 3 .... 3.125

Disability Discrimination
Act 2005 .... 3.3, 3.32, 3.41

Disability Rights Commission
Act 1999 .... 3.5
s 2(1) 3.4

Disabled Persons (Employment)
Act 1944 .... 3.1, 3.16

Disabled Persons (Employment)
Act 1958 .... 3.1

Employment Act 1989
s 1(3) 8.60
4 .... 8.60
5(1) 8.57
  (3) 8.57
8 .... 5.8, 8.64
11 .... 6.52
12(1) 7.12
  (2) 6.52
Sch 1 .... 8.60

Employment Act 2002 .... 8.126, 8.140,
                                    10.24
s 31 .... 1.117, 2.44
32(4) 1.23
45 .... 10.1, 10.5
51(1) 10.5
Sch 2 .... 11.41
Sch 3 .... 2.44, 10.35
Sch 4 ...... 2.44, 2.53, 2.57, 3.117, 10.35

Employment and Training Act 1973
s 2 .... 2.14, 8.47
10 .... 8.48

Employment Relations Act 1999
s 10 .... 2.44
20, 21 .... 10.23

Employment Rights Act 1996 ... 1.7, 7.19,
                                    8.101, 8.112, 8.126
s 13 .... 8.108
36–43 .... 7.15
47(c) 8.78
47E 8.149
48, 49 .... 8.78

Table of Statutes

Employment Rights Act 1996 – *contd*
s 55(1) 8.79
   (2) 8.81
  56(1) 8.79
   (6) 8.83
  57(1)(a), (b) 8.84
   (3), (4) 8.84
  57A 8.9, 8.134
  57B 8.9, 8.135
  66 .... 8.91
   (2) 8.78
  67 .... 8.91, 8.92
  68 .... 8.91, 8.93
  71 .... 8.74, 8.78, 8.96, 8.100, 8.117
   (4), (5) 8.107
  72 .... 8.96, 8.100
   (1) 11.18
  73 .... 8.96, 8.100, 8.107
  74, 75 .... 8.96
  75A–75D 8.9
  76, 77 .... 8.131
  78(7) 8.131
  79, 80 .... 8.131
  80A–80E 8.9
Pt VIIIA (ss 80F–80I) 8.9
s 80F 8.142
  80G 8.142, 8.144
  80H 8.142, 8.146, 8.147
  80I 8.142, 8.146
  86 .... 2.50, 8.76, 8.110, 10.17
  87–91 .... 8.76, 8.110
  92 .... 10.12
   (1) 10.33
   (4), (5) 8.77
Pt X (ss 94–134A) 2.39, 10.14
s 98 .... 2.39
   (1) 10.34
   (3A) 2.47
   (4) 3.66
  98A 2.41, 2.44
  98B–98F 2.41
  98ZA–98ZF 2.20, 2.39, 2.40, 2.41,
                2.44, 2.45, 2.47
  98ZG 2.44, 2.48
  98ZH 2.13, 2.41, 2.44, 2.46
  99 .... 8.73, 8.74, 8.119, 8.123
  104C 8.149
  108 .... 10.34
   (1) 1.23
  109 .... 2.38, 2.39, 2.41, 2.45, 2.46
  111 .... 1.23
  114, 115 .... 1.115
  123(1) 1.118
Pt XI (ss 135–181) 2.49

Employment Rights Act 1996 – *contd*
s 135 .... 2.24
  136(1)(b) 10.14
  139 .... 2.39
  155 .... 2.23, 2.24
  156 .... 2.38, 2.39
  162(1)(a)–(c) 2.24
   (2), (3) 2.24
  163(2) 2.39
Pt XIV Ch I (ss 210–219) 10.16
s 210–214 .... 2.24
  218 .... 2.23
  227 .... 2.24
   (1) 2.44
   (ZA) 8.146
  230 .... 7.9
   (1) 2.14, 2.20

Equal Pay Act 1970 .... 1.2, 1.23, 1.44,
               1.56, 1.75, 1.126,
             4.5, 6.16, 8.8, 8.23,
             8.42, 8.52, 8.113,
            10.3, 10.11, 10.32,
            11.4, 11.10, 11.11,
           11.12, 11.19, 11.20,
                     11.41
s 1(1) 11.3
   (2) 11.3, 11.17
   (a) 11.13, 11.16
   (b) 11.14, 11.16
   (c) 11.14, 11.15, 11.16, 11.25
   (d)–(f) 11.18
   (3) 1.93, 8.39, 11.3, 11.20, 11.23,
             11.24, 11.25, 11.29,
             11.30, 11.31, 11.33,
             11.34, 11.35, 11.36
   (4) 11.13
   (5) 11.14
   (6) 11.17
   (a) 11.7
   (6A), (6B) 11.7
   (7A) 11.7
   (8) 11.7
   (10)–(10B) 11.7
   (12) 11.8
  2(1) 1.115
   (4) 11.42
   (5) 11.38
  2A(2)–(3) 11.14
  2ZA 11.39, 11.42
  2ZB 11.39
   (3), (4) 11.38
  2ZC 11.38
  4 .... 11.2

Equal Pay Act 1970 – *contd*
s 6(1)(b) 8.39, 11.18
  (1AA) 11.18
  7A(5) 11.7
  7B(4) 1.126, 11.41
  7AA, 7AB 11.39

Equality Act 2006 ... 1.101, 6.70, 7.3, 8.17
s 2(1)(c), (d) 7.6
  14 .... 1.4, 3.6, 8.18
    (1) 6.68
    (h) 7.4
  15(4) 3.6, 6.68
  20 .... 1.125
  21(1) 1.125
    (4) 1.125
  22–24 .... 1.125
  25 .... 1.11, 1.125, 6.38, 6.39
    (1)(c) 3.89
  26 .... 1.125
  27 .... 1.125
  28 .... 1.125
  29, 30 .... 1.125
  31 .... 1.125
  32 .... 1.125, 8.66
  42 .... 8.18
  Pt 2 (ss 44–80) 1.2
  s 46, 47 .... 7.11
  57–62 .... 7.12
  Pt 3 (ss 81, 82) 9.21
  Sch 1
    Pt 5 .... 3.5

European Communities Act 1972 ..... 2.41
s 2(2) 2.1, 9.21

Factories Act 1961
s 175 .... 8.100

Gender Recognition Act 2004 ...... 4.4, 4.7
s 22(1), (2) 4.11
  (3)(b) 4.11

Health and Safety at Work etc.
  Act 1974 .... 1.53
  Pt I (ss 1–54) 8.60
  s 33(1)(a) 8.95
    (c) 8.95

Human Fertilisation and
  Embryology Act 1990
  s 27(1) 8.138
  28(2) 8.138
  30 .... 8.138

Human Fertilisation and Embryology
  Act 1990 – *contd*
  s 30 (6) 8.139

Human Rights Act 1998 .... 1.53, 7.13, 9.2
s 3 .... 7.6
  6 .... 8.66
    (1) 7.2
  Sch 1
    art 8–10 .... 1.3
    14 .... 1.3

Immigration Act 1971
s 3(4) 1.36

Income Tax (Earnings and
  Pensions) Act 2003 .... 8.102

Law Reform (Contributory
  Negligence) Act 1945 .... 1.118

Local Government and Housing
  Act 1989
  s 7 .... 3.7

Malicious Communications
  Act 1998 .... 1.53

Mental Health Act 1983 .... 3.16

National Minimum Wage Act 1998
s 1(3) 2.21

Northern Ireland Fair Employment
  Act 1976 .... 1.8

Pensions Act 1995 .... 1.56, 7.12, 8.52,
                                         11.19
s 62–65 .... 8.23

Police Act 1996 .... 8.59

Protection from Harassment
  Act 1997 .... 6.34
  s 3 .... 1.53
  7 .... 1.53

Public Health Act 1936
s 205 .... 8.100
  343 .... 8.100

Public Order Act 1986
s 4A 6.35

Table of Statutes

Race Relations Act 1965 .... 6.1, 6.6

Race Relations Act 1968 .... 6.1, 6.6

Race Relations Act 1976 .... 1.2, 1.5, 1.14,
1.37, 1.47, 1.92,
1.104, 1.107, 1.108,
1.125, 2.6, 2.9, 2.28,
3.7, 3.41, 3.56,
3.113, 3.120, 6.6,
6.16, 6.18, 6.20,
6.46, 6.49, 6.52,
6.53, 6.54, 7.5, 7.11,
9.5, 9.7
s 1(1) 1.34
   (a) 1.27, 1.30, 3.48, 6.7, 6.9,
6.10, 6.12, 6.13,
6.22, 6.28, 6.29,
6.39, 6.43, 7.7
   (b) **1.43**, 3.59, 6.15, 6.17, 6.37
    (ii) 1.44
  (1A) ... 1.41, 3.59, 6.1, 6.15, 6.37, 7.7
   (c) 1.44
  (1C) 6.15
  (2) 6.8
1A 1.34
2 .... **1.56**, 6.39, 7.8
  (1) 6.19, 9.12
   (c) 6.21
3 .... 1.50
  (1) 6.3, 6.11, 7.2
  (4) 1.34, 1.59, 3.48, 6.10
3A **1.48**, 1.49, 1.50, 1.114, 6.1,
6.10, 6.22, 6.23,
6.24, 6.30, 6.32,
6.39, 6.43, 7.8
  (1)(b) 6.26, 6.27
  (2) 6.26, 6.31
  (5) 1.31, 6.27
Pt II (ss 4–16) 6.59, 6.62
s 4 .... 1.14, 6.64, 7.9
  (1) 1.9, 1.11, 6.23, 6.28, 6.47
   (a) 1.60
  (2) 1.9
   (c) 6.22, 6.28, 6.31, 6.39
  (2A) 1.11, 6.23
  (3) 1.76
  (4) 1.68, 6.55
4A 1.96, 6.1, 6.7, 6.66
  (2) 6.47
   (a) 1.97
5 .... 1.96, 1.100, 6.7, 6.66, 8.55
  (1)–(3) 6.47
  (4) 1.97, 6.47

Race Relations Act 1976 – *contd*
s 6 .... 1.76, 6.48
7 .... 1.10, 3.112
8 .... 1.24
  (1) 6.53
9 .... 1.76
  (1)–(4) 6.50
10(1) 1.12
  (1A) 1.12, 6.66
  (1B) 1.12
  (2) 1.12
11 .... 6.67
  (2)–(4) 1.13
12 .... 6.67, 8.65
13 .... 6.67
  (3) 1.14
14 .... 6.67
  (4) 1.26
  (6) 1.26
15 .... 6.67
Pt III (ss 17–27) 1.23
s 17, 18 .... 1.14
26A 6.65
  (3) 1.20
26B 1.20, 6.65
27A 1.25
28 .... 6.37
29(1) 1.9, 6.38
  (2)(a), (b) 6.38
  (3) 6.38
  (4), (5) 1.11, 6.38
30 .... 1.26, 6.39
31(1), (2) 6.40
32 .... 1.110, 6.45
  (1) 1.21, 1.117, 6.41
  (2) 1.21, 1.26, 1.114, 6.42
  (3) 1.13, 1.53, 1.111, 6.41, 6.44
33 .... 1.13, 1.26, 1.117
  (1) 6.44
  (2) 1.21, 6.44
  (3) 6.44
  (4) 6.42, 6.44
35 .... 3.69
36 .... 1.103
37 .... 1.102, 1.107, 7.14
38 .... 1.102, 1.107, 3.69, 7.14
39 .... 1.72, 6.51
41 .... 1.69, 2.17
  (1)(a)–(c) 6.56
  (1A) 6.56
  (2)(d) 6.56
42 .... 1.67, 6.57
  (2)(d), (e) 6.56
43 .... 6.68

Race Relations Act 1976 – *contd*
s 47 .... 1.4, 6.68
(10) 6.2
54(2) 1.15
54A 1.64, 1.89, 1.94, 6.1, 6.7, 6.12
56(1) 1.115
(b) 1.117
(4) 1.117
57(4) 1.119
57ZA 1.90
58(2) 1.125
62, 63 .... 1.125
65(1) 1.126
(2)(a), (b) 1.126
68(6) 1.23
71(7) 6.69
71C, 71D 6.69
75 .... 1.16
(2)(c) 6.64
(5) 6.63
(8) 1.18
(9) 1.18, 6.64
(9A), (9B) 1.18
75A, 75B 1.16, 6.63, 6.65
76(12) 6.61
(14) 6.61
76A 1.17, 6.45
76B 1.17
76ZA 1.19
(7) 6.62
(9) 6.62
78 .... 1.50, 6.22, 6.32
(1) 1.7, 1.11, 1.26
Sch 1
para 1(2) 6.69

Reserve Forces Act 1996
Pt 11 (ss 110–119) 10.7

Road Traffic Act 1988
s 101 .... 2.17

**Selective Employment Payments
Act 1966** 11.8

Sex Discrimination Act 1975 ...... 1.2, 1.5,
1.81, 1.108, 1.125,
2.9, 2.12, 2.28, 3.7,
3.41, 3.52, 3.86,
3.113, 3.120, 4.1,
4.2, 4.3, 5.9, 6.8,
6.16, 6.54, 6.61, 7.5,
7.11, 8.7, 8.8, 8.20,
8.49, 8.57, 8.63,
8.113, 9.2, 9.4, 9.5,
9.7, 11.19, 11.29
s 1 .... 8.73, 8.112, 8.119
(1)(a) 1.27, 1.30, 1.31, 3.48, 4.5,
5.1, 5.7, 7.7
(b) 3.59, 8.22, 10.3
(2) 1.47
(a) 7.7, 8.3, 8.21
(b) 1.41, **1.42**, 7.7, 8.3, 8.22,
8.147
(iii) 1.44
2 .... 5.7, 8.5, 8.21, 8.68, 8.72, 8.128
(1) 1.27, 1.30, 1.31
2A 4.6
(1)–(3) 4.5
3 .... 5.1, 5.3, 5.7, 8.64
(1)(a) 1.27, 1.30, 1.31, 5.4
(b) 1.30, 1.41
(iii) 5.5
(2)(a), (b) 5.1
3A 5.7, 8.71, 8.73, 8.78, 8.108,
8.112, 8.118, 8.119
(1) 8.73
(a), (b) 1.27, 1.30, 8.69
(2) 8.69
(3) 8.70
4 .... 1.56, 7.8
(1) 8.3, 8.23
(d) 1.62
4A 7.8, 8.3
(1) **1.48**, 5.7, 8.24
(a)–(c) 1.50
(i)(a) 8.24
(2) **1.48**, 8.24
(3) **1.48**, 4.5
(b) 1.50
(4), (5) **1.48**
5(1) 5.7
(a)
(b) 5.8
(3) 1.34, 1.59, 3.48

Table of Statutes

Sex Discrimination Act 1975 – *contd*

Pt II (ss 6–21) 8.1, 8.6, 8.21, 8.22,
8.24, 8.29, 8.34,
8.35, 8.44, 8.60,
8.61, 8.65, 8.67, 8.69
s 6 .... 1.14, 7.9, 8.2, 8.35, 8.47, 8.64
(1) 1.9, 1.11
(a) 8.39
(2) 1.9, 8.40, 8.44
(a) 8.42
(b) 1.82, 5.7, 6.31
(2A) 1.11, 5.7, 8.3, 8.39
(3) 8.43
(4) 1.75, 8.52
(5) 1.75, 8.39
(6) 1.75, 8.42, 11.2
(7) 1.68, 1.75, 8.50
(8) 1.75, 4.5
6A 8.108
7 .... 1.96, 1.100, 4.7
(1) 5.8, 8.55
(2)(a)–(e) 8.55
(g) 8.55
(h) 5.8, 8.55
(3) 8.55
(4) 1.97, 8.55
7A 1.96, 4.7
(1)(b) 1.97
7B 1.96, 1.100, 4.7
8(3) 8.39
(5) 8.39, 8.42
9 .... 1.10, 3.112, 8.118
(3) 8.36, 8.55
(3A)–(3D) 8.55
(4) 8.36
10 .... 1.24, 3.110
(1), (1A) **11.8**
(2)–(5) 8.30, 11.8
(6) 8.30
10A, 10B 1.19, 8.35
11(1), (2) 1.12
(2A) 1.12, 8.37
(3) 8.37, 8.55
(3A)–(3D) 8.55
12 .... 8.64, 8.65
(1) 8.45
(2), (3) 1.13, 8.45
(3A) 1.13
13 .... 1.15, 8.55, 8.65
(1) 8.46
(3)(a), (b) 8.46
(4), (5) 8.46
14 .... 8.55
(1A) 1.14, 8.47

Sex Discrimination Act 1975 – *contd*

s 14 (1B) 8.47
15 .... 1.26
(1)(b) 8.48
(1A) 8.48
(2), (3) 8.48
(4) 1.26, 8.48
(5) 8.48
16(1), (1A) 8.47
Pt IV (ss 37–42) 8.21, 8.22, 8.24,
8.34, 8.35, 8.61, 8.65
s 17 .... 1.75, 8.33
(1A) 1.17, 8.33
(2) 8.59
18 .... 1.75, 8.58
19 .... 1.75
(1)(c) 5.8
(2) 8.46
(3)(c), (d) 5.8
20A 1.25, 8.44
Pt III (ss 21A–36) 1.23, 4.5, 8.1,
8.21, 8.22, 8.24,
8.60, 8.61, 8.65, 8.67
s 22 .... 1.14, 1.110, 8.47
(1) 1.117
(2) 1.114
(3) 1.111
23 .... 1.14, 1.117, 8.47
30(1) 1.115
(b) 1.117
(2) 1.118
(3) 1.117
33(2)(a), (b) 1.126
35(3) 8.38
35A 8.22, 8.29
(1)–(3) 1.20, 8.38
35B 8.22, 8.29, 8.38
35C 1.25, 8.38
37 .... 8.22
38(1) 1.9, 8.39
(2) 8.39
(4), (5) 1.11, 8.39
(6) 8.39
39 .... 1.26, 2.10, 8.67
41 .... 1.110, 4.10
(1) 1.21, 1.117, 8.67
(2) 1.14, 1.21, 1.26, 1.114, 6.42,
8.29, 8.47, 8.67
(3) 1.13, 1.111, 8.67
42 .... 1.13, 1.26, 1.117, 8.29
(1) 8.67
(2) 1.21
(3) 8.67
(4) 1.26

Sex Discrimination Act 1975 – *contd*
s 42A 1.15, 1.75, 8.65
43 .... 1.74
  (2), (3) 8.62
44 .... 1.72, 8.54
45 .... 1.75, 8.53
46 .... 1.75, 8.54
47 .... 1.75, 1.107
  (3), (4) 8.64
48 .... 1.75, 1.107, 3.69
  (1)–(3) 8.64
49 .... 1.75
51 .... 1.67
  (1) 8.60
51A 1.67, 2.17
52 .... 8.61
  (1) 1.67
Pt VI (ss 53–61) 8.17
s 53(2) 8.61
56A 1.4, 11.5
  (10) 8.39
63 .... 4.8
  (2) 1.15, 8.46
63A **1.89**, 1.92, 4.8
  (2) 8.29
65(1) 1.115
  (b) 1.117
  (1B) 1.118
  (3) 1.117
66(4) 1.119
66A 1.90
74(1) 1.126
  (2)(a), (b) 1.126
76(5) 1.23
76A(3) 8.66
  (6) 8.66
76D, 76E 8.66
82 .... 1.50, 4.4

Sex Discrimination Act 1975 – *contd*
s 82 (1) 1.7, 1.11, 1.14, 1.26, 5.7,
                        8.31, 8.35, 8.47,
                        8.118
  (1A) 8.37, 8.43
85 .... 1.16, 8.35
  (2)(a), (b) 8.35
  (c) 8.34
  (4) 1.18, 1.73, 8.34
  (9B)–(9E) 1.18, 8.34
  (10) 8.32
85A, 85B 1.16, 8.32

**Sex Discrimination (Election
  Candidates) Act 2002** 1.15

Social Security Act 1989
Sch 5 .... 8.52, 8.109, 8.110, 8.117
  para 5 .... 8.23
    (1), (2) 8.109
    (3)(a) 8.109
  6 .... 8.23
  7(a), (b) 8.109
  (e) 8.109

**Social Security Contributions and
  Benefits Act 1992** 8.126
Pt VII (ss 123–137) 8.101
s 171(1) 8.101, 8.102
  171ZL 8.122

State Immunity Act 1978 .... 6.58
s 1, 2 .... 1.81

**Tribunals, Court and Enforcement
  Act 2007 (Not yet in force)**
s 27 .... 1.117

Work and Families Act 2006 .... 8.100,
                                      8.121

Table of Statutory Instruments

Paragraph references printed in **bold** type indicate where the Statutory Instrument is set out in part or in full.

ACAS (Flexible Working)
Arbitration Scheme (England
and Wales) Order 2004,
SI 2004/2333 .... 8.149

Companies Act 2006
(Commencement No 1,
Transitional Provisions and
Savings) Order 2006,
SI 2006/3428
art 4 .... 2.17

Court Funds Rules 1987,
SI 1987/821
r 27(1) 1.122

Disability Discrimination Act 1995
(Amendment)
Regulations 2003,
SI 2003/1673 .... 3.3, 3.7, 3.8, 3.10,
3.41, 3.42, 6.15,
6.22, 6.28, 6.47,
6.48, 6.56
reg 7 .... 3.110
24(d) 3.110

Disability Discrimination (Blind and
Partially Sighted Persons)
Regulations 2003,
SI 2003/712 .... 3.19

Disability Discrimination
(Employment Field) (Leasehold
Premises) Regulations 2004,
SI 2004/153 .... 3.102

Disability Discrimination
(Employment)
Regulations 1996,
SI 1996/1456 .... 3.102

Disability Discrimination (Meaning
of Disability)
Regulations 1996,
SI 1996/1455
reg 5 .... 3.19, 3.29

Disability Discrimination (Public
Authorities) (Statutory Duties)
Regulations 2005,
SI 2005/2966 .... 3.96

Employment Act 2002 (Dispute
Resolution) Regulations,
SI 2004/752
reg 4(1)(h) 2.44, 2.47
6(1) 2.44
(5) 3.117
11(3)(b) 1.1.53
15 .... 1.23

Employment Equality (Age)
Regulations 2006,
SI 2006/1031 .... 1.2, 1.4, 1.5, 1.44,
1.66, 1.98, 2.1, 2.2,
2.3, 2.4, 2.12, 2.28,
2.30, 2.38, 2.45, 6.61
reg 2 .... 1.50
(2) 1.7, 2.13, 2.14, 2.20
3 .... 2.5, 2.8, 2.14, 2.16, 2.41
(1) 1.44, 2.5, 2.8, 2.14, 2.20,
2.22, 2.23
(a) 1.27, 1.30, 1.31, 2.6, 2.7
(b) 1.41
(2) 1.34, 2.6
(3)(a) 2.7
(b) 1.31, 2.6
4 .... 1.56, 2.5
(1) **2.9**
(2) 2.9
5 .... 2.5, 2.10
6 .... 1.48, 2.5
(1) 1.11, 2.11
(3) 2.11
Pt 2 (regs 7–24) 2.17
reg 7 .... 2.14, 2.37
(1) 1.9, 1.11, **2.13**, 2.27
(a) 2.16
(c) 2.16

Table of Statutory Instruments

Employment Equality (Age)
Regulations 2006, SI 2006/1031 –
contd

reg 7 (2) 1.9
    (b), (c) 2.16
    (d) 2.13, 2.16
    (3) 2.13
    (4) 2.13, 2.27, 2.39, 2.41
    (5) 2.13, 2.27, 2.41
    (6) 1.68, 2.13
    (a)–(c) 2.36
    (7) 2.13
8 .... 1.96, 2.14, 2.16
    (2)(b) 1.97
9 .... 1.10, 2.14
    (1) **2.14**
    (2)–(5) 2.14
10 .... 1.24, 2.13, 2.14
11 .... 2.37
    (1) 2.14
    (3)(b) 2.14
12 .... 1.19
    (1) 2.14
    (5) 2.14
13 .... 1.17, 2.13
    (1) 2.14
14 .... 2.13, 2.14
15 .... 2.14
    (1)–(3) 2.14
    (4) 1.20, 2.14
    (6) 2.14
16 .... 1.20, 2.14
17 .... 2.14
    (2), (3) 1.12
18 .... 2.19
    (1)–(3) 1.13, 2.14
    (4) 2.14
19(1)–(3) 2.14
20 .... 1.14, 2.20
    (1) **2.14**
    (2) 2.14
    (3) **2.14**
    (4) 2.14
21(1), (2) 2.14
    (6) 1.26
22(1) 2.14
23 .... 2.14
    (3) 2.14
24 .... 1.25, 2.51
    (3) 2.13
Pt 3 (regs 25, 26) 2.17
reg 25 .... 1.110
    (1) 1.21, 1.117
    (2) 1.21, 1.26, 1.114, 2.32

Employment Equality (Age)
Regulations 2006, SI 2006/1031 –
contd

reg 25 (3) 1.13, 1.111
26 .... 1.13, 1.26, 1.117
    (2) 1.21
    (4) 1.26
27 .... 1.69, 2.16, 2.17, 2.50
    (1) 2.49
28 .... 1.67, 2.18
29 .... 1.105, 2.27
    (1), (2) **2.19**
    (3) 2.19
30 .... 1.79, 2.13, 2.14, 2.34, 2.39,
                         2.40, 2.41, 2.42,
                               2.43, 2.47
    (1) 2.20
31 .... 1.79
    (1)–(3) 2.21
32 .... 1.79, 2.35
    (1) 2.22
    (2) 2.22, 2.23
    (3), (4) **2.23**
    (5) 2.23
    (7) 2.23, 2.49, 2.50
33 .... 1.79, 2.23, 2.35, 2.49
    (1)(a) 2.24
    (2) **2.24**
    (4)(b)(i), (ii) 2.24
    (c) 2.24
    (5) 2.24
34 .... 1.79, 2.34
    (1)(a), (b) **2.25**
36 .... 2.53
    (2)(a) 1.15
37 .... 1.89, 2.54
38 .... 2.56
    (1) 1.115
    (b) 1.117
    (3) 1.117
40 .... 1.90
41 .... 2.55
    (1) 1.126
    (2)(a), (b) 1.126
42(3) 1.23
    (4) 2.57
43 .... 2.52
44 .... 1.16
    (2) 1.18, 2.13
    (4) 1.73, 2.13
45, 46 .... 1.16, 2.13
47 .... 2.39, 2.43
Sch 2 .... 2.13, 2.14, 2.26, 2.37
    Pt 1 .... 2.56

Employment Equality (Age) Regulations 2006, SI 2006/1031 – *contd*

Sch 2 – *contd*
para 6 .... 2.56
Sch 3, 4 .... 1.126, 2.55
Sch 5 .... 2.33
Pt 1 .... 2.52
para 1(1) 2.52
3 .... 2.52
Pt 2 .... 2.52
para 4(2) 2.52
5–7 .... 2.52
8(1) 2.52
9 .... 2.52
Sch 6 .... 2.13, 2.39, 2.43
para 1(2) 2.44
2 .... 2.42, 2.47
(c)–(e) 2.44
4 .... 2.44, 2.47, 2.48
5(1) 2.44
(4) 2.44
6 .... 2.44, 2.48
7 .... 2.47, 2.48
(1)–(8) 2.44
8 .... 2.48
(1) 2.44
(5), (6) 2.44
(9), (10) 2.44
9(3) 2.44
10(1), (2) 2.44
(4) 2.44
11–13 .... 2.44
Sch 7 .... 2.44
Sch 8 .... 2.13

Employment Equality (Religion or Belief) Regulations 2003,
SI 2003/1660 .... 1.2, 1.4, 1.5, 1.23,
1.31, 1.51, 1.66,
1.69, 1.102, 1.105,
1.108, 2.5, 2.6, 2.9,
2.13, 2.19, 6.16,
6.61, 7.4, 7.13, 7.18,
9.1, 9.3, 9.19
reg 1(2) 7.1
2 .... 1.50
(1) 7.3, 7.6
(3) 1.7, 7.8, 7.9
3 .... 7.10
(1)(a) 1.27, 1.30, 1.50, 7.3, 7.6,
7.7
(b) 1.41, 7.7
(ii) 7.12

Employment Equality (Religion or Belief) Regulations 2003, SI 2003/1660 – *contd*

reg 3(1)(b) (iii) 1.44
(2) 7.7
(3) 1.34, 7.7
4 .... 1.56, 7.8
5 .... 1.48, 7.8
(1) 1.11
6 .... 7.9, 7.10
(1) 1.9, 1.11
(2) 1.9
(4) 1.68
7 .... 1.96, 1.99
(1) 7.10
(2)(a) 7.10
(b) 1.97, 7.10
(c) 7.10
(3) 7.10
8 .... 1.10, 2.14, 7.4, 7.10
9 .... 1.24, 2.14, 7.9
9A 7.12
10 .... 1.19, 2.14, 7.10
11 .... 1.17, 2.14
12 .... 2.14, 7.11
(4) 1.20
13 .... 1.20, 2.14
14 .... 2.14, 7.10
(2), (3) 1.12
(8) 1.12
15 .... 2.14, 7.11
(1)–(3) 1.13
16 .... 2.14, 7.11
17 .... 1.14, 7.10, 7.11
(3) 2.14
18 .... 2.14, 7.10, 7.11
(6) 1.26
19 .... 2.14
20 .... 2.14, 7.10, 7.11
21 .... 1.25, 2.14
22 .... 2.14
(1) 1.21
(2) 1.21, 1.26
(3) 1.13
23 .... 1.13
(2) 1.21
(4) 1.26
24 .... 1.67
25 .... 1.104, 7.14, 7.17
26 .... 1.78, 6.52, 7.17
(1) 7.12
29 .... 1.89
32 .... 1.90
34(3) 1.23

Table of Statutory Instruments

Employment Equality (Religion or Belief) Regulations 2003, SI 2003/1660 – *contd*

reg 36 .... 1.16
    (7)–(10) 1.18
    37, 38 .... 1.16

Employment Equality (Religion or Belief) (Amendment) Regulations 2003, SI 2003/2828 .... 7.3

Employment Equality (Religion or Belief) (Amendment) Regulations 2004, SI 2004/437 .... 7.3

Employment Equality (Religion or Belief) (Amendment) (No 2) Regulations 2004, SI 2004/2520 .... 7.3

Employment Equality (Sexual Orientation) Regulations 2003 SI 2003/1661 .... 1.2, 1.4, 1.5, 1.31,
    1.51, 1.69, 1.98,
    1.105, 2.5, 2.6, 2.9,
    2.13, 2.19, 6.61, 7.1,
    7.4, 9.1, 9.2, 9.3, 9.6,
    9.19, 9.21

reg 2 .... 1.50
    (1) **9.4**
    (3) 1.7, 9.14
  3 .... 9.14
    (1)(a) 1.27, 1.30, 9.5, 9.7, 9.8
    (b) 1.41, 9.7, 9.9
      (iii) 1.44
    (2) 9.7
    (3) 1.34
  4 .... 1.56, 9.14
    (1)(a) 9.12
    (c) 9.12
    (2) 9.12
  5 .... 1.48, 9.14
    (1) 1.11
    (a) 9.13
    (2) 9.13
Pt II (regs 6–21) 9.14
reg 6(1) 1.9, 1.11, 9.14
    (2) 1.9
    (a)–(d) 9.14
    (3) 9.13
    (c) 9.14
    (4) 1.68

Employment Equality (Sexual Orientation) Regulations 2003 SI 2003/1661 – *contd*

reg 6 (5)(b) 9.14
  7 .... 1.96, 1.99
    (1) 9.14
    (2)(a) 9.14
    (b) 1.97, 9.14
    (c)(ii) 9.14
    (3) 7.10
    (b), (c) 9.14
  8 .... 1.10, 2.14, 7.4
  9 .... 1.24, 2.14
  10 .... 1.19, 2.14
  11 .... 1.17, 2.14
  12 .... 2.14
    (4) 1.20
  13 .... 1.20, 2.14
  14 .... 2.14
    (2), (3) 1.12
    (8) 1.12
  15 .... 2.14
    (1)–(3) 1.13
  16 .... 2.14
  17 .... 1.14
    (3) 2.14
  18 .... 2.14
    (6) 1.26
  19, 20 .... 2.14
  21 .... 1.25, 2.14
    (1) 9.14
  22 .... 1.110, 2.14
    (1) 1.21, 1.117, 9.14
    (2) 1.21, 1.26, 1.114, 9.14
    (3) 1.13, 1.111, 9.14
  23 .... 1.13, 1.117
    (1) 9.14
    (2) 1.21, 9.14
    (3) 9.14
    (4) 1.26
  24 .... 1.67, 9.16
  25 .... 5.8, 9.18
  26 .... 1.104
    (1) 9.17
  28(2)(a) 1.15
  29 .... 1.89
  30(1) 1.115
    (b) 1.117
    (2) 1.117, 1.118
  32 .... 1.90
  33 .... 9.20
    (2)(a), (b) 1.126
  34(3) 1.23
  36 .... 1.16

Employment Equality (Sexual Orientation) Regulations 2003 SI 2003/1661 – *contd*
reg 36 (7)–(10) 1.18
  37, 38 .... 1.16

Employment Protection (Recoupment of Jobseeker's Allowance and Income Support) Regulations 1996, SI 1996/2349 .... 1.118

Employment Tribunals (Constitution and Rules of Procedure) Regulations 2004, SI 2004/1861
Sch 1
  r 50 .... 3.119
Sch 6 .... 11.44

Employment Tribunals (Constitution and Rules of Procedure) (Amendment) Regulations 2004, SI 2004/2351
Sch 6 .... 11.44
  r 4(3)(a) 11.45
  5 .... 11.45
  6(2), (3) 11.45
  7(3) 11.45
    (4)(c) 11.45
    (5), (6) 11.45
  8(1)(a) 11.45
  10 .... 11.45
  11(1)–(3) 11.45
  12(1) 11.45

Employment Tribunal (Interest on Awards in Discrimination Cases) Regulations 1996, SI 1996/2803 .... 1.122

Equal Pay (Questions and Replies) Order 2003, SI 2003/722 .... 1.126, 11.41

Equality Act (Sexual Orientation) Regulations 2007, SI 2007/1263 .... 1.2, 9.21

Fixed-term Employees (Prevention of Less Favourable Treatment) Regulations 2002, SI 2002/2034 .... 1.2, 1.126, 10.1, 10.3, 10.4, 10.5
reg 1(2) 10.6

Fixed-term Employees (Prevention of Less Favourable Treatment) Regulations 2002, SI 2002/2034 – *contd*
reg 2(1) 10.7
    (a)(ii) 10.8
  (2) 10.8
  3 .... 10.12
  (1) 10.13
    (a), (b) 10.9
  (2) 10.9
  (3) 10.10
    (b) 10.11
  (4) 10.9
  (6) 10.13, 10.15
  (7) 10.13
  4(1) 10.11, 10.27, 10.32
  5 .... 10.12, 10.14
  6(1)–(4) 10.14
  7(2) 10.15
  (7) 10.15
  8 .... 10.12, 10.16
  9 .... 10.14
  (1)(b) 10.12
  (5) 10.12
  12(2) 10.18
  13–17 .... 10.7
  18(1), (2) 10.7
  19, 20 .... 10.7
Sch 1 .... 10.14

Flexible Working (Eligibility, Complaints and Remedies) Regulations 2002, SI 2002/3236 .... 8.9
reg 3 .... **8.141**

Flexible Working (Procedural Requirements) Regulations 2002, SI 2002/3207 .... 8.9, 8.142

Management of Health and Safety at Work Regulations 1999, SI 1999/3242 .... 1.107, 8.86
reg 1(2) 8.88
  16(1) 8.87
  (2), (3) 8.91
  17 .... 8.93
  18(1) 8.88, 8.94, 8.95
  (2)(a)(ii) 8.89

Table of Statutory Instruments

Maternity and Parental Leave etc.
Regulations 1999,
SI 1999/3312 .... 8.9, 8.96, 8.118
reg 1 .... 8.117
2 .... 8.122
(1) 8.98
4(1)(a), (b) 8.98
(1A) 8.99
(2)(a) 8.98
6 .... 8.99
7(6) 8.98
(7)(a) 8.98
8 .... 8.100
9 .... 8.74, 8.78
(3) 8.108
10 .... 8.75
11(5) 8.98
12A(1), (2) 8.115
(4) 8.116
(5)–(7) 8.115
13(1)(b) 8.139
16 .... 8.131
17 .... 8.108
18 .... 8.133
(3) 8.117
18A 8.117
19 .... 8.78, 8.98, 8.108
(2)(eee) 8.115
20 .... 8.74, 8.98, 8.119
(1)(b) 8.75
(2) 8.75
(3)(eee) 8.115
21 .... 8.108
(4) 8.74
Sch 2 .... 8.131

National Minimum Wage
Regulations 1999, SI 1999/584
reg 12(3) 2.21

Occupational Pension Schemes
(Equal Treatment)
Regulations 1995,
SI 1995/3183 .... 3.113

Part-time Workers (Prevention of
Less Favourable Treatment)
Regulations 2000,
SI 2000/1551 .... 1.2, 1.19, 1.126,
10.5, 10.20, 10.21,
10.22, 10.32, 10.35,
10.38
reg 1(2) 10.28
2(1) 10.25

Part-time Workers (Prevention of Less
Favourable Treatment)
Regulations 2000, SI 2000/1551 –
contd
reg 2 (2) 10.24, 10.25
(3)(a)–(d) 10.25
(4)(a)(i), (ii) 10.25
(b) 10.25
3 .... 10.26
4 .... 10.26
5 .... 10.34
(1)(b) 10.27
(2)(a) 10.31
(3) 10.28
(4) 10.29
6 .... 10.34
(1) 10.33
7 .... 10.27
(1) 10.34
(2) 10.34, 10.37
8(11) 10.37

Paternity and Adoption Leave
Regulations 2000,
SI 2002/2788 .... 8.9, 8.126
reg 2(a)(i) 8.139
11 .... 8.122
19–27 .... 8.121
28, 29 .... 8.123

Paternity and Adoption Leave
(Adoption from Overseas)
Regulations 2003,
SI 2003/921 .... 8.125

Paternity and Adoption Leave
(Amendment)
Regulations 2006,
SI 2006/2014 .... 8.121

Race Relations Act 1976
(Amendment)
Regulations 2003,
SI 2003/1626 .... 1.43, 6.7

Race Relations Act 1976 (Statutory
Duties) Order 2006,
SI 2006/2471 .... 6.70

Race Relations (Complaints to
Employment Tribunals) (Armed
Forces) Regulations 1997,
SI 1997/2161 .... 6.64

Disability Discrimination
(Questions and Replies)
Order 2004, Si 2004/1168
art 4(b) 1.126

Sex Discrimination Act 1975
(Application to Armed Forces
etc.) Regulations 1994,
SI 1994/3276 .... 8.34

Sex Discrimination Act 1975
(Public Authorities) (Statutory
Duties) Order 2006,
SI 2006/2930 .... 8.66

Sex Discrimination (Amendment)
Order 1988, SI 1988/249 .... 8.61

Sex Discrimination and Equal Pay
(Off-Shore Employment)
Order, 1987, SI 1987/930 ...... 3.110,
11.8

Sex Discrimination and Equal Pay
(Remedies) Regulations 1993,
SI 1993/2798 .... 1.117

Sex Discrimination (Gender
Reassignment)
Regulations 1999,
SI 1999/1102 .... 4.4

Sex Discrimination (Indirect
Discrimination and Burden of
Proof) Regulations 2001,
SI 2001/2660 .... 8.29
reg 2 .... 1.89
5 .... 1.89

Sex Discrimination (Northern
Ireland) Order 1976,
NI 1976/1042
art 12 .... 8.118

Social Security (Categorisation of
Earners) Regulations 1978,
SI 1978/1689 .... 8.102, 8.122

Social Security Contributions and
Benefits Act 1992 (Application
of Parts 12za and 12zb to
Adoptions from Overseas)
Regulations 2003,
SI 2003/499 .... 8.125

Statutory Maternity Pay (General)
Regulations 1986
SI 1986/1960 .... 8.101
reg 3(1), (2) 8.102
9A 8.115
Pt III (regs 11–16A) 8.102
reg 21(7) 8.105
22, 23 .... 8.103
27 .... 8.105

Statutory Maternity Pay (Medical
Evidence) Regulations 1987,
SI 1987/235 .... 8.103
reg 2 .... 8.98

Statutory Maternity Pay (Persons
Abroad and Mariners)
Regulations 1987,
SI 1987/418 .... 8.102

Statutory Paternity Pay and
Statutory Adoption Pay
(General) Regulations 2002,
SI 2002/2822
reg 11 .... 8.122, 8.126
23, 24 .... 8.122

Statutory Paternity Pay (Adoption)
and Statutory Adoption Pay
(Adoption from Overseas)
(No 2) Regulations 2003,
SI 2003/1194 .... 8.125

Transfer of Undertakings
(Protection of Employment)
Regulations 2006,
SI 2006/246 .... 1.23, 11.42

Working Time Regulations 1998,
SI 1998/1833 .... 8.111, 10.30

Table of EU Legislative Material

Paragraph references printed in **bold** type indicate where the legislation is set out in part or in full.

Primary Legislation

Treaties and Agreements

Treaty establishing the European Community (Treaty of Rome, 1957)
art 2, 3 .... 8.63
13 .... 6.1
39 .... 3.110
48 .... 1.24
119 .... 1.19
141 .... 2.3, 2.23, 4.5, 8.11, 8.34,
8.52, 11.2, 11.10,
11.11, 11.12, 11.13,
11.17, 11.20, 11.23,
11.25, 11.29, 11.30,
11.38
(1) 8.42, **11.4**
(2) 8.42, **11.4**, 11.7, 11.19
(3) 1.19, 10.29, 11.4
(4) 8.63, 11.4
224 .... 8.61

Conventions

Convention on Human Rights and Fundamental Freedoms (Rome) 1950 .... 1.3
art 6(1) 1.81
8 .... 9.2, 9.15
9 .... 7.16
(1), (2) 7.2, 7.6
14 .... 7.2, 9.2, 9.15

Secondary Legislation

Directives

Council Directive 75/117/EEC (Equal Pay Directive) 4.5, 8.12
art 1 .... 11.4

Council Directive 76/207/EEC (Equal Treatment Directive) 1.42,
1.44, 4.2, 5.7, 8.12,
8.15, 8.20, 11.10,
11.19
art 1(2) 8.63
2(2) 1.19, 1.45, 8.34, 8.61
(6) 8.55, 8.61
(7) 8.60
(8) 8.63
3 .... 1.14, 8.47
7 .... 1.57

Council Directive 79/7/EEC (Equal Treatment Directive) 11.19

Council Directive 86/378/EEC (Equal Treatment Directive) 8.13,
11.19

Council Directive 89/391/EEC (Health and Safety Framework Directive)
art 6 .... 8.91

Council Directive 92/85/EEC (Pregnant Workers Directive) ... 8.13,
8.74, 8.86, 8.107
art 10(2) 8.77
Annex I, II 8.87

Council Directive 93/104/EEC (Working Time Directive) 8.111

Council Directive 96/34/EC (Parental Leave Directive) 8.13

Council Directive 96/71/EC (Posting of Workers Directive) 6.53

Council Directive 97/80/EC (Burden of Proof in Sex Discrimination Cases Directive) 1.30, 8.13, 8.29,
10.3, 11.26
art 2(2) 3.74

Table of EU Legislative Material

Council Directive 97/80/EC (Burden of Proof in Sex Discrimination Cases Directive) – *contd*
art 4(1) 1.85, 1.86, 1.87, 1.88

Council Directive 97/81/EC (Framework Agreement on Part-Time Work) 1.19, 8.13, 10.20, 10.22, 10.25, 10.27, 10.32
Annex
  cl 4(1) 10.31
  (2) 10.28

Council Directive 98/23/EC (Concerning the extension of Directive 97/81/EC on the Framework Agreement on Part-Time Work) 10.20

Council Directive 1999/70/EC (Concerning the Framework Agreement on Fixed-Term Work) 10.1
art 1, 2 .... 10.2
Annex
  cl 1 .... 10.2
  4 .... 10.2, 10.10
  5 .... 10.2

Council Directive 2000/43/EC (Discrimination Based on Racial or Ethnic Origin) 1.43, 1.45, 1.48, 6.7, 6.17, 6.28
art 1 .... 1.87
  2 .... 1.44, 6.15
  (3) 6.22, 6.24, 6.27
  3(2) 6.1, 6.32
  8(1) 1.87, 1.88
  9 .... **1.57**

Council Directive 2000/78/EC (Equal Treatment Framework Directive) ... 1.31, 1.48, 2.4, 2.5, 2.20, 2.23, 2.49, 3.3, 3.13, 3.14, 3.48, 3.58, 3.108, 3.110, 7.1, 7.3, 8.13, 8.148, 9.1
Recital 14 .... 2.41, 2.42
  17 .... 3.49
  25 .... 2.2

Council Directive 2000/78/EC (Equal Treatment Framework Directive) – *contd*
art 1 .... 3.7, 7.6
  (1)(b)(i) 3.59
  2 .... 1.44, 3.7
  (1) 3.42, 3.70
  (2) 2.6
  (a) 3.42, 3.45
  (2)(b) 3.70, 3.74, 3.79
  (i) 2.8, 3.42, 3.113
  (ii) 3.42, 3.113
  2(3) 1.45
  (5) 3.42, 3.46, 3.56, 3.111
  3(1) 2.14
  (c) 3.42
  4(1) 3.42
  5 .... 2.42, 3.73
  6 .... 2.22, 2.24
  (1) 2.2, 2.8, 2.41
  (c) 2.42
  10(1) 1.88
  11 .... 1.57
  13 .... 2.12
  18 .... 2.1, 2.3

Council Directive 2002/73/EC (Equal Treatment Amendment Directive) 1.48, 8.13, 8.20
art 2(2) 8.22, 8.24
  3 .... 1.19

Council Directive 2006/54/EC (Consolidated Equal Treatment Directive) 8.13, 8.14, 11.25
art 2(1)(b) 11.27
  14(2) 8.55
  19(1) 1.86
  33 .... 1.86, 8.13

Regulations

Council Regulation (EEC) 1408/71 .... 8.102

Recommendations

Commission Recommendation 92/131/EEC 1.46, 1.111, 8.16

Table of Cases

A

A v Chief Constable of West Yorkshire Police [2004] UKHL 21, [2005] 1 AC 51, [2004] 3 All ER 145, [2004] 2 WLR 1209, [2004] 2 CMLR 884, [2004] ICR 806, [2004] IRLR 573, [2004] 2 FCR 160, [2004] 20 LS Gaz R 34, [2004] NLJR 734, (2004) Times, 7 May, 148 Sol Jo LB 572, 17 BHRC 585, [2004] All ER (D) 47 (May) 4.5

Abadeh v British Telecommunications plc [2001] IRLR 23, [2001] ICR 156, EAT 3.14, 3.26, 3.27

Abbey Life Assurance Co Ltd v Tansell. See MHC Consulting Services Ltd v Tansell

Abbey National plc v Formoso [1999] IRLR 222, EAT 8.73

Abbott v Cheshire and Wirral Partnership NHS Trust [2006] EWCA Civ 523, [2006] ICR 1267, [2006] IRLR 546, (2006) Times, 10 May, 150 Sol Jo LB 471, [2006] All ER (D) 32 (Apr) 1.93, 6.16

Abrahamsson v Fogelquist: C-407/98 [2000] IRLR 732 .... 1.101, 8.63

Abrahamsson v Fogelqvist [2002] ICR 932 .... 9.17

Adebayo v Dresdner Kleinwort Wasserstein Ltd [2005] IRLR 514, [2005] All ER (D) 371 (Mar), EAT 1.9, 1.126, 6.7

Adeneler v Ellinikos Organismos Galaktos: C-212/04 [2007] All ER (EC) 82, [2006] 3 CMLR 867, [2006] IRLR 716, [2006] All ER (D) 25 (Jul), ECJ 10.5

Advocate (Lord) v Babcock and Wilcox (Operations) Ltd [1972] 1 All ER 1130, [1972] 1 WLR 448, HL 11.8

Afolabi v Southwark London Borough Council [2003] EWCA Civ 15, [2003] ICR 800, [2003] IRLR 220, [2003] 11 LS Gaz R 32, (2003) Times, 30 January, 147 Sol Jo LB 115, [2003] All ER (D) 217 (Jan) 1.23

Ahmad v United Kingdom (1981) 4 EHRR 126 .... 7.2, 7.15

Aina v Employment Service [2002] DCLD 103D 1.108

Ainsworth v IRC [2005] EWCA Civ 441, [2005] IRLR 465, [2005] NLJR 744, (2005) Times, 16 May , [2005] All ER (D) 328 (Apr), sub nom IRC v Ainsworth [2005] ICR 1149 .... 8.111

Alabaster v Woolwich plc: C-147/02 [2004] ECR I-3101, [2005] All ER (EC) 490, [2004] 2 CMLR 186, [2005] ICR 695, [2004] IRLR 486, [2004] All ER (D) 558 (Mar), ECJ 8.105, 8.106, 8.107, 11.18

Allan v GMB, UKEAT/0425/06 (31 July 2007, unreported) 1.13

Allan v Newcastle-upon-Tyne City Council [2005] ICR 1170, [2005] IRLR 504, [2005] NLJR 619, [2005] All ER (D) 197 (Apr), EAT 11.39

Allen v National Australia Group Europe Ltd [2004] IRLR 847, [2004] All ER (D) 13 (Sep) 10.5, 10.6

Allonby v Accrington and Rossendale College [2001] EWCA Civ 529, [2001] 2 CMLR 559, [2001] ICR 1189, [2001] IRLR 364, [2001] All ER (D) 285 (Mar); refd C-256/01 [2004] ECR I-873, [2005] All ER (EC) 289, [2004] 1 CMLR 1141, [2004] ICR 1328, [2004] IRLR 224, [2004] All ER (D) 47 (Jan), ECJ 1.44, 6.16, 8.36, 11.7, 11.10, 11.17

Anya v University of Oxford [2001] EWCA Civ 405, [2001] ICR 847, [2001] IRLR 377, [2001] All ER (D) 266 (Mar) 1.29, 6.9, 6.12

Apelogun-Gabriels v Lambeth London Borough Council [2001] EWCA Civ 1853, [2002] ICR 713, [2002] IRLR 116, [2001] All ER (D) 350 (Nov) 1.23

Table of Cases

Appiah v Bishop Douglass Roman Catholic High School [2007] EWCA Civ
  10, [2007] ICR 897, [2007] IRLR 264, [2007] All ER (D) 240 (Jan) 1.90, 1.92,
  6.12
Applin v Race Relations Board [1975] AC 259, [1974] 2 All ER 73,
  [1974] 2 WLR 541, 72 LGR 479, 138 JP 522, 118 Sol Jo 311, HL 1.37
Archibald v Fife Council [2004] UKHL 32, (2004) Times, 5 July,
  [2004] 4 All ER 303, [2004] ICR 954, [2004] IRLR 651, 82 BMLR 185,
  [2004] 31 LS Gaz R 25, 2004 SC 942, 2004 SCLR 971, 148 Sol Jo LB
  826, [2004] All ER (D) 32 (Jul) 3.69, 3.74, 3.77, 3.78, 3.80, 3.85
Armitage v Relate [1994] DLCD 26 .... 1.8
Armstrong v Newcastle Upon Tyne NHS Hospital Trust [2005] EWCA Civ
  1608, [2006] IRLR 124, [2005] All ER (D) 341 (Dec) 1.93, 11.17, 11.25, 11.28,
  11.29, 11.31
Arthur v A-G [1999] ICR 631, EAT 1.15
Atkins v Gregory Ltd, EAT (5 July 2006, unreported) 1.92
Attridge Law v Coleman [2007] IRLR 88 .... 3.7, 3.48
Aziz v Trinity Street Taxis Ltd [1989] QB 463, [1988] 2 All ER 860,
  [1988] 3 WLR 79, [1988] ICR 534, [1988] IRLR 204, 132 Sol Jo 898,
  [1988] 26 LS Gaz R 42 .... 1.60, 1.62, 6.21
Azmi v Kirklees Metropolitan Borough Council [2007] ICR 1154,
  [2007] IRLR 484, (2007) Times, 17 April, [2007] All ER (D) 528
  (Mar), EAT 6.16, 7.6, 7.7, 7.19, 9.7

B

B v A [2007] IRLR 576 .... 1.30
B v Ontario (Human Rights Commission) [2002] 3 SCR 403 .... 5.9
BL Cars Ltd v Brown [1983] ICR 143, [1983] IRLR 193, 80 LS Gaz
  R 94, EAT 1.9
Badeck, Re [2000] All ER (EC) 289; [2000] IRLR 432 .... 1.101
Baggs v Fudge v Fudge, 400114/05 (2005), unreported 7.6
Bahl v Law Society [2004] EWCA Civ 1070, [2004] NLJR 1292, [2004] IRLR
  799, 148 Sol Jo LB 976, [2003] All ER (D) 570 (Jul) 1.29, 1.92, 6.9
Bailey v Home Office [2005] EWCA Civ 327, [2005] ICR 1057, [2005] IRLR
  369, (2005) Times, 8 April, [2005] All ER (D) 356 (Mar) 1.93, 11.26, 11.28
Bainbridge v Redcar & Cleveland Borough Council [2007] IRLR 494 ...... 11.14, 11.43
Balamoody v United Kingdom Central Council for Nursing, Midwifery and
  Health Visiting [2001] EWCA Civ 2097, [2002] ICR 646, [2002] IRLR
  288 .... 1.38, 6.10
Baldwin v Brighton and Hove City Council [2007] ICR 680, [2007] IRLR
  232, [2006] All ER (D) 220 (Dec), EAT 1.28, 4.6, 6.8
Balgobin v Tower Hamlets London Borough Council [1987] ICR 829,
  [1987] IRLR 401, [1987] LS Gaz R 2530, EAT 1.111, 6.8
Banks v Tesco Stores Ltd [2000] 1 CMLR 400, [1999] ICR 1141, EAT 8.107
Barber v Guardian Royal Exchange Assurance Group: C-262/88 [1991] 1 QB
  344, [1990] 2 All ER 660, [1990] ECR I-1889, [1991] 2 WLR 72,
  [1990] 2 CMLR 513, [1990] ICR 616, [1990] IRLR 240, [1990] NLJR
  925, ECJ 11.19, 11.20
Barber v Staffordshire County Council [1996] 2 All ER 748, [1996] IRLR
  209, [1996] 06 LS Gaz R 26, sub nom Staffordshire County Council v
  Barber [1996] ICR 379, CA 11.2
Barclays Bank plc v Kapur (No 2) [1995] IRLR 87 .... 1.9
Bari v General Medical Council, UKEATPA/0660/05/LA (28 September
  2005, unreported) 1.15

Barry v Midland Bank plc [1999] 3 All ER 974, [1999] 1 WLR 1465,
    [1999] ICR 859, [1999] IRLR 581, [1999] 31 LS Gaz R 36, [1999] NLJR
    1253, 143 Sol Jo LB 221, HL 1.44, 11.27
Barton v Investec Henderson Crosthwaite Securities Ltd [2003] ICR 1205,
    [2003] IRLR 332, [2003] 22 LS Gaz R 29, (2003) Times, 16 April, [2003]
    All ER (D) 61 (Apr), EAT 1.30, 1.92, 1.126, 8.21, 11.22
Bayliss v Hounslow London Borough Council [2002] EWCA Civ 354, [2002]
    All ER (D) 332 (Mar) 6.31
Beardmore v South West Trains, ET 2305257/00 (2001), unreported 1.58
Beardmore v WE Hamilton, ET 2305257/00 (2001), unreported 1.58
Bellamy v American Airlines, UKEAT/0542/05 (2005), unreported 8.75
Bentley v Body Shop International plc, 3100348/00 (2000), unreported 8.75
Bentwood Bros (Manchester) Ltd v Shepherd [2003] EWCA Civ 380,
    [2003] ICR 1000, [2003] IRLR 364, [2003] All ER (D) 398 (Feb) 1.118
Benveniste v University of Southampton [1989] ICR 617, [1989] IRLR
    122, CA 11.35
Best v Tyne and Wear Passenger and Transport Executive (t/a Nexus)
    [2007] ICR 523, [2006] All ER (D) 362 (Dec), EAT 1.44
Bhakerd v Famous Names Ltd, ET Case No 19289/87 (1987), unreported 7.16
Bick v Royal West of England Residential School for the Deaf [1976] IRLR
    326, Ind Trib 5.2
Biggs v Somerset County Council [1996] 2 All ER 734, [1996] 2 CMLR 292,
    [1996] ICR 364, [1996] IRLR 203, [1996] 06 LS Gaz R 27, [1996] NLJR
    174, 140 Sol Jo LB 59, CA 11.2
Bilka-Kaufhaus GmbH v Weber von Hartz: C-170/84 [1986] ECR 1607,
    [1986] 2 CMLR 701, [1987] ICR 110, [1986] IRLR 317, ECJ 1.44, 6.16, 9.11,
                                                                         11.19, 11.23, 11.25
Bird v Silvester [2007] EWCA Civ 1052 .... 1.61
Birds Eye Walls Ltd v Roberts: C-132/92 [1993] ECR I-5579, [1993] 3 CMLR
    822, [1994] IRLR 29, sub nom Roberts v Birds Eye Walls Ltd: C-132/92
    [1994] ICR 338, ECJ 11.19
Birmingham City Council v Equal Opportunities Commission [1989] AC
    1155, [1989] 2 WLR 520, 87 LGR 557, [1989] IRLR 173, 133 Sol Jo 322,
    [1989] 15 LS Gaz R 36, [1989] NLJR 292, sub nom Equal Opportunities
    Commission v Birmingham City Council [1989] 1 All ER 769, HL 1.29, 6.8
Birmingham City Council v Samuels (24 October 2007, unreported) 1.92
Blundell v Governing Body of St Andrews Catholic Primary School
    [2007] ICR 1451, [2007] IRLR 652, [2007] All ER (D) 159
    (May), EAT 8.117
Bossa v Nordstress Ltd [1998] ICR 694, [1998] IRLR 284, EAT 1.24, 6.53
Boukhalfa v Germany: C-214/94 [1996] ECR I-2253, [1996] 3 CMLR 22,
    ECJ 3.110
Boyle v Equal Opportunities Commission: C–411/96 [1998] All ER (EC) 879,
    [1998] ECR I–6401, [1998] 3 CMLR 1133, [1999] ICR 360, [1998] IRLR
    717, [1999] 1 FCR 581, [1999] 1 FLR 119, 52 BMLR 169, 608 IRLB 5,
    [1998] All ER (D) 500, ECJ 8.107, 8.108
Bracebridge Engineering Ltd v Darby [1990] IRLR 3, EAT 1.51
Bradford Hospitals NHS Trust v Al-Shabib [2003] IRLR 4, [2002] All ER
    (D) 68 (Oct), EAT 6.9
Brash-Hall v Getty Images Ltd [2006] EWCA Civ 531, [2006] All ER (D) 111
    (May) 8.120
Brennan v J H Dewhurst Ltd [1983] IRLR 357 .... 1.11, 8.39
Briheche v Ministre de l'Interieur [2004] ECR 1–8807 .... 1.101

Table of Cases

British Airways (European Operations at Gatwick) Ltd v Moore and
  Botterill [2000] 2 CMLR 343, [2000] ICR 678, [2000] IRLR 296, EAT 8.92
British Airways plc v Boyce [2001] IRLR 157 .... 6.11
BBC Scotland v Souster [2001] IRLR 150, Ct of Sess 6.6
British Coal Corpn v Keeble [1997] IRLR 336, EAT 1.23
British Coal Corpn v Smith [1996] 3 All ER 97, [1996] ICR 515,
  [1996] IRLR 404, [1996] NLJR 843, HL 11.17
British Gas Services Ltd v McCaull [2001] IRLR 60, EAT 3.81
British Judo Association v Petty [1981] ICR 660 , [1981] IRLR 484, EAT 1.15, 8.46
British Medical Association v Chaudhary [2003] EWCA Civ 645, [2003] ICR
  1510, (2003) Times, 21 May, 147 Sol Jo LB 629, [2003] All ER (D) 208
  (May) 1.15
BP Chemicals Ltd v Gillick [1995] IRLR 128, EAT 1.8, 1.26, 8.36, 8.118
Brocklebank v Silveira, UKEAT/571/05 (11 January 2006, unreported) 1.26
Bromley v H & J Quick Ltd [1988] 2 CMLR 468, [1988] ICR 623,
  [1988] IRLR 249, CA 11.15
Brown v Croydon London Borough Council [2006] All ER (D) 320 (May) 1.27
Brown v London Borough of Croydon [2007] EWCA Civ 32, [2007] IRLR
  259, [2007] All ER (D) 239 (Jan) 6.7
Brown v Rentokil Ltd: C–394/96 [1998] ECR I–4185, [1998] All ER (EC)
  791, [1998] 2 CMLR 1049, [1998] ICR 790, [1998] IRLR 445,
  [1999] 1 FCR 49, [1998] 2 FLR 649, [1998] Fam Law 597, 48 BMLR
  126, [1998] 34 LS Gaz R 34, [1998] All ER (D) 313, ECJ 3.54, 8.73
Brown v London Borough of Croydon [2007] EWCA Civ 32, [2007] IRLR
  259, [2007] All ER (D) 239 (Jan) 1.92
Bruce v Addleshaw Booth & Co, UKEAT/0404/03 (11 February 2004,
  unreported) 1.65
Brumfitt v Ministry of Defence [2005] IRLR 4, 148 Sol Jo LB 1028, [2004]
  All ER (D) 479 (Jul), EAT 1.47, 1.50
Brunnhofer v Bank der österreichischen Postsparkasse AG: C-381/99
  [2001] ECR I-4961, [2001] All ER (EC) 693, [2001] 3 CMLR 173,
  [2001] IRLR 571, (2001) Times, 9 July, [2001] All ER (D) 273 (Jun),
  ECJ 11.4, 11.13, 11.25, 11.32
BUPA Care Homes (BNH) Ltd v Cann [2006] ICR 643, [2006] IRLR 248,
  [2006] All ER (D) 299 (Feb), EAT 1.23
Burke v British Council [2006] UKEAT/0125/06 .... 3.110
Burton v De Vere Hotels Ltd [1997] ICR 1, [1996] IRLR 596, EAT 1.47, 1.114,
                                                              6.27, 6.29, 6.43
Buxton v Equinox Design Ltd [1999] ICR 269, [1999] IRLR 158, EAT 1.116

                                    C
Cadman v Health and Safety Executive: C-17/05 [2007] All ER (EC) 1,
  [2007] 1 CMLR 530, [2006] ECR I-9583, [2006] ICR 1623, [2006] IRLR
  969, (2006) Times, 6 October, [2006] All ER (D) 17 (Oct), ECJ ... 1.44, 2.23, 2.35,
                                              11.25, 11.29, 11.30, 11.36
Caisse Nationale d'Assurance Vieillesse des Travailleurs Salaries v Thibault:
  C-136/95 [1998] ECR I-2011, [1998] All ER (EC) 385, [1998] 2 CMLR
  516, [1998] IRLR 399, [1998] All ER (D) 167, sub nom Thibault v
  Caisse Nationale d'Assurance Viellesse des Travailleurs Salaries
  (CNAVTS) [1999] ICR 160, ECJ 8.78, 8.107
Caledonia Bureau Investment and Property v Caffrey [1998] ICR 603,
  [1998] IRLR 110 .... 8.73
Calor Gas Ltd v Mrs D Bray, UKEAT/10633/04 (2005), unreported 8.75

Campbell and Cosans v United Kingdom (1982) 4 EHRR 293, ECtHR 7.2, 7.6
Caniffe v East Riding of Yorkshire Council [2000] IRLR 555 .... 1.111
Capper Pass Ltd v Lawton [1977] QB 852, [1977] 2 All ER 11, [1977] 2 WLR
    26, [1977] ICR 83, [1976] IRLR 366, 11 ITR 316, 120 Sol Jo 768, EAT 11.13
Carden v Pickerings Europe Ltd [2005] IRLR 720, [2005] All ER (D) 145
    (May), EAT 3.27
Carrington v Helix Lighting Ltd [1990] ICR 125, [1990] IRLR 6,
    [1990] 1 LS Gaz R 30, EAT 1.126
Caspersz v Ministry of Defence, UKEAT/0599/05/LA (3 March 2006,
    unreported) 1.111
Chacon Navas v Eurest Colectividades SA [2006] IRLR 706 .... 3.13, 3.24, 3.42
Chamberlin Solicitors v Emokpae [2004] ICR 1476, [2004] IRLR 592, [2004]
    All ER (D) 110 (Jun), EAT; revsd sub nom Emokpae v Chamberlin
    Solicitors [2005] EWCA Civ 142, [2005] ICR 931, 149 Sol Jo LB 264,
    [2005] All ER (D) 300 (Feb) 1.30
Chaudhary v Secretary of State for Health [2007] EWCA Civ 788,
    [2007] IRLR 800, 97 BMLR 15, [2007] All ER (D) 455 (Jul) 1.44, 1.93
Chessington World of Adventures Ltd v Reed, ex p News Group
    Newspapers Ltd [1998] ICR 97, [1998] IRLR 56, EAT 4.3, 4.6
Chief Constable of Avon and Somerset Constabulary v Chew, EAT/503/00
    (2001), unreported 8.147
Chief Constable of Avon and Somerset Constabulary v Chew [2001] All ER
    (D) 101 (Sep), EAT 1.44
Chief Constable of Bedfordshire Police v Liversidge [2002] EWCA Civ 894,
    [2002] ICR 1135, [2002] IRLR 651, [2002] All ER (D) 395 (May) 1.17, 2.14,
                                                                        6.45, 8.33
Chief Constable of Cumbria v McGlennon [2002] ICR 1156, [2002] All ER
    (D) 231 (Jul), EAT 1.17, 8.33
Chief Constable of Kent Constabulary v Kufeji EAT 1135/00 (4 May 2001,
    unreported) 6.26, 6.31
Chief Constable of Lincolnshire Police v Stubbs [1999] ICR 547,
    [1999] IRLR 81, EAT 1.110
Chief Constable of Greater Manchester Police v Hope [1999] ICR
    338, EAT 1.119
Chief Constable of West Midlands Police v Blackburn &
    Manley, EAT/0007/07 (11 December 2007, unreported) 11.25, 11.27, 11.29
Chief Constable of West Yorkshire Police v Khan [2001] UKHL 48,
    [2001] 1 WLR 1947, [2001] ICR 1065, [2001] IRLR 830,
    [2001] 42 LS Gaz R 37, 145 Sol Jo LB 230, [2001] All ER (D) 158 (Oct),
    sub nom Khan v Chief Constable of West Yorkshire Police
    [2001] 4 All ER 834 ... 1.9, 1.28, 1.39, 1.59, 1.61, 1.62, 6.8, 6.12, 6.20, 10.10, 10.31
Chief Constable of West Yorkshire Police v Vento [2002] IRLR 177, [2001]
    All ER (D) 20 (Dec), EAT; revsd sub nom Vento v Chief Constable of
    West Yorkshire Police [2002] EWCA Civ 1871, [2003] ICR 318,
    [2003] IRLR 102, [2003] 10 LS Gaz R 28, 147 Sol Jo LB 181, [2002] All
    ER (D) 363 (Dec) 1.119, 8.120
Chief Constable of West Yorkshire v Vento [2001] IRLR 124, EAT 1.38, 6.10
Chin v Post Office, Bedford Industrial Tribunal (12 December 1996,
    unreported) 6.24, 6.31
Christie v Department for Constitutional Affairs, UKEAT/0140/07/ZT
    (17 July 2007, unreported) 1.19
Christie v John E Haith Ltd [2003] IRLR 670, [2003] All ER (D) 267
    (Jul), EAT 11.25
Clark v Kings College London [2003] All ER (D) 118 (Oct), EAT 11.34

Table of Cases

Clark v TDG Ltd (t/a Novacold)[1998] ICR 1044, [1998] IRLR 420, 586
 IRLB 11, EAT; on appeal [1999] 2 All ER 977, [1999] ICR 951,
 [1999] IRLR 318, 48 BMLR 1, CA 3.41, 3.42, 3.59, 3.62, 11.29
Clarke v Telewest Communications plc, ET 1301034/2004 (June 2005,
 unreported) 8.147
Clayton v Vigers [1989] ICR 713, [1990] IRLR 177 .... 8.74
Clymo v Wandsworth London Borough Council [1989] 2 CMLR 577,
 [1989] ICR 250, [1989] IRLR 241, [1989] 19 LS Gaz R 41, EAT ... 1.9, 1.29, 8.42,
 8.43
Coker v Lord Chancellor [2001] EWCA Civ 1756, [2002] ICR 321,
 [2002] IRLR 80, (2001) Times, 3 December, 145 Sol Jo LB 268, [2001]
 All ER (D) 334 (Nov) 1.11, 1.26, 1.44, 8.39
Coleman v Attridge Law, ET2303745/2005 (23 May 2006, unreported) 1.31, 8.148
Coleman v Attridge Law: Case C-303/06 [2007] ICR 654 .... 2.6
College of Ripon and York St John v Hobbs [2002] IRLR 185, [2001] All ER
 (D) 259 (Nov) 3.18
Collins v Royal National Theatre Board Ltd [2004] EWCA Civ 144,
 [2004] 2 All ER 851, [2004] IRLR 395, 78 BMLR 62, 148 Sol Jo LB
 236, [2004] All ER (D) 279 (Feb) 3.67, 3.82, 3.84
Commission for Racial Equality v Dutton [1989] IRLR 8, CA 6.5
Commission for Racial Equality v Imperial Society of Teachers of Dancing
 [1983] ICR 473, EAT 6.40
Commissioner of Police of the Metropolis v G S Virdi [2007]
 UKEAT/0338/06 .... 3.28
Commotion Ltd v Rutty [2006] ICR 290, sub nom Rutty v Commotion Ltd
 [2006] IRLR 171, [2006] All ER (D) 122 (Jan), EAT 8.144, 8.149
Community Task Force v Rimmer [1986] ICR 491, [1986] IRLR 203 .... 8.75
Connolly v HSBC Bank plc, ET 3202622/2001 (12 May 2003, Unreported) 8.112
Coote v Granada Hospitality Ltd: C-185/97 [1998] ECR I-5199, [1998] All
 ER (EC) 865, [1998] 3 CMLR 958, [1999] ICR 100, [1998] IRLR 656,
 [1998] All ER (D) 423, ECJ 1.25, 1.61, 8.44
Copsey v WWB Devon Clays Ltd [2005] EWCA Civ 932, [2005] ICR 1789,
 [2005] IRLR 811, [2005] NLJR 1484, (2005) Times, 25 August, [2005]
 All ER (D) 350 (Jul) 1.108
Cosgrove v Caesar & Howie (a firm) [2001] IRLR 653, [2001] All ER (D)
 118 (Jun), EAT 3.81
Coulombeau (Anna) v Enterprise Rent-A-Car (UK) Ltd, ET 2600296/06
 (10 February 2007, unreported) 8.123
Coutts & Co Plc v Cure [2005] ICR 2098 .... 10.5, 10.10, 10.15
Croft v Royal Mail Group plc [2003] EWCA Civ 1045, [2003] ICR 1425,
 [2003] IRLR 592, (2003) Times, 24 July, 147 Sol Jo LB 904, [2002] All
 ER (D) 179 (Sep) 1.111, 4.6, 4.11
Crofton v Yeboah [2002] EWCA Civ 794, [2002] IRLR 634, (2002) Times,
 20 June, [2002] All ER (D) 512 (May) 1.112
Croke v Hydro Aluminium Worcester Ltd [2007] ICR 1303 .... 3.112
Cross v British Airways plc [2005] IRLR 423, [2005] All ER (D) 10
 (Apr), EAT; affd [2006] EWCA Civ 549, [2006] ICR 1239, [2006] IRLR
 804, [2006] 21 LS Gaz R 24, (2006) Times, 5 June, [2006] All ER (D)
 148 (May) 2.8, 2.46, 11.31
Crown Suppliers (Property Services Agency) v Dawkins [1993] ICR 517, sub
 nom Dawkins v Department of the Environment [1993] IRLR
 284, CA 6.5
Cruickshank v VAW Motorcast Ltd [2002] ICR 729, [2002] IRLR 24, EAT 3.25

Cumbria County Council v Dow, EAT/0148/06 (12 Novemver 2007,
unreported) 11.26, 11.29, 11.31, 11.35

D

Dacas v Brook Street Bureau (UK) Ltd [2004] EWCA Civ 217, [2004] ICR
1437, [2004] IRLR 358, (2004) Times, 19 March, [2004] All ER (D) 125
(Mar) 1.8
Daley v Allied Suppliers Ltd [1983] ICR 90, [1983] IRLR 14, EAT 1.8
Dance v Dorothy Perkins Ltd [1978] ICR 760, sub nom Dorothy Perkins Ltd
v Dance [1977] IRLR 226, EAT 11.13
Danmark v Dansk Industri, acting for Royal Copenhagen A/S: C-400/93
[1995] EWCR I-1275 .... 11.31
Dattani v Chief Constable of West Mercia Police [2005] IRLR 327, [2005]
All ER (D) 95 (Feb), EAT 1.126
Dave v Robinska [2003] ICR 1248, [2003] NLJR 921, [2003] All ER (D) 35
(Jun), EAT 1.12
Davies v McCartneys [1989] ICR 705, [1989] IRLR 439, EAT 11.24
Day v T Pickles Farms Ltd [1999] IRLR 217 .... 8.89
De Keyser Ltd v Wilson [2001] IRLR 324, [2001] All ER (D) 237
(Mar), EAT 1.116, 3.39
Deane v Ealing London Borough Council [1993] ICR 329, [1993] IRLR
209, EAT 1.121
Defrenne v Belgium: 80/70 [1971] ECR 445, [1974] 1 CMLR 494, ECJ 11.19
Defrenne v Sabena: 43/75 [1981] 1 All ER 122, [1976] ECR 455,
[1976] 2 CMLR 98, [1976] ICR 547, ECJ 11.2
Defrenne v Sabena: 149/77 [1978] ECR 1365, [1978] 3 CMLR 312, ECJ 8.12
Degnan v Redcar and Cleveland Borough Council [2005] IRLR 179, [2004]
All ER (D) 55 (Nov), EAT; affd [2005] EWCA Civ 726, [2005] IRLR
615, [2005] All ER (D) 167 (Jun) 11.20
Dekker v Stichting Vormingscentrum voor Jong Volwassenen (VJV –
Centrum) Plus: C-177/88 [1990] ECR I-3941, [1992] ICR 325,
[1991] IRLR 27, ECJ 8.67, 8.73, 8.107
Department for Work and Pensions v Hall, UKEAT/0012/05/DA (2005),
unreported 3.16, 3.73
Department of Constitutional Affairs v Jones [2007] EWCA Civ 894, [2008]
All ER (D) 43 (Jan) 3.118
Department of the Environment v Fox [1980] 1 All ER 58, [1979] ICR 736,
123 Sol Jo 404, EAT 8.35
Derby Specialist Fabrication Ltd v Burton [2001] 2 All ER 840, [2001] IRLR
69, [2000] All ER (D) 1348, EAT 1.9
Derbyshire v St Helens Metropolitan Borough Council [2007] UKHL 16,
[2007] 3 All ER 81, [2007] ICR 841, [2007] IRLR 540, [2007] NLJR 635,
(2007) Times, 27 April, 151 Sol Jo LB 573, [2007] All ER (D) 207
(Apr) 1.61, 6.21
De Souza v Automobile Association [1986] ICR 514, [1986] IRLR 103, 130
Sol Jo 110, [1986] LS Gaz R 288, CA 1.9, 6.31
Dhanjal v British Steel plc, IT/50740/91 (1993), unreported 7.12
Dhatt v McDonald's Hamburgers Ltd [1991] 3 All ER 692, [1991] 1 WLR
527, [1991] ICR 238, [1991] IRLR 130, CA 1.36, 6.10
Diakou v Islington Unison 'A' Branch [1997] ICR 121, EAT 1.13
Dibro Ltd v Hore [1990] ICR 370, [1990] IRLR 129,
[1990] 13 LS Gaz R 43, EAT 11.15

Table of Cases

Difolco v NTL Group Ltd [2006] EWCA Civ 1508, 150 Sol Jo LB 1393, sub
  nom Difalco v NTL Group Ltd [2006] All ER (D) 136 (Oct) 3.72
Din v Carrington Viyella Ltd (Jersey Kapwood Ltd) [1982] ICR 256,
  [1982] IRLR 281, EAT 6.12
Dolphin v Hartlepool (2006) 150 Sol Jo LB 1290 .... 11.8
Dorothy Perkins Ltd v Dance. See Dance v Dorothy Perkins Ltd
Driskel v Peninsular Business Services Ltd [2000] IRLR 151 ...... 1.51, 6.25, 6.26, 6.31
D'Souza v London Borough of Lambeth [1997] IRLR 677, EAT; revsd sub
  nom Lambeth London Borough v D'Souza [1999] IRLR 240, CA 1.118
Dunham v Ashford Windows [2005] IRLR 608, [2005] All ER (D) 104
  (Jun), EAT 3.22, 3.38
Dunnachie v Kingston-Upon-Hull City Council [2004] EWCA Civ 84,
  [2004] 2 All ER 501, [2004] ICR 481, [2004] IRLR 287, [2004] NLJR
  248, (2004) Times, 26 February, 148 Sol Jo LB 233, [2004] All ER (D)
  185 (Feb); revsd [2004] UKHL 36, [2005] 1 AC 226, [2004] 3 All ER
  1011, [2004] 3 WLR 310, [2004] ICR 1052, [2004] IRLR 727,
  [2004] 33 LS Gaz R 34, [2004] NLJR 1156, 148 Sol Jo LB 909, [2004]
  All ER (D) 251 (Jul) 1.118, 10.37

E

Ealing London Borough v Race Relations Board [1972] AC 342,
  [1972] 1 All ER 105, [1972] 2 WLR 71, 116 Sol Jo 60, HL 6.6
East and North Hertfordshire NHS Trust v Dr A Fernando,
  UKEAT/0727/04/DM (10 March 2005, unreported) 1.23
Eaton Ltd v Nuttall [1977] 3 All ER 1131, [1977] 1 WLR 549, [1977] ICR
  272, [1977] IRLR 71, 12 ITR 197, 121 Sol Jo 353, EAT 11.13
EB v BA [2006] EWCA Civ 132, [2006] IRLR 471, [2006] All ER (D) 300
  (Feb) 1.92, 4.8
Edmund Nuttall Ltd v Butterfield [2006] ICR 77, [2005] IRLR 751, [2005]
  All ER (D) 488 (Jul), EAT 3.20
Ekpe v Metropolitan Police Comr [2001] ICR 1084, [2001] IRLR
  605, EAT 3.14, 3.25, 3.26
Electrolux Ltd v Hutchinson [1977] ICR 252, [1976] IRLR 410, 12 ITR
  40, EAT 11.13
Electronic Data Systems Ltd v Travis [2004] EWCA Civ 1256, 148 Sol Jo LB
  1033, [2004] All ER (D) 142 (Aug) 3.120
Elsner-Lakeberg v Land Nordrhein-Westfalen: C-285/02 [2004] 2 CMLR 874,
  [2005] IRLR 209, [2004] All ER (D) 423 (May), ECJ 11.20
Emokpae v Chamberlin Solicitors. See Chamberlin Solicitors v Emokpae
Enderby v Frenchay Health Authority [1994] ICR 112, [1992] IRLR 15, CA;
  refd sub nom Enderby v Frenchay Health Authority: C-127/92
  [1994] 1 All ER 495, [1993] ECR I-5535, [1994] 1 CMLR 8, [1994] ICR
  112, [1993] IRLR 591, ECJ 1.44, 11.25, 11.28, 11.35
England v The Governing Body of Turnford School [2003] All ER (D) 105
  (May) 10.25
Enterprise Glass Co Ltd v Miles [1990] ICR 787, EAT 1.111
Environment Agency v Rowan [2008] IRLR 20 .... 3.69, 3.81
Equal Opportunities Commission v Secretary of State for Trade and
  Industry [2007] EWHC 483 (Admin), [2007] 2 CMLR 1351, [2007] ICR
  1234, [2007] IRLR 327, [2007] All ER (D) 183 (Mar) 1.50, 3.86, 8.13, 8.24,
                                                    8.71, 8.73, 8.78, 8.108, 8.112

Essa v Laing Ltd [2004] EWCA Civ 02, [2004] ICR 746, [2004] IRLR 313,
(2004) Times, 29 January, (2004) 148 Sol Jo LB 146, [2004] All ER (D)
155 (Jan) 1.120, 3.120
Estorninho v Zoran Jokic (t/a Zorans Delicatessan), ET 2301487106
(18 August 2006, unreported) 1.9
Etam plc v Rowan [1989] IRLR 150, EAT 8.55
European Roma Rights Centre v Immigration Officer at Prague Airport
(United Nations High Commissioner for Refugees intervening)
[2004] UKHL 55, [2005] 2 AC 1, [2005] 1 All ER 527, [2005] 2 WLR 1,
[2005] IRLR 115, [2004] NLJR 1893, (2004) Times, 10 December, 149
Sol Jo LB 27, 18 BHRC 1, [2005] 3 LRC 657, [2004] All ER (D) 127
(Dec) 1.32
Evesham v North Hertfordshire Health Authority 2000] ICR 612 .... 11.16

F

Falkirk Council v Whyte [1997] IRLR 560, EAT 6.17
Famy v Hilton UK Hotels Ltd [2006] All ER (D) 112 (Oct), EAT 6.10
Farmiloe v Lane Group plc [2004] All ER (D) 08 (Mar) 3.111
Farthing v Ministry of Defence. See Ministry of Defence v Farthing
Fasuyi v Greenwich London Borough Council, EAT1078/99 (20 October
2000, unreported) 1.124
Faulkner v Chief Constable of Hampshire Constabulary, [2007]
UKEAT/0505/05/LA (1 March 2007, unreported) 1.44
Fearon v The Chief Constable of Derbyshire, UKEAT/0445/02/RN
(14 October 2003, unreported) 1.62
Félix Palacios de la Villa pret Cortefiel Servicios SA: C-411/05 [2007] IRLR
989 .... 2.3, 2.5, 2.8, 2.41
Fernandez v Parliamentary Commission for Administration, EAT (28 July
2006, unreported) 1.92
Fletcher v Blackpool Fylde & Wyre Hospitals NHS Trust. See Fletcher v
NHS Pensions Agency
Fletcher v NHS Pensions Agency [2005] ICR 1458, sub nom Fletcher v
Blackpool Fylde & Wyre Hospitals NHS Trust [2005] IRLR 689, [2005]
All ER (D) 57 (Jun), EAT 1.14, 8.47
Fletcher-Cooke v The Board of Governors of Hampton School, WL 504753
(2007), unreported 8.120
Fogarty v United Kingdom (Application 37112/97) (2001) 12 BHRC 132,
(2001) Times, 26 November, [2001] ECHR 37112/97, [2002] IRLR 148,
ECtHR 1.81
Forster v Cartwright Black [2004] ICR 1728, [2004] IRLR 781, [2004] All ER
(D) 93 (Aug), EAT 8.134
Foster v British Gas plc [1991] ICR 84, [1990] IRLR 353, ECJ; apld [191]
ICR 463, [1991] IRLR 268, HL 3.111
Fox v Rangecroft [2006] EWCA Civ 1112 .... 1.92
Francovich and Bonifaci v Italy: C-6/90 and C-9/90 [1991] ECR I-5357,
[1993] 2 CMLR 66, [1995] ICR 722, [1992] IRLR 84, ECJ 8.13
Fugler v Macmillan-London Hair Studios Ltd, ET 2205090/04 (15 July 2005,
unreported) 7.15
Furniture, Timber and Allied Trades Union v Modgill [1980] IRLR 142 .... 6.8

Table of Cases

G

GMB v Susie Radin Ltd [2004] EWCA Civ 180, [2004] 2 All ER 279,
[2004] ICR 893, [2004] 11 LS Gaz R 34, 148 Sol Jo LB 266, [2004] All
ER (D) 353 (Feb), sub nom Susie Radin Ltd v GMB [2004] IRLR 400,
(2004) Times, 16 March 10.14
GUS Home Shopping Ltd v Green [2001] IRLR 75 .... 8.112, 8.113
Gabri v Sun Hydraulics Limited, ET11301796/07 (25 June 2007,
unreported) 2.44
Garland v British Rail Engineering Ltd: 12/81 [1983] 2 AC 751,
[1982] 2 All ER 402, [1982] 2 WLR 918, [1982] 2 CMLR 174,
[1982] ICR 420, [1982] IRLR 257, 126 Sol Jo 309, HL 11.19
Garry v Ealing London Borough Council [2001] EWCA Civ 1282,
[2001] IRLR 681, [2001] All ER (D) 361 (Jul) 1.9, 6.17
Gbaja-Biamila v DHL International (UK) Ltd [2000] ICR 730 .... 1.117
Gerster v Freistaat Bayern: C-1/95 [1997] ECR I-5253, [1998] 1 CMLR 303,
[1998] ICR 327, [1997] IRLR 699, ECJ 11.30
Gibson v Scottish Ambulanc Service, UKEAT/0052/02 (31 October 2003,
unreported) 10.30, 10.31
Gibson Shipbrokers Ltd v Staples, UKEAT/0263/07 (18 September 2007,
unreported) 3.68
Gilbank v Miles [2006] EWCA Civ 543, [2006] ICR 1297, [2006] IRLR 538,
[2006] All ER (D) 160 (May) 1.112
Giles v Cornelia Care Homes, ET (August 2005, unreported) 8.147
Gillespie v Northern Health and Social Services Board: C-342/93 [1996] ECR
I-475, [1996] All ER (EC) 284, [1996] 2 CMLR 969, [1996] ICR 498,
[1996] IRLR 214, ECJ 8.68, 8.107, 8.128, 11.18, 11.19
Glasgow City Council v McNab [2007] IRLR 476, EAT 7.10
Glasgow City Council v Marshall [2000] 1 All ER 641, [2000] 1 WLR 333,
[2000] LGR 229, [2000] ICR 196, [2000] IRLR 272,
[2000] 07 LS Gaz R 39, 2000 SC (HL) 67, 2000 SLT 429, [2000] All ER
(D) 119, HL 11.25
Glasgow City Council v Zafar [1998] ICR 120, [1997] IRLR 231 .... 1.29, 1.30, 1.33,
1.84, 1.92, 1.94, 6.7, 6.9
Gloucester Working Men's Club and Institute v James [1986] ICR 603,
[1986] LS Gaz R 1803, EAT 5.2
Gómez v Continental Industrias del Caucho SA: C-342/01 [2004] ECR
I-2605, [2004] 2 CMLR 38, [2005] ICR 1040, [2004] IRLR 407, [2004]
All ER (D) 350 (Mar), ECJ 8.111
Goodwin v Patent Office [1999] ICR 302, [1999] IRLR 4, EAT ... 3.14, 3.18, 3.25, 3.26
Goodwin v United Kingdom (Application 28957/95) [2002] IRLR 664,
[2002] 2 FCR 577, [2002] 2 FLR 487, [2002] Fam Law 738, 13 BHRC
120, 67 BMLR 199, [2002] NLJR 1171, (2002) Times, 12 July, [2002] All
ER (D) 158 (Jul), ECtHR 4.4
Grant v United Kingdom (Application No 32570/03) [2006] All ER (D) 337
(May), ECtHR 4.4
Gravell v London Borough of Bexley, UKEAT/0587/06/CEA (2 March 2007,
unreported) 6.24, 6.27, 6.43
Gravell v Bexley London Borough Council [2007] All ER (D) 229
(May), EAT 1.49, 1.114
Green v DB Group Services (UK) Ltd [2006] EWHC 1898 (QB),
[2006] IRLR 764, [2006] All ER (D) 02 (Aug) 1.113
Greenhoff v Barnsley Metropolitan Borough Council [2006] ICR 1514,
[2006] All ER (D) 300 (Jun), EAT 1.117

Greenwood v British Airways plc [1999] ICR 969, [1999] IRLR 600, 625
    IRLB 3, EAT 3.36
Gregory v Tudsbury Ltd [1982] IRLR 267 .... 8.80, 8.82
Grieg v Community Industry [1979] ICR 356, [1979] IRLR 158, EAT 1.39, 8.55
Griffiths-Henry v Network Rail Infrastructure Ltd [2006] IRLR 865, [2006]
    All ER (D) 15 (Jul), EAT 1.92
Grundy v British Airways plc [2007] EWCA Civ 1020, [2007] All ER (D) 345
    (Oct) 1.44, 11.27
Grundy v British Airways plc [2008] IRLR 74 .... 11.27
Gunning v Mirror Group Newspapers Ltd [1986] 1 All ER 385, sub nom
    Mirror Group Newspapers Ltd v Gunning [1986] 1 WLR 546,
    [1986] ICR 145, [1986] IRLR 27, 130 Sol Jo 242, CA 1.8
Gwynedd county Council v Jones [1986] ICR 833 .... 6.5

H
Hall v. Woolston Hall Leisure Ltd [2001] ICR 99 .... 1.82, 6.54
Hallam v Avery [2001] UKHL 15, [2001] 1 WLR 655, [2001] LGR 278,
    [2001] ICR 408, [2001] 21 LS Gaz R 39, 145 Sol Jo LB 116,
    [2001] IRLR 312, [2001] All ER (D) 273 (Mar) 1.26
Hammersmith and Fulham London Borough Council v Farnsworth (EAT
    461/99) [2000] IRLR 691 .... 3.73
Hampson v Department of Education and Science [1990] 2 All ER 25,
    [1989] ICR 179, [1989] IRLR 69, 133 Sol Jo 151,
    [1989] 13 LS Gaz R 43, CA; revsd [1991] 1 AC 171, [1990] 2 All ER 513,
    [1990] 3 WLR 42, [1990] ICR 511, [1990] IRLR 302, 134 Sol Jo 1123,
    [1990] 26 LS Gaz R 39, [1990] NLJR 853, HL 1.44, 3.56, 3.111, 6.17
Handels-og Kontorfunktionaererernes Forbund i Danmark v Dansk
    Arbejdsgiverforening, acting on behalf of Danfoss: 109/88 [1989] ECR
    3199, [1991] 1 CMLR 8, [1991] ICR 74, [1989] IRLR 532, ECJ 2.23, 2.35,
                                                        11.30
Hardman v Mallon (t/a Orchard Lodge Nursing Home) [2002] 2 CMLR
    1467, [2002] IRLR 516, EAT 8.95
Hardwick v Football Association, UKEAT/1036/97 (1997), unreported 1.15, 8.46
Hardys & Hansons plc v Lax [2005] EWCA Civ 846, [2005] IRLR 726,
    (2005) Times, 26 July, [2005] All ER (D) 83 (Jul) 1.44, 2.8, 6.16, 8.147
Hardy & Hansons v Lax [2005] ICR 1565, [2005] IRLR 256 .... 11.25
Harris v NKL Automotive Limited, EAT/134/07/DM (3 October 2007,
    unreported) 6.5, 7.6
Harrods Ltd v Remick [1998] 1 All ER 52, [1998] ICR 156, [1997] IRLR
    583, CA 1.10, 8.36
Hart v Secretary of State foe Education and Skills, ET 2304973/2004
    (8 September 2005, unreported) 10.8, 10.9, 10.11, 10.19
Haughton v Olau Line (UK) Ltd [1986] 2 All ER 47, [1986] 1 WLR 504,
    [1986] 1 CMLR 730, [1986] ICR 357, [1986] IRLR 465, 130 Sol Jo
    356, CA 11.8
Hawkins v Darken (t/a Sawbridgeworth Motorcycles) [2004] EWCA Civ
    1755, [2004] All ER (D) 186 (Dec) 1.8
Hayward v Cammell Laird Shipbuilders Ltd [1988] AC 894, [1988] 2 All ER
    257, [1988] 2 WLR 1134, [1988] ICR 464, [1988] IRLR 257, 132 Sol Jo
    750, [1988] NLJR 133, HL 11.20
Heinz (HJ) Co Ltd v Kenrick [2000] IRLR 144 .... 3.64

Table of Cases

Hendricks v Metropolitan Police Comr [2002] EWCA Civ 1686,
[2003] 1 All ER 654, [2003] ICR 530, [2003] IRLR 96,
[2003] 05 LS Gaz R 30, (2002) Times, 6 December,146 Sol Jo LB 274,
[2002] All ER (D) 407 (Nov) 1.17, 1.23, 8.33

Hendrickson Europe Ltd v Christine Pipe [2003] All ER (D) 280 (Apr) 10.27, 10.31

HM Prison Service v Johnson EAT/0420/06 (3 April 2007, unreported) 3.81

HM Prison Service v Johnson [2007] IRLR 951 .... 3.64

Heron Corpn Ltd v Commis [1980] ICR 713, EAT 6.49

Herrero v Instituto Madrileno de la Salud (Imsalud): C-294/04 [2006] IRLR
296, [2006] All ER (D) 220 (Feb), ECJ 8.78

Hewett v Motorola Ltd [2004] IRLR 545, [2004] All ER (D) 190
(Mar), EAT 3.24

Hickman v Prest Ltd, ET 59236/95 (13 May 1996, unreported) 8.136

High Quality Lifestyles Ltd v Watts [2006] IRLR 850, [2006] All ER (D) 216
(Apr), EAT 3.50, 3.51

Higham v Meurig Lestyn Horton. See Horton v Higham

Higland Council v TGWU/Unison, GMB & Others, EATS/0020/07
(18 December 2007, unreported) 11.41

Hilde Schönheit v Stadt Frankfurt am Main: C-4/02 and C-5/02 [2003] ECR
I-12575, [2004] IRLR 983, [2003] All ER (D) 401 (Oct), ECJ 1.44, 2.8, 11.31,
11.36

Hill v Clacton Family Trust Ltd [2005] EWCA Civ 1456, [2005] All ER (D)
170 (Oct) 3.16, 3.38

Hill v Revenue Comrs: C-243/95 [1998] ECR I-3739, [1998] All ER (EC) 722,
[1998] 3 CMLR 81, [1999] ICR 48, [1998] IRLR 466,
[1998] 34 LS Gaz R 33, [1998] All ER (D) 277, ECJ 10.32, 11.30

Holc-Gale v Makers UK Ltd, UKEAT/0625/05/SM (30 November 2005,
unreported) 1.126

Home Office v Bailey [2005] IRLR 757, [2005] All ER (D) 499 (Jul), EAT 11.14,
11.35

Holmes v Active Sensors Limited, ET3100214/2007 (2007), unreported 2.44

Horsey v Dyfed County Council [1982] ICR 755, [1982] IRLR 395, EAT ... 1.32, 3.52,
5.6, 8.41

Horton v Higham [2004] EWCA Civ 941, [2004] 3 All ER 852, [2004] All ER
(D) 261 (Jul), sub nom Higham v Meurig Lestyn Horton [2005] ICR
292, 148 Sol Jo LB 911, sub nom 1 Pump Court Chambers v Horton
[2004] 33 LS Gaz R 34 .... 3.113

Hoyland v Asda Stores Ltd [2006] CSIH 21, [2006] IRLR 468, 2006 SLT
524, [2006] All ER (D) 133 (Apr) 8.42, 8.112, 8.113, 11.19

Hudson v University of Oxford [2007] EWCA Civ 336, [2007] All ER (D)
356 (Feb) 10.24, 10.25

Hughes v London Borough of Hackney (1986), unreported 1.102

Humphries v Chevler Packaging, UKEAT/0224/06/2407 (24 July 2006,
unreported) 3.118

Hurley v Mustoe [1981] ICR 490, [1981] IRLR 208, 125 Sol Jo 374, EAT 5.5

Hussain v Elonex plc [1999] IRLR 420 .... 6.29

Hussain v Midland Cosmetic Sales plc, EAT 915/00 (9 May 2002,
unreported) 6.17, 7.16

Hutchinson v Westward Television Ltd [1977] ICR 279, [1977] IRLR 69, 12
ITR 125, EAT 1.23

I

Ice Hockey Super League v Henry, EAT/1167/99 (2 March 2000,
  unreported) 1.36
IRC v Morgan [2002] IRLR 776, [2002] All ER (D) 67 (Feb), EAT 1.61
Insitu Cleaning Co Ltd v Heads [1995] IRLR 4 .... 1.51, 6.25, 6.31

J

James v Eastleigh Borough Council [1990] ICR 554, [1990] IRLR 288 .... 1.30, 1.36
James v Great North Eastern Railways [2005] All ER (D) 12 (May) 10.28, 10.29
James v Greenwich London Borough Council [2007] ICR 577, [2007] IRLR
  168, [2007] All ER (D) 12 (Jan), EAT 1.8
James v MSC Cruises Ltd, ET 2203173/05 (12 April 2006, unreported) 7.15
Jangra v Gate Gourmet London Ltd, EAT/608/01 (3 October 2002,
  unreported) 3.67
Jeffery v Secretary of State for Education [2006] ICR 1062, [2006] All ER
  (D) 99 (Jun), EAT 11.42
Jepson and Dyas-Elliot v Labour Party [1996] IRLR 116 .... 1.15, 8.65
Jenkins v Kingsgate (Clothing Production) [1981] 1 WLR 1485,
  [1980] 1 CMLR 81, [1981] ICR 715, [1980] IRLR 6, 125 Sol Jo
  587, EAT 11.23
Jeremiah v Ministry of Defence. See Ministry of Defence v Jeremiah
Johns v Solent SD, UKEAT/0499/07/MAA (30 October 2007, unreported) 2.41
Johnston v Chief Constable of the Royal Ulster Constabulary: 222/84
  [1987] QB 129, [1986] 3 All ER 135, [1986] ECR 1651, [1986] 3 WLR
  1038, [1986] 3 CMLR 240, [1987] ICR 83, [1986] IRLR 263, 130 Sol Jo
  953, [1987] LS Gaz R 188, ECJ 8.60, 8.61
Jones v Post Office [2001] EWCA Civ 558, [2001] ICR 805, [2001] IRLR
  384 .... 3.66
Jones v Tower Boot Co Ltd [1997] 2 All ER 406, [1997] ICR 254,
  [1997] IRLR 168, [1997] NLJR 60, CA 1.110, 6.31, 9.14
Jones v University of Manchester [1993] ICR 474, [1993] IRLR 218,
  [1993] 10 LS Gaz R 33, 137 Sol Jo LB 14, CA 1.44
Jørgensen v Foreningen af Speciallæger [2000] IRLR 726 .... 1.44
Joyce v Northern Microwave Distributors Ltd, ET/5564/93 (16 August 1993,
  unreported) 8.136

K

KB v National Health Service Pensions Agency: C-117/01 [2004] ECR I-541,
  [2004] All ER (EC) 1089, [2004] 1 CMLR 931, [2004] ICR 781,
  [2004] IRLR 240, [2004] 1 FLR 683, (2004) Times, 15 January, [2004]
  All ER (D) 03 (Jan), ECJ 4.5, 5.3
Kalanke v Freie Hansestadt Bremen: C-450/93 [1995] ECR I-3051, [1996]
  All ER (EC) 66, [1996] 1 CMLR 175, [1996] ICR 314, [1995] IRLR 660,
  ECJ 1.101, 8.63
Kapadia v Lambeth London Borough Council [2000] IRLR 14, 625 IRLB
  2, EAT; affd [2000] IRLR 699, 57 BMLR 170, CA 3.17, 3.27, 3.37
Kaveri v Bermingham Power Ltd, ET 08037/95 (27 March 1996,
  unreported) 8.136
Kells v Pilkington plc [2002] IRLR 693, [2002] All ER (D) 33 (May), EAT 11.11
Kelly v Northern Ireland Housing Executive [1999] 1 AC 428, [1998] 3 WLR
  735, [1998] ICR 828, [1998] IRLR 593, [1998] 36 LS Gaz R 31, 142 Sol
  Jo LB 254, HL 1.8, 1.15

Table of Cases

Kenny v Hampshire Constabulary [1998] ICR 27, [1999] IRLR 76, EAT 3.74
Khan v G and J Spencer Group (t/a NIC Hygeine Limited), ET 1803250/04
   (9 January 2005, unreported) 7.15
Khan v General Medical Council [1996] ICR 1032, [1994] IRLR 646, CA 1.15
Khan v Royal Mail Groupl, UKEAT/0480/06/DA (5 December 2007,
   unreported) 3.68
Kidd v DRG (UK) Ltd [1985] IRLR 190 .... 5.5
Kiiski v Tampereen kaupunki: C-116/06 [2007] All ER (D) 120 (Sep) 8.131
King v Great Britain-China Centre [1992] ICR 516, [1991] IRLR 513, CA 1.84,
   1.92, 1.94, 6.7
Kingston and Richmond Area Health Authority v Kaur [1981] ICR 631,
   [1981] IRLR 337, EAT 6.17, 7.16
Kirby v Manpower Services Commission [1980] 3 All ER 334, [1980] 1 WLR
   725, [1980] ICR 420, [1980] IRLR 229, 124 Sol Jo 326, EAT 1.62, 6.19
Kirby v National Probation Service [2006] IRLR 508, [2006] All ER (D) 111
   (Mar), EAT 6.19
Kirton v Tetrosyl Ltd [2003] EWCA Civ 619, [2003] IRLR 353, 147 Sol Jo
   LB 474, [2003] All ER (D) 190 (Apr) 3.30
Knight v A-G [1979] ICR 194, 123 Sol Jo 32, EAT 8.35
Kokkinakis v Greece (1993) 17 EHRR 397, ECtHR 7.6
Kuddus v Chief Constable of Leicestershire Constabulary [2001] UKHL 29,
   [2002] 2 AC 122, [2001] 3 All ER 193, [2001] 2 WLR 1789,
   [2001] 28 LS Gaz R 43, [2001] NLJR 936, 145 Sol Jo LB 166, [2001] All
   ER (D) 30 (Jun) 1.121

L

Laing v Manchester City Council [2006] ICR 1519, [2006] IRLR 748, [2006]
   All ER (D) 452 (Jul), EAT 1.92
Lambeth London Borough Council v Commission for Racial Equality
   [1990] ICR 768, [1990] IRLR 231, CA 1.102, 6.47, 8.55
Lambeth London Borough v D'Souz10. See D'Souza v London Borough of
   Lambeth
Lana v Positive Action Training In Housing (London) Ltd [2001] IRLR 501,
   [2001] All ER (D) 23 (Jun), EAT 1.14, 1.114, 6.42, 8.47
Land Brandenburg v Sass: C-284/02 [2005] IRLR 147, [2004] All ER (D) 310
   (Nov), ECJ 8.78, 8.108, 11.31
Lane Group plc v Farmiloe, UKEAT 0352/03/2201 (2004), unreported 3.56, 3.111
Lasertop Ltd v Webster [1997] ICR 828, [1997] IRLR 498, 572 IRLB
   14, EAT 8.55
Latchman v Reed Business Information Ltd [2002] ICR 1453, [2002] All ER
   (D) 287 (Feb), EAT 3.36
Law Hospital NHS Trust v Rush [2001] IRLR 611, 2002 SC 24, 2002 SLT 7,
   Ct of Sess 3.25
Lawrence v Regent Office Care Ltd: C-320/00 [2002] ECR I-7325,
   [2002] 3 CMLR 761, [2003] ICR 1092, [2002] IRLR 822, (2002) Times,
   10 October, [2002] All ER (D) 84 (Sep), ECJ 11.17
Lawson v Serco Ltd [2006] UKHL 3, [2006] 1 All ER 823, [2006] IRLR 289,
   [2006] 06 LS Gaz R 36, [2006] NLJR 184, 150 Sol Jo LB 131, [2006] All
   ER (D) 184 (Jan) 1.24, 3.110
Leeds Rhinos Rugby Club v Sterling, EAT/267/01 (9 September 2002,
   unreported) 1.124
Leighton v Michael [1995] ICR 1091, [1996] IRLR 67, EAT 6.54

Leonard v Southern Derbyshire Chamber of Commerce [2001] IRLR
19, EAT 3.26, 3.28

Leverton v Clwyd County Council [1989] AC 706, [1989] 1 All ER 78,
[1989] 2 WLR 47, 87 LGR 269, [1989] ICR 33, [1989] IRLR 28, 133 Sol
Jo 45, [1989] 19 LS Gaz R 41, HL 11.17

Levez v TH Jennings (Harlow Pools) Ltd: C-326/96 [1998] ECR I-7835,
[1999] All ER (EC) 1, [1999] 2 CMLR 363, [1999] ICR 521,
[1999] IRLR 36, 608 IRLB 3, [1998] All ER (D) 662, ECJ 11.38

Lewen v Denda: C-333/97 [1999] ECR I-7243, [2000] All ER (EC) 261,
[2000] 2 CMLR 38, [2000] IRLR 67, ECJ 8.107, 8.112, 8.113

Lewisham London Borough Council v Malcolm [2007] EWCA Civ 763,
[2007] 32 EG 88 (CS), (2007) Times, 28 August, [2007] All ER (D) 401
(Jul) 3.62, 3.64

Lindsay v Alliance & Leicester plc [2000] ICR 1234, [2000] All ER (D)
282, EAT 6.18

Lisk-Carew v Birmingham City Council [2004] EWCA Civ 565,
[2004] 20 LS Gaz R 35, (2004) Times, 7 June, [2004] All ER (D) 215
(Apr) 1.60

Litster v Forth Dry Dock and Engineering Co Ltd [1990] 1 AC 546,
[1989] 1 All ER 1134, [1989] 2 WLR 634, [1989] ICR 341, [1989] IRLR
161, 133 Sol Jo 455, [1989] NLJR 400, 1989 SC (HL) 96, HL 1.110, 5.2

Litster v Forth Dry Dock and Engineering Co Ltd [1990] 1 AC 546,
[1989] IRLR 161, HL 5.2

Lloyd-Briden v Worthing College [2007] 3 CMLR 27 .... 2.3

Lloyd-Briden v Worthing College UKEAT/0065/07/RN (22 June 2007,
unreported) 2.41

Lommers v Minister van Landbouw, Natuurbeheer en Visserij: C-476/99
[2002] ECR I-2891, [2004] 2 CMLR 1141, [2002] IRLR 430, [2002] All
ER (D) 280 (Mar), ECJ 1.101, 8.63, 11.19

London Borough of Camden v Price-Job, UKEAT/0507/06/DM
(18 December 2007, unreported) 3.81

London Borough of Greenwich v Robinson, EAT 745/94 (1995),
unreported 8.136

London Clubs Management Ltd v Hood [2001] IRLR 719, EAT 3.60

London Underground Ltd v Edwards [1995] ICR 574, [1995] IRLR
355, EAT 1.44

London Underground Ltd v Edwards (No 2) [1999] ICR 494, [1998] IRLR
364, [1998] 25 LS Gaz R 32, [1998] NLJR 905, 142 Sol Jo LB 182,
[1998] All ER (D) 231, CA 1.44, 8.147, 11.27

Loughran v Northern Ireland Housing Executive [1999] 1 AC 428,
[1998] 3 WLR 735, [1998] ICR 828, [1998] IRLR 593,
[1998] 36 LS Gaz R 31, 142 Sol Jo LB 254, HL 1.8, 1.15

M

MHC Consulting Services Ltd v Tansell [2000] ICR 789, 144 Sol Jo LB 205,
sub nom Abbey Life Assurance Co Ltd v Tansell [2000] IRLR 387,
[2000] All ER (D) 483, CA 1.10, 3.112, 8.36

Table of Cases

Macarthys Ltd v Smith: 129/79 [1979] 3 All ER 325, [1979] 1 WLR 1189,
   [1979] 3 CMLR 44, [1979] ICR 785, [1979] IRLR 316, 123 Sol Jo
   603, CA; refd [1981] QB 180, [1981] 1 All ER 111, [1980] ECR 1275,
   [1980] 3 WLR 929, [1980] 2 CMLR 205, [1980] ICR 672, [1980] IRLR
   210, 124 Sol Jo 808, ECJ; apld [1981] QB 180, [1981] 1 All ER 111,
   [1980] 3 WLR 929, [1980] 2 CMLR 217, [1980] ICR 672, [1980] IRLR
   210, 124 Sol Jo 808, C 11.10, 11.11
McDonagh and Triesman v Ali [2002] EWCA Civ 93, [2002] ICR 1026,
   [2002] IRLR 489, (2002) Times, 11 March, [2002] All ER (D) 87 (Feb) 1.15,
                                                                                       8.65
Macdonald v Advocate General for Scotland [2003] UKHL 34,
   [2004] 1 All ER 339, [2003] ICR 937, [2003] IRLR 512,
   [2003] 29 LS Gaz R 36, (2003) Times, 20 June, 2003 SLT 1158, 2003
   SCLR 814, 147 Sol Jo LB 782, [2004] 2 LRC 111, [2003] All ER (D) 259
   (Jun) 1.44, 1.50, 1.114, 6.27, 6.43, 9.2
McDougall v Richmond Adult Community College [2007] ICR 1567,
   [2007] IRLR 771 .... 3.16, 3.36
McDougall v Richmond Adult Community College [2008] EWCA Civ 4,
   [2008] All ER (D) 54 (Jan) 3.36
McLean v Paris Travel Service Ltd [1976] IRLR 202, Ind Trib 5.2, 5.4
McClintock v. Department of Constitutional Affairs [2008] IRLR 29 .... 7.6, 7.7
McMenemy v Capita Business Services Limites [2007] IRLR 400 .... 10.28, 1130, 10.31
McNicol v Balfour Beatty Rail Maintenance Ltd [2002] ICR 381,
   [2001] IRLR 644, [2001] All ER (D) 404 (Jul), EAT; affd [2002] EWCA
   Civ 1074, [2002] ICR 1498, [2002] IRLR 711, 71 BMLR 1, (2002)
   Times, 26 August, [2002] All ER (D) 407 (Jul) 3.18, 3.21
Madarassy v Nomura International plc [2007] EWCA Civ 33, [2007] ICR
   867, [2007] IRLR 246, [2007] All ER (D) 226 (Jan) 1.29, 1.38, 1.39, 1.83, 1.92,
                                                                                 6.7, 8.95
Madden v Preferred Technical Group CHA Ltd [2004] EWCA Civ 1178,
   [2005] IRLR 46, 148 Sol Jo LB 1064, [2004] All ER (D) 153 (Aug) 1.38, 6.10
Maidment v Cooper & Co (Birmingham) Ltd [1978] ICR 1094, [1978] IRLR
   462, 13 ITR 458, EAT 11.13
Majrowski v Guy's and St Thomas' NHS Trust [2006] UKHL 34,
   [2006] 4 All ER 395, [2006] 3 WLR 125, [2006] ICR 1199, [2006] IRLR
   695, [2006] NLJR 1173, (2006) Times, 13 July, 150 Sol Jo LB 986, [2006]
   All ER (D) 146 (Jul) 1.53, 1.113, 6.31
Malik v British Home Stores (ET Case No 29014/79) (1980), unreported 7.16
Mandla v Dowell Lee [1983] 2 AC 548, [1983] 1 All ER 1062, [1983] 2 WLR
   620, [1983] ICR 385, [1983] IRLR 209, 127 Sol Jo 242, HL 6.5, 7.2
Mangold v Helm: C-144/04 [2006] All ER (EC) 383, [2006] IRLR 143, [2005]
   All ER (D) 287 (Nov), ECJ 2.3, 2.8, 2.41, 8.13
Marks & Spencer v Martins [1998] ICR 1005, [1998] IRLR 326 .... 6.9
Marks & Spencer plc v Williams-Ryan [2005] EWCA Civ 470, [2005] ICR
   1293, [2005] IRLR 562, 149 Sol Jo LB 511, [2005] All ER (D) 248
   (Apr) 1.23
Marleasing SA v La Comercial Internacional de Alimentacion SA: C-106/89
   [1990] ECR I-4135, [1992] 1 CMLR 305, [1993] BCC 421, 135 Sol Jo 15,
   ECJ 2.4
Marschall v Land Nordrhein-Westfalen: C-409/95 [1997] ECR I-6363, [1997]
   All ER (EC) 865, [1998] 1 CMLR 547, [1998] IRLR 39, ECJ 1.101, 8.63

1

Marshall v Southampton and South West Hampshire Area Health Authority
(Teaching): 152/84 [1986] QB 401, [1986] 2 All ER 584, [1986] ECR 723,
[1986] 2 WLR 780, [1986] 1 CMLR 688, [1986] ICR 335, [1986] IRLR
140, 130 Sol Jo 340, [1986] LS Gaz R 1720, ECJ 1.19
Marshall v Southampton and South West Hampshire Area Health Authority
(No 2): C-271/91 [1994] QB 126, [1993] 4 All ER 586, [1993] ECR
I-4367, [1993] 3 WLR 1054, [1993] 3 CMLR 293, [1993] ICR 893,
[1993] IRLR 445, ECJ; apld sub nom Marshall v Southampton and
South-West Hampshire Area Health Authority (Teaching) (No 2)
[1994] 1 AC 530n, [1994] 1 All ER 736n, [1994] 2 WLR 392, [1994] ICR
242n, HL 8.15
Martin v Lancehawk Ltd (trading as European Telecom Solutions) [2004] All
ER (D) 400 (Mar), EAT 1.30
Matthews v Kent and Medway Towns Fire Authority [2004] ICR 257,
[2003] IRLR 732, [2003] All ER (D) 90 (Aug), EAT; affd [2004] EWCA
Civ 844, [2004] 3 All ER 620, [2005] ICR 84, [2004] IRLR 697, (2004)
Times, 8 July, 148 Sol Jo LB 876, [2004] All ER (D) 47 (Jul); revsd in
part [2006] UKHL 8, [2006] 2 All ER 171, [2006] ICR 365, [2006] IRLR
367, [2006] NLJR 420, (2006) Times, 2 March, [2006] All ER (D) 15
(Mar) 10.8, 10.9, 10.25, 10.27, 10.28, 10.32
Mattis v Pollock (trading as Flamingos Nightclub) [2003] EWCA Civ 887,
[2004] 4 All ER 85, [2003] 1 WLR 2158, [2003] ICR 1335, [2003] IRLR
603, (2003) Times, 16 July, 147 Sol Jo LB 816, [2003] All ER (D) 10
(Jul) 1.110
Mayuff v The Governing Body of Bishop Challoner Catholic Collegiate
School, ET 3202398/04 (21 December 2005, unreported) 1.9, 7.15
Mayuff v The Mayor and Burgesses of the London Borough of Tower
Hamlets, ET 3202398/04 (21 December 2005, unreported) 7.15
Meade-Hill and National Union of Civil and Public Servants v British
Council [1996] 1 All ER 79, [1995] ICR 847, [1995] IRLR 478, CA 1.11, 1.44,
8.39
Meer v Tower Hamlets London Borough Council [1988] IRLR 399, CA 6.17
Meikle v Nottinghamshire County Council [2004] EWCA Civ 859,
[2004] 4 All ER 97, [2005] ICR 1, [2004] IRLR 703 .... 3.67
Metropolitan Police Comr v Harley [2001] ICR 927, [2001] IRLR 263, [2001]
All ER (D) 216 (Feb), EAT 1.9
Mid-Staffordshire General Hospitals NHS Trust v Cambridge [2003] IRLR
566, [2003] All ER (D) 06 (Sep) 3.81
Middlesbrough Borough Council v Surtees [2007] ICR 1644 .... 11.25, 11.26, 11.28,
11.29, 11.33
Millar v IRC [2005] CSIH 71, [2006] IRLR 112, 2005 SLT 1074, [2005] All
ER (D) 205 (Oct) 3.22
Mingeley v Pennock & Ivory (t/a Amber Cars) [2004] EWCA Civ 328,
[2004] ICR 727, [2004] IRLR 373, [2004] 11 LS Gaz R 33, (2004) Times,
4 March, [2004] All ER (D) 132 (Feb) 1.8
Minister of Home Affairs v Fourie (Case CCT 60/04, Judgment 1 December
2005) 5.9
Ministry of Defence v Bristow [1996] ICR 544, EAT 1.118
Ministry of Defence v Cannock [1995] 2 All ER 449, [1994] ICR 918,
[1994] IRLR 509, EAT 8.120
Ministry of Defence v Farthing [1980] ICR 705, sub nom Farthing v
Ministry of Defence [1980] IRLR 402, CA 11.33

Table of Cases

Ministry of Defence v Gandiya [2004] ICR 1708, [2004] All ER (D) 54
  (Jul), EAT; revsd sub nom Saggar v Ministry of Defence [2005] EWCA
  Civ 413, [2005] ICR 1073, [2005] IRLR 618, (2005) Times, 9 May, [2005]
  All ER (D) 382 (Apr) 1.24
Ministry of Defence v Hunt [1996] ICR 554, [1996] IRLR 139 .... 8.120
Ministry of Defence v Jeremiah [1980] QB 87, [1979] 3 All ER 833,
  [1979] 3 WLR 857, [1980] ICR 13, 123 Sol Jo 735, sub nom Jeremiah v
  Ministry of Defence [1979] IRLR 436, CA 1.9, 1.28, 6.8, 6.9
Miron v Trundel [1995] SCR 418 .... 5.9
Mirror Group Newspapers Ltd v Gunning. See Gunning v Mirror Group
  Newspapers Ltd
Morgan v Staffordshire University [2002] ICR 475, [2002] IRLR 190, EAT 3.22
Mowat-Brown v University of Surrey [2002] IRLR 235, EAT 3.31, 3.32
Moyhing v Barts and London NHS Trust [2006] IRLR 860, [2006] All ER
  (D) 64 (Jun), EAT 1.14, 8.47, 8.55
Moyhing v Homerton University Hospitals NHS Trust [2005] All ER (D) 03
  (Sep), EAT 8.47
Murphy v Bort Telecom Eireann: 157/86 [1988] ECR 673, [1988] 1 CMLR
  879, [1988] ICR 445, [1988] IRLR 267, (1988) Times, 6 February, ECJ 11.16
Murray v Newham Citizens Advice Bureau Ltd [2003] ICR 643, [2003] IRLR
  340, [2003] All ER (D) 138 (Mar) EAT 3.20

N

Nagarajan v London Regional Transport [2000] 1 AC 501, [1999] 4 All ER
  65, [1999] 3 WLR 425, [1999] ICR 877, [1999] IRLR 572,
  [1999] 31 LS Gaz R 36, 143 Sol Jo LB 219, HL 1.11, 1.30, 1.52, 1.60, 6.12,
                                                              6.21, 8.39, 10.31
National Federation of Self-Employed and Small Businesses Ltd v Philpott
  [1997] ICR 518, [1997] IRLR 340, EAT 8.13
NUT v Watson, EAT (13 June 2006, unreported) 1.92
National Vulcan Engineering Insurance Group Ltd v Wade [1979] QB 132,
  [1978] 3 All ER 121, [1978] 3 WLR 214, [1978] ICR 800, [1978] IRLR
  225, 13 ITR 212, 122 Sol Jo 470, CA 11.22
Nelson v Carillion Services Ltd [2003] EWCA Civ 544, [2003] ICR 1256,
  [2003] IRLR 428, [2003] 26 LS Gaz R 36, (2003) Times, 2 May, 147 Sol
  Jo LB 504, [2003] All ER (D) 253 (Apr) 1.93, 11.26
Nelson v Tyne and Wear Passenger Transport Executive [1978] ICR 1183,
  122 Sol Jo 642, EAT 1.124
New Southern Railway Ltd v Quinn [2006] ICR 761, [2006] IRLR 266,
  [2005] All ER (D) 367 (Nov), EAT 8.92, 8.93
New Southern Railway Ltd v Quinn, UKEAT/0313/05 (28 November 2005,
  unreported) 8.91
New Southern Railways Ltd (formerly South Central Trains) v Rodway
  [2005] EWCA Civ 443, [2005] ICR 1162, sub nom Rodway v New
  Southern Railways Ltd [2005] IRLR 583, (2005) Times, 21 April, [2005]
  All ER (D) 216 (Apr) 8.131, 8.132
Nimz v Freie und Hansestadt Hamburg: C-184/89 [1991] ECR I-297,
  [1992] 3 CMLR 699, [1991] IRLR 222, ECJ 11.30
Noone v North West Thames Regional Health Authority. See North West
  Thames Regional Health Authority v Noone
North West Thames Regional Health Authority v Noone [1988] ICR 813,
  sub nom Noone v North West Thames Regional Health Authority
  (No 2) [1988] IRLR 530, CA 1.124

North Western Health Board v McKenna: C-191/03 [2006] All ER (EC) 455,
[2006] ICR 477, [2005] IRLR 895, [2005] All ER (D) 47 (Sep), ECJ 8.107
North Yorkshire County Council v Ratcliffe. See Ratcliffe v North Yorkshire
County Council

O

O'Brien v Sim-Chem Ltd [1980] 3 All ER 132, [1980] 1 WLR 1011,
[1980] ICR 573, [1980] IRLR 373, 124 Sol Jo 560, HL 11.14
O'Flynn v Adjudication Officer: C-237/94 [1996] ECR I-2617, [1996] All ER
(EC) 541, [1996] 3 CMLR 103, [1998] ICR 608, ECJ 1.44
O'Hanlon v Revenue and Customs Comrs [2007] EWCA Civ 283, [2007] ICR
1359, [2007] IRLR 404, (2007) Times, 20 April, [2007] All ER (D) 516
(Mar) 3.60, 3.66, 3.68, 3.78, 3.79, 3.85
O'Hanlon v Revenue and Customs Comrs [2006] ICR 1579, [2006] IRLR
840, [2006] All ER (D) 53 (Aug), EAT; affd [2007] EWCA Civ 283,
[2007] IRLR 404, [2007] All ER (D) 516 (Mar) 11.31
Ojinnaka v Sheffield College, UKEAT/0201/00 (2001), unreported 8.78
Ojutiku v Manpower Services Commission [1982] ICR 661, [1982] IRLR
418, CA 6.17
1 Pump Court Chambers v Horton. See Horton v Higham
O'Neill v Bedfordshire County Council [1997] ICR 33, [1996] IRLR 372 ..... 3.20, 8.73
O'Neill v Governors of St Thomas More RCVA Upper School [1997] ICR
33, [1996] IRLR 372, EAT 1.30, 8.73
O'Shea (CJ) Construction Ltd v Bassi [1998] ICR 1130, EAT1.10
Owen and Briggs v James [1982] ICR 618, [1982] IRLR 502, CA 6.12
Oyarce v Chesire County Council [2007] ICR 1693, [2007] All ER (D) 101
(Aug) 1.64, 1.94

P

P v Cornwall County Council [1996] IRLR 347 .... 4.2
P v S: C–13/94 [1996] All ER (EC) 397, [1996] ECR I–2143, [1996] 2 CMLR
247, [1996] ICR 795, [1996] IRLR 347, sub nom P v S (sex
discrimination): C–13/94 [1997] 2 FCR 180, [1996] 2 FLR 347,
[1996] Fam Law 609, ECJ 4.2, 4.3, 4.4
P Lindorfer v Council: C-227/04 (11 September 2007, unreported) 2.4, 2.5, 2.8
Padgett v Serota and the Board of Trustess of the Tate Gallery, EAT/97/07 &
EAT/99/07 (2007), unreported 7.9
Page v Freight Hire (Tank Haulage) Ltd [1981] 1 All ER 394, [1981] ICR
299, [1981] IRLR 13, EAT 8.60
Panesar v Nestlé Co Ltd [1980] ICR 144n, [1980] IRLR 64, 130 NLJ
139, CA 6.14, 6.17
Paquay v Societe d'architectes Hoet & Minne SPRL: C-460/06 [2007] All ER
(D) 137 (Oct), ECJ 8.74
Parliamentary Comr for Administration v Fernandez [2004] 2 CMLR 59,
[2004] ICR 123, [2004] IRLR 22, [2003] All ER (D) 115 (Oct), EAT 11.25,
11.29
Partnership in Care v Laing, UKEAT/0622/06/0102 (2007), unreported 3.112
Patefield v Belfast City Council [2000] IRLR 664, CA 8.118
Paterson v Commissioner of Police of the Metropolis [2007] ICR 1522,
[2007] IRLR 763 .... 3.18, 3.26

Table of Cases

Patterson v Legal Services Commission [2003] EWCA Civ 1558, [2004] ICR
312, [2004] IRLR 153, [2004] 02 LS Gaz R 28, (2003) Times,
20 November, 147 Sol Jo LB 1364, [2003] All ER (D) 140 (Nov) 1.8, 1.15

Peake v Automotive Products Ltd [1978] QB 233, [1978] 1 All ER 106,
[1977] 3 WLR 853, [1977] ICR 968, 121 Sol Jo 644, sub nom
Automotive Products Ltd v Peake [1977] IRLR 365, 12 ITR 428, CA 1.98.43

Peake v Automotive Products Ltd [1977] QB 780, [1977] 2 WLR 751,
[1977] ICR 480, [1977] IRLR 105, 12 ITR 259, 121 Sol Jo 222, EAT;
revsd [1978] QB 233, [1978] 1 All ER 106, [1977] 3 WLR 853,
[1977] ICR 968, 121 Sol Jo 644, sub nom Automotive Products Ltd v
Peake [1977] IRLR 365, 12 ITR 428, CA 8.42, 11.2

Pearce v Governing Body of Mayfield School [2003] UKHL 34,
[2004] 1 All ER 339, [2003] ICR 937, [2003] IRLR 512,
[2003] 29 LS Gaz R 36, (2003) Times, 20 June, 2003 SLT 1158, 2003
SCLR 814, 147 Sol Jo LB 782, [2004] 2 LRC 111, [2003] All ER (D) 259
(Jun) 6.27, 6.29, 6.43

Perceval-Price v Department of Economic Development [2000] IRLR 380 .... 1.19

Perera v Civil Service Commission (No 2) [1983] ICR 428, [1983] IRLR
166, CA 1.44

Peterson v Hewlett-Packard, USA Court of Appeals, 9th Circuit, January
2004 .... 9.19

Pickering v Kingston Mobile Unit [1978] IRLR 10 .... 5.2

Pickstone v Freemans plc [1989] AC 66, [1987] 3 All ER 756, [1987] 3 WLR
811, [1987] 2 CMLR 572, [1987] ICR 867, [1987] IRLR 218, 131 Sol Jo
538, [1987] LS Gaz R 1409, [1987] NLJ Rep 315, CA; affd [1989] AC 66,
[1988] 2 All ER 803, [1988] 3 WLR 265, [1988] 3 CMLR 221,
[1988] ICR 697, [1988] IRLR 357, 132 Sol Jo 994, [1988] NLJR
193, HL 11.15

Pointon v University of Sussex [1979] IRLR 119, CA 11.16

Porcelli v Strathclyde Regional Council [1986] ICR 564, sub nom Strathclyde
Regional Council v Porcelli [1986] IRLR 134, Ct of Sess 1.47

Post Office v Chin, EAT162/97 (24 February 1998, unreported) 6.24, 6.31

Power v Panasonic UK Ltd [2003] IRLR 151, 72 BMLR 1, EAT 3.20

Powerhouse Retail Ltd v Burroughs. See Preston v Wolverhampton
Healthcare NHS Trust

Preston v Wolverhampton Healthcare NHS Trust and Secretary of State for
Health [1998] 1 All ER 528, [1998] 1 WLR 280, [1998] ICR 227,
[1998] IRLR 197, [1998] 08 LS Gaz R 33, 142 Sol Jo LB 82, 566 IRLB
12, HL; refd C-78/98 [2001] 2 AC 415, [2000] ECR I-3201, [2000] All ER
(EC) 714, [2001] 2 WLR 408, [2000] 2 CMLR 837, [2000] ICR 961,
[2000] IRLR 506, [2000] All ER (D) 663, ECJ; apld sub nom Preston v
Wolverhamptom Healthcare NHS Trust (No 2) [2001] UKHL 5,
[2001] 2 AC 455, [2001] 3 All ER 947, [2001] 2 WLR 448, [2001] ICR
217, [2001] IRLR 237, (2001) Times, 8 February, 145 Sol Jo LB 55,
[2001] All ER (D) 99 (Feb) 11.42

Preston v Wolverhampton Healthcare NHS Trust [2006] UKHL 13,
[2006] 3 All ER 193, [2006] ICR 606, (2006) Times, 13 March, [2006] All
ER (D) 102 (Mar), sub nom Powerhouse Retail Ltd v Burroughs
[2006] IRLR 381, 150 Sol Jo LB 364 .... 1.23, 11.42

Price v Civil Service Commission (No 2) [1978] IRLR 3, Ind Trib 8.39

Project Management Institute v Latiff [2007] IRLR 57 .... 1.93

Q

Qua v John Ford Morrison Solicitors [2003] ICR 482, [2003] IRLR 184,
(2003) Times, 6 February, [2003] NLJR 95, [2003] All ER (D) 29
(Jan), EAT 8.134
Quinnen v Hovells [1984] ICR 525, [1984] IRLR 227, 128 Sol Jo 431, EAT ... 1.8, 11.7
Qureshi v Victoria University of Manchester [2001] ICR 863 .... 6.31

R

R v Department of Health, ex p Gandhi [1991] 4 All ER 547, [1991] 1 WLR
1053, [1991] ICR 805, [1991] IRLR 431, DC 1.15
R (on the application of Begum) v Headteacher and Governors of Denbigh
High School [2006] UKHL 15, [2007] AC 100, [2006] 2 All ER 487,
[2006] 2 WLR 719, [2006] 2 FCR 613, [2006] NLJR 552, (2006) Times,
23 March, 150 Sol Jo LB 399, [2006] 4 LRC 543, [2006] All ER (D) 320
(Mar), sub nom R (on the application of SB) v Governors of Denbigh
High School [2007] 1 AC 100 .... 7.16
R (on the application of Playfoot) v Governing Body of Millais School
[2007] EWHC 1698 (Admin), [2007] 3 FCR 754, (2007) Times, 23 July,
[2007] All ER (D) 234 (Jul) 7.16
R (on the application of Manson) v Ministry of Defence [2005] EWHC 427
(Admin), [2005] All ER (D) 270 (Feb); affd [2005] EWCA Civ 1678,
[2006] ICR 355, [2005] All ER (D) 69 (Nov) 10.24
R (on the application of Elias) v Secretary of State for Defence
[2006] EWCA Civ 1293, [2006] 1 WLR 3213, [2006] IRLR 934, (2006)
Times, 17 October, [2006] All ER (D) 104 (Oct) 6.16
R (on the application of Mohammed) v Secretary of State for Defence
[2007] EWCA Civ 983, (2007) Times, 9 May, 151 Sol Jo LB 610, [2007]
All ER (D) 09 (May) 6.56
R (on the application of Pretty) v DPP (Secretary of State for the Home
Dept intervening) [2001] UKHL 61, [2002] 1 AC 800, [2002] 1 All ER 1,
[2001] 3 WLR 1598, [2002] 2 Cr App Rep 1, [2002] 1 FCR 1,
[2002] 1 FLR 268, [2002] Fam Law 170, 11 BHRC 589, 63 BMLR 1,
[2001] NLJR 1819, (2001) Times, 5 December, [2002] 3 LRC 163, [2001]
All ER (D) 417 (Nov) 7.2
R (on the application of Williamson) v Secretary of State for Education and
Employment [2005] UKHL 15, [2005] 2 AC 246, [2005] 2 All ER 1,
[2005] 2 WLR 590, [2005] 1 FCR 498, [2005] 2 FLR 374, [2005] NLJR
324, (2005) Times, 25 February, 149 Sol Jo LB 266, 19 BHRC 99,
[2005] 5 LRC 670, [2005] All ER (D) 380 (Feb) 7.2, 7.6
R v Secretary of State for Education and Science, ex p Keating
(1985) 84 LGR 469 .... 1.30
R v Secretary of State for Employment, ex p Seymour-Smith: C-167/97
[1999] 2 AC 554, [1999] ECR I-623, [1999] All ER (EC) 97,
[1999] 3 WLR 460, [1999] 2 CMLR 273, [1999] ICR 447, [1999] IRLR
253, ECJ; apld sub nom R v Secretary of State for Employment,
ex p Seymour-Smith (No 2) [2000] 1 All ER 857, [2000] 1 WLR 435,
[2000] 1 CMLR 770, [2000] ICR 244, [2000] IRLR 263,
[2000] 09 LS Gaz R 40, HL 1.44, 2.7, 11.19, 11.27
R (on the application of the Incorporated Trustees of the National Council
for Ageing (Age Concern for England)) v Secretary of State for
Business, Enterprise and Regulatort Reform: C-388/07 .... 2.2, 2.8, 2.20, 2.41

Table of Cases

R (on the application of Amicus – MSF section) v Secretary of State for
Trade and Industry [2004] EWHC 860 (Admin), [2007] ICR 1176,
[2004] IRLR 430, [2004] All ER (D) 238 (Apr) 7.6, 7.11, 9.15
R (on the application of Carson) v Secretary of State for Work and Pensions
[2005] UKHL 37, [2006] 1 AC 173, [2005] 4 All ER 545, [2005] 2 WLR
1369, (2005) Times, 27 May, [2005] All ER (D) 397 (May) 9.19
R v Taylor [2001] EWCA Crim 2263, [2002] 1 Cr App Rep 519,
[2002] Crim LR 314, [2001] 45 LS Gaz R 25, (2001) Times,
15 November, 145 Sol Jo LB 252, [2001] All ER (D) 330 (Oct) 37.2
Race Relations Board v Applin [1973] QB 815, [1973] 2 All ER 1190,
[1973] 2 WLR 895, 117 Sol Jo 417, CA; affd sub nom Applin v Race
Relations Board [1975] AC 259, [1974] 2 All ER 73, [1974] 2 WLR 541,
72 LGR 479, 138 JP 522, 118 Sol Jo 311, HL 1.37
Rainey v Greater Glasgow Health Board [1987] AC 224, [1987] 1 All ER 65,
[1986] 3 WLR 1017, [1987] 2 CMLR 11, [1987] ICR 129, [1987] IRLR
26, 130 Sol Jo 954, [1987] LS Gaz R 188, [1986] NLJ Rep 1161, 1987 SC
(HL) 1, 1987 SLT 146, HL 11.23, 11.31
Raja v National Council for Voluntary Organisations, 43786/96 ET 1.63
Ramdoolar v Bycity Ltd [2005] ICR 368, [2004] All ER (D) 21 (Nov), EAT 8.74
Ratcliffe v North Yorkshire County Council [1995] 3 All ER 597, 93 LGR
571, 159 LG Rev 1009, [1995] IRLR 439, [1995] 30 LS Gaz R 34,
[1995] NLJR 1092, 139 Sol Jo LB 196, sub nom North Yorkshire
County Council v Ratcliffe [1995] ICR 833, HL 11.29, 11.31
Raval v Department of Health and Social Security [1985] ICR 685,
[1985] IRLR 370, [1985] LS Gaz R 1333, EAT 6.17
Redcar and Cleveland Borough Council v Bainbridge [2007] EWCA Civ 929,
[2007] IRLR 984 .... 11.16
Redcar and Cleveland Borough Council v Bainbridge [2007] IRLR 91, [2006]
All ER (D) 197 (Nov), EAT 11.25, 11.33
Redfearn v Serco Ltd (t/a West Yorkshire Transport Service) [2005] IRLR
744, [2005] All ER (D) 98 (Sep), EAT; revsd [2006] EWCA Civ 659,
[2006] ICR 1367, [2006] IRLR 623, (2006) Times, 27 June, 150 Sol Jo
LB 703, [2006] All ER (D) 366 (May) 1.31, 1.37, 1.44, 6.13, 6.16, 9.8
Redland Roof Tiles v Harper [1977] ICR 349, EAT 11.13
Reed v Stedman [1999] IRLR 299 .... 1.51, 6.31, 9.13
Rees v Apollo Watch Repairs plc [1996] ICR 466, EAT 8.117
Relaxion Group plc v Rhys-Harper [2003] UKHL 33, [2003] 4 All ER 1113,
[2003] 2 CMLR 1329, [2003] ICR 867, [2003] IRLR 484, 74 BMLR 109,
[2003] 30 LS Gaz R 30, 147 Sol Jo LB 782, [2003] All ER (D) 258
(Jun) 1.9, 1.25, 3.108
Richards v Secretary of State for Work and Pensions: C-423/04 [2006] All
ER (EC) 895, [2006] ICR 1181, [2006] 3 FCR 229, [2006] 2 FLR 487,
[2006] Fam Law 639, (2006) Times, 5 May, [2006] All ER (D) 249 (Apr),
ECJ 4.2
Ridout v TC Group [1998] IRLR 628 .... 3.98
Rihal v Ealing London Borough Council [2004] EWCA Civ 623,
[2004] IRLR 642, [2004] All ER (D) 314 (May) 6.12
Rinner-Kühn v FWW Spezial-Gebäudereinigung GmbH & Co KG: 171/88
[1989] ECR 2743, [1993] 2 CMLR 932, [1989] IRLR 493, ECJ 11.19
Roadburg v Lothian Regional Council [1976] IRLR 283, Ind Trib 1.11, 8.39, 8.55
Robertson v Department for Environment Food and Rural Affairs
[2005] EWCA Civ 138, [2005] ICR 750, [2005] IRLR 363, (2005) Times,
2 March, [2005] All ER (D) 335 (Feb) 11.17

Rockfon A/S v Specialarbejderforbundet i Danmark: C-449/93 [1995] ECR
I-4291, [1996] ICR 673, [1996] IRLR 168, ECJ 11.8
Romec Ltd v Rudham, UKEAT/0069/07/DA (13 July 2007, unreported) 3.83
Rookes v Barnard [1964] AC 1129, [1964] 1 All ER 367, [1964] 2 WLR 269,
[1964] 1 Lloyd's Rep 28, 108 Sol Jo 93, HL 1.121
Rooproy v Rollins-Elliott [2001] All ER (D) 91 (Jul), EAT 1.112
Rothwell v Pelikan Hardcopy Scotland Ltd [2006] IRLR 24, EAT 3.79
Rovenska v General Medical Council [1998] ICR 85, [1997] IRLR 367, CA 1.23
Royal and Sun Alliance Insurance Group v Payne [2005] IRLR 848, (2005)
Times, 12 October, [2005] All ER (D) 07 (Aug), EAT 2.46
Royal Liverpool Children's NHS Trust v Dunsby, UKEAT/0426/05/LA
(1 Decmber 2001, unreported) 3.68, 3.85
Royal Mail Group plc v Lynch, UKEAT/0426/03 (8 August 2003,
unreported) 10.25
Royal Mail Group plc v Sharma, UKEAT/0839/04/ILB (22 February 2005,
unreported) 3.120
Ruby Schembri v HSBC, ET3301361/05 (14 July 2006, unreported) 6.27
Rutherford v Secretary of State for Trade and Industry [2004] EWCA Civ
1186, [2004] 3 CMLR 1158, [2004] IRLR 892, (2004) Times,
4 November, [2004] All ER (D) 23 (Sep), sub nom Secretary of State for
Trade and Industry v Rutherford (No 2) [2005] ICR 119, sub nom
Rutherford v Towncircle Ltd 148 Sol Jo LB 1065; affd sub nom
[2006] UKHL 19, [2006] ICR 785, [2006] IRLR 551, (2006) Times,
8 May, [2006] All ER (D) 30 (May), sub nom Secretary of State for
Trade and Industry v Rutherford [2006] 4 All ER 577 .... 1.44, 2.3, 11.27
Rutherford v Towncircle Ltd. See Rutherford v Secretary of State for Trade
and Industry

S

SITA UK Ltd v Hope, UKEAT/0787/04 (8 March 2005, unreported) 11.16
S and U Stores Ltd v Wilkes [1974] 3 All ER 401, [1974] ICR 645,
[1974] IRLR 283, [1975] KILR 117, 9 ITR 415, NIRC 8.92
Saggar v Ministry of Defence [2005] EWCA Civ 413, [2005] ICR 1073,
[2005] IRLR 618, (2005) Times, 9 May, [2005] All ER (D) 382 (Apr) 1.24,
3.110, 6.53, 8.30
St Helens Metropolitan Borough Council v Derbyshire [2005] EWCA Civ
977, [2006] ICR 90, [2005] IRLR 801, (2005) Times, 26 August, [2005]
All ER (D) 468 (Jul); revsd sub nom Derbyshire v St Helens
Metropolitan Borough Council [2007] UKHL 16, [2007] NLJR 635, 151
Sol Jo LB 573, [2007] All ER (D) 207 (Apr) 1.61, 1.62
Saunders v Richmond-upon-Thames London Borough Council [1978] ICR
75, [1977] IRLR 362, 12 ITR 488, EAT 1.26, 8.39
Sawyer v Ahsan [2000] ICR 1, [1999] IRLR 609, EAT 1.15
Scott v IRC [2004] EWCA Civ 400, [2004] ICR 1410, [2004] IRLR 713,
(2004) Times, 19 April, 148 Sol Jo LB 474, [2004] All ER (D) 46 (Apr) 1.121
Scottish and Southern Energy plc v Mackay, UKEAT/0075/06/MT
(30 August 2007, unreported) 3.81
Secretary of State for Employment and Productivity v Vic Hallam Ltd (1969)
5 ITR 108, HL 11.8
Secretary of State for Justice v Slee, UKEAT/10349/06 (20 July 2007,
unreported) 8.75
Secretary of State for Trade and Industry v Rutherford. See Rutherford v
Secretary of State for Trade and Industry

Table of Cases

Securicor Custodial Services Ltd v Williams, EAT 0442/02 (29 January 2003, unreported) 6.12
Seide v Gillette Industries Ltd [1980] IRLR 427, EAT 6.5, 6.12, 7.2
Shaikh v Department for Constitutional Affairs, UkEAT/0234/05 (31 August 2005, unreported) 11.10
Shamoon v Chief Constable of the Royal Ulster Constabulary [2003] UKHL 11, [2003] 2 All ER 26, [2003] ICR 337, [2003] IRLR 285, (2003) Times, 4 March, 147 Sol Jo LB 268, [2003] All ER (D) 410 (Feb) 1.9, 1.27, 1.30, 1.33, 1.35, 1.38, 1.50, 1.59, 1.92, 2.6, 9, 6.17, 6.31
Sharp v Caledonia Group Services Ltd [2006] ICR 218, [2006] IRLR 4, [2005] All ER (D) 09 (Nov), EAT 11.25
Shaw v CCL Ltd, UKEAT/0512/06/DM (22 May 2007, unreported) 8.20
Sheriff v Klyne Tugs (Lowestoft) Ltd [1999] ICR 1170, [1999] IRLR 481, 625 IRLB 6, [1999] All ER (D) 666, CA 1.120
Shields v E Coomes Holdings Ltd [1978] 1 WLR 1408 .... 11.13
Showboat Entertainment Centre Ltd v Owens [1984] 1 All ER 836, [1984] 1 WLR 384, [1984] ICR 65, [1984] IRLR 7, 128 Sol Jo 152, [1983] LS Gaz R 3002, 134 NLJ 37, EAT 1.31, 1.37, 1.39, 6.13, 6.39, 9.8
Sidhu v Aerospace Composite Technology Ltd [2001] ICR 167, [2000] IRLR 602, [2000] 25 LS Gaz R 38, CA 1.110, 6.10
Silveira v Brocklebank [2006] All ER (D) 157 (Feb), EAT 8.48
Simon v Brimham Associates [1987] ICR 596, [1987] IRLR 307, CA 6.8, 6.12
Sinclair Roche & Temperley v Heard [2004] IRLR 763, [2004] All ER (D) 432 (Jul), EAT 1.44, 8.147
Singh v RHM Bakeries (Southern) Ltd, EAT 818/77 (1978), unreported 7.16
Singh v Rowntree MacKintosh Ltd [1979] ICR 554, [1979] IRLR 199, EAT 6.14, 6.17, 7.16
Sirdar v Army Board and Secretary of State for Defence: C-273/97 [1999] ECR I-7403, [1999] All ER (EC) 928, [1999] 3 CMLR 559, [2000] ICR 130, [2000] IRLR 47, 7 BHRC 459, [1999] All ER (D) 1156, ECJ 1.18, 8.34
Sisley v Brittania Security Systems Ltd [1983] ICR 628, [1983] IRLR 404, EAT 8.55
Skyrail Oceanic Ltd v Coleman [1981] ICR 864, sub nom Coleman v Skyrail Oceanic Ltd (t/a Goodmos Tours) [1981] IRLR 398, 125 Sol Jo 638, CA 5.6
Smith v Churchills Stairlifts plc [2005] EWCA Civ 1220, [2006] ICR 524, [2006] IRLR 41, [2005] All ER (D) 318 (Oct) 3.77, 3.82
Smith v Gardner Merchant Ltd [1998] 3 All ER 852, [1999] ICR 134, [1998] IRLR 510, [1998] 32 LS Gaz R 29, 142 Sol Jo LB 244, [1998] All ER (D) 338, CA 6.29
Smith v Safeway plc [1996] ICR 868, [1996] IRLR 456, CA 1.29
Smith and Grady v United Kingdom (1999) 29 EHRR 493, [1999] IRLR 734, EctHR 9.2
Smiths Detection v Berriman, UKEAT 0712/04/CK (2005), unreported 3.69, 3.76
Smyth v Croft Inns Ltd [1996] IRLR 84, NI CA 1.39
Sorbie v Trust Houses Forte Hotels Ltd [1977] QB 931, [1977] 2 All ER 155, [1976] 3 WLR 918, [1977] ICR 55, [1976] IRLR 371, 12 ITR 85, 120 Sol Jo 752, EAT 11.11
South East Sheffield Citizens Advice Bureau v Grayson [2004] ICR 1138, [2004] IRLR 353, [2004] All ER (D) 398 (Feb), EAT 1.8
South Tyneside Metropolitan Borough Council v Anderson [2007] EWCA Civ 643, [2007] IRLR 715 .... 11.17

Southampton City College v Randall [2006] IRLR 18, [2005] All ER (D) 87
(Nov), EAT 1.106, 3.74, 3.78, 3.85
Spence v Intype Libra, UKEAT 0617/06/2704 (2007), unreported 3.78, 3.81
Spillett v Tesco Stores Ltd [2006] ICR 643, [2006] IRLR 248, [2006] All ER
(D) 299 (Feb), EAT 1.23
Springboard Sunderland Trust v Robson [1992] ICR 554, [1992] IRLR
261, EAT 11.14
Stadt Lengerich and others v Helmig: C-399/92, C-409/92, C-425/92,
C-34/93, C-50/93, and C-78/93 [1994] ECR I-5727, [1995] 2 CMLR 261,
[1996] ICR 35, [1995] IRLR 216, ECJ 10.29
Staffordshire County Council v Barber. See Barber v Staffordshire County
Council
Starmer v British Airways plc [2005] IRLR 862, [2005] All ER (D) 323
(Jul), EAT 1.44, 8.147
Stedman v United Kingdom (1997) 23 EHRR CD 168, [1997] EHRLR
545 .... 7.2
Steel v Union of Post Office Workers and the General Post Office
[1978] 1 WLR 64 .... 11.2
Steele v Optika Limited, 20614/95/ET (1997), unreported 1.51
Strathclyde Regional Council v Porcelli. See Porcelli v Strathclyde Regional
Council
Strathclyde Regional Council v Wallace [1998] 1 All ER 394, [1998] 1 WLR
259, [1998] ICR 205, [1998] IRLR 146, [1998] 07 LS Gaz R 32, 1998 SC
(HL) 72, 142 Sol Jo LB 83, sub nom West Dunbartonshire Council v
Wallace 1998 SLT 421, HL 11.25
Surrey Police v Marshall [2002] IRLR 843, EAT 3.52, 3.79
Susie Radin Ltd v GM11. See GMB v Susie Radin Ltd
Swift v Chief Constable of Wiltshire Constabulary [2004] ICR 909,
[2004] IRLR 540, [2004] All ER (D) 299 (Feb), EAT 3.35
Sykes v JP Morgan, EAT/279/00 (12 July 2002, unreported) 1.44

T
Tanna v Post Office [1981] ICR 374, EAT 1.8
Tarbuck v Sainsbury Supermarkets Ltd [2006] IRLR 664, [2006] All ER (D)
50 (Jun), EAT 3.78, 3.81
Tattari v Private Patients Plan Ltd [1997] IRLR 586 .... 1.15
Taylor v OCS Group Ltd [2006] EWCA Civ 702, [2006] ICR 1602,
[2006] IRLR 613, (2006) Times, 12 July, 150 Sol Jo LB 810, [2006] All
ER (D) 51 (Aug) 3.64
Tejani v Superintendent Registrar for the District of Peterborough
[1986] IRLR 502 .... 6.6
Tele Danmark A/S v Handels- og Kontorfunktionærernes Forbund i
Danmark (HK): C-109/00 [2001] ECR I-6993, [2001] All ER (EC) 941,
[2002] 1 CMLR 105, [2004] ICR 610, [2001] IRLR 853, [2001] All ER
(D) 37 (Oct), ECJ 8.73, 8.107
Ten Oever v Stichting Bedrijfspensioenfonds voor het Glazenwassers- en
Schoonmaakbedrijf: C-109/91 [1993] ECR I-4879, [1995] 2 CMLR 357,
[1995] ICR 74, [1993] IRLR 601, [1995] 42 LS Gaz R 23, ECJ 11.19
The Chief Constable of the Bedfordshire Constabulary v Graham
[2002] IRLR 239, [2001] All ER (D) 89 (Sep), EAT 5.4
Thomas v London Borough of Hackney, UKEAT 461/95 (13 March 1996,
unreported) 6.31

Table of Cases

Thomas v National Coal Board [1987] ICR 757, [1987] IRLR 451,
[1987] LS Gaz R 2045, EAT 11.13
Thomas v Robinson [2003] IRLR 7, [2002] All ER (D) 303 (Oct), EAT 6.31
Thorndyke v Bell Fruit (North Central) Ltd [1979] IRLR 1, Ind Trib 5.5
Timex Corpn v Hodgson [1982] ICR 63, [1981] IRLR 530, EAT 8.55
Tottenham Green Under Fives' Centre v Marshall [1989] ICR 214,
[1989] IRLR 147, [1989] 15 LS Gaz R 39, EAT 6.47, 8.55
Tottenham Green Under Fives' Centre v Marshall (No 2) [1991] ICR 320,
[1991] IRLR 162, EAT 6.47
Tower Hamlets London Borough Council v Rabin [1989] ICR 693, EAT 6.8
Training Commission v Jackson [1990] ICR 222,
[1990] 13 LS Gaz R 43, EAT 5.8
Treasury Solicitors Departmen v Chenge [2007] IRLR 386, [2007] All ER (D)
203 (Feb) 8.47
Truelove v Safeway Stores plc [2005] ICR 589, [2005] All ER (D) 343
(Feb), EAT 8.134
Tudor v Spen, ET/2404211/05 (21 June 2006, unreported) 3.52, 3.56
Tyldesley v TML Plastics Ltd [1996] ICR 356, [1996] IRLR 395, EAT 11.25, 11.26,
11.34
Tyson v Concurrent Systems Incorporated Ltd, EAT/0028/03 (9 April 2003,
unreported) 10.25

U
Unison v Allen [2007] IRLR 975 .... 11.42

V
Vakante v Addey & Stanhope School [2004] EWCA Civ 1065,
[2004] 4 All ER 1056, [2005] 1 CMLR 62, [2005] ICR 231,
[2004] 36 LS Gaz R 33, (2004) Times, 28 September, [2004] All ER (D)
561 (Jul) 1.82
Van Duyn v Home Office: 41/74 [1975] Ch 358, [1975] 3 All ER 190,
[1974] ECR 1337, [1975] 2 WLR 760, [1975] 1 CMLR 1, 119 Sol Jo 302,
ECJ 6.53
Vento v Chief Constable of West Yorkshire Police [2002] EWCA Civ 1871,
[2003] ICR 318, [2003] IRLR 102, [2003] 10 LS Gaz R 28, (2002) Times,
27 December, 147 Sol Jo LB 181, [2002] All ER (D) 363 (Dec) 1.120, 3.121,
8.120
Vicary v British Telecommunications plc [1999] IRLR 680, EAT 3.14, 3.24, 3.26,
3.27, 3.28
Villalba v Merrill Lynch & Co Inc [2004] UKEAT/0461/04 (1 July 2004,
unreported) 11.17, 11.44
Villalba v Merrill Lynch & Co Inc [2007] ICR 469, [2006] IRLR 437, 150 Sol
Jo LB 742, [2006] All ER (D) 486 (Mar), EAT 1.44, 1.60, 11.22, 11.25, 11.28,
11.29, 11.32
Virdee v EEC Quarries Ltd [1978] IRLR 295, Ind Trib 1.126
Virdi v Metropolitan Police Comr [2007] IRLR 24, [2006] All ER (D) 214
(Oct), EAT 1.23
Virgo Fidelis Senior School v Boyle [2004] ICR 1210, [2004] IRLR 268,
(2004) Times, 26 February, [2004] All ER (D) 214 (Jan), EAT 1.121, 10.37
Visa International Service Association v Paul [2004] IRLR 42, [2003] All ER
(D) 265 (May), EAT 1.117, 8.78, 8.114, 8.116

Voß v Land Berlin (Case C-300/06) [2007] ECR 00, [2007] All ER (D) 87
(Dec) 10.29, 12.27

W

Waddington v Leicester Council for Voluntary Services [1977] 2 All ER 633,
[1977] 1 WLR 544, [1977] ICR 266, [1977] IRLR 32, 12 ITR 65, 121 Sol
Jo 84, EAT 11.13
Wadman v Carpenter Farrer Partnership [1993] 3 CMLR 93, [1993] IRLR
374, EAT 1.51
Waite v Government Communications Headquarters [1983] 2 AC 714,
[1983] 2 All ER 1013, [1983] 3 WLR 389, 81 LGR 769, [1983] ICR 653,
[1983] IRLR 341, 127 Sol Jo 536, [1983] LS Gaz R 2516, 133 NLJ
745, HL 2.46
Wakeman v Quick Corpn [1999] IRLR 424, [1999] All ER (D) 158, CA 6.10
Walker (J H) Ltd v Hussain [1996] ICR 291, [1996] IRLR 11, EAT 1.52, 6.5, 7.2,
7.15
Walkinshaw v John Martin Group, S/401126/00 (15 November 2001,
unreported) 8.148
Wandsworth NHS Primary Care Trust v Obonyo (No 1)
UKEAT/0237/05/SM (8 February 2006, unreported) 6.24
Waters v Commissioner of Police of the Metropolis [2000] IRLR 720 .... 1.110
Waters v Metropolitan Police Comr [1997] ICR 1073, [1997] IRLR 589, CA;
revsd [2000] 4 All ER 934, [2000] 1 WLR 1607, [2000] ICR 1064, HL ... 1.62, 6.19
Watches of Switzerland v Savell [1983] IRLR 141, EAT 8.41
Way v Crouch [2005] ICR 1362, [2005] IRLR 603, [2005] NLJR 937, [2005]
All ER (D) 40 (Jun), EAT 1.112, 1.117, 1.118
Weathersfield Ltd v Sargent [1999] ICR 425, [1999] IRLR 94, CA 1.31, 6.13, 6.39
Webb v EMO Air Cargo (UK) Ltd: C-32/93 [1994] QB 718, [1994] 4 All ER
115, [1994] ECR I-3567, [1994] 3 WLR 941, [1994] 2 CMLR 729,
[1994] ICR 770, [1994] IRLR 482, [1994] NLJR 1278, ECJ; apld sub
nom Webb v EMO Air Cargo (UK) Ltd (No 2) [1995] 4 All ER 577,
[1995] 1 WLR 1454, [1996] 2 CMLR 990, [1995] ICR 1021, [1995] IRLR
645, [1995] 42 LS Gaz R 24, 140 Sol Jo LB 9, HL 8.13, 8.68, 8.73, 8.107
Webley v Department for Work and Pensions [2004] EWCA Civ 1745,
[2005] ICR 577, [2005] IRLR 288, (2005) Times, 17 January, [2004] All
ER (D) 368 (Dec) 10.5, 10.9
West Dunbartonshire Council v Wallace. See Strathclyde Regional Council v
Wallace
Wetstein v Misprestige Management Services, EAT/523/91 (19 March 1993,
unreported) 7.7
Whiffen v Milham Ford Girls' School [2001] EWCA Civ 385, [2001] LGR
309, [2001] ICR 1023, [2001] IRLR 468, [2001] All ER (D) 256 (Mar) 10.3,
10.9, 10.19
Whitehead v Brighton Marine Palace and Pier Company Ltd, C-3102595/04
(5 May 2005, unreported) 1.9
Williams v Greater London Citizens Advice Bureaux Service [1989] ICR
545, EAT 1.126
Williams v J Walter Thompson Group Ltd [2005] EWCA Civ 133,
[2005] IRLR 376, (2005) Times, 5 April, 149 Sol Jo LB 237, [2005] All
ER (D) 261 (Feb) 3.66
Williams v Richmond Court (Swansea) Ltd [2006] EWCA Civ 1719, (2006)
Times, 29 December, [2006] All ER (D) 218 (Dec) 3.59

Table of Cases

Williams v University of Nottingham, UKEAT/0124/07RN (8 June 2007,
 unreported) 1.24
Williams v University of Nottingham [2007] IRLR 660 .... 3.110
Williams-Drabble v Pathway Care Solutions, ET 2601718/04 (10 January
 2005, unreported) 7.15
Wippel v Peek & Cloppenburg Gmbh & Co Kg: C-313/02 [2005] IRLR 211,
 ECJ 1.8, 1.19, 10.25, 10.31
Wong v Igen Ltd (Equal Opportunities Commission intervening)
 [2005] EWCA Civ 142, [2005] ICR 931, [2005] IRLR 258, (2005) Times,
 3 March, 149 Sol Jo LB 264, [2005] All ER (D) 300 (Feb),
 [2005] 3 All ER 812 .... 1.30, 1.29, 1.60, 1.92, 6.7, 6.9, 6.21
Woodrup v Southwark London Borough Council [2002] EWCA Civ 1716,
 [2003] IRLR 111, 146 Sol Jo LB 263 .... 3.27
Wylie v Dee & Co (Menswear) Ltd [1978] IRLR 103, Ind Trib 8.55

X

X v United Kingdom (1977) 11 DR 55 .... 7.6
X and Church of Scientology v Sweden (1979) 16 DR 68 .... 7.6

Y

YL v Birmingham City Council [2007] UKHL 27, [2007] 3 All ER 957,
 [2007] 3 WLR 112, 96 BMLR 1, [2007] NLJR 938, 151 Sol Jo LB 860,
 [2007] All ER (D) 207 (Jun) 8.66
Younis v Trans Global Projects Ltd, WL 3661965 (2005), unreported 1.8
Youri v Glaxo Wellcome Operations UK Ltd, EAT/448/99 (3 August 1999,
 unreported) 6.31
Youri v Smith, EAT/448/99 (3 August 1999, unreported) 6.31

Z

Zarczynska v Levy [1979] 1 All ER 814, [1979] 1 WLR 125, [1979] ICR 184,
 [1978] IRLR 532, 143 JP 297, 122 Sol Jo 776, EAT 1.31, 6.13, 6.39

Decisions of the European Court of Justice are listed below numerically.
These decisions are also listed alphabetically in the preceding Table of Cases.

80/70: Defrenne v Belgium [1971] ECR 445, [1974] 1 CMLR 494, ECJ 11.19
43/75: Defrenne v Sabena [1981] 1 All ER 122, [1976] ECR 455,
 [1976] 2 CMLR 98, [1976] ICR 547, ECJ 11.2
149/77: Defrenne v Sabena [1978] ECR 1365, [1978] 3 CMLR 312, ECJ 8.12
129/79: Macarthys Ltd v Smith [1981] QB 180, [1981] 1 All ER 111,
 [1980] ECR 1275, [1980] 3 WLR 929, [1980] 2 CMLR 205, [1980] ICR
 672, [1980] IRLR 210, 124 Sol Jo 808, ECJ; apld [1981] QB 180,
 [1981] 1 All ER 111, [1980] 3 WLR 929, [1980] 2 CMLR 217,
 [1980] ICR 672, [1980] IRLR 210, 124 Sol Jo 808, CA 11.10, 11.11
12/81: Garland v British Rail Engineering Ltd [1983] 2 AC 751,
 [1982] 2 All ER 402, [1982] 2 WLR 918, [1982] 2 CMLR 174,
 [1982] ICR 420, [1982] IRLR 257, 126 Sol Jo 309, HL 11.19

152/84: Marshall v Southampton and South West Hampshire Area Health
    Authority (Teaching) [1986] QB 401, [1986] 2 All ER 584, [1986] ECR
    723, [1986] 2 WLR 780, [1986] 1 CMLR 688, [1986] ICR 335,
    [1986] IRLR 140, 130 Sol Jo 340, [1986] LS Gaz R 1720, ECJ 1.19
C-170/84: Bilka-Kaufhaus GmbH v Weber von Hartz [1986] ECR 1607,
    [1986] 2 CMLR 701, [1987] ICR 110, [1986] IRLR 317, ECJ 1.44, 6.16, 9.11,
                                                                    11.19, 11.23, 11.25
C-222/84: Johnston v Chief Constable of the Royal Ulster Constabulary
    [1987] QB 129, [1986] 3 All ER 135, [1986] ECR 1651, [1986] 3 WLR
    1038, [1986] 3 CMLR 240, [1987] ICR 83, [1986] IRLR 263, 130 Sol Jo
    953, [1987] LS Gaz R 188, ECJ 8.60, 8.61
109/88: Handels-og Kontorfunktionaererenes Forbund i Danmark v Dansk
    Arbejdsgiverforening, acting on behalf of Danfoss [1989] ECR 3199,
    [1991] 1 CMLR 8, [1991] ICR 74, [1989] IRLR 532, ECJ 2.23, 2.35, 11.30
171/88 Rinner-Kühn v FWW Spezial-Gebäudereinigung GmbH & Co KG
    [1989] ECR 2743, [1993] 2 CMLR 932, [1989] IRLR 493, ECJ 11.19
C-177/88: Dekker v Stichting Vormingscentrum voor Jong Volwassenen (VJV
    – Centrum) Plus [1990] ECR I-3941, [1992] ICR 325, [1991] IRLR 27,
    ECJ 8.67, 8.73, 8.107
C-262/88: Barber v Guardian Royal Exchange Assurance Group [1991] 1 QB
    344, [1990] 2 All ER 660, [1990] ECR I-1889, [1991] 2 WLR 72,
    [1990] 2 CMLR 513, [1990] ICR 616, [1990] IRLR 240, [1990] NLJR
    925, ECJ 11.19, 11.20
C-184/89: Nimz v Freie und Hansestadt Hamburg [1991] ECR I-297,
    [1992] 3 CMLR 699, [1991] IRLR 222, ECJ 11.30
C-109/91: Ten Oever v Stichting Bedrijfspensioenfonds voor het
    Glazenwassers- en Schoonmaakbedrijf 1 [1993] ECR I-4879,
    [1995] 2 CMLR 357, [1995] ICR 74, [1993] IRLR 601,
    [1995] 42 LS Gaz R 23, ECJ 11.19
C-127/92: Enderby v Frenchay Health Authority [1994] 1 All ER 495,
    [1993] ECR I-5535, [1994] 1 CMLR 8, [1994] ICR 112, [1993] IRLR
    591, ECJ
C-132/92: Birds Eye Walls Ltd v Roberts [1993] ECR I-5579, [1993] 3 CMLR
    822, [1994] IRLR 29, sub nom Roberts v Birds Eye Walls Ltd: C-132/92
    [1994] ICR 338, ECJ 11.19
C-399/92, C-409/92, C-425/92, C-34/93, C-50/93, and C-78/93: Stadt
    Lengerich and others v Helmig [1994] ECR I-5727, [1995] 2 CMLR 261,
    [1996] ICR 35, [1995] IRLR 216, ECJ 10.29
C-32/93: Webb v EMO Air Cargo (UK) Ltd [1994] QB 718, [1994] 4 All ER
    115, [1994] ECR I-3567, [1994] 3 WLR 941, [1994] 2 CMLR 729,
    [1994] ICR 770, [1994] IRLR 482, [1994] NLJR 1278, ECJ; apld sub
    nom Webb v EMO Air Cargo (UK) Ltd (No 2) [1995] 4 All ER 577,
    [1995] 1 WLR 1454, [1996] 2 CMLR 990, [1995] ICR 1021, [1995] IRLR
    645, [1995] 42 LS Gaz R 24, 140 Sol Jo LB 9, HL 8.68, 8.73, 8.107
C-342/93: Gillespie v Northern Health and Social Services Board [1996] ECR
    I-475, [1996] All ER (EC) 284, [1996] 2 CMLR 969, [1996] ICR 498,
    [1996] IRLR 214, ECJ 8.68, 8.107, 11.18, 11.19
C-400/93: Danmark v Dansk Industri, acting for Royal Copenhagen A/S
    [1995] EWCR I-1275 .... 11.31
C-449/93: Rockfon A/S v Specialarbejderforbundet i Danmark [1995] ECR
    I-4291, [1996] ICR 673, [1996] IRLR 168, ECJ 11.8
C-450/93: Kalanke v Freie Hansestadt Bremen [1995] ECR I–3051, [1996]
    All ER (EC) 66, [1996] 1 CMLR 175, [1996] ICR 314, [1995] IRLR 660,
    ECJ 8.63

Table of Cases

C–13/94: P v S [1996] ECR I–2143, [1996] All ER (EC) 397, [1996] 2 CMLR
    247, [1996] ICR 795, [1996] IRLR 347, sub nom P v S (sex
    discrimination): C–13/94 [1997] 2 FCR 180, [1996] 2 FLR 347,
    [1996] Fam Law 609, ECJ 4.2, 4.3, 4.4
C–214/94: Boukhalfa v Germany [1996] ECR I-2253, [1996] 3 CMLR 22,
    ECJ 3.110
C–1/95: Gerster v Freistaat Bayern [1997] ECR I-5253, [1998] 1 CMLR 303,
    [1998] ICR 327, [1997] IRLR 699, ECJ 11.30
C–136/95: Caisse Nationale d'Assurance Vieillesse des Travailleurs Salaries v
    Thibault [1998] ECR I-2011, [1998] All ER (EC) 385, [1998] 2 CMLR
    516, [1998] IRLR 399, [1998] All ER (D) 167, sub nom Thibault v
    Caisse Nationale d'Assurance Viellesse des Travailleurs Salaries
    (CNAVTS) [1999] ICR 160, ECJ 8.78, 8.107
C–243/95: Hill v Revenue Comrs [1998] ECR I-3739, [1998] All ER (EC) 722,
    [1998] 3 CMLR 81, [1999] ICR 48, [1998] IRLR 466,
    [1998] 34 LS Gaz R 33, [1998] All ER (D) 277, ECJ 10.32, 11.30
C–409/95: Marschall v Land Nordrhein-Westfalen [1997] ECR I–6363, [1997]
    All ER (EC) 865, [1998] 1 CMLR 547, [1998] IRLR 39, ECJ 8.63
C–394/96: Brown v Rentokil Ltd [1998] ECR I–4185, [1998] All ER (EC)
    791, [1998] 2 CMLR 1049, [1998] ICR 790, [1998] IRLR 445,
    [1999] 1 FCR 49, [1998] 2 FLR 649, [1998] Fam Law 597, 48 BMLR
    126, [1998] 34 LS Gaz R 34, [1998] All ER (D) 313, ECJ 3.54, 8.73
C–411/96: Boyle v Equal Opportunities Commission [1998] All ER (EC) 879,
    [1998] ECR I–6401, [1998] 3 CMLR 1133, [1999] ICR 360, [1998] IRLR
    717, [1999] 1 FCR 581, [1999] 1 FLR 119, 52 BMLR 169, 608 IRLB 5,
    All ER (D) 500, ECJ 8.107, 8.108
C–167/97: R v Secretary of State for Employment, ex p Seymour-Smith
    [1999] 2 AC 554, [1999] ECR I-623, [1999] All ER (EC) 97,
    [1999] 3 WLR 460, [1999] 2 CMLR 273, [1999] ICR 447, [1999] IRLR
    253, ECJ; apld sub nom R v Secretary of State for Employment,
    ex p Seymour-Smith (No 2) [2000] 1 All ER 857, [2000] 1 WLR 435,
    [2000] 1 CMLR 770, [2000] ICR 244, [2000] IRLR 263,
    [2000] 09 LS Gaz R 40, HL 1.44, 2.7, 11.19, 11.27
C–185/97: Coote v Granada Hospitality Ltd [1998] ECR I-5199, [1998] All
    ER (EC) 865, [1998] 3 CMLR 958, [1999] ICR 100, [1998] IRLR 656,
    [1998] All ER (D) 423, ECJ 1.25, 8.44
C–273/97: Sirdar v Army Board and Secretary of State for Defence
    [1999] ECR I-7403, [1999] All ER (EC) 928, [1999] 3 CMLR 559,
    [2000] ICR 130, [2000] IRLR 47, 7 BHRC 459, [1999] All ER (D) 1156,
    ECJ 1.18, 8.34
C–333/97: Lewen v Denda [1999] ECR I-7243, [2000] All ER (EC) 261,
    [2000] 2 CMLR 38, [2000] IRLR 67, ECJ 8.107, 8.112, 8.113
C–78/98: Preston v Wolverhampton Healthcare NHS Trust [2001] 2 AC 415,
    [2000] ECR I-3201, [2000] All ER (EC) 714, [2001] 2 WLR 408,
    [2000] 2 CMLR 837, [2000] ICR 961, [2000] IRLR 506, [2000] All ER
    (D) 663 .... 11.42
C–407/98: Abrahamsson v Fogelquist [2000] IRLR 732 .... 1.101, 8.63
C–381/99: Brunnhofer v Bank der österreichischen Postsparkasse AG
    [2001] ECR I-4961, [2001] All ER (EC) 693, [2001] 3 CMLR 173,
    [2001] IRLR 571, (2001) Times, 9 July, [2001] All ER (D) 273 (Jun),
    ECJ 11.4, 11.13, 11.25, 11.32
C–476/99: Lommers v Minister van Landbouw, Natuurbeheer en Visserij
    [2002] ECR I-2891, [2004] 2 CMLR 1141, [2002] IRLR 430, [2002] All
    ER (D) 280 (Mar), ECJ 8.63, 11.19

C-109/00: Tele Danmark A/S v Handels- og Kontorfunktionærernes Forbund
    i Danmark (HK) [2001] ECR I-6993, [2001] All ER (EC) 941,
    [2002] 1 CMLR 105, [2004] ICR 610, [2001] IRLR 853, [2001] All ER
    (D) 37 (Oct), ECJ 8.73, 8.107
C-256/01: Allonby v Accrington and Rossendale College [2004] ECR I-873,
    [2005] All ER (EC) 289, [2004] 1 CMLR 1141, [2004] ICR 1328,
    [2004] IRLR 224, [2004] All ER (D) 47 (Jan), ECJ ... 1.44, 6.16, 8.36, 11.7, 11.10,
                                                                                              11.17
C-4/02 and C-5/02: Hilde Schönheit v Stadt Frankfurt am Main [2003] ECR
    I-12575, [2004] IRLR 983, [2003] All ER (D) 401 (Oct), ECJ 1.44, 2.8, 11.31,
                                                                                              11.36
C-147/02: Alabaster v Woolwich plc [2004] ECR I-3101, [2005] All ER (EC)
    490, [2004] 2 CMLR 186, [2005] ICR 695, [2004] IRLR 486, [2004] All
    ER (D) 558 (Mar), ECJ 8.105, 8.106, 8.107, 11.18
C-284/02: Land Brandenburg v Sass [2005] IRLR 147, [2004] All ER (D) 310
    (Nov), ECJ 8.78, 8.108
C-313/02: Wippel v Peek & Cloppenburg Gmbh & Co Kg [2005] IRLR 211,
    ECJ 1.8
C-191/03: North Western Health Board v McKenna [2006] All ER (EC) 455,
    [2006] ICR 477, [2005] IRLR 895, [2005] All ER (D) 47 (Sep), ECJ 8.107
C-144/04: Mangold v Helm [2006] All ER (EC) 383, [2006] IRLR 143, [2005]
    All ER (D) 287 (Nov), ECJ 2.3, 2.8, 2.41, 8.13
C-212/04: Adeneler v Ellinikos Organismos Galaktos [2007] All ER (EC) 82,
    [2006] 3 CMLR 867, [2006] IRLR 716, [2006] All ER (D) 25 (Jul),
    ECJ 10.5
C-227/04: P Lindorfer v. Council (11 September 2007, unreported) 2.3, 2.5, 2.8
C-294/04: Herrero v Instituto Madrileno de la Salud (Imsalud) [2006] IRLR
    296, [2006] All ER (D) 220 (Feb), ECJ 8.78
C-423/04: Richards v Secretary of State for Work and Pensions [2006] All
    ER (EC) 895, [2006] ICR 1181, [2006] 3 FCR 229, [2006] 2 FLR 487,
    [2006] Fam Law 639, (2006) Times, 5 May, [2006] All ER (D) 249 (Apr),
    ECJ 4.2
C-17/05: Cadman v Health and Safety Executive [2007] All ER (EC) 1,
    [2007] 1 CMLR 530, [2006] ICR 1623, [2006] IRLR 969, (2006) Times,
    6 October, [2006] All ER (D) 17 (Oct), ECJ 1.44, 2.23, 2.35, 11.25, 11.29,
                                                                                              11.30, 11.36
C-411/05: Félix Palacios de la Villa pret Cortefiel Servicios SA [2007] IRLR
    989 .... 2.3, 2.5, 2.8
C-116/06: Kiiski v Tampereen kaupunki [2007] All ER (D) 120 (Sep) 8.131
C-303/06: Coleman v Attridge Law [2007] ICR 654 .... 2.6
C-460/06: Paquay v Societe d'architectes Hoet & Minne SPRL [2007] All ER
    (D) 137 (Oct), ECJ 8.74
C-388/07: R (on the application of the Incorporated Trustees of the National
    Council for Ageing (Age Concern for England)) v Secretary of State for
    Business, Enterprise and Regulatort Reform 2.2, 2.8, 2.20, 2.41

List of Abbreviations

GENERAL

AAL	=	Additional adoption leave
ACAS	=	Advisory, Conciliation and Arbitration Service
All ER	=	All England Law Reports
AML	=	Additional maternity leave
BMA	=	British Medical Association
BNP	=	British National Party
CA	=	Court of Appeal
CEHR	=	Commission for Equality and Human Rights
CIPD	=	Chartered Institute of Personnel and Development
CML	=	Compulsory maternity leave
CRE	=	Commission for Racial Equality
DBERR	=	Department for Business, Enterprise and Regulatory Reform
DRC	=	Disability Rights Commission
DTI	=	Department of Trade and Industry
EAT	=	Employment Appeal Tribunal
ECJ	=	European Court of Justice
EEC citizens	=	European Economic Community
EHRC	=	Equality and Human Rights Commission
EOC	=	Equal Opportunities Commission
ET	=	Employment Tribunal
ETS	=	Employment Tribunal Service
EWC	=	Expected week of childbirth (or confinement)
EWCA	=	England and Wales Court of Appeal
GMF	=	Genuine material factor
GOQ	=	Genuine occupational qualification
GOR	=	Genuine occupational requirement
IRLR	=	Industrial Relations Law Reports
JES	=	Job evaluation study
KIT	=	Keeping in touch (days)
LIFO	=	Last in, first out
NMW	=	National minimum wage
OML	=	Ordinary maternity leave
PILON	=	Payment in lieu of notice
PRP	=	Performance-related pay
QB	=	Queen's Bench Division
SAP	=	Statutory adoption pay
SGO	=	Special guardianship order
SMP	=	Statutory maternity pay
SOCA	=	Serious Organised Crime Agency
SPP	=	Statutory paternity pay
SSAT	=	Social Security Appeals Tribunal
TUPE	=	Transfer of Undertakings (Protection of Employment)

Abbreviations and References

LEGISLATION

AR 2006	=	Employment Equality (Age) Regulations 2006 (SI 2006/1031)
CDA 1998	=	Crime and Disorder Act 1998
CPA 2004	=	Civil Partnerships Act 2004
DDA 1995	=	Disability Discrimination Act 1995
DPA 1998	=	Data Protection Act 1998
DPEA	=	Disabled Persons (Employment) Acts 1944 and 1958
DRCA 1999	=	Disability Rights Commission Act 1999
EA 2002	=	Employment Act 2002
EA(SO) Regs 2007	=	Equality Act (Sexual Orientation) Regulations 2007 (SI 2007/1263)
ECHR	=	European Convention on Human Rights
EqA 2006	=	Equality Act 2006
ERA 1996	=	Employment Rights Act 1996
FTR 2002	=	Fixed-term Employees (Prevention of Less Favourable Treatment) Regulations 2002 (SI 2002/2034)
GRA 2004	=	Gender Recognition Act 2004
HFEA 1990	=	Human Fertilisation and Embryology Act 1990
HRA 1998	=	Human Rights Act 1998
MPL Regulations	=	Maternity and Parental Leave etc Regulations 1999
PHA 1997	=	Protection from Harassment Act 1997
PTWR 2000	=	Part-time (Prevention of Less Favourable Treatment) Regulations 2000 (SI 2000/1551)
RBR 2003	=	Employment Equality (Religion or Belief) Regulations 2003 (SI 2003/1660)
RRA 1976	=	Race Relations Act 1976
SSCBA 1992	=	Social Security Contributions and Benefits Act 1992
SDA 1975	=	Sex Discrimination Act 1975
SOR 2003	=	Employment Equality (Sexual Orientation) Regulations 2003 (SI 2003/1661)
WTR 1998	=	Working Time Regulations 1998

1   Common Concepts

1.1   INTRODUCTION

Under UK law there is no general prohibition against discrimination. Instead, UK legislation makes discrimination on certain grounds and in certain fields unlawful. UK law has evolved over many years in piecemeal fashion, together with EU discrimination law, but not always in tandem.

1.2   The principal UK discrimination legislation

(a) The *Equal Pay Act 1970* ('*EqPA 1970*') gives a man or a woman a right to the same contractual pay and benefits as a person of the opposite sex in the same employment, where the man and the woman are doing like work, work rated as equivalent, or work of equal value.

(b) The *Sex Discrimination Act 1975* ('*SDA 1975*') prohibits discrimination on the grounds of gender in employment, education, the provision of goods, facilities and services and in the disposal or management of premises; it also prohibits some forms of discrimination on the grounds of marital or civil partnership status discrimination. It prohibits discrimination on the grounds of pregnancy in employment related fields. *SDA 1975* does not cover discrimination in relation to pay or pensions.

(c) The *Race Relations Act 1976* ('*RRA 1976*') prohibits discrimination on racial grounds in employment, education, the provision of goods and services and the disposal or management of premises.

(d) The *Disability Discrimination Act 1995* ('*DDA 1995*') prohibits discrimination against disabled person in employment, education, the provision of goods, facilities, services and premises.

(e) The *Part-time (Prevention of Less Favourable Treatment) Regulations 2000 (SI 2000/1551)* ('*PTWR 2000*') give part-time workers the right not to be treated less favourably than full-time workers.

(f) The *Fixed-term Employees (Prevention of Less Favourable Treatment) Regulations 2002 (SI 2002/2034)* ('*FTR 2002*') make it unlawful to treat fixed-term employees less favourably than comparable permanent employees and limit the use of successive fixed-term contracts.

(g) The *Employment Equality (Sexual Orientation) Regulations 2003 (SI 2003/1661)* ('*SOR 2003*') prohibit discrimination on the grounds of sexual orientation in employment and vocational training.

(h) The *Employment Equality (Religion or Belief) Regulations 2003 (SI 2003/1660)* ('*RBR 2003*') prohibit discrimination in employment and vocational training on the grounds of religion or belief.

(j) The *Equality Act 2006, Part 2* ('*EqA 2006*') prohibits discrimination on the grounds of religion or belief in the provision of goods, facilities and services, education, disposal and management of premises and the exercise of public functions.

1.3 Common Concepts

(k)   The *Employment Equality (Age) Regulations 2006 (SI 2006/1031)* ('*AR 2006*') prohibit discrimination on the grounds of age in employment and vocational training. There is no corresponding legislation in relation to goods and services.

(l)   The *Equality Act (Sexual Orientation) Regulations 2007 (SI 2007/1263)* ('*EA(SO) Regs 2007*') prohibit discrimination on the grounds of sexual orientation in the provision of goods, facilities and services, education, disposal and management of premises and the exercise of public functions.

1.3 The Human Rights Act

The *Human Rights Act 1998 (HRA 1998)* gives effect in the UK to the *European Convention on Human Rights (ECHR)* and enables individuals to enforce the rights contained in *HRA 1998, Sch 1* in the UK either directly, in the case of public authorities, or indirectly through obligations on courts, tribunals and public authorities, to give effect to convention rights. In the discrimination context, the most important convention rights contained in *Sch 1* are the right to respect for private and family life (*Article 8*) the rights to freedom of thought, conscience and religion (*Article 9*), freedom of expression (*Article 10*) and (but only in conjunction with one or more other convention rights) the prohibition of discrimination (*Article 14*). These rights are not absolute rights; each is restricted or qualified.

HRA 1998 also requires UK primary and subordinate legislation to be read and given effect to in a way which is compatible with Convention rights.

1.4 Codes of Practice

Under *SDA 1975, s 56A, RRA 1976, s 47* and *DDA 1995, s 53A* the Equal Opportunities Commission (EOC), Commission for Racial Equality (CRE) and Disability Rights Commission (DRC) were empowered to issue Codes of Practice containing practical guidance in specific fields. Failure on the part of any person to observe any provision of a Code of Practice is not of itself unlawful, but in any proceedings under the statute to which the code relates, a Code of Practice shall be admissible in evidence. If any provision of such a Code appears to the tribunal to be relevant to any question arising in the proceedings it shall be taken into account in determining that question.

Following dissolution of the EOC, CRE and DRC on 1 October 2007, the Codes of Practice remain in force unless and until replaced by the EHRC (Equality and Human Rights Commission) in accordance with its powers under *EqA 2006, s 14*. *Section 14* also empowers the EHRC to issue codes of practice in connection with *SOR 2003, RBR 2003* and *AR 2006*.

1.5 Northern Ireland

DDA 1995 extends to Northern Ireland. While *SDA 1975, RRA 1976, SOR 2003, RBR 2003* and *AR 2006* do not, there are comparable legislative provisions in Northern Ireland.

There are two areas of Northern Irish employment law which are substantially different to the rest of the UK.

The first concerns the detailed provisions requiring employers of more than ten people in Northern Ireland to maintain detailed information in relation to the

2

religious background and sex of job applicants and employees for monitoring purposes and to register and file an annual return to the Equality Commission of Northern Ireland.

The second area is the obligation in Northern Ireland which requires public authorities to have due regard to the need to promote equality of opportunity between people of different religious beliefs and political opinions, race and age and between disabled and non-disabled people, and people with dependents and people without.

1.6   Scope of this book

This book covers only those provisions of UK discrimination legislation which relate to employment and related fields. It does not cover discrimination in the provision of goods and services.

Principles and concepts which are common to all or most of the UK discrimination legislation are discussed in this chapter. Those which are not, and those which require specific consideration in different contexts, are covered in the chapters which follow.

The derivation of the UK legislation and, where applicable, its EU sources is detailed in the following chapters.

1.7   COMMON CONCEPTS

Employees

Only employees and certain other specified categories of workers are protected against unlawful discrimination. 'Employment' in the UK legislation (*SDA 1975, s 82(1), RRA 1976, s 78(1), RBR 2003, reg 2(3), SOR 2003, reg 2(3), AR 2006, reg 2(2)*) is defined as:

> 'employment under a contract of service or apprenticeship or a contract personally to [execute any work or labour] (*SDA 1975, RRA 1976*) [do any work] (*RBR 2003, SOR 2003, AR 2006, DDA 1995*)' (see 'Personal work or services' at 1.8).

This is a significantly wider definition than for purposes of rights under the *Employment Rights Act 1996* ('*ERA 1996*') or other employment protection legislation. There is no requirement for a minimum qualifying period of service in respect of the protection afforded by the legislation. In addition to current employees, applicants for employment and, where there is sufficient connection, former employees, are also protected under the legislation (see 1.25).

1.8   *Employees*

In *Mirror Group Newspapers Ltd v Gunning* [1986] 1 WLR 546, [1986] ICR 145, [1986] IRLR 27 the Court of Appeal held that three conditions must be satisfied in the second limb of the definition – 'a contract personally':

(a)   there must be a contract;

(b)   under the contract, the claimant must have personally undertaken to execute any work or labour, rather than employing others to do it (applied in *Loughran & Kelly v Northern Ireland Housing Executive* [1999] 1 AC 428, [1998] 3 WLR 735, [1998] ICR 828; *Patterson v Legal Services Commission* [2003] EWCA Civ 1558, [2004] ICR 312, [2004] IRLR 153);

3

(c)   the personal obligation to execute work or labour must be the dominant purpose of the contract.

'Contract of service or apprenticeship'

For a contract to exist, the parties must be subject to sufficient mutuality of obligation (*Mingeley v Pennock* [2004] EWCA Civ 328, [2004] ICR 727). Sufficient mutuality existed in the following scenarios:

(a)   a volunteer provided with training in return for which he had to provide a minimum time commitment (*Armitage v Relate* [1994] DLCD 26);

(b)   workers who provided services on an 'on demand' basis and were not obliged to take work offered (*Wippel v Peek & Cloppenburg GmbH & Co kg C-313/02* [2005] IRLR 211);

(c)   a sales consultant who undertook to introduce contracts to a company with no minimum time commitment but in practice rendered monthly invoices (*Younis v Global Projects Ltd* [2005] WL 3661965).

A contract under which there was no obligation to offer work to a taxi driver, or for him to accept it, did not amount to employment (*Mingeley v Pennock*, *supra*) and nor did a work experience arrangement under which there were only limited mutual obligations to provide work experience and training on one side, and, on the worker's side, to comply with instructions should she attend work (*Daley v Allied Suppliers Ltd* [1983] ICR 90).

In relation to volunteers, where a charity used the words 'reasonable expectations' to describe what was expected of volunteers, and volunteers could take holiday whenever they wished, there was no obligation to work. The fact volunteers were 'usually' expected to commit to six hours' work per day and were provided with training, expenses and protection against legal liability for error did not indicate employment (*South East Sheffield CAB v Grayson* [2004] IRLR 353).

Where a worker provides services to an end user under a contract between the end user and the third party, there is no contract between the worker and the end user (*BP Chemicals Ltd v Gillick* [1995] IRLR 128), although a contract of employment has been implied between the end user and the worker (see *Dacas v Brook Street* [2004] EWCA CIV 217, [2004] ICR 1437, but contrast *James v London Borough of Greenwich* [2007] ICR 577, on appeal to the Court of Appeal at the time of writing) which suggests that an employment relationship will only be implied in more limited circumstances, where the relationship cannot be understood in any other way. In the discrimination law context, the public policy considerations which have led the courts to feel the need to confer rights via the vehicle of an implied contract are less of an imperative because, where a worker provides services through the medium of a third party, he should in any event be protected under the provisions protecting against discrimination by 'principals' without the need to establish a contractual relationship (see 1.10). As a result, both end users and employment agencies will want indemnity protection in respect of the other's discriminatory acts, given the likelihood in this scenario that a worker will name each of them in proceedings.

Personal work or services

The dominant purpose of the contract must be to execute personal work or services: see *Mirror Group Newspapers Ltd v Gunning* [1986] IRLR 27, where the purpose was the distribution of newspapers rather than personal service by the agent; *Tanna v Post Office* [1981] ICR 374, where the purpose was to provide facilities for a post office rather than to personally staff it; and *Hawkins v Darken* [2004] EWCA Civ 1755, [2004] All ER (D) 186 (Dec), where a delivery agent was able to delegate the performance of the services although he did not do so in practice (although query whether recent case law in relation to *ERA 1996* regarding the existence of mutuality where there is only a limited right to delegate where the individual themselves is unavailable would extend to the discrimination statutes). Contrast a self-employed salesman who was providing services personally (*Quinnen v Howels* [1984] IRLR 227).

The predominant purpose of the contract must be to provide work or labour

The individual must be obliged to work on a personal basis, rather than having a general contractual duty to provide services. Where the work could be provided by any staff within the individual's company, this test was not met (*Patterson v Legal Service Commission* [2003] EWCA Civ 1558, [2004] ICR 312, in respect of a tender process for legal services). By contrast, where legal services were to be provided personally by a sole practitioner, and by a partner nominated in the response for tender in a firm where she was not the only partner, they were both 'employed' for purposes of the *Northern Ireland Fair Employment Act 1976* (*Loughram and Kelly v Northern Ireland Housing Executive* [1998] ICR 828, HL(NI)).

1.9   *Scope of protection*

It is unlawful for an employer to discriminate, directly or indirectly:

(a)   in the arrangements he makes for the purpose of determining who should be offered employment;

(b)   in the terms on which he offers employment; or

(c)   by refusing or deliberately omitting to offer employment (*SDA 1975, s 6(1); RRA 1976, s 4(1), DDA 1995, s 4(1),(2); RBR 2003, reg 6(1); SOR 2003, reg 6(1); AR 2006, reg 7(1)*).

It is also unlawful to publish, or cause to be published, an advertisement which indicates, or might reasonably be understood as indicating, an intention to discriminate unlawfully (*SDA 1975, s 38(1); RRA 1976, s 29(1); DDA 1995, s 16B*) (see 1.11 and 6.38).

Once a person is in employment, it is also unlawful for an employer to discriminate against him:

(d)   in the terms of employment which he affords him (save under *SDA 1975*, on the basis that *EqPA 1970* covers pay and contractual terms);

(e)   in the way it affords him access to opportunities for promotion, transfer or training, or to any other terms, benefits, facilities or services, or by refusing or deliberately omitting to afford him with access; or

(f)   by dismissing him or subjecting him to any other detriment (*SDA 1975, s 6(2); RRA 1976, s 4(2); DDA 1995 s 4(2); RBR 2003, reg 6(2); SOR 2003, reg 6(2); AR 2006, reg 7(2)*).

The 'detriment' suffered in the case of opportunities for promotion, training, transfer or other benefits is simply the lack of access to the opportunity; the employee, for example, would not need to demonstrate that he would have been successful in his application.

Dismissal includes constructive dismissal (*Derby Specialist Fabrication Ltd v Burton* [2001] 2 All ER 840, [2001] IRLR 6, the failure to renew a fixed-term contract (*Metropolitan Police Comr v Harley* [2001] IRLR 263, EAT), and compulsory retirement.

Detriment

The House of Lords has considered the meaning of 'detriment' in two recent cases. In *Chief Constable of West Yorkshire Police v Khan* [2001] IRLR 830 and *Shamoon v Chief Constable of the Royal Ulster Constabulary* [2003] UKHL 11, [2003] 2 All ER 26, [2003] ICR 337, the House of Lords upheld earlier judgments of the Court of Appeal in *Jeremiah v Ministry of Defence* [1979] IRLR 436 and *De Souza v Automobile Association* [1986] IRLR 103, which stated that 'detriment' is established if a reasonable worker would or might take the view that he had been disadvantaged in the circumstances in which he had to work.

The test is, in part, objective, so an unjustified sense of grievance is not sufficient to establish a detriment (*Barclays Bank plc v Kapur* [1995] IRLR 87). The fact that an employee is unaware of the detriment at the time is not a defence (*Garry v Ealing London Borough Council* [2001] EWCA Civ 1282, [2001] IRLR 681). It was held in *Shamoon* that it was not necessary to demonstrate physical disadvantage or financial loss.

An employee does not suffer a 'detriment' if he is denied a benefit which is not provided to others in the same grade of employment. In *Clymo v Wandsworth London Borough Council* [1989] 2 CMLR 577, [1989] ICR 250, the EAT held that Mrs Clymo was not subjected to a detriment when she was refused permission to job share, as no one else in her grade was entitled to do so. In *Relaxion Group plc v Rhys-Harper* [2003] UKHL 33, [2003] 4 All ER 1113, [2003] 2 CMLR 1329, [2003] ICR 867, the House of Lords held that failure to provide a non-contractual benefit will not normally be a 'detriment' unless it is one which is normally provided to others in comparable circumstances.

Where the detriment suffered is sufficiently 'trivial' it may not amount to discrimination (*Peake v Automotive Products Ltd* [1978] QB 233, [1978] 1 All ER 106, where women were allowed to leave work five minutes before their male colleagues to avoid a crush and, more recently, *Khan v Direct Line Insurance plc* ET (22 November 2005, unreported), where an alternative to a sales incentive of a bottle of wine was not offered to a Muslim).

Detriment may include any aspect of the role such as work scheduling (both breaks during the working day: *Mayuuf v Governing Body of Bishop Challoner Catholic Collegiate School* 3202398/2004, and rota-setting: *Estorninho v Zoran Jokic t/a Zorans Delicatessen* 2301487106, 18 August 2006); the way in which discipline and grievances are handled (*Dresdner Kleinwort Wassenstein Ltd v Adebago* [2005] IRLR 514, and others); taking away responsibility for conducting staff appraisals (*Shamoon v Chief Constable of the Royal Ulster Constabulary* (Northern Ireland, *supra*); carrying out security checks only on employees of a particular colour (*BL Cars Limited v Brown* [1983] ICR 143); and the requirement to work voluntary overtime in less pleasant conditions, even when compensated by an extra payment (*Ministry of Defence v Jeremiah* [1980] QB 87, [1979] 3 All ER 833, [1980] ICR 13); together with the withholding of benefits properly due, such as a reference (*Khan v Chief Constable of West Yorkshire Police* [2001] UKHL 48, [2001] 4 All ER 834, [2001] 1 WLR 1947), pay rise or promotion. Only benefits offered by the employer which an employee enjoys by virtue of his employment, rather than benefits which he enjoys because they are also made available to members of the public at large, are covered (see 1.68).

De Souza v Automobile Association [1986] ICR 514, where a racist comment made about an employee by her manager to another manager did not amount to a detriment, is probably no longer good law where the comment made is sufficiently offensive, even if an isolated incident (*Whitehead v Brighton Marine Palace and Pier Company Ltd, C-3102595/04* (5 May 2005, unreported), where a one-off but very offensive remark made to a third party constituted harassment).

1.10 Contract workers/principals

It is unlawful for a principal (the end user who contracts with another person for the supply of contract workers) to discriminate against those workers in the work he provides to them (*SDA 1975, s 9; RRA 1976, s 7; DDA 1995, s 4B; RBR 2003, reg 8; SOR 2003, reg 8; AR 2006, reg 9*). The principal is treated as if it were the employer for purposes of the non-discrimination provisions in each of the statutes, extending the protection, for example, to a prohibition on harassment, victimisation and, under the *DDA 1995*, the positive duty to make reasonable adjustments. The same exemptions also apply (see 1.66–1.82).

There is no requirement that the principal 'control' the worker for these provisions to apply. Employees of concessionaires in a department store who were required to have 'store approval' from the department store, which included complying with the store's dress code, were able to bring claims for race discrimination (*Harrods Ltd v Remick* [1998] 1 All ER 52, [1998] ICR 156, [1997] IRLR 583) as was a contractor who was harassed by a customer (*CJ O'Shea Construction Ltd v Basti* [1998] ICR 1130). The work was done both for the principal and the concessionaire, and any other result would leave those employees without a personal remedy in the event of discrimination by the principal.

In the common situation where a worker provides their services to an end user via both an employment agency and their own personal company, the Court of Appeal has confirmed that they will still be deemed to be a contract worker with protection against discrimination by that end user (*Abbey Life v Tansell* [2000] IRLR 387). The only requirement is that the worker is supplied under a contract between the end user and a third party; there is no requirement that the end user and the personal company directly contract.

1.11 Job applicants

Under *SDA 1975, s 6(1); RRA 1976, s 4(1); DDA 1995, s 4(1); RBR 2003, reg 6(1); SOR 2003, reg 6(1)*, and *AR 2006, reg 7(1)* it is unlawful for an employer to discriminate against an applicant for employment:

(a)   in the arrangements he makes for the purpose of determining who should be offered that employment (eg recruitment procedures); or

(b)   in the terms on which he offers him that employment (eg lower pay, fewer benefits); or

(c)   by refusing to deliberately omitting to offer him that employment.

Liability can be established under any one of the grounds set out above. Thus, it is sufficient to prove that the interview was conducted in a discriminatory manner, without showing that the interview arrangements were discriminatory (*Nagarajan v London Regional Transport* [2000] 1 AC 501, [1999] 4 All ER 65, [1999] 3 WLR 425, [1999] ICR 877, approving *Brennan v JH Dewhurst Ltd* [1983] IRLR

357, EAT, at 20). If the employer has made discriminatory arrangements for recruitment, a claim may be made even if the post was not filled for other reasons (*Roadburg v Lothian Regional Council* [1976] IRLR 283).

'Word of mouth' recruitment may be indirectly discriminatory (*Coker v Lord Chancellor* [2001] EWCA Civ 1756, [2002] ICR 321, [2002] IRLR 8 (see 'Methods of recruitment' at 1.26).

The terms on which a job is offered may be indirectly discriminatory. In *Meade-Hill v British Council* [1996] 1 All ER 79, [1995] ICR 847, [1995] IRLR 47 a mobility clause requiring the employee to relocate to anywhere in the UK was held to discriminate on grounds of sex and marital status against a woman because a greater proportion of women are secondary earners and their husbands cannot move with them.

There is a separate requirement not to publish an advertisement which indicates an intention to discriminate. 'Advertisement' covers any form of advertisement or notice, whether to the public or not (*DDA 1995, s 16B(4)*; also *SDA 1975, s 82(1)* and *RRA 1976, s 78(1)*, where the form of words is slightly different). The publisher of an advertisement can rely, as a defence, on placing reasonable reliance on a statement by the author that the publication was not unlawful (*SDA 1975, s 38(4)*; *RRA 1976, s 29(4)*; *DDA 1995, s 16B(2A)*). The publishing of unlawful advertisements is a criminal offence under *SDA 1975, s 38(5)*; *RRA 1976, s 29(5)* and *DDA 1995, s 16B(2B)*). Proceedings can only be brought by the EHRC, as prescribed under *EqA 2006, s 25*.

Under *SDA 1975, s 6(2A)*; *RRA 1976, s 4(2A)*; *DDA 1995, s 4(3)*; *RBR 2003, reg 5(1)*; *SOR 2003, reg 5(1)* and *AR 2006, reg 6(1)* it is unlawful for an employer to harass a woman who has applied to him for employment (see 1.45ff).

1.12   Partnerships

Insofar as a worker is employed by a partnership he will receive precisely the same protection against discrimination as if he were employed by a limited company or an individual (see 1.9, 1.11 and 1.25).

As a matter of partnership law, however, a partner is not an employee of a partnership, but rather a principal within it. For a definition of 'partnership', and for the incidents and liabilities of partnerships in general, see Lindley and Banks, *Partnership* (2002) 18th ed. The discrimination statutes therefore make specific provision for partners. This protection can be summarised as follows.

The general prohibition

It is unlawful for a firm of partners, including a limited liability partnership (LLP), to discriminate on ground of race (*RRA 1976, s 10(1)*), sex (*SDA 1975, s 11(1)*), disability (*DDA 1995, s 6A(1)*), sexual orientation (*SOR 2003, reg 14(8)*), religious belief (*RBR 2003, reg 14(8)*) or age (*AR 2006, reg 17*), 'in relation to a position as partner in the firm':

(a)   in the arrangements for the purpose of determining who should be offered that position;

(b)   in the terms on which that position may be offered;

(c)   by refusing or deliberately omitting to offer that position; or

(d)   in a case where the partner in question already holds that position:

(i)   in the way access is afforded to any benefits, facilities or services, or by refusing or deliberately omitting to afford access to them; or

(ii) by expelling the partner from that position, or subjecting him to any other detriment.

As in the employment context, this protection includes within its scope proposed partners, existing partners and former partners. Furthermore, it includes partnerships which have not yet been formed (*SDA 1975, s 11(2); RRA 1976, s 10(2); DDA 1995, s 6C(1)); RBR 2003, reg 14(3); SOR 2003, reg 14(3); AR 2006, reg 17(3)*), and two-member partnerships which have, by reason of an expulsion, technically ceased to exist (*Dave v Robinska* [2003] ICR 1248, EAT).

Discrimination for these purposes includes harassment (*SDA 1975, s 11(2A); RRA 1976, s 10(1B); DDA 1995, s 6A(2); RBR 2003, reg 14(2); SOR 2003, reg 14(2); AR 2006, reg 17(2)*) and, where the relevant statute or regulations prohibit it for the purposes of employment, indirect discrimination also.

As in the employment context, it is possible for partnerships to rely on GOQ and GOR defences in respect of partners.

Anomalies with regard to race

There are two anomalous but important exceptions in relation to discrimination on ground of race in the context of partnerships, which arise from *RRA 1976, ss 10(1)* and *10(1A)*. They are that:

(a)   a partnership of fewer than six members cannot be liable for direct discrimination on grounds of nationality or colour; and

(b)   a partnership of fewer than six members cannot be liable for indirect discrimination at all.

1.13   *Disability discrimination*

Whilst direct discrimination on ground of disability is, as set out above, prohibited, indirect discrimination is not. This is, as discussed elsewhere in this work, replaced by the duty to make reasonable adjustments. That duty falls on a partnership in respect of a disabled partner in precisely the same manner as in respect of a disabled employee (*DDA 1995, s 6B*).

Trade organisations

All of the discrimination statutes apply to what are described as 'trade organisations' (*SDA 1975, s 12; RRA 1976, s 11; DDA 1995, s 13; RBR 2003, reg 15; SOR 2003, reg 15 and AR 2006, reg 18*). Insofar as a worker is employed by a trade organisation, he will receive precisely the same protection against discrimination as if he were employed by a limited company or an individual (see 1.9, 1.11 and 1.25). However, if a member of a trade organisation wishes to make a claim of discrimination, he will have to rely on the specific provisions laid out in the discrimination statutes. Those protections can be summarised as follows.

What is a 'trade organisation'?

A trade organisation is defined in the discrimination statutes as:

(a)   an organisation of workers;

(b)   an organisation of employers; or

(c)   any other organisation whose members carry on a particular profession or trade for the purposes of which the organisation exists.

It will be noted immediately that this is a broad definition. Whilst the most obvious organisations included are trade unions, the phrase 'organisation of workers' would appear to include, for instance, a factory football team, or an office hobby club.

The phrase 'trade organisation' has also been held to be wide enough to include organisations whose membership include the self-employed (*National Federation of Self-Employed and Small Businesses Limited v Philpott* [1997] ICR 518, EAT), and organisations of professional persons such as doctors (*Sadek v Medical Protection Society* [2005] IRLR 57, CA).

Prospective members

In relation to those who are not yet members, a trade organisation may not discriminate on grounds of race (*RRA 1976, s 11(2)*), sex (*SDA 1975, s 12(2)*), disability (*DDA 1995, s 13(1)*), sexual orientation (*SOR 2003, reg 15(1)*), religion or belief (*RBR 2003, reg 15(1)*), or age (*AR 2006, reg 18(1)*):

(a)   in the terms on which it is prepared to admit a person to membership; or

(b)   by refusing, or deliberately not accepting, a person's application for membership.

Discrimination in this context is given the same meaning as in respect of employment. Accordingly, it includes harassment (*SDA 1975, s 12(3A); RRA 1976, s 11(4); DDA 1995, s 13(3); SOR 2003, reg 15(3); RBR 2003, reg 15(3); AR 2006, reg 18(3)*) and (in all but the case of disability) indirect discrimination. In the case of disability discrimination, indirect discrimination is, broadly speaking, replaced with the duty to make reasonable adjustments (see 3.69).

Present members

A different set of duties fall on trade organisations in respect of their present members. In relation to an existing member, the organisation may not discriminate on ground of sex (*SDA 1975, s 12(3)*), race (*RRA 1976, s 11(3)*), disability (*DDA 1995, s 13(2)*), sexual orientation (*SOR 2003, reg 15(2)*), religion or belief (*RBR 2003, reg 15(2)*), or age (*AR, reg 18(2)*):

(a)   in the way it affords that member access to any benefits, or by refusing or deliberately omitting to afford that member access to them;

(b)   by depriving that member of membership, or varying the terms on which he is a member; or

(c)   by subjecting that member to any other detriment.

There are number of points to note with regard to the way in which these provisions are applied:

(a)   The shifting burden of proof provisions apply to complaints of discrimination by trade organisations as they do in respect of employers.

(b)   Any detriment alleged must have been suffered at the time the claimant was a member of the organisation (*Diakou v Islington Unison 'A' Branch* [1997] ICR 121, EAT).

(c)   Discrimination in this context includes indirect discrimination (*Allan v GMB* UKEAT/0425/06).

(d)   The protection offered by the legislation can in principle extend to control-
ling the terms on which a Union negotiates collective agreements, if such
terms be discriminatory (*Allan* op cit).

Individual liability

Where a trade organisation is found liable for unlawful discrimination under the
provisions outlined above, it is possible for individual office-holders or members
within the organisation also to be personally liable. Indeed, they will usually be so
liable unless they can establish that they reasonably relied on a statement by the
trade organisation that the action in question would not be unlawful (*SDA 1975,
s 42*; *RRA 1976, s 33*; *DDA 1995, s 57*; *SOR 2003, reg 23*; *RBR 2003, reg 23*; *AR
2006, reg 26*). Furthermore, since the 'employer's defence' (see 1.111) has been
drafted so as to refer only to 'employees' (*SDA 1975, s 41(3)*; *RRA 1976, s 32(3)*;
DDA 1995, s 58(5); *SOR 2003, reg 22(3)*; *RBR 2003, reg 22(3)*; *AR 2006,
reg 25(3)*), it would appear that it would not be open to a trade organisation in the
case of an office-holder who was not employed by the trade organisation to argue
that it took all reasonable steps to prevent the act on its behalf.

1.14   Vocational training providers

In addition to those provisions of the discrimination statutes which make
discrimination unlawful in the area of education, there are provisions making
such discrimination unlawful when committed by vocational training providers.
'Vocational training' is defined in *SDA 1975, s 82(1)* (also *RRA 1976*) as including
'all types and all levels of vocational training, advanced vocational training and
retraining' , 'vocational guidance' and 'practical work experience undertaken for a
limited period for the purposes of a person's vocational training'. This definition
has been held to include everything from work experience (*Lana v Positive Action
Training in Housing (London) Limited* [2001] IRLR 501) to formal professional
training (*Fletcher v Blackpool Fylde and Wyre Hospitals NHS Trust* [2005] IRLR
689, EAT).

Sex and race

A vocational training provider may not discriminate on ground of sex (*SDA 1975,
s 14*) or race (*RRA 1976, s 13*):

(a)   in the arrangements for selection;

(b)   in the terms on which access is afforded;

(c)   by refusing or omitting to afford such access;

(d)   by terminating the training; or

(e)   by subjecting the trainee to any detriment during the course of the training.

Harassment on sexual (*SDA 1975, s 14(1A)*) or racial (*RRA 1976, s 13(3)*) grounds
by a provider of vocational training is also prohibited.

In *Fletcher v Blackpool Fylde and Wyre Hospitals NHS Trust* [2005] IRLR
689, EAT, trainee midwives were entitled to claim under *SDA 1975, s 14* when
their bursaries were terminated during maternity absence from their course. The
bursary was held to be a facility connected with training, falling within the scope
of a 'working condition' under *Equal Treatment Directive 76/207/EEC, Art 3*.

In *Lana v Positive Action Training in Housing (London) Ltd* [2001] IRLR
501, EAT the respondents were liable for the termination of the claimant's work

placement with a firm on grounds of her pregnancy. By authorising the unlawful termination, the respondents were liable under *SDA 1975, s 41(2)*.

The above prohibition does not apply to discrimination against job applicants and employees (which is covered by *SDA 1975, s 6* and *RRA 1976, s 4*), nor to educational establishments (which are covered by *SDA 1975, ss 22* and *23* and *RRA 1976, ss 17* and *18*). See on jurisdiction, *Moyhing v Barts and London NHS Trust* [2006] IRLR 860, [2006] All ER (D) 64 (Jun) and the second decision in *Moyhing* on detriment at [2006] IRLR 860).

Religion or belief, sexual orientation and age

A vocational training provider also may not discriminate on ground of sexual orientation (*SOR 2003, reg 17*), religion or belief (*RBR 2003, reg 17*) or age (*AR 2006, reg 20*) against a trainee:

(a)   in the terms on which the training provider affords him access to any training;

(b)   by refusing or deliberately not affording him such access;

(c)   by terminating his training; or

(d)   by subjecting him to any other detriment during his training.

1.15   *Disability*

The *DDA 1995* does not make specific reference to vocational training providers. Instead, it covers the same territory by prohibiting discrimination on ground of disability in: (i) practical work experience placements (*s 14C*); and (ii) the provision of goods, facilities and services (*s 19*). Harassment on ground of disability is also prohibited by such organisations.

Qualifications bodies

Authorities or bodies which can confer an authorisation or qualification which is needed for, or facilitates, engagement in a particular profession or trade will be liable to an individual for sex, race, disability, sexual orientation, religion or belief or age discrimination (*SDA 1975, s 13*):

(a)   in the terms on which it is prepared to confer on him that authorisation or qualification; or

(b)   by refusing or deliberately omitting to grant his application for it; or

(c)   by withdrawing it from him or varying the terms on which he holds it.

Additional provision is made in the *DDA 1995* to outlaw discrimination by a qualifications body in the arrangements which it makes for the purpose of determining upon whom to confer a professional or trade qualification (*s 14A(1)(a)*).

'Qualification'

The word 'qualification' in this context implies some status conferred on a person in relation to his work which is either necessary or advantageous to the lawful carrying on of that work (*Loughran & Kelly v Northern Ireland Housing Executive* [1999] 1 AC 428, [1998] 3 WLR 735, [1998] ICR 828).

'Qualifying body'/'qualifications body'

The question of what is a 'qualifying body' (the term used in *SDA 1975* and *RRA 1976*) or 'qualifications body' (the term used in *SDA 1995, SOR 2003, RBR 2003* and *AR 2007*) has attracted a significant body of case law. The leading cases are three Court of Appeal decisions:

(a) In *Tattari v Private Patients Plan Ltd* [1997] IRLR 586, CA, the Court of Appeal considered the question of whether a commercial provider of medical and health insurance was a 'qualifying body' insofar as it stipulated that particular qualifications were necessary in order for doctors to be included on its list of specialist practitioners. The Court held that it was not, since the insurance provider was not in itself authorised or empowered to confer a qualification or permission.

(b) In *McDonagh and Triesman v Ali* [2002] EWCA Civ 93, [2002] ICR 1026, [2002] IRLR 489, the Court of Appeal held that the Labour Party, in selecting a candidate for local government elections, was not a qualifying body, thereby overturning previous EAT decisions to the contrary (*Sawyer v Ahsan* [1999] IRLR 609, EAT; *Jepson and Dyas-Elliott v Labour Party* [1996] IRLR 116, EAT). (Note, however, that the *Sex Discrimination (Election Candidates) Act 2002* amended the *SDA 1975* by adding *s 42A* which provides an exception for action taken by political parties in the selection of candidates for parliamentary, European Parliament, Scottish Parliament, National Assembly for Wales and local government elections, for the purpose of reducing inequality in the numbers of members of the body concerned.)

(c) In *Patterson v Legal Services Commission* [2003] EWCA Civ 1558, [2004] ICR 312, [2004] IRLR 153 the Court of Appeal distinguished *Tattari* and *Triesman*, and held that the Legal Services Commission, in its role of awarding legal aid franchises to solicitors, *was* a qualifications body, since it was assessing the solicitor's suitability to perform the work and conferring 'some sort of status' on her, as well as selecting a person to perform services on its behalf.

In line with the relatively strict approach taken by the Court of Appeal in the *Tattari* and *Triesman* cases, the EAT subsequently decided in the case of *Arthur v Attorney General* [2002] IRLR 489, EAT that an appointer of magistrates was not a qualifying body for the purposes of *RRA 1976*.

'Facilitates'

In *British Judo Association v Petty* [1981] IRLR 484, the EAT held that the word 'facilitates' covers all cases where the qualification in fact facilitates employment, whether or not it is intended by the authority or body which confers the authorisation so to do. It was not necessary to show detriment or loss. See also *Hardwick v Football Association* EAT/1036/97.

Appeals

Where there is a statutory right of appeal, or proceedings in the nature of an appeal, against a particular act, a complaint cannot be made to a tribunal concerning a qualifications body (*SDA 1975, s 63(2); RRA 1976, s 54(2); DDA 1995, s 17A(1A); SOR 2003, reg 28(2)(a); RBR 2003, reg 28(2)(a); AR 2006, reg 36(2)(a)*). See *British Medical Association v Chaudhary* [2003] EWCA Civ 645, [2003] ICR 1510; *Bari v General Medical Council* UKEATPA/0660/05/LA; *Khan v*

1.16   Common Concepts

General Medical Council [1996] ICR 1032, CA; *R v Department of Health, ex p Ghandi* [1991] 4 All ER 547, [1991] 1 WLR 1053, [1991] ICR 805.

1.16   **Crown employment**

The discrimination laws bind the Crown and apply to Crown employment, and to House of Commons and House of Lords staff (*SDA 1975, ss 85–85B; RRA 1976, ss 75–75B; DDA 1995, ss 64–65; RBR 2003, regs 36–38; SOR 2003, regs 36–38; AR 2006, regs 44–46*). Ministers of the Crown are excluded.

1.17   *Police*

Although the holding of an office within the police is not 'employment' for the purposes of the *ERA 1996*, the discrimination laws deem the holding of such office to be 'employment' for their own purposes (*SDA 1975 s 17; RRA 1976, ss 76A–76B; RBR 2003, reg 11; SOR 2003, reg 11; AR 2006, reg 13*). A new *subsection 17(1A)* was inserted into the *SDA 1975* in 2003 to confirm that Chief Officers of police are vicariously liable for the acts and omissions of police officers as employers, reversing the effect of *Chief Constable of Bedfordshire Police v Liversidge* [2002] EWCA Civ 894, [2002] ICR 1135. Proceedings should be brought against the Chief Constable and/or the police authority and individual officers who have discriminated.

Chief Officers of police may be directly liable for management decisions on matters such as recruitment and postings (*Hendricks v Metropolitan Police Comr* [2002] EWCA Civ 1686, [2003] 1 All ER 654, [2003] ICR 530 endorsing *Chief Constable of Cumbria v McGlennon* [2002] ICR 1156, EAT).

1.18   **Armed forces**

Members of the armed forces are in the service of the Crown. They are therefore subject to and protected by discrimination laws (see above), with the following exceptions.

The armed forces enjoy a total exemption from liability for disability or age discrimination (*DDA 1995, s 64(7); AR 2006, reg 44(2)*).

A partial exemption exists in respect of sex discrimination where an act is done in the interests of 'combat effectiveness'; *SDA 1975, s 85(4)* provides: 'Nothing in this Act shall render unlawful an act done for the purpose of ensuring the combat effectiveness of the armed forces'.

Internal complaints procedures must be invoked before a claim to the ET is made (*SDA 1975, s 85(9B)–9(E); RRA 1976, s 75(8)–(9B); RBR 2003, reg 36(7)–36(10); SOR 2003, reg 36(7)–36(10)*).

In *Sirdar v Army Board and Secretary of State for Defence C-313/02* [2005] IRLR 211, the ECJ rejected the submission that matters relating to national security fell outside EU anti-discrimination provisions, but held that exclusion of women from special combat units such as the Royal Marines may be justified under the *Equal Treatment Directive, Article 2(2)*, which exempts occupational activities for which the sex of the worker is a determining factor.

1.19   **Office-holders**

The discrimination laws apply to persons who are not (or might not be) 'employees', but are rather private or public 'office-holders' (*SDA 1975, ss 10A– 10B; RRA 1976, s 76ZA; DDA 1995, s 4C–4F; RBR 2003, reg 10; SOR 2003,*

14

reg 10; AR 2006, reg 12). Protection for office-holders was introduced following the broadening of the application of the principle of equal treatment in the *Treaty on European Union* ('EC Treaty'), *Article 141(3)* and *Directive 2002/73/EC, Article 3* beyond 'employment' to 'self-employment and occupation'. Those appointed, recommended or approved by central government are included. Elected and appointed members of central or local government are expressly excluded.

The particular case of employment tribunal chairmen (known, since 1 December 2007, as Employment Judges) has given rise to considerable dispute:

(a)   In *Perceval-Price v Department of Economic Development* [2000] IRLR 380, NICA it was held that tribunal chairmen claiming discrimination in connection with pension rights were 'workers' in 'employment' within the meaning of *Article. 119* of the *EC Treaty* and the *Directives*, even though they were excluded from the NI equal pay and sex discrimination legislation as holders of a statutory office. The Court of Appeal disapplied domestic law because of the conflict with EU law, following *Marshall v Southampton and South West Hampshire Area Health Authority* [1986] IRLR 140. This was only possible because the defendant was an 'emanation of the State'.

(b)   In *Christie v Department for Constitutional Affairs & Anor* UKEAT/0140/07/ZT the EAT recently rejected a similar challenge to the statutory exclusion brought by a part-time tribunal chairman under the *Part-time Workers (Prevention of Less Favourable Treatment) Regulations 2000* and the *Part-time Workers Framework Directive (97/81/EC)*. The EAT held, relying on *Wippel v Peek & Cloppenburg GmbH & Co KG* [2005] ICR 1604, (1) that there was no autonomous meaning of 'worker' in EU law; (2) under the *Framework Directive*, Member States had a discretion to determine how 'worker' and 'employment' should be defined; (3) alternatively, the *Regulations* clearly excluded holders of a statutory office, and therefore could not be read compatibly with the *Directive*, and could not be disapplied.

1.20   Barristers and advocates

It is unlawful for a barrister or a barrister's clerk to discriminate on ground of sex (*SDA 1975, s 35A(1)(2)*), race (*RRA 1976, ss 26A* and *26B*), disability (*DDA 1995, s 7A*), sexual orientation (*SOR 2003, regs 12* and *13*), religion or belief (*RBR 2003, regs 12* and *13*) or age (*AR 2006, regs 15* and *16*) in relation to:

(a)   arrangements for offering pupillage or tenancy;

(b)   the terms on which pupillage or tenancy is offered;

(c)   refusing or deliberately omitting to offer pupillage or tenancy;

(d)   the terms applicable to a pupil or tenant;

(e)   opportunities for training or gaining experience, and benefits, facilities or services;

(f)   termination of pupillage or tenancy;

(g)   any other detriment.

Furthermore, it is unlawful for any person to discriminate against a barrister on ground of sex (*SDA 1975, s 35A(3)*), race (*RRA 1976, s 26A(3)*), disability (*DDA 1995, s 7A(4)*), sexual orientation (*SOR 2003, reg 12(4)*), religion or belief (*RBR*

2003, reg 12(4)) or age (*AR 2006, reg 15(4)*) in the giving, withholding or acceptance of instructions. Harassment is also prohibited.

1.21   Personal liability

Anything done by a person in the course of his employment shall be treated as done not only by his employer (whether or not it was done with the employer's knowledge and approval) but also by him personally (*SDA 1975 s 41(1)*; *RRA 1976 s 32(1)*; *DDA 1995 s 58(1)*; *RBR 2003, reg 22(1)*; *SOR 2003, reg 22(1)*; *AR 2006, reg 25(1)*). Similarly, anything done by a person as agent for another person with the authority (express or implied, precedent or subsequent) of that other person shall be treated as done by him as well as that other person (*SDA 1975, s 41(2)*; *RRA 1976, s 32(2)*; *DDA 1995, s 58(2)*; *SOR 2003, reg 22(2)*; *RBR 2003, reg 22(2)*; *AR 2006, reg 25(2)*). In such circumstances, the individual is deemed to aid the employer or principal (*SDA 1975, s 42(2)*; *RRA 1976, s 33(2)*; *DDA 1995, s 57(2)*; *SOR 2003, reg 23(2)*; *RBR 2003, reg 23(2)*; *AR 2006, reg 26(2)*).

1.23   Work-seekers dealing with employment agencies

1.22   Workers supplied by employment agencies are likely to enjoy protection against discrimination as a 'worker', either of the agency or the end user for which they work (see 1.10). They are also protected against discrimination by the employment agency which supplies them under specific provisions in the legislation, as are work-seekers seeking employment services from an employment agency (see 1.26).

Jurisdiction

Limitation period

Claimants normally have three months from the date of the act complained of (or the last in a series of connected acts) in which to present a claim. A series of acts will be seen as connected where amounting to 'an act extending over a period', for example the application of a consistent policy or practice (*East and North Hertfordshire NHS Trust v Dr A Fernando* UKEAT/0727/04/DM; but contrast *Rovenska v General Medical Council* [1998] ICR 85, [1997] IRLR 36, where a series of rejected applications for registration were each discrete acts). The guidance of Mummery J, as he was then in *Hendricks v Metropolitan Police Commissioner* [2002] EWCA Civ 1686, [2003] All ER 654, [2003] ICR 530, is helpful: 'The focus should be on ... [whether the respondent] was responsible for an ongoing situation or a continuing state of affairs in which [the protected group] were treated less favourably'.

The three-month time limit may be extended where there has been concealment of facts giving rise to the claim by the employer, or where it is 'just and equitable' to do in the circumstances of the case (*SDA 1975, s 76(5)*; *RRA 1976, s 68(6)*; *DDA 1995, Sch 3, para 3(2)*, *SOR 2003, reg 34(3)*; *RBR 2003, reg 34(3)*; *AR 2006, reg 42(3)*). This is much broader than the reasonably practicable test which applies under *ERA 1996, s 108(1)*, and includes failure to comprehend the time limit even where in receipt of legal advice and a right of action only arising outside the time limit as a result of a judicial decision (*British Coal Corporation v Keeble* [1997] IRLR 336), although an active decision by a claimant to delay is likely to mean the tribunal will refuse to extend time (*Hutchinson v Westward Television Ltd* [1977] IRLR 69, [1977] ICR 279). Other examples include where the applicant only became aware of facts that would found a complaint after expiry of the usual time limit (*London Borough of Southwark v Afolabi* [2003] EWCA Civ 15, [2003]

ICR 800), where an applicant's lawyers mistakenly failed to comply with the time limit (*Virdi v Commissioner of Police of the Metropolis & Anr*, [2007] IRLR 24), and where the applicant reasonably waited for the outcome of an internal grievance (*Marks & Spencer plc v Williams-Ryan* [2005] EWCA Civ 470, [2005] ICR 1293, [2005] IRLR 562) (in respect of the normally stricter test under *ERA 1996, s 111*); *Apelogun-Gabriels v Lambeth London Borough Council* [2001] EWCA Civ 1853, [2002] ICR 713).

Different rules apply to claims under the *EqPA 1970*, where claims must be brought within six months of employment ending (which includes a change of employer by operation of TUPE (*Powerhouse Retail Ltd v Burroughs* [2006] UKHL 13, [2006] IRLR 381), and time can be extended in cases of concealment or disability but not on a just and equitable basis (see 11.42).

Where a claimant has submitted a written grievance relating to facts which would give rise to a claim within one month of the expiry of the normal time limit to present that claim to the employment tribunal, the time limit to commence tribunal proceedings will be extended by a further three months (*Employment Act 2002, s 32, Employment Act 2002 (Dispute Resolution) Regulations 2004, reg. 15*). The deadline for submitting a statutory grievance can be extended on a 'just and equitable' basis in the same way as the deadline for the related tribunal claim (*BUPA Care Homes Ltd v Cann and Spillett v Tesco Stores Ltd* [2006] ICR 643, [2006] IRLR 248). At the time of writing, government proposals were awaited regarding increasing time limits which formed part of the consultation following the Gibbons review.

Complaints of breach under the discrimination statutes are brought in the employment tribunal, other than complaints outside the employment field (ie under *SDA 1975, Part III*; *RRA 1976, Part III*; and *DDA 1995, Part III*, in respect of public authorities, the provision of goods, facilities and services etc, and complaints under *SOR 2003, RBR 2003* and *AR 2006*, in respect of qualifying bodies and higher education (see 1.115).

1.24   *Territorial scope*

The legislation (except certain strands of discrimination under the *RRA 1976* (see RACE DISCRIMINATION (6)) applies to 'employment at an establishment in Great Britain', meaning:

(a)   work wholly or partly in Great Britain; or

(b)   work wholly outside Great Britain where the following additional conditions are satisfied:

    (i)   the employer has a place of business at an establishment in Great Britain;

    (ii)   work is done for purposes of that business carried out in Great Britain; and

    (iii) the individual in question is ordinarily resident in Great Britain either when he applies for or is offered employment, or at any time during the employment (*SDA 1974, s 10*; *RRA 1976, s 8*; *DDA 1995, s 68*; *RBR 2003, reg 9*; *SOR 2003, reg 9*; *AR 2006, reg 10*).

The individual's entire period of employment is taken into account in assessing his place of work, rather than just the period in which the acts of discrimination took place (*Saggar v Ministry of Defence* [2005] EWCA Civ 413, [2005] IRLR 618, [2005] ICR 1073). Where an employee is based abroad but visits Great Britain, he may be protected if the visits are for essential work purposes and are not *de minimis* (*Ministry of Defence v Gandiya* [2004] ICR 1708, where one day's required attendance in the UK and two voluntary visits related to the role were insufficient to establish employment in the UK).

Williams v The University of Nottingham UKEAT/0124/07/RN held that whether work was done 'for the purposes of the employer's business carried on at its establishment in Great Britain' was the same question as that considered by the House of Lords in *Lawson v Serco Ltd* [2006] UKHL 3, [2006] 1 All ER 823, [2006] IRLR 289 in an unfair dismissal claim, ie whether work was done 'for the purposes of a business carried on in Great Britain'.

These rules will, however, be disapplied where they are in conflict with *Article 48* of the *EC Treaty* relating to free movement of workers (*Bossa v Nordstress Ltd* [1998] IRLR 284, where an Italian national was entitled to claim in the employment tribunal for discrimination against him by an Italian employer whilst he was resident in the UK).

1.25   Former employees

An individual is protected against discriminatory acts where the detriment complained of 'arises out of or is closely connected to' a previous relationship which falls within one of the protected categories outlined at (see 1.7–1.22) (*SDA 1975, ss 20A, 35C; RRA 1976, s 27A; DDA 1995, s 16A; RBR 2003, reg 21; SOR 2003, reg 21; AR 2006, reg 24*). This statutory protection codifies the House of Lords' decision in *Relaxion Group plc v Rhys-Harper* [2003] UKHL 33, [2003] 4 All ER 1113, [2003] 2 CMLR 1329, [2003] ICR 867, although claimants alleging discrimination on grounds of colour or nationality must still rely on the *Relaxion* test because of a lacuna in the *RRA 1976*.

The most common type of post-termination discrimination complained of is victimisation, where an individual is treated less favourably, for example a reference denied or outstanding pay withheld, because they have raised a complaint of discrimination (whether by way of informal complaint, statutory grievance or litigation) (see, for example, *Coote v Granada Hospitality Ltd C-185/97* [1998] ECR I-5199, [1998] All ER (EC) 865, [1998] 3 CMLR 958). All acts of discrimination or harassment are covered provided they are sufficiently connected to the previous relationship, for example, failure to pay expenses or commission, or a dispute relating to pensions entitlement. Where an employee has commenced proceedings or has raised a grievance as a precursor to submitting a claim, employers can face a difficult choice between creating disclosable documentation that may prejudice their defence in the litigation, and having a victimisation claim added to the previous grounds as a result of their failure to progress the grievance, or give a reference (see 1.55ff).

Note the duty under the *DDA 1995* to make reasonable adjustments continues after employment ends (see DISABILITY DISCRIMINATION (3)).

1.26   Employment agencies

In addition to protection as 'workers' of the end user, and potentially as 'employees' of an employment business which supplies them, individuals who use the services of employment agencies are protected against discrimination by that agency under specific provisions in the legislation (*SDA 1975, s 15; RRA 1976, s 14; DDA 1995, s 21A; RBR 2003, reg 18; SOR 2003, reg 18; AR 2006, reg 21*):

(a)   in the terms on which the agency offers to provide any of its services;

(b)   by refusing or deliberately not providing any of its services;

(c)   in the way it provides any of its services; or

(d)   by harassing any work-seeker.

An employment agency is defined for these purposes as a person who, whether for profit or not, provides services for the purpose of finding employment for workers or supplying employers with workers (but excluding school and further education institutions which are covered separately, and which are outside the scope of this work) (*SDA 1975, s 82(1); RRA 1976, s 78(1); RBR 2003, reg 18(6); SOR 2003, reg 18(6); AR 2006, reg 21(6)*). Employment agencies can also be liable where they knowingly aid the end user's act of unlawful discrimination (*SDA 1975, s 42; RRA 1976, s 33; DDA 1995, s 57; RBR 2003, reg 23; SOR 2003, reg 23; AR 2006, reg 26*).

Conversely, the client instructing the agency will be liable where they have authorised or instructed the agency to discriminate (*SDA 1975, ss 39, 41(2); RRA 1976, ss 30, 32(2); DDA 1995, ss 16C, 58(2)*). Note the newer anti-discrimination legislation does not separately prohibit the giving of discriminatory instructions (*RBR 2003, reg 22(2); SOR 2003, reg 22(2); AR 2006, reg 25(2)*).

The provisions of the *DDA 1995* are differently framed, but the prohibition against discrimination in the provision of 'employment services' which includes vocational guidance and training also extends to employment agencies as the providers of 'services to assist a person to obtain or retain employment, or to establish himself as self-employed' (*DDA 1995, s 21A*). In this regard, agencies must not harass disabled candidates or workers (see 3.86ff), and must take reasonable steps to prevent their practices, policies and procedures from placing that person at a substantial disadvantage. The following are specific areas of the recruitment process where an agency may be exposed to liability.

Accepting client instructions

To establish a defence against a claim that they 'knowingly aided' the unlawful acts of their clients, agencies should seek a statement from the client that the instructions are not unlawful. Even with the benefit of such a statement, it must still be reasonable for the agency to rely on it in order to accept the client's instructions, and so it would be well advised either to take its own legal advice or to seek a written legal opinion from the client where it believes instructions may not be lawful. However, to be liable, the agency must either have wanted the discriminatory act to occur, or have had actual knowledge that the client would or was contemplating treating the worker in that way: a reasonable suspicion that it might take place was not enough (*Hallam v Avery* [2001] UKHL 15, [2001] 1 WLR 655). Where the client knowingly or recklessly makes a false or misleading statement that the instructions are not unlawful, and the agency relies on this, the client is liable to a fine (*SDA 1975, s 42(4); RRA 1976, s 14(6); RBR 2003, reg 23(4); SOR 2003, reg 23(4); AR 2006, reg 26(4)*). However, the agency itself may still be liable. The safest course for the agency is to obtain an indemnity in respect of liability arising out of the client providing discriminatory instructions, but this does not address the reputational issues of an agency being found to have discriminated both in respect of potential candidates and clients.

Clearly, where it would be lawful for the client not to employ or engage the candidate, the instructions will not be discriminatory and so the agency will bear no liability. However, only some of the legislation states this expressly (*SDA 1975, s 15(4)*; *RRA 1976, s 14(4)*). Lawfulness in this context is not limited to GOQs and GORs (see 1.95ff).

Methods of recruitment

Executive search firms typically do not use advertisements to carry out recruitment for their clients in the private sector, although they are generally required to do so for public sector bodies, which will have a duty to promote equality of opportunity (which is outside the scope of this book). Recruitment by way of contacting specific targeted individuals involves a more limited pool of potential candidates, both in terms of number and the protected characteristics they share (such as age and race). This argument was considered by the Court of Appeal in relation to the Lord Chancellor's recruitment of a personal acquaintance as special advisor, where it found no disproportionate impact on the claimants on the basis that the correct pool of comparators was made up of individuals known to the Lord Chancellor, which was a legitimate requirement of the role (*Coker v Lord Chancellor* [2001] EWCA Civ 1756, [2002] ICR 321, [2002] IRLR 80). In that case, the pool of comparators comprised solely the successful candidate, who satisfied the requirement of being known to the Lord Chancellor whilst also having the other necessary skills. The Court of Appeal nonetheless stated that recruitment from a pool of those known to the employer or by 'word of mouth' was not best practice in accordance with the EOC and CRE Codes and could result in unlawful discrimination. This is more likely to be the case where an employer does not impose a requirement that it personally knows the candidate, but instead relies on head-hunting or recruitment through personal contacts where, in contrast to the *Coker* case, it is likely that a wider group of candidates could meet its requirements and so disproportionate impact on a group protected under the statutes would be shown.

Selection

An employment agency may interview candidates, either to consider whether to accept them for job-seeking services, to compile a shortlist or even to select the successful candidate on behalf of its client. In doing so the same obligations apply to it as to the prospective employer, namely to avoid unlawful discrimination in the way the recruitment process is operated. This encompasses all steps in the recruitment process, from arrangements for interview (see in particular 3.69 with regard to reasonable adjustments), establishing non-discriminatory job criteria (see for example, 2.28ff with respect to the setting of requirements for minimum age or experience), ensuring consistent selection processes and assessment of all candidates (Britannia Products Ltd, Brooke Street Bureau (Bradford) and Network Industrial Recruitment, CRE formal investigation 1994) and avoiding asking questions or making comments that give rise to an inference of unlawful discrimination (*Saunders v Richmond-upon-Thames London Borough Council* [1977] IRLR 362, [1978] ICR 75). The agency should also consider, and refer to its client, any questions raised by candidates with regard to adjustments to the role where refusal may potentially give rise to indirect discrimination (see for example 3.69 with regard to reasonable adjustments such as working hours or location, provision or modification of equipment and changes to job duties, and 8.39, 8.147ff and 2.28ff with regard to changes to working hours or location to accommodate caring responsibilities).

Terms of supply

Employment businesses, which supply temporary workers, continue to be under a duty not to discriminate throughout the term of the contract (and potentially beyond; see 1.25). So an employment agency breached the *SDA 1975* as a result of its failure to carry out a risk assessment when placing a pregnant work-seeker with a client (*Brocklebank v Silveira* UKEAT/571/05), and when it failed to allow a worker to return to the temporary post which she had occupied following her return from maternity leave (*BP Chemicals Ltd v Gillick and Roevin Management Services* [1995] IRLR 128).

1.27   DIRECT DISCRIMINATION

Introduction

The statutory definition of 'direct discrimination' is essentially the same for all grounds of prohibited discrimination (with one significant exception):

> 'A discriminates against B when A treats B less favourably than he treats or would treat another, and does so on a prohibited ground.'

[*SDA 1975, ss 1(1)(a), 2(1), 3(1)(a), 3A(1)(a), 3A(1)(b); RRA 1976, s 1(1)(a); DDA 1995, s 3A(5); RBR 2003, reg 3(1)(a); SOR 2003, reg 3(1)(a).*]

The test which the tribunal will usually apply is to consider whether the two key elements of the statutory definition are met: has there been less favourable treatment and, if so, was that treatment on a prohibited discriminatory ground? In other words, what was the reason for the treatment in question?

Although it is useful for the tribunal to ask the two questions sequentially, there is scope for a tribunal to consider these as one issue where the less favourable treatment cannot be determined without first examining the reasons for the treatment.

The facts of cases are not always capable of division into neat sub-headings and sequential analysis may give rise to problems where, for example, it is the appropriate comparator which is in question. For these reasons, as the House of Lords found in *Shamoon v Chief Constable of the Royal Ulster Constabulary* [2003] UKHL 11, [2003] 2 All ER 26, [2003] ICR 33, in determining whether there has been direct discrimination, if the statutory test is treated as two parts, rather than one question, problems may arise – per Lord Nicholls, paras 7 and 8: 'Sometimes the less favourable treatment issue cannot be resolved without, at the same time, deciding the reason why issue. The two issues are intertwined'. (In reality, this is how evidence will be presented at a tribunal (see 1.83). *Shamoon* was followed in *Brown v Croydon London Borough Council* [2006] All ER (D) 320 (May). Elias LJ indicated that 'it is not necessary for a tribunal, in each and every case, specifically to identify the two-stage process.'

Direct discrimination on grounds of age is distinct from other strands, in that A will not unlawfully discriminate against B if A can objectively justify the discrimination by demonstrating that it was a proportionate means of achieving a legitimate aim (*AR 2006, reg 3(1)(a)*) (see AGE DISCRIMINATION (2)). The defence of justification is not available for direct discrimination on any other prohibited ground.

1.28   Less favourable treatment

The comparator must be someone whose relevant circumstances are the same or not materially different from B's circumstances. These circumstances will be those considered by A in treating B in the way that he did, discounting the alleged discriminatory factor (*Shamoon*). In reality, it may be difficult to identify a real comparator possessing the same characteristics and so, often, B will identify several people who provide useful evidence of how A might have treated a real comparator. These comparators are often referred to as 'evidential' comparators. For a discussion of comparators see 1.33–1.39, but in many cases, focusing on the correct comparator will reveal the reason for the treatment and so the elements of the claim are inextricably linked.

In many cases less favourable treatment will be easy to identify. Significantly, it need not be the sole or principal reason for A's behaviour, but must be an important factor. Obvious behaviour, such as failing to promote, depriving someone of a pay rise, or dismissal, will be caught, as may be less obvious treatment, such as discouraging an employee or treating others preferentially.

Less favourable treatment must have occurred. Although the statutory test for direct discrimination considers how the employer treats or would treat a comparator, it does require B *to have suffered* the less favourable treatment. An employer does not discriminate if B can only argue that A *would* have treated him less favourably. In *Baldwin v Brighton and Hove City Council* [2007] ICR 680, EAT, B was a transsexual. B argued that unlawful discrimination took place when he perceived that, if he attended an interview, he would be less favourably treated by a clergyman, whom he believed to be a transphobe. The EAT acknowledged this argument could only succeed if B's manager had knowledge of B's gender reassignment and, with that in mind, had selected this interviewer. But the interviewer did not treat B any less favourably than an actual or hypothetical comparator simply by agreeing to join the interview panel.

It is not necessary for a tribunal to examine the consequences of the less favourable treatment, or determine whether objectively B is worse off because of it. In *Chief Constable of West Yorkshire Police v Khan* [2001] UKHL 48, [2001] 1 WLR 1947, [2001] ICR 1065, HL the West Yorkshire Police refused to give K a reference, and K claimed race discrimination. The West Yorkshire Police argued that the reference they would give would have been poor and therefore not helpful to K. The House of Lords held that the tribunal need not consider the consequences of a reference which might, when given, be unhelpful to K. What mattered was that K 'would have preferred not to have been treated differently' from others. The bar is therefore relatively low.

An employer cannot defend less favourable treatment by arguing that the overall benefits offered to the employee compensate for any less favourable treatment (*Ministry of Defence v Jeremiah* [1980] QB 87, [1979] 3 All ER 833, [1979] 3 WLR 857, [1980] ICR 13, CA): where men were paid an enhanced overtime rate to undertake 'dirty work' there was still less favourable treatment on the grounds of sex. It was a detriment to the men to be required to do dirty work which the women were not.

1.29   *Unreasonable or poor treatment distinguished from less favourable treatment*

The test in *Shamoon* requires a comparison; it is not enough to show unfavourable treatment. A's treatment of B will not be unlawful discrimination if it is not less favourable than the way he treats or would treat others. To determine whether it is less favourable, B must identify a real or hypothetical comparator (C) and show that A did or would treat B less favourably than C (see 1.33ff).

A will not discriminate simply because his behaviour is unreasonable. The complainant will not prove less favourable treatment simply by comparing the treatment with that of a reasonable employer: an employer's unreasonableness does not mean that an employee has been treated less favourably (*Glasgow City Council v Zafar* [1998] ICR 120, [1997] IRLR 231). The extent to which unreasonable behaviour may be relevant in drawing inferences of discrimination was considered by the Court of Appeal in *Bahl v Law Society* [2004] EWCA 1070, [2004] IRLR 799, and *Wong v Igen Ltd (Equal Opportunities Commission intervening)* [2005] EWCA Civ 142, [2005] ICR 931, [2005] IRLR 258.

If A can show that he treats all employees equally badly he may escape liability for discrimination. This argument was successfully run in *Madarassy v Nomura International plc* [2007] EWCA Civ 33, [2007] ICR 867, [2007] IRLR 246, para 93, in which M complained that her manager intimidated and threatened her. The tribunal found on the evidence that he treated all staff this way, regardless of gender, and the Court of Appeal observed, 'This was the culture of this workplace. It might be horrible, but it was not sexist'.

There are limits to this 'defence'. A may need to adduce evidence of universally bad treatment (*Anya v University of Oxford* [2001] EWCA Civ 405, [2001] ICR 847, [2001] IRLR 377, para 14). Further, the courts have considered the circumstances in which a tribunal may draw inferences where there is no explanation for the unreasonable treatment. In *Bahl* the Court of Appeal confirmed that unreasonable behaviour alone will not create an inference of discrimination, but the absence of an alternative explanation may do so (para 101). In *Igen*, the Court of Appeal acknowledged that a tribunal may draw such inferences in these circumstances, but nevertheless cautioned against drawing them too readily (para 76).

An employer does not discriminate if it fails to provide an advantage in circumstances where it does not offer that advantage to other employees (*Clymo v Wandsworth London Borough Council* [1989] 2 CMLR 577, [1989] ICR 250). In *Clymo*, a female employee argued she was treated less favourably when after the birth of her child her application for a job-share was refused. The employer did not offer job-sharing to anyone of her grade, and consequently the EAT held she did not suffer a detriment.

An employer does not discriminate simply because it treats two employees differently. For instance, where an employer introduced a dress code which required its employees to dress in a smart and conventional way, but the dress code requirements for male and female employees were the same, there was no less favourable treatment (*Smith v Safeway Plc* [1996] ICR 868, CA).

Whether the treatment is regarded as less favourable is essentially an objective consideration although, inevitably, depending on the nature of the alleged less favourable treatment, subjective elements do come into it. *Khan* is an illustration of this, as (although outside the employment sphere) is *Birmingham City Council v Equal Opportunities Commission* [1989] AC 1155, [1989] 2 WLR 520, 87 LGR 557, [1989] IRLR 173, where the House of Lords took into consideration the subjective preference of parents to send their girls to grammar schools. There were more single sex boys' schools than girls' schools in the relevant area. The House of Lords held that it was not necessary for B to prove objectively that grammar schools were better than non-selective schools to demonstrate less favourable treatment, rather that girls had fewer opportunities to attend grammar schools than boys.

1.30 *The reason for the less favourable treatment*

To establish whether there has been less favourable treatment one must look at the reasons for that treatment.

Where B can show he has suffered less favourable treatment by A, compared with an actual or hypothetical comparator, C, his claim for direct discrimination will not succeed if that treatment was not on a prohibited ground (sex; during a 'protected period', ie pregnancy; exercising or seeking to exercise a right to statutory maternity leave; married or civil partnership status; gender reassignment; race, colour, nationality, or ethnic or national origin; religion or belief; sexual orientation; disability; or age: *SDA 1975, ss 1(1)(a), s 2(1), s 3(1)(a), s 3(1)(b), 3A(1)(a), (b), s 3A(1); RRA 1976, s 1(1)(a); DDA 1995, s 3A(5); RBR 2003, reg 3(1)(a); SOR 2003, reg 3(1)(a); AR 2006, reg 3(1)(a)*). The tribunal must consider *why* B was treated less favourably.

(a) 'But for' test or 'reasons why'

The orthodox test for establishing the reason for the treatment is one of *classic causation*, ie for the tribunal to ask whether, 'but for' B's particular characteristic (ie his age, sex, race, etc) the less favourable treatment would have occurred. The 'but for' test was approved by the House of Lords in *James v Eastleigh Borough Council* [1990] ICR 554, HL. The Council gave women over 60 free access to the swimming pool while charging men full price until they were 65; the Council argued that the reason for the policy was that men did not reach pensionable age until 65. The House of Lords found that these reasons were irrelevant: J was able to show that 'but for' his sex, a man between the ages of 60 and 65 would not have had to pay for access to the swimming pool, and this was discriminatory. The 'but for' test excludes an examination of motive or intention.

In *O'Neill v Governors of St Thomas More RCVA Upper School* [1996] IRLR 372, [1997] ICR 33, EAT, the guidance given was that the tribunal should adopt a simple, commonsense approach, asking what was the 'effective and predominant cause' or 'real and efficient cause' of the treatment complained of.

More recently, the tribunals have moved away from the 'but for' test in favour of the 'reasons why' test, which involves the tribunal in a consideration of A's conscious or subconscious reasons for treating B less favourably.

One reason for this trend away from the 'but for' test is that it may not in fact reveal the reason for the treatment. In *Shamoon*, S was a Chief Inspector who had certain responsibilities under the appraisal process as a counselling officer. Complaints were made about the way she conducted the appraisals, and her counselling role was withdrawn. S complained that she had been treated less favourably than two male Chief Inspectors.

The House of Lords said that the tribunal must enquire why the claimant received the less favourable treatment noting that 'save in obvious cases, answering the crucial question will call for some consideration of the mental process of the alleged discriminator'. This reflects the shift in the burden of proof (see 1.83ff and is a more sophisticated approach than the application of the 'but for' test. It can, however, on first sight create confusion as the older authorities are peppered with references to the fact that the employer's intention or motivation should be irrelevant. The authors believe, however, that in *Shamoon* the House of Lords does not advocate that it is relevant to consider whether the employer intended to discriminate – a lack of intention would indeed be irrelevant if the impact was to discriminate – but to examine the underlying reasons for the less favourable treatment.

The problem is illustrated by *B v A* [2007] IRLR 576, EAT, in which a solicitor, B, had a relationship with a female personal assistant, A. When the affair ended, A was dismissed. The tribunal concluded that the dismissal would not have occurred but for the fact that A was a woman. However, the EAT upheld B's appeal and found that the issue was not merely one of 'but for' causation. It held that the test has a subjective element, and a court must ask itself why, as a matter of fact, the alleged discriminator acted the way he did. The 'but for' test revealed nothing about the motives of B.

See also *Martin v Lancehawk Ltd t/a European Telecom Solutions* [2004] All ER (D) 400 (Mar) (approved in *Igen*), in which the employer's male managing director had an affair with a female employee, M. The tribunal concluded that the reason for the dismissal was the breakdown in the relationship and not her gender. She argued that if she had not been female she would not have been dismissed. The EAT found that the 'but for' test is sometimes inappropriate – the hypothetical comparator proffered by M was a heterosexual male with whom the managing director did not have an affair. However, this did not explain *why* M had been dismissed. The EAT held if there were an appropriate comparator in this case (and the EAT noted that there might not) it would be a hypothetical male employee with whom the managing director had an affair, following which the male employee was dismissed. On the facts before the EAT there was no evidence that the managing director would treat the hypothetical comparator any differently. In any event, M's sex was not the motivating factor behind her dismissal, but the affair which had led to a breakdown in the relationship, and the managing director to hold that the employee was untrustworthy.

In light of *Shamoon, Khan* and *Igen*, it seems that there will be limited circumstances where the 'but for' test will now be applied. This is more so since the shift in the burden of proof following implementation of *Directive 97/80/EC* (see 1.85ff) as tribunals increasingly look for and/or receive from the employer an explanation for the conduct complained of an initial stage of the proceedings.

(b) No requirement for discriminatory motivation or intent

As stated above, although the recent trend is to consider the reasons why less favourable treatment occurred, this was motivated by a concern that the 'but for' test could lead to a finding of direct discrimination, where there was no discriminatory *reason* for the treatment. There is, however, no requirement for a tribunal to find a discriminatory *motive* or *intent* for the less favourable treatment to constitute direct discrimination, if the reasons why A acted in the way he did lead to a finding of discrimination (*R v Secretary of State for Education and Science, ex parte Keating (1985)* 84 LGR 469; *Glasgow City Council v Zafar* [1998] ICR 20, HL; *Nagarajan v London Regional Transport* [1999] ICR 877, HL).The courts have recognised that there will be limited circumstances when A acknowledges that the reason for the treatment was an individual's sex or race, etc. In so far as it can, the tribunal must consider what subconscious motivation can be inferred from the evidence before it.

(c) Prohibited ground need not be the only reason for discrimination

The prohibited ground need not be the sole or main reason for the less favourable treatment. It might be one of several reasons, although the discriminatory reason must be a significant cause of the unlawful discrimination (*Nagarajan*, in which Lord Nicholls said, at para 886: 'decisions are frequently reached for more than one reason. Discrimination may be on racial grounds even though it is not the sole ground for the decision ... If racial grounds or protected acts had a significant influence on the outcome, discrimination is made out').

The statutory burden of proof provisions mean, strictly, that, 'it is necessary for the employer to prove, on the balance of probabilities that the treatment was in no sense whatsoever on the grounds of sex, since "no discrimination whatsoever" is compatible with the Burden of Proof Directive' (per Judge Ansell at para 25, *Barton v Investec Henderson Crosthwaite Securities Ltd* [2003] IRLR 332, [2003] ICR 1205, EAT). The Court of Appeal in *Igen*, while approving this (and rejecting the modification suggested by HH Judge McMullen in *Emokpae v Chamberlin Solicitors* [2004] IRLR 592, that the respondent need only prove that the treatment was 'significantly influenced by' grounds of [sex] – as in *Nagarajan*) stated that, '… we doubt if Lord Nicholls' wording is in substance different from the "no discrimination whatsoever" formula. A "significant" influence is an influence which is more than trivial. We find it hard to believe that the principle of equal treatment would be breached by the merely trivial' (per Peter Gibson LJ at para 37).

1.31   **Discrimination by association or perception**

To whom must the protected characteristic apply?

The specific wording of the legislation is key. Because of the way in which direct discrimination is defined, it will extend to a broader range of treatment in some contexts than the claimant's own characteristics. Thus, discrimination may occur where there is less favourable treatment 'on grounds of the particular characteristic' or, depending on the context, of 'on grounds of B's particular characteristic'.

Under *SDA 1975* the prohibited characteristic must be that of B herself – that is, the case for discrimination on grounds of sex, marital and civil partnership status, gender reassignment and disability (*SDA 1975, ss 1(1)(a), 2(1), 3(1)(a); DDA 1995, s 3A(5)*).

Under *RRA 1976* the race need not be the race of the employee who is discriminated against. There may be unlawful discrimination on racial grounds if B suffers less favourable treatment because he refuses to discriminate against another (*Showboat Entertainment Centre Ltd v Owens* [1984] 1 All ER 836, [1984] 1 WLR 384, [1984] ICR 65; *Weathersfield Ltd t/a Van and Truck Rentals v Sargent* [1999] IRLR 94, [1999] ICR 425, CA; *Zarczynska v Levy* [1979] 1 All ER 814, [1979] 1 WLR 125, [1979] ICR 184). In *Showboat* a white manager of an entertainment centre was dismissed for refusing to obey an instruction to exclude all black customers. Browne Wilkinson J (para 70) explained the rationale for this interpretation of the *RRA 1976*: 'the words "on racial grounds" are perfectly capable in their ordinary sense of covering any reason or action based on race, whether it be the race of the person affected by the action or others.' The EAT was persuaded that this was the correct interpretation because there is nothing in the legislation which suggests the words 'on racial grounds' are intended only to cover the race of B, and it did not think Parliament could have intended that where B is dismissed for refusing to obey an unlawful discriminatory instruction he should be without a remedy, and otherwise placing him in the position of choosing being party to unlawful discrimination or losing his job.

In *Weathersfield* (para 96) the Court of Appeal acknowledged that while considering 'on racial grounds' to cover discrimination by association entails giving a broad meaning to that expression, such an interpretation is 'justified and appropriate'. In *Redfearn v Serco Ltd (t/a West Yorkshire Transport Service)* [2006] EWCA Civ 659, [2006] ICR 1367 a BNP councillor was dismissed – his job involved driving disabled passengers who were predominantly Asian. His employer dismissed him because they feared for the health and safety of bus passengers, from racial reprisals. The Court of Appeal refused to extend the meaning of 'on racial grounds' to these circumstances. He was, they said, dismissed because of his membership of BNP, a non-racial characteristic, and thus on political grounds. *RBR 2003* does not demand such interpretation as the wording is different (see RELIGION AND BELIEF (7)). *SOR 2003*, like *RRA 1976*, simply refers to discrimination 'on grounds of sexual orientation', and it is likely that the interpretation in *Weathersfield* and *Showboat* will apply.

Under *AR 2006, regs 3(1)(a)* and *3(3)(b)*, A can discriminate against B on the grounds of his age or his 'apparent age' (for details, see AGE (3)).

DDA 1995 refers to less favourable treatment on the grounds of B's disability. A current reference to the European Court of Justice (ECJ) from the UK asks the ECJ to consider whether *DDA 1995* appropriately implements *Framework Directive 2000/78/EC* ('the *Framework Directive*') and, if not, whether *DDA 1995* can be read purposively by the courts to protect B because of his association with a disabled person (*Coleman v Attridge Law and another* ET2303745/2005). In *Coleman*, C was the primary carer for her disabled son. She alleged that she had been subject to disability and disability-related discrimination because of her son's disability. *DDA 1995, s 3A(1)(a)* provides that 'a person discriminates against a disabled person if, for a reason which relates to the disabled person's disability, he treats him less favourably ...'.

The implications for other strands of discrimination legislation, if 'associative discrimination' is introduced into UK discrimination legislation, is likely to be limited. *RRA 1976*, *RBR 2003* and *SOR 2003* are, as discussed above, drafted broadly enough to allow for that interpretation.

1.32   Stereotypical assumptions

Stereotypical assumptions can constitute direct discrimination: 'The words "on the grounds of" also cover cases where the reason for discrimination was a generalised assumption that people of a particular sex, marital status or race possess or lack certain characteristics ...' (*Horsey v Dyfed County Council* [1982] ICR 755, [1982] IRLR 395).

The fact that a stereotypical assumption contains an element of truth, or that it was at some time in the past true, does not alter this (In *European Roma Rights Centre v Immigration Officer at Prague Airport (United Nations High Commissioner for Refugees intervening)* [2004] UKHL 55, [2005] 2 AC 1, [2005] 1 All ER 52, Baroness Hale said (at para 74), 'The individual should not be assumed to hold the characteristics which the supplier associates with the group, whether or not most members of the group do indeed have such characteristics ...').

1.33   COMPARATORS

Introduction

The legal concept of discrimination has at its heart the task of *comparison*. The discrimination law of the United Kingdom does not prohibit the unfair or unreasonable treatment of minorities *per se*. Indeed, as Lord Browne-Wilkinson observed in *Zafar v Glasgow City Council* [1998] ICR 120, [1998] IRLR 36, HL, the fact that an employer (or other alleged discriminator) has acted unreasonably in its treatment of an alleged victim of discrimination is technically irrelevant. Rather, the question always is whether the alleged victim has or has not been treated *less favourably* than someone else, on a prohibited ground.

That 'someone else', actual or hypothetical, with whom a claimant in a discrimination case compares his treatment, is known as a 'comparator'. The task of identifying actual or hypothetical comparators, and comparing their treatment with that of the alleged victim, is a central task in any direct discrimination case.

Indeed, as the House of Lords observed in *Shamoon v Chief Constable of the Ulster Constabulary* [2003] UKHL 11, [2003] 2 All ER 26, [2003] ICR 337, the question whether a particular person is or is not a proper comparator can often be determinative of the outcome of a case.

1.34   *The statutory requirement*

The discrimination statutes now all lay down a definition of the characteristics which are required in order for someone to be a proper comparator, actual or hypothetical, for the purposes of a discrimination case. *RRA 1976, s 3(4)*, which is materially mirrored in all the other discrimination statutes (see *SDA 1975, s 5(3), DDA 1995, s 3A(5), RBR 2003, reg 3(3), SOR 2003, reg 3(3)* and *AR 2006, reg 3(2)*), provides as follows (emphasis added):

> 'A comparison of the case of a person of a particular racial group with that of a person not of that group under *s 1(1)* or *1A* must be such that the relevant circumstances in the one case are the same, or not materially different, in the other.'

1.35   *'Relevant circumstances'*

The formula '… such that the relevant circumstances in the one case are the same, or not materially different, in the other' was considered in detail in the decision of the House of Lords in *Shamoon* (see 1.33). The ratio, in short, of their Lordships' decision was that the 'relevant circumstances' which cannot be 'materially different' if someone is to constitute a proper comparator are:

(a)   all those circumstances that *were* taken into account when the allegedly discriminatory decision was made (aside of course from the prohibited grounds); and

(b)   all those circumstances that *would have been* taken into account if the alleged comparator had been in the position of the alleged victim.

The importance of the second category of relevant circumstances identified above was illustrated by the particular facts of the *Shamoon* case itself. In that case, a female police officer argued that she had been discriminated against on ground of her sex because she had had the task of performing staff appraisals taken away from her after a complaint was made against her. She compared herself with two male police officers of the same rank who continued to perform such appraisals. However, it was held that those male police officers were *not* proper comparators, because: (i) neither had had a complaint made about them; and (ii) both worked in a different department. Those two circumstances *would have been* taken into account had those men been in the claimant's position and were therefore, to put the House of Lords' decision in terms of the statute, 'relevant circumstances' which were 'materially different'.

The characteristics of a comparator are not subject to any further limitation than that in *s 3(4)* and its analogues. Accordingly, where that test is met, comparison is possible with employees in associated companies, as opposed to the same company.

1.36   *Discriminatory relevant circumstances*

A significant problem is posed when an alleged discriminator seeks to rely, in an attempt to argue that a nominated comparator is not a proper one, on an allegedly materially different 'relevant circumstance' which is *in itself* discriminatory. The two leading cases in this area do not speak with one voice by any means:

(a)   *James v Eastleigh Borough Council* [1990] IRLR 288, HL. The respondent
      Council permitted free access to a swimming pool for women at the age of
      60, but for men at the age of 65. The respondent argued that the reason for
      this distinction was the difference in 'pensionable age', ie the age at which
      men and women received state pensions, and therefore the difference in
      treatment was not 'on ground of sex'. The House of Lords rejected this
      argument, holding that it is impossible to defend a discriminatory act as not
      being 'on ground of sex' when it is based on a statutory scheme which *itself*
      discriminates on ground of sex. At least one way of understanding the
      James case would be that a person (in that case a woman aged 60 to 64)
      cannot be prohibited from being a legitimate comparator by virtue of a
      'relevant circumstance' (in that case pensionable age) which is in itself
      discriminatory.

(b)   *Dhatt v McDonald's Hamburgers Ltd* [1991] 3 All ER 692, [1991] 1 WLR
      527, [1991] ICR 238. The applicant was of Indian nationality and, under
      the *Immigration Act 1971*, was entitled to live and work in the United
      Kingdom without restriction or need for a work permit. He was given a job
      but was dismissed for failing to provide evidence of his right to work. He
      complained that he had been unlawfully discriminated against on the
      ground of his race by comparison with citizens of Member States of the
      European Economic Community ('EEC citizens'), who were not required
      to produce evidence of their entitlement to work. The Court of Appeal,
      however, held that EEC citizens were *not* proper comparators within the
      meaning of *section 3(4)*, since Parliament, by giving a right of freedom to
      work in the United Kingdom to British and EEC citizens, had distin-
      guished between them and nationals of other states so that a comparison
      between the applicant and those groups was not a comparison of like with
      like. In other words, the Court of Appeal held that the difference in
      treatment between EEC citizens and non-EEC citizens was a 'relevant
      circumstance' that was 'materially different'.

It is often argued that the *Dhatt* decision is incompatible with the *James* decision
and therefore wrong. This is a jurisprudentially difficult argument, since: (i) the
Court of Appeal in *Dhatt* both considered and distinguished the *James* decision;
and (ii) the *Dhatt* decision has since been followed by the EAT, in *Ice Hockey
Super League Ltd v Henry* EAT/1167/99.

The basis for the Court of Appeal's distinction between the facts of the *Dhatt* and
James cases was that in *Dhatt*, nationality was a relevant circumstance '... because
Parliament itself recognises and seeks to enforce by reference to nationality a
general division between those who by reason of their nationality are free to work
and those who require permission' (per Neill LJ at 535), whereas in *James*,
Parliament had *not* in any way enacted 'that concessions granted by local
authorities on the ground of age should depend on the attainment of pensionable
age' (per Neill LJ at 534), and therefore 'pensionable status' could not be a
materially relevant circumstance since it was in itself discriminatory. Although it
is difficult to find any basis for this distinction in the discrimination legislation, it
is nevertheless conceptually tenable.

Until a further appellate case resolves the tension between the *James* and *Dhatt*
cases, therefore, the law would appear to be that it *is* possible to rely on a
materially different relevant circumstance which is in itself discriminatory but *only*
where the difference in treatment itself arises directly from legislation.

The characteristics of a comparator are not subject to any further limitation than that in *s 3(4)* and its analogues. Accordingly, where that test is met, comparison is possible with employees in associated companies as opposed to the same company.

1.37 *Comparisons where own membership of protected class not relied on*

A further difficulty with regard to the comparative exercise arises where a claimant alleges discrimination on ground of *someone else's* membership of a protected class. Where such a claim is brought, the comparative exercise can be modified.

The leading case is *Showboat Entertainment Centre Ltd v Owens* [1984] 1 WLR 384, EAT, in which a white manager was dismissed for refusing to obey an instruction to exclude all black customers from an entertainment centre. The respondent argued that it was necessary to compare how it treated the applicant with the way in which it would have treated another manager who also refused to carry out the instruction. The EAT robustly rejected this argument, holding that (emphasis added):

> 'Although one has to compare like with like, in judging whether there has been discrimination you have to compare the treatment actually meted out with the treatment which would have been afforded to a man having all the same characteristics as the complainant except his race *or his attitude to race*. Only by excluding *matters of race* can you discover whether the differential treatment was on racial grounds. Thus, the correct comparison in this case would be between the applicant and another manager who did not refuse to obey the unlawful racialist instructions.'

It would therefore appear that where a person is treated less favourably on ground of someone else's membership of a protected class, the court must exclude that person's 'attitude to' members of that protected class when assessing whether an actual or hypothetical comparator is a proper one. Further (obiter) examples of the application of the principle were given in:

(i)   the decision of the House of Lords in *Race Relations Board v Applin* [1975] AC 259, 289–290, in which Lord Simon observed that the dismissal of a white employee by a white employer for marrying a black person was plainly within the 'mischief' which the *RRA 1976* was intended to address; and

(ii) the decision of the Court of Appeal in the same case (*Race Relations Board v Applin* [1973] QB 815, 828a–e), in which Lord Denning MR observed that a white publican who refused to admit or serve a white customer on the ground that she was accompanied by a black person would be liable in principle for race discrimination. In both of these cases, the judges approached the matter on the basis that the correct comparison was with someone who had *not* married a black person and/or was *not* accompanied by a black person.

This rule of law presented the Court of Appeal in the subsequent case of *Redfearn v Serco Ltd* [2006] ICR 1367, CA with some difficulty. In that case, Mr Redfearn, who was white, had been employed by Serco as a bus driver and escort for people with disabilities. A local newspaper identified him as a British National Party (BNP) candidate in forthcoming local elections. The BNP sought the restoration of Britain as a predominantly white nation. Mr Redfearn was elected as a BNP councillor and was subsequently summarily dismissed by Serco on the basis that his employment would present a risk to the health and safety of its employees and passengers and would jeopardise Serco's reputation. Mr Redfearn, relaying heavily on the *Showboat* case, argued that he had been treated less favourably on ground of race because Serco had employed a race-based criterion in his dismissal. The Court of Appeal firmly rejected this argument, and in doing so significantly narrowed the ambit of the ratio in the *Showboat* case. The relevant passage of the judgment of Mummery LJ reads as follows:

'**44** The essence of *Showboat* is that an employee who refuses to implement his employer's racially discriminatory policy is entitled to be protected from less favourable treatment under the 1976 Act. The use of the employee to implement the employer's racially discriminatory policy means that "racial grounds" operate directly in the less favourable treatment of the employee, whether the race or colour in question be that of the employee or that of a third party. Mr Bowers's proposition goes far wider so as to embrace cases in which the employer, far from seeking to implement a racially discriminatory policy contrary to the policy of the 1976 Act, is acting to eliminate race discrimination in accordance with the policy of the 1976 Act. According to Mr Bowers (subject to his points on causation and remedy) the employee would be entitled to receive the same protection under the 1976 Act from unfavourable treatment, such as dismissal, however racially discriminatory he was towards third parties contrary to his employer's instructions.

'**45** Mr Bowers's proposition turns the ratio of *Showboat* and the policy of the race relations legislation upside down. It would mean that any less favourable treatment brought about because of concern about the racist views or conduct of a person in a multi-ethnic workplace would constitute race discrimination. The ratio of *Showboat* is that the racially discriminatory employer is liable "on racial grounds" for the less favourable treatment of those who refuse to implement his policy or are affected by his policy. It does not apply so as to make the employer, who is not pursuing a policy of race discrimination or who is pursuing a policy of anti-race discrimination, liable for race discrimination.

'**46** In this case it is true that the circumstances in which the decision to dismiss Mr Redfearn was taken included racial considerations, namely the fact that Serco's customers were mainly Asian and that a significant percentage of the workforce was Asian. Racial considerations were relevant to Serco's decision to dismiss Mr Redfearn, but that does not mean that it is right to characterise Serco's dismissal of Mr Redfearn as being "on racial grounds". It is a non sequitur to argue that he was dismissed "on racial grounds" because the circumstances leading up to his dismissal included a relevant racial consideration, such as the race of fellow employees and customers and the policies of the BNP on racial matters. Mr Redfearn was no more dismissed "on racial grounds" than an employee who is dismissed for racially abusing his employer, a fellow employee or a valued customer. Any other result would be incompatible with the purpose of the 1976 Act to promote equal treatment of persons irrespective of race by making it unlawful to discriminate against a person on the grounds of race.

'**47** In my judgment, the employment tribunal was correct in law in deciding that Mr Redfearn was not dismissed "on racial grounds". The grounds of dismissal were not racial. They did not become racial grounds because Serco dismissed him in circumstances in which it wished to avoid the perceived detrimental effects of Mr Redfearn's membership of, and election to office representing, the BNP, which propagated racially discriminatory policies concerning non-white races who formed part of Serco's workforce and customer base.'

1.38   *Hypothetical comparators*

It is important to note that, apart from in equal pay cases where an actual comparator is obligatory, a claimant is not obliged to name an actual comparator in order to have a viable discrimination case. Where there is no actual comparator who meets the statutory requirements, a tribunal or court is instead obliged to consider what would have happened to a hypothetical comparator (*Balamoody v UK Central Council for Nursing, Midwifery and Health Visiting* [2001] EWCA Civ 2097, [2002] IRLR 288, CA).

The hypothetical comparator is *not* required to be '... a clone of the applicant in every respect (including personality and personal characteristics) except that he or she is or a different race' (*Madden v Preferred Technical Group CHA Ltd* [2004] EWCA Civ 1178, [2005] IRLR 46 per Wall LJ, 87)). Rather, as with an actual comparator, the only requirement is that the relevant circumstances of the hypothetical comparator should not be materially different.

In considering whether a hypothetical comparator has been treated less favourably than a claimant, there are two (not necessarily alternative) approaches that a tribunal can adopt.

The first approach is to consider the alleged discriminator's treatment of other actual persons who are not proper comparators within the meaning of the discrimination statutes ('evidential comparators'). From the treatment of these people it is said to be possible to infer how the hypothetical comparator would have been treated. The leading case is *Chief Constable of West Yorkshire v Vento* [2001] IRLR 124, in which the EAT approved a process by which a tribunal had used four persons who were not actual comparators '... as if building blocks in the construction of the neighbourhood in which the hypothetical male officer was to be found' (at 15). The *Vento* case was approved by the Court of Appeal in *Balamoody* (cited above). See also *Shamoon* at 1.35, per Lord Scott at 109.

The second approach has become known as the 'reason why' approach. Why was the claimant treated in the fashion he was treated? This was the approach recommended by the House of Lords in the *Shamoon* case. The relevant passage of the speech of Lord Bingham warrants quotation:

'... in practice tribunals in their decisions normally consider, first, whether the claimant received less favourable treatment than the appropriate comparator (the "less favourable treatment" issue) and then, secondly, whether the less favourable treatment was on the relevant proscribed ground (the "reason why" issue). Tribunals proceed to consider the reason why issue only if the less favourable treatment issue is resolved in favour of the claimant. Thus the less favourable treatment issue is treated as a threshold which the claimant must cross before the tribunal is called upon to decide why the claimant was afforded the treatment of which she is complaining.

'... No doubt there are cases where it is convenient and helpful to adopt this two-step approach to what is essentially a single question: did the claimant, on the proscribed ground, receive less favourable treatment than others? But, especially where the identity of the relevant comparator is a matter of dispute, this sequential analysis may give rise to needless problems. Sometimes the less favourable treatment issue cannot be resolved without, at the same time, deciding the reason why issue. The two issues are intertwined.

'... employment tribunals may sometimes be able to avoid arid and confusing disputes about the identification of the appropriate comparator by concentrating primarily on why the claimant was treated as she was. Was it on the proscribed ground which is the foundation of the application? That will call for an examination of all the facts of the case. Or was it for some other reason? If the latter, the application fails. If the former, there will be usually be no difficulty in deciding whether the treatment, afforded to the claimant on the proscribed ground, was less favourable than was or would have been afforded to others.

'The most convenient and appropriate way to tackle the issues arising on any discrimination application must always depend upon the nature of the issues and all the circumstances of the case. There will be cases where it is convenient to decide the less favourable treatment issue first. But, for the reason set out above, when formulating their decisions employment tribunals may find it helpful to consider whether they should postpone determining the less favourable treatment issue until after they have decided why the treatment was afforded to the claimant.'

It is submitted that the 'reason why' approach is, in hypothetical comparator cases, preferable. The artificiality of the hypothetical exercise is kept to a minimum if the tribunal starts by asking itself, on the basis of all the evidence before it, whether a claimant would have been treated any differently but for their membership of a protected class. This can include even disregarding the burden of proof provisions and adopting a one-stage approach by '... acting on the assumption that the burden may have shifted to the respondent and then considering the explanation put forward by the respondent' (*Madarassy v Nomura International plc* [2007] EWCA Civ 33, [2007] ICR 867).

1.39   *Illegitimate hypotheses*

The hypothetical approach does, however, have an important limitation, namely that the tribunal or court must not hypothesise as to what might have happened to the claimant or some other person in an admittedly different situation which seems, in a broad sense, comparable. In particular, it is generally not appropriate for tribunals to consider 'mirror image' scenarios whereby, for instance, a female applying for a job at a male-dominated employer would be compared with a male applying for a job at a female-dominated employer. The tribunal must not be dragged into considering apparent converses of the facts before it. The task of a tribunal or court is to consider the case before it. The point can be illustrated by reference to three cases in particular:

(a)   *Chief Constable of West Yorkshire Police v Khan* [2001] UKHL 48, [2001] 1 WLR 1947, [2001] ICR 1065. The claimant, Sergeant Khan, started proceedings in an employment tribunal alleging racial discrimination against his employer. He then asked for a reference, which request was refused. Mr Khan argued that his request had been refused because of his protected act. The Chief Constable argued that the court ought to compare Mr Khan with a hypothetical police officer who: (i) had not lodged the proceedings; and instead (ii) had brought proceedings against the Chief Constable on some other ground, such as libel or wrongful dismissal. The House of Lords comprehensively rejected the second half of this submission, holding that the statute called for a simple comparison between the treatment given to Sergeant Khan and the treatment which would have been given to a police officer who had not done a protected act. It was not appropriate to speculate as to what might have happened has Sergeant Khan made some other complaint.

(b)   *Smyth v Croft Inns Ltd* [1995] NI 292, [1996] IRLR 84, CA (Northern Ireland). S, a Roman Catholic, was employed as a barman in a pub with Protestant customers in a loyalist area of Belfast. A message was delivered to the pub saying that S should be advised not to be in the bar in the following week. The employers took no action. S, believing that his life was at risk, resigned and claimed that he had been discriminated against on grounds of religious belief in that he had been constructively dismissed. The Court of Appeal in Northern Ireland held that the relevant comparison was *not* a hypothetical Protestant barman working in a Catholic bar in a nationalist area, but rather simply between S and a hypothetical Protestant barman working in the *same bar*.

(c)   *Grieg v Community Industry* [1979] ICR 356, [1979] IRLR 158, EAT. The applicant, a woman, was refused work in a painting and decorating department as she would be the only woman in a team of men and that would cause an 'unacceptable imbalance in the group's composition'. The EAT held that '... the relevant employment to consider is not some hypothetical employment with the personnel concerned totally different, but is the employment for which the applicant applied', and that it was therefore irrelevant to speculate what might have happened had the claimant been a man applying for a job in an all-woman department. Something of the flavour of this case can be detected from the fact that the EAT was also required to reject a submission to the effect that, if it was '... in the applicant's best interests that she should not be offered the job', then there would be no discrimination at all.

The one caveat to enter in respect of the above is that whilst a hypothetical 'mirror image' comparison is not appropriate for determining whether there has been less favourable treatment, such a comparison *can* be legitimate as a way for a court or tribunal to determine what the real reason for the treatment in question was. See the *Showboat* and *Madarassy* cases cited above.

1.40   INDIRECT DISCRIMINATION

Introduction

There have been changes to the statutory tests for indirect discrimination, which are addressed in more detail below. The three essential elements of indirect discrimination have remained the same:

(a)   there is a measure by the employer which puts a group of people within a protected group at a disadvantage;

(b)   the complainant, who falls within that group, suffers that disadvantage; and

(c)   the employer cannot objectively justify its practice.

Note there is no concept of indirect discrimination in respect of disability or gender reassignment.

1.41   The statutory definition (for all grounds except nationality or colour)

The statutory definition to be applied in cases of sex, marital and civil partnership status, race (meaning race or ethnic or national origins), gender reassignment, religion or belief, sexual orientation, or age discrimination is:

'A discriminates against B if A applies to B a provision, criterion or practice which he applies or would apply equally to persons not of the same particular feature, but

(i)   which puts or would put persons with the same characteristic as B at a particular disadvantage when compared with other persons;

(ii)   which puts B at that disadvantage; and

(iii)   which A cannot show to be a proportionate means of achieving a legitimate aim.'

The precise formulations for the strands of discrimination law covered by this test vary slightly, but are essentially the same (see *SDA 1975, ss 1(2)(b)* and *3(1)(b)*; *RRA 1976, s 1(1A); RBR 2003, reg 3(1)(b); SOR 2003, reg 3(1)(b))* and *AR 2006, reg 3(1)(b))*. See following chapters for detail.

1.42   Sex discrimination: the situation prior to 1 October 2005

On 1 October 2005 the statutory definition of indirect discrimination was amended in order to implement the definition contained in the *Equal Treatment Directive (Directive 2000/43/EC)* as amended by *Council Directive 2002/73* and to harmonise definitions across other grounds of unlawful discrimination. The current test is that in 1.41.

Under *SDA 1975 s 1(2)(b)* the test in respect of acts of discrimination which occurred between 12 October 2001 and 1 October 2005 is:

'... a person discriminates against a woman if he applies to her a requirement or condition which he applies or would apply equally to a man but–

(i)   which is such that the proportion of women who can comply with it is considerably smaller than the proportion of men etc;

(ii)   which he cannot show to be justifiable irrespective of the sex of the person to whom it is applied; and

(iii)   which is to her detriment.'

1.43   The statutory test for racial group (nationality or colour)

There are two definitions of indirect race discrimination. In July 2003 the *Race Relations Act 1976 (Amendment) Regulations 2003 (SI 2003/1626)* implemented the test of indirect discrimination applicable under the *Race Discrimination Framework Directive*. The *Directive* does not apply to discrimination on the grounds of colour or nationality, whereas *RRA 1976* covers discrimination on the grounds of colour, race, nationality or ethnic or national origins (see RACE DISCRIMINATION (6)).

Under *RRA 1976* the test for discrimination on grounds of race and ethnic or national origin is as described at 1.41. The test applicable to indirect discrimination on the grounds of nationality and colour (*RRA 1976, s 1(1)(b)*) is that:

'A person ... discriminates if ... he applies a requirement or condition which he applies or would apply equally to persons not of the same racial group as [B] but:

(i)   which is such that the proportion of persons in that racial group who can comply with it is considerably smaller than the proportion of persons not of that racial group who can comply with it; and

(ii)   which he cannot show to be justifiable irrespective of the colour, race, nationality or ethnic or national origins of the person to whom it is applied; and

(iii)   which is to the detriment of [B] because he cannot comply with it.'

Rather than replace *RRA 1976* with new primary legislation to make it compatible with the European legislation, the Government used secondary regulations to introduce the amendments. However, these were only capable of amending *RRA 1976* in so far as it was incompatible with European Community law. The 'colour and nationality' strands of race discrimination remain covered by the pre-July 2003 definition. The Government has indicated an intention to harmonise and simplify legislation in the future. In June 2005 the Government, as part of the Discrimination Law Review, published a green paper 'Discrimination Law Review – A Framework for a Fairer Future: Proposals for a Single Equality Bill for Great Britain', in which it set out the Government's proposed strategy for harmonising the definitions of indirect discrimination. The impact of the different tests is examined further in RACE DISCRIMINATION (6).

1.44   Meeting the definition of indirect discrimination

(a) 'Provision, criterion or practice'

B must show that A applied a provision, criterion or practice (or 'requirement or condition' (see above)). There is no statutory definition of 'provision, criterion or practice'. Each has been given a broad construction ranging from laws applicable to all employees in the UK, to a measure by one employer regarding the working patterns of one section of its workforce.

A provision includes a condition or requirement (such as a contractual term), and can extend to non-contractual policies, collective agreements, rules and guidelines.

Criteria are applied at all stages of the employment relationship, from the criteria which a prospective employer chooses to apply when selecting candidates for employment, to decisions to promote or reward existing employees, and the criteria by which an employer decides to select an employee for dismissal, in other words the standards used by the employer in exercising his judgement. A criterion need not be an absolute requirement or a complete bar to obtaining a benefit or avoiding a disadvantage, only something which is desirable. A 'practice' can be something quite informal. The combination of these terms results in a test which is much easier for the claimant to satisfy than the old 'test' which called for a 'requirement or condition' (and still does in the case of colour or nationality). The effect may be to subject more internal procedures to enquiry although, of course, the 'justification' defence is available to employers (see below). The statutory definition also permits claims to be brought about effects which will only be felt in the future as indeed they could before – see *Meade-Hill and National Union of Civil and Public Servants v British Council* [1996] 1 All ER 79, [1995] ICR 847, [1995] IRLR 478, where the Court of Appeal found that a mobility clause, not yet relied on by the employer, amounted to a requirement or condition.

Although tribunals are willing to take a broad view of what amounts to a provision, practice or criterion, the claimant must identify the measure complained of (*Allonby v Accrington and Rossendale College* [2001] EWCA Civ 529, [2001] IRLR 364, [2001] ICR 1189, CA). If a claimant fails to identify a measure which could amount to a provision, criterion or practice, his claim will fail (*Redfearn*, para 51). The exception to this general rule is in cases brought under *EqPA 1970*, where it is recognised that there will be circumstances where no provision, criterion or practice can be identified, but there is nonetheless a finding of indirect discrimination on the basis that there is cogent and compelling evidence that women suffer a disparate impact than men in respect of their pay arrangements (*Villalba v Merrill Lynch* [2006] IRLR 437, [2007] ICR 469, EAT; *Tyne and Wear Passenger Transport Authority (t/a Nexus) v Best and others* [2007] ICR 523, EAT, *Enderby v Frenchay Health Authority* [1994] ICR 112, ECJ) (see also EQUAL PAY (11)). In *Starmer v British Airways plc* [2005] IRLR 862, [2005] All ER (D) 323 (Jul), the EAT, considering the case where an employee asking to work 50 per cent of full-time hours was offered a reduction to 75 per cent, held the employer's stipulation was a provision, criterion or practice – even though it had been applied only to the claimant.

(b) B, and others in the protected group suffer a 'particular disadvantage'

B must be able to show that the application by A of the provision, practice, or criterion puts him, and others in his protected class, at a 'particular disadvantage'. This necessarily requires a comparison between the advantaged and disadvantaged groups. Before that comparison can be made, B must identify the proper pool for comparison, so that a tribunal can assess whether or not there was a disparate impact between those who were and were not disadvantaged by the provision, practice or criterion.

The pool for comparison

It is for B to advance what he believes to be the appropriate pool. This will depend on the nature of the provision, criterion or practice itself, and those who are affected or potentially affected by the application of the measure in question. The pool can vary greatly in size. For instance, where the measure is national employment legislation, the appropriate pool is likely to be all employed people who can avail themselves of rights under that legislation (*R v Secretary of State for Employment, ex p Seymour-Smith* [2000] 1 All ER 857, [2000] 1 WLR 435; *Rutherford v Secretary of State for Trade and Industry* [2006] UKHL 19, [2006] ICR 785, HL), ie the working population of the United Kingdom. Where the measure challenged is applied by one employer to one section of his workforce, the appropriate pool may be the employer's entire workforce, or just that section of it.

Although in the absence of agreement, B must advance what he believes to be the appropriate pool or pools, the tribunal may substitute in its own pool if B's choice is not appropriate. Although the pool used to be a matter for the tribunal's discretion, in *University of Manchester v Jones* [1993] ICR 474 the Court of Appeal expressed the view that a broad pool is desirable and that there will usually be one pool (but there may be more). That said, the higher courts have resisted the temptation to lay down guidance. Selection of the wrong pool will invalidate the finding and consequently the pool selection is often appealed (*London Underground v Edwards (No 1)* [1995] ICR 574, CA; *University of Manchester v Jones* [1993] ICR 474, CA; *Perera v Civil Service Commission (No 2)* [1983] ICR 428, CA). However, it is not the case that there is only one suitable pool in each case; B must advance a legitimate pool for comparison, but a finding of discrimination cannot be challenged solely on the basis that a different, also legitimate, pool would have produced a different result (*Grundy v British Airways Plc* [2007] All ER (D) 345, para 31).

The pool 'must be one which suitably tests the particular discrimination complained of' (per Sedley LJ in *Grundy*, para 27); it should not include those 'who have no interest in the advantage or disadvantage in question', ie the pool should not be wider than necessary (per Baroness Hale of Richmond in *Rutherford*, para 82), nor should it be 'narrowed by reference to qualifications or conditions which are not logically relevant' (per Lord Walker of Gestingthorpe in *Rutherford*, para 66; see also University of Manchester v Jones [1993] ICR 474, 495 and 505; *London Underground Ltd v Edwards (No 2)* [1999] ICR 494, CA, 508–509; and *Barry v Midland Bank Plc* [1999] 3 All ER 974, [1999] 1 WLR 1465, [1999] ICR 859, HL, 869–870). Thus it should be limited by factors which affect the claimant's ability to satisfy the measure.

Thus, the pool should consist of all those to whom the provision, criterion or practice does or can apply. In a case concerning indirect discrimination on the grounds of sex where the employer applied a policy to all employees that it would not allow employees who were in a partnership (ie an emotional relationship) also to be in a supervisor/subordinate relationship, the complainant identified the wrong pool for comparison when she argued for a pool comprising those people who had partners who were working for the employer (*Faulkner v Chief Constable of Hampshire Constabulary* [2007] UKEAT/0505/05/LA). The EAT held that the appropriate pool should be the whole of the Hampshire Police workforce, as the policy applied to all employees.

Similarly, when the British Medical Association (BMA) refused to support a member's race discrimination claim against a regulatory body, the Court of Appeal found that the tribunal and the EAT had erred in identifying the correct pool as limited to those affected by the BMA's practice of not supporting claims made against regulatory bodies (*BMA v Chaudhary* [2007] EWCA Civ 788, [2007] IRLR 800, CA). Such a pool, which focuses only on those disadvantaged by the employer's policy, allows no room for comparison and yet indirect discrimination requires precisely that. The Court of Appeal in *Chaudhary* held that the appropriate pool was all BMA members who wanted support in race discrimination claims against a regulatory body.

Disparate impact

Once the pool for comparison has been determined, B must undertake the comparative exercise and demonstrate that because he belongs to a protected group, he has suffered a particular disadvantage compared with those others in the pool who do not. Particular disadvantage is not defined. There is no case law as yet, but it seems that the test for particular disadvantage will depend less, if at all, on statistics – although in some cases these may be relevant and persuasive. Other cases may depend more on the evidence of expert and other witnesses. The particular disadvantage test does not require a tribunal to compare the proportions of those who can or cannot comply with a particular measure – or indeed for it to consider the meaning of can comply. Thus arguments such as those in *Sykes v JP Morgan* EAT/279/00 (July 12, 2002, unreported), where a highly paid woman who could afford to employ a nanny was found able (albeit unwilling) to comply with a requirement to work full-time, will be of much less relevance.

A critical issue in many cases may now be not whether the claimant is in theory able to comply with a particular measure, but the degree of disadvantage he suffers by so doing, whether and how the disadvantage suffered relates to the protected ground, and whether the tribunal considers that the disadvantage suffered merits redress.

It is not yet known whether tribunals will interpret 'particular' as meaning 'specific', ie peculiar to a particular protected group, and/or whether 'particular' simply means significant or identifiable. It is possible that there is no single answer. The test, like the 'considerably smaller proportion' test, while serving as a means of filtering out trivial claims, is flexible – probably more so than the older test.

Statistics

The authorities prior to the implementation of the new test tell us that the typical way to determine whether B had been put at a disadvantage was by statistical analysis of the proportions of advantaged and disadvantaged people in the pool. There will, however, be many cases where the disparity of treatment is marginal, and depending on whether the statistical analysis focuses on those who are advantaged or disadvantaged within the pool, the results can lead to starkly different conclusions.

The trend was to undertake an 'advantaged-led' analysis, considering the relevant percentages of those who are advantaged. Take as an example a situation where all employees must have 15 years' employment as a full time-employee with A in order to secure a particular benefit from A, which is potentially indirectly discriminatory on the grounds of sex (or age) as potentially fewer women will be able to satisfy the length of service requirement. The statistical analysis requires an assessment of the number of women in the pool that can comply, compared with the number of men that can comply. The two percentages are then compared to each other rather than to the whole pool. More recently, it was recognised that while it could be a useful starting point to look at this percentage it may also be relevant to consider the disadvantaged group. In *Rutherford* the majority of the House of Lords preferred to resolve the case by reference to broad principles rather than looking at statistical evidence – and assessing whether the difference indicates a 'particular disadvantage' (*Rutherford v Secretary of State for Trade and Industry (No 2)* [2006] UKHL 19, [2006] ICR 785, HL). This is not to say that there is no place for considering the disadvantaged groups, and it will not be an error of law if a tribunal does not make an advantaged-led analysis (*Grundy v British Airways Plc* [2007] All ER (D) 345, para 35).

A narrow pool which focuses on the disadvantaged will usually assist the complainant in demonstrating a disparate impact, and it is likely that these arguments will continue to be run (on the basis of Lord Nicholls judgment in *Seymour-Smith* and Lord Walker of Gestingthorpe (obiter) in *Rutherford*, para 67).

In *R v Secretary of State for Employment (ex parte Seymour-Smith)* [1999] 2 AC 554, [1997] ICR 447, ECJ, paras 61–62 the ECJ ruled that it is for a national court to determine whether the statistics used are 'relevant and sufficient for the purposes of resolving the case before it'. In particular, the ECJ noted that there will be cases where the statistics illustrate 'purely fortuitous or short-term phenomena'. Statistical data will be open to challenge if it is out of date, or for other reasons distorts the proper comparison.

Where the pool for comparison involves a large workforce, of which the disadvantaged group is a small proportion, it may be appropriate to express the proportions in the disadvantaged group as a ratio of each other (*Barry*, para 36).

In *Coker v Lord Chancellor* [2001] EWCA Civ 1756, [2002] ICR 321, CA the Lord Chancellor had appointed a friend as his special advisor. C claimed she should have been considered for the position. The pool for comparison comprised those who were appropriately qualified for the position of special adviser, and the allegedly discriminatory requirement was that applicants needed to be known personally to the Lord Chancellor. On the facts, nearly the entire pool of comparators was excluded from being considered for appointment (as very few were personally known to the Lord Chancellor). Consequently it was not possible for the requirement to have a disproportionate impact on different groupings within the pool.

Given the difficulties, a flexible approach to the assessment of the disparate impact issue is now favoured, particularly in situations where on the advantaged-led analysis, the statistics demonstrate a marginal percentage difference between the advantaged groups, and yet there is demonstrable indirect discrimination. In *London Underground Ltd v Edwards (No 2)* [1999] ICR 994, [1998] IRLR 364, a case involving a change to a shift rota system, E, for childcare reasons, could *not* comply with the change to the rota system. London Underground employed 2,023 male train drivers and 21 female drivers; all men could comply with the new rota system and only one female driver (the complainant) could not comply. On pure numbers alone, the fact that only one woman could not comply was not persuasive on the issue of disparate impact. The statistical analysis of those advantaged by the rota system (ie those who could comply with it) showed that 95.2% of women could comply, compared with 100% of men, a disparate impact of 4.8%. The EAT and the Court of Appeal found indirect discrimination. Although the statistical evidence was not necessarily compelling, it was right for the tribunal to focus on the percentage discrepancy between the numbers of male and female operators (demonstrating the job was difficult or unattractive to women), despite the numerical evidence that only one woman could be found unable to comply.

It may be appropriate to consider whether there is an intrinsic risk that someone with a particular characteristic is disadvantaged. In *Chief Constable of Avon and Somerset Constabulary v Chew* [2001] All ER (D) 101 (Sep) a police officer's application to work part-time was rejected because she was unable to comply with the roster shifts cycle. She claimed indirect sex discrimination. The chosen pool for assessing the disparate impact was all police officers in that constabulary. Of the pool of 3016 police officers, only 11 could not comply with the requirement to work the shift roster: ten women and one man. 99.96% of male officers and 97.7% of female police officers were able to comply. On a pure statistical analysis there was a disparate impact of only 2.26%. The tribunal and EAT found that although a disparate impact of 2.26% was, at face value, insufficient to establish indirect discrimination, the tribunal was entitled to take into other factors, as the requirement to comply with a roster shift cycle was intrinsically more likely to impact on women more than men because women tend to have the main childcare responsibility. Relying on the ECJ decisions in *O'Flynn v Adjudication Officer C-237/94* [1996] ECR I-2617, [1996] All ER (EC) 541, [1996] 3 CMLR 103 and *Seymour-Smith*, the EAT found that a rigid statistical analysis will not always suffice to reveal underlying indirect discrimination.

National statistics

Even where relevant and reliable national statistics are available, a purely mathematical approach may not be appropriate (see *Seymour-Smith* [1999] ICR 447). Expert evidence may be used to displace or call into question the relevance of statistical evidence.

On occasion, a tribunal may take into account matters considered to be of common or general knowledge. For example, in *London Underground v Edwards (No 2)* [1999] ICR 494, [1998] IRLR 364, CA, a tribunal acknowledged that more single parents are female than male. Such assumptions may be challenged, however, if, for example, they are without foundation, are outdated, or are themselves based on stereotypical beliefs (as in *Sinclair, Roche & Temperley and Others v Heard and Fellowes (No 1)* [2004] IRLR 763 EAT, where the tribunal should not have concluded that because more women than men had responsibility for childcare, fewer high-paid senior women executives could work long hours).

(c) Personal disadvantage

As with a finding of direct discrimination, B will only be able to found a claim of discrimination if he can show that he has suffered the disadvantage. It is not enough to point to a disadvantage suffered by others who share the protected characteristic. To take an obvious example, a woman who claims that the imposition of a shift system into her work pattern is indirectly discriminatory against women with child-caring responsibilities will not be able to claim indirect discrimination if she does not have child-care responsibilities which prevent her from complying with the shift system.

Justification

Where B has demonstrated that the provision criterion or practice (or requirement or condition) has the requisite disparate impact, the burden of proof shifts to the employer. A may be able to justify the application of the provision, practice or criterion. (Justification is also available for cases of direct age discrimination; see AGE DISCRIMINATION (2)). The test for objective justification in all relevant strands of discrimination law, with one exception, is:

> 'A must show that the provision, criterion or practice is 'a proportionate means of achieving a legitimate aim.' (*SDA 1975, s 1(2)(b)(iii); RRA 1976, s 1(1A)(c); RBR 2003, reg 3(1)(b)(iii); SOR 2003, reg 3(1)(b)(iii); AR 2006, reg 3(1)*)

In cases of indirect discrimination on grounds of nationality or colour, the application of the provision, criterion or practice by A must be 'justifiable irrespective of' B's particular characteristic (*RRA 1976, s 1(1)(b)(ii)*).

The test for objective justification in relation to indirect discrimination is a codification of the decision in *Bilka-Kaufhas GmbH v Weber von Hartz C-170/84* [1986] ECR 1607, [1986] 2 CMLR 701.

In all the Directives, the test is that indirect discrimination will occur unless 'that provision, criterion or practice is objectively justified by a legitimate aim and the means of achieving that aim are appropriate and necessary' (*Race Directive, 2000/43/EC, Article 2; Framework Directive 2000/78/EC, Article 2; Equal Treatment Directive 76/207/EC* as amended by *2002/73/EC, Article 2*). In *Bilka-Kaufhaus* a department store had a policy of requiring employees to have worked full-time in 15 of their 20 years' service in order to qualify for an occupational pension scheme – the rationale was to discourage part-time work, as part-time employees tended to refuse to work less sociable hours at which times the store nevertheless needed staff cover. The policy was indirectly discriminatory to women, but could it be justified? The ECJ held that this was a matter for national courts to determine, and in doing so they should consider whether the measures taken (i) correspond to a *real need* on the part of the employer; (ii) whether they are *appropriate* with a view to achieving the objectives pursued; and (iii) whether they are *necessary* to that end (para 36). In all cases it is a matter for the employer to prove justification.

The UK legislation expresses justification by reference to 'proportionality' rather than what is 'appropriate' and necessary'. The principle of proportionality applies to interpretation of all Community law and the ECJ requires national courts to apply the 'proportionality test' (*Cadman v Health and Safety Executive* [2007] All ER (EC) 1, [2006] ICR 1623, ECJ; *Enderby*). The Government has argued that the terms 'appropriate and necessary' and 'proportionality' can be used interchangeably, therefore, despite the legislature's literal departure from the EC legislation, its implementation of the justification test reflects the interpretation of the test in European case law. (See Notes to the (then) draft *Employment (Age) Regulations 2006*.)

Whether the Government's view is correct depends on the interpretation of 'necessary'. Necessity (at least in the UK) does not mean absolute necessity; the principle of proportionality inherently involves a balance between the interests of the employer and the employee and therefore the employer is required to show that its actions were 'reasonably necessary'; see, for example, *Barry*.

The ECJ decisions are clear that whether or not a discriminatory practice can be justified is a matter for the national courts.

The principle of proportionality requires consideration of whether the objective pursued is sufficient to override the indirect discrimination (*Enderby*). The greater the disparate impact on the disadvantaged group, the stronger the objective justification must be (*Barry*, para 40; *Starmer*; *Allonby v Accrington and Rossendale College* [2001] IRLR 364, paras 26–29; *Hampson v Department of Education and Science* [1989] IRLR 69, [1990] ICR 511, HL).

This balancing exercise requires the tribunal to consider whether the means chosen by the employer are suitable, and whether or not the employer could achieve its aim by other means. This is not to say that the employer must show that the means chosen are the only way to meet that aim (*Seymour-Smith* [2000] ICR 244). In *London Underground Ltd v Edwards (No 1)* [1995] ICR 574, EAT the employer sought to argue before the tribunal and the EAT that the introduction of a new shift roster for its train drivers (which the tribunal, EAT and Court of Appeal found to be indirectly discriminatory to women) was justifiable as it would allow costs savings of £10 million per year. The tribunal (with whom the EAT agreed) took into account the costs savings, and found that provision could have been made for single parents who were disadvantaged by the shift roster without a significant detriment to the savings sought. This approach is consistent with the ECJ's position that budgetary considerations alone cannot justify discrimination on grounds of sex (*Hilde Schönheit v Stadt Frankfurt am Main C-4/02* and *C-5/02* [2003] ECR I-12575, [2004] IRLR 983; *Jorgensen v Foreningen af Speciallaeger* [2000] IRLR 726 ECJ, para 39). It does not follow that where there is an alternative means of achieving an objective, the employer should always take that route – if the means chosen are proportionate and the aim legitimate then the employer's practice will be justified (*Redfearn v Serco Ltd* [2006] EWCA Civ 659, [2006] ICR 1367; *Allonby*) In *Redfearn* the employer argued that R's presence created a risk. Although ultimately it was not necessary for Court of Appeal to reach a conclusion on justification, it found that the tribunal's decision (that the dismissal was justified on health and safety grounds) was not perverse simply because it had not considered other non-discriminatory ways in which the employer could achieve its aim.

The grounds for justification need not have 'consciously and contemporaneously featured in the decision-making process of the employer' (*Starmer v British Airways Plc* [2005] All ER (D), at para 42; *Schonheit v Stadt Frankfurt am Main* [2004] IRLR 983, at 86–87). In *Starmer*, where an employee pilot's application to work part-time hours was refused, the employer was allowed to advance arguments that its refusal was justified on health and safety grounds when the decision to refuse her application had been based on the employer's resourcing requirements. This means that the employer must not simply assert its reasons but must show evidence of the need for the measure.

Thus, an employer will not justify a discriminatory measure by reference to mere generalisations – he must produce cogent factual evidence that demonstrates why the aim he pursues is legitimate and necessary (*Seymour-Smith* [1999] ICR 447, para 76). The tribunal is required to carry out a critical evaluation of the facts (*Redfearn* [2005] IRLR 744 at 59; *Hardys & Hansons plc v Lax* [2005] EWCA Civ 846, [2005] IRLR 726, at 19–34; *Cadman* [2004] IRLR 971, [2005] ICR 1546 at 31; *Barry v Midland Bank plc* [1999] IRLR 582, [1999] ICR 859, HL at 587). In *Cadman*, it was argued before the ECJ that pay rates based on length of service (which were found to indirectly discriminate against women) could be justified by generalisations (for instance it is legitimate to reward loyalty, or an experienced worker will usually be more productive at work as he will be more familiar with the employer's business and its clients). The ECJ following *Seymour-Smith* found that the proportionality test requires an employer to demonstrate that the practice he adopts, even where based on a legitimate aim, is conceived so as to minimise its disparate impact on the disadvantaged group (*Cadman*, at 58).

It is for the tribunal to decide whether an objective is justifiable In *Hardys & Hansons plc*, a full-time female employee applied to job-share her current role, her employer refused and she subsequently claimed indirect sex discrimination. Considering the employer's justification arguments, the Court of Appeal found that the tribunal was in such cases required to undertake a very careful, critical analysis of the reasons put forward by the employer, demonstrating such in its own reasoned decision. While acknowledging that the word 'necessary' used in *Bilka-Kaufhaus* is to be qualified by the word 'reasonably', Pill LJ said:

'That qualification does not, however, permit the margin of discretion or range of reasonable responses for which the appellants contend. The presence of the word 'reasonably' reflects the presence and applicability of the principle of proportionality. The employer does not have to demonstrate that no other proposal is possible. The employer has to show that the proposal, in this case for a full-time appointment, is justified objectively notwithstanding its discriminatory effect. The principle of proportionality requires the tribunal to take into account the reasonable needs of the business. But it has to makes its own judgment, upon a fair and detailed analysis of the working practices and business considerations involved, as to whether the proposal is reasonably necessary. I reject the ... submission ... that, when reaching its conclusion, the employment tribunal needs to consider only whether or not it is satisfied that the employer's views are within the range of reasonable responses' (para 32).

'The power and duty of the employment tribunal to pass judgment on the employer's attempt at justification must be accompanied by a power and duty in the appellate courts to scrutinise carefully the manner in which its decision has been reached.' (para 34)

1.45   **HARASSMENT**

Statutory harassment: EU sources

Directives

Council Directive 2000/43/EC ('the *Race Directive*') implementing the principle of equal treatment between persons irrespective of racial or ethnic origin provides that:

> 'Harassment shall be deemed to be discrimination ... when an unwanted conduct related to racial or ethnic origin takes place with the purpose or effect of violating the dignity of a person and of creating an intimidating, hostile, degrading, humiliating or offensive environment ... the concept of harassment may be defined in accordance with the national laws and practice of the Member States.'(*Article 2.3*)

Council Directive 2000/78/EC ('the *Framework Directive*'), establishing a general framework for equal treatment in employment and occupation in respect of discrimination based on religion or belief, disability, age or sexual orientation, contains a virtually identical provision (*Article 2.3*), as does the *Equal Treatment Directive* (*ETD*) *76/207/EEC* (as amended by *Directive 2002/73, Article 2.2*) in respect of discrimination based on gender. However, the *ETD* also contains an additional, separate definition of sexual harassment:

> '... where any form of unwanted verbal, non-verbal or physical contact of a sexual nature occurs with the purpose or effect of violating the dignity of a person, in particular when creating an intimidating, hostile, degrading, humiliating or offensive environment.' (*Article 2.2*)

On 26 April 2007 the EU-level social partner organisations concluded a framework agreement on harassment and violence at work. The agreement, which is due to be implemented by April 2010 at national level by the signatories' member trade unions and employers' organisations, sets out to raise awareness and understanding of the problem and provide a framework for action. While the agreement may lead to collective agreements at national, sectoral and major employer level, it is unlikely to lead to specific new legislation.

1.46   *Commission Code*

Annexed to Commission Recommendation of 27 November 1991 on the protection of the dignity of women and men at work (92/131/EEC), the *Commission Code of Practice on protecting the dignity of women and men at work – A code of practice on measures to combat sexual harassment* ('the Commission Code'), para 2 provides:

> 'Sexual harassment means "unwanted conduct of a sexual nature, or other conduct based on sex affecting the dignity of women and men at work". This can include unwelcome physical, verbal or non-verbal conduct.

> 'The essential characteristic of sexual harassment is that it is unwanted by the recipient, that is it is for each individual to determine what behaviour is acceptable to them and what they regard as offensive. Sexual harassment becomes sexual harassment if it is persisted in once it has been made clear that it is regarded by the recipient as offensive, although one incident may constitute sexual harassment if sufficiently serious. It is the unwanted nature of the conduct which distinguishes sexual harassment from friendly behaviour, which is friendly and mutual.'

1.47 **UK law**

The old law

UK tribunals acknowledged harassment as a very easily recognisable form of direct discrimination under *SDA 1975* and *RRA 1976* many years before harassment was specifically addressed in any of the EU Directives and despite the fact that there was no statutory definition of harassment. There is a considerable body of UK case law, much of which remains relevant.

The basis on which such claims were (and still may be made in some cases) is that the victim of the harassment has been subjected to less favourable treatment which amounts to a detriment because of their sex/race etc. The victim would also have to compare his treatment with that of an actual or hypothetical comparator.

That said, in *Porcelli v Strathclyde Regional Council* [1986] ICR 564 the Court of Session indicated that if the type of harassment was 'gender specific' no comparator was needed. In that case, a woman was subjected to a sustained campaign of bullying by two male colleagues, some of it of a sexual nature. (An employment tribunal found that a male colleague who was disliked would also have been treated badly, although the treatment would have been different, and had dismissed the sex discrimination claim.)

However, the House of Lords in *MacDonald v Advocate General for Scotland* [2003] UKHL 34, [2004] 1 All ER 339, [2003] ICR 937 and *Pearce v Governing Body of Mayfield School* [2003] IRLR 512 emphasised that *SDA 1975* did not (then) acknowledge any separate concept of sexual harassment and that to succeed, the claimant would have to prove that she was treated less favourably than a man had, or would have been, treated in the same circumstances.

In *Pearce*, the House of Lords questioned the decision in *Burton and Rhule v De Vere Hotels* [1996] IRLR 596, EAT, in which the EAT had held that an employer could be liable for the harassment of its employees by third parties not in its employment. The House of Lords in *Pearce* indicated that an employer can only be liable if its failure to take steps to prevent harassment was itself motivated by the applicant's race, etc (see also 1.49).

The EAT applied *MacDonald* in *Brumfitt v Ministry of Defence and anor* [2005] IRLR 4, rejecting a direct discrimination claim from a woman who was part of a group of men and women exposed to sexually explicit language and abuse by a supervisor. She claimed that although both sexes had been exposed to the language the effect on her, as a woman, was worse. The EAT held that unless she could show less favourable treatment than a male comparator, the abuse would not constitute direct discrimination. Her claim failed: she could not demonstrate that her gender was the reason for the words used.

1.48 *Statutory harassment: UK law*

The *SDA 1975, RRA 1976* and *DDA 1995* were amended in order to implement the *Race Directive, Framework Directive* and amended *Equal Treatment Directive* and now contain separate, statutory, definitions of harassment:

- at *SDA 1975, s 4A (1)* and *(3)* on grounds of sex and gender reassignment (commencement: 1 October 2005);

- at *RRA 1976, s 3A* on grounds of race or ethnic or national origins (but not colour/nationality) (commencement: 19 July 2003);

- *DDA 1995, s 3B* (commencement: 1 October 2004).

So, from their implementation dates, have *SOR 2003, reg 5*, *RBR 2003, reg 5* and *AR 2006, reg 6*.

There are small but significant differences in the ways in which the provisions of the Directives are implemented in the UK discrimination legislation. These differences are noted at 1.50.

The UK statutes provide:

SDA 1975

4A Harassment, including sexual harassment

(1)   For the purposes of this Act, a person subjects a woman to harassment if–

   (a)   on the ground of her sex, he engages in unwanted conduct that has the purpose or effect–

      (i)   of violating her dignity; or

      (ii)   of creating an intimidating, hostile, degrading, humiliating or offensive environment for her.

   (b)   he engages in any form of unwanted verbal, non-verbal or physical conduct of a sexual nature that has the purpose or effect–

      (i)   of violating her dignity; or

      (ii)   of creating an intimidating, hostile, degrading, humiliating or offensive environment for her; or

   (c)   on the ground of her rejection of or submission to unwanted conduct of a kind mentioned in paragraph (a) or (b), he treats her less favourably than he would treat her had she not rejected, or submitted to, the conduct.

(2)   Conduct shall be regarded as having the effect mentioned in sub-paragraph (i) or (ii) of subsection (1)(a) or (b) only if, having regard to all the circumstances, including in particular the perception of the woman, it should reasonably be considered as having that effect.

(3)   For the purposes of this Act, a person ('A') subjects another person ('B') to harassment if–

   (a)   A, on the ground that B intends to undergo, is undergoing or has undergone gender reassignment, engages in unwanted conduct that has the purpose or effect–

      (i)   of violating B's dignity; or

      (ii)   of creating an intimidating, hostile, degrading, humiliating or offensive environment for B; or

   (b)   A, on the ground of B's rejection of or submission to unwanted conduct of a kind mentioned in paragraph (a) treats B less favourably than A would treat B had B not rejected or submitted to, the conduct.

(4)   Conduct shall be regarded as having the effect mentioned in sub-paragraph (i) or (ii) of subsection (3)(a) only if, having regard to all the circumstances, including in particular the perception of B, it should reasonably be considered as having the effect.

(5)   Subsection (1) is to be read as applying equally to the harassment of men, and for that purpose shall have effect with such modifications as are requisite.

RRA 1976

3A Harassment

(1)   A person subjects another to harassment ... where on grounds of race or ethnic or national origin he engages in unwanted conduct which has the purpose or effect of–

(a)   violating that other person's dignity; or

(b)   creating an intimidating, hostile, degrading, humiliating or offensive environment for him.

(2)   Conduct shall be regarded as having the effect specified ... only if, having regard to all the circumstances, including in particular the perception of that other person, it should reasonably be considered as having that effect.

DDA 1995

3B Meaning of 'harassment'

(1)   For the purposes of this Part, a person subjects a disabled person to harassment where, for a reason which relates to the disabled person's disability, he engages in unwanted conduct which has the purpose or effect of–

(a)   violating the disabled person's dignity; or

(b)   creating an intimidating, hostile, degrading, humiliating or offensive environment for him.

(2)   Conduct shall be regarded as having the effect referred to in paragraph (a) or (b) of subsection (1) only if, having regard to all the circumstances, including in particular the perception of the disabled person, it should reasonably be considered as having that effect.

The harassment provisions of *RBR 2003, SOR 2003* and *AR 2006* follow the format in *RRA 1976*.

1.49   *Statutory harassment: common elements*

While the Directives all provide that harassment will be deemed to be discrimination where the unwanted conduct has the purpose or effect of violating dignity *and* creating an intimidating, etc environment, all the UK implementing provisions, which provide two separate alternative routes, cover conduct that falls within either (and not necessarily both) limb (a) or (b). Therefore, under the UK legislation, harassment can occur in one of two ways: A engages in unwanted conduct which (a) has the purpose of violating B's dignity, etc or (b) has the effect of violating B's dignity, etc. Thus, consistent with pre-existing UK case law, it may be easier for a claimant to satisfy this element of a harassment claim under UK legislation than under the Directives which they implement.

The Directives permit Member States to define the concept of harassment in accordance with their own national laws and practice. All the UK implementing legislation provides that conduct will only be regarded as having the effect specified in (a) or (b) if, in all the circumstances, including *in particular* the (subjective) opinion of the person, the conduct should reasonably (that is, objectively) be considered as having that effect. This 'reasonableness test' is consistent with pre-existing UK case law and is not a new development (see *Shamoon*: '... if the victim's opinion that the treatment was to his or her detriment is a reasonable one to hold, that ought, in my opinion, to suffice ... while an unjustified sense of grievance ... cannot constitute a detriment, a justified and reasonable sense of grievance ... may well do so.').

The provision also derives in part from the *Commission Code of Practice on protecting the dignity of women and men at work* (see 1.46).

It is a composite, flexible test which gives tribunals some latitude and considerable discretion. It remains to be seen how it will be used under the newer discrimination strands, particularly age.

According to the EAT in *Gravell v London Borough of Bexley* [2007] All ER (D) 2009, the House of Lords judgment in *Pearce* did not necessarily preclude a statutory harassment race claim against an employer who had permitted or countenanced racial harassment by a third party. G, who is white, claimed racial harassment where her employer maintained a policy of ignoring racist comments from customers. G had to listen to such comments and was told that she should not tell customers that such comments were unacceptable. Reversing a tribunal decision to strike out the claim, the EAT observed that statutory racial harassment had been introduced after the House of Lords judgment and 'there is considerable scope for argument as to whether the observations of the House of Lords on *Burton* in *Pearce* [based on the direct discrimination provisions of the *RRA 1976*] also hold good in a claim of *s 3A* harassment.'

Judge Clark suggested also that if the employer council had had such a policy this might have amounted to racial harassment by creating an offensive environment for the claimant.

1.50   UK statutory definitions: the differences

RRA 1976, s 3A provides there may be harassment where 'on grounds of race or ethnic or national origins' the unwanted conduct occurs.

SDA 1975, s 4A(1)(a) provides that there may be harassment of a woman where 'on the ground of her sex' the unwanted conduct occurs.

SDA 1975, s 4A (1)(b) provides that there may be harassment where a person engages in any form of unwanted verbal, non-verbal or physical conduct of a sexual nature that has the purpose or effect of violating the woman's dignity or creating an intimidating, hostile, degrading, humiliating or offensive environment for her. This provision is not replicated in any other statute or regulations. Where conduct is *of a sexual nature* there will be no need to compare the treatment of a woman with that of a man, or vice versa. While there may be debate as to whether conduct is of a sexual nature – for example whether certain commonly used swear words will be considered as being sexual in nature – the conduct need not be directed at a specific person to constitute harassment under this head. A number of claims which failed under the old test following the *MacDonald* judgment (for example *Brumfitt*) might have succeeded if brought under this head. People of either sex can complain under this provision. While the statutory wording is new, much old law will be of relevance here, also pre-existing guidance on sexual harassment, primarily the European Commission Code of Practice on sexual harassment. Guidance in relation to the new statutory provision includes a fact sheet produced by Women and Equality, which provides that it is expected that the courts will construe 'conduct of a sexual nature' widely, in accordance with the facts of each case.

SDA 1975, s 4A(1)(c) and *4A(3)(b)* also have no counterparts elsewhere. *S 4A(1)(c)* provides protection from harassment where on the grounds of her rejection of or submission to sex-related harassment or sexual harassment the person is treated less favourably than she would have been had she not rejected or submitted to the conduct. *S 4A(3)(b)* provides similar protection in respect of gender reassignment. While both provisions resemble victimisation provisions in some ways, a victimisation claim can only be brought after the woman has done a 'protected act' (see 1.55ff): claims under these provisions may be brought where she has not. However, to succeed, the claimant will have to show that there has been conduct which meets the definition of harassment, that she received less favourable treatment than she would have otherwise and that there is a causal link between the two.

DDA 1995, s 3B provides that there may be harassment where a disabled person is subjected to harassment 'for a reason which relates to the disabled person's disability'.

RRB 2003, SOR 2003 and *AR 2006* follow the same format as *RRA 1976* – 'on grounds of religion or belief/sexual orientation/age. (Since amendment of *RBR 2003, reg 3(1)(a)* – see RELIGION AND BELIEF (7) – the harassment provision here may now be wider than the direct discrimination provision in those Regulations.)

Of note:

- none of these provisions uses the corresponding wording of the Directives, which seek to prohibit unwanted conduct which is 'related to' the particular type of discrimination protected;

- the wording in some of the UK statutes (particularly in *DDA 1995*) is more specific and restrictive than in others, eg *SDA 1975, s 4A (1)*;

- while generally the words used in the harassment provisions in each statute replicates exactly that used in the direct discrimination provision, this is not the case in *RRA 1976* where the words 'on racial grounds' are used in the direct discrimination provision, which is defined (*s 3*) to also include grounds of colour and nationality, whereas the statutory harassment provision extends only to harassment on grounds of race, ethnic or national origins;

- the *SDA 1975* provision contained in *s 4(A)(1)(a)* was challenged by the Equal Opportunities Commission in *Equal Opportunities Commission v Secretary of State for Trade and Industry* [2007] EWHC 483 (Admin), [2007] 2 CMLR 1351, [2007] ICR 1234. In this case, the DTI maintained that the *SDA 1975* provision, if interpreted correctly, did not have the limiting effect claimed by the EOC and therefore there was no failure to implement the ETD correctly in this regard. The High Court ruled that this (and other) provisions did not comply with the Directive. The Government has stated its intention to amend the UK legislation.

It may also be that the wording used variously in the UK statutes imports a requirement for a comparator where there is no such requirement in the Directives, as it may prove impossible in some cases (although not in others) to prove, for example that harassment was on the ground of a woman's sex without comparing the treatment of a man. The Government's intention is to clarify that this is not required.

There is much case law on the meaning of 'on [the] grounds of' in the context of direct discrimination. The definitive position for the present is that set out by the House of Lords in *Shamoon v Chief Constable of the Royal Ulster Constabulary* [2003] IRLR 285: generally, it will be necessary to establish the *real reason for* the conduct. There may be several different reasons for conduct; the reason need not be the only reason for there to be found discrimination.

The differences between these provisions are discussed further in the relevant chapters.

The old formulation and the statutory definitions are mutually exclusive. Where the new definition/s of harassment apply, it is in each case provided that detriment does not include conduct of a nature such as to constitute harassment (*SDA 1975, s 82*; *RRA 1976, s 78*; *DDA 1995, s 18D*; *RBR 2003, reg 2*; *SOR 2003, reg 2*; *AR 2006, reg 2*). Where a claimant relies on the statutory definition, he no longer has to show that the conduct complained of constituted a detriment amounting to less favourable treatment, thereby meeting the definition of direct discrimination. However, while statutory harassment and direct discrimination claims are mutually exclusive and therefore the same facts cannot amount to both statutory harassment and direct discrimination, claimants are able and may be well-advised to claim in the alternative less favourable treatment should the harassment claim fail. This will be of particular relevance in claims under *RRA 1976*, where the scope of the harassment and direct discrimination provisions is different (see above).

Because the amendments to UK discrimination legislation went no further than was necessary to implement EU law, and the new or amended Directives above do not cover all forms of discrimination covered by UK law, the separate definition/s of harassment do not apply specifically to discrimination on the grounds of nationality or colour (under *RRA 1976*), marital status, pregnancy and maternity leave or civil partnership (under *SDA 1975*). Harassment in these areas will be covered (if at all – see separate chapters) under the direct discrimination provisions. In those cases it will be necessary for the claimant to prove that he has been subjected to a detriment and has received less favourable treatment than has a comparator. It is also possible, however, that tribunals will feel able to construe some grounds of discrimination widely enough to treat some of these types of harassment under the new legislative provisions.

1.51   Unwanted conduct

A very wide range of conduct and behaviours might give rise to a harassment claim.

Under the statutory definitions as under the old case law, to amount to harassment, the conduct must be unwanted. There is no requirement under the statutory definition that the perpetrator must be aware that the conduct is unwanted. A one-off incident can constitute harassment. For example, when the proprietor's son called out to a female employee 'hiya big tits', it was readily acknowledged to be 'a form of bullying and is not acceptable in the workplace in any circumstances … such conduct is likely to create an intimidating, hostile and humiliating work environment for the victim' (*Insitu Cleaning v Heads* [1995] IRLR 4).

It will be much easier for the claimant to establish that it is unwanted if it is obvious this was or should have been the case: extreme forms of conduct, eg assault or violent and abusive language directed solely at the victim, will readily be recognised as harassment, even if the claimant does not specifically object to the behaviour or complain about it contemporaneously.

The explanatory notes to *SOR 2003* and *RBR 2003* provide that it will not always be necessary for the complainant to indicate that he finds certain conduct or language unacceptable: 'there may be cases where it will be perfectly clear that offensive remarks about persons ... are unwanted by those persons'.

Where the victim overhears dirty jokes or where he is the subject of thoughtless remarks which cause him offence or distress, it may be necessary for them to have indicated at the time, and subsequently that the conduct is unwanted. For example, in a case under the old law, where a woman chose to participate in and appeared to enjoy sexual activity at the time, she failed to show that the conduct was unwanted (*Steele v Optika Ltd* [1997] 20614/95/ET).

In *(1) Reed and (2) Bull Information Systems Ltd v Stedman* [1999] IRLR 299, the EAT gave guidance to employment tribunals on what might constitute unwanted behaviour, noting (in a sexual harassment case) that while a woman might appear to be unduly sensitive to what otherwise might be regarded as unexceptional behaviour, 'it is for each person to define their own levels of acceptance, the question would be whether by words or conduct she had made clear that she found such conduct unwelcome. It is not necessary to make a public fuss to indicate her disapproval, walking out of the room may be sufficient. Tribunals will be sensitive to the problems that victims may face in dealing with a man, perhaps in a senior position to herself, who will be likely to deny that he was doing anything untoward and may say the victim was over-sensitive ...'

In *Bracebridge Engineering Ltd v Darby* [1990] IRLR 3 two male colleagues indecently assaulted D. She reported this but no action was taken. She resigned and claimed constructive dismissal. The EAT held that a single incident of sexual harassment of this severity would amount to discrimination.

In *Driskell v Peninsula Business Services Ltd & Others* [2000] IRLR 151, EAT, D claimed that her manager, who had a history of making sexually explicit comments and banter, advised her to wear a short skirt and a see-through blouse when he interviewed her for a position. Her complaints about him were investigated but rejected. When the company failed to move him she refused to work and was as a consequence dismissed. The EAT held that where there is a series of alleged incidents, a tribunal should not consider the effect of each incident in isolation but should assess the situation only after considering all the relevant facts. Also, when deciding whether sexual banter amounts to sex discrimination, the sex of the parties involved should be taken into account as sexual comments by a male manager may be more intimidating when directed towards a woman than towards a man.

In *Wadman v Carpenter Farrer Partnership* [1993] IRLR 374, EAT, where W complained of sexual harassment after she was singled out for sexual comments of a personal nature made by male colleagues, the EAT advised tribunals to refer to the European Commission Code of Practice for definitions of sexual harassment, and for the steps employers should take to meet their obligations.

1.52   The harasser's purpose

As stated above, to meet the statutory definition, the harasser's conduct must either have the purpose of violating the claimant's dignity or of creating an intimidating, hostile, degrading, humiliating or offensive environment for the victim or have such an effect.

We do not yet know what must be established to prove that the harasser had such a purpose. There is no corresponding provision under the old law, but one of the few authorities on intention to discriminate in relation to indirect race discrimination may assist (see, generally, RACE DISCRIMINATION (6)). For example, in *JH Walker v Hussain and others* [1996] ICR 291, the EAT found that 'intention' signified that at the time the relevant act was done the person both wanted to bring about a state of affairs that constitutes the unfavourable treatment, and also knew that the unfavourable treatment would result from his actions. It is also possible that purpose will be regarded as synonymous with such words as motive and reason (see *Nagarajan v London Regional Transport* [2000] 1 AC 501, [1999] 4 All ER 65, [1999] 3 WLR 425, [1999] ICR 877, in the context of a direct discrimination claim).

Under the first limb of each of the new definitions of harassment, the purpose must be to violate dignity, etc – strong words indicating, it might be thought, the need to show the victim has suffered serious injury or affront. These words, however, taken straight from the Directives, cannot, given the principle of non-regression, ie reducing the protections already available in EU Member States, have the effect of restricting the types of conduct or the effect on the victim which may give rise to a harassment claim in the UK.

If the harasser's purpose can be proved and is held to injure the other person's dignity, the claimant need go no further: there is no qualifying provision.

However, in other cases, the claimant will need to show that the treatment created an intimidating, etc environment for him (presumably it will not be sufficient to show that the environment was made intimidating generally, or for others, if the claimant is not also specifically adversely affected by it – although this may be readily inferred).

1.53   *Other relevant legislation*

In addition to claims under the *Human Rights Act 1998, Health and Safety at Work Act 1974, Criminal Justice and Public Order Act 1994* and *Malicious Communications Act 1998*, harassment claims may be made in appropriate circumstances, under the *Protection from Harassment Act 1997 (PHA 1997)*

PHA 1997 makes harassment both a civil tort and a criminal offence. Initially introduced to protect victims from stalking, it has been used by complainants in harassment claims. Employers can also be found vicariously liable where the harassment occurs in the course of employment (*Majrowski v Guy's and St Thomas's NHS Trust* [2006] IRLR 695).

PHA 1997 prohibits conduct which amounts to harassment or which a person knows or ought to know amounts to harassment of the victim, but only where the harassment takes the form of a course of conduct. Course of conduct is defined as involving conduct on 'at least two occasions' and harassment includes alarming the person or causing distress (*s 7*).

The offence is committed where the course of conduct 'amounts' to harassment. The effect on the person being harassed is therefore the relevant consideration and not the harasser's motive. The test in the second limb where the person ought to know that it amounts to harassment is an objective one and will be satisfied if a reasonable person in the possession of the same information would think that the course of conduct amounted to harassment. If the harasser can show that the conduct was for the prevention and detection of crime or was reasonable in the circumstances in the case, he will have a defence.

The victim can also bring civil proceedings for damages for any anxiety caused by the harassment and to cover any financial loss which has resulted from the harassment (*s 3*). He can also seek an injunction order to stop the harassment (backed by powers of arrest) (*s 3*). These remedies are not available in the employment tribunal.

Penalties on conviction are imprisonment for up to six months and/or a fine of up to £5,000. Where the harasser puts the victim in fear of violence, or where the harasser breaches an injunction, the offence is triable either way. If the harasser is convicted on indictment, the maximum penalty is five years' imprisonment and/or a fine.

A claim under *PHA 1997* must be brought in the County Court or High Court – the employment tribunals have no jurisdiction to hear the claim. The time limit for bringing a civil claim under the *PHA 1997* is six years. A complainant might therefore consider taking this action if the time limit under *RRA 1976* has expired.

In contrast to claims for harassment under the statutory definition or the direct discrimination provisions under *RRA 1976*, employers will not be able to rely on the statutory defence (in *RRA 1976, s 32(3)*) of showing that they took such steps as were reasonably practicable to prevent the harasser doing that or those acts in the course of his employment.

Harassment and the statutory dispute resolution procedures

The Employment Act 2002 (Dispute Resolution) Regulations 2004, reg 11(3) provide that where:

'(a)   the party has reasonable grounds to believe that commencing the procedure or complying with the subsequent requirement would result in a significant threat to himself, his property, any other person or the property of any other person; [or]

(b)   the party has been subjected to harassment and has reasonable grounds to believe that commencing the procedure or complying with the subsequent requirement would result in his being subjected to further harassment,'

the statutory procedures do not apply. Harassment is defined, the definition matching that of the statutory definitions. A complainant can only rely on *reg 11 (3)(b)* if he *has been* subjected to conduct which meets the definition and believes on reasonable grounds that he would suffer further harassment, again as defined. There are no reported cases on this provision.

1.54   **Harassment: sources of further information**

●   ACAS – The Advisory, Conciliation and Arbitration Service's 'Bullying and harassment at work: a guide for employees', available at http://www.acas.org.uk/index.aspx?articleid=797

- ACAS – 'Bullying and harassment at work: a guide for managers and employers', available at http://www.acas.org.uk/index.aspx?articleid=794

- CIPD – The Chartered Institute of Personnel and Development's Fact Sheet on 'Harassment and Bullying at Work', available at http://www.cipd.co.uk/subjects/dvsequl/harassmt/harrass.htm?IsSrchRes=1

- CIPD –'Bullying at Work: Beyond Policies to a Culture of Respect', available at http://www.cipd.co.uk/NR/rdonlyres/D9105C52–7FED-42EA-A557-D1785DF6D34F/0/bullyatwork0405.pdf

- CRE – The Commission for Race Equality's 'Statutory Code of Practice on Racial Equality in Employment', sample anti-harassment policy at Appendix 3, available at http://www.cre.gov.uk/downloads/employmentcode.pdf

- CRE – Fact sheet on 'Preventing harassment at work: A note for employers', available at http://www.cre.gov.uk/gdpract/preventingharassment.html

- DRC – The Disability Rights Commission's 'Code of Practice – Employment and Occupation', section 4, available at http://www.drc-gb.org/library/publications/employment/code_of_practice_-_employment.aspx

- European Commission – Commission Recommendation of 27 November 1991 on the protection of the dignity of women and men at work (92/131/EEC), available at http://eur-lex.europa.eu/LexUriServ/LexUriServ.do?uri=CELEX:31992H0131:EN:HTML

- EOC – The Equal Opportunity Commission's 'Brief Guide to Equality in the Workplace for Employers', pp 8 and 21, available at http://www.eoc.org.uk/PDF/A_brief_guide_to_equality_in_the_workplace_for_employers.pdf

- EOC – Sample Harassment and Bullying Policy contained in its publication 'Gender Equality Matters', available at http://www.eoc.org.uk/PDF/Guidance_on%20policies_and_good_practice_for_employers.pdf

1.55   VICTIMISATION

All the UK, discrimination legislation contains specific protection against victimisation, prohibiting less favourable treatment by reason that the claimant has done (etc) one of the things specified in the legislation: the protected act.

Victimisation is one form of discrimination. It is a separate claim which may be made and can succeed independently of, or in addition to, other discrimination claims. It is therefore not necessary to show that the underlying complaint had any merit.

A victimisation claim differs from other forms of discrimination in that the proscribed ground is the commission of the protected act, not the sex, race etc of the claimant.

1.56   UK legislation

Discrimination by way of victimisation

RRA 1976, s 2 provides:

> 'A person ("the discriminator") discriminates against another person ("the person victimised") in any circumstances relevant for the purposes of any

provision of this Act if he treats the person victimised less favourably than in those circumstances he treats or would treat other persons, and does so by reason that the person victimised has–

(a)   brought proceedings against the discriminator or any other person under this Act; or

(b)   given evidence or information in connection with proceedings brought by any person against the discriminatory or any other person under this Act; or

(c)   otherwise done anything under or by reference to this Act in relation to the discriminator or any other person; or

(d)   alleged that the discriminator or any other person has committed an act which (whether or not the allegation so states) would amount to a contravention of this Act,

or by reason that the discriminator knows that the person victimised intends to do any of those things, or suspects that the person victimised has done, or intends to do, any of them.'

This does not apply to treatment of a person by reason of any allegation made by him if the allegation was false and not made in good faith.

Corresponding provisions are to be found in *SDA 1975, s 4* (which covers also victimisation under *EqPA 1970* and the *Pensions Act 1995*); *DDA 1995, s 55* (which differs slightly in form: see DISABILITY DISCRIMINATION (3)); *RBR 2003, reg 4; SOR 2003, reg 4; AR 2006, reg 4.*

1.57   EC legislation

The Race Directive

The *Race Directive 2000/43/EC* provides:

'Article 9

'Victimisation

'Member States shall introduce into their legal systems such measures as are necessary to protect individuals from any adverse treatment or adverse consequence as a reaction to a complaint or to proceedings aimed at enforcing compliance with the principle of equal treatment.'

The *Framework Directive 2000/78/EC, Article 11* contains an identical provision. The *Equal Treatment Directive 76/207/EEC, Article 7*, its corresponding provision, also contains specific protection for employees' representatives.

1.58   Less favourable treatment

The concept of less favourable treatment is the same as in direct discrimination claims. To be unlawful under the victimisation provisions, the less favourable treatment must also amount to detrimental treatment (see 1.27ff). Many different types of acts, some of them relatively insignificant, can amount to less favourable treatment. In *Beardmore v (1) South West Trains (2) WE Hamilton* [2001] ET 2305257/2000 a notice posted by a respondent thanking 'the vast majority of staff' for their support during an investigation into allegations of sexual harassment made against him was considered to be victimisation of the claimant, whose grievance had been upheld.

A number of claims arise out of the conduct of ongoing litigation and/or the provision of references.

1.59   *The correct comparator*

To establish whether there has been less favourable treatment, a comparison must be made. The relevant circumstances must in each case be 'the same or not materially different'. Although this form of words does not strictly apply to victimisation under *SDA 1975* and *RRA 1976* (where *s 5(3)* and *s 3(4)* respectively apply only to direct and indirect discrimination), Lord Nicholls in *Shamoon v Chief Constable of the Royal Ulster Constabulary* [2003] UKHL 11, [2003] 2 All ER 26, [2003] ICR 337 considered that the comparison exercises should be the same for each form of discrimination:

> 'What is required is a simple comparison between the treatment of the claimant and a comparator. Protected act aside, the comparator should be in the same position as the claimant, "not in an admittedly different but allegedly comparable position".'

In victimisation cases, it can be particularly difficult to select or construct an appropriate comparator. The leading case is the House of Lords judgment in *Chief Constable of West Yorkshire Police v Khan* [2001] IRLR 830, [2001] ICR 1065, HL.

K claimed race discrimination, following a number of unsuccessful applications for promotion. Before the tribunal hearing, he applied to another police force, which asked West Yorkshire Police for references and staff appraisals. West Yorkshire Police refused to supply them, stating that, on legal advice, providing the documents might prejudice their case. K claimed victimisation.

The House of Lords held that:

- to identify the less favourable treatment, the tribunal must find the appropriate comparator, actual or hypothetical, who had not carried out the protected act. This comparator *should not be* an employee who had brought discrimination proceedings against the employer or an employee who had brought a different type of employment claim against the employer but, in this case, a police officer in the same position as the applicant who had not done the protected act – ie another officer in the West Yorkshire force;

- only then should the tribunal seek to establish less favourable treatment, which in this case would be found, as the request would have been granted in the case of the correct comparator.

'By reason that'

In *Khan* the House of Lords held also that:

- K's request was not refused 'by reason that' he brought proceedings, but so that the employer could protect itself from further tribunal claims and preserve its position in the ongoing litigation. The employer and employee were engaged in litigation and an employer acting honestly and reasonably should be able to preserve its position and protect itself from further claims which might arise from the contents of any reference;

- to determine whether an employer treated an employee less favourably 'by reason that' he has done a protected act, the tribunal must identify the real reason for the treatment. This was not a 'but for' test, which was insufficient for these purposes.

- the 'by reason that' test should be a subjective one that scrutinises the reasons for the alleged discriminator's acts.

1.60   **Conscious or unconscious motivation**

In *Nagarajan v London Regional Transport* [1999] IRLR 572, HL a former employee with a long history of bringing race discrimination claims against his employers applied for new employment, was rejected and claimed victimisation against London Regional Transport and a personnel manager. From the facts, the tribunal inferred that the interviewing panel was consciously or subconsciously influenced by the applicant's history of making claims. However, the EAT, relying on *Aziz v Trinity Street Taxis Ltd* [1989] QB 463, [1988] 2 All ER 860, [1988] 3 WLR 79, and the Court of Appeal, found that for there to be victimisation, there must be conscious motivation on the part of the respondent – mere knowledge that the claimant had carried out the protected acts did not permit the inference that this affected the decision to treat the claimant less favourably.

The Court of Appeal also found that there was no victimisation under *RRA 1976, s 4(1)(a)* unless it could be shown that the person victimising the claimant had also been responsible for making the arrangements for selection under that provision.

By a majority, the House of Lords held that conscious or unconscious motivation on the part of the respondent was sufficient to found a victimisation claim and that the claimant need only establish that the fact that the employee had carried out a protected act was a significant influence on the alleged victimisation. The House of Lords also held that the fact that different employees had been involved in the decision-making process did not preclude a finding of victimisation – acts carried out by one employee were held to be those of the employer and where one employee does not discriminate or victimise but others do, the employer will still be vicariously liable (see 1.109ff).

In *Lisk-Carew v Birmingham City Council* [2004] EWCA Civ 565, [2004] 20 LS Gaz R 35 the claimant was dismissed for misconduct (He had 'repeatedly failed to comply with reasonable management direction', 'failed to withdraw unsubstantiated allegations against management and other colleagues' and had been 'offensive and uncooperative towards management'). He brought unfair dismissal, race discrimination and victimisation claims. The tribunal held that the dismissal was fair and there was no direct discrimination. However, it found that allegations the claimant had made had had 'a significant influence on the decision to dismiss even if that influence was subconscious rather than conscious'. The tribunal had also concluded that, with one exception, the allegations made by the claimant had not been both false and made in bad faith and the dismissal had not been by reason of the one allegation which did not pass this test. There was therefore victimisation. The EAT and Court of Appeal upheld the decision.

Nagarajan was considered in light of the (subsequent) *Burden of Proof Directive* in *Wong v Igen Ltd (Equal Opportunities Commission intervening)* [2005] EWCA Civ 142, [2005] ICR 931, [2005] IRLR 258, where Peter Gibson LJ stressed that because EU law principles required the eradication of 'all discrimination whatsoever', 'significant influence' must mean an influence which is more than trivial. In *Villalba v Merrill Lynch and Co Inc* [2006] IRLR 437 the EAT confirmed that, where proper consideration had been given to the possibility of subconscious prejudice, one particular incident among many others might properly be considered 'not a significant influence' in the decision to dismiss Ms Villalba.

1.61   Limit to 'honest and reasonable' exception

In *Commissioners of Inland Revenue and another v Morgan* [2002] IRLR 776 victimisation was found when, after Miss Morgan brought a race discrimination claim, her employer circulated a memorandum advising her colleagues that as a result of her request for information on alleged comparators, confidential data might become public. The EAT rejected the argument that the memo was not sent by reason that the claimant had brought proceedings, but by reason that the respondents wished to preserve their position in the litigation. The EAT acknowledged the 'honest and reasonable' employer test created by the House of Lords in *Khan*, but held that circulating the memo fell outside this exception.

In *St Helens Metropolitan Borough Council v Derbyshire* [2005] EWCA Civ 977, [2006] ICR 90, school dinner ladies brought equal pay claims and most settled, but some did not. The Council wrote to all staff and to the claimants individually (although they were represented by their union) indicating that if the claims continued and succeeded many redundancies might result. The claimants brought victimisation claims. The Court of Appeal (Mummery LJ dissenting) held that the tribunal had been wrong to find that the *Khan* 'honest and reasonable' test did not apply because here the employer was seeking to persuade the employees to settle their case, whereas in *Khan* the employer was seeking to preserve its position in ongoing litigation. The majority held that while the *Khan* 'honest and reasonable' test had no legislative basis, employers in such situations should be able to encourage employees to settle claims without risking victimisation claims.

The House of Lords ([2007] ICR 841, [2007] IRLR 540) agreed that the correct comparators were employees who had not brought or continued equal pay claims, sending the letters amounted to less favourable treatment, and that each claimant had suffered detriment.

The House of Lords (Lord Neuberger) found, however, that the 'honest and reasonable' test placed a 'somewhat uncomfortable and unclear meaning' on 'by reason that'. Their Lordships thought that the reasoning in *Khan*, which predated implementation of the *Race Directive* should be reconsidered in the light of, in particular, the ECJ decision in *Coote v Granada Hospitality Ltd C-185/97* [1998] ECR I-5199, [1998] All ER (EC) 865, [1998] 3 CMLR 958, where it was held that employees should be protected against measures taken 'as a reaction to proceedings brought by the employer'.

The House of Lords preferred that the 'honest and reasonable' test be directed not at 'by reason that', but at the issue of detriment, which must be judged from the viewpoint of the claimant. Thus the integrity of the employer's actions should not be assessed by examining its reasons for pursuing the litigation but instead by considering whether the employer did anything which might make a reasonable employee feel unduly pressured, given that litigation will ordinarily cause anxiety, to settle her claim. Lord Neuberger believed that the analysis in *Khan* distorted the meaning of 'by reason that', which should simply be read as 'because'. Baroness Hale referred to the corresponding wording in the *Equal Treatment Directive* (*76/207/EEC*), which required consideration whether the employer's behaviour was 'a reaction to' the employees' claims – which in this case it clearly was.

For further consideration of victimisation claims in the context of ongoing proceedings, and a different conclusion, now see *Bird v Sylvester and anor* [2007] EWCA Civ 1052, CA (reported post-1 January 2008).

1.62   **Protected acts**

A victimisation claim will fail if the claimant cannot show that his actions amount to a protected act or because he cannot prove it.

There are five ways in which a claimant might gain protection. These are where *the victim* has:

(a)   *Brought proceedings* – A distinction may be made between bringing proceedings and their continued existence: see *Khan* and *St Helens*, above. It may be that an employer that acts in connection with ongoing litigation in an honest and reasonable way does not victimise if the employee is not unduly prejudiced or disadvantaged by the acts or by the manner in which they are done.

(b)   *Given evidence or information in connection with proceedings* – This provision gives protection in connection with proceedings brought under the particular act or regulations against the discriminator or any other person and so is very wide. There must, however, be actual proceedings.

(c)   *Otherwise done anything under or by reference to* – For something to be done 'under the Act' a specific statutory provision must be identifiable (*Kirby v Manpower Services Commission* (1980) 1 WRL 730 (although it is arguable that the acts here were done 'by reference to' and should have qualified for protection anyway).

In *Aziz v Trinity Street Taxis Ltd* [1989] QB 463, [1988] 2 All ER 860, [1988] 3 WLR 79, a race case, the Court of Appeal held that 'by reference to' is much wider than 'under' and should be construed accordingly. 'An act can properly be said to be done by reference to the Act if it is done by reference to the race relations legislation in the broad sense even though the doer does not focus his mind specifically on any provision of the Act.'

(d)   *Alleged that the discriminator or any other person has committed an act which would contravene the legislation* – In *Waters v Commissioner of the Metropolis* [1997] IRLR 589 a policewoman who had been sexually assaulted off-duty complained that her employers failed to respond to and investigate her complaint and that she had been victimised. The Court of Appeal ruled that *SDA 1975, s 4(1)(d)* only applied where the act was one for which the employer would have been liable. The sexual assault was not committed during the course of employment, the employer was not liable and there was therefore no victimisation.

No actual allegation need have been made (*Fearon v The Chief Constable of Derbyshire* UKEAT/0445/02/RN).

(e)   *Or by reason that the discriminator knows the person victimised intends to do any of those things, or suspects the person victimised has done, or intends to do, any of them.*

What is important here is what *the discriminator* knows or suspects, not what the victim has done. Here, a much broader approach is permitted:

'It requires a state of mind in the discriminator relating to what the victim has done or intends to do ... for a protected act to fall within this second category, it is not necessary that it take the form of an allegation, or the doing of anything by reference to the Act.' (*Fearon*)

In this case, where senior police officers formed a view that the applicant was or might be aggrieved by his treatment on account of his race, this provision applied.

1.63 Good faith

There is no protection against victimisation if the allegation is false *unless* it was made in good faith. In *Raja v National Council for Voluntary Organisations* 43786/96 ET a male employee responded to a sexual harassment allegation made by female colleague by claiming she had sexually harassed him. The tribunal found that the allegation was both false and made in bad faith.

1.64 Burden of proof

The reversal of the burden of proof (see 1.83ff) does not apply to claims of victimisation under *RRA 1976*, given the wording in *RRA 1976, s 54A* (*Oyarce v Cheshire County Council* [2007] ICR 1693).

1.65 A separate, but not standalone, claim

In *Bruce v Addleshaw Booth & Co* UKEAT/0404/03 B alleged victimisation contrary to *DDA 1995, s 55* (the victimisation claim), claiming that the firm treated him less favourably than they treated others who applied for employment but who were not disabled.

The tribunal held that *s 55* itself 'creates no cause of action. It is not a free-standing provision'. B could not rely on *s 55* because none of the provisions set out in *DDA 1995, ss 4–7* (the general discrimination provisions) applied. The EAT upheld the decision to strike out the claim, finding that not only was no express reference made by the claimant to the relevant provisions, he did not even plead facts which set up an arguable case of unlawful discrimination.

1.66 EXCEPTIONS

Note that, at the time of writing, the Discrimination Law Review conducted in preparation for the Single Equality Act, proposed unifying the various defences and exceptions available under discrimination legislation, by providing general tests and specific exemptions 'to clarify the circumstances in which different treatment is allowed'. Although this would involve removing a number of the specific exceptions, those in respect of *RBR 2003* and *AR 2006* would generally be retained (see 1.78–1.79). As with the other proposals arising from the Discrimination Law Review, the question of which exceptions should be retained will be subject to consultation prior to the introduction of the Single Equality Act.

1.67 Statutory exceptions common to two or more strands of discrimination legislation

National security

In all strands, discrimination will not be unlawful if it was done for the purpose of safeguarding national security (*SDA 1975, s 52(1)*; *RRA 1976, s 42*; *DDA 1995, s 59(3)*; *SOR 2003, reg 24*; *RBR 2003, reg 24*; *AR 2006, reg 28*). In all cases except sex discrimination, the doing of the act in question must be justified by that purpose.

1.68 *Benefits to the public*

In all strands, an employee will not be able to claim that his employer has discriminated against him in the provision of facilities or services where such facilities or services are provided to the public at large (*SDA 1975, s 6(7); RRA 1976, s 4(4); DDA 1995, s 4(4); SOR 2003, reg 6(4); RBR 2003, reg 6(4); AR 2006, reg 7(6)*). This might be the case, for example, where the owner of a leisure centre allows its employees to use its facilities, or where an employee of a bank takes out a mortgage with his employer. This exception will not, however, prevent an employee from bringing a discrimination claim where he is able to do so outside the employment field, for example, in the field of goods and services (applicable to race, sex and disability strands).

1.69   *Compliance with statutory provision*

The *SDA 1975, RRA 1976, DDA 1995* and *AR 2006* all contain an exception where the potentially discriminatory act was necessary in order to comply with a requirement of a statutory provision (*SDA 1975, ss 51–51A; RRA 1976, s 41; DDA 1995, s 59; AR 2006, reg 27*). Neither the *SOR 2003* nor the *RBR 2003* contain such an exception.

The operation of the exception in *SDA 1975* is slightly more complex that in *RRA 1976, DDA 1995* and *AR 2006*. In the fields of employment and vocational training the statutory provisions which will trigger the exception are limited to statutory provisions aimed at protecting women (as regards pregnancy or maternity or other circumstances giving rise to risks specifically affecting women) (*SDA 1975, s 51*). There is then a separate (non-restricted) exception for certain other parts of the *SDA 1975* which do not fall within the employment and vocational training fields (for example in the field of goods and services) (*SDA 1975, s 51A*).

1.70   *Genuine occupational reason*

See 1.95ff.

1.71   *Positive action*

See 1.101ff.

1.72   *Sport*

Confining sporting activities to one particular sex is permitted where the reason for this discrimination is that strength/stamina of an average woman puts her at a disadvantage to the average man (*SDA 1975, s 44*). The exception only applies in respect of individuals who are competing in sporting events. So, for example, discriminating on the basis of sex in choosing a coach would not come within the exception (see SEX DISCRIMINATION (8)).

Discrimination on the grounds of nationality, birth place or length of residency is permitted in order to select someone to represent a country or area, or, where the rules of a competition relating to a sport or game require it (*RRA 1976, s 39*) (see RACE DISCRIMINATION (6)).

1.73   *Armed forces*

Acts done for ensuring combat effectiveness are outside the scope of the *SDA 1975 (s 85 (4))* (see SEX DISCRIMINATION (8)). None of the regulations contained in the *AR 2006* apply to the armed forces (*AR 2006, reg 44(4)*) (see AGE DISCRIMINATION (2)). The *DDA 1995* does not apply to the armed forces within the field of employment (*DDA 1995, s 64(7)*) (see DISABILITY DISCRIMINATION (3)).

1.74 *Charities*

Acts done in order to give effect to a provision contained in a 'charitable instrument' are excluded from the scope of the *SDA 1975* (*s 43*). 'Charitable instrument' is defined as an enactment or other instrument made for charitable purposes (in England and Wales the purposes must be exclusively charitable). Acts done by a charity pursuant to a charitable purpose are outside scope of *DDA 1995* employment provisions (*DDA 1995, s 18C*).

1.75 **Specific exceptions**

Sex

See also SEX DISCRIMINATION (8).

- pay – discrimination relating to pay will not fall under *SDA 1975* but may fall under *EqPA 1970*. Note, however, that in the case of gender reassignment, discrimination relating to pay will still fall within *SDA 1975* (*s 6(4)–(8)*).

- police officers – height requirements and uniform allowances (*s 17*);

- prison officers – height requirements (*s 18*);

- ministers of religion (*s 19*);

- insurance (*s 45*);

- communal accommodation and related benefits (*s 46*);

- the special regime in respect of maternity leave;

- public authorities (see 1.101 and 8.66ff).

Separate provisions deal with the selection of political candidates and trade union offices (*ss 42A* and *49*), but these are outside the scope of this work. For provisions in respect of discriminatory training (*ss 47–48*), see 1.101.

1.76 *Race*

See also RACE DISCRIMINATION (6).

- training where skills are to be exercised outside Great Britain (relevant to colour and nationality grounds only) (*RRA 1976, s 6*);

- employment for the purposes of a private household (relevant to colour and nationality grounds only) (*s 4(3)*);

- pay for seamen recruited abroad to work on a ship (relevant to nationality ground only) (*s 9*);

- public authorities (see 1.101 and 6.69ff).

1.77 *Disability*

See also DISABILITY DISCRIMINATION (3).

- public authorities (see 1.101 and 3.96).

1.78 *Religion and belief discrimination*

See also RELIGION AND BELIEF (7).

- wearing of turbans by Sikhs on construction sites (*RBR 2003, reg 26*).

1.79   *Age*

See also AGE DISCRIMINATION (2).

- retirement (*AR 2006, reg 30*);

- national minimum wage (*reg 31*);

- benefits based on length of service (*reg 32*);

- enhanced redundancy payments (*reg 33*);

- life assurance and retired workers (*reg 34*).

1.81   **Excluded persons**

1.80   The statutes will not apply to employees who work outside their territorial scope (see 1.24).

Other defences

State immunity

As a matter of general law, where a claim is brought against a foreign sovereign state or its Head of State, that party is entitled to claim immunity from the jurisdiction of the courts of the United Kingdom (*State Immunity Act 1978, s 1*). This rule also extends to, for example, ambassadors, embassies and ministers.

The case of *Fogarty v UK* [2002] IRLR 148 confirms that state immunity is available in respect of discrimination claims. In *Fogarty*, an administrative assistant had successfully claimed discrimination under the *SDA 1975* after being dismissed from her job at the US embassy in London. She brought a further claim alleging victimisation, following the embassy's refusals to re-deploy her. The US Government, however, invoked state immunity and as a result her further claim could not be heard.

Ms Fogarty also argued breach of her right to a fair trial before the European Court of Human Rights, but the European Court found that the imposition of state immunity did not constitute a breach of the *Convention for the Protection of Human Rights and Fundamental Freedoms 1950, Article 6(1)*.

It should be noted that parties can waive state immunity by acts of submission, which include instituting proceedings or intervening in or taking any step in proceedings (except such steps as are necessary to claim immunity) (*State Immunity Act 1978, s 2*).

1.82   *Illegal contracts/conduct*

As a matter of general law, illegality bars a claim based on a contract which was illegal when it was formed or which became illegal through its performance.

Illegality can in certain circumstances constitute a bar to discrimination, but the threshold for illegality in this context is a high one and the general rules relating to contractual illegality are not determinative. In order for illegality to be an effective bar, it is necessary for the claim to be clearly and inextricably connected with the illegal conduct.

In *Hall v Woolston Hall Leisure Limited* [2001] ICR 99, an employee claimed that she was dismissed because of her pregnancy, contrary to *SDA 1975, s 6(2)(b)*. The tribunal upheld her claim but the Court of Appeal was subsequently charged with considering whether the claim failed as a result of the illegality of the employment contract. On the facts, the court found that the employee had turned a blind eye to her employer defrauding the Inland Revenue by failing to deduct tax and national insurance. The court stated that, in a discrimination claim relating to a dismissal, the employee must to some extent rely on a contract of employment. However, the employee's complaint was not so closely connected with or inextricably bound up with the employee's acquiescence in her employer's defrauding of the Inland Revenue that to award compensation would be to condone her illegal conduct. Accordingly, the employee was entitled to bring the sex discrimination claim.

By contrast, in a race discrimination case (*Vakante v Addey & Stanhope School* [2004] EWCA Civ 1065, [2004] 4 All ER 1056, [2005] 1 CMLR 62, [2005] ICR 231), the claim was found to be inextricably linked to the illegality. The employee was a Croatian asylum seeker who had been granted asylum in the UK on terms that he could not take up employment without the consent of the Home Office. He obtained a position as a trainee teacher after misrepresenting his immigration status, and his employer was permitted to rely on the defence of illegality in respect of his dismissal. The court held that to find otherwise would have been to condone the employee's conduct in misrepresenting his immigration status.

1.83 BURDEN OF PROOF

Introduction

The burden of proof is extremely important in discrimination cases. As Lord Justice Mummery stated in *Madarassy v Nomura International plc* [2007] ICR 867, [2007] IRLR 246, para 12:

> 'There is probably no other area of the civil law in which the burden of proof plays a larger part than in discrimination case ... Most cases turn on the accumulation of multiple findings of primary fact, from which the court or tribunal is invited to draw an inference of a discriminatory explanation of those facts. It is vital that, as far as possible, the law on the burden of proof applied by the fact-finding body is clear and certain.'

1.84 Law prior to the introduction of the statutory reversal of proof

Prior to the introduction of the statutory reversal of proof in the various pieces of anti-discrimination legislation, the issue of burden of proof was governed by case law. In *King v Great Britain-China Centre* [1992] ICR 516, a race discrimination case, Lord Justice Neill, giving the judgment of the court, set out five key principles extracted from the case law. He emphasised, in particular, that a finding of discrimination and a finding of a difference in race would often point to the possibility of racial discrimination. In such circumstances the tribunal would look to the employer for an explanation. If no such explanation was then put forward or if the tribunal considered the explanation to be inadequate or unsatisfactory it would be legitimate for the tribunal to infer that the discrimination was on racial grounds.

He also indicated that, on the basis of the case law, it was unnecessary and unhelpful to introduce the concept of a shifting burden of proof. At the conclusion of all the evidence the tribunal should make findings as the primary facts and draw such inferences as they consider proper from those facts. They should then reach a conclusion on the balance of probabilities, bearing in mind both the difficulties which face a person who complains of unlawful discrimination and the fact that it is for the complainant to prove his case.

The *King* guidance was approved by the House of Lords in *Glasgow City Council v Zafar* [1998] ICR 120, 125D–126B (Lord Browne-Wilkinson, with whom the other Law Lords agreed).

1.85 **European legislation**

Burden of Proof Directive

On 15 December 1997 the Council of the EU adopted *Directive 97/80/EC* on the burden of proof in cases of discrimination based on sex ('the *Burden of Proof Directive*') (OJ L14, 20 January 1998, p 6). The Directive was adopted under the Social Chapter, which did not cover the United Kingdom at that time. The Directive was subsequently extended to the United Kingdom with effect from 13 July 1998 by Directive 98/52/EC (OJ L205, 22 July 1998, p 66).

The *Burden of Proof Directive, Article 4(1)* required the United Kingdom, on or before 22 July 2001, to take any measures necessary to ensure that:

'... when persons who consider themselves wronged because the principle of equal treatment has not been applied to them establish, before a court or other competent legal authority, facts from which it may be presumed that there has been direct or indirect discrimination, it shall be for the respondent to prove that there has been no breach of the principle of equal treatment.'

1.86 *The Consolidated Equal Treatment Directive*

On 5 July 2006, the *Burden of Proof Directive* and the other major directives on gender equality were consolidated in *Directive 2006/54/EC* ('the *Consolidated Equal Treatment Directive*') on the implementation of the principle of equal opportunities and equal treatment of men and women in matters of employment and occupation (OJ L204, 26 July 2006, p 23). *Article 19(1)* of the Directive mirrors the *Burden of Proof Directive, Article 4(1)*. The deadline for implementation of the Directive is 15 August 2008, but Member States are only required to transpose into national law those provisions which 'represent a substantive change as compared with the earlier Directives' (*Article 33*). It is unlikely, in the circumstances, that any changes will be made to the domestic burden of proof provisions in the light of the Directive.

1.87 *Race Directive*

On 29 June 2000, the Council of the EU adopted *Directive 2000/43/EC* ('the *Race Directive*'), implementing the principle of equal treatment between persons irrespective of racial or ethnic origin (OJ L180, 19 July 2000, p 22). This Directive was expressly limited to 'discrimination on the grounds of racial or ethnic origin' (*Article 1*). The *Race Directive, Article 8(1)* mirrors the *Burden of Proof Directive, Article 4(1)*.

1.88 *Framework Directive*

On 27 November 2000, the Council of the EU adopted *Directive 2000/78/EC* ('the *Framework Directive*') establishing a common framework for equal treatment in employment and occupation (OJ L303, 2 December 2000, p 16). This Directive laid down a general framework for combating discrimination on the grounds of religion or belief, disability, age or sexual orientation. The *Framework Directive, Article 10(1)* mirrors the *Burden of Proof Directive, Article 4(1)* and the *Race Directive, Article 8(1)*.

1.89   **Domestic legislation**

Burden of proof in employment tribunals

The following are the applicable statutory provisions where a claim of discrimination is appropriately brought before an employment tribunal.

The *Burden of Proof Directive* was implemented by the Sex *Discrimination (Indirect Discrimination and Burden of Proof) Regulations 2001 (SI 2001/2660), reg 5*, which amended *SDA 1975* to insert a new *s 63A* as follows:

'(1)   This section applies to any complaint presented under *section 63* to an employment tribunal.

'(2)   Where, on the hearing of the complaint, the complainant proves facts from which the tribunal could, apart from this section, conclude in the absence of an adequate explanation that the respondent – (a) has committed an act of discrimination against the complainant which is unlawful by virtue of *Part 2*, or (b) is by virtue of *section 41* or *42* to be treated as having committed such an act of discrimination against the complainant, the tribunal shall uphold the complaint unless the respondent proves that he did not commit, or, as the case may be, is not to be treated as having committed, that act.'

By *reg 2* of those Regulations, the amendment was effective from 12 October 2001. It applied to proceedings commenced, but not determined, before that date.

SDA 1975, s 63A is mirrored in the other domestic legislative provisions on burden of proof, namely:

(a)   *RRA 1976, s 54A*, inserted by the *Race Relations Act 1976 (Amendment) Regulations 2003 (SI 2003/1626), reg 41*. It was inserted with effect from 19 July 2003, but applies to proceedings commenced, but not determined, before that date: *ibid, reg 2(1)*. It is expressed only to apply to complaints that a respondent has committed an act of discrimination 'on grounds of race or ethnic or national origin': the significance of this wording is considered further at 1.94.

(b)   *DDA 1995, s 17A(1C)*, inserted by the *Disability Discrimination Act 1995 (Amendment) Regulations (SI 2003/1673), regs 3(1)* and *9(2)(c)*, with effect from 1 October 2004, but, again, with application to proceedings commenced but not determined before that date.

(c)   *SOR 2003, reg 29*. *SOR 2003* entered substantially into force on 1 December 2003, and the burden of proof provisions therefore only apply from that date.

(d)   *RBR 2003, reg 29*. *RBR 2003* entered substantially into force on 2 December 2003, and the burden of proof provisions therefore only apply from that date.

(e)   *AR 2006, reg 37*. *AR 2006* entered substantially into force on 6 April 2006 and the burden of proof provisions therefore apply only from that date.

1.90   *Burden of proof in county courts*

Where a claim is appropriately brought in a county court in England or Wales or a sheriff court in Scotland, materially identical statutory provisions concerning the burden of proof apply. These were introduced to the legislation in materially identical ways to the burden of proof provisions applicable to employment tribunal claims.

These are contained in *SDA 1975, s 66A*; *RRA 1976, s 57ZA* (for the practical application of which see *Appiah v Bishop Douglass Roman Catholic High School* [2007] EWCA Civ 10, [2007] ICR 897, [2007] IRLR 264); *SOR 2003, reg 32*; *RBR 2003, reg 32*; and *AR 2006, reg 40*.

1.91   **The interpretation of the statutory burden of proof provisions by the courts**

General principles: the two-stage process

The statutory burden of proof provisions contemplate a two-stage process. At stage 1, the claimant is required to prove facts from which the tribunal could conclude, in the absence of an adequate explanation, that the respondent has committed an act of unlawful discrimination. If the claimant is able to satisfy this evidential burden, the evidential burden moves to the respondent for stage 2. At stage 2 the respondent is required to explain the basis of the alleged act and, in particular, to demonstrate that it was not discriminatory.

1.92   Direct discrimination

What the claimant needs to prove. This means, in direct discrimination cases, that the claimant will be required to prove, at stage 1, facts from which the tribunal could conclude, in the absence of an adequate explanation, that:

(a)   in circumstances relevant for the purposes of any provision of *RRA 1976* (for example, in relation to employment),

(b)   the alleged discriminator has treated another person less favourably; and

(c)   has done so on a prohibited ground (*Igen (Formerly Leeds Careers Guidance) and ors v Wong* [2005] ICR 931, at paras 28 and 29).

Current judicial guidance. The current essential judicial guidance on the application of the statutory burden of proof provisions is contained in the decisions of the Court of Appeal in *Igen v Wong* and *Madarassy v Nomura International plc* [2007] EWCA Civ 33, [2007] ICR 867, [2007] IRLR 246. *Madarassy v Nomura* should be read in conjunction with the decisions of the Court of Appeal in two further cases, heard and decided at the same time, namely *Appiah v Bishop Douglass Roman Catholic High School* [2007] ICR 897, [2007] IRLR 264 and *Brown v London Borough of Croydon* [2007] ICR 909, [2007] IRLR 259.

Igen v Wong. *Igen v Wong* and the other cases with which it was joined concerned both sex and race discrimination, although it is clear from the judgment that the Court of Appeal (Peter Gibson LJ, giving the judgment of the court) also had in mind the burden of proof provisions in the other pieces of domestic legislation. According to the Court of Appeal the correct approach to the application of the statutory burden of proof was as follows (references in brackets to paragraphs are to paragraphs of the Court's judgment):

(a)   The statutory amendments changed the law as laid down in *King* and *Zafar*, in that, if stage 2 is reached, and the respondent's explanation is inadequate, it is not merely legitimate, but necessary for the employment tribunal to conclude that the complaint should be upheld (paragraph 18).

(b)   In applying the burden of proof provisions tribunals must obtain their main guidance from the statutory language itself (paragraph 16).

(c)   At stage 1, as set out at 1.91, the claimant is required to prove facts from which the tribunal could conclude, in the absence of an adequate explanation, that there has been discrimination by the respondent (paragraphs 28 and 29).

(d)   In considering what inferences may be drawn from the primary facts, the tribunal must assume that the respondent has no adequate explanation for those facts (paragraphs 21 and 22).

(e)   To discharge the burden at stage 2 the respondent is required to prove, on the balance of probabilities, that the treatment established by the claimant at stage 1 was not on the ground of sex, race, etc (Annex).

The 'Barton' guidance. The most significant early case on the application of the statutory burden of provisions in direct discrimination cases was the sex discrimination case of *Barton v Investec Securities Ltd* [2003] ICR 1205. In *Barton* the EAT (Judge Ansell presiding) gave guidance as to how a tribunal should approach the task of applying the statutory burden of proof provisions. This guidance was subsequently approved, with modifications, by the Court of Appeal in *Igen v Wong*. The revised guidance is set out in the Annex to *Igen v Wong*. A tribunal is not required, however, to set out this guidance or to go through it paragraph by paragraph in its decision (*Igen v Wong*, para 16).

Case law post-*Igen* and pre-*Madarassy*. Following *Igen v Wong* the EAT considered the effect of *Igen* on a number of occasions. It was evident from these cases that there were a number of practical issues concerning how the burden of proof provisions should operate in practice which had been left unresolved. The most significant decisions were the following: *Network-Rail Infrastructure Ltd v Griffiths-Henry* [2006] IRLR 865, EAT (Elias J) decision of 23 May 2006; *NUT v Watson*, decision of EAT (Elias J) of 13 June 2006; *Li v Atkins v Gregory Ltd*, EAT (Elias J) of 5 July 2006; *Fox v Rangecroft and anor* [2006] EWCA Civ 1112, CA of 13 July 2006; *Laing v Manchester City Council* [2006] IRLR 748, EAT (Elias J) of 28 July 2006; and *Fernandez v Parliamentary Commission for Administration and anor*, EAT (Bean J) of 28 July 2006. These decisions illustrated some of the practical difficulties which tribunals were having with the application of the burden of proof provisions. They were cited with approval by Mummery LJ for the court in *Madarassy v Nomura* (paragraph 14).

In *EB v BA* [2006] EWCA Civ 132, [2006] IRLR 471, a case concerning discrimination on the ground of gender reassignment, the Court of Appeal held, importantly, that the approach reflected in *SDA 1975, s 63A* may be relevant at an interlocutory stage as well as at the final hearing. The claimant contended that she had been excluded from consultancy work following her transition from male to female. The respondent successfully resisted disclosure of documents relating to work not allocated to her, on the basis that it was for the claimant to particularise her case. The claimant failed to establish her sex discrimination claim at the final tribunal hearing. Despite the tribunal's decision being upheld by the EAT (HHJ Ansell QC), the respondent's approach was criticised on appeal by Lord Justice Hooper, with whom the other Lords Justices agreed. Allowing the appeal against the dismissal of her claim of sex discrimination, he noted (paragraphs 51–55) that it was important that tribunals bear in mind the objectives of the shifting burden of proof at the pre-hearing, as well as at the hearing stage: 'employers should not be permitted to escape the provisions of *section 63A* [of *SDA 1975*] by leaving it to the employee to prove her case'. A respondent who fails to make documentary evidence available at a preliminary stage may, therefore, be unable to satisfy stage 2 of the process if the burden shifts.

EB v BA exemplifies the difficulties faced by tribunals in dealing with the burden of proof in complex cases, and of balancing the significant cost and burden imposed on a respondent against the overriding objective. One way of dealing with the evidential burden in a complicated case may be by way of preparation by the respondent of a 'Scott' schedule, summarising, for example, work not allocated to the claimant and the reason for the non-allocation: the Court of Appeal in *EB v BA* suggested this should have taken place. This approach, however, is not without its own difficulties. At a further appeal by the claimant in *EB v BA* against case management orders made by the tribunal managing the proceedings after remission by the Court of Appeal, the EAT (HHJ Burke QC, sitting alone) on 28 June 2007 indicated that, once the claimant had such a schedule, it was legitimate to require her (in effect) to particularise her case through service of a counter-schedule. The EAT commented that:

> 'it is common in many types of litigation where complex issues of fact arise that 1) one party, usually the party bearing the burden of proof, is required to draw up a schedule and to set out its case in brief as to each item on that schedule and 2) thereafter the opposing party is required to set out either on that schedule or in a separate counter schedule its response to each such item. This exercise is a normal and standard aspect of case management in cases appropriate for a schedule … It does not involve any reversal of the burden of proof or any injustice to the party required to respond.'

Madarassy v Nomura. A number of the practical issues raised in the post-*Igen* case law were resolved by the Court of Appeal in *Madarassy v Nomura*, *Appiah* and *Brown v Croydon*. After approving *Igen v Wong*, Lord Justice Mummery, giving the judgment of the Court, indicated that the value of *Madarassy*, taken together with *Appiah* and *Brown v Croydon*, was in 'showing how the burden of proof should work'. In particular, the Court clarified the following important practical issues concerning the operation of the burden of proof (references to paragraphs are to paragraphs of the various judgments of the Court of Appeal):

(a) Proof of a difference in status and a detriment at stage 1 is not sufficient to shift the burden to the respondent:

> 'The bare facts of a difference in status and a difference in treatment only indicate a possibility of discrimination. They are not, without more, sufficient material from which a tribunal "could conclude" that, on the balance of probabilities, the respondent had committed an unlawful act of discrimination' (*Madarassy v Nomura*, paragraph 56).

(b) 'Could conclude' at stage 1 means that a reasonable tribunal 'could properly conclude' from all the evidence before it. This includes all relevant evidence, including evidence adduced by the respondent. It would include evidence as to whether the act complained of occurred at all; evidence as to any comparators relied on by the claimant; or (controversially) evidence as to the reasons for the less favourable treatment (*Madarassy v Nomura*, paragraphs 57, 67–72; *Appiah*, paragraph 43). So, to adopt one example suggested by Mr Justice Elias in *Laing v Manchester City Council* (above), if an employer withheld money from a number of employees, one of whom was black, for working to rule, and did not withhold money from those who were not working to rule, it would be open to the employer to adduce evidence at stage 1 that many white employees had also had money withheld. This would not be 'explanation', but 'factual evidence presenting a fuller picture of the material facts and putting the evidence of the claimant in context' (*Laing* (above), paragraph 62).

(c)   While there is a distinction between 'fact' and 'explanation', these categories are not hermetically sealed, however, and there is plainly a relationship between them (*Appiah*, paragraph 43, approving *Laing* (above), paragraph 68, in which Elias J noted that 'facts will frequently explain, at least in part, why someone has acted as they have'). It will not always be easy, in the circumstances, to tell when evidence is 'fact' and when it is 'explanation'. So, for example, if an employee complains that she was shouted at by her line manager when pregnant, is the fact that he shouted at everyone in his department, male or female, pregnant or non-pregnant, an 'explanation' for prima facie less favourable treatment, admissible only at stage 2, or 'factual evidence putting the evidence of the claimant into context', admissible at stage 1?

(d)   Although the application of the statutory burden of proof provisions involves a two-stage process, the tribunal is not required, in practice, to hear the evidence and argument in two stages. It will have heard all the evidence in the case before it embarks on the two-stage analysis. Additionally, although it will generally be good practice to apply the two-stage test there will be cases, particularly where a hypothetical comparator is relied on, where it may be appropriate for the tribunal to move directly to stage 2. Again, however, it is not required to do so (*Brown v Croydon*, para 41; *Madarassy v Nomura*, paragraphs 80–84; applying the reasoning of Lord Nicholls in *Shamoon v Chief Constable of the Royal Ulster Constabulary* [2003] ICR 337, paragraphs 7–12).

Reasonableness. One issue not fully resolved by the case law is the issue of the extent to which unreasonable behaviour on the part of a respondent will be sufficient to satisfy stage 1 such that explanation from the respondent in required. In *Bahl v Law Society* [2004] EWCA Civ 1070, [2004] NLJR 1292, [2004] IRLR 799, a case decided on facts occurring before the changes to the burden of proof, the Court of Appeal (Peter Gibson LJ, giving the judgment of the court) emphasised that unreasonable treatment does not of itself justify an inference of discrimination, although unexplained unreasonable treatment may justify the drawing of such an inference. To what extent does this reasoning survive the introduction of the statutory burden of proof provisions? Is unreasonable treatment sufficient to shift the burden?

Bahl was cited with approval by the Court of Appeal in *Madarassy v Nomura* (paragraph 14). The Court was not required to consider its application to the specific facts of the case, however. The facts of *Igen v Wong* suggest, however, that unreasonable conduct, at least where it is 'strikingly unreasonable' (paragraph 46) may be sufficient to cause the burden of proof to shift. The Court of Appeal in *Igen v Wong* did, however, caution tribunals generally against 'too readily inferring unlawful discrimination on a prohibited ground merely from unreasonable behaviour where there is no evidence of other discriminatory behaviour on such ground' (paragraph 51).

For a post-*Madarassy* example of unreasonable behaviour being held to satisfy stage 1, see *Birmingham City Council and anor v Samuels* UKEAT/0208/07 (McMullen J).

1.93   Indirect discrimination; duty to make reasonable adjustments

The application of the two-stage test appears to have given rise to fewer problems in indirect discrimination cases and cases of alleged failure to make reasonable adjustments contrary to *DDA 1995*. This is, no doubt, because the statutory components of these claims themselves contemplate a multi-stage approach, with the respondent required, where appropriate, to establish justification.

What the claimant needs to prove. In indirect discrimination cases the claimant is required to prove disparate adverse impact at stage 1 (*Nelson v Carillion Services Ltd* [2003] EWCA Civ 544, [2003] ICR 1256, [2003] IRLR 428) (Simon Brown LJ, with whom the other Lords Justices agreed); *Chaudhary v Secretary of State for Health* [2007] EWCA Civ 789, decision of 27 July 2007, paragraphs 66, 75 (Mummery LJ, giving the judgment of the court).

In 'reasonable adjustments' cases Elias J has suggested (*Project Management Institute v Latif* [2007] IRLR 579, paragraph 45) that the claimant is required, at stage 1:

(a)   to establish the provision, criterion or practice relied on; and

(b)   to demonstrate substantial disadvantage.

The burden then shifts to the respondent to show that no adjustment or further adjustment should be made.

Equal pay. The application of the two-stage test appears, in practice, however, to have given rise to greater problems in the field of equal pay. The claimant must identify the comparator group and produce the statistical evidence to show an appreciable difference in pay for jobs of equal value (Abbott v Cheshire and Wirral Partnership NHS Trust [2006] EWCA Civ 523, [2006] ICR 1267, [2006] IRLR 546, paragraph 17 (Lord Justice Keen, with whom the other Lords Justice agreed)). In *Bailey v Home Office* [2005] EWCA Civ 327, [2005] ICR 1057, [2005] IRLR 369 Lord Justice Peter Gibson and Lord Justice Waller, with both of whom Sir Martin Nourse agreed, doubted whether claimants in equal pay litigation bore the burden of demonstrating that the relevant difference in pay had a disparate adverse impact on women, and, therefore, whether *Carillion* was appropriately applied in this type of case (paragraphs 9, 37). They concluded that, in any event, *EqPA 1970, s 1(3)* did not demand a high threshold for the establishment of disparity. Waller LJ suggested (paragraph 39) that where a difference in pay was established, and statistics seemed to indicate a *possibility* of a disproportionate adverse impact, the burden should shift. In *Armstrong v Newcastle Upon Tyne NHS Hospital Trust* [2005] EWCA Civ 1608, [2006] IRLR 12, however, Arden LJ endorsed *Carillion* and noted that the burden shifted where the figures *demonstrated* a disproportionate adverse impact (paragraph 103).

1.94 Discrimination by way of victimisation under the RRA 1976

As mentioned in 1.89, *RRA 1976, s 54A* only applies where the complaint is that the respondent has committed an act of discrimination 'on grounds of race or ethnic or national origins'. In *Oyarce v Cheshire County Council* [2007] IRLR 1693, the EAT (Mr Justice Wilkie presiding) found that this wording applied to qualify the type of claim to which the statutory burden of proof provisions applied. The effect of this approach is to exclude claims of discrimination by way of victimisation in race cases from the scope of these provisions. The previous approach to burden of proof, as laid down in *King* and *Zafar* (see 1.84) will apply to these claims.

1.95 GENUINE OCCUPATIONAL REQUIREMENTS/GENUINE OCCUPATIONAL QUALIFICATIONS

Note that, at the time of writing, the Discrimination Law Review conducted in preparation for the Single Equality Act proposed unifying exceptions and defences across discrimination legislation, in particular by introducing a genuine Occupational Requirement test to apply to all the legislation (bar *DDA 1995*) and removing specific job-related GOQs. The proposals will be subject to consultation.

1.96   Application of GORs and GOQs

All the legislation (save *EqPA 1970*, *SDA 1975* and *DDA 1995*) provides that acts that would otherwise be unlawful under them are permitted where necessary because of the GORs of the role (*RRA 1976, s 4A*; *SOR 2003, reg 7*; *RBR 2003, reg 7*; *AR 2006, reg 8*). In addition, there are further exemptions under *SDA 1975* and *RRA 1976* for GOQs in respect of the specific types of work listed in those statutes (*SDA 1975, ss 7–7B*; *RRA 1976, s 5*). The exemptions apply to employment, contract work, partnerships, office-holders, the provision of vocational work providers and other training and to employment agencies. They apply to recruitment, opportunity for promotion, training and other benefits during employment, and (GORs only) dismissal. They do not apply to the terms and conditions offered or to other types of detriment in employment including, importantly, victimisation and harassment.

The employer will generally bear the burden of proving that the relevant GOR or GOQ applies, and the tribunal will apply an objective test of which the employer's assessment of the requirements of the job is only one piece of evidence to be taken into account.

Where an employer (or employment agency) believes a GOR or GOQ applies on recruitment, the CRE and EOC advise that the specific exemption should be specified in the advertisement for the job in question to help substantiate the employer's GOR or GOQ defence at a later date. This will also help to avoid the risk that a publisher may refuse to accept the advert for fear of being liable under the prohibition of publishing unlawfully discriminatory adverts (see 1.9).

At the time of writing, the Discrimination Law Review conducted in preparation for the Single Equality Act proposed replacing GORs and GOQs with a uniform test applying to all the statutes (save *DDA 1995*) which would provide 'greater flexibility'.

1.97   Differences between GORs and GOQs

There are a number of practical differences between GORs and GOQs, some seemingly purely down to the vagaries of the draftsman, as follows:

(a)   A GOR will only apply where it is a 'genuine *and determining* requirement', meaning that the GOR must be the key requirement of the role rather than just one of several factors of equal importance.

(b)   As set out at 1.98(e), the employer must act proportionately in order to rely on a GOR (*RRA 1976 4A(2)(a)*; *SOR 2003, reg 7(2)(b)*; *RBR 2003, reg 7(2)(b)*; *AR 2006, reg 8(2)(b)*). There is no overall requirement of proportionality of the GOQs in relation to race and gender, but an employer must consider whether work can be allocated amongst his existing employees in order to avoid the need for a new recruit to be of a particular gender, race etc (*SDA 1975, s 7(4)*; *RRA 1976, s 5(4)*). An employer must act 'reasonably' in order to rely on the GOQ in respect of gender reassignment (*SDA 1975, s 7A(1)(b)*).

(c)   GORs provide a defence in relation to dismissal, whereas GOQs do not.

(d)   GORs apply to a post whereas GOQs apply to an individual, which could become relevant where the requirements of a role change. A GOR in this circumstance might justify termination of employment whereas a GOQ may require continued employment of the individual. So, for example, if a person changes their faith, the GOR under *RBR 2003* may permit termination, whereas the GOQ under *SDA 1975* would not allow dismissal for example of a person who changes gender. A GOQ must be reassessed on each occasion a post becomes vacant to ensure that it can still be validly claimed. Circumstances may have changed, rendering the GOQ inapplicable (EOC).

1.98 General GOR

The definition that must be met in order for a GOR to apply is that the relevant criterion which applies to the role is a 'genuine occupational requirement'. The following principles are key:

(a)   that the protected characteristic (for example, race) is a *requirement* of the role. This means that it must be *necessary* in order to perform the role as legitimately specified by the employer, rather than simply preferable in the employer's eyes;

(b)   that the characteristic is determining (see 1.97(a)).

(c)   that the characteristic is genuinely required meaning it was, in fact, a legitimate requirement, rather than that the employer applied it on a whim (DTI Guidance to *SOR 2003* and *AR 2006*);

(d)   that the characteristic is linked to duties which are fundamental to the role. The EOC guidance also stresses that the characteristic must be required for the role in question, meaning that each role must be looked at on an individual basis rather than assuming it applies to all roles within a certain function on a uniform basis;

(e)   that the requirement is proportionate, meaning that the employer must pursue any alternatives to satisfy the specific requirement short of taking the potentially unlawful action which requires him to rely on the GOR. Where there is another way to fulfil the objectives of the role, the employer will not then be able to rely on the GOR. The obvious example, mirrored in the language of the GOQs, is that the employer should consider whether the requirement can be satisfied among his existing staff, including reallocating duties where necessary, before seeking to rely on a GOR in respect of recruitment.

1.99 Specific GORs

Specific exemptions also apply in respect of sexual orientation (*SOR 2003, reg. 7*) and religion and belief (*RBR 2003, reg 7*). In respect of religion, the *SOR 2003* applies in respect of relevant employment for purposes of an organised religion and *RBR 2003* to employers who have an ethos based on religion or belief. The principles of the exemption differ slightly from the general GOR referred to above (see 1.98). (See also SEXUAL ORIENTATION (9) and RELIGION AND BELIEF (7).)

1.100 Job-specific GOQs

For GOQs applying to specific types of job under *RRA 1976, s 5*, and *SDA 1975, ss 7* and *7B*, see SEX DISCRIMINATION (8), RACE DISCRIMINATION (6) and GENDER REASSIGNMENT (4). Note that the GOQ under *RRA 1976* only applies where the GOR does not, which may mean an employer who unsuccessfully argues that a GOR does not apply cannot then try to rely on a GOQ.

1.101   POSITIVE ACTION

Positive action is a limited exemption to the general rule that discrimination is unlawful in the UK, whatever its motivation. The legislation allows certain specified action to promote under-represented groups in the workplace, stopping short of actual discrimination in their favour. Arguably the UK's anti-discrimination legislation does not include as wide an exemption for positive action as permitted under EU law. *Equal Treatment Directives 76/2007/EC* and *2000/43/EC* allow Member States to maintain or adapt measures to prevent or compensate for disadvantages linked to racial or ethnic origin or gender, 'with a view to ensuring full equality in practice'. Note: in respect of race/ethnic origin the Directive permits 'specific' measures but query the difference this makes in practice. The distinction between lawful positive action and unlawful positive discrimination has been considered by the ECJ in *Kalanke v Freie Hansestadt Bremen* C–450/93 [1995] ECR I–3051, [1996] All ER (EC) 66, [1996] 1 CMLR 175; *Marschall v Land Nordrhein-Westfalen C-409/95* [1997] ECR I-6363, [1997] All ER (EC) 865, [1998] 1 CMLR 547; *Badeck* [2000] IRLR 432; *Abrahamsson and Anderson v Forelqvist* [2000] IRLR 732; *Lommers v Minister Van Landbouw, Natuurbeheer en Visserij* [2002] IRLR 430. The case law was reviewed in *Briheche v Ministre de l'Interieur* [2004] ECR 1–8807, the ECJ stating at [23]:

> 'A measure which is intended to give priority in promotion to women in sectors of the public service must be regarded as compatible with Community law if it does not automatically and unconditionally give priority to women when women and men are equally qualified, and the candidatures are the subject of an objective assessment which takes account of the specific personal situations of all candidates.'

The UK Government is under pressure both to extend the current scope for positive action, and to introduce a mandatory rather than permissive regime, as part of the Discrimination Law Review recently undertaken at the time of publication of this book.

In addition to the very limited exemptions which apply in respect of training and encouragement of job applications (see 1.102 and 1.107), positive action is permissible in three other key areas. *DDA 1995* imposes positive obligations on employers to help overcome the disadvantages encountered by disabled employees and does not prohibit discrimination in favour of disabled employees. To avoid indirect discrimination, the other legislation can also be seen to impose a limited duty to take positive steps in certain circumstances, of which examples are given at 1.108. Lastly, the legislation, including *EqA 2006*, places a positive duty to promote equal opportunities including public authorities, in respect of race, gender and disability, which is currently under review by the Government; however, these are beyond the scope of this work.

1.102   Race, religion and belief

Employees ordinarily resident in Great Britain

Both *RRA 1976* and *RBR 2003* allow the following positive action:

   (i)   providing access to work-related training; and

(ii)   encouraging a person 'to take advantage of opportunities for doing that work',

where the person in question is from a racial group which is under-represented in that type of work (*RRA 1976, ss 37–38*). The CRE Code of Guidance gives as examples of encouragement the wording of job advertisements, mentoring opportunities, shadowing schemes, open days, and career fairs, and information about careers and vacancies provided to schools in areas with large ethnic minority populations. This exemption applies to employers, trade unions, employers' associations and trade or professional organisations in respect of both their employees and members and the training exemption also applies in respect of other training providers.

Under *RRA 1976*, the relevant racial group will be considered under-represented where, at any time in the 12 months prior to the positive action being taken:

(a)   there were no persons of that racial group doing that work at that workplace; or

(b)   the number of persons from that group who were doing that work was small when compared with the overall number of employees at that workplace; or

(c)   the proportion of persons from that group who were doing that work at that establishment was small in comparison with the number of persons in that group as a proportion of the population from which the employer normally recruited.

Where there is under-representation where compared to the national population (examples (a) or (b)), training or encouragement can be provided on an exclusive basis to the racial group (or groups) in question. However, where the under-representation is local (as in example (c)), the training or opportunity must be made available to all groups although some places can be reserved for the under-represented group. Ethnic monitoring within the workforce can help to provide data in this regard, where it distinguishes between specific functions and levels of seniority, and is now strongly recommended by the CRE and (in respect of gender and marital status) the EOC. Other than public authorities, employers are not under an active duty to take positive action, although where data suggest inequalities and remedial action is not taken this may lend support to a discrimination claim arising out of other acts or omissions.

In addition, providing special access to facilities or services to a particular racial group, where linked to its 'special needs' in respect of education, training or welfare, is permitted under *RRA 1976, s 35*. The Court of Appeal has, however, confirmed that the scope of this permissible positive action does not extend to making offers of employment (*Lambeth London Borough Council v Commission for Racial Equality* [1990] ICR 768, [1990] IRLR 231) This exemption is, unlike *RRA 1976, ss 37–38*, unqualified by the need to show that the racial group in question is under-represented within the employer's workforce. However, an employer would need to show that the disadvantages he was seeking to overcome were specific to the racial group in question, for example, language problems.Training in skills specifially required by his organisation may be equally relevant to the wider population.

As set out above, the positive action exemption does not extend to permitting positive discrimination. So, in a case reported in the CRE Code of Practice, whilst it was lawful for a local authority in a job advertisement to encourage 'black and ethnic minorities' to apply, it unlawfully discriminated on racial grounds, when it refused to accept applications from three white candidates (*Hughes and others v London Borough of Hackney* [1986] (unreported)). The CRE Code also makes the point that employers making use of the positive action provisions exemption under *RRA 1976* should take care that the training or encouragement provided as a form of positive action does not constitute employment, or lead automatically to employment; the CRE give as an example 'on-the-job' training or apprenticeships, which amount to employment and not training, and so cannot lawfully form part of an employer's positive action programme. The CRE Code does, however, give useful practical examples of the types of training and encouragement that have been developed under the positive action exemption.

1.103   *Employees not ordinarily resident in Great Britain*

RRA 1976, s 36 also sets out an exemption for the provision of education or training or 'ancillary benefits' where the employer or training provider believes the person will leave Great Britain after the period of employment of training in question.

1.104   **Religion or belief, and sexual orientation**

The test under *RBR 2003, reg 25* and *SOR 2003, reg 26* is potentially wider than that under *RRA 1976*: the positive action detailed at 1.102 can be taken by an employer or trade organisation where it 'reasonably appears' to them that it will prevent or compensate for disadvantages linked to religion or belief, or sexual orientation, suffered by a person doing that work or likely to take up that work.

As such, the emphasis is on showing likely practical difficulties for the person in taking up that job, of which numerical disadvantage when compared to the relevant population might be evidence, but is not in itself required. Other examples might include acting on employee comments (such as exit interviews) or published research showing that employees face difficulties in certain roles, for example because of the prejudices of colleagues or customers (although disadvantages that are only *perceived* by the employee to exist do not fall within the positive action exemption).

1.105   **Age**

AR 2006, reg 29 allows the following positive action:

(a)   providing access to facilities for training, and

(b)   encouraging job applications,

where the person in question is of a particular age or age group that is disadvantaged in relation to that particular work.

The test for the particular age or age group being disadvantaged is the same as for *RBR 2003* and *SOR 2003*: that it reasonably appears to the employer that the positive action will prevent or compensate for disadvantages linked to religion or belief suffered by a person doing that work or likely to take up that work. It may again be more difficult to show actual 'disadvantage' than simple numerical under-representation (see 1.102). Unlike the other statutes, direct discrimination under *AR 2006* can be justified where a 'proportionate means of achieving a legitimate end'; however, given that *reg 29* specifically addresses positive action, it may be difficult for an employer to show it was justified in taking positive action that falls outside this narrow exception.

1.106 **Disability discrimination**

DDA 1995 makes discrimination against disabled persons unlawful but does not apply the reverse obligation, so that disability against persons who are not disabled, on those grounds, is not unlawful. *DDA 1995, reg 4A* in fact requires acts of positive discrimination from employers, in respect of their positive duty to make reasonable adjustments. This duty extends, in limited circumstances, to considering creating a new role where a person is unable to perform their current role owing to disability (*Southampton City College v Randall* [2006] IRLR 18). See DISABILITY DISCRIMINATION (3).

1.107 **Sex, maternity and pregnancy**

The extent of permitted positive action under *SDA 1975* (*ss 47–48*) is the same as under *RRA 1976* (see 1.102). There is also a separate exemption for training where a man or woman has a 'special need' as a result of being out of regular full-time employment because of domestic or family responsibilities.

The EOC recommends a variety of different types of training, such as work experience or work shadowing to gain experience of a new type of work, and training in specific skills and techniques and career counselling and guidance to encourage women to apply for promotion where they are under-represented at senior levels. In terms of encouraging job applications from women, the EOC recommends a statement in job advertisements that applications from women are welcomed, and providing 'taster days' to give women experience of the role. The EOC suggest these steps will help to counter general skills shortages; however, they would of course only be lawful for areas where women are under-represented.

As under *DDA 1995*, the *Management of Health and Safety at Work Regulations 1999* require an employer to take positive steps to protect its pregnant workers, for example by undertaking a risk assessment and making any necessary modifications to her working conditions (see SEX DISCRIMINATION (8)) This may be viewed as treating the pregnant worker more favourably than her non-pregnant colleague, but is an attempt to remove the disadvantage the pregnant employee may otherwise be under, akin to the effect of *DDA 1995* in respect of disabled workers. A similar rationale informs the duty under the *Maternity and Paternity Leave etc Regulations 1999* (*SI 1999/3312*) to give preferential treatment to an employee on or returning from maternity leave in a redundancy situation, by appointing her to a vacant role for which she is qualified in preference to a colleague who is also at risk of redundancy, and may be better skilled for the role, but is not on maternity leave, albeit this provision seems to go further than strictly necessary to overcome the disadvantage suffered by an employee who has been out of the workplace for reason of her maternity leave (see SEX DISCRIMINATION (8)).

1.108 **Avoiding indirect discrimination**

The duty to avoid indirect discrimination may extend to taking positive steps in some circumstances that may be seen as a type of positive action. So, although there is no reference to positive action under *SDA 1975*, to avoid a finding of indirect sex discrimination on the basis that women proportionately bear greater caring responsibilities, an employer will need to accommodate a female employee's flexible working request where this is to allow her to care for a child or dependent relative save where his refusal is objectively justified (see SEX DISCRIMINATION (8)). Where black employees were not represented in senior management, it was indirectly discriminatory in breach of *RRA 1976* to require an applicant for the role of Equal Opportunities Manager to be of senior management grade (*Aina v Employment Service* [2002] DCLD 103D). And to avoid breach of *RBR 2006*, an employer will need to give careful consideration to an observant Christian employee's request not to work Sundays, including rearranging shifts were reasonably practicable (*Copsey v WWB Devon Clays Limited* [2005] EWCA Civ 932, [2005] ICR 1789, [2005] IRLR 811; (see RELIGION AND BELIEF (7)).

1.109   VICARIOUS LIABILITY

Employers can be vicariously liable for acts of discrimination committed by their employees or agents both under UK legislation and under common law.

1.110   Liability for an employee's acts under the legislation

Liability

The legislation shares common provisions on vicarious liability. Anything done by a person in the course of his employment is treated as if done by both him and his employer, whether or not done with the employer's knowledge and approval (*SDA 1975, s 41; RRA 1976, s 32; DDA 1995, s 58; RBR 2003, reg 22; SOR 2003, reg.22; AR 2006, reg 25*).

The meaning of 'in the course of employment' is widely construed, relying both on the broad definition of 'employment' under the legislation (see 1.7ff) and the fact that the legislation makes clear that an employer will be vicariously liable regardless of whether he condoned or even was aware of the unlawful acts. In the leading case *Jones v Tower Boot Co Ltd* [1997] 2 All ER 406, the Court of Appeal also held that to apply the principle that vicarious liability should not extend to more extreme examples of harassment and discrimination, on the basis they were outside the usual course of employment, would undermine the purpose of the legislation. Not only acts at the workplace, but at work-related social events are covered, for example at post-work drinks and a work leaving party held in a pub (*Chief Constable of the Lincolnshire Police v Stubbs* [1999] IRLR 81). Whether the circumstances show that the acts were an extension of employment is largely a question of fact for the tribunal to decide: an offsite 'family fun day' organised by an employer but to which staff were accompanied by family and friends was not an extension of the workplace (*Sidhu v Aerospace Composite Technology Ltd* [2000] IRLR 602) and nor were police living quarters (*Waters v Commissioner of Police the Metropolis* [2000] IRLR 720).

This test is similar to, but still slightly wider than, the approach taken in respect of common law negligence claims, where an employer will not liable where there is a sufficiently close connection between the nature of the employee's job and be unlawful acts carried out by him, even when clearly unauthorised (*Lister v Forth Dry Dock and Engineering Co Ltd* [1990] 1 AC 546, [1989] 1 All ER 1134; *Mattis v Pollock (trading as Flamingos Nightclub)* [2003] EWCA Civ 887, [2004] 4 All ER 85, [2003] 1 WLR 2158).

1.111   *Defence*

The legislation also shares a common defence, which is that the employer 'took such steps as were reasonably practicable to prevent the employee from doing that act or from doing in the course of his employment acts of that description' (*SDA 1975, s 41(3); RRA 1976, s 32(3); DDA 1995, s 58(5); RBR 2003, reg 22(3); SOR 2003, reg 22(3); AR 2006, reg 25(3)*).

The courts approach the defence by (i) identifying whether the employer took any steps to prevent the employee whose acts are complained of from carrying out those acts in the course of his employment; and (ii) considering whether the employer could have taken any further acts which were reasonably practicable (*Caniffe v East Riding of Yorkshire Council* [2000] IRLR 555). In *Caniffe*, the EAT also confirmed that the fact that the acts complained of were so serious that the employee who committed them would have been aware that their conduct was unacceptable without the need for instruction, or that the steps were not realistically likely to succeed, did not of itself mean the employer could rely on the 'reasonable steps' defence, for the policy reasons given by the House of Lords in *Jones v Tower Boot Co* (see 1.110). The fact that those steps were unsuccessful does not, however, mean that the defence will fail, or it would never be relied on: by definition the defence is only needed where an act of discrimination has, in fact, taken place.

The test of reasonable practicality equates to proportionality. It involves a balancing exercise between the extent of the difference the employer's steps are likely to take, and the time, effort and expense of the suggested measures. In *Croft v Royal Mail Group plc* [2003] EWCA Civ 1045, [2003] ICR 1425, [2003] IRLR 592, the employer in briefing staff of a colleague's sex change reminded them of their duty of non-harassment, and issuing an informal warning when subsequent verbal harassment took place (which had the effect of preventing that harassment), had taken reasonably practicable steps. The tribunal took into account the fact there was no evidence that the employees complained of did not know their acts constituted harassment, and that further education would have been unlikely to have resulted in their accepting the claimant's decision to undergo gender reassignment. In *Caspersz v Ministry of Defence* UKEAT/0599/05/LA the fact that the employer had in place a 'dignity at work' policy which was 'conscientiously implemented' was sufficient to establish the 'reasonable steps' defence. The tribunal and EAT judgments provide little guidance as to what on those facts amounted to 'conscientious implementation', save that the harasser in that case was aware of the policy, the respondent had apologised for a previous potential breach of that policy (where the individual complained of had already left its employment and so could not be disciplined), and, that, in relation to the incidents that founded the tribunal complaint, it had promptly investigated and had dismissed the employee who had breached that policy.

Whether reasonable steps have been taken is largely a question of fact to be determined by the tribunal, and as such the case law is somewhat inconsistent. In *Enterprise Glass Co Ltd v Miles* [1990] ICR 787, an oral warning was insufficient to establish the defence. In *Balgobin and Francis v London Borough of Tower Hamlets* [1987] ICR 829, EAT, the EAT refused to interfere with a decision of the tribunal that notwithstanding the fact that there was no evidence that the employer trained staff on its equal opportunities policy or even brought it to their attention, and that it failed to act on prior complaints before the particular sexual harassment complained of, it had taken 'reasonable steps'. More extensive steps will, however, generally be expected of an employer where he is aware that an employee presents a particular risk, in particularly where that employee is in a senior role compared to the complainant (*Caniffe* and *Caspersz, supra*).

In order to rely on this defence, an employer should draw up an equal opportunities policy which complies with the minimal provisions of the Commission Code of Practice (Commission Recommendation number 92/131/ECC) and relevant CRE, EOC and ACAS Codes. In particular, the policy should state that breach may amount to gross misconduct, require employees to report their concerns as to breach of the policy (*Caniffe, supra*) and set out alternative personnel with whom complaints should be raised (to avoid the possibility that the individual named may in fact be the subject of the complaint) (as noted in *Caspersz, supra*). Employers should also demonstrate that they are not simply paying 'lip service' to their obligations by running regular training sessions for staff on the policy, and, most importantly, to consistently investigate and, where appropriate, discipline where either formal or informal complaints of breach of the policy are made. A person of appropriate seniority and character should be given overall responsibility for the policy: the EAT in *Caspersz* noted *obiter* that if evidence had been put to it that the employer had been aware of the character of the harasser in the case at the time it have him overall responsibility for the employer's equal opportunities policy, it may not have been able to rely on the defence. Monitoring of the effectiveness of the policy is also advisable (this was expressly not considered so did not form part of the decision to exonerate the employer in *Caspersz*).

1.112 *Personal liability of employees*

An employee can be liable personally for carrying out the employer's discriminatory act, and for knowingly aiding the employer's unlawful act, even where the employer is able to rely on the 'reasonable steps' defence (see 1.111) (*Crofton v Yeboah* [2002] EWCA Civ 794, [2002] IRLR 634). Where employees have been required to pay part or all of an award, these have generally been cases where the defendant employee's conduct has been egregious.

Although rarer, awards may also be made on a joint and several basis (see *Way v Crouch* [2005] ICR 1362, [2005] IRLR 603, where the defendant employee was a major shareholder with influence over the employer's decisions, and *Gilbank v Miles* [2006] EWCA Civ 543, [2006] IRLR 538, where the defendant employee was the employer's manager and fostered a culture of discrimination). Apportionment of liability is linked to responsibility for the damage incurred and culpability, and not to ability to pay (*Rooproy v Rollins-Elliott* [2001] All ER (D) 91 (Jul)).

1.113 **Liability for an employee's acts under the Protection from Harassment Act 1997**

An employer can also be vicariously liable for harassment by its employees in breach of *PHA 1997* where the unlawful act complained of is committed in the course of employment (*Majrowski v Guy's and St Thomas's NHS Trust* [2006] UKHL 34, [2006] 4 All ER 395). This route is potentially easier for an employee than a claim under the discrimination legislation, for the following reasons among others: the common law rather than the statutory test of 'in the course of employment' applies; the 'reasonable steps' defence is not open to the employer; a six-year limitation period applies and the requirement to raise a statutory grievance does not; and, lastly, there is no need to show the harassment was on protected grounds, such as gender or race.

In *Majrowski* the House of Lords emphasised that the conduct complained of must be sufficiently serious to amount to what is a criminal act under *PHA 1997*. Given that the wording of the statute in fact appears to impose a low hurdle, it may be that the severity of the conduct will in fact be reflected in the level of damages awarded. The measures of damages is not, however, yet clear: the substantive hearing in the *Majrowski* case did not take place (presumably because the case settled), and the significant award made in *Green v DB Group Services (UK) Limited* [2006] All ER (D) 02 Aug, [2006] EWHC 1898, QB constituted compensation for common law personal injury with an unspecified amount for damages under the *PHA 1997*.

1.114 **Liability for acts of third parties**

An employer may also be liable towards its employees where its employees suffer discrimination from third parties in the course of their employment which it was within the employer's power to prevent (*Burton and Rhule v De Vere Hotels* [1996] IRLR 596). While this principle has been disapproved by the House of Lords (*Pearce v Governing Body of Mayfield Secondary School* [2003] UKHL 34, [2004] 1 All ER 339, [2003] ICR 937) on the basis that the employer was not motivated by unlawfully discriminatory reasons in failing to protect its employees, this decision should now be applied with care following the extension of the legislation in respect of harassment: in a case under *RRA 1976, s 3A* the EAT has held that an employer's failure to address an employee's complaints of racist language by her colleagues and customers could result in an offensive (etc) environment (*Gravell v Bexley London Borough Council* [2007] All ER (D) 229 (May)) (see 1.45ff).

Where an agent has implied or express authority to act on behalf of a principal (and whether that authority is given before or after the act in question), the principal will be liable for his acts of unlawful discrimination (*SDA 1975, s 41(2)*; *RRA 1976, s 32(2)*; *DDA 1995, s 58(2)*; *RBR 2003, reg 22(2)*; *SOR 2003, reg 22(2)*; *AR 2006, reg 25(2)*). This included liability for the discriminatory decision of a training provider to terminate a contract (*Lana v Positive Action Training in Housing (London) Ltd* [2001] IRLR 501). The only exception is for acts which in themselves amount to an offence under *RRA 1976*.

1.115 **SANCTIONS, REMEDIES AND ENFORCEMENT**

Summary

The primary remedy for claims for unlawful discrimination brought in the employment tribunal is monetary compensation. Declarations and recommendations for action are also available but reinstatement or re-engagement are not (save where a discrimination claim is brought with a successful unfair dismissal claim pursuant to *ERA 1996, ss 114–115*). The decision as to which remedies (compensation, declaration, recommendation) are awarded is in the tribunal's discretion. It must order whichever of the available remedies that it considers to be 'just and equitable' (*SDA 1975, s 65(1)*; *RRA 1976, s 56(1)*; *DDA1995, s 17A(2)*; *RBR 2003, reg 30(1)*; *SOR 2003, reg 30(1)*; *AR 2006, reg 38(1)*).

In equal pay claims, where an equality clause is implied into the contract in successful claims, arrears of remuneration are payable for the six years prior to the date that the claim was received by the tribunal (*EqPA 1970, s 2(1)*).

1.117 **Procedure**

1.116 The parties may agree the amount of any financial remedy between themselves or the question of remedy may be decided at a remedies hearing. This may be relatively informal, simply involving submissions on the schedule of loss and counter-schedule of loss. The higher the value of the claim, however, the more formal the proceedings are likely to become, to the extent of requiring directions for the exchange of witness statements, cross-examination, expert evidence and a separately listed hearing. See *Buxton v Equinox Design Ltd* [1999] IRLR 158 at [16] per Morison J and *De Keyser v Wilson* [2001] IRLR 324 on expert evidence.

Compensation

Pecuniary loss

The following general principles apply:

(a)   There is no ceiling to the award that can be made. The ceiling was abolished in sex discrimination cases by the *Sex Discrimination and Equal Pay (Remedies) Regulations 1993 (SI 1993/2798).*

(b)   Pecuniary awards are made according to the tortious measure of civil damages. This is expressed in the legislation as compensation corresponding to any damages that could have been awarded by a county court or a sheriff court to pay to the complainant if the complaint had been brought in a county court, save in respect of compensation for disability discrimination, which is expressed as being calculated by applying the principles to the calculation of damages in claims in tort or (in Scotland) in reparation for breach of statutory duty. [*SDA 1975, s 65(1)(b); RRA 1976, s 56(1)(b); DDA1995, s 17A(2)(b), (3); RBR 2003, reg 30(1)(b); SOR 2003, reg 30(1)(b); AR 2006, reg 38(1)(b).*]

(c)   Compensation on the tortious measure must therefore aim to put the employee in the position which they would have been in had the discrimination not occurred (*Ministry of Defence v Cannock* [1994] IRLR 509 per Morison J at 517).

(d)   The ordinary rules of mitigation in tort apply.

(e)   Employers may be vicariously liable for the acts of their employees. [*SDA 1975, s 41(1); RRA 1976, s 32(1); DDA1995, s 58(1); RBR 2003, reg 22(1); SOR 2003, reg 22(1); AR 2006, reg 25(1).*]

(f)   Individual employees against whom a claim is brought may be personally liable to pay compensation, whether or not their employer is vicariously liable. A finding against an individual employee can be made under the provisions for 'aiding unlawful acts' in each discrimination statute. See *Gbaja-Biamila v DHL International (UK) Ltd* [2000] ICR 730 at [33]–[35]. [*SDA 1975, s 42; RRA 1976, s 33; DDA1995, s 57; RBR 2003, reg 23; SOR 2003, reg 23; AR 2006, reg 26.*]

(g)   Where the employer is also liable, liability of employer and employee is joint and several. A tribunal should take into account the considerations set out in *Way v Crouch* [2005] IRLR 603 at [23] if it is considering making a joint and several award.

(h)   Compensation can be increased or a compensatory award made if an employer fails to implement a recommendation ordered by the tribunal. [*SDA 1975, s 65(3); RRA 1976, s 56(4); DDA1995, s 17A(5); RBR 2003, reg 30(3); SOR 2003, reg 30(2); AR 2006, reg 38(3).*]

(j)   Compensation should be calculated on a net rather than gross basis (*Visa International Service Association v Paul* [2004] IRLR 42).

(k)   Loss of pension rights should be approached in accordance with the current tribunal guide to Compensation for Loss of Pension Rights (3rd ed, 2003). Two approaches are set out in that guide: the simplified approach and the substantial loss approach. Guidance as to their application can be found in *Greenhoff v Barnsley Metropolitan Borough Council* [2006] ICR 1514 per Silber J.

(l)   Pursuant to *EA 2002, s 31*, the tribunal must reduce any award of compensation by 10% and has discretion to reduce it by 50% where just and equitable, if the failure to complete the statutory dispute resolution procedures was attributable to the employee. Conversely, compensation must be increased by 10% and may be increased by 50% if the failure to complete is the fault of the employer.

(m)   Note that the *Tribunals, Courts and Enforcement Act 2007* was given Royal Assent in July 2007. When it comes into force (date not yet known), *s 27* of this Act will make a tribunal award enforceable as if it were payable under a county court order in England, Wales and Northern Ireland, and as if it were a extract registered decree arbitral bearing a warrant for execution issued by a sheriff court in Scotland.

1.118 *Indirect discrimination*

This applies to sex, sexual orientation and religion and belief only. The tribunal's power to award compensation is different to that for direct discrimination in these cases:

(a)   *Intentional discrimination*: compensation can be awarded where the tribunal is satisfied that the respondent intended the discriminatory consequences of the provision, criterion or practice.

(b)   *Unintentional discrimination*: from 25 March 1996, save in race discrimination claims, compensation can be awarded where the tribunal has considered whether to make a declaration of the rights of the complainant and/or a recommendation for action and the tribunal considers that it is just and equitable to award compensation as well. Note, however, that the 'just and equitable' test, which is also the basis for assessing the compensatory award for unfair dismissal under *ERA 1996, s 123*, is not the measure of compensation in discrimination awards.

[*SDA 1975, s 65(1B)*; *RBR 2003, reg 30(2)*; *SOR 2003, reg 30(2)*.]

Successful discrimination claims will often be accompanied by successful claims for unfair dismissal on grounds of discrimination. Complainants will commonly elect to have their compensation assessed under the discrimination provisions because there is no ceiling on the award that can be made (*D'Souza v London Borough of Lambeth* [1997] IRLR 677). Further, the recoupment provisions under the *Employment Protection (Recoupment of Jobseeker's Allowance and Income Support) Regulations 1996 (SI 1996/2349)* which apply to compensation for unfair dismissal do not apply to compensation under the discrimination provisions.

To reflect the tortious measure, losses must flow from the act of discrimination itself. In contrast, under *ERA 1996, s 123(1)*, the tribunal must have regard to the losses sustained by the complainant in consequence of the dismissal in so far as that loss is attributable to the to action taken by the employer. Although, the *s 123(1)* test appears broader, since the decision in *Dunnachie v Kingston upon Hull City Council* [2005] 1 AC 226 in which it was held, amongst other things, that employees should not receive more than their actual losses as compensation for unfair dismissal, the difference in sums awarded for reasons of causation is likely to be minimal, although the statutory cap on unfair dismissal awards will continue to make a remedy under discrimination legislation more attractive.

In most cases, the following are the most common heads of loss:

(a)   the employee's loss of earnings to date of tribunal hearing;

(b)   the employee's loss of future earnings;

(c)   the employee's expenses in bringing tribunal claim (other than legal expenses, eg photocopying costs).

The sum awarded may be adjusted to take account of the following factors:

(i)   the percentage likelihood of future events occurring. Cumulative percentage chances can be calculated (*Ministry of Defence v Hunt* [1996] ICR 544);

(ii)   a reasonable length of time within which an employee could regain employment (in dismissal cases) subject to the ordinary rules of mitigation in tort. The complainant must take reasonable steps to procure further employment;

(iii)   contributory negligence: see *Way v Crouch* [2005] IRLR 603 applying the approach of the *Law Reform (Contributory Negligence) Act 1945* in tort claims to sex discrimination claims;

(iv)   Discount for accelerated receipt in larger award cases (*Bentwood Bros (Manchester) Ltd v Shepherd* [2003] EWCA Civ 380, [2003] ICR 1000);

(v)   The discriminator's motives: this factor, whilst not relevant to a finding of discrimination, may be relevant to an award of compensation. In *Chief Constable of Manchester v Hope* [1999] ICR 338, no compensatory award was made where there was a finding of no discriminatory intent.

1.119 *Injury to feelings*

Since awards for injury to feelings are recoverable in tortious claims, they are also recoverable in discrimination cases, although this is only made express in relation to claims relating to discrimination outside the employment field for sex and race cases (*SDA 1975, s 66(4)*; *RRA 1976, s 57(4)*). In *Vento v Chief Constable of West Yorkshire Police* [2002] EWCA Civ 1871, [2003] ICR 31, the Court of Appeal set out three bands of awards linked to the degree of seriousness of the discrimination to guide tribunals. The lowest band range is from £500 to £5,000 for less serious cases involving one-off or isolated incidents. The middle band range is from £5,000 to £15,000 for serious cases not meriting an award in the highest band. The highest band range is from £15,000 to £25,000 for where there has been, for example, a lengthy campaign of discriminatory harassment. It is now rare for awards to be below £500 and, equally, awards above £25,000 are exceptional.

1.120 *Personal injury*

Compensation is also available for personal injury (most commonly psychiatric injury) subject to the ordinary principles for recovery for such a claim in tort:

(a)   the injury must flow from the act(s) of discrimination;

(b)   employers must take employees as they find them.

It was suggested by Stuart-Smith LJ in *Sheriff v Klyne Tugs (Lowestoft) Ltd* [1999] IRLR 481, CA at [21] that an employee claiming for personal injury in a discrimination case might well wish to obtain a medical report. It is submitted that a tribunal is unlikely properly to conclude that an injury, particularly a psychiatric injury (as opposed to injury to feelings not amounting to a clinical condition), was caused by an act of discrimination in the absence of a medical report.

However, in *Essa v Laing Ltd* [2004] EWCA Civ 02, [2004] IRLR 31 per Pill LJ at [34] to [39] it was held that it was not necessary for the injury to be reasonably foreseeable, and was probably sufficient if the injury was a direct consequence of the act(s) of discrimination (note the dissenting view of Rix LJ at [106]).

Awards for both injury to feelings and for psychiatric injury may be awarded as in *Vento v The Chief Constable of West Yorkshire Police* [2002] EWCA Civ 1871, [2003] ICR 318, [2003] IRLR 102 in which the award included sums for both psychiatric damage (clinical depression and adjustment disorder) and injury to feelings, although the award for injury to feelings was substantially reduced.

1.121 *Aggravated and exemplary damages*

Aggravated damages are available for discrimination claims in England and Wales and should not be incorporated into an award for injury to feelings (*Scott v IRC* [2004] EWCA Civ 400, [2004] ICR 1410, [2004] IRLR 713). In Scotland, however, aggravated damages are not part of the law of tort and are not recoverable for discrimination claims. However, in contrast to the approach in England and Wales, account may be taken of the way in which an employee was treated in setting the level of an award for injury to feelings. See *Virgo Fidelis Senior School v Boyle* [2004] IRLR 268 for a successful award (on appeal) of aggravated damages.

In theory, exemplary damages are also available for discrimination claims other than equal pay claims, although in very narrow circumstances. Those circumstances are, firstly, where there has been oppressive, arbitrary or unconstitutional action by agents of the Government and, secondly, where the tortfeasor's conduct was calculated to make a profit for himself which would exceed any compensation payable to the complainant (*Kuddus v Chief Constable of Leicestershire Constabulary* [2001] UKHL 29, [2002] 2 AC 122). Prior to *Kuddus*, exemplary damages were not available for any torts, including discrimination, which did not exist at the time of *Rookes v Barnard* [1964] AC 1129, although tribunals compensated for this lacuna by reflecting unmeritorious conduct by public bodies in increased awards for injury to feelings (see *Deane v London Borough of Ealing* [1993] IRLR 209).

1.122 *Interest*

Simple interest should be added to the net sum of an award pursuant to the *Employment Tribunals (Interest on Awards in Discrimination Cases) Regulations 1996 (SI 1996/2803)* save where the tribunal considers that (i) there are exceptional circumstances, whether relating to the claim as a whole or to a particular element of the award; and (ii) those circumstances are such that serious injustice would be caused if interest were to be awarded by reference to the periods set out in the regulations. If those circumstances apply, the award of interest is in the tribunal's discretion.

The rate to be applied in England and Wales is that of the Special Investment Account pursuant to the *Court Funds Rules 1987 (SI 1987/821), rule 27(1)*.

1.123 *Declaration of rights*

The tribunal may state the rights of the complainant and the respondent in relation to the act to which the complaint relates. Rarely, where the employee is still employed, it may be sufficient remedy for the employer to agree to put right the discriminatory act.

1.124   Common Concepts

1.124 *Recommendation for action*

The tribunal may make a recommendation that the respondent take within a specified period action appearing to the tribunal to be practicable for the purpose of obviating or reducing the adverse effect on the complainant of any act of discrimination to which the complaint relates. The remedy for non-compliance is, as set out above, increasing or substituting a compensatory award (*Nelson v Tyne and Wear Passenger Transport Executive* [1978] ICR 1183). Tribunals have a broad discretion to make recommendations although it has been held not to extend to the recommending of appointments to available jobs for those who have been denied them through discrimination (*Noone v North West Thames Regional Health Authority (No 2)* [1988] IRLR 530). Practicality has to be decided by reference to the effect on the complainant and the discriminator; compare *Fasuyi v Greenwich London Borough Council* EAT/1078/99 per Lindsay J at para 24 with *Leeds Rhinos Rugby Club v Sterling* EAT/267/01 (9 September 2002) at para 6.1 per HH Judge Reid QC.

1.125 *EOC/CRE/DRC/EHRC*

The Commission for Equality and Human Rights was established by the EqA 2006, replacing the Equal Opportunities Commission, Commission for Racial Equality and Disability Rights Commission. The CEHR's powers to intervene in legal proceedings, instigate investigations and seek remedies are wider than those enjoyed by the bodies it replaces. Sections 20–32 which set out these powers came into force on 1 October 2007:

(a)   The CEHR may investigate if it suspects that a person has committed an unlawful act (*Eq Act 2006 s 20*)

(b)   It may give a notice of unlawful action being committed to a person and require the person to prepare an action plan to avoid repetition of the unlawful act or recommend action to be taken by that person. There is a right of appeal (*Eq Act 2006 s 21(1) and 21(4)*).

(c)   It may agree with a person not to investigate or issue a notice if the person undertakes not to commit an unlawful act (*Eq Act 2006 s 23*).

(d)   It may apply to court for an injunction to restrain a person it thinks likely to commit an unlawful act (*Eq Act 2006 s 24*).

(e)   It may bring a complaint to a tribunal or court to prevent unlawful advertising by injunction (*Eq Act 2006 s 25*).

(f)   It may provide legal assistance to an individual who is a party to legal proceedings relating to the equality enactments (*Eq Act 2006 s 28*).

(g)   It may intervene in any legal proceedings if they are relevant to the CEHR's functions.

(h)   It may assess the extent to which public authorities have complied with duties under the SDA 1975, RRA 1976 and DDA 1995 (*Eq Act 2006 s 31*) and issue s compliance notice to a public authority if there has been a failure to comply (*Eq Act 2006 s 32*).

1.126 **QUESTIONNAIRES**

A claimant who believes that he has been discriminated against can serve a questionnaire under *EqPA 1970, s 7B*; *SDA 1975, s 74(1)*; *RRA 1976, s 65(1)*; *DDA 1995, s 56(2)*; *SOR 2003, reg 33*; *RBR 2003, reg 33* or *AR 2006, reg 41(1)* or to elicit further information from the respondent/intended respondent before or shortly after tribunal proceedings have commenced.

Standard questionnaires and reply forms have been prescribed by the *Secretary of State* (*Schedules to the Equal Pay* (*Questions and Replies*) *Order 2003* (*SI 2003/722*); *Sex Discrimination* (*Questions and Replies*) *Order 1975* (*SI 1975/2048*); *Race Relations* (*Questions and Replies*) *Order 1977* (*SI 1977/842*); *AR 2006, reg 41, Schs 3* and *4*; the *Disability Discrimination* (*Questions and Replies*) *Order 2004* (*SI 2004/1168*); and *SOR 2003, Sch 2*). There is no standard form procedure available under *PTWR 2000* or *FTR 2002*.

The purpose of serving the questionnaire is to enable the claimant to assess the merits of his claim and to decide how to conduct the case properly depending on the replies received. A claimant will usually serve the questionnaire before submitting a claim in the employment tribunal. If, after receiving a reply to the first, it appears that further questions need to be asked, the claimant can ask the employment tribunal to grant leave to serve another questionnaire. *In Carrington v Helix Lighting Ltd* [1990] IRLR 6, EAT, the EAT stated, albeit obiter, that 'It is a sensible and necessary part of the procedure that after an initial questionnaire an applicant should be able to seek leave, on notice, to administer a further questionnaire.' However, if any questions (either in the first or any subsequent questionnaire) are irrelevant, the respondent may refuse to reply on the grounds that the questions are irrelevant or oppressive and ask the tribunal not to draw inferences from the refusal to respond to such questions.

Provided a questionnaire has been served within the relevant time limits laid down in the discrimination legislation, the questions and the replies will be admissible as evidence, regardless of whether the questionnaire or replies follows the format prescribed by the Secretary of State (*EqPA 1970, s 7(B)(3)*; *SDA 1975, s 74(2)(a)*; *RRA 1976, s 65(2)(a)*; *DDA 1995, s 56(3)(a)*; *SOR 2003, reg 33(2)(a)*; *RBR 2003, reg 33(2)(a)* and *AR 2006, reg 41(2)(a)*). In *Dattani v Chief Constable of West Mercia Police* [2005] IRLR 327, the EAT confirmed that an employer, asked a direct question in writing by an aggrieved person, who failed to respond, or did so evasively, ought to be treated in the same way irrespective of whether a question had been asked under the statutory procedure.

The relevant time limit will depend on whether the claimant has submitted his claim form to the employment tribunal and the type of discrimination complained of. In general, if the claimant has not lodged his claim form, the time limit for serving the questionnaire is three months from the date of the complained act, or within any extension of time permitted by the *Dispute Resolution Regulations 2004, reg 15*. The exception to the general rule is a claim brought under *EqPA 1970* where the claimant can serve a questionnaire at any time on the intended respondent before the claim form is lodged (*Equal Pay* (*Questions and Replies*) *Order 2003* (*SI 2003/722*)). If the claim has been presented to the employment tribunal, in general, the claimant must serve the questionnaire within 21 days of lodging the claim form. The exception to the general rule is a claim brought under *DDA 1995* where the claimant has up to 28 days from the lodging of the claim form to serve the questionnaire on the respondent (*Disability Discrimination* (*Questions and Replies*) *Order 2004, reg 4(b)*). The employment tribunal has discretion to grant an extension to the time limits stated above. In *Williams v Greater London Citizens Advice Bureaux Service* [1989] ICR 545, the EAT upheld the tribunal's decision not to grant an extension of time to the claimant. The claimant had not given a reason for the delay and had not produced a copy of the proposed questionnaire, and the employment tribunal was entitled to exercise its discretion and refuse leave.

Both questions and replies are admissible as evidence, as stated above. Inferences may be drawn by the employment tribunal or court if the tribunal is of the view that the respondent has deliberately and without reasonable excuse, failed to reply within eight weeks of service of the questionnaire, or given evasive responses to the questions asked. In *Virdee v ECC Quarries Ltd* [1978] IRLR 295, it was held that one answered question out of nine questions asked constituted an evasive reply.

If the employment tribunal draws an inference that the employer has discriminated unlawfully, the burden of proof is reversed and it will be the employer to show that the less favourable treatment was not because of or related to the prohibited grounds (*SDA 1975, s 74(2)(b)*; *RRA 1976, s 65(2)(b)*; *DDA 1995, s 56(3)(b)*; *EqPA 1970, s(7B)(4)*; *SOR 2003, reg 33(2)(b)*; *RBR 2003, reg 33(2)(b)* and *AR 2006, reg 41(2)(b)*). In *Dresdner Kleinwort Wasserstein Ltd v Adebayo* [2005] IRLR 514, the EAT confirmed that equivocal or evasive answers to legitimate queries in statutory questionnaires will properly assume a greater significance in cases where the burden of proving that no discrimination has occurred is found to have passed to the employer. In *Barton v Investec Henderson Crosthwaite Securities Ltd* [2003] IRLR 332, EAT, the EAT held that the employment tribunal had erred in failing to draw adverse inferences from the employer's failure to deal properly with the statutory questionnaire procedure – there were a number of serious matters arising out of the failure of the employer to deal properly with the questionnaire procedure and/or to give clear and consistent replies that required the tribunal to draw adverse inferences such that they could conclude, in the absence of an adequate explanation, that an act of discrimination had occurred. Thus, the burden of proof passed to the employer to prove that sex was not a reason for the claimant's less favourable treatment.

A standard discrimination questionnaire will generally not be held to be a 'stage 1 grievance letter' for the purposes of the statutory grievance procedure which employees must normally commence before an employment tribunal will hear most claims (*Holc-Gale v Makers UK Ltd* UKEAT/0625/05/SM). However, where claimants submit written documents in a different format to the standard questionnaire which contains a mixture of grievances and questions, the position may be different.

2   Age Discrimination

2.1   LEGISLATIVE BACKGROUND

The Age Regulations 2006

On 1 October 2006, the *Employment Equality (Age) Regulations 2006 (SI 2006/1031)* (*'AR 2006'*) came into force, making certain types of discrimination on the ground of age unlawful in Great Britain for the first time. Provisions in *AR 2006* relating to occupational pensions came into force two months later, on 1 December 2006.

Although there had been domestic discussion of legislation to prohibit age discrimination, the ultimate impetus for the *Regulations* came from the European Union. *AR 2006* implement *Council Directive 2000/78/EC* establishing a general framework for equal treatment in employment and occupation ('*Framework Directive 2000/78/EC*'). As regulations implementing an EC Directive, *AR 2006* were made under the powers in of the *European Communities Act 1972, s 2(2)*, without the need for primary legislation.

The UK approved the *Framework Directive 2000/78/EC* (which also required Member States to provide for the prohibition of discrimination on grounds of disability, sexual orientation, and religion or belief) on 17 October 2000, but secured a long implementation period: Member States had until 2 December 2003 to implement the Directive, with the option of taking a further three years (until 2 December 2006) in the case of age and disability discrimination (*Framework Directive 2000/78/EC, Article 18*).

The UK Government opted to take almost the full six years to implement the Directive in relation to age discrimination, and embarked upon a lengthy and extensive consultation process that included the key consultation documents *Equality and Diversity: Age Matters*, Department of Trade and Industry, July 2003 ('*Age Matters*'), and *Equality and Diversity: Coming of Age*, Department of Trade and Industry, July 2005 ('*Coming of Age*').

2.2   The Framework Directive 2000/78/EC

The *Framework Directive 2000/78/EC* recognises at *Recital 25* that age discrimination is special among the strands of discrimination:

> 'The prohibition of age discrimination is an essential part of meeting the aims set out in the Employment Guidelines [agreed by the European Council at Helsinki on 10 and 11 December 1999] and encouraging diversity in the workforce. However, differences in treatment in connection with age may be justified under certain circumstances and therefore require specific provisions which may vary in accordance with the situation in Member States. It is therefore essential to distinguish between differences in treatment which are justified, in particular by legitimate employment policy, labour market and vocational training objectives, and discrimination which must be prohibited.'

Article 6(1) accordingly allows Member States to provide that differences of treatment on grounds of age

2.3   Age Discrimination

'shall not constitute discrimination, if, within the context of national law, they are objectively and reasonably justified by a legitimate aim, including legitimate employment policy, labour market and vocational training objectives, and if the means of achieving that aim are appropriate and necessary.'

However, *AR 2006* have been challenged on the basis that they go too far in sanctioning discrimination on age grounds, and thus fail properly to implement the Directive (*R (on the application of the Incorporated Trustees of the National Council for Ageing (Age Concern for England) v Secretary of State for Business, Enterprise and Regulatory Reform CO/5485/2006*, (the '*Heyday*' case). A reference to the ECJ is pending.

2.3   Before AR 2006

Before 1 October 2006, discrimination on age grounds had, at least as a matter of domestic law, never been unlawful in the United Kingdom. In 1999, the Government published a voluntary *Code of Practice on Age Diversity in Employment*, Department of Trade and Industry, 14 June 1999 ('The Code of Practice') as part of a broader public awareness campaign entitled *Age Positive*. There was, however, no legal remedy for those discriminated against on the ground of age.

In the case of *Secretary of State for Trade and Industry v Rutherford (No 2)* [2006] 1 ICR 785, an attempt was made to use the EC law on equal pay (*Article 141, EC Treaty*) to mount an indirect challenge to the discriminatory age cap in the unfair dismissal legislation – but despite initial success in the employment tribunal, the challenge failed in the EAT, Court of Appeal and House of Lords.

In *Mangold v Helm Case C-144/04* [2006] IRLR 143, involving a challenge to German legislation on the grounds that it was age discriminatory, the ECJ appeared to hold that the principle of non-discrimination on grounds of age had to be regarded as a general principle of Community law, and the German court should disapply national legislation conflicting with it, albeit that the time period for the implementation of the *Framework Directive 2000/78/EC* had not expired in Germany (see *Mangold* especially at [75] to [77]). That is a highly controversial proposition, analysed and doubted by Advocate General Mazak in his opinion in *Félix Palacios de la Villa v Cortefiel Servicios SA Case C-411/05* [2007] IRLR 989 at [78] to [99]; the ECJ, however, in its judgment of 16 October 2007, did not criticise *Mangold*, mentioning it only in passing, and deciding the case simply on the basis of the Directive. The proposition in *Mangold* thus remains binding on a UK court (see *Lloyd-Briden v Worthing College* [2007] 3 CMLR 27, EAT at [19], per Wilkie J). On that basis, one might expect it to be possible for a claimant to base a claim involving facts prior to 1 October 2006 (where *AR 2006* do not assist) on a general EC principle against age-discrimination. However, in *Lloyd-Briden* itself, the EAT distinguished *Mangold* on the ground that in that case, the Member State in question (Germany) had enacted age discriminatory legislation during the implementation period, in breach of its implied obligations under the *Framework Directive 2000/78/EC Article 18*; Wilkie J at [21] held that the general principle of non-discrimination on grounds of age was only effective where the Member State's obligations under the Directive had been broken – and that was not the case in the UK.

2.4   Interpretation of AR 2006

There is a dearth of UK appellate authority to assist with interpreting *AR 2006*. Tribunals must interpret *AR 2006* as far as possible in the light of the wording and purpose of the *Framework Regulation 2000/78/EC* (see *Marleasing SA v La*

90

Comercial Internacional de Alimentación SA (Case C-106/89) [1990] ECR I-4135), and so that Directive and judgments of the ECJ interpreting it will provide critical guidance. *Mangold* and Palacios have, however, been the only relevant ECJ decisions to date, and the ECJ has not taken other opportunities to give guidance on age discrimination (e g *Lindorfer v Council of the European Union Case C-227/04*, where the Advocates General, but not the ECJ, addressed the issue of age discrimination). For the time being, further guidance may be found in the following sources:

(a)   *Age and the Workplace*, guidance for employers published by ACAS and available at www.acas.org.uk/media/pdf/r/j/Age_and_the_Workplace.pdf. The ACAS guidance is not binding and does not have the status of a statutory code (to which employment tribunals must have regard), but it is likely that tribunals will turn to it for assistance, particularly while binding authority remains scarce.

(b)   The UK government's *Notes on the Regulations*, published March 2006 and available at http://www.berr.gov.uk/files/file27136.pdf, which have no binding authority but provide a regulation-by-regulation commentary on (and a useful guide to the thinking behind) *AR 2006*.

(c)   The consultation papers *Age Matters* and *Coming of Age*, which show the development of the government's thinking.

(d)   The DTI's eight Age Legislation Factsheets, now made available by the new Department for Business, Enterprise and Regulatory Reform at http://www.berr.gov.uk/employment/discrimination/age-discrimination/index.html.

(e)   The DTI's *Impact of the Age Regulations on Pension Schemes*, published December 2006, available at www.berr.gov.uk/files/file35877.pdf.

2.5   THE MEANING OF AGE DISCRIMINATION AND HARASSMENT

Age discrimination in context

AR 2006, in common with other discrimination legislation, create various types of discriminatory conduct: direct discrimination and indirect discrimination (*reg 3*), victimisation (*reg 4*), harassment (*reg 6*), and instructions to discriminate (*reg 5*). Conceptually, these categories are broadly very similar to those created under other discrimination legislation.

However, there are two fundamental differences between discrimination under *AR 2006* and other forms of discrimination. First, unlawful discrimination is narrower in scope under *AR 2006* than under any other UK discrimination legislation. This is a function of the additional latitude given by the *Framework Article 2000/78/EC* to the objective justification of age discrimination, which is translated in *AR 2006* into the exceptional justifiability of direct discrimination under *reg 3(1)*, and into a considerably greater range of exceptions to the prohibition of discrimination than are found in any other discrimination legislation (see 2.15).

The second fundamental difference is conceptual. Age is not a discrete characteristic; a person's age falls somewhere on a continuum (see the observations of AG Mazak in his Opinion in *Félix Palacios de la Villa* at [61] and of AG Jacobs in *Lindorfer* at [84], although the ECJ made no comment in either case). On the other hand, sex, race, sexual orientation, religion, belief and even disability fall relatively easily into socially or legally defined, discrete categories.

2.6 Age Discrimination

Principally as a result of these two features *AR 2006* operate quite differently, in important respects, to the otherwise very similar *Employment Equality* (*Sexual Orientation*) *Regulations 2003* (*SI 2003/1661*) (*'SOR 2003'*; see RELIGION AND BELIEF (7)) and *Employment Equality* (*Religion or Belief*) *Regulations 2003* (*SI 2003/1660*) (*'RBR 2003'*; see SEXUAL ORIENTATION (9)).

2.6 Direct discrimination

Direct discrimination is defined by *reg 3(1)(a)*: A discriminates against B if, on grounds of B's age, A treats B less favourably then he treats or would treat other persons, and he cannot show the treatment to be a proportionate means of achieving a legitimate aim. That final element of the definition – allowing objective justification of what would otherwise be discrimination – is common to legislative definitions of other forms of discrimination, but only in *AR 2006* applies to direct discrimination.

Less favourable treatment

Less favourable treatment is a concept common to all UK discrimination legislation, and will bear the same meaning in *AR 2006* as it does elsewhere (see 1.28ff).

'On grounds of B's age'

Direct discrimination must involve treatment 'on grounds of B's age'. This differs from the position under *SOR 2003* (which read 'on grounds of sexual orientation'), *RBR 2003* and the *Race Relations Act 1976* (*'RRA 1996'*), which reads 'on racial grounds'); none of those formulations require the particular characteristic to belong to B. Less favourable treatment of B on the grounds that B associates with people of a certain age does not amount to direct discrimination (compare, in relation to associative sexual orientation discrimination, the DTI guidance at www.berr.gov.uk/employment/discrimination/emp-equality-regs-2003/Introduction/page24669.html). In this respect, *AR 2006* arguably fail to implement the *Framework Directive 2000/78/EC*, which at *Article 2(2)* defines prohibited direct discrimination as treatment 'on any of the grounds referred to in *Article 1'*, including age. Compare, in relation to disability discrimination, the pending reference to the ECJ in *Coleman v Attridge Law Case C-303/06*, discussed at 3.7.

For the purposes of direct discrimination, B's age includes B's apparent age (*reg 3(3)(b)*). This would seem to cover cases both where, for example, B appears 'too young' to A and where A considers that B appears to others to be 'too young'.

Comparators

Less favourable treatment is a comparative concept: a claimant must demonstrate less favourable treatment by comparison with some other person. That other person, known as a comparator, may be actual or hypothetical; for a general discussion, see 1.33ff.

AR 2006, reg 3(2), in common with other discrimination legislation, requires that a comparison of B's case with the comparator's be such that 'the relevant circumstances in the one case are the same, or not materially different, in the other': like must be compared with like (compare *Shamoon v Chief Constable of the Royal Ulster Constabulary* [2003] ICR 337, [2003] IRLR 285 at [4]).

In some circumstances, the proper comparator in an age discrimination case will be simple: where a person is less favourably treated on grounds of having reached a fixed trigger age (for example, if a firm of solicitors compels a partner to retire on his 65th birthday because it insists on partners retiring on reaching 65), the comparator should be aged anything below that age, but otherwise in the same position in all material respects.

The selection of the appropriate comparator has caused some difficulty elsewhere in discrimination law, but the fact that age is not a discrete characteristic (see 2.5) creates a difficulty peculiar to *AR 2006*. If a man is treated less favourably on the grounds of his sex, it is clear that the appropriate comparator is a woman who is otherwise in the same position in all material respects. However, if a woman aged 60 seeks to show that she has been treated less favourably because she is 'too old', how young the appropriate comparator should be is a difficult question.

In other discrimination strands, the traditional approach has been first to identify the comparator, and then to ask whether the claimant was treated less favourably 'on grounds of age'. However, it has been recognised that this is not always appropriate. See *Shamoon* at [8], per Lord Nicholls:

> 'No doubt there are cases where it is convenient and helpful to adopt the two-step approach to what is essentially a single question: did the claimant, on the proscribed ground, receive less favourable treatment than others? But, especially where the identity of the relevant comparator is a matter of dispute, this sequential analysis may give rise to needless problems. Sometimes the less favourable treatment issue cannot be resolved without, at the same time, deciding the reason why issue. The two issues are intertwined.'

It is submitted that in direct age discrimination cases, at least where no fixed trigger age is involved, it will rarely, if ever, be helpful to address the identification of a comparator before the issue of whether there was less favourable treatment 'on grounds of age' because the two issues will generally *always* be intertwined. Age is not a discrete characteristic, and so a distinction between people on grounds of age will, unless some particular trigger age is involved, necessarily be arbitrary. Direct discrimination is a process of putting people into discrete categories and treating them differently in accordance with their category (the words 'discrete' and 'discrimination' are conceptually as well as etymologically related). In the case of age discrimination, unless a particular trigger age is involved, the categorisation process is an entirely arbitrary one within the mind of the discriminator; as a result, one cannot determine the appropriate comparator without establishing the grounds for treatment. The fact that age includes apparent age for the purposes of *reg (1)(a)* (see above) is consistent with the subjective nature of direct age discrimination.

2.7   *Justification*

As noted above, direct age discrimination can be justified: conduct which is a proportionate means of achieving a legitimate aim does not fall within the definition of discrimination at all. See below for a detailed discussion of justification.

Indirect discrimination

Under *reg 3(b)(i)*, A discriminates against B if A applies to B a provision, criterion or practice which he applies or would apply to persons not of the same age group as B, but which puts or would put persons of the same age group as B at a particular disadvantage when compared with other persons, and which puts B at that disadvantage, unless A can show that the provision, criterion or practice is a proportionate means of achieving a legitimate aim. For a discussion of the general principles of indirect discrimination, see 1.40ff.

Provision, criterion or practice

The language of 'provision, criterion or practice' is common to the European discrimination directives and their implementing UK legislation. What is meant by a 'provision, criterion or practice' is explored fully at 1.44.

Age group

'Age group' is defined by *reg 3(3)(a)* as a group of persons defined by reference to age, whether by reference to a particular age or a range of ages. The fact that age is a characteristic that falls along a continuum creates a problem: where are the limits of any particular age group to be drawn? In the case of direct discrimination, the grounds for less favourable treatment and the mind of the discriminator make it possible to draw a dividing line between people of different ages. But if an age group is to be defined in order to assess the impact of a provision on that group, objective criteria are required.

Drawing a line in indirect discrimination cases is a problem even outside age discrimination where the alleged discrimination is between discrete categories. Statistics may demonstrate, for example, that in practice a provision has a greater impact on women than on men, but the question remains whether that disparate impact is sufficient to show indirect discrimination – that was the question with which the House of Lords was tasked in *R v Secretary of State for Employment, ex p Seymour-Smith* [2000] ICR 244.

In cases of indirect age discrimination, two line-drawing exercises are necessary: not only to determine whether there is a sufficient disparate impact, but to establish the appropriate group. In Figure 1 below, illustrating the adverse effect of a provision on members of a pool of different sex, there are two columns to be compared. In Figure 2, which illustrates the adverse effect of a provision on members of a pool aged between 20 and 72, there are no columns, but a line; the relevant groups for comparison if the claimant is, say, aged 50 are not obvious at all.

Of course, depending on the provision, criterion or practice applied, the graph in Figure 2 might be much sharper (as it might, for example, in the case of a stipulation that a job applicant should have GCSEs, equivalent qualifications – like O-levels – not being accepted. In that case one would expect the graph to show an obvious body of disadvantaged older people).

The ECJ has proved unhelpful in offering guidance on how significant a disparate impact must be to constitute indirect sex discrimination. It is likely that the establishment of age groups will also remain largely a matter of impression for tribunals.

It should be noted that only actual, and not apparent, age is relevant to indirect age discrimination.

Figure 1: Adverse effect by sex

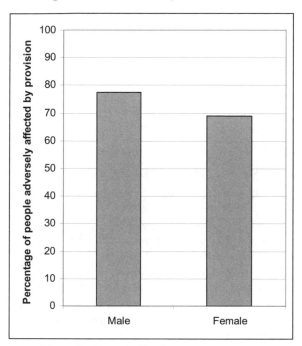

Figure 2: Adverse effect by age

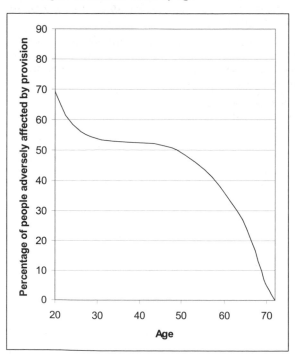

2.8 Age Discrimination

2.8 Objective justification

As highlighted above, both indirect and, unusually, direct discrimination are capable of justification under *AR 2006*, by showing that the provision, criterion or practice, or the less favourable treatment, is a proportionate means of achieving a legitimate aim. It does not appear that the justification need have been in the potential discriminator's mind at the time; compare *Schönheit v Stadt Frankfurt am Main Case C4/02* [2006] 1 CMLR 51 at [86].

Objective justification of indirect discrimination is discussed generally at 1.44ff. The following discussion considers the justification of direct age discrimination, and features of the justification of indirect discrimination that are special to age.

Objective justification under the Framework Directive 2000/78/EC

Unlike *AR 2006*, the *Framework Directive 2000/78/EC* creates separate provisions to allow for the objective justification of indirect and of direct discrimination:

(a) The application of a provision, criterion or practice that puts people of a particular age at a particular disadvantage compared with others is excepted from the definition of indirect discrimination in *Article 2(2)(b)* if:

> 'that provision, criterion or practice is objectively justified by a legitimate aim and the means of achieving that aim are appropriate and necessary.'

(*Article 2(2)(b)(i)*). This provision for objective justification is common to religion or belief, sexual orientation, age and disability.

(b) *Article 6(1)* permits Member States to provide that differences of treatment on grounds of age (which would otherwise constitute direct discrimination) shall not constitute discrimination if:

> 'within the context of national law, they are objectively and reasonably justified by a legitimate aim, including legitimate employment policy, labour market and vocational training objectives, and if the means of achieving that aim are appropriate and necessary.'

This provision is special to age discrimination. Apart from the proviso 'within the context of national law', and the (apparently non-exhaustive) examples of legitimate aims, the language of objective justification in *Article 6(1)* is nearly identical to that in *Article 2(2)(b)(i)*; but *Article 6(1)* does require that the differences of treatment be 'objectively *and reasonably*' justified (emphasis supplied). The significance of those additional words has not been directly considered in the ECJ decisions to date.

Objective justification under AR 2006, reg 3(1)

The UK government has reflected both the above provisions of the *Framework Directive 2000/78/EC* in *Reg 3(1)*, taking the view that *Article 6(1)* allows it to create a general objective justification exception for direct discrimination. The *Heyday* challenge (see 2.2) includes a challenge to the correctness of that view, and to the legality of the general exception; it is argued that *Article 6(1)* permits only the creation of specific exceptions to the direct discrimination prohibition, which the *Member State* must justify.

The UK government has, in addition, relied on *Article 6* to create a series of specific exceptions in *AR 2006*. See 2.15.

A lower standard for justification of age discrimination?

Certain comments in Opinions of Advocates General might be interpreted as suggesting that justifying age discrimination may be easier than justifying discrimination of other forms. See the Opinion of AG Jacobs in *Lindorfer* at [84] to [85]:

> 'Sex is essentially a binary criterion, whereas age is a point on a scale. Sex discrimination based on actuarial tables is thus an extremely crude form of discrimination, involving very sweeping generalisations, whereas age discrimination may be graduated and may rely on more subtle generalisations.

> 'Moreover in law and in society in general, equality of treatment irrespective of sex is at present regarded as a fundamental and overriding principle to be observed and enforced whenever possible, whereas the idea of equal treatment irrespective of age is subject to very numerous qualifications and exception ...'

AG Sharpston did not take issue with AG Jacobs on this point in her Opinion in the same case following the judgment in *Mangold*; and AG Mazak expressed an arguably consistent, though more cautious, view in his Opinion in *Félix Palacios de la Villa* at, eg, [62]:

> 'whilst the application of the prohibition of discrimination on grounds of age ... requires a complex and subtle assessment, age-related distinctions are very common in social and employment policies.'

It is suggested, however, that it would be unwise to conclude that a lower standard of objective justification is required in the case of age discrimination. In fact Advocates General Jacobs and Mazak both appear to address two distinct issues: the difficulty of establishing discrimination due to the fact that age is a continuous variable (as discussed above at 2.5), and the widespread social and political acceptance of direct age discrimination in certain forms. While it is recognised in EC law that direct age discrimination may be socially necessary, or even beneficial, it by no means necessarily follows that if an age group can be identified as particularly disadvantaged by the application of a provision, that indirect discrimination ought to be any more readily justifiable than indirect discrimination against, for example, a racial group. Indirect discrimination on age grounds may well be harder to demonstrate, for the reasons discussed above, but once demonstrated it may be no easier to justify.

A higher standard of objective justification for direct age discrimination?

The *ACAS Guidance* at page 30 suggests that direct discrimination will only be permissible exceptionally. It is possible, but by no means clear, that if direct age discrimination is to be objectively justified, a higher standard of justification will be required than in the case of indirect discrimination. The question whether there is any significant practical difference between the standards is the third of the questions that have been referred to the ECJ in the *Heyday* case (where the claimant appears to rely on the additional requirement of reasonableness in *Article 6(1)*).

Legitimate aims

AR 2006 do not give examples of legitimate aims that may objectively justify age discrimination under *reg 3(1)*. *Article 6(1)* of the *Framework Directive 2000/78/EC* sets out an apparently non-exhaustive list of legitimate aims for direct discrimination ('legitimate employment policy', and 'labour market and vocational training objectives'), but these are rather vague.

Possible legitimate aims have been variously suggested in guidance and consultation documents:

(a)   business needs, efficiency, reducing staff turnover or providing promotion opportunities to retain good people (*Impact of the Age Regulations on Pension Schemes*, page 7);

(b)   health, welfare and safety; facilitation of employment planning; particular training requirements; encouraging and rewarding loyalty; the need for a reasonable period of employment before retirement; recruiting or retaining older people (*Coming of Age*, page 33; encouraging the recruitment of older people has the approval of the ECJ in *Mangold* as a potential legitimate aim);

(c)   economic factors such as business needs and efficiency; health, welfare and safety (including protection of young people or older workers); the particular training requirements of the job (ACAS Guidance, page 31).

The same broad themes occur: business needs; health, welfare and safety; and particular training requirements. Despite the references to business efficiency, the *ACAS Guidance* suggests that cost-saving alone will not be a legitimate aim, and this is surely right; compare *Cross and others v British Airways* [2005] IRLR 423. The EAT did, however, hold in *Cross*, after reviewing the ECJ case law, that cost may be taken into account so long as some other, legitimate aim is advanced. In some cases it may prove difficult to draw the line between a permissible attempt to achieve a legitimate aim in an affordable way and an impermissible attempt to save money because discrimination is cheaper than non-discrimination. If an employer can show that non-discrimination would be catastrophically expensive for its business, it may be possible to rely on the need to keep the business running, in combination with the cost of the non-discriminatory alternative, as a legitimate aim.

It is expected that any aim which is itself tainted by age discrimination will be illegitimate. *Coming of Age* at page 34 gives the example of a fashion retailer that seeks to employ young shop assistants in order to attract young buyers. This particular example is curious, in that the discrimination which taints the objective is age discrimination in the provision of goods and services, which is not unlawful – yet. An aim is not a 'legitimate aim' simply because it is not unlawful, but if an aim is otherwise legitimate, it is not clear that it should be tainted (and rendered illegitimate) by lawful discrimination.

Proportionality

Even if a potential discriminator can establish a legitimate aim, it must establish that the treatment or the provision, criterion or practice is a proportionate means of achieving that end. The *Notes on the Regulations* explain at [14] that 'appropriate and necessary' (the language used in the objective justification provisions of the *Framework Directive 2000/78/EC*) is used interchangeably both in the Directive and in ECJ jurisprudence. The UK Government has adopted the term 'proportionate' for the sake of consistency throughout *AR 2006*, and presumably as a convenient shorthand.

The ECJ in its decision in *Palacios* has held that in selecting means to achieve a legitimate aim, Member States enjoy broad discretion in deciding whether those means are appropriate and necessary: [68]. The ECJ, it appears, will only interfere if the Member State's decision has been unreasonable: [72]. However, it should not be expected that the courts will adopt a similarly generous approach in relation to individual employers. Proportionality requires the tribunal to make its own judgment on justification and not simply to consider whether the employer's view is reasonable (see *Hardys and Hansons plc v Lax* [2005] IRLR 726 at [32], and the general discussion of proportionality at 1.44).

The principles of proportionality are helpfully set out for employers at page 30 of the *ACAS Guidance*, echoing *Coming of Age* at page 34:

'•   what you are doing must actually contribute to a legitimate aim, e g if your aim is to encourage loyalty then you ought to have evidence that the provision or criterion you introduce is actually doing so;

'•   the discriminatory effect should be significantly outweighed by the importance and benefits of the legitimate aim;

'•   you should have no reasonable alternative to the action you are taking. If the legitimate aim can be achieved by less or non-discriminatory means then these must take precedence.'

It is debatable whether the requirements of proportionality in relation to direct discrimination require the directness of the discrimination to be factored into the balance (described in the second of the ACAS bullet points), such that it is harder to justify direct discrimination than indirect discrimination even where the adverse effect is the same. It would seem clear, however, that in cases of direct discrimination, it will be more likely that a legitimate aim can be achieved by alternative, less discriminatory means, and direct discrimination will be less often proportionate for that reason.

Relationship with exemptions

AR 2006 establishes an extensive set of exceptions to age discrimination which the United Kingdom has itself sought to justify under the terms of the *Framework Directive 2000/78/EC*. A potential discriminator does not need to rely on an objective justification if it can bring itself within one of the exceptions, which remain safe havens unless they are shown to be unlawful because the UK's justification is inadequate (an exercise which will be considerably more difficult than attacking an employer's proffered objective justification).

If, as *AR 2006* provide, it is permissible for employers to justify direct discrimination in specific cases, there is no reason in principle why the creation of a 'ready made' justification by the legislature by way of an exception should make it any harder for employers to justify a practice simply because it comes close to, but falls outside, that exception. Indeed, if a potential discriminator falls outside the exceptions, but seeks to rely on a legitimate aim in circumstances very close to one of the exceptions, proximity to the exception may, at least in rhetoric and analogy if not as a matter of strict law, assist in legitimacy and proportionality arguments before a tribunal.

2.9   **Victimisation**

Victimisation under *AR 2006* is an identical concept to victimisation under *SOR 2003*, *RBR 2003*, *SDA 1975*, *RRA 1976* and *DDA 1995*. For the common concepts see the discussion at 1.55.

Reg 4(1) provides that A discriminates against B if A treats B less favourably than he treats or would treat other persons in the same circumstances, and does so by reason that B has:

(a)   brought proceedings against A or any other person under or by virtue of *AR 2006*;

(b)   given evidence or information in connection with proceedings brought by any person against A or any other person under or by virtue of *AR 2006*;

(c)   otherwise done anything under or by reference to *AR 2006* in relation to A or any other person; or

(d)   alleged that A or any other person has committed an act which (whether or not the allegation so states) would amount to a contravention of *AR 2006*,

or by reason that A knows that B intends to do any of (a) to (d), or suspects that B has done or intends to do any of (a) to (d).

Reg 4(2) creates an exception to *reg 4(1)* where B's allegation, information or evidence is false and not given or made in good faith.

2.10   Instructions to discriminate

By *reg 5*, A discriminates against B if he treats B less favourably than he treats or would treat other persons in the same circumstances, and does so by reason that:

(a)   B has not carried out (in whole or in part) an instruction to do an act which is unlawful by virtue of *AR 2006*; or

(b)   B, having been given an instruction to do such an act, complains to A or to any other person about that instruction.

Reg 5 requires a comparator. The appropriate comparator would be a person who complied with or did not complain about the instruction.

There is no requirement that A be a person in authority (compare the position under similar provisions in other discrimination legislation, e g *SDA 1975, s 39*).

2.11   Harassment

Like victimisation, the concept of harassment under *AR 2006* is identical to that found in other discrimination legislation: see, for a general discussion, 1.45ff.

A subjects B to harassment where, on grounds of age, A engages in unwanted conduct which has the purpose or effect of violating B's dignity, or creating an intimidating, hostile, degrading, humiliating or offensive environment for B (*reg 6(1)*). Conduct is to be regarded as having those effects only if, having regard to all the circumstances, including in particular the perception of B, it should reasonably be considered as having that effect (*reg 6(3)*).

2.12   DISCRIMINATION IN EMPLOYMENT

Scope of AR 2006

AR 2006 only apply to employment, occupation and training, like the *Framework Directive 2000/78/EC* they implement. As yet, age discrimination in the provision of goods, services and facilities other than for training is not prohibited. If, as provided for by draft regulations, *SDA 1975* is amended to prohibit such discrimination on the grounds of gender reassignment, age will remain the only strand in which it is permitted.

Change is possible but not an immediate prospect. *Article 13* is not limited to the employment field, but allows the Council, on a proposal from the Commission

and after consulting the European Parliament, to take action against age discrimination generally. However, at present, the Commission is not minded to initiate
any legislation prohibiting age discrimination in the provision of goods and
services: see the Commission's *Non-discrimination and Equal Opportunities for All*,
COM (2004) 224 final, published 1 June 2005.

More likely than a European initiative is domestic legislation. The proposed
Single Equality Bill, when it eventually materialises (see FOREWORD), may contain
a prohibition on age discrimination in goods, facilities and services. But the issue
remains open. The *Equalities Review*, published in February 2007 (see http://
archive.cabinetoffice.gov.uk/equalitiesreview) did not express a view on whether
age discrimination should be so extended; and the *Discrimination Law Review*,
which has invited consultation on the question, has yet to be published.

2.13 Discrimination in employment

Scope of the concept of employment

AR 2006, reg 7 prohibits discrimination against employees and applicants for
employment at establishments in Great Britain. 'Employment' under *AR 2006*
(except in the context of *reg 30*, the retirement exception, and *Schs 2, 6*, and *8*) is
defined broadly, as it is in *RBR 2003* and *SOR 2003*, as employment under a
contract of service or apprenticeship, or a contract personally to do any work (see
reg 2(2) and the discussion at 1.8). An establishment at Great Britain is defined by
reg 10; the definition is the same as in other discrimination legislation (see 1.24).

By *reg 44(2)*, the regulations apply to Crown employment as they do to private
employment, but service in any of the naval, military or air forces of the Crown is
excepted (*reg 44(4)*).

By *regs 45* and *46*, the Regulations apply to House of Commons and House of
Lords staff as they apply in relation to other employment.

In addition, police constables (*reg 13*) and Serious Organised Crime Agency
(SOCA) secondees (*reg 14*) are deemed, subject to various provisos, to be
employees for the purposes of *AR 2006*, and thus fall within *reg 7*, although they
would not meet the statutory definition of 'employees' (see below).

Applicants

It is unlawful for an employer, in relation to employment by him at an establishment in Great Britain, to discriminate against a person (*reg 7(1)*):

(a)   in the arrangements he makes for the purposes of determining to whom he
       should offer employment;

(b)   in the terms on which he offers that person employment; or

(c)   by refusing to offer or deliberately not offering him employment;

and *para (3)* makes it unlawful for an employer to harass an applicant. These are
identical to the other legislative provisions on discrimination against job applicants: see the general discussion at 1.11.

However, *paras (4)* and *(5)* create an exception which is special to *AR 2006*: where
reg 30, the retirement exception, would apply to an applicant if he were recruited,
para (1)(a) and *(c)* does not apply if:

(a)   the person's age is greater than the employer's normal retirement age, or if
       the employer does not have one, 65; or

(b)   the person would, within six months from the date of his application to the employer, reach the employer's normal retirement age, or if the employer does not have one, 65.

A 'normal retirement age' is defined by *para* (*8*) as an age of 65 or more which meets the requirements of *ERA 1996, s 98ZH*, for which section see 2.38. The controversy surrounding *reg 30* applies equally to this exception. See the discussion at 2.41.

Employees

It is unlawful for an employer, in relation to a person whom he employs at an establishment in Great Britain, to discriminate against that person (*regulation 7(2)*) –

(a)   in the terms of employment which he affords him;

(b)   in the opportunities he affords him for promotion, a transfer, training, or receiving any other benefit;

(c)   by refusing to afford or deliberately not affording him any such opportunity; or

(d)   by dismissing him or subjecting him to any other detriment;

and harassment of employees by employers is unlawful under *para* (*3*).

By *para* (*6*), *para* (*2*) does not apply to benefits if the employer is concerned with the provision of benefits of that description to the public or to a section of the public including the employee, subject to certain exceptions. *Para* (*7*) provides that dismissal within para (*2*)(*d*) includes the termination of a person's employment by the expiration of any period (unless the employment is immediately renewed on the same terms), and termination by the employee's act in circumstances where the employee is entitled to terminate it without notice by reason of the conduct of his employer.

These provisions are identical to those in *SOR 2003* and *RBR 2003*. For a general discussion, see 1.27ff. For the practical issues raised in the context of age discrimination, see below at 2.27ff.

Former employees

If there has been a relationship between A and B in which it would be unlawful for A to discriminate against or harass B under the Regulations (a 'relevant relationship', ie an employment relationship or any other relationship covered by *AR 2006*), then where that relationship has come to an end, it is unlawful for A to discriminate against B by subjecting him to a detriment or harassment, where the discrimination arises out of and is closely connected to the relationship (*reg 24*). For the possible practical consequences of this for employers and employees, see below at 2.51.

It is immaterial for the purposes of *reg 24* that the relevant relationship has ended before the coming into force of *AR 2006*, so long as the discrimination would have been unlawful after that date (see *reg 24(3)*).

These provisions are substantially identical to those under *SOR 2003* and *RBR 2003*. See the discussion at 1.25.

2.14   **Protection outside the employment relationship**

AR 2006, regs 9–23 prohibit discrimination outside employment in a number of work- and education-related settings. These Regulations are in very nearly identical terms to *SOR 2003, regs 8–22* and the equivalent regulations of *RBR 2003*; where reference is made below to discussion elsewhere it is to discussion of the terms common to these sets of regulations. *Regs 9–23* are required to implement the full scope of the *Framework Directive 2000/78/EC*, which applies not only to employment but to 'occupation', vocational training, working conditions and trade organisations (*Framework Directive 2000/78 EC, Article 3(1)*).

In relation to those provisions that prohibit discrimination in work-based relationships, it should be noted that all such relationships fall outside the narrow definition of employment in *ERA 1996, s 230(1)*, and so the retirement exception in *reg 30* (see 2.39) will not apply. Thus mandatory retirement of partners or of office-holders, for example, will be unlawful direct discrimination unless it can be objectively justified.

Contract workers

It is unlawful for a principal, in relation to contract work at an establishment in Great Britain, to discriminate against a contract worker (*reg 9(1)*):

(a)   in the terms on which he allows him to do that work;

(b)   by not allowing him to do it or continue to do it;

(c)   in the way he affords him access to any benefits or by refusing or deliberately not affording him access to them; or

(d)   by subjecting him to any other detriment.

That proposition is subject to two provisos. First, *para (3)* provides that a principal does not contravene *para 1(b)* by doing any act in relation to a contract worker, where in the employment context the act would be lawful by virtue of *reg 8* (the exception for GORs, etc – see 2.16). Secondly, *para (4)* provides that *para (1)* does not apply to benefits of any description if the principal is concerned with the provision, for payment or not, of such benefits to the public, or to a section of the public to which the contract worker belongs, unless that provision differs in a material respect from the provision of the benefits by the principal to his contract workers.

It is unlawful for a principal, in relation to contract work at an establishment in Great Britain, to subject a contract worker to harassment (*reg 9(2)*).

Reg 9(5) defines 'principal' as a person who makes work available for doing by individuals who are employed by another person who supplies them under a contract made with the principal, and defines 'contract work' and 'contract worker' accordingly.

For a discussion of the terms and concepts in *regs 9* and *10* (defining an establishment in Great Britain), which are common also to *SOR 2003* and *RBR 2003*, see 1.24.

Pension schemes

Certain types of discrimination in relation to occupational pension schemes are prohibited by *reg 11*. *Reg 11* is very similar to the corresponding prohibitions on discrimination in pension schemes under *RBR 2003* and *SOR 2003*. By *para (1)*, it is unlawful, except in relation to benefits that have accrued before the coming into force of the regulation (NB the date on which *reg 11* came into force was postponed until 1 December 2006), for the trustees or managers of an occupational pension scheme, or any employer in relation to such a scheme to discriminate against a member or prospective member in carrying out their functions in relation to the scheme. The main difference to *RBR 2003* and *SOR 2003* is the extension of the prohibition to employers. While it is unlawful for an employer to discriminate against its employees in the provision of pension benefits in all discrimination strands, it appears that by operation of *reg 11* it is possible for employers to be liable for age discrimination against members or prospective members of pension schemes, even if they are not their employees.

The critical difference between *AR 2006* and *SOR 2003* and *RBR 2003* is that *AR 2006, Sch 2*, which is given effect by *reg 11(3)* to regulate the detail of the discrimination prohibition in pension schemes, also has the purpose of creating exemptions for certain rules and practices (*reg 11(3)(b)*), exemptions that are special to age discrimination.

A discussion of the detail of *Sch 2* is beyond the scope of this work.

Office-holders

Reg 12 applies to any office or post to which persons are appointed to discharge functions personally under the direction of another person (and in respect of which they are entitled to pay) and to any office or post to which appointments are made by, or on the recommendation or subject to the approval of, a Minister of the Crown, a government department, or the Welsh and Scottish devolved equivalents, but not to a political office, nor in any case where *regs 7* (applicants and employees), *9* (contract workers), *15* (barristers), *16* (advocates) or *17* (partnerships) apply or would apply but for any exception (see *para 8*).

Reg 12 creates prohibitions on discrimination against office-holders (or applicants for posts) that are analogous to the prohibitions on discrimination against other workers. For a discussion of the detail, see the general discussion at 1.19.

The GOR exception in *reg 8* is applied by analogy to *reg 12* by *reg 12(5)*.

Police

Special provision for police constables is made in *reg 13*. By *para (1)*, the holding of the office of constable is to be treated as employment by the Chief Officer of Police as respects any act done by him in relation to a constable or that office, and as employment by the police authority as respects any act done by it in relation to a constable or that office.

Plainly, *reg 13(1)* has the effect that a police constable falls within *reg 7*, and is to be treated like an employee for the purposes of that regulation. It is less immediately clear whether a police constable is intended to be deemed an employee for the purposes of *reg 30*, the retirement exception, which applies only to an employee within the meaning of *ERA 1996, s 230(1)*. It is thought that since *AR 2006* contain a general definition of 'employee' that is specifically disapplied in the case of *reg 30* (see the interpretation provisions in *reg 2(2)*), the deeming provision in *reg 12(1)* must be construed as a reference to the general definition, and inapplicable to *reg 30*.

If this construction is correct, a police constable does not fall within *reg 30* at all. *Reg 30* covers Crown employees as well as employees within the meaning of *ERA 1996, s 230(1)*, but Crown employment in the definition at *AR 2006, reg 2(2)* covers holders only of statutory, not common law offices. The office of police constable is a common law office: see *Liversidge v Chief Constable of Bedfordshire Police* [2002] EWCA Civ 894, [2002] IRLR 651 at [63]ff, per Peter Gibson LJ. Thus mandatory retirement of a police officer on the grounds of age will amount to unlawful direct discrimination unless it can be objectively justified under *reg 3(1)*.

The remaining paragraphs of *reg 13* include provisions for the liability of Chief Officers of Police liable for the acts of constables and for the payment of compensation, costs and expenses out of the police fund, which are common to this and other discrimination legislation.

Serious Organised Crime Agency

Reg 14 provides that any constable or other person who has been seconded to SOCA to serve as a member of its staff shall be treated as employed by SOCA. Those seconded to SOCA are thus protected from discrimination by *reg 7*.

Barristers

Broadly, it is unlawful for a barrister or barrister's clerk to discriminate in offering pupillage or tenancy and in treatment of pupils and tenants (*reg 15(1)* and (*2*)). It is unlawful for a barrister or clerk to subject a pupil or tenant (or an applicant for pupillage or tenancy) to harassment (*para (3)*). *Para (4)* makes it unlawful, in relation to the giving, withholding or acceptance of instructions to a barrister, to discriminate against any person by subjecting him to a detriment or harassment. See the general discussion of these provisions, common to this and other discrimination legislation, at 1.20.

Advocates

Reg 15 applies only to England and Wales (*reg 15(6)*). *Reg 16* makes equivalent provision for Scottish advocates. See the general discussion at 1.20.

Partnership

AR 2006 prohibit age discrimination against partners and potential partners, in identical terms to those in other discrimination legislation (*reg 17*). For the structure and operation of the discrimination provisions, see the discussion at 1.12.

Trade organisations

It is unlawful for a trade organisation:

(a)   to discriminate against a person in the terms on which it admits him to membership or by refusing to accept or deliberately not accepting his application for membership (*reg 18(1)*);

(b)   to discriminate against one of its members in the way it affords (or refuses or deliberately omits to afford) the member access to benefits, by depriving him of membership or varying the terms of his membership, or by subjecting him to any other detriment (*reg 18(2)*); and

(c)   to subject a member (or applicant for membership) to harassment (*reg 18(3)*).

For discussion of these provisions and the definition of 'trade organisation' in *reg 18(4)*, see 1.13.

Qualifications bodies

Under *reg 19(1)* it is unlawful for a qualifications body to discriminate against a person:

(a)   on the terms in which it is prepared to confer a professional or trade qualification;

(b)   by refusing or deliberately not granting his application for such a qualification; or

(c)   by withdrawing the qualification or varying the terms on which he holds it.

It is also unlawful for a qualifications body to subject a holder of a professional or trade qualification (or an applicant for one) to harassment (*reg 19(2)*). For discussion of these provisions and the associated definitions in *reg 19(3)*, see 1.15.

Provision of vocational training

Reg 20 creates prohibitions against discrimination in the provision of vocational training. By *para (1)*, it is unlawful, in relation to a person seeking or undergoing training, for any training provider to discriminate against him:

(a)   in the terms on which the training provider affords him access to any training;

(b)   by refusing or deliberately not affording him such access;

(c)   by terminating his training; or

(d)   by subjecting him to any other detriment during his training.

It is unlawful for a training provider, in relation to a person seeking or undergoing training which would help fit him for any employment, to subject him to harassment (*reg 20(2)*).

Para (3) creates an exception related to GORs:

'Paragraph (1) does not apply if the discrimination concerns training that would only fit a person for employment which, by virtue of regulation 7 (exception for genuine occupational requirement) the employer could lawfully refuse to offer the person seeking training.'

There is a subtle difference between the wording of *para (3)* and the wording of *reg 17(3)* in *RBR 2003* and in *SOR 2003*. In both of those sets of regulations, the provision reads:

'Paragraph (1) does not apply if the discrimination *only concerns training for employment which* ...' (emphasis supplied).'

While the *Notes on the Regulations* observe at [65] that there are 'technical differences', and state that the DfES was understood to be planning to bring *SOR 2003* and *RBR 2003* in line with *AR 2006*, this has not yet happened. As matters stand, the language of *AR 2006* would appear to be more restrictive. The GOR exception in *reg 20(3)* seems to be limited to training the only purpose or effect of which is to fit a person for employment in respect of which an employer could rely on a GOR. If the training has any incidental purpose or effect (eg improving the person's literacy skills generally), it would not appear to fall within the exception. Under *RBR 2003* and *SOR 2003*, on the other hand, the exception seems to cover all 'training for employment' in respect of which employment a GOR could be relied upon. The *Notes on the Regulations* state at [62] that *AR 2006, reg 20*:

'does allow a training provider to refuse to offer training to a person where the employment for which the training is to be undertaken is employment for which possession of a characteristic related to age is a GOR,'

but it is to be doubted whether this is in fact the effect of the regulation's language.

AR 2006, reg 20(4) defines 'training' and 'training provider'. It should be noted that the definition of 'training provider' differs slightly from that in *RBR 2003* and *SOR 2003* in that the exclusion of educational governing bodies and proprietors of schools from the definition is not subject to any exception in relation to a person who is undertaking practical work experience at the educational establishment or school and is not a student or pupil there. It thus appears that such a person (who not being a student is not protected by *reg 23*) falls outside the scope of the protection afforded by *AR 2006*.

For a discussion of the definitions and the provisions common to other discrimination legislation, see 1.14.

Employment agencies, careers guidance, etc

Reg 21 prohibits, in identical terms to the prohibitions under *SBR 2003* and *RBR 2003* (as amended), discrimination by employment agencies in providing or refusing to provide any of their services (see *reg 21(1)*), and harassment (see *reg 21(2)*). For a general discussion of the provisions see 1.26.

Assisting persons to obtain employment, etc

Reg 22(1) prohibits discrimination by the Secretary of State (by subjection to a detriment or by harassment) of any person in the provisions of facilities or services under the *Employment and Training Act 1973, s 2* (ie facilities or services to assist people to obtain employment). Such discrimination is likewise prohibited in the case of Scottish Enterprise and Highlands and Islands Enterprise in relation to the provision of such facilities of services under the analogous statutes for Scotland. The provisions are in substance identical to those under *RBR 2003* and *SOR 2003*.

Institutions of further and higher education

Reg 23 applies to certain educational establishments, and prohibits a variety of discriminatory conduct by the governing bodies of those establishments against students or prospective students. *Reg 23* is almost identical to the equivalent provisions in other discrimination legislation.

Reg 23 diverges from *RBR 2003* and *SOR 2003* only in one respect: the GOR exception at *para (3)* is, just like the exception in *reg 20(3)* (see **2.14**) more restrictive than that in the equivalent provisions in those other regulations. Thus, again, training which has effects incidental to fitting the person for employment which might be subject to a GOR arguably falls outside the scope of the exception.

2.15 **Exceptions to the prohibition of age discrimination**

The exceptions to the prohibition of discrimination on grounds of age are the most extensive of any British discrimination legislation.

2.16   Age Discrimination

2.16   *Genuine occupational requirement*

Reg 8 provides that in relation to discrimination falling within *reg 3* (ie indirect or direct discrimination on grounds of age), the provisions of *reg 7* that would prohibit discrimination in recruitment arrangements and the decision whether to recruit (*reg 7(1)(a)* and *7(1)(c)*), in promotion or transfer to, or training for, employment (*reg 7(2)(b)* and (*c*)), and in dismissal (*reg 7(2)(d)*), do not apply where there is a GOR that needs to be met: ie where, having regard to the nature of the employment or the context in which it is carried out,

(a)   possessing a characteristic related to age is a genuine and determining occupational requirement;

(b)   it is proportionate to apply that requirement in the particular case; and

(c)   either:

    (i)   the person to whom that requirement is applied does not meet it; or

    (ii)   the employer is not satisfied, and in all the circumstances it is reasonable for him not to be satisfied, that the person meets it.

The concept of a GOR is common to discrimination legislation and is discussed at 1.95ff. The importance of the GOR exception in the context of age discrimination is doubtful. Where a characteristic related to age is indeed 'genuine and determining' (e g a requirement that a person hold a valid, full driving licence), the requirement will usually be a statutory one, and so discrimination on that basis is permitted under *reg 27* (see 2.17). However, the classic example of an engagement that may be subject to a GOR – that of a part for an actor – will generally still hold for age discrimination: a child must be played by a child.

2.17   *Statutory authority*

Reg 27 provides that nothing in *AR 2006, Pt 2* or *3* shall render unlawful any act done in order to comply with a requirement of any statutory provision. Similar provision is made in, eg, *SDA 1975, s 51A* and *RRA 1976, s 41*; see generally, and in particular for the meaning of 'in order to comply', 6.56.

Statutory authority for age discrimination is, however, much more extensive than in other forms of discrimination. By way of example:

● *Children and Young Persons Act 1933, s 18(1)* prohibits the employment of children under the age of 14;

● *Road Traffic Act 1988, s 101* disqualifies persons under certain ages from driving classes of motor vehicles;

● *Companies Act 2006, s 157(1)* will create a minimum age of 16 for company directors (though note that the maximum age of 70 for directors of public companies or their subsidiaries under *Companies Act 1985, s 293* has been repealed: *SI 2006/3428, Article 4*).

2.18   *National security*

Reg 28 creates an exception for acts done for the purpose of safeguarding national security, if the doing of the act was justified by the purpose. For a discussion of the national security exception, which is common to *AR 2006* and other discrimination legislation, see 1.67. Circumstances where safeguarding national security would justify age discrimination in the fields of employment, occupation and training are difficult to envisage.

2.19   *Positive action*

Reg 29(1) creates an exception for acts done in or in connection with:

(a)   affording persons of a particular age or age group access to facilities for training which would help fit them for particular work; or

(b)   encouraging persons of a particular age or age group to take advantage of opportunities for doing particular work,

where it reasonably appears to the person doing that act that it prevents or compensates for disadvantages linked to age suffered by persons of that age or age group doing that work or likely to take up that work.

Likewise, *reg 29(2)* excepts acts done by a trade organisation (as defined in *reg 18*, for which see 2.14) in or in connection with:

(a)   affording only members of the organisation of a particular age or age group access to facilities for training which would help fit them for holding a post of any kind in the organisation; or

(b)   encouraging only members of the organisation of a particular age or age group to take advantage of opportunities for holding such posts in the organisation,

where it reasonably appears to the organisation that the act prevents or compensates for disadvantages linked to age suffered by those of that age or age group holding such posts or likely to hold such posts.

Para (3) creates a further exception for acts of a trade organisation done in or in connection with encouraging persons of a particular age or age group to become members of the organisation, where it reasonably appears to the organisation that the act prevents or compensates for disadvantages linked to age suffered by persons of that age or age group who are, or are eligible to become, members.

For general discussion of these provisions, which are very similar to equivalent provisions in *SOR 2003* and *RBR 2003*, see 1.101. The concept of an 'age group' is nebulous (see the discussion at 2.7). An age group may have to be identified for the purposes of *reg 29* by reference to the incidence of the disadvantages in question.

2.20   *Retirement*

The compulsory retirement of workers at a set age (whether by an employer or by a state) is perhaps the most conspicuous example in the world of work of direct discrimination – in a non-technical sense – upon grounds of age. However, *AR 2006, reg 20* creates an exception to the prohibition of discrimination on grounds of age in the case of dismissal for the reason of retirement, in the case of employees at or over the age of 65. There are several points to note:

(a)   *Reg 30* does not apply where an employee is compulsorily retired before the age of 65. Such a retirement dismissal must be justified in the ordinary way, in accordance with the final clause of *reg 3(1)* (see 2.5ff).

(b)   A complex set of provisions (discussed in detail below at 2.38) are introduced into *ERA 1996*, as *ss 98ZA* to *98ZF*, to determine whether the reason for a dismissal is in fact retirement for the purposes of *reg 30*.

(c)   The definition of an employee for the purposes of *reg 30* is narrower than that used generally in *AR 2006*, including in the *reg 3(1)* prohibition on discrimination. While an employee in general is anyone employed under a contract of service or of apprenticeship, under a contract personally to do any work (see *reg 2(2)*), the retirement exception applies only to employees within the meaning of *ERA 1996, s 230(1)* (ie individuals who have entered into or work under contract of employment), to people in Crown employment and to relevant members of the House of Lords and House of Commons staff (*reg 30(1)*). In particular:

(i)   the retirement exception does not apply to workers who are not employees in the narrower sense;

(ii)   the retirement exception does not apply to partners, or to office holders who do not fall within the definition of Crown employment.

In such cases, the direct discrimination involved in compulsory retirement on grounds of age will have to be justified in the ordinary way, in accordance with the final clause of *reg 3(1)*.

Reg 30, and the issue of compulsory retirement in general, are highly controversial. It has been argued that the blanket retirement exception in *reg 30* represents a failure by the United Kingdom properly to implement the age discrimination protections required by the *Framework Directive*. That argument is the subject of the current *Heyday* judicial review proceedings (*R (on the application of the Incorporated Trustees of the National Council for Ageing (Age Concern for England) v Secretary of State for Business, Enterprise and Regulatory Reform* CO/5485/2006) and the pending reference to the ECJ in that case. For discussion, see below at 2.41.

2.21   *National minimum wage*

By *reg 31(1)*, it is not unlawful to remunerate A at a lower rate than B where the hourly rate of the national minimum wage (NMW) for a person of A's age is lower than that for a person of B's age, and A is remunerated at a rate lower than the single hourly rate for the NMW prescribed by the Secretary of State under the *National Minimum Wage Act 1998, s 1(3)*, and where A and B are both 'relevant persons' under *para (3)*, ie qualify for the NMW.

In the case of an apprentice who does not qualify for the NMW and is thus not a relevant person, there is an alternative exception in *reg 31(2)*: it is not unlawful under *AR 2006* for such an apprentice to be remunerated at a lower rate than an apprentice who is a relevant person. An apprentice is defined by *para (3)* as a person who is employed under a contract of apprenticeship, or who is to be treated as so employed in accordance with the *National Minimum Wage Regulations 1999 (SI 1999/584), reg 12(3)*.

2.22   *Benefits based on length of service*

Reg 32 creates a qualified exception to the prohibition against age discrimination in the case of provision to workers of benefits based on length of service.

By *para (1)* it is not unlawful under the Regulations for A, in relation to the award of any benefit by him, to put B at a disadvantage when compared to C, if and to the extent that the disadvantage suffered by B is because B's length of service is less than that of C.

However, *para (1)* is qualified by *para (2)*, which provides that if B's length of service exceeds five years, it must reasonably appear to A that his use of the length of service criterion fulfils a business need of his undertaking.

The government suggests in the *Notes on the Regulations* that the purpose of *reg 32* is to retain service related benefits, which it says at [113] is justified under the *Framework Directive 2000/78/EC, Article 6* by the legitimate aim of:

> 'employment planning, in the sense of being able to attract, retain and reward experienced staff. [Service related benefits] help maintain workforce stability by rewarding loyalty as distinct from performance and by responding to employees' reasonable expectation that their salary should not remain static.'

If B's service exceeds five years, however, it falls upon the employer or principal to 'top-up', as it were, the government's objective justification: it must 'reasonably appear' to A that the use of the length of service criterion fulfils a business need of his undertaking. It seems that A is under a double burden. First, he must show that it in fact appears to him (or appeared at the relevant time) that the use of the criterion fulfils or fulfilled a business need. Secondly, he must show that his subjective view was reasonable, a word which inevitably imports some sort of objective test.

The degree of stringency of the objective test requires consideration and may be open to argument. Outside the context of EC-based discrimination law, a reasonableness requirement might require no more than that the employer's view was a view open to a reasonable employer. Here, however, the context might tend to require reasonableness informed by proportionality – but proportionality is the standard of the objective justification test in *reg 3(1)*.

On the face of *AR 2006* alone, it does not appear that it was intended that the objective element of the test would be of the same rigour as the objective justification test: the opportunity for objective justification is already built in to the definition of discrimination in *reg 3(1)*. *Reg 32(2)* adds nothing if objective justification is required; indeed, it is more stringent than *reg 3(1)* since, unlike what appears to be the case in that regulation (see 2.8), A must hold the view in question at the time: a retrospective rationalisation is impermissible.

The government seems to have aimed at a halfway house, where it provides part of the objective justification, and the employer provides the rest. It may be that the correct standard of reasonableness lies somewhere between common law reasonableness and proportionality. The regulation is not wholly satisfactory and it remains to be seen how it works in practice.

2.23 *Business needs*

Para (2) lists encouraging the loyalty or motivation, or rewarding the experience, of some or all of the employer's workers as examples of business needs. It is submitted that apart from 'rewarding loyalty', none of the examples is particularly convincing: length of service based benefits do not motivate except insofar as they reward loyal employees, and a new employee might have just as much experience as a long serving employee (though nonetheless, rewarding experience was accepted as a legitimate expectation in the *Article 141* cases *Handels-og Kontorfunktionaererernes Forbund I Danmark v Dansk Arbejdsgiverforening, acting on behalf of Danfoss C-109/88* [1991] ICR 74 and *Cadman v Health and Safety Executive* [2006] 1 ICR 1623: 'Length of service goes hand in hand with experience', *Cadman*, [35]). While the list is non-exclusive, it may be that further examples of business needs are few and far between. The language of 'business needs' does not accommodate intentions that are laudable but unnecessary.

Calculating the length of service

Reg 32, paras (*3*)–(*5*) establishes a compulsory mechanism for calculating a worker's length of service. *By para* (*3*), A must calculate either:

(a)   the length of time the worker has been working for him doing work which he reasonably considers to be at or above a particular level (assessed by reference to the demands made on the worker, for example, in terms of effort, skills and decision-making); or

(b)   the length of time the worker has been working for him in total;

and A must choose between these modes on each occasion when he decides to use the length of service criterion in relation to the award of a benefit to workers.

By *para* (*4*),

(a)   A must calculate the time as a number of weeks during the whole or part of which the worker was working for him;

(b)   A may discount any period during which the worker was absent from work (including absences which A or the worker thought were permanent at the time) unless in all the circumstances (including how A deals with other workers' absences in similar circumstances) it would not be reasonable for him to do so;

(c)   A may discount any period of time during which the worker was present at work ('the relevant period'), where:

   (i)   the relevant period preceded a period during which the worker was absent from work; and

   (ii)   in all the circumstances (including the length of and reason for absence, and the effect of the absence on his ability to discharge his duties, and the way A treats other workers in similar circumstances) it is reasonable for A to discount the relevant period.

Para (*5*) provides that for the purposes of *para* (*3*)(*b*), a worker shall be treated – and so A must treat him – as having worked for A during any period during which he worked for another if that period is treated as a period of employment with A under *ERA 1996, s 218*, or if the period would count as 'relevant service' under *ERA 1996, s 155* if A made the worker redundant.

Para (*7*) provides that 'benefit' does not include any benefit awarded to a worker by virtue of ceasing to work for A. The *Notes on the Regulations* point out at [126] that enhanced redundancy payments, for which *reg 33* makes an exception, are not covered by *reg 32*.

Cadman

In *Cadman* [2006] 1 ICR 1623, in the context of a challenge to length of service based benefits on the basis of Equal Pay rights (*Article 141*), the ECJ was referred the question, as it described it at [26],

   'whether, and if so in what circumstances, article 141 EC requires an employer to provide justification for recourse to the criterion of length of service as a determinant of pay where use of that criterion leads to disparities in pay between the men and women to be included in the comparison.'

The Court held that its ruling in *Danfoss* [1991] ICR 74 had established that as a general rule, recourse to the criterion of length of service is appropriate to attain the legitimate objective of rewarding employees' experience: the employer does not generally have to show the importance of rewarding length of service in the case of an employee's specific tasks (*Cadman* [36]). However, where the worker produces evidence capable of giving rise to serious doubts as to whether length of service is, in the circumstances, appropriate to obtain the legitimate objective, the employer must show that the general rule holds true as regards the job in question (*Cadman* [38]). See the discussion of *Cadman* at 11.25.

While the ECJ did not refer to age discrimination in its judgment, the case was decided at a time when the *Framework Directive 2000/78/EC* had become effective, and the Advocate General adverted to the possibility of indirect age discrimination in his Opinion (at [23]; reported at [1991] ICR 74). There is nothing in *Cadman* to suggest that the same approach should not apply under *AR 2006*. Thus if an employer seeks to rely on rewarding experience as a legitimate aim under *reg 3(1)*, it need not establish that the general justification holds true as regards the job in question, unless the worker produces evidence capable of giving rise to serious doubts to the contrary.

This would produce the curious result that under *AR 2006*, where an employer seeks to rely on a *reg 3(1)* defence of his use of the length of service criterion, on the basis of *Danfoss* and *Cadman*, the burden is on the employee to produce evidence capable of giving rise to serious doubts of the criterion's appropriateness, but where the employer relies on the appearance of a business need under *reg 32(2)*, the burden is upon the employer to establish that there reasonably appeared to it to be a business need.

This analysis suggests a further limitation on the usefulness of *reg 32(2)* for employers.

2.24 *Enhanced redundancy benefits*

An exception for the provision of enhanced redundancy payments to 'qualifying employees' is created by *reg 33(1)*. For redundancy payments generally, see TOLLEY'S EMPLOYMENT HANDBOOK (REDUNDANCY – I).

Qualifying employees

A 'qualifying employee' is an employee who (see *para (2)*)

(a)   is entitled to a redundancy payment by virtue of *ERA 1996, s 135*, ie is dismissed by reason of redundancy or is laid off, is eligible for a redundancy payment by reason of being laid off or kept on short-time;

(b)   would have been so entitled but for the operation of *ERA 1996, s 155*, which makes entitlement to a redundancy payment conditional on a minimum of two years' continuous employment; or

(c)   agrees to the termination of his employment in circumstances where, had he been dismissed, would have been a qualifying employee by virtue of (a) or (b).

AR 2006 do not render it unlawful for an employer to pay a qualifying employee an enhanced redundancy payment which is less than the enhanced redundancy payment he gives to another qualifying employee, provided that both amounts are calculated in the same way (*reg 33(1)(a)*). Nor do the regs render it unlawful for an employer to give enhanced redundancy payments only to qualifying employees who qualify by *reg 33(2), paras (a)* and (c)(i), ie who had a minimum of two years' continuous employment.

Calculation of enhanced redundancy payments

An 'enhanced redundancy payment' is defined as a payment calculated in one of two ways (*reg 33(2)*):

(a)   In accordance with *para (3)*: ie, in accordance with *ERA 1996, s 162(1)–(3)*, and not in fact making an *enhanced* payment at all. There are three steps to that calculation:

    (i)   The period during which the employee has been continuously employed (as defined for these purposes by *ERA 1996, ss 210–214*; see TOLLEY'S EMPLOYMENT HANDBOOK (CONTINUOUS EMPLOYMENT)) must be determined (*ERA 1996, s 162(1)(a)*). Where the employee is a 'qualifying employee' under *AR 2006* who agrees to the termination of his employment, the period ends on the date on which the termination takes effect (*reg 33(5)* and *ERA 1996, s 162(1)(a)*).

    (ii)   By reckoning backwards from the end of that period, the number of years' employment falling within that period is counted (*ERA 1996, s 162(1)(b)*), up to a maximum of 20 years (*s 162(3)*).

    (iii)   The appropriate amount is allowed for each of those years (*s 162(1)(c)*), ie one and a half weeks' pay for each year of employment in which the employee was forty-one or older, a week's pay for each year of employment in which the employee was twenty-two or older but younger than forty-one, and half a week's pay for each year the employee was younger than twenty-two (*s 162(2)*).

A week's pay for these purposes is subject to the statutory maximum (at present £310) laid down in *ERA 1996, s 227*.

(b)   In accordance with *para (4)*, ie in the same manner as *para (3)*, but with the employer having the options of enhancing the payment by doing one or more of the following:

    (i)   setting its own higher maximum than the statutory maximum in *ERA 1996, s 227*, or disapplying the statutory maximum altogether (*reg 33(4)(b)(i)*);

    (ii)   applying a multiplier (greater than one) to the appropriate amount allowed for each year of employment (*reg 33(4)(b)(ii)*),

    (iii)   applying a multiplier (greater than one) to the sum yielded by the previous calculation (*reg 33(4)(c)*).

The UK Government has suggested that *reg 34(b)(ii)* will not permit an employer to apply differential multiples to the different 'appropriate amounts' under *ERA 1996, s 162(2)*: see www.berr.gov.uk/files/file28606.pdf. That is not clear from the face of the regulation, but since the retention of an age-differential scheme is itself a derogation from the principle of non-discrimination, which the government has sought to justify under the *Framework Directive 2000/78/EC, Article 6*, it is a convincing argument that the terms of the regulation should not be construed to allow employers to amplify its discriminatory effect. On the other hand, an employer might seek to obviate the discriminatory effect, for example by applying a multiplier of 3.3 to the appropriate amount for years when an employee was younger than 22, a multiplier of 1.65 for years when an employee was older than 21 but younger than 41, and a multiplier of 1.1 for years when an employee was 41 or older, with the effect that all employees would receive 1.65 times a week's pay per year of employment, regardless of their age in each year. Since this would avoid the discriminatory effect of the regulation rather than amplifying it, the construction argument identified above does not apply. Thus it may be that the government's interpretation of *reg 34(b)(ii)* will not hold true in cases where the application of differential multipliers would decrease the discriminatory effect of the redundancy provisions. It should, however, be noted that the *AR 2006, reg 33(4)(c)* require that any multiplier be a figure greater than one.

2.25 *Provision of life assurance cover to retired workers*

Where A arranges for workers to be provided with life assurance cover after their early retirement on grounds of ill health, it is not unlawful under *AR 2006:*

(a)   for A to arrange such cover to cease when the workers reach their normal retirement age, if a normal retirement age applied in relation to them at the time they took early retirement (*reg 34(1)(a)*);

(b)   for A to arrange such cover to cease at the age of 65, in relation to any other workers (*reg 34(1)(b)*).

'Normal retirement age' means the age at which workers in A's undertaking who held the same kind of position as the worker held at the time of his retirement were normally required to retire. Compare the discussion of retirement at 2.38ff.

2.26 *Pensions*

The prohibition on discrimination in occupational pension schemes is subject to detailed exceptions set out in *AR 2006, Sch 2*. A discussion of these is beyond the scope of this work.

2.27 **DISCRIMINATION IN RECRUITMENT**

AR 2006 contain a limited number of provisions which deal directly with issues arising on the recruitment of employees as follows:

○   the prohibition on unlawful discrimination against applicants contained in *reg 7(1)*;

○   the exception contained in *reg 7(4)* and *reg 7(5)* permitting the rejection of an applicant who has reached the employer's normal retirement age (65 if the employer does not have a normal retirement age) or who will reach this age within six months of the application date (see 2.39);

○   the application of a genuine occupational requirement contained in *reg 8* (see 2.16); and

○   the exception for positive action contained in *reg 29* (see 2.19).

The general principle on recruitment (as reflected in the Government's 2003 *Age Matters* consultation paper) is that decisions should be based on considerations other than age, for example the skills needed for the role.

2.28 **Advertisements and job specifications**

AR 2006 do not include specific provisions making it unlawful to publish discriminatory advertisements, in contrast to *SDA 1975, RRA 1976* and *DDA 1995*. The key danger area with respect to job advertisements is the use of language or descriptions which may lead an employment tribunal to infer that an employer intended to discriminate against a particular age group when recruiting, whether on a direct or indirect basis. An applicant who was then turned down for a role could rely on the advertisement to support a claim that the failure to offer him the role was discriminatory. It could be argued that a person who did not actually apply for a role but was deterred from doing so by a discriminatory advertisement could bring a claim on the basis that they were discriminated against by the 'arrangements made' for the purposes of determining to whom employment should be offered, although this argument has been rejected at employment tribunal level.

In Ireland, where age discrimination has been outlawed since 1998, there has been a series of cases focussing on the content of employers' job advertisements, and it is apparent that the use of descriptions such as 'young', 'mature', 'senior' and 'dynamic' risk potential applicants concluding that the employer is targeting a particular age range to the exclusion of others. The fact that an employer has used such a description in the context of the advertisement will provide useful evidence to an unsuccessful job applicant who is claiming that age played a role in the decision to reject their application. The key for an employer when preparing an advert is to consider how it will be perceived by the public, regardless of the intent. In practice, this will involve focussing on the objective skills and experience which are required by the role, rather than the characteristics of the candidate which are subjectively desirable.

The imposition of a 'wish list' of specific requirements when preparing job specifications will often give rise to considerations of indirect discrimination. For example, the requirement for all applicants to hold a particular academic qualifi-cation such as 'GCSE maths' will potentially discriminate indirectly against older applicants who may have attended school before GCSEs were introduced. The potential discrimination in this instance could perhaps easily be avoided by broadening the requirement to include qualifications equivalent to the GCSE maths.

A more tricky issue arises with respect to length of experience requirements, which are a common feature of job specifications, for example the requirement for the successful candidate to have at least 'five years' project management experi-ence'. Such requirements will often discriminate indirectly against younger candi-dates who have been working for a shorter period of time, and therefore unable to meet the requirement. In the light of this risk, an employer should carefully consider if the length of experience is genuinely required for the candidate to perform the role successfully, and if there are any alternatives such as listing the types of experience required by the role (which will generally be easier to objectively justify).

2.29   **Job titles**

Similar to job advertisements, the terminology used in job titles could lead to an inference being drawn that the employer was seeking candidates within a particu-lar age group when recruiting. For example, job titles such as 'junior administra-tor' or 'senior accounts executive' are open to the interpretation that the employer will only consider applications based on a perception of the suitable age range for the available role. Instead of using such descriptions within job titles, it is preferable for employers to adopt an objective grading system for all job titles based on the level of the employee within the particular organisation.

2.30   **Application forms**

Asking all candidates to disclose their age or date or birth as part of a standard application form will not, of itself, constitute unlawful discrimination. The risk of requesting this information at an early stage in the recruitment process is that an employment tribunal may be invited to draw an adverse inference about the employer's reasons for requesting this information when candidates' ages should be irrelevant to the recruitment decision. In this regard, the risk of asking such questions is similar to the risk asking questions around race, religion, etc. Since the introduction of *AR 2006*, many employers have removed standard questions on age or date of birth from their application forms. Instead, these details are now often requested for the sole purpose of equal opportunities monitoring as part of a detachable equal opportunities monitoring form. It is generally advisable for employers to collate and monitor information relating to applicants' ages (on an anonymised basis) to assist with demonstrating compliance with equal opportunities principles on recruitment and this is recommended in the ACAS Guidance.

Requests for chronological information, for example dates of previous employment, also risk adverse inferences being drawn, as in many cases it will be possible to discern the applicant's age from this information. The Employer's Forum on Age (an employer's network dedicated to tackling age discrimination in the workplace) recommends the use of an 'age neutral' application form which separates *all* chronological information into a specific section for HR to review, with the recruiting managers having access only to information relating to the candidates' competencies, such as their skills and abilities for the role. This approach has not to date proved popular, but employers who continue to consider such chronological information as part of the recruitment process should be prepared to explain the rationale for requesting these details in order to rebut any adverse inferences which may otherwise be drawn.

2.31   **Interviews**

Employers face various pitfalls during the interview stage due to the unpredictable nature of the discussion which can take place during the course of an interview. Interviewers should be trained to avoid questions which are based on a stereotypical assumption about the candidate's suitability for the role based on his age. Obvious examples are questions addressed to older candidates about their views on reporting to a younger manager, or their ability to learn new skills. Again, the fact that such questions were asked may be used as evidence by an unsuccessful candidate that their age was a reason for their not being offered a role. Comments relating to age in an interview could also give rise to a claim for harassment. Ideally, interviewers should follow a set script of questions wherever possible and take careful notes of the interview in case the basis for the recruitment decision comes under scrutiny at a later stage.

2.32   **Recruitment methods**

The methods adopted by employers in order to recruit may inadvertently exclude or disadvantage applicants within specific age groups, for example recruitment through word of mouth, which may disadvantage younger candidates who have not had the opportunity to build a network of contacts. Employers would be well advised to take appropriate steps to ensure that their recruitment methods do not discriminate directly or indirectly against applicants within particular age groups, for example by ensuring job advertisements are placed in a range of publications which target all different age groups and also the inclusion of clear diversity statements in recruitment literature.

Particular attention has been placed on the role of graduate recruitment schemes which are targeted at university leavers, and regarded by many employers as a key tool to attracting talent. The imposition of an age limit for graduate recruits is direct discrimination, whereas the requirement for a recruit to have completed university studies within a particular timeframe is likely to amount to indirect discrimination. In both cases, it will be difficult to justify the imposition of the requirement. Accordingly, graduate recruitment literature should make it clear that the employer invites applications from candidates of all ages, and the shortlisting and selection decisions should reflect this position.

Further to *reg 25(2)*, employers are potentially liable for the acts of their agents, for example the discriminatory practices of a recruitment agency, provided that the agent is acting under the authority of the employer (whether express or implied, and whether precedent or subsequent). To address this risk an employer should seek assurances about the agency's compliance with equal opportunities principles, ideally backed by an appropriate indemnity from the agency for any liability which is incurred.

2.33   DISCRIMINATION DURING EMPLOYMENT

Pay and benefits: common potentially discriminatory features

In the context of pay and benefits, there are a number of criteria which have commonly been included in remuneration packages which could, potentially, amount to age discrimination. If employers wish to continue to include these criteria they need to consider whether they fall within any of the specific exemptions included in *AR 2006* and, if not, whether they can be objectively justified. If discriminatory provisions are included, employees could bring a claim for compensation. Alternatively, where the provisions are contractual, included in a collective agreement or amount to a rule of the undertaking employees could seek to rely on the provisions of *Sch 5* to argue that the discriminatory provisions are void or unenforceable and seek a declaration to that effect, even without having suffered any loss.

2.34   *Age conditions*

Age has often been included as either a condition for access to a particular benefit or as a criterion in determining the level of benefits to which an employee is entitled. For example, age has frequently been used in determining the level of redundancy payments. Certain benefits, such as health checks, might only have been made available to older workers. Other benefits, such as life assurance, might only have been available to employees who were members of a pension scheme with minimum and maximum ages for admission. Other commonly used age conditions include providing beneficial treatment under share schemes or bonus schemes to employees who leave service after a particular age, and not providing certain benefits (such as income protection policies) to employees who have passed normal retirement age. All of these provisions will be directly discriminatory unless one of the exemptions applies or the criterion can be objectively justified.

A number of specific exemptions might be relevant. There is a specific exemption for setting pay rates by reference to the age bands used for the purposes of the National Minimum Wage (see 2.21). Using age as a criterion for access to training might fall within the exception for positive action where it compensates for age-related disadvantages suffered by actual or potential employees of a particular age or age group (see 2.19). Age criteria might also fall within the specific exemption for statutory authority (see 2.17) where, for example, they are required to be included to take advantage of beneficial tax treatment for a particular benefit scheme (as is the case with the share incentive plan and sharesave legislation). There is also a specific exception in *reg 34* which permits an employer to stop life assurance cover for workers who have taken early retirement on grounds of ill health when they reach normal retirement age or (if there is none) age 65 (see 2.25). Note though that the exception for retirement in *reg 30* (see 2.38ff) only protects employers from claims that *the dismissal* of an employee is discriminatory. If an employee remains in employment after the normal retirement age then any less favourable treatment in relation to the terms and conditions on which his employment is extended or the benefits afforded to him could amount to discrimination.

If no specific exemption applies, an employer will need to prove an objective justification if it wishes to retain an age condition (see 2.8). One particular difficulty in the field of pay and benefits is that the cost of providing benefits to all employees on the same basis may well be the only reason for the employer wishing to retain age conditions. Existing case law on the other strands of discrimination suggests that there might be difficulties in relying on cost as an objective justification (see 'Justification' under 1.44).

2.35   *Length of service*

Length of service has frequently been used as a criterion for eligibility for particular benefits. Insurance schemes (such as private health insurance, permanent health insurance or life insurance) frequently have a 'qualifying period' or 'waiting time' before employees are eligible to join, as do benefits such as enhanced maternity pay, enhanced redundancy payments or a staff discounts.

Length of service requirements also frequently determine the level of benefit to which an employee is entitled. For example, the level of holiday or sick pay to which an employee is entitled may increase with length of service. Similarly, the level of redundancy payment to which an employee is entitled is typically determined by length of service. Pay scales also frequently reward length of service. This will be the case where a pay scale for a particular grade of employee is expressly related to length of service in that grade. It might also arise less directly where employees in a particular post receive annual pay increases without reference to a particular pay scale for a post, so that longer serving employees tend to earn more than more recent joiners.

Some benefits, such as long service awards, are specifically designed to reward length of service.

Using length of service as a criterion, unless one of the exemptions applies or the criterion can be objectively justified, is potentially indirectly discriminatory on grounds of age because it will be more difficult for younger workers to satisfy the length of service criterion than for older workers. The longer the length of service criterion which is applied, the more likely it is that it will put employees in a younger age group at a 'particular disadvantage' so as to require objective justification.

The first consideration in deciding whether a length of service criterion is unlawful is likely to be *AR 2006, reg 32* (see 2.22), which provides a specific exemption which allows employers to retain length of service criteria of up to five years in relation to any benefits which they award. It also allows employers to justify length of service criteria of more than five years by reference to a test which is likely to be easier to satisfy than the test of objective justification. However, to rely on the exception an employer will need to comply with the strict provisions of *reg 32*, for example as to how length of service is calculated. Also the exemption does not apply to 'benefits awarded to a worker by virtue of his ceasing to work' (see 2.23), although the exception in *reg 33* for redundancy payments may be relevant here (see 2.24).

Where a 'waiting period' is provided for by statute, e g the qualifying period for statutory maternity pay, an employer will be able to rely on the exception for statutory authority (see 2.17), although in many cases the provision will be justified by *reg 32* in any event.

Even where an exemption does not apply, an employer may be able to show an objective justification for using length of service in pay and benefits by showing that it amounts to a proportionate means of achieving a legitimate aim (see 2.8). A number of potentially legitimate aims can be identified.

- *Rewarding experience*

    The aim of including a length of service criterion, particularly in a pay scale, may be to reward experience acquired which better enables a worker to perform his duties. In *Cadman*, the ECJ held, in the context of a complaint of sex discrimination in pay, that this constitutes a legitimate objective of pay policy. It also held, following its earlier decision in *Danfoss*, that as a general rule, use of the criterion of length of service is an appropriate way to achieve that objective, since length of service goes hand in hand with experience, and experience generally enables the worker to perform his duties better. The ECJ therefore held that an employer is free to reward length of service without having to establish the importance it has in the performance of an employee's specific tasks. However, elaborating on its decision in *Danfoss*, the ECJ held that where a worker provides evidence capable of giving rise to serious doubts as to whether recourse to the criterion of length of service was an appropriate way to achieve the aim in question, then the employer would have to show that length of service does in fact go hand in hand with experience and that experience enables the employee to perform his duties better, as regards the job in question.

    Age discrimination was not directly considered by the ECJ in *Cadman*. However, the decision that rewarding experience which better enables a worker to perform his duties is a legitimate aim of pay policy seems equally applicable to age discrimination.

- *Retaining employees*

    Another common aim of length of service criteria is staff retention. This may be valued by employers as it reduces recruitment and training costs and retains knowledge and experience within an organisation. Retaining employees (or rewarding loyalty) was identified as a legitimate aim in *Coming of Age* and (as part of a wider aim of 'employment planning') in the *Notes on Regulations*.

- *Rewarding loyalty*

    It may be that some benefits, such as long service awards which tend to be relatively modest and awarded after many years' service, do not have much of an effect on retaining employees (unless perhaps as part of a contribution to an overall workplace culture) and are in fact designed to recognise and reward loyalty. Rewarding loyalty was also identified as a legitimate aim in *Coming of Age*.

In any case, the employer will need to be able to prove the aim of using the length of service criterion and that the criterion does contribute to achieving that aim. The decision of the ECJ in *Cadman* and the approach of the Government in including the exemption in *reg 32* indicates that tribunals might take a benevolent approach to the use of length of service in benefit schemes.

Length of service criteria can also be indirectly discriminatory on grounds of sex and so give rise to a claim of sex discrimination or for equal pay, because statistically the length of service of female workers tends to be less than that of male workers. The question of whether it does so will need to be considered separately from whether it amounts to age discrimination. The specific exemptions which apply under *AR 2006* do not provide a defence to a claim of indirect sex discrimination and, whilst it might be expected that a tribunal would take the same approach to objective justification for both age and sex discrimination, this will not necessarily be the case. In considering whether a criterion is a proportionate means of achieving a legitimate aim, the discriminatory effect will need to be taken into account and the discriminatory effect on women may be different from the effect on younger workers in any particular case. See also the comments above in relation to *Cadman*.

2.36   Medical criteria

Access to certain insured benefits, such as health insurance, permanent health insurance, critical illness cover and life insurance will often be subject to passing a health check. Such criteria, unless one of the exemptions apply or the criterion can be objectively justified, are likely to be indirectly discriminatory on grounds of age because it may be more likely that older workers will have difficulty in satisfying the criteria. Such criteria might also be discriminatory on grounds of disability (see DISABILITY DISCRIMINATION (3)).

Insured benefits

Employers frequently provide employees with insurance as a benefit, e g life assurance, private health insurance, permanent health insurance, critical illness insurance or travel insurance.

AR 2006 do not extend to the provision of goods and services and so insurance providers are not covered by *AR 2006*. This means that they can continue to apply age-related criteria, whether in relation to the benefits provided, the employees who they are prepared to cover or the premiums which they will charge.

However, employers, in choosing the schemes that they offer and the terms of those schemes, could be liable under *AR 2006*. The draft Regulations included a specific exemption for 'work-related invalidity schemes' but this was not included in the final draft of *AR 2006*. Therefore where an insurance provider seeks to include age-related criteria, an employer will have to consider whether any of the exemptions apply (see 2.15ff) and, if not, whether there is an objective justification for providing the benefit with those criteria.

In some schemes, age criteria might be objectively justified by the nature of the benefit or some other legitimate aim. For example, it might be possible to argue that ceasing cover under a particular permanent health insurance scheme after an employee reaches an age where they could draw a pension, if they became long-term sick, might be objectively justified in the circumstances of a particular scheme. However, if the age criteria cannot be justified by the nature of the benefit, employers will have to consider whether the benefit can be procured or provided on a non-discriminatory basis.

In some cases, it will be possible to obtain insurance cover which does not contain age-related criteria, but that cover may be more expensive. On the basis of the current authorities it is likely to be difficult to objectively justify retaining age-related criteria on the basis of cost alone (see 1.44).

In other cases, it may be that particular cover is not available in the market place without age-related restrictions. In those circumstances the only way to provide benefits equally to all staff would be to remove the benefit entirely or to self-insure for older workers. An employer who nevertheless provided the benefit with age-related restrictions could potentially be challenged both in relation to the decision to provide the benefit to some but not all and the decision not to self-insure. In relation to these:

- If there is a good business reason for providing a particular benefit, then it should be possible to objectively justify the decision to continue providing the benefit. The employer would need to identify the 'legitimate aim' which was the reason for providing the particular benefit. The employer would also need to show that the scheme in question was a proportionate means of achieving that aim. That would involve considering alternative ways of achieving the aim and ensuring that any element of discrimination is minimised. It might also be necessary to ensure that older employees had some replacement benefit of equivalent value to that provided to younger employees.

- Again, current authorities suggest that it might be difficult to justify not self-insuring because of the cost alone. However, it might be argued that self-insurance in effect requires the employer to provide a benefit of a different nature and so would not be providing equal treatment (indeed it may treat older employees more favourably).

Where an employer provides benefits of a particular kind to the public or a section of the public, which includes its employees, *reg 7(6)* provides that it will not be liable to those employees for provision of those benefits unless (a) the provision differs in a material respect from the provision of the benefits by the employer to his employees; or (b) the provision of the benefits to the employee in question is regulated by his contract of employment; or (c) the benefits relate to training.

2.37   Pension schemes

Employers can be liable for discriminatory pension schemes in the same way as other benefits (*reg 7*). In addition, *reg 11* also provides that anyone who is the trustee or manager of or an employer in relation to an occupational pension scheme can be liable for age discrimination. *Reg 11* and *Sch 2* set out a number of detailed exemptions in relation to pension schemes (whether occupational or not). It also sets out special rules in relation to occupational pension schemes including implying a non-discrimination rule, a power for trustees and managers to amend the scheme and special procedural rules and provisions as to remedy in relation to proceedings in the employment tribunal. A detailed consideration of these provisions is outside the scope of this work.

2.38   DISCRIMINATION ON TERMINATION OF EMPLOYMENT

Retirement

During consultation on *AR 2006* one of the most disputed issues was whether employers should be permitted to force employees to retire. The meaning of retirement is considered below, but the issue in dispute was essentially whether it should be possible for employers to dismiss employees because they had reached a particular age.

Prior to *AR 2006* coming into effect, *ERA 1996, s 109* provided that employees could not claim unfair dismissal if they were dismissed at or after the 'normal retiring age' for their position or, if there was no normal retiring age, age 65. Nor were such employees entitled to a statutory redundancy payment (*ERA 1996, s 156*). This meant that an employer could force employees to retire, on grounds of their age, at or above the normal retiring age or (where there is none) age 65, subject only to complying with any contractual obligations (e g to give notice of dismissal, if the contract did not expire automatically).

On the face of it, this practice amounts to direct discrimination on grounds of age, unless there is an objective justification. However, following consultation, the Government decided to continue to provide a 'default retirement age' of 65, allowing employers to force employees to retire at or above age 65 without the need to show objective justification. To do so, employers must follow a specified retirement procedure which includes a right for employees to request to continue working beyond the proposed retirement date. This approach was taken primarily because the Government concluded that a significant number of employers use a set retirement age as a necessary part of their workforce planning and also to avoid an adverse impact on the provision of occupational pensions and other work-related benefits (see *Coming of Age*, and also the *Notes on Regulations*). The Government has said that it will monitor the situation and will review whether it is still appropriate to have a default retirement age in 2011 and has set out in *Coming of Age* the factors which it will take into account in deciding whether to retain a default retirement age at that stage. As set out below, the default retirement age is being challenged in the *Heyday* case.

2.39   *Default retirement age – overview*

The default retirement age is implemented by various provisions:

- *Reg 30* provides a defence against claims of age discrimination in relation to the dismissal of employees at or above age 65 where the reason for dismissal is retirement (see 2.47).

- *Reg 7(4)* provides a defence against claims of age discrimination where an employer refuses to offer employment to an employee whose age is (or would, within six months of the application, be) greater than the employer's normal retirement age or, if none, age 65 (see 2.13).

- *Reg 47* and *Sch 6* set out the retirement procedure, including a duty to notify an employee of an intended retirement and a duty to consider a request from an employee to work beyond the intended retirement date (see 2.43).

- *ERA 1996, ss 109* and *156*, which imposed maximum ages for unfair dismissal and redundancy, have been repealed, but *ERA 1996, s 98* has been amended to add 'retirement' as a potentially fair reason for dismissal (see 2.38).

- *ERA 1996, ss 98ZA–98ZF* apply to determine whether the reason for dismissal is retirement for the purposes of *reg 30* and unfair dismissal. These provisions are unusual in that they focus primarily upon the procedure which an employer follows in dismissing an employee, rather than what motivates the employer to dismiss.

The combined effect of the provisions is that, if an employer complies with the retirement procedure in relation to an employee who is above a normal retirement age (which, if it is under 65 is objectively justified) or, where there is no normal retirement age, is above age 65, then the dismissal will be deemed to be by reason of retirement. In addition, the dismissal will be fair and it will not give rise to a claim for age discrimination.

It appears to be the case that the dismissal will be by reason of retirement and fair even if the employer actually decided to follow the retirement procedure for a reason unrelated to age, eg because of the employee's performance or a redundancy situation, although this was apparently not the Government's intention and a contrary argument can be made (see 2.47).

However, following the retirement procedure will not give the employer a defence against a claim based on one of the other strands of discrimination (eg sex, race, disability, sexual orientation, religion or belief) arising out of the dismissal. It also appears that employees will still be entitled to a statutory redundancy payment if the reason why the employer 'retired' them was redundancy. This is because, although *ss 98ZA–98ZF* provide that retirement shall be taken to be the only reason for dismissal in certain circumstances, *ERA 1996, Pt X* (which sets out the entitlement to a redundancy payment) does not refer to *ss 98ZA–98ZF*. Therefore it appears that, for the purposes of establishing entitlement to a redundancy payment, the reason for dismissal will continue to be determined in accordance with the definition of redundancy in *ERA 1996, s 139* and the presumption of redundancy in *ERA 1996, s 163(2)*.

Employees might also have contractual entitlements arising out of their 'retirement' dismissal. This might include payments under benefit schemes such as redundancy or severance schemes. Benefit schemes frequently make special provision for employees who 'retire'. This might be more favourable treatment (eg good leaver status under a benefit scheme) or less favourable treatment (eg exclusion from entitlement to a redundancy payment). The application of such provisions will depend on the interpretation of the terms of the particular benefit scheme. If contractual provisions do not expressly refer to *s 98ZA–98ZF*, then 'retirement' might be interpreted differently in such schemes, particularly where the schemes were put in place prior to 1 October 2006, when *AR 2006* came into effect. In addition, such provisions could give rise to claims for age discrimination; the exception in *reg 30* only provides a defence against claims that the dismissal itself amounts to unlawful age discrimination.

Employees who remain in employment past any 65 (or any other mandatory retirement age which an employer might have) will continue to be protected against discrimination by *AR 2006* in relation to the terms of their ongoing employment.

2.40   *Retirement in other circumstances – objective justification*

Where *reg 30* does not apply, it will be unlawful age discrimination to 'retire' an individual (ie to dismiss him on grounds of his age), unless an objective justification can be shown. This might arise in a number of situations, eg:

- Where an employer wishes to adopt a mandatory retirement age of less than 65. It is likely to be difficult to put forward an objective justification in most cases.

- Where the individual does not fall within the limited definition of 'employee' in *reg 30* (see 2.13ff), eg partners, directors (as office-holders) and independent contractors. This is likely to make the once common practice of allowing employees to continue working after normal retirement age – but as contractors rather than employees – unattractive, as employers will not be able to rely on the retirement procedure to prevent claims for age discrimination if their contracts are later terminated on grounds of age. It could also give rise to difficulties in dealing with executive directors, where their employment can lawfully be terminated by reason of retirement, but removing them from office requires objective justification (although this is often likely to be relatively easy to establish where the executive role is terminating and, in any event, executive directors often do not have any remuneration attached to their office holding, as opposed to their employment which would limit any compensation).

- Where an employee is dismissed after age 65 or normal retirement age but the reason for dismissal is not 'retirement' within the meaning of *ERA 1996, ss 98ZA–98ZF.*

There is nothing to prevent an employer allowing an employee to 'retire' at any age if this is at the request of the employee.

2.41   *Legal challenge to default retirement age*

The legality of the default retirement age (as set out in *regs 30* and *7(4)–(5)*) has been challenged in judicial review proceedings brought by Heyday, a branch of Age Concern for England, on the basis that the provisions fail to give effect to the UK's obligations under the *Framework Directive (R (on the application of the Incorporated Trustees of the National Council for Ageing (Age Concern for England) v Secretary of State for Business, Enterprise and Regulatory Reform* CO/5485/2006). *Heyday* is also challenging the legality of the provisions relating to the justification of direct discrimination in *reg 3* in those proceedings. *Heyday's* argument is that these provisions are ultra vires the *European Communities Act 1972*, which is the enabling Act relied upon for the authority to introduce *AR 2006.*

The UK Government is defending the challenge to the default retirement age on two bases:

- Firstly, *recital 14* of the *Framework Directive* provides that the directive shall be 'without prejudice to national provisions laying down retirement ages'. The Government argues that the effect of this is that the Directive does not apply to national provisions laying down retirement ages, and the default retirement provisions in the UK fall within this exclusion. Heyday argue that *recital 14* only allows Member States to leave in place national provisions which laid down retirement ages which were already in place before the making of the *Framework Directive* and, in any event, *regs 30* and *7(4)–(5)* do not amount to national provisions which lay down retirement ages.

- Alternatively, the Government argues that the provisions fall within the scope of *Article 6(1)* of the *Framework Directive* which permits differences on treatment on grounds of age if, within the context of national law, they are objectively and reasonably justified by a legitimate aim and if the means of achieving that aim are appropriate and necessary. The Government relies here on the aims set out in *Coming of* Age and the *Notes on Regulations*, ie workforce planning and avoiding an adverse impact on the provision of occupational pensions and other work-related benefits. *Heyday* argues that the default retirement age provisions are not proportionate and do not meet the standards which are required to justify direct discrimination under *Article 6(1)*, which *Heyday* argues are exceptional and higher than are required to justify indirect discrimination.

The High Court has referred to the ECJ the question of whether the *Framework Directive* extends to national rules permitting employers to dismiss employees aged 65 or over by reason of retirement, and whether *regs 30* and *7* amount to national provisions laying down retirement ages. They have also referred questions regarding *reg 3* and the standard of objective justification required for direct discrimination.

A decision from the ECJ is not expected until 2009. However, the ECJ has recently considered the legality of mandatory retirement provisions under Spanish law in the case of *Felix Palacios de la Villa v Cortefiel Servicious SA C-411/05*. The ECJ (disagreeing with the opinion of the Advocate General on this point) rejected the argument that the *Framework Directive* did not apply to the provision in question, as it fell within the scope of *recital 14*. The ECJ concluded that:

> '... recital [14] merely states that the directive does not affect the competence of the Member States to determine retirement age and does not in any way preclude the application of that directive to national measures governing the conditions for termination of employment contracts where the retirement age, thus established, has been reached.'

It therefore appears that the first of the Government's arguments referred to above will fail and the legality of the default retirement age will depend on the High Court's assessment of whether the provisions are objectively justified, within the scope of *Article 6(1)* in the light of the ECJ's guidance on the interpretation of *Article 6(1)*.

The decision of the ECJ in *Palacios* also considered whether the mandatory retirement provisions in Spanish law were objectively justified, within the meaning of *Article 6(1)* and concluded that they were. The ECJ identified the aim of the Spanish provision as regulating the national labour market and in particular, checking unemployment. It concluded that this was a legitimate aim as employment policy is specifically listed as a legitimate aim in *Article 6(1)*. It also concluded that it was not unreasonable for the Spanish authorities to take the view that the measure in question was appropriate and necessary to achieve its aim. The ECJ emphasised that Member States enjoy a broad discretion in deciding to pursue a particular aim in the field of social and employment policy and in deciding the measures capable of achieving it. However, whilst this measure of discretion is helpful to the UK Government's argument on justification, the court did base its decision on a consideration of particular features of the Spanish provisions. Therefore the fact that the Spanish mandatory retirement provisions were justified does not mean that the UK default retirement age will be justified. This will depend on a consideration of the Government's justification by the High Court, which might of itself be subject to appeal to the Court of Appeal and House of Lords.

If the default retirement age is ultimately found to be contrary to the *Framework Directive* then employees who are retired in accordance with the retirement procedure could have claims for age discrimination, even if they are retired before the decision in *Heyday* and/or any consequent changes to *AR 2006*. If the relevant provisions of *AR 2006* are found to be ultra vires then, arguably at least, they will have been void from the outset so that employers will not be able to rely on the relevant provisions to provide a defence to a claim of age discrimination. This would mean that employees of private sector employers would be able to succeed in claims, irrespective of whether the *Framework Directive* or a general principle prohibiting age discrimination can have horizontal direct effect (as was found by the ECJ in *Mangold*).

Until the *Heyday* challenge is decided, employees who are retired and wish to bring a claim should not delay in presenting their claims. The EAT in the case of *Johns v Solent SD* UKEAT/0499/07/MAA concluded that a claim against a private employer arising out of compulsory retirement in accordance with the default retirement age should be stayed pending the decision of the ECJ in *Heyday*, overturning the decision of the employment tribunal to strike the claim out. That case has now been appealed to the Court of Appeal but in the meantime, the President of the Employment Tribunals in England and Wales has ordered that all claims regarding *reg 30* should be stayed. The order will be reviewed following the decision of the Court of Appeal in *Johns*.

A challenge has also been made to the law as it existed before *AR 2006*. In *Lloyd Briden v Worthing College* UKEAT/0065/07/RN an employee who was dismissed above the age of 65 before 1 October 2006 attempted to argue, on the basis of *Mangold*, that *ERA 1996, s 109* (which imposed the maximum age for claiming unfair dismissal) should be set aside as being inconsistent with the *Framework Directive* and general principles of EU law. The EAT refused to do so, distinguishing *Mangold* on the basis in that case the national law in question had been introduced during the transposition period for the directive, whereas *s 109* pre-dated the Directive.

2.42　*Meaning of 'retirement'*

The terms 'retirement' or 'retire' are used in several places in *AR 2006*, but are not defined. For the purposes of *reg 30*, unfair dismissal and determining whether the statutory dismissal procedure applies to a dismissal, *ERA 1996, ss 98A–98F* apply to determine whether the reason for dismissal was retirement. These sections are unusual in that they focus on the procedure followed in relation to a dismissal, rather than the motivation of the employer. However, in other parts of *AR 2006* it is necessary to determine the meaning of 'retirement' without reference to *ERA 1996, ss 98ZA–98ZF*, for example, the duty to notify under *Sch 6, para 2*, the definition of 'normal retirement age' in *ERA 1996, s 98ZH* and in applying *ERA 1996, ss 98A–98F*, where retirement is not conclusively deemed to be the reason for a dismissal.

It is likely that the tribunals will approach the question in the light of the Government's justification for introducing the default retirement age provisions, particularly since the provisions may be contrary to the *Framework Directive* if they go further than is necessary to achieve those objectives. The primary justification put forward is that permitting a default retirement age allows workforce planning, ie it allows employers to set a target age against which an employers can plan their work and employees can plan their careers and retirement (see *Notes on Regulations*). This, together with the fact that there is a defence to a claim for age discrimination suggests that 'retirement' means termination of employment on grounds of an employee's (old) age. In ordinary usage 'retirement' is often associated with stopping work altogether and/or drawing a pension, but there seems no reason for these elements to be relevant to retirement for the purposes of *AR 2006*.

The term 'retirement' is also used in the *Framework Directive* (eg in *recital 14* and *Article 6(1)(c)*), but again is not defined.

The meaning of retirement in other contexts (eg pension and benefit schemes) will not necessarily be the same as under *AR 2006*. In drafting benefit schemes employers would be well advised to specifically define 'retirement' to avoid uncertainty.

2.43 Retirement procedure: the duty to notify and the right to request not to retire

Reg 47 and *Sch 6* set out a detailed retirement procedure which must be followed where an employer intends to retire an employee. There is no definition of 'retire' for these purposes in *AR 2006*, but the most natural interpretation appears to be that the procedure applies where an employer intends to dismiss an employee on grounds of his (old) age. The procedures only apply to employees as narrowly defined in *reg* 30. Therefore the procedures do not apply to, eg, partners, non-executive directors or independent contractors.

There are two aspects to the procedure. Firstly, there is a duty on the employer to notify the employee of an intended retirement. Secondly, there is a right on the part of the employee to request not to retire and the employer has a duty to consider any such request in line with a procedure involving meeting with the employee and giving a right to appeal, where a request is not agreed to. The procedures, and the consequences of failure to comply with them, are very complex. Details of the procedures are set out below, along with the consequences of not following the procedure. The consequences of even a minor failure to comply can be quite severe and employers who wish to rely on the retirement procedure to force employees to retire would be well advised to diarise key dates and have standard documentation to ensure that they comply with the procedure. The ACAS guidance includes draft documentation which employers and employees can use in following the procedures. For a discussion of the effect of following the procedure see above at 2.39.

2.44 *Definitions*

There are two terms which are defined in *AR 2006* which are key to understanding the operation of the retirement procedures.

'Intended date of retirement' is, broadly speaking, the date on which an employer intends to retire an employee, established in accordance with *Sch 6, para 1(2)*. It is used in determining whether an employee has the right to request not to retire (*Sch 6, para 5*; see below). Generally, an employee has the right to make such a request once in relation to each intended date of retirement. It is also used in determining whether retirement is the reason for dismissal under *ERA 1996, ss 98ZA–98ZF*; dismissal before the intended date of retirement will not be by reason of retirement. It is defined in *Sch 6, para 1(2)*:

- Where an employer complies with the duty to notify (whether under *Sch 6, para 2* or *para 4*; (see below)), before the employee has made a valid request not to retire, the date specified in the employer's notification is the intended date of retirement.

- Where an employer has failed to notify in accordance with *Sch 6, para 2* and before the employer notifies in accordance with *Sch 6, para 4*, the employee, having reasonable grounds for believing that the employer intends to retire him on a certain date, makes a request not to retire which specifies that date, the date so specified will be the intended date of retirement.

- Where following notification by an employer or a valid request not to retire, the employer and employee agree an earlier retirement date than that notified, or the employer extends employment by six months or less, in accordance with the right to request procedure, the new termination date replaces the original intended date of retirement (*Sch 6, para 2(d)*). In those circumstances any dismissal can still be fair without the need to repeat the retirement procedure.

- Finally, where employment is extended because the employer has not responded to a request not to retire by the termination date (see below) the new date of termination is the intended retirement date (*Sch 6, para 2(e)*).

'Operative date of termination' is the date on which termination of employment by an employer takes effect, save where employment is automatically extended in accordance with *Sch 6, para 10* (see below). It is used in determining whether retirement is the reason for dismissal under *ERA 1996, ss 98ZA–98ZF*. Retirement will not be the reason for dismissal where the operative date of termination is before the normal retirement age or, where there is no normal retirement age, age 65.

Duty to notify

An employer who intends to retire an employee has a duty to notify the employee in writing of:

- the date on which he intends the employee to retire; and

- the employee's right to request not to retire.

This notification must be given not more than one year but not less than six months before the date on which he intends the employee to retire (*Sch 6, para 2*). This duty to notify applies irrespective of any provisions in an employee's contract or any handbook or policy which set out when an employee can expect to retire.

The duty to notify generally arises on each occasion when an employer intends to retire an employee, so that if an employee's request not to retire is granted, a new notification will have to be given if the employer subsequently wants to retire the employee at a later date. However, there is an exception to the duty to notify where the employer has complied with duty to notify in relation to a particular intended retirement date or the employee has made a valid request not to retire, before the duty to notify was complied with and, in accordance with the right to request procedure, the employer either (i) agrees to a retirement date which is earlier than the original intended retirement date; or (ii) agrees or notifies a new retirement date which is within six months after the original date. In those circumstances, no further duty to notify arises in relation to the revised intended retirement date.

If the employer fails to notify between 12 and six months before the intended date of retirement, the duty to notify continues until the fourteenth day before the 'operative date of termination' (*Sch 6, para 4*).

Right to request not to retire

An employee has a right to request not to retire on the intended date of retirement. This right arises even if the employer does not comply with its duty to notify, although it appears that an employee can only make a request if he has reasonable grounds for believing that the employer intends to retire him on a certain date. This is because, although it is not expressly stated, it appears that the right to request only arises where there is an intended date of retirement (see *Sch 6, paras 5(1)* and *(4)*). Where an employer has not complied with its duty to notify, there will only be an intended date of retirement if the employee has requested retirement having reasonable grounds for believing that the employer intends to retire him on a particular date (see *Sch 6, para 2(c)*). This might arise where an employee's contract automatically expires at age 65 or where an employee's employment has been extended for a fixed term after the normal retirement age.

There are a number of formal requirements for a request to be valid:

- it must be in writing;

- it must state that it is made under *Sch 6, para 5*;

- it must propose that the employee's employment should continue, following the intended date of retirement, either (i) indefinitely, (ii) for a stated period, or (iii) until a stated date.

- if the request is made before the employer has complied with its duty to notify, it must identify the date on which the employee believes the employer intends to retire him.

If the employer has complied with its primary obligation to notify an employee of the right to request between six and 12 months (inclusive) before the intended date of retirement, the request must be made more than three months, but not more than six months, before the intended date of retirement. If the employer has not complied with that duty, the request can be made at any time up to the intended retirement date.

Only one request can be made in relation to any one intended date of retirement.

However, there is no new right to request where the employer has complied with the duty to notify in relation to a particular intended retirement date or the employee has made a valid request not to retire, before the duty to notify was complied with and, in accordance with the right to request procedure, the employer either (i) agrees to a retirement date which is earlier than the original intended retirement date; or (ii) agrees to or notifies a new retirement date which is within six months after the original date.

The employee's right is to request extended employment on the same terms and conditions, although there is nothing to prevent the parties agreeing different terms for ongoing employment.

Duty to consider

If a valid request is made, an employer is under a duty to consider the request in accordance with the procedure laid down in *Sch 6, paras 7–9* (see *Sch 6, para 6*). Although there is a duty to consider a request, *AR 2006* do not set out any circumstances in which a request must be accepted. Nor is there a duty on employers to give reasons for refusing a request. The original draft of *AR 2006* provided that a request had to be considered in 'good faith'. These words were dropped from the final version of *AR 2006*. However, it seems likely that tribunals will nevertheless find that it is implied that the duty to consider must be exercised in good faith. It is also implicit in *Sch 6, para 7(5)* that any representations which the employee makes in support of a request must be considered. However, it is not entirely clear what this will require and the duty is still likely to be a low one. An employer who, despite holding the relevant meetings, never gave any consideration to an employee's request on the basis that it operated a policy of never allowing employees to work beyond their normal retirement age would appear to have failed to comply with the duty (making the dismissal of the employee unfair under *ERA 1996, s 98ZG* (see below). However, there would appear to be nothing to prevent an employer from operating a policy of not allowing employees to work beyond normal retirement age provided it considers whether it should abandon or make an exception to that policy when it receives a request. Evidentially, the difference between the two situations will be difficult to prove.

Where an employer wishes to operate a default retirement age, in considering the approach it takes to requests to work beyond the normal retirement age, it should consider the effect which regularly accepting requests might have on its 'normal retirement age' (see 2.46). If it regularly allows employees to work beyond 65 but regularly requires them to retire at a later age (eg it allows them to remain on a one-year contract to age 66) then the later age could become a 'normal retirement age' making dismissals at age 65 unfair and unlawful age discrimination (unless objectively justified). Allowing employees to stay on to different ages, depending on their individual circumstances, or allowing them to stay on indefinitely should not have this effect, although it might mean that an employer did not have a 'normal retirement age'.

Although there is no duty to give reasons for refusing a request not to retire, ACAS guidance states that giving reasons may enable the employee to leave with dignity and respect and help an employer to maintain good working relationships with other employees, which it states would be in line with normal good practice recommended by ACAS. In considering whether to give reasons, or at least to document them, an employer should also consider that a retirement dismissal could give rise to a claim for discrimination on grounds other than age, or for a redundancy payment (see 2.49ff) as well as a claim for unfair dismissal on the basis of the failure to consider the request (as set out above). Therefore there may be circumstances in which an employer needs to be able to demonstrate the reason for its decision not agree to a request not to retire.

Meeting

Where a valid request is made, an employer must hold a meeting within a reasonable period after receiving it (*Sch 6, para 7(1)*). The employer and the employee must take all reasonable steps to attend the meeting (*Sch 6, para 7(2)*).

The duty to hold a meeting does not apply if:

- before the end of the period that is reasonable, the employer and employee agree that the employee's employment will continue either indefinitely or for an agreed period and the employer gives notice to the employee of that and (in the latter case) of the length of the agreed period or the date on which employment will end (*para 7(3)*); or

- it is not practicable to hold a meeting within a period that is reasonable and the employer considers the request and any representations made by the employee (*para 7(4)*).

The employer must give the employee notice of his decision as soon as is reasonably practical after the date of the meeting or, where it was not reasonably practicable to hold a meeting, his consideration of the request. This notice must:

- where the decision is that the employee's employment will continue indefinitely, state that fact;

- where the decision is that the employee's employment will continue for a further period (which may be shorter than the period requested), state that fact and specify the length of the period or the date on which it will end;

- where the decision is to refuse the request (and not allow any extension of employment), confirm that the employer wishes to retire the employee and the date on which the dismissal is to take effect;

- where the decision is to refuse the request (including where the decision is to allow employment to continue for a further period, which is shorter than requested by the employee) inform the employee of his right to appeal;

- be in writing and dated.

(See *Sch 6, para 7(7)–(8)*)

The notice does not need to state a reason (see 2.47).

If this notification has not been given by the date when the employee's employment would otherwise end, employment might be extended (see below).

Appeals

An employee is entitled to appeal against a refusal of a request or a decision to allow employment to continue for a further period which is shorter than requested by the employee. To do so the employee must give notice to the employer setting out the grounds of appeal. The notice must be given as soon as is reasonably practicable after the notice giving the employer's decision and must be dated and in writing (*para 8(1)*).

If a notice of appeal is given, the employer must hold a meeting with the employee to discuss an appeal within a reasonable period after the date of the notice of appeal. The employer and employee must take all reasonable steps to attend the meeting. The same exceptions to the duty to hold a meeting apply as in the case of the initial meeting (*para 8(5)–(6)*; and see above).

The employer must give the employee notice of his decision on the appeal as soon as is reasonably practicable after the appeal meeting or, where it was not reasonably practicable to hold a meeting, his consideration of the request. The notice must again be in writing and be dated and must contain the same information as the decision following the initial meeting (see above) except that there is no right to appeal (*para 8(9)–(10)*).

Consequences of failure to comply

If an employer complies with the duty to notify and the right to request procedure in relation to an employee who is above a normal retirement age (which, if it is less than 65 is objectively justified) or, where there is no normal retirement age, is above age 65, then the dismissal will be by reason of retirement. In those circumstances, the dismissal will be fair and it will not give rise to a claim for age discrimination.

If the employer does not comply with the retirement procedure, then the consequences depend on which duty the employer has failed to comply with.

If an employer does not comply with the duty to notify six to 12 months before the intended date of retirement, then the following consequences apply:

- The employee may present a complaint to an employment tribunal and the tribunal will award compensation of such amount as it considers just and equitable, not exceeding eight weeks' pay (subject to the statutory cap on a weeks' pay under *ERA 1996, s 227*). The complaint must be presented before the end of the period of three months beginning with the last day permitted to the employer for complying with the duty to notify under *para 2* (ie six months before the intended date of retirement) or, if the employee did not then know the intended date of retirement, the first day on which he knew or would have known that date. A tribunal can extend this time limit by such period as it considers reasonable where it is satisfied that it was not reasonably practicable for the complaint to be presented before the end of that period (see *Sch 6, para 11*).

• The dismissal will not be automatically deemed to be by reason of retirement under *ERA 1996, ss 98ZA–98ZF*. Whether it will be by reason of retirement will depend, in part, on whether the employer complies with the duty to notify at all and, if so, how long before the intended date of retirement (see *s 98ZF*). If retirement is not the reason for dismissal then the dismissal might be unfair and amount to unlawful age discrimination. In addition, if retirement is not the reason for dismissal, the statutory dismissal procedures will apply to the dismissal, and if the employer has not complied with that procedure then the dismissal will be automatically unfair and any compensation awarded in respect of the dismissal (whether for unfair dismissal or discrimination) can be uplifted by 10% to 50% (see below).

• If the reason for dismissal is retirement and the employer has failed to comply with its duty under *para 4* (ie to notify prior to the fourteenth day before the operative date of termination) then the dismissal will be auto-matically unfair.

• The employee has additional rights under the right to request procedure. In particular, he may submit a request not to be retired at any point up to the intended date of retirement (otherwise it has to be submitted more than three months before). If the request is submitted before the employer complies with its duty to notify and the employee has reasonable grounds to believe that the employer intends to retire him on a particular date, the employee can define the intended date of retirement. It would then be difficult for the employer to 'retire' the employee before that date.

If the employer does not comply with the duty to notify before the 14th day before the operative date of termination, in accordance with *Sch 6, para 4* then:

• retirement is unlikely to be found to be the reason for dismissal under *ERA 1996, s 98ZF* (see above);

• if retirement is found to be the reason for dismissal, the dismissal will be automatically unfair, under *ERA 1996, s 98ZG* (see above).

If the employer does not comply with any part of the duty to consider procedure then there is no direct claim which an employee can present, but there may be an impact on the reason for the dismissal and its fairness. In particular:

• If an employer has not complied with its duty to notify six to 12 months prior to the intended retirement date, then whether the employer has followed the procedures in *Sch 6, para 7* (holding a meeting to consider a request not to retire and giving a decision) will be taken into account in determining whether the reason for dismissal is retirement (see above).

- If the reason for dismissal is retirement, then the dismissal will be auto-matically unfair if an employer has not complied with *Sch 6, paras 6–8*. This includes the duty to 'consider' a request as well as the procedural requirements in relation to the initial meeting and decision and the appeal. Therefore even a small technical breach (e g not dating a notification) would appear to make the dismissal unfair.

Early indications from employment tribunals suggest that they will take a very technical approach to the question of whether the parties have followed the retirement procedure (see e g *Gabri v Sun Hydraulics Limited* ET11301796/2007 and *Holmes v Active Sensors Limited* ET3100214/2007).

Correcting a failure to comply

Where an employer realises that it has failed to comply with the duty to notify within the period six to 12 months before it intends to retire an employee then, given the consequences of failure to comply, it might consider putting back the date on which it intends to retire the employee so as to allow it to give six months' notice, as required by *para 2*. If it does so, it can benefit from the conclusive presumption that retirement is the reason for dismissal, avoiding the adverse consequences referred to above. This will be the case even if the new termination date falls after the employer's normal retirement age.

If notice of dismissal has already been given to an employee, or if an employee's employment terminates automatically (under the terms of the contract) when he reaches normal retirement age, then the employee's consent would be required to continue employment. However, where the employee wants to remain in employ-ment this is likely to be forthcoming. Where the employee does not agree to extend employment then, even if a dismissal is technically unfair, the fact that the employee has chosen not to have employment extended could help to reduce any compensation payable.

Where an employer has failed to comply with the duty to notify six to 12 months before termination, but does not wish to extend employment, then it appears that the more closely it complies with its duties, the more likely it is that retirement will be the reason for dismissal. If there is any doubt as to whether a dismissal will constitute a retirement, the employer should also consider complying with the statutory dismissal procedure, to avoid the risk of an uplift if the reason for dismissal is found not to be retirement. Where an employee makes a request not to retire, it should be possible to ensure that the retirement procedure also satisfies the statutory dismissal procedure without the need for any additional meetings.

Right to be accompanied

Employees have the right to be accompanied at both the initial meeting and the appeal meeting if they 'reasonably' request it (*Sch 6, para 9*). Where such a request is made the employer must permit the employee to be accompanied by a worker of his choice employed by the same employer. The chosen companion is permitted to confer with the employee during the meeting and to address the meeting, but not to answer questions on behalf of the employee. If the chosen companion will not be available at the time proposed for the meeting and the employee proposes an alternative time for the meeting which is within seven days after the original time and is convenient for all parties, the employer must postpone the meeting to that time (*para 9(3)*).

Note that, unlike the right to be accompanied at a disciplinary or grievance hearing under *ERA1999, s 10*, there is no right to be accompanied by a trade union representative unless he is also a worker employed by the same employer.

An employee may present a complaint to an employment tribunal that his employer has failed or threatened to fail to comply with his obligation to allow him to be accompanied, or to postpone a meeting so that he can be accompanied. A complaint must be presented before the end of the period of three months beginning with the date of the failure or threat, or within such further period as the tribunal considers reasonable in a case where it is satisfied that it was not reasonably practicable for the complaint to be presented before the end of that period of three months. Where a tribunal finds that the complaint is well founded it will order the employer to pay compensation of an amount not exceeding two weeks' pay, subject to the statutory cap in *ERA 1996, s 227(1)* (*Sch 6, para 12*).

Employees have the right not to be subjected to any detriment by their employer on the ground that they have exercised their right to be accompanied and any dismissal on that ground will be automatically unfair. Workers have the right not to be subjected to any detriment by their employer by reason of having accompanied or sought to accompany an employee and, where the worker is also an employee, any dismissal of an employee on that ground will be automatically unfair (*Sch 6, para 13*).

Dismissal before request considered

Where an employer has received a valid request not to retire in relation to a proposed dismissal and the employer has not given notice of its decision in relation to that request in accordance with *para 7(6)* (see above) before the day on which that dismissal would otherwise take effect, the employee's employment is automatically extended until the day after that notice is given (*Sch 6, para 10(1)–(2)*).

The new termination date then becomes the 'intended date of retirement'. It also becomes the 'operative date of termination' for all purposes except that it is disregarded for the purposes of *ERA 1996, ss 98ZA–98ZH* (*para 10(4)*), which determine whether the reason for dismissal is retirement for certain purposes (see 2.44). This means that, for the purposes of considering whether the operative date of retirement was before the normal retirement age or age 65 under *ss 98ZA–ZH* (which would mean that retirement was deemed not to be the reason for dismissal) the dismissal date originally proposed would be considered, rather than the extended date. Therefore an employer who had sought to dismiss an employee before the normal retirement age or age 65, but where the statutory extension had the effect that employment actually terminated after the normal retirement age or age 65, could not take advantage of that fact to argue that retirement was actually the reason for dismissal.

Relationship with statutory dismissal, disciplinary and grievance procedures

The statutory dismissal procedures set out in the *Employment Act 2002* (*Dispute Resolution*) *Regulations 2004* (*SI 2004/752*) (*'Dispute Regulations'*) do not apply to a dismissal where the reason for dismissal is retirement, determined in accordance with *ERA 1996, ss 98ZA–98ZF* (see *Dispute Regulations, reg 4(1)(h)*). However, if the reason for dismissal is ultimately found not to be 'retirement' and the employer has not complied with the statutory procedures in relation to the dismissal, then the dismissal will be unfair (*ERA 1996, s 98A*) and any compensation awarded in relation to the dismissal (eg for unfair dismissal or discrimination) would be uplifted by 10% to 50% in accordance with *EA 2002, s 31*.

The statutory grievance procedure does not apply to claims for failure to notify or refusal of the right to be accompanied under *Sch 6, para 10* or *11*, as they are not listed in the *EA 2002, Sch 3* or *4* (see *Dispute Regulations, reg 6(1)*).

2.45   Transitional provisions

Transitional provisions were included dealing with retirement of employees between 1 October 2006 and 1 April 2007. These are set out in *AR 2006, Sch 7* and summarised in the ACAS guide but are not considered further.

Unfair dismissal

AR 2006 repealed the maximum age for bringing an unfair dismissal claim which was contained in *ERA 1996, s 109*, but introduced 'retirement' as a new, potentially fair reason for dismissal, as one of the provisions to introduce a default retirement age (see 2.38). *AR 2006* also inserted new provisions into the *ERA 1996* to determine whether the reason for a dismissal is retirement for these purposes and a new test of fairness which applies only to retirement dismissals (*ss 98ZA–98ZF*). These are set out below, after a consideration of the meaning of 'normal retirement age' in *AR 2006*.

2.46   *Normal retirement age*

The concept of the normal retirement age is key to understanding the provisions of the *ERA 1996* relating to retirement dismissals. 'Normal retirement age' is defined as 'the age at which employees in the employer's undertaking who hold, or have held, the same kind of position as the employee are normally required to retire' (*ERA 1996, s 98ZH*). There is no definition of 'retire' here but the most natural interpretation appears to be termination of employment on grounds of (old) age.

Prior to its repeal, *ERA 1996, s 109* provided that employees could not bring a claim for unfair dismissal if they were above the 'normal retiring age for an employee holding the position of the employee' at the effective date of termination. Although the wording is slightly different, and there was no statutory definition of normal retiring age, it is likely that the case law on the meaning of 'normal retiring age' will be followed in interpreting 'normal retirement age'.

The leading case on the meaning of normal retiring age is *Waite v Government Communications Headquarters* [1983] 2 AC 714, where the House of Lords held that the normal retiring age is the age at which employees in a particular position can reasonably expect to be compelled to retire, unless there is some special reason in a particular case for a different age to apply. The House of Lords held that, where there is a contractual retiring age applicable to all or nearly all the employees holding a particular position, there is a presumption that the contractual retiring age is the normal retiring age. However, that presumption could be rebutted by evidence that there is in practice some higher age at which employees holding the position are regularly retired, and which they have reasonably come to regard as their normal retiring age. The correct approach to what is 'normal' was not merely statistical – the tribunal should ascertain what would be the reasonable expectation or understanding of the employees holding that position at the time of their dismissal. There is conflicting case law on whether a normal retiring age could be lower than the contractual retiring age (compare *Royal and Sun Alliance Group plc v Payne* [2005] IRLR 848 and *Cross v British Airways plc* [2006] EWCA Civ 549).

2.47 *Reason for dismissal*

For the purposes of unfair dismissal (*ERA 1996, s 98(3A)*), the application of the exemption from age discrimination for retirement dismissals (*reg 30*) and the application of the statutory dismissal procedures (*Dispute Regulations, reg 4(1)(h)*) the question whether the reason for dismissal was retirement is to be determined in accordance with *ERA 1996, ss 98ZA–98ZF.*

The provisions are unusual in that, unlike the general approach in unfair dismissal claims, the focus is not on what motivates the employer to dismiss, but on the procedure. Depending on the age of the employee, the existence of a normal retirement age, the date of termination and the extent to which the retirement procedure has been complied with (see below) , there will be one of four conclusions:

(a) **Retirement will be deemed to be the only reason for dismissal and any other reason shall be disregarded.** The test for whether the presumption applies appears to be purely procedural (see below) and so in these circumstances, on the face of it, there is no scope for considering the employer's actual motive. The fact that an employer actually followed the retirement procedure because of the employee's performance or a redundancy procedure is irrelevant. However, in the *Coming of Age* consultation paper the Government stated clearly that if an employer used the retirement procedure and the employee felt that the 'retirement' was for other reasons (e g redundancy or competency) then the employee could challenge the dismissal as unfair. It could be argued though, that an employer's motive should be taken into account in deciding whether retirement is the reason for dismissal. This is because retirement will only be deemed conclusively to be the reason for dismissal if the employer has notified the employee 'in accordance with' *Sch 6, para 2*. The duty to notify applies where an employer 'intends to retire' an employee. It could be argued, therefore, that an employer who does not 'intend to retire' an employee does not notify the employee in accordance with *para 2* so that the presumption of retirement does not arise. However, it is also clear from *Coming of Age* that the purpose of the retirement procedure was to provide employers with a high degree of certainty as to the reason for dismissal, provided they comply with the retirement procedure. If an employer had to establish that it intended to dismiss by reason of retirement, before being able to establish that retirement was deemed to be the reason for dismissal, this whole purpose would be undermined and the procedures would actually make it more difficult to prove that retirement was the reason for dismissal than if motive alone was considered.

(b) **Retirement will be deemed not to be the reason (or a reason) for dismissal.** In these circumstances, it would be open to the employer to try to prove another potentially fair reason for dismissal. In circumstances where the actual reason why the employee was dismissed is because he had reached the employer's retirement age, it is not clear whether the tribunal is required to ignore this reason (in which case there may be no reason for dismissal or a subsidiary reason might become the principal reason) or whether the tribunal must look at the employer's actual motivation (i e the employee reaching normal retirement age) and consider whether it falls into another potentially fair reason (e g some other substantial reason). The former interpretation appears more likely (and is consistent with the position where retirement is deemed to be the only reason for dismissal and other actual motivations are ignored). However, this would mean that the tribunal had to decide what 'retirement' meant in order to exclude that part of the employer's motivation.

(c) **The tribunal must determine the reason (or principal reason) for dismissal having particular regard to the matters set out in *ERA 1996, s 98ZF*.** These are:

- whether or not an employer has notified the employee in accordance with *Sch 6, para 4* (ie complied with the duty to notify more than 14 days before the operative date of termination);

- if so, how long before the notified retirement date the notification was given; and

- whether or not the employer has followed, or sought to follow, the procedures in *Sch 6, para 7* (ie the duty, which arises where an employee has requested not to retire, to hold a meeting (where reasonably practicable) and notify the employee of a decision in relation to his request).

Presumably, the more closely an employer has complied with the retirement procedure, the more likely it is that retirement will be found to be the reason for dismissal. However, *s 98ZF* does not preclude other factors from being taken into account and, indeed, the reference to determining whether retirement is the 'principal' reason suggests that other reasons which motivated the dismissal should be taken into account. However it is not clear how a tribunal should balance the procedural requirements (to which it must have particular regard) with the employer's motive (which may suggest other 'reasons' for the dismissal) or other matters such as the employer's reasons for not following the procedure. For example, will a tribunal disregard clear evidence that an employer's decision to dismiss was based on a redundancy situation or performance concerns, where the employer has complied with the duty to notify almost six months prior to the intended date of retirement and complied with *Sch 6, para 7*? Conversely, if an employer has clearly dismissed the employee because of the employee having reached retirement age but has taken no steps to comply with the procedure, will the tribunal ignore the employer's motive and find that retirement was not the reason for dismissal? A finding that retirement was the reason for dismissal in these circumstances would give the employer a defence against an age discrimination claim (*reg 30*) but mean that the dismissal was unfair, applying the test of fairness set out below. It seems likely that a tribunal will take all the circumstances into account, giving particular weight to the degree of compliance with the retirement procedure as evidence that retirement is the reason for dismissal, but not treating this as conclusive in the face of clear evidence to the contrary.

(d) **The tribunal must determine the reason (or principal reason) for dismissal and may have regard to the matters set out in *ERA 1996, s 98ZF*, but need not.** This category is not expressly identified in *ss 98ZA–98ZF*, but is referred to in the *Notes on Regulations*. In these circumstances it appears that a tribunal could have regard to any circumstances which appeared to be relevant, in determining the principal reason for dismissal and would not have to have particular regard (or any regard) to the factors set out in *s 98ZF*.

Which of the above conclusions applies in any particular situation is determined as follows:

No normal retirement age: dismissal before 65 OR Normal retirement age: dismissal before retirement age

Where there is no normal retirement age and the operative date of termination is before the employee is aged 65, the dismissal is not by reason of retirement. This is also the case where there is a normal retirement age and the operative date of termination is before the normal retirement age (even if the operative date of termination is after the employee reaches age 65).

No normal retirement age: dismissal at or after 65 OR Normal retirement age of 65 or above: dismissal at or after retirement age

Where there is no normal retirement age and the operative date of termination falls on or after the date when the employee reaches age 65, or the employee has a normal retirement which is 65 or higher, and the operative date of termination falls on or after the date when the employee reaches the normal retirement age:

- If the employer has notified the employee in accordance with *Sch 6, para 2* (ie complied with the duty to notify six to 12 months before the intended date of retirement) and the employment terminates on the intended date of retirement, retirement will be the (only) reason for dismissal.

- If the employer has notified the employee in accordance with *Sch 6, para 2* and the employment terminates *before* the intended date of retirement, retirement will not be the (or a) reason for dismissal.

- If the employer has not notified the employee in accordance with *Sch 6, para 2* and there is an intended date of retirement (because the employer has notified more than 14 days but less than six months before the operative date of termination in accordance with *Sch 6, para 4* or where the employee has made a valid request not to retire before the duty to notify has been complied with) and the employment terminates *before* the intended date of retirement, retirement will not be the (or a) reason for dismissal.

- In all other cases where the employer has not notified in accordance with *para 2* the tribunal must determine the reason (or principal reason) for dismissal in accordance with *s 98ZF*.

- If the employer notified in accordance with *Sch 6, para 2* but the dismissal takes effect after the intended date of retirement, the *Notes on Regulations* state that the tribunal may (but not must) take the factors referred to in *ERA 1996, s 98ZF* into account in determining the reason for dismissal.

Normal retirement age below 65: dismissal at or after retirement age

Where the employee has a normal retirement age which is below 65 and the operative date of termination falls on or after the date when the employee reaches normal retirement age:

- If the normal retirement age is unlawful under *AR 2006* (note that the exception in *reg 30* does not apply to retirements under the age of 65) then retirement is not the (or a) reason for dismissal. In these circumstances retirement can never be the reason for dismissal (even after an employee reaches age 65).

- If the normal retirement age is lawful (ie because it is objectively justified) then the position is the same as if the normal retirement age were 65 or above (see above).

2.48   *Fairness*

If the reason for dismissal is retirement, then the only factors which are relevant in deciding whether the dismissal is fair are whether the employer has complied with particular requirements of the retirement procedure (*ERA 1996, s 98ZG*). In particular the dismissal will be fair if the employer has complied with all of the following requirements, and unfair if it has not:

- the duty to notify of retirement under *Sch 6, para 4* (which only arises if an employer has not complied with the duty to notify six to 12 months prior to the intended date of retirement);

- the right to request procedure set out in *Sch 6, paras 6–8*, (including the duty to consider a request not to retire and any appeal against a decision on that request, and compliance with the procedural requirements in relation to the meeting and appeal).

The requirements of *paras 4* and *6–8* are set out in detail above (see 2.44ff). It appears that any failure to comply, no matter how trivial (eg not dating a notification), will render the dismissal unfair. However, the approach which the tribunal will take to compensation is not clear. At present, where a dismissal is only procedurally unfair, a tribunal will reduce any compensation for unfair dismissal to reflect the chances that a fair dismissal would have occurred had a fair procedure been followed. A retirement dismissal would always be fair if the employer complied with the procedural requirements of the duty to notify more than 14 days before the operative date of termination and followed the right to request procedure. Therefore, arguably, compensation should be limited to any additional time which the employee would have been employed whilst the employer complied with those procedures, unless the tribunal concludes that the employer has failed to comply with its duty to consider and that, had it done so, it would have allowed the employee to continue in employment. Given the apparently wide scope for an employer to reject a request not to retire, it should be relatively easy for an employer to show that it would not have agreed to allow an employee to remain in employment.

2.49   **Redundancy schemes**

(*a*) *Statutory redundancy pay*

The statutory redundancy payments scheme, originally introduced in 1965, has historically contained a number of age-related aspects. These included differentiating between three age bands (under 21, 21 to 40, and 41 and over) when calculating redundancy pay, discounting service below the age of 18, imposing an age limit of 65 on the entitlement to redundancy pay and tapering the value of the redundancy payment for employees aged 64. As part of the *Age Matters* consultation, the Government proposed a broad range of changes to the scheme, including the removal of the age band 'multipliers' and also the abolition of the upper and lower age limits on the entitlement to redundancy pay. The Government revised its position on the age band multipliers when publishing the final draft of *AR 2006* in March 2006, announcing that the retention of multipliers which favoured workers as they became older could be objectively justified under the EU's *Equal Treatment Framework Directive 2000/78/EC* on the basis that older workers were more likely to become long-term unemployed and also experience a substantial fall in earnings in any future employment (see the written statement to Parliament from Mr Gerry Sutcliffe, Parliamentary Under-Secretary of State for Trade and Industry dated 2 March 2006).

The changes to the statutory redundancy payment scheme introduced on 1 October 2006 were therefore limited to the removal of the lower and upper age limits on the entitlement to receive redundancy pay, and the elimination of the tapering of redundancy payments for employees aged between 64 and 65. Other potentially discriminatory aspects of the scheme such as calculating redundancy pay according to each employee's length of service, limiting the relevant period of service to 20 years and applying the age band multipliers have all been retained. An employer who makes redundancy payments to its employees in accordance with the statutory scheme set out in *ERA 1996, Part XI* will be exempt from claims of age discrimination by virtue of the statutory authority exception set out in *AR 2006, reg 27(1)* (see 2.17) and/or *reg 33* (see 2.24).

(b) Enhanced redundancy schemes

AR 2006, reg 33 provides a specific exemption for enhanced redundancy schemes which closely mirror the calculation used in the statutory redundancy scheme (see 2.24). However, many enhanced redundancy schemes operated by employers prior to the introduction of *AR 2006* did not fall within the parameters of this exception. To the extent that an employer has continued to operate an enhanced redundancy scheme which does not comply with the provisions of *AR 2006, reg 33*, it will need to objectively justify any elements of the scheme which discriminate against employees directly or indirectly on the grounds of age (for example, using length of service to calculate the amount of the payment, which tends to favour older employees).

A further point to note is that the exception for the provision of certain benefits based on length of service (as set out in *AR 2006, reg 32*; see 2.22) does not apply to redundancy payments as a consequence of *reg 32(7)*, which specifically excludes from the scope of this exception benefits awarded by virtue of an employee ceasing his employment.

(c) Redundancy criteria

AR 2006 do not contain specific provisions dealing with the criteria used by employers when selecting employees for redundancy. Clearly, any selection which is based on the ages of the employees will amount to direct discrimination and objective justification is likely to prove extremely difficult. The use of length of service in the form or 'last in first out' or 'LIFO' is likely to disadvantage younger employees with shorter periods of service and therefore constitute indirect discrimination, unless it can be objectively justified. Given the availability of other objective redundancy criteria, it is likely to be difficult for an employer to objectively justify the use of LIFO except, perhaps, as a tie breaker where two employees have identical scores. The *ACAS Guidance* comments that practices such as LIFO or the use of length of service in any selection criteria are likely to be age discriminatory.

2.50   **Notice periods**

The statutory minimum periods of notice required to terminate employment (as set out in *ERA 1996, s 86*) increase according to the employee's length of service. The calculation of notice based on length of service will potentially amount to indirect discrimination against younger employees who are likely to have shorter periods of service. However, the provision of statutory minimum notice falls within the general exception for acts done with statutory authority set out in *AR 2006, reg 27*, so any resulting discrimination is deemed lawful.

Of course, many employers provide for contractual notice periods which are more generous than the statutory minima. It is unclear whether contractual notice periods fall within the scope of the exception for certain service related benefits set out in *AR 2006, reg 32* (see 2.22) on the basis that the definition of 'benefits' for these purposes excludes benefits provided by virtue of an employee ceasing employment (*reg 32(7)*). The *Notes on the Regulations* do not address this issue, and the point is certainly arguable where the notice period for employees increases with length of service, particularly where the employer has an established practice of making a payment in lieu of notice. Until this issue is clarified through case law, an employer may need to consider whether it can objectively justify increasing the period of notice according to length of service, given the resulting adverse impact on the younger members of the workforce.

2.51   DISCRIMINATION FOLLOWING THE END OF EMPLOYMENT

As referred to in 2.13, *AR 2006, reg 24* sets out specific provisions dealing with relationships which have come to an end, including employment relationships. Accordingly, it is unlawful for an employer to subject a former employee to a detriment or harassment contrary to *AR 2006* where such discrimination or harassment arises out of and is closely connected to the relationship. For example, it would be unlawful to refuse to provide a reference, or to provide an unfavourable reference, to a former employee on the grounds of their age. These provisions extend to the circumstances where the employment relationship in question came to an end before *AR 2006* came into force on 1 October 2006.

2.52   VALIDITY OF DISCRIMINATORY TERMS

AR 2006, reg 43 and *Sch 5* contain various provisions relating to the validity of contracts (*Part 1*), collective agreements and rules of undertaking (*Part 2*). Under *Part 1* and further to *Sch 5, para 1(1)*, a contractual term will be rendered void where (i) the making of the contract is unlawful under *AR 2006* as a consequence of including the term; (ii) the term is included in furtherance of an act which is unlawful; or (iii) where the term provides for the doing of an act which is unlawful under *AR 2006*. However, if the term in question amounts to unlawful discrimination against or harassment of a party to the contract in question, then rather than being deemed to be void, it will be enforceable only on the part of the 'victim' of the discrimination. Pursuant to *Sch 5, para 3*, a county court or sheriff court has the power to remove or modify a provision rendered void or unenforceable under *Sch 5*. The fact that a contract was entered into before 1 October 2006 when *AR 2006* came into force is irrelevant for these purposes.

Sch 5, Part 2 contains broadly similar provisions relating to the terms of collective agreements (whether legally binding, or otherwise), employers' rules applicable to employees or prospective employees and rules imposed by trade organisations and qualifications bodies. Further to *Part 2, Sch 5, para 4(2)*, such terms and rules will be void where (i) the making of the collective agreement is, by reason of the inclusion of the term, unlawful under *AR 2006*; (ii) the term or rule is included or made in furtherance of an act which is unlawful under *AR 2006*; or (iii) the term or rule provides for the doing of an act which is unlawful under *AR 2006*. Again, it is irrelevant for these purposes whether the term was agreed, or the rule was made, before *AR 2006* came into force on 1 October 2006. The employment tribunal has the power to declare that a rule or term is void further to *Part 2,*

Sch 5, para 8(1) on the application of an employee or member within certain criteria set out in *Part 2, Sch 5, paras 5, 6 and 7. Para 9* contains provisions to prevent the avoidance of a rule or term from depriving the person discriminated against or any person more favourably treated by the term or rule of any rights conferred by or in respect of a contract made or modified in pursuance of or by reference to the term or rule in question. These provisions could impact age-related benefits or other terms which are incorporated into collective agreements, such as enhanced redundancy formulas or redundancy selection criteria.

2.53 ENFORCEMENT

Jurisdiction of employment tribunals

AR 2006, reg 36 provides for the jurisdiction of the employment tribunals to hear any complaint based on unlawful discrimination and harassment in the employment context.

Unless the claimant's complaint is that the respondent has dismissed, or is contemplating dismissing, him, it will be necessary for the claimant to raise a grievance under *EA 2002, Sch 4* before filing a claim before the employment tribunals.

Further details relating to the jurisdiction of the employment tribunals in discrimination claims can be found at 1.24.

2.54 Burden of proof

AR 2006, reg 37 sets out provisions relating to the burden of proof in cases which appear before the employment tribunals, which mirror the provisions found in other strands of discrimination legislation.

In summary terms, *reg 37* provides that once a complainant had proven facts from which a tribunal could conclude, in the absence of an adequate explanation from the respondent, that discrimination or harassment has taken place, the tribunal must uphold the complaint unless the respondent proves to the contrary.

Further details relating to the burden of proof in employment tribunal claims can be found at 1.83.

2.55 Questionnaires

AR 2006, reg 41 provides for a questionnaire procedure. As with other strands of discrimination legislation, the purpose of the questionnaire procedure is to enable the aggrieved person to obtain information which may assist with pursuing a claim under *AR 2006*. A sample questionnaire on the part of the person aggrieved is included at *Sch 3*, and a sample reply by the respondent is included at *Sch 4*.

Further details relating to the questionnaire procedure can be found at 1.126.

2.56 Remedies

AR 2006, reg 38 sets out the remedies open to an employment tribunal if it considers that a complaint under *AR 2006* is well founded. As with other discrimination legislation, these include a declaration based on its findings and an award of compensation as the tribunal determines is just and equitable (including compensation for loss of past and future earnings, and injury to feelings).

Further details relating to the remedies open to an employment tribunal can be found at 1.115.

The remedies related to a breach of the pensions provisions in *AR 2006, Sch 2* are dealt with separately in *Part 1, Sch 2, para 6*.

2.57 Time limits

The provisions relating to time limits for pursuing a claim before the employment tribunals mirror the provisions for other discrimination claims and are set out in *AR 2006, reg 42*. A complaint to a tribunal must be brought within a period of three months from the date that the act was committed, subject to the tribunal's discretion to hear a complaint which is out of time if it considers that it is just and equitable to do so. Specific provisions relating to continuing acts are set out in *reg 42(4)*. In cases where the statutory grievance procedures apply under *EA 2002, Sch 4*, and the employee submits a grievance within three months of the date on which the act occurred, the time limit for bringing a tribunal claim is extended to six months.

Further details relating to the time limits for pursuing tribunal claims can be found at 1.23.

3   Disability Discrimination

3.1   INTRODUCTION

Position before 2 December 1996

Prior to 2 December 1996, there was no specific anti-discrimination legislation which prohibited employment-related discrimination against disabled people.

Measures such as the *Disabled Persons (Employment) Acts ('DPEA') 1944* and *1958* established a system under which employers with more than 20 employees had to employ a quota of registered disabled people (usually at least three per cent of the employer's workforce) and reserved certain occupations for disabled workers. The quota system included criminal sanctions, but overall was not very effective because it was rarely enforced and it did not afford disabled people any individual rights.

The failure of the quota system to provide an effective means of protection meant that between 1979 and 1993 there were various attempts to introduce more comprehensive legislation aimed at preventing disability discrimination. This included a number of private members' bills, all of which failed.

3.2   Development of the Disability Discrimination Act 1995

The *Disability Discrimination Act 1995 ('DDA 1995')* was the result of a government initiative in response to a campaign both inside and outside Parliament for equality and greater protection for disabled people. A consultation document entitled 'Government Measures to Tackle Discrimination Against Disabled People' was issued in July 1994. This was followed by a White Paper, 'Ending Discrimination Against Disabled People', and a Disability Bill (published in January 1995) committing the Government to addressing, amongst other things, disability-related discrimination in employment. This Disability Bill became *DDA 1995*, receiving Royal Assent on 8 November 1995. *DDA 1995* repealed the *DPEA* and the quota system and in its place established a framework, supplemented by secondary legislation, for targeting discrimination faced by disabled persons in employment, access to goods, facilities and services, and the purchase or renting of property.

3.3   Position after 2 December 1996

The employment provisions of *DDA 1995, Part II* came into force on 2 December 1996 and have been significantly amended since then. The majority of these changes were made from 1 October 2004 by the *Disability Discrimination Act 1995 (Amendment) Regulations 2003 (SI 2003/1673) ('2003 Regulations')*, which implemented the changes needed to make *DDA 1995* consistent with the EC Equal Treatment Framework Directive 2000/78/EC (*'Framework Directive'*) (see COMMON CONCEPTS (1)). Additional changes were made in 2005 by the *Disability Discrimination Act 2005 ('DDA 2005')* to general concepts, such as the definition of disability.

3.4 Disability Discrimination

3.4 Disability Rights Commission

The Disability Rights Commission (DRC) was an independent statutory body set up to oversee the operation of *DDA 1995*, and to promote equality of opportunity for disabled people. The DRC was established under the *Disability Rights Commission Act 1999* ('*DRCA 1999*'). Under *DRCA 1999, s 2(1)* the DRC had the following four general duties:

(a) to work towards the elimination of discrimination and harassment of disabled persons;

(b) to promote the equalisation of opportunities for disabled persons;

(c) to take such steps as it considered appropriate with a view to encouraging good practice in the treatment of disabled persons;

(d) to keep the working of *DDA 1995* and *DRCA 1999* under review.

Like the Equal Opportunities Commission (EOC) and the Commission for Racial Equality (CRE), the DRC had a number of specific powers, relating to areas including research, the provision of assistance to individual complainants and enforcement, enabling it to carry out its general duties.

3.5 Commission for Equality and Human Rights

From 1 October 2007, the EHRC (see FOREWORD) took over the work of the DRC, and the *DRCA 1999* was repealed in its entirety. The EHRC derives its powers from *Equality Act 2006* ('*EqA 2006*') (see FOREWORD). Insofar as the EHRC's duties in respect of equality and diversity groups relate to disability matters, these duties will be delegated to a disability decision-making committee (*EqA 2006, Sch 1, Part 5*). The disability committee will be empowered, among other things, to monitor the law, give information and advice, offer legal assistance and conciliation and institute judicial reviews. These duties will be delegated to the disability committee for at least five years, at the end of which period the EHRC will review its activities and will recommend to the Secretary of State how long the committee should continue in existence.

3.6 Code of Practice

In carrying out its duties under the *EqA 2006*, the EHRC will have a range of general and enforcement powers (see FOREWORD). These powers will include the power to issue statutory Codes of Practice. In relation to disability discrimination in the employment context, the EHRC inherits the current DRC Code of Practice: Employment and Occupation (2004) ('*Code*'). The *Code*, which was first published in 1996, was updated in 2004 to take account of the changes to *DDA 1995* made by the *2003 Regulations*, as well as case law developments. All references to the *Code* in this chapter are to the 2004 version. The *Code* sets out practical guidance on how to prevent discrimination against disabled people in employment or when seeking employment. It also contains guidance on the law, which is designed to help employers, tribunals and others understand and apply the provisions of *DDA 1995* (see further *EqA 2006, ss 14* and *15*).

The substantive part of the *Code* is divided into the following sections:

(a) Section 2 contains general guidance on how disability discrimination can be avoided;

(b) Section 3 provides a general overview of the main provisions of *DDA 1995* in relation to employment (and occupation);

(c)   Section 4 explains how *DDA 1995* defines discrimination and harassment;

(d)   Section 5 explains how the duty to make reasonable adjustments operates in practice;

(e)   Section 6 explains when disability related discrimination can be justified;

(f)   Section 7 explains how employers can avoid discrimination during recruitment;

(g)   Section 8 explains how employers can avoid discrimination during employment;

(h)   Section 9 explains the provisions of *DDA 1995* which apply to certain occupations, including contract workers;

(i)   Section 10 explains the particular provisions of *DDA 1995* which apply in relation to occupational pension schemes and group insurance services;

(j)   Section 11 explains how discrimination can be avoided in the provision of employment services;

(k)   Section 12 explains how the duty to make reasonable adjustments applies in relation to making alterations to premises; and

(l)   Section 13 explains how other particular provisions of *DDA 1995* are relevant to understanding how the legislation works, how it interacts with other legislation, and focuses in particular on ways to resolve disputes.

The *Code* is a key aid to interpretation of *DDA 1995* for employers and their advisors. A failure to comply with the *Code* does not of itself give rise to liability in civil or criminal proceedings, but its provisions may be used in evidence and must be taken into account by courts and tribunals if relevant to a question in proceedings (*DDA 1995, s 53A (8A*; see now *EqA 2006, s 15(4)*).

3.7   **SCOPE**

Comparison between DDA 1995 and other discrimination legislation

DDA 1995 shares some similarities with the *Sex Discrimination Act 1975* ('*SDA 1975*'), the *Race Relations Act 1976* ('*RRA 1976*') and the regulations prohibiting discrimination on the grounds of sexual orientation, religion or belief and age, such as the types of job applicants, employees and contract workers who are covered, and the circumstances in which employers can be liable for unlawful discrimination. (Generally, see COMMON CONCEPTS (1)). However, in other ways *DDA 1995* is a distinct piece of legislation.

Crucially, rather than providing protection to all from discrimination if it is on the ground of 'disability', *DDA 1995* is asymmetric in the way it operates. Unless the claim is one of victimisation (see 3.88), the employment and occupation provisions of *DDA 1995, Part II* only protect those who have, or have had, a disability which meets the definition in *DDA 1995, s 1(1)* and does not prohibit discrimination against non-disabled people. It follows that, in general, more favourable treatment of disabled people is not prohibited by *DDA 1995* (although such treatment is not *required* except in the case of the duty to make reasonable adjustments). (Note, however, that other legal requirements may impact upon a decision to treat a disabled applicant or employee more favourably than a non-disabled comparator: see for example the *Local Government and Housing Act 1989, s 7*, which requires all appointments of local authority staff to be made 'on merit'.)

3.8 Disability Discrimination

DDA 1995 also differs significantly from the other discrimination strands in its definition of discrimination. In its original form, *DDA 1995* provided for two kinds of discrimination (less favourable treatment and failure to make reasonable adjustments), as well as victimisation, but did not explicitly contain prohibitions of either direct or indirect discrimination as defined in the other strands. From 1 October 2004, the *2003 Regulations* amended *DDA 1995* so that it now provides for the following kinds of unlawful discrimination in the employment field:

(a)   direct discrimination on grounds of disability (see 3.45);

(b)   disability-related discrimination – that is, less favourable treatment for a disability-related reason not amounting to direct discrimination (see 3.57);

(c)   breach of a duty to make reasonable adjustments in relation to a disabled person (see 3.69); and

(d)   victimisation (see 3.88).

The concepts of less favourable treatment, discrimination and the duty to make reasonable adjustments are unique to *DDA 1995*, but the changes made by the *2003 Regulations* mean that on the whole there is more consistency between *DDA 1995* and the other discrimination strands in other areas. However, even in its amended form, *DDA 1995* still does not expressly prohibit indirect disability discrimination (though most instances of indirect discrimination will be covered by the concepts of disability-related discrimination and the duty to make reasonable adjustments) or expressly provide protection against discrimination by association with a disabled person.

The scope of *DDA 1995* regarding associative discrimination was considered by the EAT in *Attridge Law and Another v Coleman* [2007] IRLR 88. The case involved a claim under *DDA 1995* brought by a carer of a disabled person. *Framework Directive 2000/78/EC* prohibits discrimination in employment and occupation 'on the grounds of' religion or belief, disability, age or sexual orientation'. See 1.31 for a discussion on discrimination by association or perception generally. *DDA 1995* only expressly protects a disabled person from the various forms of disability discrimination on the grounds of their own disability. Having decided that on a literal interpretation *DDA 1995* did not cover associative discrimination, the tribunal decided to make a reference to the ECJ for guidance as to the scope of protection under *Framework Directive* against this type of discrimination, and how *DDA 1995* should be interpreted in light of that. Following an appeal by the employer, the EAT upheld the decision to make this reference. The ECJ decision will have important implications for both carers, and individuals claiming that they have been discriminated against because they are *perceived* to be disabled when in fact they are not (for example, in the case of an employee dismissed because his employer mistakenly believes him to be HIV positive).

3.8 Protected categories

Even if a person meets the definition of a disabled person, in order to bring a claim of direct discrimination, disability-related discrimination or breach of a duty to make reasonable adjustments, they must also show that they fall into a category which is protected under *DDA 1995*. The protected categories under *DDA 1995, Part II*, were significantly extended by the *2003 Regulations* to cover both employment and certain occupations. The protected categories under *DDA 1995* are currently:

(a)   job applicants and employees (*ss 4–4A*);

(b)   contract workers (*s 4B*);

(c)   office-holders (*ss 4C–4F*);

(d)   members or prospective members of occupational pension schemes (*ss 4G–4K*);

(e)   partners or prospective partners in a partnership (*ss 6A–6C*);

(f)   barristers, advocates and pupils (*ss 7A–7D*);

(g)   members or applicants for membership of trade organisations (*ss 13–14*);

(h)   holders or applicants for professional or trade qualifications (*ss 14A–14B*);

(i)   those undertaking or seeking practical work experience against placement providers (*ss 14C–14D*);

(j)   members of locally electable authorities such as a county council (*ss 15A–15C*).

This chapter will only consider in detail the position of job applicants and employees under *DDA 1995, Part II*. (See 3.113 for a summary of the provisions which are applicable to other individuals and categories of activity. A full analysis of these provisions is, however, outside of the scope of this work.)

3.9   **Employment**

The prohibition on discrimination in employment is contained in *DDA 1995, s 4*. *DDA, s 68(1)* defines employment as 'employment under a contract of service or of apprenticeship or a contract personally to do any work'. This provision has the same meaning as under the other discrimination statutes (see COMMON CONCEPTS (1)) and 3.95ff for details of the scope of liability of employers and principals towards job applicants and employees before, during and after employment under *DDA 1995*).

3.10   **Exceptions and special cases**

DDA 1995, Part II applies to all private employers irrespective of their size. Prior to 1 October 2004, employers with fewer than 15 employees were exempt from *DDA 1995*. However, this exemption was repealed by the *2003 Regulations*. The *2003 Regulations* also extended the protection of *DDA 1995* to previously excluded Crown employments such as the police, fire fighters, and prison officers. For the most part, *DDA 1995, Part II* now applies to the Crown and to Crown employment in the same way as it applies to private employers. There are, however, still some specific circumstances where the employment and occupation provisions either do not apply (such as service or practical work experience in any of the armed forces (*DDA 1995, ss 14C(5)* and *64(7)*), or where the legislation makes special provision, for example in relation to contract workers (see 3.109) on exceptions and special cases).

3.11   **MEANING OF DISABILITY AND DISABLED PERSON**

General

DDA 1995 only prohibits discrimination against those persons who are, or have been, disabled within the meaning of the legislation (the only exception being for those claiming victimisation (see 3.88).

3.12   Disability Discrimination

It is not enough that a claimant is unwell or is disabled in a general sense. In order to claim protection under *DDA 1995*, claimants must have a disability within the meaning of *DDA 1995, s 1(1)* which provides:

> 'Subject to the provisions of Schedule 1, a person has a disability for the purposes of this Act if he has a physical or mental impairment which has a substantial and long-term adverse effect on his ability to carry out normal day-to-day activities.'

3.12   *Present and past disabilities*

DDA 1995, s 1(2) provides that a disabled person is a person who has a disability. It is, thus, clear that *DDA 1995* protects those who have a disability at the time of any alleged discrimination, but provision is also made protecting those who have had a disability within the meaning of *DDA 1995* in the past provided that that disability had a substantial adverse effect for at least 12 months (*s 2(1)* and *Sch 2, para 5(1)*).

3.13   *Definition of disability under Framework Directive 2000/78/EC*

The approach of the UK legislation that mere sickness is not a disability is consistent with the approach taken by the ECJ in relation to the meaning of the concept under *Framework Directive*. In *Chacón Navas v Eurest Collectividades SA* [2006] IRLR 706 the ECJ considered whether a person dismissed by their employer because of sickness was protected by the disability provisions of the *Framework Directive*. The ECJ held that such a person was not protected because for the purposes of the *Framework Directive*, the concept of disability refers to a limitation which results from physical, mental or psychological impairments, which hinders the participation of the person concerned in their professional life (which is somewhat different from *DDA 1995*, which focuses on the concept of 'normal day-to-day activities' rather than employment activities (see 3.23)), and which is likely to last for a long time.

3.14   *The medical model*

The definition in *DDA 1995, s 1(1)* uses what can be described as a medical model to define a disabled person as someone with a certain condition or certain limitations on their ability to carry out normal day-to-day activities. Whether a claimant meets this definition is a question of fact for a tribunal to assess (*Vicary v British Telecommunications Plc* [1999] IRLR 680; *Abadeh v British Telecommunications Plc* [2001] IRLR 23). In *Goodwin v The Patent Office* [1999] IRLR 4 the EAT stressed that because it is a piece of social legislation, tribunals should adopt a purposive approach to the language of *DDA 1995*. This will include the definition of disability, and means that in practice tribunals should interpret the language of the *Act* to give effect to the stated or presumed intention of Parliament behind the legislation (for example to facilitate the full participation of disabled people in employment and routes into employment) and construe the legislation to extend, rather than restrict, protection. Following the implementation of *Framework Directive*, tribunals are now also obliged (where appropriate) to construe *DDA 1995* purposively to give effect to European law.

In *Goodwin*, the EAT also said that the language used in *DDA 1995* should be given its 'ordinary and natural meaning'. Further, in *Ekpe v Metropolitan Police Comr* [2001] IRLR 605, the EAT said that whether a claimant is disabled within the meaning of the *DDA 1995* is a threshold provision, and that it should be viewed in that light (because meeting the definition does not mean that a claimant is automatically entitled to a remedy). However, despite this holding, and despite the requirement to take a purposive approach, in practice tribunals sometimes take a very technical approach to the definition of disability. This can make *DDA 1995* more difficult for claimants to use, because unless they can prove that they are disabled within the precise terms of *DDA 1995*, the tribunal will not go on to consider the actual allegations of discrimination. Failure to establish a disability is the single most common reason for claims under the *DDA 1995* to be dismissed.

3.15   *The social model*

The medical nature of the definition in *DDA 1995, s 1(1)* and the problem this sometimes poses for claimants, has led the DRC to recommend that the definition of disability should be changed so as to be based on what is known as a 'social model', based on the identification of disabling barriers (for example, in the workplace) and providing protection against discrimination on the grounds of 'impairment' (broadly defined), regardless of the level or type of impairment. This approach has not yet, however, found favour with the legislator.

3.16   *Meaning of disability in other legislation*

The definition in *DDA 1995, s 1(1)* is specific to the Act. This means that the fact that a person may satisfy the definition of disability in another statute or that they receive, or qualify for, a disability-related benefit does not automatically lead to the conclusion that they are disabled under *DDA 1995* (unless they were registered as disabled under DPEA (see below)). Equally, the fact that a person does not satisfy the definition of a disabled person under other legislation does not mean that they will not qualify for protection under *DDA 1995*. *DDA 1995, s 68* deals with these points expressly in connection with mental impairments and the *Mental Health Act 1983*: for discussion of the interaction between the two statutory regimes see *McDougall v Richmond Adult Community College* [2007] IRLR 771.

In *Hill v Clacton Family Trust Ltd* [2005] EWCA Civ 1456, [2005] All ER (D) 170 (Oct) the Court of Appeal held that the fact that a person was awarded disability living allowance by a Social Security Appeals Tribunal (SSAT) in relation to post-traumatic stress disorder was not definitive evidence that she was disabled for the purposes of *DDA 1995*. The Court of Appeal said there was no rule or principle of law that a tribunal is bound to follow SSAT decisions, and that it is for the tribunal to make up its own mind when deciding whether a person had suffered mental impairment for the purposes of *DDA 1995* (see also *McDougall*). However, if an employer is aware that a person is considered to be disabled for other purposes (e g that they qualify for a disability benefit), that employer may be put on notice that the person could be disabled under *DDA 1995* (*Department for Work and Pensions v Hall* UKEAT/0012/05/DA).

The only circumstance where qualifying as disabled under other legislation will be determinative is where a person was registered as disabled under *DPEA* at certain times. If a person's name appeared on the register of disabled persons under *DPEA* on both 12 January 1995 and 2 December 1996, they will be treated as disabled under *DDA 1995* for a three-year period starting on 2 December 1996, and therefore to have had a past disability during that period (*DDA 1995, Sch 1, para 7*).

3.17   *Burden of proof*

The onus has always been on claimants to prove that they meet the definition of a disabled person under *DDA 1995* (*Kapadia v London Borough of Lambeth* [2000]

IRLR 699), and to produce any necessary supporting expert evidence. The burden of proof provision in *DDA 1995, s 17(1)(c)* inserted by the *2003 Regulations* (see COMMON CONCEPTS (1)) has not changed this.

When considering whether a claimant is disabled within the meaning of *DDA 1995* in *Goodwin* (see 3.14), the EAT held that tribunals should consider the evidence by reference to the following conditions:

(a)   Does the claimant have an impairment which is either mental or physical?

(b)   Does the impairment have an effect on the claimant's ability to carry out normal day-to-day activities in one of the respects set out in *DDA 1995, Sch 1 para 4(1)*, and does it have an adverse effect?

(c)   Is the adverse effect (upon the claimant's ability) substantial?

(d)   Is the adverse effect (upon the claimant's ability) long-term?

3.18   The meaning of impairment

Guidance

DDA 1995 neither defines the term 'impairment' nor contains an exhaustive list of conditions qualifying as impairments. However, some assistance is given in the form of statutory 'Guidance on matters to be taken into account in determining questions relating to the definition of disability' (*'Guidance'*) which was issued after *DDA 1995* was introduced. Revised *Guidance* came into force on 1 May 2006, but the old *Guidance* continues to apply after 30 April 2006 in relation to any proceedings where it is alleged that a person unlawfully discriminated contrary to *DDA 1995* before 1 May 2006. All references below are to the 2006 *Guidance*.

The *Guidance* takes account of the changes made to *DDA 1995* and the developments in case law since it was first introduced. The *Guidance* does not directly impose any legal obligations, but tribunals are obliged, when determining whether a person is a disabled person within the meaning of the *Act*, to take into account any guidance appearing to be relevant (*DDA 1995, s 3(3)*). This is most likely to be in cases where whether a claimant has a disability is unclear. However, where the case is clear the *Guidance* must not be used as an additional hurdle over which claimants have to jump (*Goodwin*).

In *McNicol v Balfour Beatty Rail Maintenance Ltd* [2002] EWCA Civ 1074, [2002] ICR 1498 the Court of Appeal held that the term 'impairment' bears its 'ordinary and natural meaning' and said that when considering whether a claimant has a physical or mental impairment:

'The essential question in each case is whether, on sensible interpretation of the relevant evidence, including the expert medical evidence and reasonable inferences which can be made from all the evidence, the applicant can be fairly be described as having a physical or mental impairment.'

In answering this question in *Paterson v Commissioner of Police of the Metropolis* [2007] IRLR 763 the EAT said that tribunals must read *DDA 1995, s 1(1)* in a way which gives effect to the ECJ decision in *Chacón Navas* (see 3.13), that the concept of disability refers to a limitation which results from physical, mental or psychological impairments which hinders the participation of the person concerned in professional life.

The EAT has held that someone has a physical impairment if they have 'something wrong with them physically' (*College of Ripon & York St John v Hobbs*

[2002] IRLR 185). This is a low threshold test which applies equally to mental impairments. This means that the focus of the impairment limb of the definition is simply on whether the claimant has a condition that has a negative impact on them either physically or mentally. The severity of the impairment is dealt with by the requirement that it must have a substantial and long-term adverse effect. As a result, in many cases there will not be a dispute about whether a claimant has an impairment, but rather on whether it has the requisite effects on their ability to carry out normal day-to-day activities.

A disability can arise from a wide range of impairments, some of which may be visible and easy to identify, and others which may not be so immediately obvious. The *Guidance* (para A6) contains examples of some conditions which may qualify as impairments including:

(a)   sensory impairments, such as those affecting sight or hearing;

(b)   impairments with fluctuating or recurring effects such as rheumatoid arthritis, ME/chronic fatigue syndrome, depression and epilepsy;

(c)   progressive impairments, such a motor neurone disease, forms of dementia and muscular dystrophy;

(d)   organ specific impairments, including respiratory conditions such as asthma, thrombosis and heart disease;

(e)   developmental impairments, such as autistic spectrum disorders and dyslexia;

(f)   mental health conditions and mental illnesses, such as depression and schizophrenia;

(g)   impairments produced by injury to the body or brain.

3.19   *Deemed disabilities*

In addition to the provisions that apply to the registered disabled, a number of conditions are deemed to be disabilities under *DDA 1995, s 1(1)*. These are:

(a)   cancer, HIV and multiple sclerosis (*Sch 1, para 6A*);

(b)   blindness or partial sightedness (where the person is certified as such by an ophthalmologist, or registered as such by the local authority) (*Disability Discrimination (Blind and Partially Sighted Persons) Regulations 1996 (SI 2003/712)*);

(c)   severe disfigurements (save for those consisting of tattoos that have not been removed or body piercings used for decorative or other non-medical purposes (see 3.20)) (*Sch 1 para 3* and *Disability Discrimination (Meaning of Disability) Regulations (SI 1996/1455)* ('*Meaning Regulations*'), reg 5).

3.20   *Excluded conditions*

The *Meaning Regulations* also exclude certain conditions from *DDA 1995, s 1(1)* by deeming that they are not impairments. The excluded conditions are:

(a)   addiction to alcohol, nicotine or any other substance (unless as a result of administration of medically prescribed drugs or other medical treatment);

(b)   a tendency to set fires;

(c)   a tendency to steal;

(d)   a tendency to physical or sexual abuse of other persons;

(e)   exhibitionism;

(f)   voyeurism;

(g)   seasonal allergic rhinitis (e g hay fever), except where it aggravates the effect of another condition.

Additionally, certain disfigurements (tattoos which have not been removed and body piercings used for decorative or other non-medical purposes) are also excluded from the definition of an impairment because they are deemed not to have a substantial adverse effect on a person's ability to carry out normal day-to-day activities.

DDA 1995 is concerned with the effect of impairments rather than their cause (see 3.21), so a claimant can have a disability even if their impairment was caused by an excluded condition (see *Guidance,* para A8 and *Power v Panasonic UK Limited* [2003] IRLR 151). This means that the fact that a claimant has an excluded condition will not prevent them from being disabled under *DDA 1995* if they have another legitimate impairment that meets *DDA 1995* definition in the Act. For example, someone who has paranoid schizophrenia which manifests itself as a tendency to physical abuse of other persons might have a disability on the basis of their schizophrenia (*Murray v Newham Citizens Advice Bureau* [2003] IRLR 340) and someone whose depression has been caused by alcohol abuse might have a disability on the basis of their depression (*Power*).

In cases where a claimant has both a legitimate impairment and an excluded condition it may be difficult to ascertain whether any potentially unlawful discrimination was the result of the impairment or the excluded condition. In *Murray*, the EAT resolved this by finding that only 'free-standing' conditions were excluded under the *Meaning Regulations* and that the exclusion did not apply to conditions which are the consequences of a recognised disability. However, in *Edmund Nuttall Ltd v Butterfield* [2005] IRLR 751 a different division of the EAT said that it did not find this distinction helpful. In *Nuttall* the EAT said that the critical question is one of causation and, applying the same approach taken in other discrimination jurisdictions, held that the tribunal should ask itself whether the legitimate impairment was an 'effective cause' of the less favourable treatment (*O'Neill v (1) Governors of St Thomas More RCVA Upper School (2) Bedfordshire County Council* [1996] IRLR 372). A decision from the Court of Appeal is needed to resolve the tension between *Murray* and *Nuttall*.

Applying *Nuttall*, if the legitimate impairment is the effective cause of the less favourable treatment then, subject to any defences available under *DDA 1995*, unlawful discrimination will be made out even if the excluded condition also formed part of the employer's reason for the treatment. It is only if the effective cause for the less favourable treatment was the excluded condition that the claim will fail. In a case involving reasonable adjustments, this approach would mean that the employer would only be under an obligation to make adjustments to prevent a provision, criterion or practice or physical feature of premises from placing the claimant at a substantial disadvantage in so far as the disadvantage results from a legitimate impairment. These distinctions will often be difficult to draw, particularly where the legitimate impairment and the excluded condition are causally related. Pending a decision from the Court of Appeal on the point, in these circumstances a tribunal may have to consider whether the excluded condition is 'free-standing' as it did in *Murray*.

3.21   **Physical impairment**

Cause and effect

In some cases, it will be obvious whether a claimant has a physical impairment. However, difficulties can arise when a claimant has physical symptoms, but is unable to show that they are caused by an identifiable condition or disease. Similarly, some physical conditions may give rise to a mental impairment. In *Rugamer v Sony Music Entertainment UK Ltd; McNicol v Balfour Beatty Rail Maintenance Ltd* [2001] IRLR 644 both claimants claimed to have physical impairments, but there was no evidence that their pain had a physical cause. It was accepted that pain can have a psychological rather than a physical cause, but neither claimant had claimed to have a mental impairment. The EAT said that they were not disabled because the correct approach was to focus on the cause rather than the effect of an impairment and a mental condition which causes pain was not a physical impairment.

The EAT took a different approach on similar facts in *Hobbs* (see 3.18). There was evidence that the claimant's mobility problems were caused by symptoms including muscle cramps and twitching, but there was no proof that these problems were caused by a physical condition. Again, the claimant had not claimed that she had a mental impairment. The EAT nevertheless held that the claimant had a physical impairment because there was no need to distinguish between the cause of an impairment on one hand and the evidence of the effects of that impairment on the other. The Court of Appeal endorsed this approach on appeal in *McNicol* and held that it is not necessary to consider how an impairment has been caused (see Court of Appeal decision in *McNicol v Balfour Beatty Rail Maintenance Limited* [2002] IRLR 71; *Millar v Commissioners of Revenue & Customs* [2006] IRLR 112 and *Guidance*, para A8). All of these cases are good examples of the need for claimants to be clear about the nature of the impairment they are relying on (or if there is any doubt to plead that they have both a physical and a mental impairment).

3.22   **Mental impairment**

Historically, one of the most difficult aspects of *DDA 1995* was its application to mental impairments. Up until 5 December 2005, *DDA 1995, Sch 1 para 1(1)* provided that a mental impairment included an impairment resulting from or consisting of a mental illness only if the illness is a 'clinically well-recognised illness'. The *Guidance* in force at that time stated that:

'a clinically well-recognised illness is a mental illness which is recognised by a respected body of medical opinion. It is very likely that this would include those specifically mentioned in publications such as the World Health Organisation's International Classification of Diseases.'

There was no equivalent requirement that physical impairments had to be clinically well-recognised. This is why prior to 5 December 2005 it was important, in cases like *McNicol* (see 3.21), for the courts to decide whether the claimant had a physical or mental impairment.

Morgan v Staffordshire University [2002] IRLR 190 shows how *Sch 1, para 1(1)* operated in practice. The claimant suffered stress and anxiety and was depressed after an assault at work. The claimant claimed that she had a mental impairment based on a mental illness, and that her employer had failed to make reasonable adjustments, but did not produce any medical evidence to substantiate her claim apart from her medical notes which contained various references to 'stress', 'anxiety' and 'depression'. The EAT held that these vague references were not enough to prove that she had a mental illness that was clinically well-recognised, and her claim failed.

Sch 1, para 1(1) put the focus in claims involving mental illnesses on proving that the claimant had a clinically well-recognised condition rather than simply whether they had a condition which had a negative impact on them mentally. *S 18(2)* removed this requirement from *DDA 1995* from 5 December 2005. This change means that rather than finding a clinically well-recognised categorisation for mental illnesses, the focus is on establishing the effect the illness is having on the claimant's ability to carry out normal day-to-day activities.

The removal of *Sch 1, para 1(1)* is likely to mean that more employees with mental impairments will be able to satisfy the definition of disability for the purposes of *DDA 1995*. However, even prior to December 2005, *Dunham v Ashford Windows* [2005] IRLR 608 had already established that mental impairments which did not result from or consist of a mental illness could fall within the definition of a disability without the clinically well-recognised requirement needing to be addressed. Dunham claimed he was disabled as a result of a generalised effect his learning difficulties had on a number of skills rather than a specific effect on one skill area (as would be the case, for example, with dyslexia and reading). The EAT nevertheless agreed that he was disabled, and in so doing effectively widened the scope of *DDA 1995* in relation to people with generalised learning difficulties. The EAT, however, said that claimants are unlikely to establish that they have this type of mental impairment solely on the basis of difficulties at school or because they were less intelligent than average. The EAT stressed that claimants would still need to produce expert evidence as to the nature and degree of the impairment they were relying on (see 3.37).

3.23 Ability to carry out normal day-to-day activities

An impairment only affects normal day-to-day activities if it affects one or more of the capacities listed in *DDA 1995, Sch 1, para 4(1)*. These are:

(a)   mobility;

(b)   manual dexterity;

(c)   physical co-ordination;

(d)   continence;

(e)   ability to lift, carry or otherwise move everyday objects;

(f)   speech, hearing or eyesight;

(g)   memory or ability to concentrate, learn or understand; or

(h)   perception of the risk of physical danger.

These capacities apply equally to both physical and mental impairments. For example, it should not be assumed that the only category that is relevant to people with a mental impairment will be memory or ability to concentrate, learn or understand, and that mobility and physical co-ordination will only be relevant to people with physical impairments. The ability to concentrate can also be impaired by physical pain, whilst someone with a mental impairment might find it difficult to carry out activities involving mobility or other physical skills.

3.24   *Day-to-day activities*

The list of capacities in *DDA 1995* is not a list of day-to-day activities. *DDA 1995* does not define what is or is not a day-to-day activity. This is a question of fact for the tribunal to consider, using their basic common sense, rather than a matter for medical experts (*Vicary*; see 3.14). However, the *Guidance* does provide some further assistance in that it states that, in general, day-to-day activities are things people do on a regular or daily basis such as shopping, reading, and writing, having a conversation, or using the telephone, watching television, getting washed and dressed, preparing and eating food, carrying out household tasks, and taking part in social activities (*Guidance*, para D4).

The *Guidance* also stresses that the list of capacities should be looked at in a broad sense (*Guidance*, para D2). For example, mobility covers moving or changing position in a wide sense and therefore includes day-to-day activities such as sitting, standing, bending and reaching as well as walking, travelling in a car and using public transport (*Guidance*, para D20).

This broad approach is reflected in the case law. In *Hewett v Motorola* [2004] IRLR 545, the EAT held that ability to understand is not limited to understanding information, knowledge or instructions; it can also encompass difficulties suffered by someone with Asperger's Syndrome in understanding the normal social interaction or subtleties of human non-factual communication.

In *Paterson* (see 3.18), the EAT had to decide whether participation in high pressure examinations was a normal day-to-day activity. That case involved an employee with dyslexia who argued that his impairment placed him at a substantial disadvantage compared to his non-dyslexic peers when undertaking examinations as part of his employer's promotion process. The EAT held that assessments and examinations are normal day-to-day activities (as is the act of reading and comprehension) both in their own right, and the term is given a meaning which encompasses the activities which are relevant to participation in professional life (*Chacón Navas*; see 3.13). This decision will assist in other claims for disability discrimination based on learning difficulties or other mental impairments.

3.25   *Normal*

In *Goodwin* (see 3.14) the EAT stated that:

> 'a normal day-to-day activity is best left unspecified: easily recognised but defined with difficulty.'

The *Guidance* (para D5), however, does provide some clarification of what 'normal' means in this context and stresses that, like 'impairment', the term should be given its ordinary everyday meaning. It is relevant to look at how far an activity is normal for a large number of people and carried out on a daily or frequent and fairly regular basis, but this does not mean that it has to be regularly carried out by a majority of people or by both sexes. In *Ekpe* (see 3.14), the tribunal had held that wearing rollers and putting make-up on were not normal day-to-day activities because they are carried out almost exclusively by women. The EAT disagreed, on the basis that this reasoning would exclude anything done by women but not men or vice versa as not being normal. It held that what is 'normal' is best understood as anything that is not abnormal or unusual, or particular to the claimant or a particular group of people defined by reference to some singular characteristic (apart from their gender).

The concept of a normal day-to-day activity therefore does not include highly specialised activities such as a particular hobby or any particular form of work.

This is because there is no particular form of work or hobby that is normal for most people. However, whilst some jobs and pastimes might involve unusual or specialist skills, many will also still involve normal day-to-day activities such as sitting down, standing up, walking, and using everyday objects such as a keyboard. The fact that these activities are carried out during the course of a claimant's work or of a specialist pastime will not prevent their ability to do them, and the way they are performed, being relevant for the purposes of assessing whether they are disabled (*Law Hospital NHS Trust v Rush* [2001] IRLR 611 and *Guidance*, paras D7 to D9).

The effects of a person's working environment or of another location where a specialist activity is being carried out will also be relevant when determining the effect of an impairment. In *Cruickshank v VAW Motorcast Limited* [2002] IRLR 24 the claimant's asthma was caused and exacerbated by exposure to fumes when he was at work. However, the tribunal decided that he was not disabled because he showed no symptoms when he was not at work. The EAT held that it was not appropriate to confine the evaluation for the purposes of *DDA 1995* to the extent to which a claimant is disabled in a normal day-to-day environment. If a claimant shows symptoms whilst they are at work which affect their ability to carry out normal day-to-day activities then those symptoms will not be discounted just because the nature of their work is specialist or unusual. This decision may raise the (surprising) possibility that a person may be disabled for the purposes of some jobs but not others.

3.26 Substantial adverse effect

The EAT observed in *Ekpe* (see 3.14) that, in practice, if an impairment affects one of the capacities in *DDA 1995, Sch 1, para 4(1)*, then it is almost inevitable that it will have an adverse effect on normal day-to-day activities. However, to meet the definition of disability under *DDA 1995*, the adverse effect must be substantial. The *Guidance*, para B1 states that:

> 'The requirement that an adverse effect be substantial reflects the general understanding of "disability" as a limitation going beyond the normal differences in ability which may exist among people. A "substantial" effect is more than would be produced by the sort of physical or mental conditions experienced by many people which have only "minor" or "trivial" effects.'

In *Paterson* (see 3.18), the EAT interpreted this to mean that a substantial adverse effect is one that falls outside the normal range of effects to be expected from a cross-section of the population. However, when assessing whether an impairment has a substantial adverse effect, the tribunal must not draw comparisons between the performance of the claimant and that of the population at large. The relevant comparison is between the way in which the individual carries out the activity in question and the way they would carry it out if they were not impaired. If that difference is more than the kind of difference one might expect in a cross-section of the population, then the effects are substantial.

Deemed disabilities (see 3.19), progressive conditions (see 3.30) and conditions with recurring effects (see 3.35) are treated as if they have a substantial adverse effect without the need to satisfy all the requirements of *DDA 1995, s 1(1)*.

The *Guidance* (paras B1 to B15) sets out a number of factors which are relevant to considering whether there is a substantial adverse effect in other cases. These are:

(a)   the time taken to carry out an activity;

(b)   the way in which an activity is carried out;

(c)   the cumulative effects of an impairment;

(d)   the effects of behaviour (including coping strategies and medical advice);

(e)   the effects of the environment;

(f)   the effects of medical treatment (see 3.27).

The *Guidance* also contains some helpful examples (paras D15 to D27) of the types of impact it might be reasonable to regard as having a substantial adverse effect. However, these examples should not be used as a checklist (*Leonard v Southern Derbyshire Chamber of Commerce* [2001] IRLR 19). They are illustrative and non-exhaustive.

Again, it is not for a medical expert to tell the tribunal whether an impairment has or has had a substantial adverse effect on a claimant's ability to carry out normal day-to-day activities. This is a matter on which the tribunal must decide (*Vicary and Abadeh*; see 3.14). In *Goodwin* (see 3.14), the EAT gave some important guidance on how tribunals should carry out this assessment. Mr Goodwin, a paranoid schizophrenic, was dismissed after complaints about his behaviour which included auditory hallucinations (hearing voices), and thought broadcasting (when he imagined that other people could access his thoughts). All of these problems had an adverse effect on Mr Goodwin's ability to concentrate for any sustained period. Mr Goodwin, however, was able to care for himself at home, travel to and from work and carry out his work when he was there. As a result, the tribunal decided that the effect on his ability to concentrate was not substantial. The EAT held that this was the wrong approach and said that when assessing the effect of an impairment on normal day-to-day activities tribunals should focus on the effect that it has on the things a claimant either cannot do or can only do with difficulty, rather than on the things they can do. Where there are still many things that a claimant can do (as in *Goodwin*), this avoids the tribunal concluding that the adverse effect of an impairment cannot be substantial. A similar approach was taken in *Leonard*, where the EAT stressed that it was inappropriate for a tribunal to take examples of what a claimant can do and weigh these in the balance against what they cannot do. The fact that a person can carry out certain activities does not mean their ability to do other activities has not been impaired (see also *Paterson*).

3.27   *Medical treatment*

A particular issue is whether claimants whose impairments are subject to treatment or correction can still claim protection under *DDA 1995*. *DDA 1995, Sch 1, para 6(1)* provides that where an impairment would be likely to have a substantial adverse effect on the ability of the person concerned to carry out normal day-to-day activities but for the fact that measures are being taken to correct it, the impairment is to be treated as having that substantial adverse effect (ie the effect it would have if no corrective measures were being taken) (*Code*, paras B11 to B15).

Sch 1, para 6(1) states that the term 'measures':

'includes, in particular medical treatment and the use of a prosthesis or other aid.'

DDA 1995 does not define what will constitute medical treatment, nor what is or is not a 'prosthesis or other aid', but case law suggests that these are broad categories which are not just limited to medication and medical aids. Measures will include surgical plates and pins (*Carden v Pickerings Europe Ltd* [2005] IRLR

720), counselling with a consultant clinical psychologist (*Kapadia*; see 3.17) and psychotherapy (*Woodrup v London Borough of Southwark* [2002] EWCA Civ 1716, [2003] IRLR 111 and *Abadeh*; see 3.14), but are unlikely to include household objects used to mitigate the effects of a disability such as the use of an automatic can opener where a claimant has a physical impairment which has a substantial adverse effect on their manual dexterity (*Vicary*; see 3.14).

In *Goodwin* (see 3.14), the EAT held that in applying *Sch 1, para 6(1)*, tribunals should examine how the claimant's abilities have actually been affected at the material time (see 3.36) whilst on medication, and then consider what effects they think the impairment would have had but for the fact that such measures are being taken: these are then the 'deduced effects'. The question is whether the actual and deduced effects of the impairment on the claimant's ability to carry out normal day-to-day activities are substantial and adverse. In practice, this means that the beneficial effects of corrective measures should be ignored when considering whether an impairment has a substantial adverse effect. For example, the question of whether a person who wears a hearing aid is disabled is to be considered by reference to what their level of hearing would be without that aid.

The approach to corrective measures and medical treatment under *Sch 1 para 6(1)* has been described as a 'peculiarly benign doctrine' (*Woodrup*) and, as a consequence, claimants who wish to rely on these provisions must have relevant expert evidence to support their claim (see 3.37).

Sch 1 para 6(1), the concept of deduced effects, does not apply to the use of spectacles or contact lenses in relation to an impairment to a person's sight (*para 6(3)*). Further, *para 6(1)* only applies to continuing medical treatment i e measures that 'are being taken'. It does not apply to medical treatment that has ended.

3.28   *Coping strategies*

The *Guidance* (paras B7 to B9) recognises that there are coping strategies which can prevent or mitigate adverse effects so that they are no longer substantial. However, these are not treated in the same way as continuing medical treatment (*Vicary, Leonard* and *Commissioner of Police of the Metropolis v G S Virdi* UKEAT/0338/06). Whether a tribunal should take account of coping strategies will depend on the extent to which it is reasonable to expect a person to rely on such strategies. The possibility that coping strategies may cease to work in certain circumstances should also be taken into account.

3.29   *Severe disfigurements*

Under *DDA 1995, Sch 1, para 3(1)*, a severe disfigurement will be treated as having a substantial adverse effect on a person's ability to carry out normal day-to-day activities. However, under *Meaning Regulations, reg 5*, tattoos that have not been removed and body piercings for decorative or other non-medical purposes are excluded from being so treated.

3.30   *Progressive conditions*

DDA 1995, Sch 1, para 8(1) provides that:

'where–

(a)   a person has a progressive condition (such as cancer, multiple sclerosis or muscular dystrophy or HIV infection),

(b)   as a result of that condition, he has an impairment which has (or had) an effect on his ability to carry out normal day-to-day activities, but

(c)   that effect is not (or was not) a substantial adverse effect,

he shall be taken to have an impairment which has a substantial adverse effect if the condition is likely to result in his having such an impairment.'

This provision protects those with progressive conditions which are likely to worsen progressively over time, but whose effect is not a substantial adverse effect when symptoms first appear. In *Kirton v Tetrosyl Ltd* [2003] EWCA Civ 619, [2003] IRLR 353 the Court of Appeal considered the meaning of the requirement in *para 8(1)(b)* that the impairment must arise as the result of the progressive condition. The claimant developed urinary incontinence as a result of treatment for prostate cancer. However, his claim that his urinary incontinence was a disability failed because the tribunal and the EAT held that *para 8(1)(b)* did not apply. The EAT held that for *para 8(1)* to apply, the effect on normal day-to-day activities had to result from the claimant's cancer and not the surgery. The Court of Appeal overruled this decision and held that an impairment will result from a progressive condition if it follows from the condition in the ordinary course of events, even if it is not directly caused by the condition. The claimant's surgery was a standard response to prostate cancer, and so his urinary incontinence was a disability by virtue of *para 8(1)*.

3.31   *Asymptomatic progressive conditions*

To rely on *DDA 1995, Sch 1, para 8(1)*, claimants have to show not only that they have a progressive condition, and that it has, or has had, an effect on their ability to carry out normal day-to-day activities; they must also show that it is more likely than not that, at some stage in the future, the condition will have a substantial adverse effect on their ability to carry out normal day-to-day activities. This can be done by reference to medical evidence of the likely prognosis and/or statistical evidence (*Mowat-Brown v University of Surrey* [2002] IRLR 235). In *Mowat-Brown* the claimant had MS, but the medical evidence was that some years after first being diagnosed he had very few symptoms and that there were: 'grounds for optimism about his future'. In the light of this evidence the EAT held that it was not possible to conclude that the requirements of *para 8(1)* had been satisfied.

3.32   *Deemed disability*

Cases like *Mowat-Brown* led to calls for *DDA 1995* to be amended to provide more protection for those with asymptomatic progressive conditions such as multiple sclerosis. *DDA 2005* inserted *Sch 1, para 6A(1)* which provides that a person who has cancer, HIV infection or multiple sclerosis is deemed to be disabled from the point of diagnosis. This amendment came into force from 5 December 2005, but it does not apply to all progressive conditions. For example, someone with motor neurone disease or muscular dystrophy would still have to satisfy the requirements of *Sch 1, para 8(1)* if at the material time their condition did not have a substantial adverse effect on their ability to carry out normal day-to-day activities. This approach was taken because other progressive conditions which are not covered by *Sch 1, para 6A(1)* are identified when the symptoms show, so it was felt that it was not necessary to include them in a list of asymptomatic conditions.

Sch 1, para 2 provides that further disabilities can be added to the list of progressive conditions in *Sch 1, para 6A(1)*. The Government has indicated that this power could be exercised if, for example, further case law emerges to show that *Sch 1, para 8(1)* is not working as intended.

Sch 1, para 6A(2) contains a power for new regulations to be introduced to exclude certain types of cancer from being covered by *Sch 1, para 6A(1)*. It had been intended that this power would be used to exclude people with what were considered to be 'minor', easily treatable forms of cancer (such as some skin cancers) from the deemed disability provisions. However, after some considerable criticism of this approach by Parliament when debating the draft *Disability Bill* which became *DDA 2005*, and after consultation with cancer charities and other interested bodies before implementing *DDA 2005*, to date, no cancers have been excluded from *DDA 1995* under this provision.

3.33   Long term

Under *DDA 1995, Sch 1, para 2(1)* an impairment will have a long-term effect only if:

(a)   it has lasted at least 12 months;

(b)   the period for which it lasts is likely to be at least 12 months;

(c)   it is likely to last for the rest of the life of the person affected.

3.34   *Past disabilities*

DDA 1995, Sch 2, para 5 amends *DDA 1995, Sch 1, para 2(1)* in relation to past disabilities by providing that a past substantial adverse effect will have been long-term if it either:

(a)   lasted for at least 12 months; or

(b)   occurred and recurred over a period covering at least 12 months.

3.35   *Recurring effects*

DDA 1995 also makes specific provision for impairments with recurring or fluctuating effects. *DDA 1995, Sch 1, para 2(2)* provides that:

> 'Where an impairment ceases to have a substantial effect on a person's ability to carry out day-to-day activities, it is to be treated as having that effect if that effect is likely to recur.'

The effect of this provision is that the substantial adverse effect does not have to be continuous throughout the relevant period. Even if the impairment has ceased to have a substantial adverse effect it will be treated as continuing for as long as its substantial adverse effect is likely to recur. This means that conditions with effects that can recur or where effects can be sporadic, such as rheumatoid arthritis and epilepsy, as well as mental health conditions such as schizophrenia, bipolar effective disorder and certain types of depression can still be 'long-term' for the purposes of the *DDA 1995* if they are likely to recur (*Guidance*, paras C4 to C5).

In this context, something is 'likely' if it is more probable than not that it will happen (*Guidance*, para C2). In *Swift v Chief Constable of Wiltshire Constabulary* [2004] IRLR 540, the EAT said that when considering *Sch 1, para 2(2)* the tribunal should ask itself the following questions:

(a)   Was there at some stage an impairment which had a substantial adverse effect on the claimant's ability to carry out normal day-to-day activities?

(b)   Did the impairment cease to have a substantial adverse effect on the claimant's ability to carry out normal day-to-day activities, and if so when?

(c)   What was the substantial adverse effect?

(d)   Is that substantial adverse effect likely to recur?

The question for the tribunal is whether the substantial adverse effect is likely to recur, not whether the impairment is likely to recur. Unlike progressive conditions, the likely future effect must be the same as the earlier effect. However, there is no time limit on the recurrence. As long as a substantial adverse effect is likely to recur once in a person's lifetime, it will be treated as ongoing.

Where a past disability has ceased to have a substantial adverse effect on a person's ability to carry out normal day-to-day activities, it will be treated as continuing to have that substantial adverse effect if that effect recurs (*Sch 2, para 5(2)*).

3.36   *The material time*

There has been some divergence at EAT level about the point in time at which the existence of a disability, including whether an effect is long-term or likely to recur, must be assessed. In *Greenwood v British Airways Plc* [1999] IRLR 600 the EAT held that this assessment should take place based on what is known at the time of the hearing, not at the time of the alleged discriminatory act. In contrast, in *Latchman v Reed Business Information Ltd* [2002] ICR 1453 a different division of the EAT expressly disapproved this aspect of *Greenwood* and held that this assessment should take place based on what is known at the date of the alleged discrimination. The EAT reached the same conclusion in *Cruickshank*. In *McDougall v Richmond Adult Community College* [2007] IRLR 771 the EAT declined to follow *Latchman* and expressly approved the decision in *Greenwood* holding that whether an impairment had a long-term adverse effect should be determined on the basis of the facts known at the time of the hearing.

However, the Court of Appeal has recently handed down its judgment in *McDougall* on the material time for assessing whether an effect is long-term or likely to recur, and has reversed the EAT's decision (*Richmond Adult Community College v McDougall* [2008] EWCA Civ 4). The Court of Appeal found that a tribunal should decide whether a disability is long-term or likely to recur on the basis of the facts at the time of the discriminatory act, not on the basis of the facts known at the hearing. Pill LJ stated (at para 24): 'The central purpose of the [*DDA 1995*] is to prevent discriminatory decisions and to provide sanctions if such decisions are made. Whether an employer has committed such a wrong must, in my judgment, be judged on the basis of the evidence available at the time of the decision complained of.' In deciding this, the Court of Appeal followed Elias J's interpretation of the guidance in *Spence*.

3.37   **PRACTICAL ISSUES RELATING TO THE DEFINITION OF DISABILITY**

Obtaining expert evidence in cases where disability is in dispute

Medical evidence

The medical nature of the definition of disability means that in cases where disability is in dispute, the evidence of a medical expert will be crucial for both sides. Tribunals are often presented with conflicting medical evidence. It is therefore important that tribunals attach the correct weight to that evidence and are clear about their role and that of the medical expert. It is particularly important that tribunals consider the evidence and know what evidence they can accept and what evidence they can reject.

Tribunals have to consider all of the medical evidence presented to them and unless they have a good reason for doing so, they should not disregard uncontested medical evidence (*Kapadia*; see 3.17). It is appropriate for medical reports to deal with the diagnosis of the impairment, any observations of the claimant carrying out day-to-day activities and the ease with which a claimant is able to perform those functions, together with any relevant opinion as to prognosis and the effect of medication. However, although many practitioners will offer an opinion on whether a claimant has a disability within the meaning of *DDA 1995*, this a legal question for the tribunal, and one which cannot be delegated to the medical experts (*Vicary* and *Abadeh*; see 3.14).

3.38   *Evidence from other experts*

Expert evidence need not always be obtained from a medical practitioner. In *Dunham* (see 3.22), the EAT held that the evidence adduced to establish the nature of the claimant's learning difficulties could be provided by a suitably qualified psychologist, and need not come from a qualified medical practitioner. The EAT said that what was important was that there should be evidence from a suitably qualified expert who could speak, on the basis of his experience and expertise, as to the relevant condition. However, this decision contrasts sharply with *Hill* (see 3.16), where the Court of Appeal placed much greater weight on the evidence of the medically qualified experts than the evidence of a psychotherapist.

3.39   *Instructing experts to obtain medical advice*

In *De Keyser Ltd v Wilson* [2001] IRLR 324, the EAT gave some guidance on how expert evidence should be collected in tribunal cases. The guidelines provide the following advice to parties considering obtaining medical evidence:

(a)   not to assume that the tribunal will be willing to hear expert evidence. The opportunity should be taken to explore with the tribunal chairman (now Employment Judge), either at a case management discussion or in correspondence, whether expert evidence is likely to be admitted at the main hearing;

(b)   both parties should jointly instruct the same expert unless there are special circumstances in which one party is already committed to using its own expert;

(c)   the parties need to agree responsibility for payment of a jointly instructed expert's fees and disbursements;

(d)   even if a joint expert is not appointed, an expert report will carry more evidential weight if the contents of the letter of instruction to the expert have been commented on and, preferably, agreed by the other side;

(e)   a letter of instruction should:

   (i)   contain the questions which the expert has to advise on;

   (ii)   state what facts are agreed by the parties and what facts are in dispute;

   (iii) emphasise that the expert's overriding duty is to the tribunal rather than to any party;

   (iv)   state what aspects of the case the expert is required to advise on; and

    (v)   not be partisan,

(f)   to speed matters up, the tribunal can give directions where a joint expert is to be instructed; these might include the date by which the identity of the expert and letter of instruction must be agreed, and a date for production of the expert's report;

(g)   where separate experts are instructed, a timetable should be agreed between the parties or fixed by the tribunal. The timetable should include a date for exchange of experts' reports and a date for a without prejudice meeting of the experts with a view to them producing a schedule of agreed issues and points of dispute between the experts.

3.40 Meaning of disability discrimination and harassment in the employment field

Prior to 1 October 2004, *DDA 1995* prohibited two types of discrimination in the employment field (other than victimisation), namely:

(a)   less favourable treatment discrimination (*s 3A(1)*; formerly *s 5(1)*); and

(b)   failure to make reasonable adjustments (*s 3A(2)* and, in relation to applicants and employees, *s 4A*; formerly *ss 5(2)* and *6*).

From 1 October 2004, however, the *DDA 1995* prohibits three distinct types of discrimination (in addition to victimisation and harassment):

(a)   direct discrimination (*s 3A(4),(5)*);

(b)   disability-related discrimination (that is, less favourable treatment not amounting to direct discrimination) (*s 3A(1)*); and

(c)   failure to make reasonable adjustments (*ss 3A(2)* and *4A*).

In order to understand these three categories it is necessary first briefly to consider the old regime.

3.41 Meaning of discrimination prior to 1 October 2004

Generally

Prior to the *2003 Regulations*, the *DDA 2005* prohibited (a) less favourable treatment discrimination and (b) discrimination by failure to make reasonable adjustments. (It also, as now, prohibited discrimination by way of victimisation.)

Less favourable treatment

It is important to understand that less favourable treatment discrimination under *DDA 1995* is not and was not the same thing as direct discrimination under, for example, *SDA 1975* or *RRA 1976*: see *Clark v Novacold* [1999] IRLR 318, CA at s 31. As explained further below, less favourable treatment occurs where (subject to justification) a disabled person is treated less favourably for a reason *related to* his disability. While this concept is broad enough to include all cases of direct discrimination, less favourable treatment also covers many instances of what would (under *SDA 1975* or *RRA 1976*) be classed as indirect discrimination – as well as some cases which might well fall outside both the direct and indirect discrimination provisions of those Acts. References in older cases and texts equating less favourable treatment (under the 'old' *DDA*) with direct discrimination are, thus, incorrect.

3.42 Disability Discrimination

3.42 *Reasonable adjustments*

The central concept of the duty to make reasonable adjustments originally set out in the 'old' *DDA* (prior to 1 October 2004) survives in the new *DDA* provisions, but subject to a number of detailed changes, broadly serving to extend the scope of the duty and remove exceptions or defences thereto.

Requirements of the Framework Directive

The amendments made to *DDA 1995* by the *2003 Regulations* as from 1 October 2004 were made in order to comply with *Framework Directive*. That Directive, unlike the original *DDA 1995*, largely employed the conventional distinction between direct and indirect discrimination (see, respectively, *Articles 2(2)(a)* and *2(2)(b)*). Briefly, its requirements were as follows.

Direct discrimination

The *Framework Directive* requires (*Article 2(1)*) the prohibition of direct disability discrimination (*Article 2(2)(a)*) (that is, the less favourable treatment of one person, on the ground of disability, than another in a comparable situation) and does not allow for any general defence of justification to a direct discrimination claim. Note that while it might be argued that some defence to a direct discrimination claim might be afforded by *Article 4(1)* (genuine occupational requirements) of the *Directive* (see eg *Chacón Navas v Eurest*, Advocate General's opinion at 81), no such provision was made by the *2003 Regulations*: *DDA 1995*, unlike *SDA 1975* and *RRA 1976* allows for no genuine occupational requirements defence; this is because the DDA does not prohibit discrimination in favour of disabled persons or against non-disabled persons.

By contrast, the 'old' *DDA* did (implicitly) prohibit direct discrimination (because this was covered by less favourable treatment), but allowed for a defence of justification ('old' *DDA, ss 5(1)(b)* and *5(3)*). Accordingly, the *2003 Regulations* sought to remove the possibility of justification in relation to direct discrimination as defined in the *Framework Directive*, by 'carving out' this element of less favourable treatment (*DDA, s 3A(4)*, *(5)*).

One limited possibility for justification of direct discrimination does, however, remain and it derives from *Article 2(5)* of the *Framework Directive*, which makes the prohibition of disability discrimination subject to measures laid down by national law which are necessary in a democratic society for the maintenance of public order, the prevention or criminal offences, the protection of health (including safety) and the protection of the rights and freedoms of others. While that provision is not explicitly implemented in the *DDA 1995* by the *2004 Regulations* or otherwise, the possibility of the application of national legislation to 'trump' the *Framework Directive* is provided for by the maintenance in force of *DDA 1995, s 59* (statutory authority).

Indirect discrimination

The *Framework Directive* requires (*Article 2(1)*) the prohibition of indirect discrimination, defined (*Article 2(2)(b)*) as occurring where:

> 'an apparently neutral provision, criterion or practice would put persons having .. a particular disability at a particular disadvantage compared with other persons,'

unless either:

(a)   that provision, criterion or practice is 'objectively justified by a legitimate aim and the means of achieving that aim are appropriate and necessary'; or

(b)   (in relation only to the disability strand of the *Framework Directive*) the employer 'is obliged, under national legislation, to take appropriate measures in line with the principles contained in *Article 5* [reasonable accommodation for disabled persons] in order to eliminate disadvantages entailed by such provision, criterion or practice'.

The *Framework Directive* thus apparently gave Member States a legislative choice for implementation of its provisions on indirect disability discrimination: indirectly discriminatory provisions, criteria or practices could either be subject to a requirement of objective justification (*Article 2(2)(b)(i)*) or they could be subject to a duty to make reasonable adjustments/accommodation (*Articles 2(2)(b)(ii)* and *5*). It is important to understand that the UK implementing legislation (in the form of the *2003 Regulations* amending *DDA 1995*) took the latter choice – so that in general, the *Framework Directive*'s indirect discrimination requirements are met through the reasonable adjustments duty (see, in relation to employers, *DDA 1995, ss 3A(2)* and *4A*) rather than through less favourable treatment discrimination. (There is one notable exception, falling outside the employment field, to this general approach and it relates to competence standards applied by qualifications bodies; here an objective justification approach is applied: see *DDA 1995, ss 14A(3)* and *14B(1)(a)*).

In construing the reasonable adjustments duty set out in *DDA 1995, s 4A*, it is therefore important to bear in mind that the duty must be construed (in accordance with general EC law principles of construction) so as to ensure that the requirement of *Article 2(2)(b)*, that *all* potentially indirectly discriminatory provisions, criteria or practices be subject to the duty, is met.

The main alterations to the reasonable adjustments duty in the 'old' (pre-October 2004) *DDA 1995*, which were made by the *2003 Regulations* in order to comply with the *Framework Directive*, were as follows:

(a)   extension of the duty to cover all 'provisions, criteria or practices' (e g *DDA 1995, s 4A(1)(a)*) rather than merely 'arrangements' ('old' *DDA 1995, s 6(1)(a)*); note that the coverage of 'arrangements' is, however, explicitly preserved: *DDA 1995, s 18D(2)*);

(b)   removal of the limitation (formerly found in *DDA 1995, s 6(2)*) that the reasonable adjustments duty applied only to (i) arrangements for determining to whom employment should be offered; (ii) terms, conditions or arrangements on which employment, promotion, a transfer, training or any other benefit were offered or afforded. This has the effect, for example, that while under the 'old' *DDA*, a reasonable adjustments claim might not have been allowed in respect of the act of dismissal itself (e g *Clark v Novacold, per* Mummery J at ss 79, 92), under the *DDA 1995* as it now stands, it is clear that a decision to dismiss an employee *is* subject to the reasonable adjustments duty: the *Framework Directive* plainly applies to dismissals (*Article 3(1)(c)*). (Indeed, the *Framework Directive* and the application of some duty to make reasonable adjustments, extends even beyond the end of the employment relationship – see *DDA 1995, s 16A*);

(c)   removal of the exception to the reasonable adjustments duty for benefits under occupational pension schemes and other similar schemes and arrangements (formerly *DDA 1995, s 6(11)*): this means that pension benefits provided by *employers* will be subject to the reasonable adjustments duty. (Insofar as a complaint of discrimination is made in respect of acts by occupational pension scheme *trustees*, that will be governed by the provisions of *DDA 1995, ss 4G* to *4K*, including the reasonable adjustments duty in *s 4H*. Those provisions were inserted in *DDA 1995* by the *Disability Discrimination Act 1995* (*Pensions*) *Regulations 2003* (*SI 2003/2770*), with effect from 1 October 2004 – see 3.113);

(d)   the removal of the defence of justification (formerly contained in *DDA 1995, s 5(2)(b)* and *5(4)*) in respect of failure to make reasonable adjustments (although this may have a limited impact in practice: see 3.67).

The Directive and less favourable treatment

Because the *Framework Directive*'s indirect discrimination requirements were implemented by means of the reasonable adjustments duty (as explained above), the provisions of *DDA 1995* on less favourable treatment (other than in respect of direct disability discrimination) were untouched by the implementation of the *Framework Directive*, since they did not (and did not purport to) implement the *Framework Directive*'s requirements on indirect discrimination. Thus, for example, less favourable treatment discrimination continues to be subject to a defence of 'material and substantial' justification (*DDA 1995, s 3A(1)(b)* and (*3*)), which is significantly easier for an employer to satisfy than that of objective justification set out in *Article 2(2)(b)(i)* of the *Framework Directive*. But no breach of the *Framework Directive* would seem to be involved since its indirect discrimination requirements are implemented by the reasonable adjustments duty (see above). Thus, the claim for less favourable treatment not amounting to direct discrimination (characterised in the *Code of Practice* and, below, as 'disability related discrimination') continues to exist as a purely domestic law claim in addition to those for direct discrimination and for failure to make reasonable adjustments, each of which implement *Framework Directive* requirements (in relation, respectively, to direct and indirect discrimination).

3.43   Three types of disability discrimination under the DDA after 1 October 2004

As set out above, since 1 October 2004, *DDA 1995* has prohibited three types of discrimination (other than victimisation and harassment), namely:

(a)   direct discrimination;

(b)   disability-related discrimination (that is, less favourable treatment not amounting to direct discrimination); and

(c)   failure to make reasonable adjustments.

The interaction of these three concepts in practice is considered further below. It makes sense to consider the concepts in the order listed here, not least because both direct discrimination and disability-related discrimination are sub-categories of less favourable treatment – although note that the *Code* appears to suggest (section 4.1) that direct discrimination should be considered first, and reasonable adjustments second, with disability-related discrimination being considered last of the three (apparently on the basis that while direct discrimination and failure to make reasonable adjustments are not subject to justification, the same is not true of disability-related discrimination).

3.44   Less favourable treatment

DDA 1995, s 3A(1) provides that a person discriminates against a disabled person if:

(a)   for a reason which relates to the disabled person's disability, he treats him less favourably than he treats or would treat others to whom that reason does not or would not apply; and

(b)   he cannot show that the treatment in question is justified (for the elements of the justification defence, see *s 3A(3),(4)*).

Since 1 October 2004, there are (in effect) two types of less favourable treatment discrimination, namely:

(i)   direct disability discrimination – that is, less favourable treatment amounting to direct discrimination falling within *s 3A(5)*. Such discrimination cannot be justified (*s 3A(4)*); and

(ii)   disability-related discrimination – that is, less favourable treatment *not* amounting to direct disability discrimination within *s 3A(5)*. Such discrimination *can* be justified (*s 3A(2),(3)*). It should be noted that the term 'disability-related discrimination' is *not* used in the *DDA 1995* itself – it is merely a convenient shorthand for less favourable treatment not amounting to direct discrimination, and is employed in the *Code* as explained at section 4.28 thereof.

The key distinction between direct discrimination and disability-related discrimination can be simply stated as follows:

direct discrimination (which cannot be justified) occurs where the reason for the less favourable treatment suffered by a disabled person is the disability itself. By contrast, disability-related discrimination (which can be justified) occurs where the reason for such treatment is not the disability itself, but is nevertheless related to the disability (see *Code*, section 4.29).

As will be explained below, the main distinction between the two types of discrimination (other than in relation to the possibility of justification) lies in the identification of the correct comparator in each case.

3.45   Direct discrimination

Direct discrimination occurs where an employer treats a disabled person less favourably 'on the ground of the disabled person's disability' than he treats or would treat a person not having that particular disability whose relevant circumstances 'including his abilities' are the same as, or not materially different from, those of the disabled person (*DDA s 3A(5)* and see *Article 2(2)(a)* of the *Directive*).

3.46   *No justification for direct discrimination*

Under *DDA 1995, s 3A(4)*, there is, in general, no possibility of justification for direct discrimination (unless, in the particular case of conflicting legislative provision requiring such discrimination, under *s 59* construed in accordance with *Article 2(5)* of the *Directive*). See COMMON CONCEPTS (1).

3.47   *No prohibition of discrimination against non-disabled persons*

As set out above, unlike other discrimination law statutes, *DDA 1995* is asymmetrical in that it does not prohibit discrimination against persons who are non-disabled (the term 'able-bodied' is not favoured by disability groups). It is, thus, entirely lawful (so far as *DDA 1995* is concerned) for an employer to advertise for, or to recruit or promote, a disabled employee (or an employee having a particular disability) in preference to a non-disabled employee and it is for this reason that *DDA 1995* (unlike the other discrimination law strands) does not need to provide for a defence of 'genuine occupational qualification/ requirement' in relation to such cases. (Note that while *DDA 1995 permits* more favourable treatment of disabled employees, it does not *require* such treatment – save in the particular case of the duty to make reasonable adjustments: *s 18D(1)*.)

3.48 *Relevance of other discrimination 'strands'*

The drafting of the definition of direct discrimination is at *DDA 1995, s 3A(5)*; in addition to closely reflecting the wording of the *Framework Directive*, is also strikingly similar to that contained in other discrimination law statutes, notably *SDA 1975, ss 1(1)(a)* and *5(3)*. (The definitions found in other 'strands', such as the race legislation – see *RRA 1976, ss 1(1)(a)* and *3(4)* – and that relating to sexual orientation and religion, are arguably wider in covering discrimination by association and discrimination based on perceived status. As to association and perception in *DDA 1995, s 3A(5)*, and the ECJ reference in the case of *Attridge Law v Coleman* [2007] IRLR 88; see 3.7.) It seems likely, therefore, that case law on the interpretation of, in particular, *SDA 1975* definition of direct discrimination (see SEX DISCRIMINATION (8)) will be relevant in construing *DDA 1995, s 3A(5)*.

3.49 *Uniqueness of direct disability discrimination*

The application of the prohibition on direct disability discrimination poses unique challenges in practice because a 'permitted' ground for less favourable treatment (eg lack of job capability) may overlap with, or in an extreme case (eg that of a blind applicant for a job as a bus driver) even arguably be the same as, a 'prohibited' ground for less favourable treatment (eg the existence of a disability directly causing the lack of job capability). Both the *Framework Directive* (*recital 17* of which provides that the *Framework Directive* does not require the recruitment, etc of an individual who is not competent, capable and available to perform the essential functions of the post) and *DDA 1995* itself (by its comparator provisions, in relation to abilities – see 3.45) recognise and seek to deal with that overlap.

3.50 *'On the ground of': identification of comparator*

In determining whether less favourable treatment has occurred 'on the ground of' a disabled person's disability, it will often be very helpful to identify the correct comparator. *DDA 1995, s 3A(5)* provides that in carrying out a 'like-for-like' comparison for the purpose of the direct discrimination provisions, where it is alleged that a person with a particular disability has been less favourably treated on the ground of that disability, a comparator is to be identified:

(a)   who does not have the particular disability in question; and

(b)   whose relevant circumstances, *including his abilities*, are the same as, or not materially different from, those of the disabled person. The relevant circumstances are not limited to the comparator's abilities but include any other relevant circumstances (*High Quality Lifestyles Ltd v Watts* [2006] IRLR 850, EAT, at 46). The reference to abilities is at odds with the other discrimination strands, although the exercise of identifying a comparator is otherwise similar. See COMMON CONCEPTS (1).

3.51   *Comparator: practical examples*

See the *Code* at section 4.13ff. The following are practical examples of identifying a comparator in a direct discrimination claim:

(a)   A disabled person takes six months' sick leave because of his disability, and is dismissed by his employer. A non-disabled fellow employee also takes six months' sick leave (because she has broken her leg) but is not dismissed. The difference in treatment is attributable to the employer's unwillingness to employ disabled staff. The non-disabled employee is an appropriate comparator and there has been direct disability discrimination (*Code*, box after section 4.13). By contrast, the dismissal of the disabled employee pursuant to a policy of dismissing all members of staff who have been off sick for six months would not involve direct discrimination: a non-disabled employee having taken six months' sick leave (the appropriate comparator) would also have been dismissed (*Code*, box after section 4.14). Note, however, that in this example there might well be good claims for disability-related discrimination and discrimination by failure to make reasonable adjustments (see below).

(b)   A disabled person with a severe facial disfigurement, who is otherwise well qualified, is turned down for a post as a shop assistant solely because other employees would be uncomfortable working with him. The appropriate comparator is a person who does not have such a disfigurement but with the same abilities to do the job. Such a person would not have been rejected in this way – so there has been direct disability discrimination (*Code*, box after section 4.16).

(c)   In *High Quality Lifestyles v Watts*, the claimant was dismissed from his employment as a support worker for people with learning difficulties on the basis that he was HIV positive and that there was a risk of transmission of his condition to service users (who might scratch or bite him, drawing blood). The EAT held that the correct comparator was an employee who had an attribute (other than being HIV positive) carrying 'the same risk of causing to others illness or injury of the same gravity, here serious and possibly fatal'. The case was remitted to the employment tribunal to consider whether such a comparator would have been dismissed. (Note, however, that the outcome of the case may have been affected by the claimant's concession that the appropriate comparator was a person at risk of transmitting a life-threatening disease: judgment 38.)

3.52   *Direct discrimination and generalised assumptions*

It follows from the definition of direct discrimination that if less favourable treatment occurs because of the employer's generalised or stereotypical assumptions about the disability or its effects, that is likely to be direct discrimination (*Code*, section 4.8). This is because an employer would not normally make such assumptions about a non-disabled person, but would instead consider his individual abilities.

For example, suppose that a blind woman is not shortlisted for a job involving computers because the employer wrongly assumes that blind people cannot use them, and that the employer makes no attempt to consider the individual circumstances and abilities of the applicant. The employer has treated the blind applicant less favourably than others by not shortlisting her; and that treatment is 'on the ground of' her disability because it would not have been assumed that a non-disabled person was unable to use a computer (*Code*, box after section 4.8).

This was apparently also the result in the case of *Tudor v Spen* ET/2404211/05, where the claimant was dismissed from her job as an animal nursing assistant after she had a stroke and became blind. Her employer assumed, without seeking any advice, that there was no point in continuing to employ the claimant after her stroke. This was a case properly categorised as direct disability discrimination because the employer had made assumptions, on the ground of the claimant's disability, about her ability to do the job – and such assumptions would not have been made about a non-disabled person.

That this is the correct approach is underlined by, for example, *SDA 1975* case law holding that the making of generalised assumptions about women may amount to direct sex discrimination. See, for example, *Horsey v Dyfed County Council* [1982] IRLR 395; [1982] ICR 775, EAT, where the assumption by an employer that a wife would follow her husband to his place of work (rather than the husband moving to the wife's place of work) amounted to direct sex discrimination. The EAT stated that the employer 'must look at the particular circumstances of that case and not [act] on the basis of any general assumption'. See SEX DISCRIMINATION (8). It follows that some pre-October 2004 cases such as *Surrey Police v Marshall* [2002] IRLR 843, EAT would or might be differently decided under the new direct discrimination provisions. In the *Marshall* case, the employer, in refusing the applicant employment as a fingerprints recognition officer in the police force, had acted on the basis of medical opinion about bipolar affective disorder *in general* rather than on a risk assessment or expert opinion based on the applicant's own particular circumstances. Such a decision might well now amount to direct disability discrimination (and, as such, incapable of justification).

3.53   *Direct discrimination and knowledge of disability*

While many, probably most, instances of direct disability discrimination will occur in cases where the employer is aware that the disabled person has a disability, direct discrimination may sometimes occur even though the employer does not know of the disability. (This is an issue which will not, of course, normally arise in relation to the more visible grounds for discrimination such as sex and race.) To take an example given in the *Code* (box after section 4.11), suppose that an employer were to advertise an internal promotion stating that people with a history of mental illness need not apply; and that a disabled employee otherwise eligible for the promotion had a history of schizophrenia of which the employer was unaware. The employee would, notwithstanding the employer's lack of knowledge, have a good claim for direct disability discrimination in relation to the loss of promotion opportunities: the appropriate comparator would be an employee with comparable abilities but not having a history of mental illness, and such an employee would not have been automatically excluded from eligibility.

3.54   *The particular case of wheelchair users*

The *Code* suggests (second box after section 4.9) that there will be direct disability discrimination if an employer treats an employee less favourably simply on the ground that she is a wheelchair user. But it is not clear that this is correct. Being a wheelchair user is not something which by definition only applies to disabled people – a person may use a wheelchair because, for example, she has a temporary injury following an accident. (Contrast, for example, the cases about pregnancy discrimination (eg *Brown v Rentokil Ltd C-395/96* [1998] IRLR 445, ECJ): pregnancy is a condition only affecting women (see SEX DISCRIMINATION (8)), but wheelchair use is not something only affecting disabled people). Thus, while it may be that as a matter of *fact* an employer refusing to employ a wheelchair user is doing so because of prejudice against disabled people, as a matter of *law* the mere fact that treatment is based on wheelchair use may not be enough to found a successful direct discrimination claim. The situation may be different in cases where a particular auxiliary aid is only used by disabled people. Thus, for example, less favourable treatment of a person on the ground that she had an artificial leg might amount to direct disability discrimination (having an artificial leg being, by definition, a state of affairs only affecting certain disabled people – the effects of a prosthetic leg are, of course, to be disregarded in assessing disability (*DDA 1995, Sch 1, paras 6(1), (2)*).

3.55   *Direct discrimination and reasonable adjustments*

One issue which needs to be considered when analysing a direct discrimination claim is the impact of any reasonable adjustments which were, or ought to have been, made in relation to a disabled person who complains of less favourable treatment. *DDA 1995* makes no specific provision on this point, but the *Code* (section 4.22) sets out the position as follows:

(a)   In considering a direct discrimination claim, the disabled person and his abilities must be considered *as they in fact were* at the time of the alleged act of discrimination, rather than as they might have been had particular adjustments been made (or, as the case may be, had particular adjustments not been made).

(b)   If there were particular reasonable adjustments which an employer was required by *DDA 1995* to make, but in fact failed to make (and which would or might have had an impact on the disabled person's abilities to do the job), in considering a direct discrimination claim, the disabled person's abilities are nevertheless to be considered as they in fact were and not as they might have been had adjustments been made.

(c)   Similarly, if an employer did in fact make adjustments enhancing the disabled person's performance (whether or not it was required by *DDA 1995* to do so), the disabled person and his abilities is to be considered on the basis of those enhancements and not as he would or might have been without the benefit of the adjustments.

The position is more readily illustrated by examples (*Code*, boxes following section 4.22):

(i)   A disabled person applies for a typing job, but is not allowed to use her own adapted keyboard (even though the employer ought reasonably to have allowed this). She carries out a typing test at a speed of 30 words per minute (wpm). With the adapted keyboard, her speed would have been 50 wpm. A non-disabled candidate is given the job because her typing speed on the test is 45 wpm with the same accuracy rate. This is not direct discrimination (the appropriate comparator being a non-disabled candidate with a speed of 30 wpm) – but the disabled person would be likely to have good claims for failure to make reasonable adjustments and for disability-related discrimination.

(ii)   The same disabled person applies for a similar job and is allowed to use her adapted keyboard. She completes a typing test with a speed of 50 wpm. A non-disabled candidate types at 30 wpm with the same accuracy rate. The disabled candidate is rejected because of prejudice in favour of the non-disabled candidate. This is direct discrimination (the appropriate comparator being a non-disabled applicant with a speed of 50 wpm – such a comparator would have been offered the job).

3.56 *Direct discrimination: problem areas.*

The most difficult cases will probably arise in two areas:

(a) *Disability closely connected with job suitability*: because direct disability discrimination is not, in general, capable of justification, difficult cases will arise for employers where an employee's (or applicant's) disability is closely connected with his ability to do, or suitability for, the job in question. This may perhaps arise, for example, where a disabled applicant (or an employee who has become disabled) appears to the employer plainly to be incapable of the job in question as a direct result of his disability – as in the, admittedly extreme, example of the blind bus driver – or the case of a disabled person with a severe facial disfigurement applying for a job as a receptionist in a children's nursery. Two general points may be made here:

(i) *Necessary to consider disabled person's individual abilities*: on a practical level, employers should ensure that they consider a disabled employee's (or applicant's) individual abilities rather than making assumptions about what he cannot do. If the making of generalised assumptions leads to less favourable treatment, it may well amount to direct disability discrimination (see above, and in particular *Tudor v Spen*; see 3.52). By contrast, if an employer considers the disabled person's actual abilities against a set of objective criteria applied equally to other candidates, the risk of a successful claim will be much reduced.

(ii) *Need to identify comparator:* in analysing whether there has in fact been direct discrimination in difficult cases of this sort, it will be essential to identify an appropriate comparator (see above). Thus, returning to the 'blind bus driver' example, the *Code* states that the correct comparator in the case of a person with a severe visual impairment refused the job because he fails an eye test is a non-disabled person (eg a person who merely has poorer than average eyesight) who also fails to pass that test – so that there would be no direct discrimination. That said, the careful identification of a comparator will not necessarily lead to the conclusion that there has been no direct disability discrimination – in the nursery example above, it seems likely that the correct comparator is a person without any disfigurement and who is otherwise suitable for the job, so that a claim for direct discrimination would be made out.

(b) *Disability discrimination considered to be required by legislation*: this second problem area may arise more rarely. It would arise where legislation other than *DDA 1995* (for example, legislation prohibiting insulin-dependent diabetics from piloting ships) was considered to require less favourable treatment of disabled persons on the ground of their disability (often on the basis of a 'blanket ban'). Careful thought will be required in such cases:

(i) It will first be necessary to be clear that the legislation in question does in fact *require* the less favourable treatment in question (rather than, say, merely permitting such treatment). *DDA 1995, s 59(1)* is (even as a matter of domestic law) to be narrowly construed: see eg *Hampson v Department of Education and Science* [1990] ICR 511, HL (which deals with the equivalent provisions of *RRA 1976*); and see COMMON CONCEPTS (1). It is important not to assume that the legislation requires a particular result without a careful check. For a practical example (albeit pre-dating the coming into force of the *2003 Regulations*) see *Lane Group plc v Farmiloe* UKEAT/0352/03/DA, which concerned the application of health and safety legislation on the use of personal protective equipment, in particular protective shoes, to a disabled employee with psoriasis.

(ii)   It will be necessary to consider whether any reasonable adjustments could be made to avoid the impact of the conflicting legislation (see eg *Lane Group v Farmiloe*, above, at 41) – failing which, the employer will at least be liable for failure to make reasonable adjustments.

(iii) In the case where the employer is an 'emanation of the state' for EC law purposes, it will (further) be necessary to consider whether the legislation relied upon complies with the requirement of *Article 2(5)* of the *Framework Directive*, which requires such measures to be 'necessary in a democratic society' – a proportionality test – pursuant to a number of aims, including health (which would include health and safety). If the legislation does not fulfil the test in *Article 2(5)*, the employee may be able to rely upon directly effective *Framework Directive* rights to disapply the necessary legislation. Note that such rights will not, however, be available as against a purely private employer.

3.57   Disability-related discrimination

'Disability-related discrimination' is not a term found anywhere in *DDA 1995*. Rather it is a term used in the *Code* (section 4.28) to signify less favourable treatment within the meaning of *s 3A(1)* which does not amount to direct discrimination within the meaning of *s 3A(5)*. Disability-related discrimination is unjustified less favourable treatment for a *disability-related* reason – that is, a reason which relates to the disabled person's disability but is not the disability itself (*Code,* section 4.29). Thus, disability-related discrimination occurs where (paraphrasing *s 3A(1)*):

(a)   for a disability-related reason, a person treats a disabled person less favourably than he treats or would treat others to whom that reason does not apply; and

(b)   he cannot show that the treatment in question is justified (as to which, see *s 3A(3), (4)*).

3.58   *Disability-related discrimination and the Directive*

As explained above, *DDA 1995's* prohibition of disability-related discrimination does not purport to implement any requirement of the *Framework Directive*. This is because (in summary) the *Framework Directive's* requirements on direct discrimination are implemented by *s 3A(4), (5)* (direct disability discrimination) – while its requirements on indirect discrimination are implemented by the duty to make reasonable adjustments (*ss 3A(2)* and *4A*).

3.59   *Disability-related discrimination and indirect discrimination*

While disability-related discrimination is less favourable treatment not amounting to direct disability discrimination, this does not mean that it can be equated with, or properly described as, 'indirect' disability discrimination. *DDA 1995, s 3A(1)* does not mirror, for example, *SDA 1975, s 1(1)(b)* (indirect sex discrimination) or *RRA 1976, ss 1(1)(b)* or *1(1A)* (indirect racial discrimination). As will be seen further below, there are a number of key differences between disability-related discrimination and 'classic' indirect discrimination, including that:

(a)   Disability-related discrimination requires that there should have been less favourable treatment (albeit that this requirement is relatively easily satisfied because of the identity of the comparator – see below). Indirect discrimination, by contrast, occurs where a *neutral* provision or requirement has a disproportionate adverse impact on a particular group. It will not always be clear that the application of such a neutral requirement has led to less favourable treatment (although it will very frequently give rise to a reasonable adjustments claim: see further *Williams v Richmond Court (Swansea) Ltd* [2006] EWCA Civ 1719).

(b)   Indirect discrimination includes an element of group disadvantage, while disability-related discrimination may be established if a single disabled person has been less favourably treated.

(c)   The justification defence to disability-related discrimination is usually significantly easier to establish than that for indirect discrimination and, in particular, does not include any requirement of proportionality.

Many cases of disability-related discrimination could, however, be reformulated as cases of 'classic' indirect discrimination. Suppose, for example, that an employee is dismissed because (for a disability-related reason) she is unable to comply with her employer's requirement that she works full-time, 40 hours per week. That employee will (subject to justification) have a good claim for disability-related discrimination (see below). In indirect discrimination terms (for example, in terms of the definition in the *Framework Directive, Article 1(1)(b)*), the employer will have applied to her an apparently neutral provision, criterion or practice (the 40 hours per week requirement) applying equally to non-disabled persons, but which may well put persons with particular disabilities at a particular disadvantage compared with others. Subject to the different (and more stringent) test of justification (that of objective justification in *Article 1(1)(b)(i)*), the employee would also have a claim for indirect discrimination. But the point is, at present, of academic interest only given the absence of such a cause of action in *DDA 1995*.

3.60   *Disability-related discrimination: identification of comparator*

The key to understanding and correctly applying the less favourable treatment requirement in *DDA 1995, s 3A(1)* is identifying the correct comparator. What needs to be established is that, for a disability-related reason, a disabled person has been less favourably treated than a person to whom *that reason* does not apply: *Clark v Novacold; Code* section 4.30. The correct comparator is a person (who may or may not be disabled) to whom the identified disability-related reason does not apply. The comparator is *not* a non-disabled person in comparable circumstances. The position is best illustrated by examples:

(a)   A disabled employee is dismissed by his employer for taking an extended period of sick leave related to his disability. A non-disabled employee would also have been dismissed for taking a similar period of sick leave. There is a disability-related reason for the dismissal, namely the period of sick leave. The correct comparator is a person to whom *that reason* does not apply, that is, a person (whether disabled or otherwise) who has not taken the sick leave. Such a person would not have been dismissed. Therefore disability-related discrimination is established, subject to justification. The comparator is *not* a non-disabled person taking a comparable amount of sick leave: *Clark v Novacold* (above).

(b) A disabled woman is refused an administrative job because she cannot type. She cannot type because she has arthritis. A non-disabled person who was unable to type would also have been turned down. There is a disability-related reason for the refusal to employee the woman – namely the inability to type. The correct comparator is a person to whom that reason does not apply – that is, a person who can type. Such a person would not have been refused the job. Therefore, the disabled woman has been less favourably treated for a disability-related reason and disability-related discrimination is established, subject to justification. (The comparator is *not* a non-disabled person who is unable to type.)

(c) A disabled employee is on long-term sick leave, and as a result is placed on half pay after six months. She claims that she has suffered disability-related discrimination because she has received half pay instead of her ordinary pay. The correct comparator is a non-disabled employee who is not on long-term sick leave. The woman has suffered disability-related discrimination, subject to justification (which is, however, likely to be fairly readily made out): *O'Hanlon v Commissioners for HM Revenue & Customs* [2007] EWCA Civ 283 (per Hooper LJ at 86; per Sedley LJ at 96–7), where the employment tribunal had fallen into the 'trap' ([2006] IRLR 840, EAT at 83) of comparing the claimant with a non-disabled person also absent for the same length of time. Cf *London Clubs Management v Hood* [2001] IRLR 719, a highly unusual case analysed by the EAT in *O'Hanlon* as turning on the 'very narrow point indeed' that the claim was for sick pay rather than for ordinary pay. *Hood* can be regarded as having been confined to its facts; the correct approach is now that set out in *O'Hanlon*.

3.61 *Disability-related discrimination and direct discrimination*

Note that because of the different exercises to be carried out in identifying the comparator, in many cases, facts giving rise to a good claim for less favourable treatment will not also give rise to a direct discrimination claim. Thus, in the two examples given in 3.60, there is no direct disability discrimination because (in each case) a non-disabled person in comparable circumstances and with comparable abilities would have received the same treatment as the disabled person.

3.62 *What is a disability-related reason?*

The question of what is meant by a reason 'which relates to' the disabled person's disability was recently considered by the Court of Appeal in *Lewisham London Borough Council v Malcolm* [2007] EWCA Civ 763, [2007] 32 EG 88 (CS). The court held that there were two questions to consider: first, what was the reason for the less favourable treatment? And secondly, was there 'an appropriate causal link' between that reason and the disability? If the reason for the treatment 'engaged some aspect of' the disability, then this requirement would be satisfied and the reason would be 'related to' the disability. See further *Clark v Novacold*, where Mummery LJ referred to the 'requirement of a causal link with disability'. The conclusion of the court in *Malcolm* itself was that there was a disability-related reason for the defendant taking possession proceedings, which it had done because a disabled tenant with schizophrenia had sublet his premises. The court held (Toulson LJ dubitante) that the subletting was a disability-related reason because the schizophrenia gave rise to 'limited thinking' and thus to limited understanding of the legal consequences of subletting. This is an extremely broad approach which, if followed, will mean that a claimant seeking to establish a disability-related reason will have only a low hurdle to clear.

3.63   *Less favourable treatment*

For consideration of what is meant by 'less favourable treatment', see COMMON CONCEPTS (1).

3.64   *Disability-related discrimination and employer's state of mind*

Two different issues arise here.

(a)   *Disability-related reason must affect the employer's mind*: for disability-related discrimination to be made out, the employer must treat the employee less favourably for a disability-related reason which is present in the employer's mind. The reason must affect the employer's mind, whether consciously or subconsciously (the latter being relevant in cases of innate prejudice and, therefore, more likely to arise in cases of direct, rather than disability-related, discrimination). Where there is more than one reason for the dismissal, the disability-related reason must have had a significant influence on the employer's decision. In any case, unless the disability-related reason has affected the employer's mind, he will not have discriminated. See generally *Taylor v OCS Group Ltd* [2006] EWCA Civ 702, [2006] ICR 1602 and *HM Prison Service v Johnson* [2007] IRLR 951.

(b)   *Knowledge of disability not necessary*: By contrast, it is not necessary (in order for a claim of disability-related discrimination to succeed) for the employer to have knowledge of the *fact* of the employee's disability itself (as opposed to the disability-related reason for the less favourable treatment): *Heinz v Kenrick* [2000] IRLR 144, EAT. Thus, in the *Heinz* case, an employee was dismissed on the grounds of long-term absence. That absence was related to her disability (chronic fatigue syndrome), but the employer was not aware (at the time of dismissal) that the employee was suffering from that (or any) disability. The question of whether the reason for dismissal was disability-related was held to be a question of objective fact. Here, the reason for dismissal did, in fact, relate to the disability – so less favourable treatment for a disability-related reason was established.

Thus, in summary, it is not necessary for the actual disability to operate upon the employer's mind, provided that the disability-related reason has done so. On the other hand, the mere fact that the employee's disability had a causative effect on the less favourable treatment complained of will be insufficient if there is no disability-related reason operating on the employer's mind. See *Taylor v OCS*, above, *per* Smith LJ at 72–73: in that case, the fact that the claimant's deafness might have contributed to his dismissal (because it led to an inability to explain himself) was insufficient in the absence of an established disability-related reason in the employer's mind (but cf the broad pro-claimant approach in *Lewisham LBC v Malcolm* (see 3.62), which proceeded on the basis that the defendant landlord had no knowledge of the claimant's schizophrenia when starting possession proceedings on the basis that he had sublet his premises)

3.65   *Disability-related discrimination: justification*

Less favourable treatment not amounting to direct discrimination is justified if, but only if, the reason for the treatment is both material to the circumstances of the particular case and substantial (*DDA1995, s 3A(3)*) – although such treatment cannot be justified in a case where there has been a failure to make reasonable adjustments unless it would have been justified even if the employer had complied with that duty (*s 3A(6)*; see below).

3.66 *'Material and substantial' test*

While *DDA 1995* imposes no explicit overarching test of 'reasonableness' (compare, in the context of unfair dismissal, *Employment Rights Act 1996, s 98(4)*), it is for the present established (cf the reservations expressed by Sedley LJ in *Collins v Royal National Theatre Board* [2004] EWCA Civ 144, [2004] 2 All ER 851 at 25 and *O'Hanlon* at 98) that the test for justification does nevertheless involve something akin to the 'range of reasonable responses' test in unfair dismissal law (*Jones v Post Office* [2001] EWCA Civ 558, [2001] IRLR 384, CA; *Williams v J Walter Thompson Group* [2005] EWCA Civ 133, [2005] IRLR 376). Thus:

(a)   the use of the word 'material' means that there must be a 'reasonably strong connection between the employer's reason and the circumstances of the individual case' (*Jones*, per Arden LJ at 37; *Code*, section 6.3); and

(b)   'if credible arguments exist to support the employer's decision, the employment tribunal may not hold that the reason for the discrimination is not substantial. If, however, the employer's reason is outside the band of responses which a reasonable employer might have adopted, the reason would not be substantial' (*Jones*, loc cit). The *Code* states (section 6.3) that 'substantial' in this context means that 'the reason must carry real weight and be of substance'.

3.67 *Justification and reasonable adjustments*

Justification of less favourable treatment will not, however, be established in a case where there has been a failure to make reasonable adjustments unless such justification would have been established even if the reasonable adjustments duty had been complied with (*s 3A(6)*). See further *Jangra v Gate Gourmet, London Ltd*, EAT/608/01 (23 October 2002). In *Meikle v Nottinghamshire County Council* [2004] EWCA Civ 859, [2004] IRLR 703, CA, the claimant (an employee with a disability affecting her vision) was placed on half pay under her employer's sick leave policy after a certain period of absence on sick leave. The Court of Appeal held that the employer's failure to make reasonable adjustments (eg by providing enlarged written materials and by reducing contact hours) had prolonged the claimant's absence. Had the adjustments been made, the claimant would not have been absent for long enough to be put on half pay. Therefore, the less favourable treatment (the half pay) could not be justified under what is now *s 3A(6)*.

Notwithstanding the link between justification and reasonable adjustments link, it is important to appreciate that a claim for disability-related discrimination and a claim for breach of the reasonable adjustments duty each exist as free-standing claims. A failure to comply with the reasonable adjustments duty is 'discrimination' (*s 3A(2)*) and there is no need to plead or establish any other type of discrimination (eg direct discrimination or disability-related discrimination) in order to succeed in such a claim. Similarly, it is perfectly possible to bring a claim for less favourable treatment without pleading or proving a reasonable adjustments claim.

3.68   Disability Discrimination

3.68   *Justification in practice*

Questions about justification may commonly arise in the following areas.

(a)   *Absence/sick leave.* If an employee is less favourably treated (eg by being dismissed) pursuant to an absence policy, and his absence is disability-related, then this may fulfil the 'material and substantial' justification test. *DDA 1995* does not impose an absolute obligation on an employer to refrain from dismissing an employee who is absent on grounds of ill health due to disability: see *Royal Liverpool Children's NHS Trust v Dunsby* UKEAT/0426/05/LA (1 December 2005) at 16 (where the EAT recognised, at 17, that it is rare for a sickness absence procedure to require disability-related absences to be disregarded, and that the question of whether an employer acts unlawfully in taking such absences into account will depend on whether there is 'material and substantial' justification). Justification may be established provided that:

  (i)   the employer has properly considered the employee's individual circumstances and has then properly applied the relevant provisions of the policy thereto. (If he has not done these things, there is a risk that the reason for the treatment will not be 'material' in the *Jones* sense);

  (ii)   the decision to subject the employee to the treatment in question is within the range of reasonable responses in the circumstances and/or the reason for the treatment 'carries real weight' (otherwise the reason may not be 'substantial');

  (iii)   the employer has considered whether the relevant policy places the employee at a substantial disadvantage in comparison with non-disabled persons and, if so, has considered whether to make any reasonable adjustments to it to prevent it from having that effect – and has made any such adjustments. (If he has not done so, he may have failed to comply with his *s 4A* reasonable adjustments duty – in which case, as set out above, he will be unable to rely on the *s 3A* justification defence – see *s 3A(6)*). This is likely to be the most difficult area in practice. If persons with a particular disability are likely to have substantially more sickness absence than persons without that disability, then the reasonable adjustments duty is likely to come into play. Ultimately, the question for the tribunal will then be whether it is reasonable for the employer to refuse to modify a policy in a particular case.

This last point was considered, in relation to a claim for full pay while on disability-related sick leave, in *O'Hanlon*. In that case, the EAT ([2006] IRLR 840 at 67ff) held that it would be a 'very rare case indeed' where an adjustment to an agreed sick pay scheme would be required, although the EAT did not rule out the possibility that such an adjustment could be required in 'exceptional circumstances'. In the Court of Appeal, Hooper LJ (giving the leading judgment) saw 'much force' in the EAT's approach on the point (at 57). Sedley LJ held that collectively agreed pay structures for a very large establishment (while not in principle beyond the reach of the *DDA 1995*) were 'not ready candidates for individual variation' (at 99); and that while it would not be permissible or justified to construct a scheme operating arbitrarily to the disadvantage of the disabled, 'any unplanned discriminatory aspect may well be justified on the ground that such exceptions as can fairly be made in favour of disabled employees are already programmed into the scheme'. See also *Khan v Royal Mail Group*

UKEAT/0480/06/DA (5 December 2007) and *Gibson Shipbrokers Ltd v Staples* UKEAT/0263/07 (18 September 2007) – both cases where the EAT briefly considered the *O'Hanlon* principle.

(b)   *Health and safety concerns.* The key here is that the employer should avoid stereotypical assumptions that a disabled person represents a risk to health and safety (for example because he is in a wheelchair or suffers from a medical condition such as diabetes or epilepsy). If the employer makes such an assumption, and treats the employee less favourably as a result, he risks being liable to claims for both direct discrimination (see above) and disability-related discrimination (because there may well be no 'reasonably strong connection' between the employer's reason and the individual circumstances).

3.69   Duty to make reasonable adjustments

The duty to make reasonable adjustments is a unique feature of *DDA 1995*, requiring as it does that disabled employees should (in certain circumstances) be treated more favourably than their non-disabled counterparts (see *s 18D(1)* and e g *Archibald v Fife Council* [2004] UKHL 32 per Baroness Hale at 57); c f other 'strands' of discrimination law where such 'positive discrimination' is not required – nor, save in exceptional circumstances (see e g *SDA 1975 s 48*; *RRA 1976, ss 35* and *38*), permitted.

The duty is set out, in relation to employers, in *DDA 1995, s 4A*. It requires that where either (a) a provision, criterion or practice applied by or on behalf of an employer, or (b) any physical feature of premises occupied by the employer, places the disabled person concerned at a substantial disadvantage in comparison with persons who are not disabled, the employer should take such steps as it is reasonable, in all the circumstances of the case, for him to have to take in order to prevent the provision, criterion or practice (or, as the case may be, the physical feature), from having that effect. The EAT has given schematic guidance as to the course to be steered by a tribunal prior to a finding of a breach of the reasonable adjustments duty (*Smiths Detection v Berriman* UKEAT/0712/04/0908, updated in *Environment Agency v Rowan* [2008] IRLR 20). In short, a tribunal considering a reasonable adjustments claim must identify:

(a)   the provision, criterion or practice applied by or on behalf of an employer; or

(b)   the physical feature of premises occupied by the employer; or

(c)   the identity of non-disabled comparators (where appropriate); and

(d)   the nature and extent of the substantial disadvantage suffered by the claimant.

3.70   *Preliminary considerations*

In considering the duty it is necessary to bear in mind a number of preliminary points:

(a)   *Failure to make adjustments is discrimination.* A failure by an employer to comply with a duty to make reasonable adjustments is disability discrimination by that employer (*DDA 1995, s 3A(2)*). There is no need to prove any additional discriminatory act by the employer. Thus, there is no need to prove that there has additionally been direct discrimination or disability-related discrimination. A reasonable adjustments claim is free-standing.

(But note that a breach of the duty to make reasonable adjustments is not otherwise actionable (e g it is not actionable as a breach of statutory duty) –*s 18B(6)*.)

(b) *Reasonable adjustments duty implements indirect discrimination requirements of the Directive*. As set out above, the duty to make reasonable adjustments set out in *s 4A* (as amplified by *s 18B*) implements the *Framework Directive*'s prohibition of indirect disability discrimination (*Articles 2(1)* and *2(2)(b)*, in particular subparagraph (*ii*) thereof). The *Framework Directive* requires that *all* apparently neutral potentially indirectly discriminatory provisions, criteria or practices be subject to the reasonable adjustments duty. The *DDA*'s reasonable adjustments provisions are to be (broadly) construed accordingly.

(c) *Duty to make adjustments in order to prevent disadvantageous effect*. The duty is not simply a duty to make such adjustments as are reasonable in all the circumstances, but a duty to take such steps as are reasonable in those circumstances in order to prevent the provision, criterion or practice (or, as the case may be, the physical feature) from having the effect of placing the disabled person concerned at a substantial disadvantage (*s 4A(1)*).

(d) *Supplementary provision about reasonable adjustments*. It is important to note that *s 18B* makes supplementary provision about the reasonable adjustments duty on employers in *s 4A* (and about the corresponding reasonable adjustments duties elsewhere in Part 2 – see eg *s 4B(4)*, (5) (contract workers); *s 4E* (office-holders); *s 4H* (occupational pension schemes) etc). In particular, *s 18B* sets out factors to which regard is to be had in determining whether it is reasonable for a person to have to take a particular step (subsection (*1*)); gives examples of steps which may need to be taken in order to comply with a reasonable adjustments duty (subsection (*2*)); and makes provision about the alteration of premises (subsections (*3*)–(*5*)). Additionally, it is (as always) important to make reference to the *Code*, *Chapter 5* of which makes provision in relation to the reasonable adjustments duty.

3.71 *To whom is the duty owed?*

The duty to make reasonable adjustments is owed to 'the disabled person concerned' as defined in *DDA 1995, s 4A(2)* (and not to disabled persons generally: cf *DDA 1995, Part 3* (goods and services)). In the case of a provision, criterion or practice for determining to whom employment should be offered, the duty is owed to 'any person who is, or has notified the employer that he may be, an applicant for that employment'; in any other case, the duty is owed to a disabled person who is an applicant for the employment concerned or an employee of the employer concerned.

3.72 *No anticipatory duty to make adjustments*

It follows that, unlike in *DDA 1995, Part III*, there is no 'anticipatory' duty upon an employer to make reasonable adjustments – that is, there is no duty to make such adjustments in anticipation of the possibility that a person with a particular disability may apply for a job or may become an employee of the employer. There is no duty to make adjustments to a role to remedy a substantial disadvantage to a theoretical potential candidate who is disabled before that candidate has applied for the job (or notified the employer that he may do so) (and see *Difolco v NTL Group* [2006] EWCA Civ 1508, 150 Sol Jo LB 1393, at 13). Nor is there any duty on an employer to invest in equipment (such as computer voice-recognition software) or to make adjustments to premises (e g installing wheelchair ramps) in anticipation of the possibility that a person with a particular disability may apply for a job or join its staff. That is, however, subject to two provisos:

(a)   Overlap with *Part III* duties. Where an employer is also a service-provider, it will (in respect of service provision) be subject to the *Part III* 'anticipatory' duty to make adjustments (that is, a duty owed to disabled persons generally (*DDA 1995, s 21*) rather than only to 'the disabled person concerned' (*s 4A(2)*). The two types of duty will overlap where there is an overlap between service-provision and employment (for example, if an employer has an office for its employees to which members of the public have access; or if a service-provider employer provides the same material on an intranet site for employees and on an internet site for its customers). Similar overlaps may occur where the employer is a public authority subject to the *s 21E* duty to make adjustments.

(b)   Good practice. While there is no requirement to make anticipatory adjustments, the *Code* (sections 2.10–2.11) points out that it is good practice, and likely to be cost-effective, to plan ahead. It will be considerably cheaper to consider (and provide for) the needs of a range of disabled people when refurbishing a building, or when purchasing a new IT system, than it will be subsequently to attempt to modify the building or system for the needs of a particular disabled applicant or employee.

3.73   *Employer's knowledge*

No duty to make reasonable adjustments is imposed in relation to a disabled person if the employer does not know, and could not reasonably be expected to know:

(a)   in the case of an applicant or potential applicant, that the disabled person concerned is, or may be, an applicant for the employment; or

(b)   in any case, that that person has a disability and is likely to be placed at a comparative substantial disadvantage (*DDA 1995, s 4A(3)*).

This is in contrast to the position in relation to disability-related discrimination, where lack of knowledge of disability will not afford a defence provided that the disability-related reason acted on the employer's mind in meting out the less favourable treatment (see 3.64). (And note further that it may sometimes even be possible for a claim for direct discrimination to succeed notwithstanding the employer's lack of knowledge of the disability: see 3.53).

As to the question of whether an employer could 'reasonably be expected' to know that a particular person has a disability, see the *Code,* section 5.12. In *Department for Work and Pensions v Hall* UKEAT 0012/05/3108, the EAT described the question of constructive knowledge as one of 'pure fact', refusing to interfere with the employment tribunal's conclusion that there was such knowledge in a case where the claimant (i) had declined to provide any information about disability or long-term health conditions on a health declaration form; (ii) had refused permission for the employer to contact her doctor; (iii) thereafter behaved at work in a 'disruptive and volatile' manner involving 'both verbal altercations and minor physical contact'.

One particular issue which may arise for employers is the provision by employees or applicants of medical information to the employer's occupational health advisor. In general, it seems that where such information is provided to such an advisor and the advisor is an agent or employee of the employer, such knowledge will be imputed to the employer (Code, section 5.15 and *Hammersmith and Fulham London Borough Council v Farnsworth* [2000] IRLR 691, EAT). Particular difficulties will arise if the employee has not given consent to the information being passed on to the employer: in some circumstances, a line manager may find him- or herself in the situation of making adjustments without knowing precisely why they are needed. In order to avoid this, employers may wish to ensure that it is made clear to applicants and employees that information will need to be shared for *DDA 1995* purposes to the extent necessary to allow adjustments to be made. This will raise data protection issues, as to which, see the Employment Practices Code on Data Protection (Information Commissioner, June 2005), Part 4 (information about workers' health), and particularly the good practice recommendations on occupational health schemes.

It should be noted that the *Framework Directive* does not contain any similar restriction (as to employer's knowledge) on the duty to provide 'reasonable accommodation' (*Article 5*); although references to measures being 'appropriate and 'needed in a particular case' might be argued to be consistent with the restriction.

3.74   *'Provision, criterion or practice'*

As set out above, the duty to make adjustments arises where a 'provision, criterion or practice' places the disabled person concerned at a comparative substantial disadvantage. The term 'provision, criterion or practice' has been used in a number of recent EC discrimination law directives, the first occasion being in the *Burden of Proof Directive (97/80/EC)* (definition of indirect sex discrimination, *Article 2(2)*). The term is likely to be broadly construed given that it is used to define the concept of indirect discrimination for the *Framework Directive* purposes (*Article 2(2)(b)*). It is probably broader than, but includes (*DDA 1995, s 18D(2)*), the previous term 'arrangements' (formerly found in *DDA 1995, s 6(1)(a)*). As to its meaning, see further section 5.8 of the *Code*. Even before the broadening of the scope of the reasonable adjustments duty by implementation of the *Framework Directive*, recent case law developments had taken a broad approach to that scope – so that the duty can extend even to adjusting the essential requirements of a job, or to creating a new job.

In *Archibald v Fife Council* [2004] UKHL 32, [2004] IRLR 651, the claimant had been employed by the respondent as a road sweeper, but became physically disabled to the extent that she could not carry out her duties. The only suitable alternative employment, in sedentary office work, was at a slightly higher grade and the respondent required her to go through a competitive interview process. The claimant did so, but was unsuccessful in applying for more than 100 alternative posts. She claimed that the respondent's duty extended to adjusting the competitive interview requirement (so as to transfer her to a post at the slightly higher grade without an interview). The House of Lords held that it was an implied condition or 'arrangement' of the claimant's employment that (i) she should at all times be physically fit to do her job as a road sweeper; (ii) if she was physically unable to do that job she was liable to be dismissed. The employer's duty (to prevent these 'arrangements' from placing the claimant at a substantial comparative disadvantage) could therefore extend (if reasonable) to transferring the claimant to a vacant clerical post at the higher grade (and salary).

This broad approach to the reasonable adjustments duty can also be seen in *Southampton City College v Randall* [2006] IRLR 18, where the EAT held (at 22) that the *DDA 1995* provisions about reasonable adjustments did not (as a matter of law) preclude the creation of a new post in substitution for an existing post from being a reasonable adjustment.

It seems likely, however, that one limitation on this broad approach is that the courts will continue to require a provision, criterion or practice to be job-related, as did the EAT in *Kenny v Hampshire Constabulary* [1999] ICR 27, EAT: in that case, the applicant needed assistance when going to the toilet. The EAT held that 'arrangements' (old *DDA 1995, s 6(1)(a)*) must be job-related and that, therefore, the duty did not extend to attending to an employee's personal needs.

3.75 *Physical features of premises occupied by the employer*

By *DDA 1995, s 18D(2)*, 'physical feature' (in relation to any premises) includes any of the following (whether permanent or temporary):

(a) any feature arising from the design or construction of a building on the premises;

(b) any feature on the premises of any approach to, exit from, or access to such a building;

(c) any fixtures, fittings, furnishings, furniture, equipment or material in or on the premises; and

(d) any other physical element or quality of any land comprised in the premises.

This would seem to be a broad definition. According to a list, stated to be non-exhaustive, given at *Code* section 5.10, physical features will include 'steps, stairways, kerbs, exterior surfaces and paving, parking areas, building entrances and exits (including emergency escape routes), internal and external doors, gates, toilet and washing facilities, lighting and ventilation, lifts and escalators, floor coverings, signs, furniture, and temporary or movable items'.

Where an employer occupies premises under a lease preventing that employer from making particular alterations to premises in order to comply with the reasonable adjustments duty, provision is made in *DDA 1995, s 18A* about the seeking of consent from the lessor, such consent not to be unreasonably withheld. Provision is also made for cases where a binding obligation other than a lease (eg a mortgage or restrictive covenant) prevents a building being altered (*s 18B(3)*). For further detail, reference should be made to Chapter 12 of the *Code*.

3.76 *Substantial disadvantage*

The duty to make adjustments arises only where the provision, criterion or practice (or physical feature) places the disabled person concerned at a 'substantial disadvantage' by comparison with persons who are not disabled (as to the required comparison, see below.) The *Code* suggests (section 5.11) that a disadvantage is 'substantial' if it is merely 'more than minor or trivial' (and this would tie in with the meaning of 'substantial' in the definition of disability – as to which, see 3.26). It is necessary for an employment tribunal considering a reasonable adjustments claim to identify 'the nature and extent of the substantial disadvantage' suffered by the claimant, bearing in mind that identifying this disadvantage may involve considering the cumulative effect of both 'arrangements' and 'physical features' (ie looking at the overall picture) (*Smiths Detection v Berriman* UKEAT 0712/04/CK).

3.77   *Comparators*

The provision, criterion or practice (or physical feature) must place the disabled person concerned at a substantial disadvantage 'in comparison with persons who are not disabled'. In reasonable adjustments cases, the comparator should normally be readily identifiable by reference to the disadvantage caused by the relevant arrangements (*Smith v Churchills Stairlifts* [2005] EWCA Civ 1220, CA; *Archibald v Fife*). In practice, once the substantial disadvantage has been identified, the identification of a comparator is unlikely to be a significant additional hurdle.

In *Smith* itself, the 'arrangements' at issue were the requirement to carry a full-sized (and heavy) radiator cabinet and/or the fact that the offer of a place on a sales training course was subject to the condition of being able to carry such a cabinet. The claimant was unable to lift the cabinet. The tribunal found as a fact that a majority of the population would have difficulty carrying it any distance and lifting it into a car as required. However, the majority of candidates on the training course were able to lift the cabinet. The disadvantage to the claimant was that he was rejected from the course because of his inability to lift the cabinet. The Court of Appeal held (at para 40) that the proper comparators (identified by reference to the disadvantage) were the six successful candidates who were able to comply with the lifting requirement and/or the nine people who were admitted to the course. The arrangements as a whole clearly placed the claimant at a substantial disadvantage in comparison with these comparators, so the requirement of comparative substantial disadvantage was made out.

3.78   *Adjustments required – examples*

DDA 1995, s 18B(2) sets out the following 'examples of steps which [an employer] may need to take in relation to a disabled person in order to comply with a duty to make reasonable adjustments' (see also the *Code*, sections 5.18–20):

(a)   making adjustments to premises;

(b)   allocating some of the disabled person's duties to another person;

(c)   transferring him to fill an existing vacancy. (Note that (i) 'transfer' may, subject to reasonableness, include a promotion – *Archibald* (see 3.74); (ii) the duty may, again depending on the facts and upon what is reasonable, extend to requiring the creation of a new post in substitution for an existing post – *Southampton City College v Randall* [2006] IRLR 18 at 22, see 3.74);

(d)   altering his hours of working or training;

(e)   assigning him to a different place of work or training;

(f)   allowing him to be absent during working or training hours for rehabilitation, assessment or treatment;

(g)   giving, or arranging for, training or mentoring (whether for the disabled person or any other person);

(h)   acquiring or modifying equipment;

(i)   modifying instructions or reference manuals;

(j)   modifying procedures for testing or assessment;

(k)   providing a reader or interpreter;

(l)   providing supervision or other support.

The *Code* makes the commonsense point (section 5.19) that it may sometimes be necessary for an employer to take a combination of steps.

The list set out in *DDA 1995, s 18B(2)* is only a list of examples. Other steps may well be required, depending upon the 'provision, criterion or practice' (or physical feature), and the comparative substantial disadvantage, identified. Thus, the *Code* (section 5.20) identifies the following as other steps which might be required by the reasonable adjustments duty:

- conducting a proper assessment of what reasonable adjustments may be required. (But note that this may be an incorrect statement of the law: see the discussion of *Tarbuck v Sainsbury's Supermarkets* [2006] IRLR 664, EAT; *Spence v Intype Libra* UKEAT 0617/06/JOJ and related cases; see 3.81);

- permitting flexible working (as to homeworking, see *Environment Agency v Rowan*: in the circum stances of that case, the EAT expressed doubts as to whether a period of homeworking could constitute a reasonable adjustment);

- allowing a disabled employee to take a period of disability leave;

- participating in supported employment schemes, such as Workstep;

- employing a support worker to assist a disabled employee;

- modifying disciplinary or grievance procedures;

- adjusting redundancy selection criteria;

- modifying performance-related pay arrangements. (As to the position in relation to sick pay, see *O'Hanlon v Commissioners for HM Revenue & Customs Cmrs* [2007] EWCA Civ 283, [2007] ICR 1359; and 3.68).

3.79   *Adjustments to policies and procedures*

The examples given in *DDA 1995, s 18B(2)* of reasonable adjustments are, with the exception of that in *s 18B(2)(j)* (modifying procedures for testing or assessment), practical rather than procedural in nature. But, as the *Code* recognises, the duty to make reasonable adjustments can extend beyond this to include the making (in appropriate cases) of adjustments to policies and procedures (e g absence policies or disciplinary procedures) placing a disabled employee at a comparative substantial disadvantage. That this is so is particularly clear in the light of the *Framework Directive, Article 2(2)(b)*, which requires *all* potentially indirectly discriminatory provisions, practices and criteria to be subject to a duty to take appropriate measures to eliminate the disadvantages they entail. So, for example, a job applicant with a particular disability who is refused a job because of an employer's policy of making health clearance decisions based on the report of an expert who has not examined the applicant in person might bring a claim for failure to comply with the reasonable adjustments duty on the basis that the employer should have adjusted its policy (by arranging for the expert to examine her in person before reaching a decision): compare *Surrey Police v Marshall* [2002] IRLR 843, EAT, where the original tribunal had found that the reasonable adjustments duty had not arisen and there was no cross-appeal on the point. An adjustment to a dismissal procedure was required by the EAT in *Rothwell v Pelikan Hardcopy Scotland Ltd* [2006] IRLR 24, where it was held (at 23–25) that consultation with the claimant prior to the decision to dismiss would have been a reasonable adjustment (although the EAT in that case did not specify the arrangements or the comparative substantial disadvantage caused thereby). And adjustments to ill health absence procedures were discussed in *O'Hanlon v Commissioners for HM Revenue & Customs*; see 3.68).

3.80 *Adjustments to 'core' requirements of the job*

The duty to make adjustments extends to the terms, conditions and arrangements relating to the essential functions of a disabled person's employment (as well as to more peripheral matters): see *Archibald* at 41 (see 3.74), where the House of Lords identified the following as 'arrangements' placing the employee at a comparative substantial disadvantage and thus potentially requiring adjustment:

(a)   the requirement that the employee should at all times be physically fit to do her job as a road sweeper;

(b)   the fact that if she was physically unable to do the job she was employed to do she was liable to be dismissed.

Compare *Paterson*, where the EAT held that, in the special circumstances of this case, where a standard akin to a competence standard was required to be met by a probationary police officer, the employer was not required to make reasonable adjustments to certain 'irreducible minimum requirements' of the position.

3.81 *Failure to assess or consult on reasonable adjustments*

There is conflicting case law on the question of whether the reasonable adjustments duty imposes a free-standing duty to assess whether adjustments are necessary or to consult with the employee or obtain information (including medical reports) from him in order to inform the process of considering adjustments. The better (and most recent) view is that a failure to carry out such assessment or consultation is not in itself a breach of the reasonable adjustments duty: *Spence v Intype Libra Ltd* UKEAT 0617/06/2704, following *Tarbuck v Sainsbury's Supermarkets Ltd* [2006] IRLR 664, EAT and *British Gas Services v McCaull* [2001] IRLR 60, EAT and disagreeing with *Mid Staffordshire General Hospitals NHS Trust v Cambridge* [2003] IRLR 567. That this is the correct approach has recently been confirmed by the EAT in *Scottish and Southern Energy Plc v Mackay* UKEAT/0075/06/MT, following the *Tarbuck* line of cases for the reasons given in the case of *HM Prison Service v Johnson* UKEAT/0420/06 'unless and until the Court of Appeal rules otherwise'. And see to like effect *London Borough of Camden v Price-Job* UKEAT/0507/06/DM and *EA Gibson Shipbrokers*. This is because the reasonable adjustments duty is a duty to take reasonable steps to prevent the provision (etc) from placing the disabled employee at a comparative substantial disadvantage – but the carrying out of an assessment or the obtaining of a medical report 'does not of itself mitigate or prevent or shield the employee from anything' (*Spence* at 43; see further at 47). (See also *Environment Agency v Rowan*, where similar reasoning was applied to a trial period, in that case of homeworking.)The issue is whether the necessary reasonable adjustment has been made: 'whether it is by luck or judgment is immaterial' (*ibid* at 38). (Note that, because of the conflict of EAT authority, leave was given to Mr Spence to appeal to the Court of Appeal: *Spence* at 52). The *Spence* principle is, in any event, subject to the following caveats:

(a)   a failure to consult with an employee or to assess whether reasonable adjustments are necessary puts the employer at very significant risk of failing to spot that a particular (substantive) adjustment is required and therefore of failing to comply with the reasonable adjustments duty in that respect;

(b)   in particular, the mere fact that an employee (or her doctor) has not put forward any particular adjustment for the employer's consideration does not absolve the employer of its *DDA 1995, s 4A* reasonable adjustments duty (see *Cosgrove v Caesar & Howie* [2001] IRLR 653, EAT, but note that that case predated *Tarbuck v Sainsbury's* and *Spence v Intype Libra*, above, and should be read in the light of those cases);

(c)   moreover, a failure to consult prior to dismissal will very often have the consequence of rendering a potentially fair dismissal unfair for the purposes of *Employment Rights Act 1996, s 98*.

3.82   *Reasonableness*

The question for the tribunal (*DDA 1995, s 4A(1)*) is whether the step(s) in question is/are step(s) which it is 'reasonable, in all the circumstances of the case, for [the employer] to have to take' in order to prevent the provision, criterion or practice (or physical feature) from placing the disabled person at a comparative substantial disadvantage. This is an objective test – the question is what steps it is reasonable for the employer to have to take, not what steps the employer reasonably believes should be taken: see eg *Smith v Churchills Stairlifts plc* at 44–45 (citing *Collins v Royal National Theatre Board Ltd* [2004] EWCA Civ 144, [2004] IRLR 395 at 20). The tribunal's conclusion on the issue of reasonableness will, of course, depend upon the facts and context in any particular case (see the reference to 'all the circumstances of the case' in *s 4A(1)*).

3.83   *Factors to be taken into account*

DDA 1995, s 18B(1) requires regard to be had, in particular, to the following in determining whether it is reasonable for an employer to have to take a particular step in order to comply with the reasonable adjustments duty (for further guidance, see *Code,* sections 5.24–5.41):

(a)   the extent to which taking the step would prevent the effect in relation to which the duty is imposed (see, eg, *Romec Ltd v Rudham* UKEAT/0069/07/DA (13 July 2007);

(b)   the extent to which it is practicable for the employer to take the step;

(o)   the financial and other costs which would be incurred by the employer in taking the step and the extent to which taking it would disrupt any of his activities;

(d)   the extent of the employer's financial and other resources;

(e)   the availability to the employer of financial or other assistance with respect to taking the step;

(f)   the nature of the employer's activities and the size of his undertaking;

(g)   where the step would be taken in relation to a private household, the extent to which taking it would—

    (i)   disrupt that household, or

    (ii)   disturb any person residing there.

Other factors may additionally be relevant. The *Code* (section 5.42) gives the following additional examples of factors relevant to reasonableness:

- *effect on other employees.* Note in particular that (as in cases involving indirect sex discrimination and part-time working (see SEX DISCRIMINATION (8)) the fact that non-disabled employees would resent the making of adjustments is most unlikely to mean that the employer is not obliged to make them;

- *adjustments made for other disabled employees.* It would often be very difficult to justify a refusal to make an adjustment for one employee when a similar adjustment had previously been made for another working for the same employer;

- *the extent to which the disabled person is willing to co-operate.*

3.84 *Justification*

It is important to note that from 1 October 2004, there is no possibility of justifying a failure to make reasonable adjustments. (Such justification was previously provided for by *DDA 1995, ss 5(2)(b)* and *5(4)*). If an employer has failed to take such steps as the tribunal determines it is reasonable for him to have to take in accordance with *s 4A*, there will have been discrimination (*s 3A(2)*), with no possibility of justification. That said, the removal of the justification defence may have a fairly limited impact: an adjustment was in most cases unlikely to be found to be reasonable if there was some material and substantial reason why it should not be carried out (see further *Collins v Royal National Theatre Board Ltd*).

3.85 *Problem areas*

The duty to make reasonable adjustments is probably the most difficult area for employers to deal with, particularly because (a) it requires more favourable treatment of disabled than non-disabled employees and applicants; and (b) it is unique to *DDA 1995*. The duty may commonly arise, and cause difficulties, in areas such as:

(a) *Performance-related pay.* See the *Code*, section 5.20, final box, which suggests that a disabled employee paid purely on output should be paid at an agreed rate – eg her average hourly rate – during frequent short additional breaks necessitated by her disability – though whether this is required will ultimately depend (assuming that comparative substantial disadvantage is established) upon whether this is reasonable in all the circumstances. While the courts have not yet grappled with the problem of performance-related pay generally, it seems likely that they will take a fairly robust approach to implementing agreed performance-related pay schemes without modification in individual cases, provided that (i) all possible reasonable adjustments to enhance the disabled employee's performance level have been made; and (ii) the scheme has been properly applied to the employee's individual circumstances without (for example) the making of any disability-based assumptions. But much will, of course, depend on the particular circumstances of the case and the provisions of the scheme.

(b) *Absence monitoring.* See *Royal Liverpool Children's NHS Trust v Dunsby* at 3.68, where the EAT recognised that it would be rare for an absence procedure to require periods of disability-related absence to be disregarded. As always, the ultimate question will be one of reasonableness in the particular case and once again care should be taken to ensure that: (i) all possible adjustments (eg ensuring adequate rest breaks and/or shorter working hours) have been made to minimise the amount of time off sick taken by the employee; and (ii) that the absence monitoring scheme has been applied to the disabled employee as it is (or would be) applied to non-disabled employees (and without, for example, any assumption that the disabled employee is likely to take more time off or to need closer monitoring).

(c)   *Sick pay*. The Court of Appeal in *O'Hanlon v Revenue & Customs Cmrs* (see 3.60), has recently taken a robust approach to this difficult issue, recognising that in many cases an employer will readily be able to justify a refusal to depart from the provisions of an agreed sick pay scheme by making enhanced sick payments to a particular disabled employee.

(d)   *Alternative positions for disabled employees*. This issue is particularly likely to arise when an existing employee becomes disabled. As set out above, the duty to make reasonable adjustments may (depending on the facts and circumstances, and subject always to reasonableness) require an employer not only to transfer a disabled employee to an equivalent post but also: (i) to promote her to a higher grade (*Archibald v Fife*; see 3.74); or even (ii) (in particular circumstances, e g when carrying out a re-organisation) to create a post tailored to her needs (*Southampton City College v Randall*; see 3.74).

3.86   Harassment

For the purposes of the employment provisions of *DDA 1995*, an employer subjects a disabled person to harassment where, for a reason which relates to the disabled person's disability, he engages in unwanted conduct which has the purpose or effect of—

(a)   violating the disabled person's dignity, or

(b)   creating an intimidating, hostile, degrading, humiliating or offensive environment for him(*s 3B(1)*).

By *s 3B(2)*, conduct is to be regarded as having the effect in (a) or (b) only if, having regard to all the circumstances, including in particular the perception of the disabled person, it should reasonably be considered as having that effect.

See further COMMON CONCEPTS (1). Note that in *Equal Opportunities Commission v Secretary of State for Trade and Industry* [2007] EWHC 483 (Admin), [2007] 2 CMLR 1351, the High Court held that provisions in the *SDA 1975* defining harassment as unwanted conduct 'on the ground of [the complainant's] sex' did not properly implement the relevant EC Directive. The court noted (at 7) that the result of this argument was that the provisions of (*inter alia*) *DDA 1995, s 3B* implementing the *Directive* were also unlawfully formulated (although note that *DDA 1995* uses 'for a reason which relates to' rather than 'on the ground of'). It remains to be seen what action the Government will take to deal with this point.

Note that prior to 1 October 2004, harassment was rendered unlawful by *DDA 1995* insofar as it amounted to (less favourable treatment) discrimination by an employer against a disabled employee by subjecting that employee to 'any other detriment' (*s 4(2)(d)*). Harassment is now explicitly excluded from the scope of 'ordinary' discrimination by *s 18D(2)*, which provides that 'detriment' does not include harassment.

3.87   *Examples*

The following are examples given in the *Code* of behaviour amounting to harassment (see further boxes after section 4.39):

- calling a disabled employee by offensive names (whether or not in his presence) with the intention of humiliating him;

- making constant jokes about persons with particular disabilities, or circulating such jokes by e-mail;

- making references to an employee's disability in front of other members of his team, despite his requests not to do so.

Compound claims

While it is quite possible for a claimant to bring a disability discrimination claim based on only one of the three distinct types of discrimination (direct discrimination, disability-related discrimination and reasonable adjustments), it will be much more common for claims to allege more than one of these (and claims may, of course, additionally allege that there has been harassment (see 3.86) or victimisation (see 3.88)).

In the overwhelming majority of cases, however, a claimant will be well advised to plead (and to seek to prove) both disability-related discrimination and a failure to make reasonable adjustments (and, in addition, if appropriate, direct discrimination). Most cases can be pleaded in both ways. The only clear exception will be a case where it is plain that the employer did not have (either actual or constructive) knowledge of the employee's disability – so that no reasonable adjustments duty could arise. There may also be an exception in cases where the disabled employee has been treated in precisely the same way as other employees (so that less favourable treatment could not be established for disability-related discrimination purposes, while a reasonable adjustments claim could still be pleaded), but such cases are likely to be rare: in many such cases, the *result* of the treatment is less favourable for the disabled employee, even if the treatment itself is identical to that meted out to non-disabled employees.

It is undoubtedly true that some cases may 'feel' more like less favourable treatment cases, and others more like reasonable adjustments cases. For example, suppose that a disabled employee with arthritis has a slower-than-average typing speed of 20 wpm because of her disability, and consider two cases: (a) her employer runs a promotion competition for a managerial role but requires applicants to have a typing speed of 50 wpm in order to be eligible; (b) the employee requires a special keyboard in order to be able to type without suffering pain, and her employer fails to provide this. Case (a) might be more naturally categorised as a less favourable treatment case and case (b) as a reasonable adjustments case. But:

(a)   case (a) could be pleaded as a reasonable adjustments case, on the basis that the 50 wpm requirement placed the employee at a substantial comparative disadvantage and should therefore have been modified in her case;

(b)   in case (b), if the failure to provide the keyboard led to reduced performance and, thus, to a failure to receive performance-related pay or to achieve promotion (or, indeed, to dismissal), then a less favourable treatment (disability-related discrimination) claim might be pleaded and proved.

For further examples of the interaction of the three types of discrimination (and, in addition, victimisation), see section 4.37 of the *Code*.

3.88 **OTHER UNLAWFUL ACTS**

Victimisation

As with all of the other discrimination legislation, it is unlawful for an employer to treat a person less favourably than others by reason that a person performed a 'protected act' or is believed or suspected of doing or intending to do a protected act (*DDA 1995, s 55(1)*). For general principles, see 1.55ff. However, *DDA 1995* provisions differ slightly. Protected acts under *DDA 1995* are as follows:

(a)   bringing proceedings against any person under *DDA 1995* (*s 55(2)(a)(i)*);

(b)   giving evidence or information in connection with such proceedings brought by any person (*s 55(2)(a)(ii)*);

(c)   otherwise doing anything under or by reference to *DDA 1995* in relation to any other person (*s 55(2)(a)(iii)*); or

(d)   alleging that A or any other person has (whether or not the allegation so states) contravened *DDA 1995*.

Victimisation under the *DDA 1995* applies to both disabled and non-disabled persons. Both groups are also protected against victimisation from a former employer once their employment has come to an end (see COMMON CONCEPTS (1)).

3.89 **Discriminatory advertisements**

DDA 1995, s 16B(1) provides that it is unlawful for a person to publish or cause to be published an advertisement inviting applications for (amongst other things) employment, promotion or transfer of employment if it indicates or might reasonably be understood to indicate that an application will or may be determined by reference to:

(a)   the applicant not having a disability or any particular disability;

(b)   the applicant not having had any disability or any particular disability; or

(c)   any reluctance of the persons determining the application to comply with a duty to make reasonable adjustments.

An advertisement for the purposes of *DDA 1995* includes every form of advertisement or notice, whether this is made to the public or not (*s 16B(4)*).

S 16B(2) contains an exclusion for placing a discriminatory advertisement where it would not in fact be unlawful under *DDA 1995, Part II* for the application to be determined in the manner indicated. This would apply, for example, in relation to a reluctance to make reasonable adjustments because it is necessary for a person to be able to ride a bicycle in order to work as a bicycle courier (*Code*, section 7.13).

A publisher of a discriminatory advertisement may have a defence if they can show that it was published in reliance on a statement made by the person placing the advertisement that it was not unlawful and it was reasonable for them to rely on that statement (*s 16(2A)*). A person who knowingly or recklessly makes such a statement to a publisher commits a criminal offence and, if convicted, is subject to a fine not exceeding level 5 (*s 16B(2B)*). *S 16B(2B)* does not make the publisher guilty of a criminal offence, although it may still be the subject of a tribunal claim in relation to the advertisement.

S 16B does not, of course, make it unlawful for an employer to try to attract disabled candidates, and this is supported by *Code*, section 7.11. Therefore, a job advertisement can include wording such as that the employer 'would welcome applications from disabled people'. (As set out above, *DDA 1995*, unlike other discrimination law strands, operates asymmetrically in that it does not prohibit discrimination against non-disabled people – so that an employer may not only advertise for but actually appoint a disabled candidate in preference to a non-disabled candidate, subject always to other legal requirements – see 3.69).

Claims in relation to discriminatory advertisements (and instructions and pressure to discriminate (see 3.90) cannot be made by an individual. It is for the EHRC to bring these claims in the tribunal (*EqA 2006, s.25(1)(c)*).

3.91 Instructions and pressure to discriminate

3.90   It is unlawful for a person who has authority or influence over another person to instruct them or put pressure on them to commit unlawful discrimination. This covers pressure to discriminate whether applied directly to the person concerned, or indirectly but in a way in which he is likely to hear about (*DDA 1995, s 16C*). As is the case for discriminatory advertisements, a claim under *s 16C* can only be brought by the EHRC. See further COMMON CONCEPTS (1).

Liability of employers and principals for the unlawful acts of others

Employees

Anything done by a person during the course of their employment is treated for the purposes of *DDA 1995* as also done by their employer, whether or not it was done with the employer's knowledge or consent (*s 58(1)*). However, the employer will have a defence if it can show that it took 'such steps as were reasonably practicable' to prevent such actions (*s 58(5)*). For further information on liability of employers and principals see COMMON CONCEPTS (1).

3.92   *Agents*

Employers who act through agents are liable for their agents' actions where such actions are done with the express or implied authority of the employer and this is the case whether or not the authority was given before or after the act in question (*DDA 1995, s 58(2)*). For example, an employer may be liable for the acts of a contractor or consultant who discriminates or harasses an employee contrary to *DDA 1995*. For further information on liability for unlawful act of an agent, see COMMON CONCEPTS (1).

3.93 Aiding unlawful acts

A person who knowingly aids another person to do an unlawful act under *DDA 1995* is treated as doing the same kind of unlawful act (*s 57(1)*). The *Code* (section 3.25) gives the example of a recruitment consultant who refuses to consider a disabled applicant for a vacancy because his client has said that they do not want to take on anyone who is handicapped. In this scenario, in addition to the employer client's liability for its unlawful act, the recruitment consultant could be liable for aiding the employer to discriminate.

Further, where an employer or principal is vicariously liable for the acts of their employee or agent under *s 58(1)*, (2) (or would be vicariously liable but is able to establish a reasonable steps defence), the individual employee or agent is deemed to have aided that unlawful act (*s 57(2)*). Therefore, in addition to a potential claim against the employer or principal, a claimant will also be able to bring a claim against the employee or agent who committed the act of discrimination in question. See further COMMON CONCEPTS (1).

3.94   *False or misleading statements*

An employee or agent who is liable for aiding an unlawful act may have a defence if they can show that they acted in reliance on a statement made by their employer or principal that the act in question was not unlawful, and it was reasonable for them to rely on the statement (*DDA 1995, s 57(3)*). Where a person knowingly or recklessly makes such a statement that is materially false or misleading they are guilty of a criminal offence and liable on summary conviction to a fine not exceeding level 5 (*s 57(4), (5)*).

3.95   **IN PRACTICE**

General

According to the DRC (now the EHRC) there are around ten million disabled people in Great Britain. The DRC has stated that the:

> 'functional limitations arising from disabled people's impairments do not inevitably restrict their ability to participate fully in society. Rather than the limitations of an impairment, it is often environmental factors (such as the structure of a building, or an employer's working practices) which unnecessarily lead to these social restrictions.'

The potential benefits of avoiding disability discrimination and harassment, aside from legal obligations, may include making an employer's workforce more representative of the community; attracting and keeping able staff; undervaluing, under-using or losing able staff; and improving staff morale and productivity.

3.96   *Practical steps on how to avoid discrimination*

The *Code* has a number of good practice suggestions for avoiding discrimination. Although the aim of these suggestions is to avoid discrimination in the first place, in many instances having undertaken these steps will also aid an employer in defending any claims brought against it under *DDA 1995*. (Note further that in the case of an employer which is also a public authority, the general duty to promote equality (*s 49A*) and the specific duties, including the duty to prepare and implement a Disability Equality Scheme, in the *Disability Discrimination (Public Authorities) (Statutory Duties) Regulations 2005*, made under *DDA 1995, s 49D*, will in addition be relevant in this area. The detailed requirements of those duties are beyond the scope of this work).

(a)   **Implementing anti-discrimination policies and practices**

Having diversity and equality policies and incorporating anti-discrimination policies in relation to disabled employees will, if those policies are properly communicated to employees and actively put into practice, assist employers both in disseminating their commitment to equality throughout the organisation and in demonstrating to a tribunal in the event of litigation that they have taken all possible steps to avoid discrimination. The *Code* (section 2.12) makes a number of suggestions of good practice in relation to policies, which are summarised below:

(i)   establish a policy and communicate it to employees;

(ii)   provide training to all employees (and agents), whether by an external training provider or internally, so that they understand the employer's policy relating to disabled persons, the obligations under *DDA 1995* and the practice of reasonable adjustments;

(iii) inform all employees that breaches of the policy will not be tolerated and respond quickly and effectively to such breaches;

(iv)   monitor the implementation and effectiveness of the policy;

(v)   address acts of disability discrimination by employees as part of disciplinary rules and procedures;

(vi)   have complaints and grievance procedures which are easy for disabled employees to use and which are designed to resolve issues effectively;

(vii) have clear procedures to prevent and deal with harassment for a reason related to a person's disability;

(viii) establish a policy in relation to disability-related leave, and monitor the implementation and effectiveness of such a policy;

(ix)   consult with disabled employees about their experiences of working for the organisation;

(x)   regularly review the effectiveness of reasonable adjustments made for disabled people in accordance with *DDA 1995* (and act on the findings of those reviews);

(xi)   keep clear records of decisions taken in respect of the above matters.

(b)   Auditing policies and procedures

The DRC (now EHRC) recommends that policies such as flexible working arrangements and emergency evacuation procedures are audited in order to consider the needs of disabled employees.

(c)   Avoiding making assumptions

Avoiding making assumptions about employees who may or may not be disabled may also help to avoid discrimination. The *Code* (section 2.4) lists some common assumptions.

(d)   Finding out about disabled people's needs

Consultation with disabled people, whether formal or informal, can help employers comply with their legal obligations, particularly in relation to reasonable adjustments. The DRC (now EHRC) also suggests that this process can assist companies in dealing better with disabled customers while also producing commercial benefits.

(e)   Monitoring

Monitoring should ideally be carried out to establish the proportion of disabled people at certain grades or levels within the employer's organisation, as well as collating information on the number of disabled people applying for positions and, within that, the number being appointed.

The results of monitoring should enable an employer to re-evaluate its internal practices.

Confidentiality must be ensured, and questions appropriately and sensi-tively phrased. Information received will generally constitute sensitive personal data, within the meaning of the *Data Protection Act 1998* (*DPA 1998*), so an employer must ensure that one of the conditions set out in *DPA 1998, Sch 3* is fulfilled. Reference should also be made to the *Employment Practices Code on Data Protection* (Information Commis-sioner, June 2005).

3.97   **Applicants for employment**

It is unlawful for an employer to discriminate against a job applicant on the grounds of the applicant's disability in the following ways:

(a)   in the arrangements which he makes for the purpose of determining to whom he should offer employment (*DDA 1995, s 4(1)(a)*);

(b)   in the terms on which he offers that person employment (*s 4(1)(b)*); or

(c)   by refusing to offer or deliberately not offering the applicant employment (*s 4(1)(c)*).

3.98   *Arrangements made for the purpose of determining to whom he should make an offer*

For the purposes of *DDA 1995*, 'arrangements' has a wide meaning that covers all aspects of the recruitment process, from specifying the job and advertising it, to the process of assessing candidates, interview and selection.

(a)   *Advertisements* — (see 3.89).

(b)   *Application forms* — The *Code,* section 7.16 to 7.18 explains that where an employer provides information about a job, it is likely to be a reasonable adjustment for it to provide, on request, information in a format accessible to a disabled applicant, eg e-mail, Braille, large print, audio tape or computer disc. It is also likely to be a reasonable adjustment to allow an applicant to submit an application which contains necessary information in alternative accessible formats.

(c)   *Qualifications* — An employer is entitled to require applicants to have certain qualifications. However, these must be justified and necessary. The qualification must be relevant and significant for the purposes of the job and the particular applicant and there should be no reasonable adjustment which would change this. For example, an employer requiring two GCSEs would be unable to justify rejecting an applicant whose dyslexia precluded this if she could show that she had expertise required for the job in some other way (*Code,* section 7.10).

(d)   *Job specifications* — Including unnecessary or marginal requirements in a job description or person specification can be discriminatory, eg requiring an applicant to be 'energetic' where the job is actually sedentary may unjustifiably exclude applicants whose disabilities result in them tiring more easily (*Code,* section 7.7). Clear job descriptions should set out the funda-mental elements of the job to be advertised.

Job descriptions should also avoid blanket exclusions, such as would occur (for example) if an employer were to stipulate that candidates must have no history of mental illness, believing that such candidates will have poor attendance. If that employer then rejects an applicant solely because they have had a mental illness, without checking the individual's actual attendance record, this will amount to unlawful direct disability discrimination.

(e) *Interviews* — Where an employer is aware, or could reasonably be expected to be aware, that an applicant or potential applicant has a disability likely to place him at a substantial disadvantage in the employer's existing interview practices and procedures, the employer may be required to make reasonable adjustments (*Code*, section 7.19) to accommodate the applicant, eg allowing an applicant to bring a helper to an interview to assist when answering questions that are not part of the assessment (*Code*, section 7.22).

The *Code*, section 7.23, provides that it is good practice to allow an applicant to indicate any relevant effects of a disability and to suggest adjustments to help overcome any disadvantage the disability may cause at interview. However, the EAT in *Ridout v TC Group* [1998] IRLR 628, EAT stated that not too great a burden should be placed on the employer to require them to question job applicants in great detail about their disability. In this instance Ridout applied for a position with TC Group indicating on her application form that she had photosensitive epilepsy. At the interview, R said that the lighting in the interview room might cause her a problem, but that if it became an issue, she had her sunglasses with her. She did not put her sunglasses on during the interview and did not complain about the lighting. Her job application failed and she claimed that TC Group had failed to make reasonable adjustments for the interview. The EAT held that the duty to make reasonable adjustments must be assessed on the basis of what employers can reasonably be expected to do when faced with circumstances requiring detailed investigations into the effects of a rare type of disability without help from the individual telling them what her needs were. The EAT went on to say that if Ridout had informed TC Group of her needs prior to the interview, it might have been required to have done more to facilitate her.

During the interview process, employers can ask a disabled applicant about their disability and often such information will be relevant rather than discriminatory, as it may identify areas where the employer will need to make adjustments to accommodate the disability. However, disability-related questions should not be used to discriminate against a disabled person. An employer should only ask questions if they are, or may be, relevant to the person's ability to do the job after reasonable adjustments have been made. For example, asking an applicant with a visual impairment whether she was born with the condition would not be relevant to the job and therefore, is likely to be unlawful. However, asking a wheelchair user whether changes may be needed in the workplace to accommodate him would not be unlawful (*Code*, section 7.27).

(f) *Aptitude tests* — Where an employer routinely uses an aptitude or similar test as part of the interview process, they will need to consider whether they may need to make reasonable adjustments in relation to a particular disabled applicant. In such instances, it may be reasonable for the employer to assess the applicant's skills using an alternative test, or revise the test – or the way the results are assessed – to take account of a disabled candidate. The *Code* gives the following examples of adjustments that may be necessary:

(i) allowing a disabled person extra time to complete the test (as in *Paterson*);

(ii)   permitting the assistance of a reader or scribe during a test;

(iii)   accepting a lower pass rate for a person whose disability inhibits performance in such a test.

However, the extent to which such adjustments might be required would depend on how closely the test relates to the job in question. Where the nature and form of the test is necessary to assess a matter relevant to the job then an employer may not need to make any reasonable adjustments (*Code*, section 7.25).

(g)   ***Health requirements, use of health declaration forms and questionnaires —*** Stating that certain personal, medical or health-related characteristics are essential or desirable can lead to disability discrimination if the characteristic is not necessary for the job. Even when they are genuinely necessary, the employer must also consider whether it would be reasonable for it to waive such characteristics in any individual case (*Code*, section 7.9).

DDA 1995 does not prevent an employer from asking a disabled person to have a medical examination, but it is likely that the employer will discriminate unlawfully if it requires a disabled person to have medical checks but not other applicants. However, such a request may be justified in relation to certain jobs. For example, a successful job applicant indicates that he has a disabling heart condition. It is likely that the employer would be justified in requiring a medical examination provided it is restricted to assessing the implications for the particular job, eg a job that requires lifting and carrying (*Code*, section 7.31).

The *Code* suggests that asking a basic question such as whether a person is disabled is unlikely to yield any useful information and may simply lead to confusion. That such a question was asked might subsequently prove problematic for the employer as it may be used to suggest discrimination. In addition, shortlisting on the basis of an applicant's responses to a medical questionnaire may be unlawful discrimination if the employer has not ascertained the likely effects of a disability or medical condition on the applicant's ability to do the job, or whether reasonable adjustments would overcome any disadvantage it causes. The *Code* states that:

'even where there are medical requirements which must be met, it is good practice for employers not to require job applicants to answer a medical questionnaire until after a conditional job offer has been made.'

Medical information relating to applicants (and employees) will be sensitive personal data for the purposes of *DPA 1998*. The Information Commissioner (the UK's independent public body set up to promote access to official information and protect personal information) has issued guidance on the use of employees' health data, contained in Part 4 of the Employment Practices Code (2005) ('*Data Protection Code*'). *Data Protection Code*, para 4.1.5 states that health questionnaires should be designed to ensure that they only elicit information that is relevant and necessary. The supplementary guidance to the *Data Protection Code* states that this requirement implies that health questionnaires should therefore be designed by health professionals and that they should be interpreted by those who are qualified to draw meaningful conclusions from the information supplied.

3.99   *The terms on which he offers that person employment*

A disabled employee should not be offered terms and conditions of employment that are less favourable than those offered to other people (*DDA 1995, s 4(1)(b)*). For example, offering a person with a history of depression a six-month probationary period, even though other employees are only offered a three-month probationary period will amount to direct discrimination (*Code*, section 7.32).

3.100   *Refusing to offer or deliberately not offering employment*

It is unlawful for an employer to discriminate against a disabled applicant by refusing or deliberately not offering employment to them without justification (*DDA 1995, s 4(1)(c)*). The employer should not make assumptions about the applicant's capabilities to do the job or its own ability to make reasonable adjustments to accommodate his needs.

3.101   **Discrimination against employees**

It is unlawful for an employer to discriminate against a disabled employee:

(a)   in the terms of employment which the employer affords the employee (*DDA 1995, s 4(2)(a)*).

(b)   in the opportunities the employer affords the employee for promotion, a transfer, training or receiving any other benefit (*s 4(2)(b)*)

(c)   by refusing to afford the employee, or deliberately not affording the employee, any such opportunity (*s 4(2)(c)*); or

(d)   by dismissing the employee, or subjecting him to any other detriment (*s 4(2)(d)*).

3.102   *Terms and conditions of employment*

Disabled employees should not be discriminated against in relation to their terms and conditions of employment. Employers will need to consider what reasonable adjustments, if any, need to be made to a disabled employee's terms and conditions. These may include, for example, varying the contractual working hours of an employee who cannot travel on public transport during peak hours because of a disability.

Prior to 1 October 2004 the *Disability Discrimination (Employment) Regulations 1996 (SI 1996/1456)* (*'Employment Regulations'*) prevented employers from being liable for disability discrimination in relation to most performance-related pay (PRP) schemes. The *Employment Regulations* provided that as long as a PRP scheme applied to all employees, or to a class of employees which included a disabled person, then disability-related less favourable treatment in relation to the scheme would be deemed to be justified. Further, such schemes would not place disabled people at a substantial disadvantage (so there would be no duty to make reasonable adjustments). The *Employment Regulations* were revoked and partly replaced by the *Disability Discrimination (Employment Field) (Leasehold Premises) Regulations 2004 (SI 2004/153)* from 1 October 2004. However, the provisions related to PRP schemes were not replaced. As a result, PRP schemes can frequently prove difficult for employers to manage in relation to disabled employees. If, for example, in relation to a performance-related bonus, an employee fails to achieve the targets set for them in the usual manner, but the reason for this failure is disability-related absence, this could give rise to a claim of both disability-related discrimination, and failure to make a reasonable adjustment to the scheme. The employer will have to decide whether to pay a bonus and, if so, at what level. The robust approach taken in the recent sick pay cases (see 3.68) may provide some comfort to employers in these circumstances, but much will depend on the circumstances of the case and the provisions of the scheme.

3.103 *Induction, training and development*

Employers must ensure that arrangements for induction, training and development do not disadvantage disabled employees. For example, materials provided during induction to new employees may, following discussion with the employee, need to be provided in Braille, or made available via a computer equipped with a voice synthesiser or speech-enabled applications, to a blind employee.

Employers should avoid making assumptions about disabled employees' suitability for, or willingness to attend, training sessions. reasonable adjustments may need to be made to enable disabled employees to attend. For example, an employee with severe dyslexia may require the trainer to talk them through certain aspects of written training materials, or audio-visual materials may need to be provided with subtitles in the case of a deaf employee.

3.104 *Promotion, transfer and benefits*

Employees must not be treated less favourably on the grounds of a disability, or for a reason related to disability, in relation to decisions on promotions, transfers and benefits, as well as the practical arrangements made in relation to them.

An employer should evaluate whether the key skills he has determined as a requirement for a vacancy are really necessary. If a disabled employee applies, but would be unable to carry out a small part of that role due to a disability, it might well be reasonable for the employer to consider whether training would help or whether that part could be reallocated to another employee.

Employers should be careful about making assumptions in respect of a disabled employee's suitability for more senior roles. For example, an employer should not simply assume that an employee suffering from depression would not be capable of carrying out a manager's role without basing this opinion on medical evidence.

3.105 *Benefits*

Benefits, in this context, means any benefits, facilities or services which an employer provides to its employees in connection with their employment and would include items commonly thought of as benefits, such as permanent health insurance, but also car parking spaces and access to a staff restaurant or self-service refreshments. In general, benefits will be widely construed, although in most circumstances it does not include benefits which the employer is in the business of providing to the public (see 3.115).

If a disabled employee is unable to take advantage of a facility provided by an employer to its employees and the reason for this relates to that employee's disability, the employer must consider whether there are any reasonable adjustments which might remove this barrier. For example, an employer may need to make modifications for an employee in a wheelchair to access the staff restaurant.

Assumptions should not be made about disabled employees' willingness to participate in social events connected with work, or client entertainment events.

3.106   Disability Discrimination

3.106 *Managing disability*

An employer must not discriminate against an employee who becomes disabled during employment, or whose disability worsens. If the employee's condition alters during employment, the employer may need to re-evaluate the need to make reasonable adjustments and consider whether any adjustments already in place remain appropriate. The primary objective of the employer, at least to begin with, should be to consider whether any adjustments can be made to enable the employee to remain in their original role. If that is not possible, then the employer should consider alternative roles, including adjustments to such a role, should be considered before termination.

If possible, the employer should discuss the employee's needs with the employee and, in relation to progressive conditions, what the effect on the employee's ability to carry out the role in the future will or may be, so that the employer can consider and plan future reasonable adjustments. An occupational health practitioner or other suitable specialist may need to be involved, particularly where an employee is returning from a period of absence. An employer may need to consider rearranging working methods or allocating any minor parts of the disabled employee's role to another employee.

The *Code* recommends that when an employer is seeking to determine what reasonable adjustments to put in place to allow the employment of a disabled person, they may want to consider the advice available from Jobcentre Plus through the Access to Work scheme. The purpose of the Access to Work scheme is the provision of practical support to disabled people in, or entering into, paid employment to help overcome work-related obstacles resulting from disability. The Access to Work scheme can provide a grant towards these additional employment costs, although this is not automatic. It may well be a reasonable step for the employer to assist a disabled person in making an application for assistance from the Access to Work scheme and for the employer to provide ongoing administrative support (by completing claim forms, for example).

In appropriate cases, employers should also consider seeking expert advice on the extent of a disabled person's capabilities and what might be done to change premises or working arrangements. Where an employee has been off work, a phased return might be appropriate. In addition, an appropriate specialist will be able to offer an opinion on the employee's fitness to return to work; which of the employee's usual tasks should be avoided and for how long; and what adjustments can be made to the employee's physical workplace and other working conditions to facilitate the employee's return to work.

An employer cannot apply to a medical practitioner for a copy of a medical report about an employee without the employee's consent (*Access to Medical Records Act 1988, s 3(1)*). Further, the employee must be informed that he has the right to withhold his consent and request to see the report supplied in response to the employer's application before it is provided to the employer (*s 4(1)*). If the employee exercises his right to see the report, the practitioner must not supply the report to the employer until the employee has provided his consent for that to be done (*s 5(1)*).The employee can also request that amendments are made to parts of the report that the employee considers to be incorrect or misleading (*s 5(2)(a)*), and if the practitioner is not prepared to make such amendments, the employee can require the practitioner to attach to the report a statement of the employee's views in respect of the parts of the report which the practitioner is declining to amend (*s 5(2)(b)*).

Medical information relating to employees will almost certainly constitute sensitive personal data within the meaning of *DPA 1998*, and an employer must therefore ensure that one of the conditions set out in *DPA 1998, Sch 3* is fulfilled. Where the employee has given his specific informed consent this will be sufficient, but employers must be certain that all uses they make of the medical information are covered by the wording of the consent.

Many contracts of employment contain provisions allowing the employer to require that the employee attends a medical examination with a doctor chosen by the employer. This can prove a useful provision for an employer, particularly where an employee is unwilling to co-operate or the employer for whatever reason wishes to obtain a second opinion having received a report from the employee's GP.

3.107 *Termination*

Direct discrimination can occur if an employee is dismissed or selected for redundancy on the ground of their disability. If a dismissal decision is made for a reason related to a disabled employee's disability (other than the disability itself) there will be disability-related discrimination unless the employer can show that it is justified. The duty to make reasonable adjustments applies to dismissals as to other arrangements (see 3.79).

Where an employer is required to set redundancy selection criteria, the employer must consider whether any proposed criteria could disadvantage disabled employees. If so, the employer should consider whether any adjustments could reduce or remove that impact. The *Code* gives the example of a redundancy procedure which uses sickness absence as a selection criterion. It may well be a reasonable adjustment to discount disability-related sickness absence under those circumstances.

3.108 **Discrimination against former employees**

As a result of the House of Lords' finding in *Relaxion Group plc v Rhys-Harper* [2003] UKHL 33, [2003] 4 All ER 1113 that discrimination on the grounds of sex, race or disability can be unlawful where it occurs after the termination, upon implementation of the *Framework Directive, DDA 1995, s 16A* was amended with effect from 1 October 2004 to prohibit post-employment discrimination. *DDA 1995* now states that it is unlawful for a former employer to discriminate against a former employee on the grounds of his disability by subjecting him to a detriment or harassment that arises out of and is closely connected to the employment. For example, it would be unlawful to refuse to provide a reference or provide a poor reference for a former employee on the grounds of the person's disability (although a blanket policy of refusing to provide references to former employees could not normally be impugned, unless perhaps an argument could be made that the policy placed a particular person at a comparative substantial disadvantage and thus required adjustment).

A former employer may also be under a duty to make reasonable adjustments where a provision, criterion or practice applied to the disabled person in relation to matters arising out of his former employment; or any physical feature of premises occupied by a former employer, places the disabled ex-employee at a substantial disadvantage compared to those who are not disabled (*DDA 1995, s 16A(4), (5)*). For example, if a former employee is a member of a work social club and that person can no longer access the building because of a disability, once the former employer is aware of this, it will need to consider reasonable adjustments (*Code*, section 8.30).

However, the duty imposed under *s 16A(4)*, *(5)* will not apply if the employer did not know and could not have reasonably known that the disabled person has a disability and is likely to be affected as mentioned above (*s 16A(6)*).

3.109 Exceptions and special cases

This section deals with exceptions from the *DDA*'s coverage, either for particular groups of individuals (eg those in the armed forces or employed abroad), or generally (in the case of statutory authority). It also considers areas where the *DDA* makes special provision, both in the case of particular groups (such as contract workers or the police) or particular subject areas (such as charities or the provision of services to the public).

3.110 *Exceptions*

Individuals excluded from DDA protection

The 2004 amendments to *DDA 1995* to implement the *Framework Directive* significantly increased the scope of the *DDA*'s coverage (not least by abolishing the 'small employers' exception previously found in *s 7*: see the *2003 Regulations, reg 7*). Individuals will, however, be excluded from protection in the following cases:

(a) *Employment otherwise than 'at an establishment in Great Britain'.* The prohibition on discrimination by employers in *DDA 1995, s 4* applies 'only in relation to employment at an establishment in Great Britain'. (Similar provision is made in *s 4B(8)* in relation to contract workers; note that other provisions of *Part II* are not explicitly made subject to such territorial limitations.) 'Great Britain' includes such of the territorial waters of the United Kingdom as are adjacent to Great Britain (*s 68(1)*). 'Employment at an establishment in Great Britain' is to be construed in accordance with *s 68(2)–(4A)*:

    (i) *Land-based employment. DDA* protection will apply if either (*s 68(2)*): (1) the employee does his work wholly or partly in Great Britain; or (2) he does his work wholly outside Great Britain and the conditions in *s 68(2A)* are satisfied. These are that: (a) the employer has a place of business at an establishment in Great Britain; (b) the employee's work is for the purposes of the business carried on at that establishment; and (c) the employee is ordinarily resident in Great Britain either at the time when he applies for, or is offered, the employment or at any time during the course of the employment.

    (ii) *Ships, aircraft and hovercraft.* (1) *Ships. DDA* protection will apply if both of the following are satisfied: (a) the ship is registered at a port of registry in Great Britain (or belongs to or is possessed by the Queen in right of the UK Government) (*s 68(2B); s 68(2D)(a)*); (b) the employee does his work wholly or partly in Great Britain (including the territorial waters – see above) or does his work wholly outside Great Britain and satisfies the conditions in *s 68(2A)* (above) (*s 68(2)*). (2) *Aircraft and hovercraft. DDA* protection will apply if both the following are satisfied: (a) the aircraft or hovercraft is registered in the UK and operated by a person who has his principal place of business, or is ordinarily resident, in Great Britain (or belongs to or is possessed by the Queen in right of the UK Government) (*s 68(2C); s 68(2D)(b)*); (b) the employee does his work wholly or partly in Great Britain (including the territorial waters – see above) or does his work wholly outside Great Britain and satisfies the conditions in *s 68(2A)* (above) (*s 68(2)*).

(iii)   *Oil rigs etc.* Special provision is made for employment concerned with the exploration of the sea bed or sub-soil or the exploitation of their natural resources: see *s 68(4A), SDA 1975, s 10* and the *Sex Discrimination and Equal Pay (Offshore Employment) Order 1987* (which makes provision in relation to areas designated under the *Continental Shelf Act 1964, s 1(7)* and in relation to the Frigg Gas Field).

See further *Saggar v Ministry of Defence* [2005] EWCA Civ 413, [2005] ICR 1073 (dealing with the previous provisions under the *RRA*) and *Burke v British Council* UKEAT/0125/06 (dealing with the 'old' *DDA* provisions; it was accepted, at 12, that the new *DDA* provisions on overseas employment complied with the *Directive*). For the European approach, see eg *Boukhalfa v Germany C-214/94* [1996] ECR I-2253, a case under *Article 39* of the *EC Treaty* concerning a woman of Belgian nationality working at the German Embassy in Algiers. See also *Williams v University of Nottingham* [2007] IRLR 660, a case involving work outside the EU (in Malaysia), applying the same approach as in unfair dismissal cases (see *Lawson v Serco Ltd* [2006] UKHL 3, [2006] 1 All ER 823) to determining whether work was for the purposes of the employer's business carried on at establishment in UK. See generally COMMON CONCEPTS (1).

(b)   *Armed forces. DDA 1995, Part II* does not apply to 'service in any of the naval, military or air forces of the Crown' (*s 64(7)*). Further, the practical work experience provisions of *DDA 1995, ss 14C–14D* do not apply to a work placement undertaken in any of those forces (*s 14C(5)*). The provisions of *s 64(7)* were previously stated to be 'for the avoidance of doubt' ('old' *DDA 1995, s 64(7)*), because service in the forces did not amount to 'employment', but given the extended coverage of *Part II* (and in particular its coverage of office-holders), these words were removed by the *Amendment Regs 2003, reg 24(d)*.

Exception from DDA protection: statutory authority and national security

3.111   The following provision is made:

(a)   *Statutory authority.* By *DDA 1995, s 59(1)*, nothing in the *DDA* makes unlawful any act done in pursuance of any enactment, in pursuance of any instrument made under any enactment by a Minister of the Crown or member of the Scottish Executive or by the National Assembly for Wales, or to comply with any condition or requirement imposed (before or after coming into force) by virtue of any enactment by a Minister, a member of the Scottish Executive or by the Welsh Assembly. The exception in *s 59(1)* is to be narrowly construed; in particular, an act is only done 'in pursuance' of an enactment or instrument if it is specified in and required by that enactment or instrument (*Hampson v Department of Education* [1991] 1 AC 171, HL, at 181). The mere fact that an act of discrimination is permitted by the statute is insufficient. In the specific context of the *DDA*, see *Farmiloe v Lane Group plc* [2004] All ER (D) 08 (Mar), where the EAT held (at 52) that:

'Health and Safety Legislation takes precedence over the protection against disability discrimination provided that all reasonable steps have been taken to accommodate the particular needs of the individual worker.'

As set out above at 3.45ff, the *Framework Directive* (*Article 2(5)*) only allows for exceptions to its non-discrimination provisions in cases where measures are laid down by national law pursuant to a number of set aims and meet a proportionality test (of necessity in a democratic society). If reliance is placed (pursuant to *s 59(1)*) upon a statutory or other requirement requiring disability discrimination by a defendant employer which is an 'emanation of the state' for EC law purposes (see *Foster v British Gas* [1990] IRLR 353, ECJ at 20), it may therefore be possible for the claimant employee to place reliance upon any relevant directly effective provisions of the *Framework Directive* in order to override that requirement.

(b)   *National security.* By *s 59(2A)*, nothing in *Part II* (the employment field) of the *DDA* makes unlawful any act done for the purpose of safeguarding national security 'if the doing of the act was justified by that purpose'. (*S 59(2A)*, which effectively incorporates a proportionality test, was inserted by the *2003 Regulations*, presumably in order to comply with *Article 2(5)* of the *Framework Directive*: previously, the provision was not subject to a test of justification: see now *s 59(3)*.)

3.112 *Special cases*

Contract workers

By *DDA 1995, s 4B(1)*, it is unlawful for a principal, in relation to contract work, to discriminate against a disabled contract worker in the terms on which he allows him to do the contract work; by not allowing him to do it or to continue to do it; in the way he affords him access to any benefits or by refusing or deliberately omitting to afford him access to them; or by subjecting him to any other detriment. Harassment is outlawed by *s 4B(2)* and *s 4B(4)–(7)* (see below), which impose duties to make reasonable adjustments upon the employer and the principal. See generally the *Code*, sections 9.3 to 9.13.

Similar provision as to contract workers is made in *SDA* 1975, *s 9* and *RRA* 1976, *s 7* (see, respectively, 8.36 and 6.60). For consideration of the definition of 'contract worker' see most recently *Partnership in Care v Laing & anr* UKEAT/ 0622/06/0102 and cases there cited.

'Principal' is defined in the *DDA* as a person ('A') who makes work available for doing by individuals who are employed by another person who supplies them under a contract made with A. 'Contract work' means work so made available, and 'contract worker' means any individual who is supplied to the principal under such a contract (*s 4B(9)*). In *Abbey Life Assurance Co Ltd v Tansell* [2000] IRLR 387, CA, the Court of Appeal (adopting a purposive, protective approach to construction of *DDA 1995*) held that the *DDA* protection for contract workers extended to the situation where the applicant was employed by a company which supplied him to an agency, which in turn supplied him to an end-user. The applicant was (despite the extra contract in the chain) a contract worker and the end-user a principal within the meaning of the predecessor to *s 4B* ('old' *DDA 1995, s 12*). (*Tansell* was recently followed by the EAT in another context, that of whistleblowing, in the case of *Croke v Hydro Aluminium Worcester Ltd* [2007] ICR 1303, EAT.)

The position as to reasonable adjustments is that duties are owed by *both* the employer (in practice, usually the employment agency) *and* the principal (the 'host' with whom the worker is placed): see, respectively, *s 4B(4), (5)* and *s 4A* as applied by *s 4B(6)*:

(a) *Reasonable adjustments duty of the employer.* The employer (the agency) owes a duty to the disabled contract worker to make reasonable adjustments where a provision, criterion or practice applied by *most of the principals* to whom he is, or might be, supplied (or a physical feature of premises occupied by most of those principals) places the employee at a substantial comparative disadvantage (*s 4B(4), (5)*). The *Code* (box after section 9.10) gives the example of a blind secretary employed by an employment business which supplies her to other organisations for secretarial work. Her inability to access standard computer equipment places her at a comparative substantial disadvantage at the offices of all or most of the principals to whom she might be supplied. The employment business might (subject to reasonableness) be required to provide her with a specially adapted portable computer and/or Braille keyboard. It should be noted that in addition, the employer owes the contract worker the usual reasonable adjustments duty of an employer under *s 4A* (which is not disapplied by *s 4B*).

(b) *Reasonable adjustments duty of the principal.* The principal (the host organisation) is under the same reasonable adjustments duty to the disabled contract worker as he would be if he were the employer of that disabled person (*s 4B(6)*, applying *s 4A*). However, in assessing the question of reasonableness of any proposed adjustment, it might well be relevant to consider the length of the period for which the worker is appointed to work for the principal (see *Code*, section 9.8 and box).

A principal (host organisation) is not, however, required to take a step in relation to a disabled contract worker if under *s 4A* the employer (the agency) is itself required to take the step in relation to him (*s 4B(7)*). The *Code* (box after section 9.11) seeks to illustrate this by stating that in the example given above, a bank which hired the blind secretary might (subject to reasonableness) have to make any necessary changes to ensure that the computer provided by the employment business was compatible with its own system.

3.113 Other groups/categories covered by Part II

Upon implementation of the *Framework Directive, DDA 1995, Part II* was considerably expanded (it had originally dealt with employment; contract workers; trade organisations; occupational pensions; and group insurance). In addition to employees and contract workers, the following groups of individuals and categories of activity are now subject to *DDA* protection. (Note that full analysis of these provisions is, however, outside the scope of this work.)

(a) *Office holders.* Under the 'old' *DDA*, protection was extended only to appointments to an office or post by a Minister of the Crown or government department ('old' *s 66*; see now *s 4C(3)(b)*). From 1 October 2004, however, ss *4C* to *4F* extend that protection additionally (*s 4C(3)*) to:

(i) (*s 4C(3)(a)*) offices or posts to which persons are appointed 'to discharge functions personally under the direction of another person' (see further *s 4C(4)(a)*) and in respect of which they are entitled to remuneration (being more than just expenses or compensation for loss of earnings: *s 4C(4)(b)*); and

(ii)   (*s 4C(3)(c)*) offices or posts to which appointments are made 'on the recommendation of, or subject to the approval of' a Minister, a government department, any part of the Scottish Administration or the Welsh Assembly.

Discrimination and harassment by a 'relevant person' are unlawful, and 'relevant persons' are made subject to a duty to make reasonable adjustments (respectively *s 4D* and *s 4E*). 'Relevant person' is defined (in *s 4F(2)*) by reference to the function being carried out – for example, in a case relating to an appointment to an office or post, the 'relevant person' is the person with power to make that appointment. The position is slightly more complicated for a complaint in relation to a working condition, or to harassment or 'any other detriment' (see *s 4F(2)(d)–(f)*). See further the *Code,* sections 9.14–9.22.

(b)   *Occupational pension schemes.* Discrimination by an employer in the operation of an occupational pension scheme will be caught by the ordinary employment provisions of the *DDA,* namely: *s 4* – see in particular *s 4(2)(b)* (opportunities for receiving 'any other benefit'); *s 4(2)(c)* (refusing to afford, or deliberately not affording, opportunity to receive such a benefit); *s 4(2)(d)* (any other detriment); and *s 4A* (duty to make adjustments – note that the previous exception for benefits under occupational pension schemes ('old' DDA *s 6(11)*) no longer applies). But discrimination by the trustees or managers of an occupational pension scheme (who are distinct from the employer) will not be so caught and therefore requires special provision. Such provision is made in *ss 4G* to *4K*, inserted by the *Disability Discrimination Act 1995 (Pensions) Regulations 2003 (SI 2003/2770)* with effect from 1 October 2004. Note the special provision as to procedure and remedies made in (respectively) *s 4I* and *s 4J*. Note too that the provision has similarities with that made (as to sex discrimination in pensions) in the *Occupational Pension Schemes (Equal Treatment) Regulations 1995 (SI 1995/3183)*. See also Chapter 10 of the *Code.*

(c)   *Partnerships.* See *ss 6A to 6C* in relation to discrimination by a firm against a partner (or potential partner) in that firm. Special provision is made as to the cost of making the adjustment. The general rule is that the disabled person concerned is not required to contribute to the cost of making a reasonable adjustment. In the case of a partnership, however, a partner may have a share in the firm's profits. It is therefore provided by *s 6B(4)* that the cost of reasonable adjustments is to be treated as an expense of the firm, and that the extent to which such cost should be borne by the disabled person is not to exceed such cost as is reasonable having regard in particular to his share in the firm's profits. As to this, see *Code,* section 9.31 and box. See generally *Code,* sections 9.25–9.31.

(d)   *Barristers and advocates.* Because barristers and pupil barristers are not employed by their chambers, special provision is needed to extend *DDA* protection to them. Such provision is made by *ss 7A* to *7B*. (Provision is made for advocates in Scotland, as to the taking of pupils, by *ss 7C–7D*). The provision mirrors provisions in *SDA 1975* and *RRA 1976* (see 6.65 and 8.38). It should be noted in particular that by *s 7A(4)*, it is unlawful for 'any person', in relation to the giving, withholding or acceptance of instructions to a barrister, to discriminate against 'a disabled person' or to subject him to harassment (see, similarly, *s 7C(4)* (advocates)). This is of potentially wide application, given that neither the category of person who may be the discriminator nor that of persons discriminated against is delimited (compare the other provisions of *Part II*). For the position under the 'old' *DDA* (barristers not protected by 'trade organisations' provisions), see *Higham and ors v Horton* [2004] EWCA Civ 941. See generally *Code*, sections 9.32 to 9.41.

(e)   *Trade Organisations and qualifications bodies.* The existing *DDA* provisions on trade organisations ('old' *DDA, ss 13–15; DDA 1995, ss 13–14*) are, from 1 October 2004, supplemented by *ss 14A* and *14B* on qualifications bodies ('qualifying bodies' in *SDA 1975* and *RRA 1976*). Those provisions are the subject of a separate DRC (now EHRC) Code, the *Code of Practice, Trade Organisations and Qualifications Bodies*, London, TSO, 2004. Detailed consideration of the provisions is beyond the scope of this work, but note that the application by a qualifications body of a 'competence standard' (as defined in *s 14A(5)*) is subject to a test of objective justification (*Framework Directive, Article 2(2)(b)(i)*) rather than a duty to make reasonable adjustments (*Framework Directive, Article 2(2)(b)(ii)*; *DDA 1995, s 14A(3)*). Note too, however, that the question of whether a competence standard is objectively justified may nevertheless (as a matter of proportionality) turn to some extent on whether less onerous alternatives to the standard have been considered by the qualifications body and on whether the needs of disabled persons generally (or persons with particular disabilities as a group) have been taken into account in setting or maintaining the standard.

(f)   *Practical work experience. DDA* protection is extended (*ss 14C* and *14D*) to discrimination by placement providers in relation to work placements, that is 'practical work experience undertaken for a limited period for the purposes of a person's vocational training' (*s 14C(4)*) where that person is not employed by the placement provider. See generally *Code*, sections 9.42 to 9.50.

(g)   *Locally electable authorities and their members.* See *DDA 1995, ss 15A–15C*. Note that the provisions apply in relation to official, as opposed to party political, business; and that there are exclusions for election or appointment to offices and committees of the authority (*s 15B(3)*).

Special categories of employment:

(h)   *Crown employment.* By *DDA 1995, s 64(2), Part II* applies to service for purposes of a Minister of the Crown or government department (other than service of a person holding a statutory office), and to service on behalf of the Crown for purposes of a person holding a statutory office or purposes of a statutory body, as it applies to employment by a private person. This provision is necessary because of the theory that civil servants do not enjoy a contract of employment with the Crown (so that their service would otherwise fall outside the definition of 'employment' in *s 68(1)*).

(j)   *Police.* Provision is made by *DDA 1995, s 64A* treating the holding of the office of constable as employment (for the purposes of *Part II* (i) by the Chief Officer of police as respects any act done by him in relation to a constable or that office; (ii) by the police authority as respects any such act done by them. Again, the provision is necessary because the holding of the office of constable (which is held by all police officers, not just those with the *rank* of Police Constable) does not technically amount to employment.

3.114 Charities

By *DDA 1995, s 18C(1)*, nothing in *Part II* (employment) affects any charitable instrument providing for conferring benefits on one or more categories of person determined 'by reference to any physical or mental capacity' or makes unlawful any act done by a charity in pursuance of its charitable purposes so far as connected with persons so determined.

By *s 18C(2)*, nothing in *Part II* prevents a person who provides supported employment from treating members of a particular group of disabled persons more favourably than other persons in providing such employment (or the Secretary of State for agreeing to arrangements for the provision of supported employment which will, or may, have that effect).

While the necessity for *s 18C(1)* may be understandable insofar as any charitable instrument may provide for conferring benefits on a *non-disabled* person by reference to particular physical or mental capacity (eg for conferring grants upon persons fulfilling particular sporting or academic requirements), the necessity for *s 18C(2)*, and for *s 18C(1)* insofar as relating to the conferring on benefits on disabled persons or particular classes of such persons, is less apparent. Because the *DDA 1995* does not prohibit discrimination against non-disabled people, or discrimination in favour of particular categories of disabled persons, the provisions seem redundant and may have been included, and subsequently retained, out of an abundance of caution.

3.115 Facilities provided to the public

By *DDA 1995, s 4(4)*, the *Part II* prohibition on discrimination by employers against employees (*s 4(2)*) does not apply to benefits of any description if the employer is concerned with the provision (whether or not for payment) of benefits of that description, to the public or to a section of the public which includes the employee in question, unless:

(a)   that provision differs in a material respect from the provision of the benefits by the employer to his employees;

(b)   the provision of the benefits to the employee in question is regulated by the contract of employment; or

(c)   the benefits relate to training.

This provision is designed to prevent an overlap between *Part II* (employment) and *Part III* (provision of goods, facilities and services) of *DDA 1995*. Thus, for example, if a disabled wheelchair-using employee of a supermarket who also happens to shop in that supermarket while off-duty wishes to claim discrimination in relation to the lack of accessibility of goods to wheelchair users, that claim is properly brought under *Part III* rather than *Part II*.

3.116 ENFORCEMENT

Complaints to employment tribunal

DDA 1995, s 17A(1) provides that a complaint by any person that another person has discriminated against him, or subjected him to harassment, may be presented to a tribunal.

3.117 *Statutory grievance process*

In most cases, in order for an employee to be able to bring a claim under any jurisdiction listed in *Employment Act 2002, Sch 4* (which includes a claim under *DDA 1995, s 17A*), the employee must first have raised a grievance relating to the subject matter of the claim. The main exception to this is where the grievance is the fact the employer has dismissed or is contemplating dismissing the employee (*Employment Act 2002 (Dispute Resolution) Regulations 2004, reg 6(5)*).

In summary, the statutory grievance procedure has three steps. The first step is the employee informing the employer of the grievance in writing. The second step requires the employer to invite the employee to a meeting to discuss the grievance. The third step, if requested, is an appeal by the employee against the decision which followed the second step meeting

3.118 *Time limits*

Claims of disability discrimination in the tribunal should be brought within three months of the date of the alleged act of discrimination (*DDA 1995, Sch 3, para 3*). Note that this time limit can be extended in the event that the employment tribunal finds that it is just and equitable to do so. This may include where the employee has been generally reluctant to acknowledge he is or was disabled (*Department of Constitutional Affairs v Jones* [2007] EWCA Civ 894, [2008] All ER (D) 43 (Jan)).

As to the extension of time limits generally, see COMMON CONCEPTS (1).

For the purposes of the time limit, an act (or acts) of discrimination which extend over a period of time is treated as having been done at the end of that period (*DDA 1995, s 3(3)(b)*). However, the EAT has found that a failure to make reasonable adjustments is an omission and not a continuing act (*Humphries v Chevler Packaging* UKEAT/0224/06/2407).

3.119 *Restricted reporting orders*

A restricted reporting order may be made in any claim under *DDA 1995, s 17A* or *s 25(8)*, in which evidence of a personal nature is likely to be heard by the tribunal or a chairman (*Employment Tribunals (Constitution & Rules of Procedure) Regulations 2004, Sch 1, rule 50*).

3.120 *Remedies*

In the event of a successful claim of disability discrimination, the remedies are the same as under *SDA 1975* and *RRA 1976* (see COMMON CONCEPTS (1)). If the employee is successful, the tribunal will make a declaration that the employer has unlawfully discriminated against the employee.

Compensation will be awarded to a successful employee on the basis of statutory torts and is unlimited (*DDA 1995, s 25*). Compensation can therefore be very high in cases where the employee has lost his job, or future earning prospects are poor. Instances of six-figure awards are relatively frequent in *DDA 1995* cases. The possible heads for financial awards are broadly:

(a)   loss of earnings and other employment-related benefits to the date of hearing;

(b)   future loss of earnings and employment-related benefits;

(c)   injury to feelings;

(d)   personal injury;

(e)   aggravated damages;

(f)   exemplary damages.

In *Travis v Electronic Data Systems Ltd* [2004] EWCA Civ 1256, 148 Sol Jo LB 1033 an employee with schizophrenia, aged 40, had been discriminated against in a redundancy programme. The tribunal awarded compensation based on 50 per cent of salary and benefits which the employee would have earned up to his 65th birthday had he not been made redundant. Factors which the tribunal took into account are the fact that prejudice against his illness would make it difficult for him to find another job.

Tribunals may take into account future pay rises, promotions the employee may have achieved and whether the illness has been aggravated by the conduct of the employer.

The Court of Appeal has held that in discrimination cases the appropriate test for deciding whether an employer is liable to pay compensation for psychiatric injury suffered by an employee is simply whether unlawful discrimination caused it (*Essa v Laing* [2004] EWCA Civ 02, [2004] ICR 746).

Where an employee has been discriminated against but has subsequently been dismissed for a non-discriminatory reason, future loss for failure to make reasonable adjustments during employment will not be recoverable (*Royal Mail Group plc v Sharma* UKEAT/0839/04/ILB).

3.121 *Injury to feelings*

In *Vento v Chief Constable of West Yorkshire Police* [2002] EWCA Civ 1871, [2003] IRLR 102 (SEX DISCRIMINATION (8)), the Court of Appeal identified three broad bands for injury to feelings, as distinct from compensation for psychiatric or similar personal injury, and stated as follows:

'(i)   The top band should normally be between £15,000 and £25,000. Sums in this range should be awarded in the most serious cases, such as where there has been a lengthy campaign of discriminatory harassment on the ground of sex or race ... Only in the most exceptional case should an award of compensation for injury to feelings exceed £25,000.

'(ii)   The middle band of between £5,000 and £15,000 should be used for serious cases, which do not merit an award in the highest band.

'(iii)   Awards of between £500 and £5,000 are appropriate in less serious cases, such as where the act of discrimination is an isolated or one-off occurrence. In general, awards of less than £500 are to be avoided altogether, as they risk being so low as not to be a proper recognition of injury to feelings.'

3.123 **Questionnaire process**

3.122 An employee can request information from an employer through the use of a standard questionnaire, (*DDA 1995, s 56*). The questionnaire is available from the EHRC and can be submitted at any time before proceedings are instituted or within 28 days after they are instituted.

Other sources of help and advice

Equality and Human Rights Commission

As part of its general duties, the EHRC gives advice and information, not only to disabled people but also employers and service providers. It, like its predecessor body the DRC, will produce policy documents and research on disability issues and organise campaigns. Appropriate tribunal cases, primarily test cases which test the limits of the law, will also supported and funded by the EHRC.

ACAS

3.124 ACAS aims to improve organisations and working life through better employment relations. It provides information, independent advice and training and aims to work with employers and employees to solve problems and improve performance. ACAS also has a helpline which will answer employment queries in confidence. In addition, it operates a service called Equality Direct, which is a confidential advice service for small businesses on equality.

3.125 **NO CONTRACTING OUT**

General

A term of a contract is void if the making of the contract is, by reason of the inclusion of the term, unlawful by virtue of *DDA 1995*, or the term is included in furtherance of an act which is unlawful by virtue of *DDA 1995* or provides for the doing of an act which is unlawful by virtue of *DDA 1995, Part I* (*Sch 3A, para 1(1)*).

An exception to the general rule stated above is where a term, the inclusion of which constitutes, furthers, or provides for unlawful discrimination against, or harassment of, a party to the contract. In these circumstances the term is not void but it is unenforceable against that party (*Sch 3A, para 1(2)*).

4   Gender Reassignment

4.1   OVERVIEW

In the last decade, sex discrimination law has been expanded so as to prohibit certain instances of discrimination against those whose gender identity (self-perception in terms of masculinity and femininity) does not accord with their birth sex (the sex which the organs of their bodies match). Such persons are known variously as 'transpersons', 'transgender' or 'transsexuals'. The term 'transsexual' conventionally refers only to persons who have chosen to undergo medical treatment to reassign their gender.

Prior to 1999, the discrimination law of the United Kingdom provided no direct protection against discrimination on ground of gender reassignment. The *Sex Discrimination Act 1975* ('*SDA 1975*') was generally thought not to apply to such discrimination, since it was considered that discrimination on ground of gender reassignment did not constitute discrimination on ground of a person's sex.

4.2   The P v S case

Thus, in the case of *P v (1) S (2) Cornwall County Council* [1996] IRLR 347, a tribunal found that a claimant had been dismissed by reason of gender reassignment, but that this did *not* constitute discrimination on grounds of sex contrary to the 1975 Act.

This interpretation of the existing legislation was challenged before the European Court of Justice (ECJ) (*Case C-13/94*) The ECJ, effectively overturning the tribunal's understanding of the law, held that the scope of the Equal Treatment Directive [Council Directive 76/207] ('the Directive') *included* discrimination arising from gender reassignment, since such discrimination was based, essentially if not exclusively, on the sex of the person concerned. This principle continues to be applied by the ECJ today, for instance in a recent case establishing that a transsexual must be permitted to claim a retirement pension at 60: *Richards v Secretary of State for Work and Pensions (Case C-423/04)* [2006] All ER (EC) 895.

4.3   The courts' response

The courts in the United Kingdom responded quickly to the *P v S* decision. In the case of *Chessington World of Adventures Ltd v Reed ex parte News Group Newspapers Ltd* [1998] IRLR 56, which raised the question whether discrimination on ground of gender reassignment was contrary to *SDA 1975*, the English EAT reinterpreted the relevant provisions of *SDA 1975* '... consistently with the ruling of the European Court in *P v S*...'. The result of this reinterpretation was that '... where ... the reason for the unfavourable treatment is sex based, that is a declared intention to undergo gender reassignment, there is no requirement for a male/female comparison to be made', and thus there was discrimination contrary to *SDA 1975*.

4.4   The 1999 amendments

The *Chessington* decision, and a number of post-*P v S* tribunal decisions to similar effect, were, however, felt by the Government to be an insufficient response to *P v S*. With regard to *Chessington*, the then-called the Department for Education and Employment (DFEE) observed that 'the re-interpretation places a strain upon the provisions of the Sex Discrimination Act' (DFEE paper, 'Legislation regarding discrimination on the grounds of transsexualism in employment', January 1998). It was felt that there was a need for legislation to clarify the position.

After a consultation process, the government introduced the *Sex Discrimination (Gender Reassignment) Regulations 1999 (SI 1999/1102)*. These Regulations made appropriate amendments to the SDA 1975 so that, in the spheres of employment and vocational training, it is now unlawful to discriminate on grounds of gender reassignment. This chapter examines the scope of the protection offered by those amendments.

Key concepts/glossary

Gender dysphoria: The concept of 'gender dysphoria' underlies much of the academic literature on transgender issues. It describes the anxiety, uncertainty or persistently uncomfortable feelings about one's birth gender which afflict transpersons, often from an early stage in their lives.

Gender reassignment: The legal definition of 'gender reassignment' is defined in *SDA 1975, s 82* as '… a process which is undertaken under medical supervision for the purpose of reassigning a person's sex by changing physiological or other characteristics of sex, and includes any part of such a process.' This is a relatively broad definition of a process which, whilst it includes reference to 'medical supervision', does not require surgery. Accordingly, hormonal or other types of therapy, so long as undertaken with a view to reassigning a person's sex, will suffice.

Treatment: Diagnosis of transsexualism is carried out by a specialist. Preliminary diagnosis is followed by hormone therapy. If an individual has not yet changed social gender, they can be expected to start to do so at around this stage. At some point over the next few months the individual will start to live full-time as a member of their 'new' sex. The individual then usually proceeds to surgery after one or two years of hormone therapy.

Gender recognition certificates: Under a procedure governed by the *Gender Recognition Act 2004*, it is now open to a person who has undergone gender reassignment to seek legal recognition of their acquired gender. This Act was passed against a background of criticism by the European Court of Human Rights of the United Kingdom's comparative lack of legal recognition or protection for transsexuals: See *Goodwin v United Kingdom (Case 28957/95)* [2002] IRLR 664; *Grant v United Kingdom (App. No. 32570/03)* [2006] All ER (D) 337 (May). This is achieved by obtaining a gender recognition certificate from a gender recognition panel. Surgery is not necessary in order to fulfil the requirements for making an application. Rather, a person must:

(a)   have or have had 'gender dysphoria';

(b)   have lived in his or her acquired gender for two years prior to the application; and

(c)   intend to live permanently in his or her acquired gender.

The effect of a gender recognition certificate is that, for almost all legal purposes, the person concerned must be treated as if he or she had been ➡

---

born in his or her acquired gender. Consequently, it becomes possible for a transsexual to experience discrimination on the basis of his or her acquired gender, as set out elsewhere in this book.

Gender dysphoria as disability: Where a transsexual has suffered from gender dysphoria for twelve months or more, or the condition is likely to last for twelve months or more, it may constitute a disability within the meaning of the *Disability Discrimination Act 1995* ('*DDA 1995*'). In such circumstances discrimination against a transsexual could conceivably contravene both *DDA 1995* and *SDA 1975*. Issues arising from *DDA 1995* are discussed in DISABILITY DISCRIMINATION (3).

4.5 **DISCRIMINATION ON THE GROUNDS OF GENDER REASSIGNMENT (SIMILARITIES/DIFFERENCES TO SEX DISCRIMINATION)**

Discrimination: definition

The definition of discrimination on ground of gender reassignment is to be found in *SDA 1975, s 2A(1)*, which provides:

'A person ('A') discriminates against another person ('B') ... if he treats B less favourably than he treats or would treat other persons, and does so on the ground that B intends to undergo, is undergoing or has undergone gender reassignment.'

This provision is drafted in very similar fashion to *SDA 1975, s 1(1)(a)*, which deals with direct discrimination on ground of sex. The concept and parameters of 'less favourable treatment' for the purposes of discrimination on ground of sex will therefore be highly relevant when construing *s 2A(1)*.

There are, however, at least three significant differences between the definition of discrimination on ground of gender reassignment and that relating to sex discrimination in general:

(1) Only direct discrimination

Discrimination on ground of gender reassignment is prohibited only to the extent that such discrimination is *direct*; there are no indirect discrimination provisions.

(2) Absences for gender reassignment

With regard to the specific issue of gender-reassignment-related absences, *SDA 1975, s 2A(3)* provides that a person will be discriminated against only if he is treated less favourably than he would be if the absence was due to: (a) 'sickness or injury'; or (b) 'some other cause and, having regard to the circumstances of the case, it is reasonable for him to be treated no less favourably'. If, therefore, an employer would normally discipline a worker for taking a month off work because of sickness or injury, it would not be discriminatory for the same employer to discipline a worker for taking a month off work to have gender reassignment surgery. This is considerably less extensive protection than that afforded in the context of maternity.

(3) Point at which provisions engaged

Since *SDA 1975, s 2A(1)* deals with acquired gender, rather than birth sex (as with *s 1(1)(a)*), it has been necessary for the draughtsman to define when a person acquires the characteristic on the basis of which discrimination is prohibited. By using the words 'intends to undergo', *s 2A(1)* ensures that the gender-reassignment regime prohibits not merely discrimination on the ground of an *existing* gender reassignment process, but also an *intended* process. An employee or other relevant person therefore acquires the protection of *SDA 1975* as soon as they declare an intention to undergo the process.

Harassment: definition

The definition of harassment on ground of gender reassignment is to be found in *SDA 1975, s 4A(3)*:

'(3) For the purposes of this Act, a person ('A') subjects another person ('B') to harassment if—

(a)   A, on the ground that B intends to undergo, is undergoing or has undergone gender reassignment, engages in unwanted conduct that has the purpose or effect—

   (i)   of violating B's dignity, or

   (ii)   of creating an intimidating, hostile, degrading, humiliating or offensive environment for B, or

(b)   A, on the ground of B's rejection of or submission to unwanted conduct of a kind mentioned in paragraph (a), treats B less favourably than A would treat B had B not rejected, or submitted to, the conduct.'

This provision employs the same terminology as that relating to harassment on ground of sex and, accordingly, those same principles will be relevant (see COMMON CONCEPTS (1)).

Scope of application

The prohibitions on discrimination and harassment on ground of gender reassignment apply only to discrimination in the fields of employment and vocational training. Unlike discrimination on ground of sex, the prohibitions do *not* apply to discrimination in education, or in the provision of housing, goods, facilities and services. (See *SDA 1975, s 2A(1)–(2)* and *Part III.*)

Comparators

A transsexual is to be regarded in his or her reassigned gender: *A v Chief Constable of West Yorkshire Police* [2004] UKHL 21, [2005] 1 AC 51, para 58 (Baroness Hale). Accordingly, in the search for a comparator (actual or hypothetical), the correct approach is to compare a claimant's treatment with that which was afforded (or would have been afforded) to someone of the sex to which the claimant *used to* belong. In the typical case of a male-to-female transsexual, therefore, comparison must be made between the claimant and a *male* employee in an equivalent position.

4.6   Equal pay

Discrimination against transsexuals in terms of payment for work is prohibited by *Article 141* of the EC Treaty and the Equal Pay Directive 75/117: *KB v National Health Service Pensions Agency and Secretary of State for Health (Case C-117/01)* [2004] IRLR 240. Such claims must be brought under *SDA 1975, s 6(8)* rather than the *Equal Pay Act 1970*.

KEY AREAS FOR DISPUTE

In the context of employment and vocational training, there are a number of areas where the cases suggest there is a greater risk of discrimination occurring, or discrimination claims being brought.

- *Harassment by his or her colleagues or clients:* see *Chessington World of Adventures Ltd v Reed ex parte News Group Newspapers Ltd* [1998] IRLR 56), where the appellant announced a change of gender identity from male to female and changed her name to Niki by statutory declaration, which led to a concerted course of serious harassment by some of her male colleagues.

- *Making inappropriate arrangements for the use of single sex facilities, particularly, toilet facilities:* see *Croft v Royal Mail Group plc* [2003] EWCA Civ 1045, [2003] ICR 1425), which concerned a male-to-female pre-operative transsexual person who claimed she was discriminated against by being required by the employer to use the gender-neutral disabled toilet in the workplace. On the facts of this case both the EAT and the Court of Appeal found that there was no unlawful discrimination under *SDA 1975, s 2A* and it was appropriate for the employer in the particular circumstances to make separate arrangements for a transsexual employee while he or she is in the course of undergoing a gender reassignment. The protection offered in *s 2A* does not extend to giving an employee automatic entitlement to use the facilities of the new gender as soon as they start presenting themselves in that gender.

- *Gender-specific roles:* See 4.7.

- *Not permitting adequate time off work for the purposes of undergoing the required surgery*

- *Discriminatory decisions in recruitment and promotion exercises:* see *Baldwin v Brighton and Hove City Council* [2007] IRLR 232, which concerned a female-to-male transsexual person who was asked to apply for an alternative post at the expiry of his existing contract. He alleged that a member of the interview panel was 'transphobic' so did not attend the interview and alleged constructive dismissal. The EAT held that it is not sufficient to show that a respondent 'would have' treated the claimant in a less favourable way – the treatment in question must actually take place.

- *Dismissing employees who have transitioned, or intend to transition*

- *Withholding work, or changing the nature of someone's role, particularly to keep them away from client-facing roles*

- *Not ensuring that people who transition are treated equally in the provision of benefits*

For practical advice on how to deal with a member of staff who intends to transition see 4.9ff.

4.7   **GENUINE OCCUPATIONAL QUALIFICATIONS**

As with sex discrimination, there is a limited exception to the general prohibition on direct discrimination for situations where such discrimination arises from a 'genuine occupational qualification' (GOQ). The GOQs which are set out in *SDA*

1975, s 7 apply, under *s 7A*, to transsexuals as they do to others. The transsexual is regarded as having his or her acquired gender for the purposes of applying those GOQs.

In addition to the 'standard' GOQs, *SDA 1975, s 7B* provides four supplementary GOQs, which apply *only* in the case of transsexuals in the course of 'transitioning'. These apply where:

(1)   the job involves the holder being liable to be called upon to perform intimate physical searches pursuant to statutory powers;

(2)   the job entails work in a private home in an intimate context and reasonable objection is taken to a transitioning transsexual performing such work;

(3)   the nature and location of the establishment is such that it would be impracticable to live elsewhere than premises provided by the employer, reasonable objection is taken to the holder of such a job sharing accommodation and facilities with either sex, and it is not reasonable to expect the employer to alter the premises; and/or

(4)   the holder of the job provides vulnerable individuals with personal services and, in the reasonable view of the employer, those services cannot be effectively provided by a transitioning transsexual.

The *s 7B* GOQs are only available to employers whilst an employee is 'transitioning'. Once the transsexual has been registered under their acquired gender under the *Gender Recognition Act 2004* ('*GRA 2004*'), he or she must be treated on a fully equal basis with those born into his or her acquired gender. This means that the GOQ position must be assessed as if the person concerned had been born into their acquired gender.

4.8   ENFORCEMENT AND REMEDIES

Where a person has been discriminated against in an employment or vocational training context on ground of gender reassignment, he or she may bring a claim to an employment tribunal: *SDA 1975, s 63*. The reversal of the burden of proof which is provided for in *SDA 1975, s 63A* applies in the same way as a claim based on discrimination on ground of sex: *EB v BA* [2006] IRLR 471, CA.

4.9   GUIDANCE FOR EMPLOYERS

4.10   Introduction

This section provides some practical guidance for employers on how to handle issues relating to gender reassignment in the workplace. It is recommended that all employers should consider the issues addressed in 4.10 whether or not any of their staff are known to be covered by legislation. Para 4.11 addresses the issues to be considered once a member of staff has notified an employer that he or she is suffering from gender dysphoria or is considering gender reassignment.

General guidance for all employers

Policies and training

An employer may be liable for any discriminatory act done by an employee in the course of his or her employment, unless it can show that it took such steps as were reasonably practicable to prevent the act from occurring (see *SDA 1975, s 41*). Maintaining adequate policies and holding regular training can assist an employer in demonstrating that it took these preventative steps.

All relevant policies and practices should be vetted to ensure they do not discriminate on the grounds of gender reassignment. Equal opportunities policies that refer to discrimination on grounds of sex can now be considered automatically to include discrimination on grounds of gender reassignment. However, employers should, as a matter of best practice, amend their existing policies to include an express reference to gender reassignment.

Employers who have specific policies and procedures to cover, for example, sexual orientation, religion or age, should consider introducing a separate gender identity policy. General HR policies, for example those dealing with confidentiality or harassment, should be checked to ensure that they would adequately cover a transsexual employee.

Employers should include transgender issues on training programmes addressing equal opportunities and harassment.

Recruitment, selection and promotion

The process of recruitment and selection of a new employee should not be affected by an individual's transsexual status. Allowing transsexual status to influence the decision as to whether to recruit will be unlawful unless the rationale falls within one of the narrow exceptions referred to at 4.7.

The normal rules of best practice should be adopted when conducting interviews. Employers should have a job description for each role, together with a prepared set of questions relating to the job which is used consistently for all candidates. Interviewees may not want to disclose their transsexual status at interview and this is not a question that should be asked. Interviewers should receive training to ensure that they treat all applicants consistently and do not pose any inappropriate questions.

In terms of career advancement and opportunities for promotion, the employer should ensure that decisions are not influenced by someone's transsexual status.

4.11   Specific guidance for employers of transsexual employees

First approach by the employee and managing the transition

When a manager, supervisor or colleague is first approached by an employee who is suffering from gender dysphoria, or considering gender reassignment, the employer should reassure the individual that the employer will be as supportive as possible through the transition process. The employer should take all appropriate steps to ensure respect for the individual's privacy, dignity at work and confidentiality.

It is helpful if the employer nominates one person to manage the transition from the employer's perspective, with the agreement of the individual. That person should engage at an early stage with the individual to discuss the handling of the transition and the ways in which the employer can support the individual and prepare a plan for the process. This should be kept strictly confidential.

The whole process should be actively managed and kept under review, including regular meetings throughout the process.

Specific matters to be discussed at the meetings and addressed by the employer are set out below.

4.11   Gender Reassignment

Time off for medical treatment

Employers should discuss with the individual how much time off he or she will need to undergo treatment. During absence for treatment or surgery normal sick pay arrangements apply. It is likely to constitute unlawful discrimination if employers treat an individual undergoing gender reassignment treatment less favourably than someone who is absent for some other medical reason (see 4.5).

Employers should follow their normal policy for medical appointments. However, employers should try to allow some flexibility so that an employee can, for example, travel the longer distances that may be required to see a qualified professional, or attend follow-up appointments, which may take place outside the individual's home town or overseas. If complications arise from any relevant medical treatment that result in a long-term incapacity for work, then the employee should be treated in the same way as any other person who becomes unfit for duty, including complying with its duties under the *DDA 1995* where applicable, where the employee has been diagnosed as suffering from gender dysphoria and the condition is likely to last for more than 12 months (see DISABILITY DISCRIMINATION (3).

Informing colleagues, clients and customers

There is no general need or requirement to inform colleagues, clients or the public that an employee is undergoing gender reassignment. Indeed, it is not appropriate to inform anybody about this matter without the individual's explicit consent as the information is likely to constitute sensitive data under the Data Protection Act 1998.

In some circumstances, information may be necessary where the relationship with somebody who knew the person prior to their change of status is to continue. It is usually good practice for employers to agree to take responsibility for informing those who need to know, with the individual's consent, unless the employee would prefer to do this his or herself. If the individual person wishes to make personal explanations to some or all of his or her contacts, the employer should ask to know when the disclosure is to take place and offer to assist with the detail of the communication.

Dress codes

If there is a dress code, it is good practice to allow enough flexibility to accommodate the process of transition from one sex to another. The individual concerned should be given his or her new uniform early on in the process, before transition at work, to allow him or her to become used to wearing it. A new name badge should also be provided, if appropriate.

Single sex facilities

It will always be preferable for an employer and employee to agree the point at which the use of gender-split facilities such as toilets and changing rooms should change. Typically, the point at which the individual should be permitted to use the facilities of the employee's 'new' sex is likely to be the point at which the individual changes gender. While it is clearly not acceptable to insist upon a transsexual employee using separate facilities (such as a disabled toilet) in the long term, there is a period during which an employer is entitled to make separate arrangements for those undergoing gender reassignment, particularly when other employees raise objections.

In *Croft v Royal Mail Group plc* [2003] All ER (D) 319, [2003] EWCA Civ the Court of Appeal held that a formerly male employee could not, by presenting as a female, necessarily and immediately assert the right to use female toilets. On the other hand, the Court of Appeal also held that an employee could not necessarily be required, in relation to toilets, to behave as if they were not undergoing gender reassignment until they reached the post-operative stage. Pill LJ held that the moment at which a person at the pre-operative 'real life test' stage is entitled to use female toilets will depend on all the circumstances:

> 'The employers must take into account the stage reached in treatment, including the employee's own assessment and presentation. They are entitled to take into account, though not to be governed by, the susceptibilities of other members of the workforce.'

In the present case, the measures taken by the employers were held to be appropriate ones in the circumstances. They were entitled, for a period of time, to require the employee to use the unisex disabled toilet. The time had not come when they were obliged to permit her to use the female toilets.

Reactions of others

The employer should take appropriate steps to ensure that all members of staff refer to the transsexual person by their new name and use pronouns appropriate to their new gender role. This may involve having to train the individual's colleagues, but this should only be done with the individual's consent. The employer should consider agreeing in advance with the employee how they would like the situation to be managed if there are colleagues who are hostile to the change, and ensure someone is available to assist the individual if any incidents do arise.

The employer should be prepared to address the concerns of other employees, for example if concerns are raised about sharing single-sex facilities. The employer should try to determine what is at the heart of the concerns and try to resolve issues. It may be the case that issues can be dealt with relatively simply, for example by ensuring that cubicle doors offer sufficient privacy, or through training staff.

Media interest

If the gender reassignment attracts media attention, the employer should be prepared to support the employee. A single point of contact should be nominated to liaise with the media, from the press office if there is one. Other staff should be advised to maintain strict confidentiality and not to provide any information in response to media enquiries.

If an employee is being harassed by the media at the workplace or in connection with their work, the employer should try to protect him or her and consider strategies that minimise personal exposure. In extreme cases complaints can also be made to the Press Complaints Commission.

Records and personnel file

In order to protect confidentiality, employers should ensure that all documents, public references (for example, telephone directories and websites) and employment details reflect the new gender of the employee.

Under *GRA 2004, s 22(1)* it is an offence for any person who has acquired 'protected information' in an official capacity to disclose the information to any other person (subject to certain exceptions). *Section 22(2)* defines 'protected information' as information about:

- a person's application for a gender recognition certificate; or

- the gender history of a successful applicant.

Under *s 22(3)(b)* a person acquires protected information in an official capacity if the person acquires it as an employer, or prospective employer, of the person to whom the protected information relates, or as a person employed by such an employer or prospective employer. *GRA 2004* does provide some exceptions when protected information may be disclosed, for example where the person to whom the protected information relates agrees to the disclosure of the information or where the information does not enable that person to be identified.

Pensions and benefits

Employers registering staff for corporate insurance and benefits policies should be aware of whether their underwriters need to be informed of a transsexual employee's status, since some insurers may automatically invalidate a policy if gender reassignment is not disclosed.

Typical policies which may require the information to be disclosed include, for example:

- life assurance;

- permanent health or income protection;

- private medical insurance;

- personal accident insurance;

- motor vehicle insurance in the case of company cars.

Once a Gender Recognition Certificate has been obtained, an employer will need an employee's consent to disclose 'protected information' to a benefit provider unless one of the exceptions under *GRA 2004* applies. One such exception applies where a disclosure is made for the purposes of the social security system or a pension scheme.

4.12   Relocation and redeployment

The employer should ensure that, to the extent possible, it is 'business as usual' and an employee should not be shielded from contact with clients or otherwise have his or her job altered. The employer should not offer to relocate or redeploy the individual unless he or she specifically raises the issue.

However, it is possible that a transsexual employee may wish to be relocated to another workplace during the transition period, or even permanently. The employer should consider this request in the same way as it would consider any other request for relocation, but taking into account the particular sensitivities of the situation, and its obligation under *DDA 1995*, if it applies. Ultimately, a decision should be made in conjunction with the individual employee.

Checklist for employers

In summary, some of the key issues which an employer should consider with an individual who is undergoing or intends to undergo gender transitioning are:

- What is the individual's preferred timetable for the transitioning and the medical procedures?

- What time off will be required for this?

- At what point will the employee's name and social gender change?

- Have arrangements been agreed for dress code and use of single-sex facilities?

- Which clients and staff should be informed and when?

- Does the employee wish to tell his or her line manager, colleagues and clients him or herself, or does he or she prefer the employer to do so?

- Have the nature and contents of any communications to clients and staff been agreed?

- What amendments need to be made to the individual's personnel records and the employer's IT systems and other records?

- Does any special training need to be arranged for particular staff or groups of staff?

- What steps have been agreed to handle any harassment, hostile reactions or media interest?

4.13 OTHER SOURCES

There are a number of resources available to employers wishing to address these issues. Examples include:

- 'Gender Reassignment – a Guide for Employers' (January 2005), produced by the Women and Equality Unit of the Department for Trade and Industry (now Department for Business, Enterprise and Regulatory Reform).

- 'Gender Reassignment – Guidance for Managers and Supervisors' (May 2006), produced by the Equal Opportunities Commission.

- 'Transsexual People in the Workplace: PFC Code of Practice' (December 1998), produced by Press For Change (the pressure group for transsexual people).

5 Marital Status and Civil Partnership

5.1 INTRODUCTION

Discrimination against married persons and civil partners is dealt with in the *Sex Discrimination Act 1975, s 3* ('*SDA 1975*'). A person discriminates against another ('A') in any circumstances relevant for the purposes of any of the provisions relating to employment, where A is either married or a civil partner and:

(1) on the ground of being married, or being a civil partner, that person treats A less favourably than he treats or would treat a person who is not married or a civil partner (direct discrimination); or

(2) he applies to A a provision, criterion or practice which he applies or would apply equally to another, but:

> (a) which puts or would put persons who are married or civil partners at a particular disadvantage when compared with persons who are not married or civil partners; and

> (b) which puts A at that disadvantage; and

> (c) which he cannot show to be a proportionate means of achieving a legitimate aim (indirect discrimination).

The prohibition on discrimination against married persons appeared in the originally enacted version of *SDA 1975*, and it remains an uncommon subject of discussion in the law reports. This is presumably because it is a relatively unusual distinct ground of discrimination in practice and because, where it does occur, it can sometimes be subsumed within other, more familiar, discrimination provisions.

Marital discrimination is also somewhat unusual in principle, because most forms of anti-discrimination legislation were designed to protect persons who were members of groups which had been disadvantaged by society in the past, and/or which were minority groups. Nevertheless martial status discrimination has a role in anti-discrimination laws, for three principle reasons. First, it provides a short cut to exposing a type of sex discrimination which might otherwise be more difficult to expose. For example, the promotion by an employer of single women over married women within an organisation simply because the latter are not perceived as the right 'types' is an obviously suspect practice from the point of view of equality. Stated in those terms, the problem does not in fact (and conceptually it should not necessarily) require any comparison between a man and a woman (cf *SDA 1975, s 1(1)(a)*). The concept of marital status discrimination allows the married female complainant to compare herself to an unmarried *woman*, rather than to a man (actual or hypothetical). Secondly, by countering assumptions about how married people will behave at work or will contribute to their work, it has the capacity to provide, albeit in a modest and imperfect way (given the modern prevalence of unmarried families), a conceptual framework which does not focus *solely* on formal or theoretical sexual equality, but which also takes into account the practical, generalised and gendered societal problem of family responsibility versus work. Thirdly, in its recently amended form it provides some further protection for workers in non-heterosexual relationships – albeit only those who have entered into civil partnerships.

5.2 Marital Status and Civil Partnership

5.2 Married persons

Who does *SDA 1975, s 3* protect? In the first place, a person who is 'married' (*s 3(2)(a)*). In the second place, a person who is 'a civil partner' (*s 3(2)(b)*).

It has been held that the dismissal of a woman on the ground that she was *about* to get married was not an act of unlawful discrimination under *s 3*, because the woman, whilst married by the time of the termination of employment, had not been married at the time she was given notice: *Bick v Royal West of England Residential School for the Deaf* [1976] IRLR 326. It is submitted that *Bick* (a first instance decision) was wrongly decided. The intention behind the section was to protect people from being subjected to detriment on account of marital status. In principle one would have thought that this form of anti-discrimination law should at least protect people who are *about* to get married and dismissed as a direct result. It is unsatisfactory to say that a person in the position of Mrs Bick might have other remedies: eg direct sex discrimination (by comparing herself to a hypothetical male), or unfair dismissal (see *McLean v Paris Travel Service* [1976] IRLR 202 or *Pickering v Kingston Mobile Unit* [1978] IRLR 102). The tribunal's approach in *Bick* exacerbated, instead of ameliorating, the potentially incomplete protection afforded by the section as drafted. The tribunal should have held, for example, that a relevant act of discrimination occurred at the date of the termination of the employee's contract (see *Gloucester Working Men's Club and Institute v James* [1986] ICR 603, EAT) by which time the complainant was 'married'. Or it could have adopted a purposive approach to *s 3*, in line with the relevant European principles of interpretation: see eg *Litster v Forth Dry Dock and Engineering Co Ltd* [1990] 1 AC 546, [1989] IRLR 161.

There is no definition of 'married' in *SDA 1975*. The common law and statutory provisions concerning marriage apply. A person who has previously married, but is now divorced is very unlikely to be regarded as 'married' under *SDA 1975* (with the consequence that *SDA 1975* does not specifically protect people from prejudice against divorced persons even though the fact of having been divorced might be thought to be a marital 'status').

5.3 Civil partners

SDA, s 3 was amended with effect from 5 December 2005 by the Civil Partnerships Act 2004 ('*CPA 2004*'). *CPA 2004* created the civil partnership, a new legal status for relationships between homosexual couples, and it brought to an end certain discriminatory effects of the rule that under English law a marriage can only exist between a man and a woman (see eg *KB v NHS Pensions Agency and Secretary of State for Health* [2004] IRLR 240, ECJ). *CPA 2004, s 251* amends *SDA 1975, s 3* so as to include civil partners as well as married persons within its reach. So, for example, a civil partner who is treated by his employer less favourably than a person who is neither a civil partner nor a married person now has a right to make a complaint under the section.

A 'civil partner' is a person who has been registered as the civil partner of a person of the same sex (see *CPA 2004, s 1*).

It remains to be seen whether this provision might reinvigorate marital status discrimination law, which has perhaps become somewhat obscure. For now, it can simply be observed that, just as unmarried heterosexual partners remain unprotected by *SDA 1975, s 3*, so too do those homosexual partners who have chosen not to enter into a formal civil partnership. They must rely, to the appropriate extent, on the provisions dealing with discrimination on the basis of sexual orientation (see SEXUAL ORIENTATION (9)).

5.4 **DIRECT DISCRIMINATION: LESS FAVOURABLE TREATMENT ON GROUNDS OF MARITAL STATUS/CIVIL PARTNERSHIP**

The two most obvious examples of direct discrimination under *SDA 1975, s 3(1)* might be summarised by the behaviour of two theoretical and paradigmatically unenlightened employers: (1) the 'anti-family employer' and (2) the 'homophobic employer'. The anti-family employer, for example, does not want to employ anyone who is married, because he feels they will not be sufficiently dedicated to their career. Their priorities will be elsewhere. The employer is treating people less favourably on grounds of their marital status. The homophobic employer, by contrast, gladly accepts married persons, or unmarried persons, but not homosexual employees who are part of a civil partnership. Those employees are being treated less favourably than others on account of their civil partnership status. They too are protected by *s 3*.

There are relatively few examples in the case law of direct discrimination contrary to *s 3*, and such examples as exist might prove misleading to the unwary. Take for example, *Chief Constable of Bedfordshire Constabulary v Graham* [2002] IRLR 239, EAT. Here a female police inspector was promoted to the position of area inspector, only to be promptly demoted back to her former position. The reason for the demotion was that she was married to the chief superintendent of the same police force. Her complaints of indirect sex discrimination, and both direct and indirect discrimination contrary to *SDA 1975, s 3*, were upheld by a tribunal and consequently by the EAT. But was Mrs Graham in fact demoted on grounds of *marital status* (ie the fact that she was a married person), or was she demoted because of the *identity of her husband*? The two things are not necessarily the same, and the case is not, in fact, authority for the proposition that a person subjected to a detriment because of her marriage to, or partnership or relationship with, a particular person necessarily has a claim under *s 3*. (It may of course, be unfair to dismiss a person because of her relationship with a particular person, or discriminatory on grounds of sex: see e g *McLean v Paris Travel Service* [1976] IRLR 202). The EAT in *Graham* explained (at paragraph 58 of its judgment) that the reason why the claim under *s 3* succeeded was that the employer's reason for the treatment of Mrs Graham, in this particular case, was that she would not be a competent and compellable witness against her spouse in any criminal proceedings. That was a reason, thought the EAT, which (being an attempt to apply the law of evidence in relation to married persons) was *marriage-specific* (not spouse-specific), and it was therefore direct discrimination on grounds of marital status within *s 3*.

The principles relating to direct discrimination, developed in detail in the sex and race discrimination case law, will also apply here. One specific question which arises in this context (and has not yet been answered by the courts) relates to the identity of the comparator. Might a civil partner be able complain of direct discrimination under *s 3(1)(a)* by comparing himself to a married person? (For example, an applicant for a job discovers after interview that the employer believes in 'family values' and is looking to take on married persons with or without children, but no single people, or homosexual people, and definitely not people (like him) who have entered into a civil partnership, which the employer believes undermines family values). The actual wording of the section suggests otherwise. The complainant needs to satisfy the condition (*s 3(1)*) of being *either* married, *or* being a civil partner, in order to come within the section at all. The person (or hypothetical person) with whom comparison is to be made is someone who does not satisfy that condition, ie someone who is neither a married person nor a civil partner.

5.5   INDIRECT DISCRIMINATION AGAINST MARRIED PERSONS/CIVIL PARTNERS

Here the classic example, no doubt rarer these days than it was when *SDA 1975, s 3* was enacted in its original form, is the employer who firmly believes that any applicant for employment who has a child is 'unreliable' and refuses to recruit such a person, or subjects him or her to other detriments once employed. In *Hurley v Mustoe* [1981] IRLR 208 it fell to the EAT (Browne-Wilkinson J, as he then was, presiding) to correct the judgment of an industrial tribunal, who had erroneously thought that there was nothing wrong with such an attitude under *SDA 1975*. As the EAT pointed out, even if (which should not have been assumed) there might have been some individuals for whom, in the employer's experience, the very fact of having had children had caused unreliability at work, it obviously did not follow that it was justifiable for him to have excluded from his consideration the entire class of persons with children: 'a condition excluding all members of a class from employment cannot be justified on the ground that some members of that class are undesirable employees'. The practice would indirectly discriminate against married persons and would be disproportionate.

Beyond the straightforward cases, and just as in other claims of indirect sex discrimination, it will be necessary to consider carefully the evidence to be tendered about differential impact, and the correct pool to be assessed. It is no longer wise for a party to expect tribunals to assume that apparently neutral provisions, criteria or practices in fact operate to the disadvantage of married persons or persons in civil partnerships. See, for example, *Kidd v DRG (UK)* [1985] IRLR 190, EAT; to be compared with an older, and more relaxed approach in *Thorndyke v Bell Fruit* [1979] IRLR 1.

As to justification and proportionality (*s 3(1)(b)(iii)*), it is likely that the concepts and authorities which are relevant to indirect sex discrimination generally will apply here (see 7.22).

5.6   FURTHER INDICATIONS OF DISCRIMINATION: STEREOTYPING

Discriminatory attitudes to married persons can take various forms. An employer should not assume that the husband is the breadwinner, and such an assumption will be evidence of sex discrimination if applied detrimentally: see e g *Coleman v Skyrail Oceanic Ltd* [1981] IRLR 398, CA. Similarly, the mere fact that an employee's husband has relocated does not justify an assumption that the couple will necessarily live together and/or that the employee will necessarily follow the husband with no concern for her own career: *Horsey v Dyfed County Council* [1982] IRLR 395, EAT. Such generalised assumptions can constitute direct sex discrimination if they lead to less favourable treatment.

5.7   THE HARASSMENT PROBLEM

There is a potentially difficult problem about whether it is now unlawful to harass a person on grounds of their marital status. The problem arises in this way. It is specifically unlawful to harass on grounds of sex: see *SDA 1975, ss 4A* and *6(2A)*. These relatively new provisions (in force since 1 October 2005) have brought to an end the older and somewhat artificial practice of viewing sexual harassment at work as actionable as a type of 'detriment' under *s 6(2)(b)*, and as a form of 'less favourable treatment' on grounds of sex under *s 1(1)(a)*. Indeed a new *s 82(1)* of *SDA 1975* makes it clear that harassment is not a type of detriment.

However, there is no equivalent provision to *s 6(2A)*, specifically deeming harassment on the grounds of marital status (or civil partnership) as an unlawful act, and there now appears to be no scope for arguing that such harassment would be a detriment on grounds of sex. The potential answer to the problem is to suggest that *s 4A(1)*, by referring to harassment 'on grounds of sex', is potentially wide enough to include marital status discrimination. After all, the *Equal Treatment Directive (76/2007/EC)* prohibits 'discrimination ... on grounds of sex either directly or indirectly by reference in particular to marital or family status', and thus arguably views marital status discrimination as a subset of sex discrimination.

But that answer would require a very strong Euro-inspired decision from a court, since it appears to go against the grain of the domestic *SDA 1975*, in three respects. First, and unlike the Equal Treatment Directive, *SDA 1975* specifically distinguishes between 'discrimination' (clearly wide enough to include *s 3* discrimination), and 'sex discrimination' (limited to *ss 1*, *2*, and *3A* discrimination only): see *s 5(1)*. So discrimination on the grounds of marital status is not, according to *SDA 1975* itself, sex discrimination. Secondly (a similar point), if direct marital status discrimination is discrimination on grounds of sex, then why the need for *s 3* at all? Thirdly, if correct, the argument would leave civil partners stranded, and worse off than married persons: whilst married employees might be able complain about being harassed by reference to the words of the Equal Treatment Directive, civil partners probably could not. One is forced to concede that neither the problem as stated, nor the potential answer to it as formulated, are particularly attractive, and that legislative reform could and should make the position clear.

5.8 STATUTORY EXCEPTIONS

Under the *Employment Act 1989, s 8* the Secretary of State may by order provide that special treatment afforded to lone parents in connection with participation in certain training schemes will not give rise to discrimination against married persons contrary to *SDA 1975*. This provision was brought in after the EAT had held, in *Training Commission v Jackson* [1989] ICR 222, that a married woman with children had been discriminated against on grounds of marital status in the refusal of a support payment, because only lone parents (not married parents) were eligible for such a payment.

The *SDA 1975* creates a further two notable exceptions. Firstly, *s 7(2)(h)*, one of a number of situations in which sex can be a genuine occupational requirement. *Section 7* as a whole applies to 'sex discrimination' (*s 7(1)*), and therefore marital status discrimination is probably not caught (*s 5(1)(b)*). However, it is worth noting that *s 7(2)(h)* specifically allows an employer to appoint a husband and wife or civil partnership team to a position without discriminating against other applicants on the grounds of sex. Secondly, *s 19(1)*, which applies where employment is for the purposes of organised religion. The section entitles an employer to apply a requirement relating to a person not being either married or a civil partner (*s 19(3)(c)*); or, in relation to a person who is either married or a civil partner, relating to the person or their spouse or civil partner, not having a living former spouse or civil partner, or to how either the person or their spouse or civil partner ceased to be married or a civil partner (*s 19(3)(d)*). However, the requirement must be applied so as to comply with the doctrines of the religion or to avoid conflicting with the strongly held religious convictions of a significant number of the religion's followers (*s 19(1)(c)*).

There is also the exception found in the *Employment Equality (Sexual Orientation) Regulations 2003 (SI 2003/1661), reg 25* ('*SOR 2003*'), which provides that neither any prevention or restriction of access to benefits by reference to marital status, nor the conferring of a benefit on married persons and civil partners to the exclusion of all others, shall not be unlawful (see SEXUAL ORIENTATION (9)).

5.9   **COMPARATIVE JURISPRUDENCE**

Since the English jurisprudence relating to marital status discrimination is rather sparse, certainly at appellate level, it is interesting to consider briefly examples from two other jurisdictions where related issues have been judicially considered.

In *B v Ontario (Human Rights Commission)* [2002] 3 SCR 403, the Canadian Supreme Court held that non-discrimination principles concerning marital and family status set out in the Ontario Human Rights Code were broad enough to include circumstances where the discrimination resulted from the particular identity of the complainant's spouse or family member. Compare the English case of *Graham* (see 5.4). The Court justified its broad and purposive approach by reminding itself that the goal of anti-discrimination law was to prevent the drawing of negative distinctions based on irrelevant personal characteristics.

In *Miron v Trundel* [1995] SCR 418 the Supreme Court had little difficulty in finding marital status discrimination where the complaint was that a benefit accorded to married couples was denied to (same-sex) unmarried couples. The Court reasoned that the unmarried are a historically disadvantaged group (see 5.1), and whilst their characteristic of being unmarried is not immutable, the situation for them in reality is often more complex and they deserve protection under constitutional principles. In effect, therefore, 'marital status' under Canadian law included the status of being unmarried, unlike (it seems) under the English *SDA 1975* (see above).

The Constitutional Court of South Africa recently emphasised the State's responsibilities to provide persons in homosexual relationships with truly equal marriage rights: see *Minister of Home Affairs v Fourie and Bonthuys* (Case CCT 60/04, Judgment 1 December 2005). At paragraphs 150–151 Sachs J, drawing as the South African Constitutional Court often does on painful yet instructive lessons from the past, noted that the merely formalistic correction of historical and practical consequences of exclusion from marriage would not be good enough; and speculated that the creation of a separate partnership status for homosexuals only that was supposedly 'separate but equal' might still in truth be discriminatory.

6   Race Discrimination

6.1   LEGAL SOURCES AND GUIDANCE MATERIAL

Legal sources

Race discrimination has been outlawed in the UK since the introduction of the *Race Relations Acts* of *1965* and *1968*. Both these pieces of legislation were, however, considerably narrower in scope than the *Race Relations Act 1976* ('*RRA 1976*') which repealed and replaced them. It is the provisions of the *RRA 1976* that now provide the UK legislative framework for protection from discrimination on grounds of race.

Since enactment, the *RRA 1976* has been amended by numerous pieces of secondary legislation, the most significant of which has been the *Race Relations Act 1976 (Amendment) Regulations 2003 (SI 2003/1626)* ('*2003 Amendment Regulations*'). The *2003 Amendment Regulations* implement the *Race Discrimination Framework Directive (Council Directive 2000/43/EC)* which was issued by the European Council in accordance with its powers under *Article 6* of the *Treaty of Rome* (now *Article 13* of the amended *Treaty*).

The main changes introduced by the *2003 Amendment Regulations* in respect of discrimination on grounds of race, ethnic or national origins were as follows:

(a)   a new definition of indirect discrimination (*RRA 1976, s 1(1A)*);

(b)   a statutory definition of racial harassment (*RRA 1976, s 3A*);

(c)   a reversal of the burden of proof in race discrimination cases (*RRA 1976, s 54A*);

(d)   changes to the circumstances in which an employer can argue that being of a particular race, ethnic or national origin is a genuine requirement of a particular role (*RRA 1976, s 4A*);

(e)   removal of some of the historic exceptions to the anti-discrimination provisions, for example, in respect of employment in private households.

Despite strong opposition from the Commission for Racial Equality, the UK Government limited the ambit of the *2003 Amendment Regulations* to race, ethnic and national origins, in accordance with the ambit of the *Race Directive*. However, *RRA 1976* also outlaws discrimination on grounds of colour and nationality (the latter of which is expressly excluded from the scope of the *Race Directive* by *Article 3, para 2*). The *2003 Amendment Regulations* have therefore given rise to a disparity in the protection afforded to employees (and others) by the *RRA 1976*, depending upon which racial ground is under consideration. This disparity, where relevant, will be discussed further in the body of this chapter. It should, however, be noted that in practice the disparity has less impact than it might as employees seeking protection will often be able to allege discrimination on a number of different racial grounds.

A Single Equality Act (see the Foreword) is now proposed, which would have a significant impact upon the structure of race equality legislation in the UK.

6.2   Other guidance

In addition to the legislative framework described above, employers can also turn to a wide variety of guidance materials including the Commission for Racial Equality's statutory code of practice on racial equality in employment ('CRE Code') and good practice guidance produced by the Advisory Conciliation and Arbitration Service (ACAS) on tackling discrimination and promoting equality. This guidance does not have legal force; breach of its provisions does not of itself amount to unlawful discrimination. However, *RRA 1976, s 47(10)* makes clear that the contents of the CRE Code are admissible in evidence in an employment tribunal or court. Further, if any provision of the CRE Code appears to the tribunal or court to be relevant to any question arising in the proceedings before it, it *must* take that provision into account when determining that question.

6.3   RACE AND RACIAL GROUNDS

Introduction

The definitions of direct and indirect race discrimination refer to less favourable treatment 'on racial grounds' and to membership of a 'racial group' respectively. Racial grounds are defined in *RRA 1976, s 3(1)* as 'any of the following grounds, namely colour, race, nationality or ethnic or national origins'. These categories are addressed in turn in the following sub-sections. It is important to identify correctly which racial ground or grounds give rise to the claim, as the doctrine of *res judicata* will apply should the claim be unsuccessful. See 6.11.

6.4   Colour

This category is self-explanatory and has produced little case law. An employer discriminates against an employee on grounds of their colour if, for example, they treat black employees less favourably than white employees.

6.5   Race and ethnic origins

It is now clear that the concept of 'ethnic origins' is broader than race. In *Mandla v Dowell Lee* [1983] 2 AC 548, [1983] 1 All ER 1062, the House of Lords held that Sikhs could qualify as an ethnic group, even if they were not a racial group. *Mandla* concerned a headmaster's decision to refuse a Sikh boy a place at his school on the ground that the boy wished to wear a turban and refused to cut his hair. The case concerned indirect discrimination (not direct) since there were several Sikh pupils at the school. However, the requirement not to wear a turban clearly had a disproportionate impact upon Sikhs. The Court of Appeal had reasoned that ethnic origins were the same as racial origins and that Sikhs were not a racial group as they were not biologically distinguishable from other inhabitants of the Punjab. The Court went on to hold that the complaint was really of religious discrimination (which was not at the time prohibited).

In the House of Lords, Lord Fraser gave the leading speech and defined an ethnic group as one which regards itself, and is regarded by others, as a distinct community on the basis of certain characteristics. Some of these characteristics are essential and include:

(i)   a long-shared history of which the group is conscious as distinguishing it from other groups and which it keeps alive; and

(ii)   a cultural tradition of its own, including family and social customs often, but not necessarily, associated with religious observance.

Non-essential characteristics which serve as a useful guide to distinguishing ethnic groups from the broader community include:

(iii)   a common geographical origin or descent from a small number of common ancestors;

(iv)   a common language, although this need not be peculiar to the group;

(v)   a common literature which is peculiar to the group;

(vi)   a common religion which is different from that of neighbouring groups or the broader community; and

(vii)   being a minority or being an oppressed or dominant group within a larger community.

Lord Fraser also emphasised that membership of an ethnic group could occur through adherence.

On a similar basis, it has been held that Jews may be members of a racial or ethnic group (*Seide v Gillette Industries* [1980] IRLR 427). Applying *Mandla*, the Court of Appeal has also found that gypsies could constitute an ethnic group as they had not merged wholly with the majority population (*Commission for Racial Equality v Dutton* [1989] IRLR 8). This was so despite their long presence in the country and the fact that they could no longer claim common racial stock.

By contrast, Rastafarians have been found not to constitute an ethnic group (*Crown Suppliers (PSA) Ltd v Dawkins* [1993] ICR 517). In *Dawkins*, the Court of Appeal found that there were insufficient grounds to distinguish Rastafarians from the rest of the Afro-Caribbean population and the 60-year history of the Rastafarian movement did not amount to a long-shared history.

Muslims cannot be regarded as an ethnic group as they are united primarily by their religious beliefs. However, there remains the possibility that a rule which disadvantages Muslims as a class (for example, by disciplining them for taking time off to attend Eid or requiring them not to wear a headscarf) may be found to constitute indirect discrimination against a racial group (*J H Walker Ltd v Hussain* [1996] IRLR 11). Now that there is express provision on religious discrimination (see RELIGION OR BELIEF (7)), such actions are less likely under *RRA 1976*. It has now been confirmed that Rastafarianism falls within the scope of the *Employment Equality (Religion and Belief) Regulations 2003 (Harris v NKL Automotive Limited*, EAT (3 October 2007); see RELIGION OR BELIEF (7)). It is a mistake to focus on the single factor of language as sufficient to identify an ethnic group. In *Gwynedd County Council v Jones* [1986] ICR 833, the EAT held that the tribunal had erred in regarding the English-speaking Welsh as a distinct ethnic group from the Welsh-speaking Welsh.

6.6   Nationality and national origins

'Nationality' did not appear on the list of prohibited grounds in either the 1965 or 1968 predecessors of the *RRA 1976*. This created a gap in protection, as revealed by the decision in *Ealing London Borough Council v Race Relations Board* [1972] AC 342. Ealing adopted the rule that the applicant should be a British subject under the *British Nationality Act 1948* as a condition of appearing on its waiting list for council accommodation. On this basis, a Polish applicant, who was otherwise qualified, was refused council accommodation. The Race Relations

Board argued that Ealing had discriminated against the applicant on the ground of his national origins as prohibited by the 1968 Act. The House of Lords held by a majority that the term 'national' in 'national origins' referred to race and not citizenship. On that basis, Ealing did not discriminate against the applicant on the basis that he was a Polish national and would have treated him the same way regardless of his citizenship.

RRA 1976 now expressly includes nationality in the list of prohibited grounds. However, the distinction between citizenship and race remains as is clear from *Tejani v Superintendent Registrar for the District of Peterborough* [1986] IRLR 502. In *Tejani,* the Court of Appeal held that it was not unlawful racial discrimination for the Registrar to require to see the passports of those wishing to be married by him who came from abroad. The Registrar treated all persons from abroad in the same way, regardless of their national or racial origins.

'National origins' has a broader meaning than an individual's legal nationality acquired at birth. Thus, the Inner House has held that the English and Scots have different national origins, although they both share citizenship of the United Kingdom (*BBC Scotland v Souster* [2001] IRLR 150). Mr Souster claimed that his contract as a rugby journalist with BBC Scotland was not renewed on the ground that he was English. He was replaced by a Scottish woman. BBC Scotland sought to defend the proceedings on the basis that the English and the Scots were not different racial groups and so discrimination between them could not be said to be on racial grounds. The Inner House rejected this argument: 'national origins' is a broader term than nationality and could cover differences between the Scots and English. Moreover, it also held that an individual could adopt a different set of national origins in the course of their life and could adhere to a different national group by, for example, marriage. Finally, a person can be discriminated against on the grounds of their national origins because they are *perceived* to be a member of a particular group (for example, because of their accent) whether they actually are a member or not.

6.7 TYPES OF RACE DISCRIMINATION

Direct discrimination

RRA 1976, s 1(1)(a)) sets out the test for direct discrimination. It provides that a person unlawfully discriminates against another if, on 'racial grounds', he treats that person less favourably than he treats or would treat others. There is no justification defence to a claim of direct race discrimination (see COMMON CONCEPTS (1)) and so any direct race discrimination will be unlawful unless a genuine occupational requirement (GOR) or genuine occupational qualification (GOQ) applies under *RRA 1976, ss 4A* and *5*.

Despite the fact that *s 1(1)(a)* requires an answer to be given to a single question, the courts have, as with other strands of discrimination (see COMMON CONCEPTS (1)), historically followed a two-stage approach, looking first at whether the complainant was treated less favourably than others were treated or would have been treated in the same circumstances, and then at whether the reason for that less favourable treatment was on 'racial grounds' (see *Glasgow City Council v Zafar* [1998] ICR 120). Originally, *RRA 1976* placed the burden of proving both 'stages' on the claimant. However, the courts recognised the difficulty faced by claimants in producing direct evidence of racial discrimination, since those who discriminate on grounds of race 'do not in general advertise their prejudices' (*Zafar*). Case law established that where there was no direct evidence of race discrimination, the tribunal was entitled to look at all the facts and circumstances of the case and draw appropriate inferences. Furthermore, where a claimant established that he was treated less favourably, and demonstrated a difference in race pointing to the possibility of racial discrimination, the tribunal could look to the alleged discriminator for an explanation. Where the tribunal considered the explanation to be inadequate, it *could* infer that the discrimination was on racial grounds (*King v Great Britain-China Centre* [1992] ICR 516), but was not bound to do so as a matter of law (*Zafar*).

The insertion of *s 54A* into the *RRA 1976* by the *Race Relations Act 1976 (Amendment) Regulations 2003* (which implements the *Burden of Proof Directive (2000/43/EC)*) has in effect codified this two-stage approach, but only in respect of cases of discrimination on grounds of race, ethnic or national origin. Where the claimant has proved facts from which the tribunal *could*, in the absence of an adequate explanation by the respondent, conclude that the respondent had committed an act of discrimination, the burden shifts to the respondent to prove that he did not commit that act (see COMMON CONCEPTS (1)); see also *Madarassy v Nomura International plc* [2007] All ER (D) 226 (Jan) for more detail on what is needed to shift the burden of proof to the respondent). At this second stage, if the respondent is unable to prove that he did not commit the act, then the tribunal *must* uphold the claimant's complaint (for guidance on the application of *s 54A* see *Wong v Igen Ltd (Equal Opportunities Commission intervening)* [2005] EWCA Civ 142, [2005] ICR 931 and *Madarassy*).

In respect of cases of discrimination on grounds of colour and nationality, the approach adopted by pre-*section 54A* case law continues to apply. In practice, the distinction in relation to different racial grounds is unlikely to come into play very often, as different grounds will frequently be inextricably linked. It has also been suggested by the Court of Appeal that the *s 54A* approach should be followed in any event (see *Adebayo v Dresdner Kleinwort Wasserstein Ltd* [2005] IRLR 514).

It was established prior to the inclusion of *RRA 1976, s 54A* that a two-stage approach may not always be appropriate in every case as the issues of less favourable treatment and racial grounds may be intertwined, particularly, for example, where the identity of the relevant comparator is a matter of dispute (see *Shamoon v Chief Constable of the Royal Ulster Constabulary* [2003] UKHL 11, [2003] 2 All ER 26 and COMMON CONCEPTS (1)). The Court of Appeal has now confirmed that this remains the position under *s 54A*; failure to follow a two-stage test will not automatically mean that a tribunal has erred in law, provided that it placed the burden of explaining the differential treatment on the alleged discriminator (*Brown v Croydon London Borough Council and another* [2007] All ER (D) 239 (Jan)).

For convenience however, the two questions are dealt with separately below.

6.8 **Less favourable treatment**

Treatment

Treatment has been interpreted widely, to include not only obvious behaviour (such as failing to promote an employee or dismissing an employee), but also, for example, acts or words of discouragement (in appropriate circumstances) (*Simon v Brimham Associates* [1987] ICR 596; *Tower Hamlets London Borough Council v Rabin* [1989] ICR 693) or a denial of choice (*Birmingham City Council v Equal Opportunities Commission (No 1)* [1989] AC 1155). The less favourable treatment must actually have taken place; it is not enough for a complainant to show that he 'would have' been treated less favourably, for example, if he had attended a job interview (*Baldwin v Brighton and Hove City Council* [2007] ICR 680; EAT decision under *SDA 1975*).

Paying someone who is being less favourably treated extra does not make the treatment lawful (*Jeremiah v Ministry of Defence* [1980] QB 87; per Lord Denning and Lord Justice Brightman in a Court of Appeal decision under *SDA 1975*).

It is the treatment itself rather than the consequences of that treatment that the tribunal must look at (*Balgobin and Another v Tower Hamlets London Borough Council* [1987] ICR 829; EAT decision relating to the *SDA 1975*). The case of *Chief Constable of West Yorkshire v Khan* [2001] UKHL 48, [2001] 1 WLR 1947 (a victimisation case) illustrates the point. In that case, the House of Lords held that the claimant was treated less favourably where his employer refused his request to provide a reference to support his application for a promotion, even though the consequences of providing that reference would have been seriously damaging to his application.

It is less favourable treatment to segregate someone from others based on the grounds of race (*RRA 1976, s 1(2)*; *Furniture, Timber & Allied Trades Union (FTATU) v Modgill* [1980] IRLR 142, EAT). This is the case regardless of whether the facilities are equal for both sets of employees. In other words, the separation on racial grounds is itself less favourable treatment. However, *Modgill* established that it is not discriminatory for an employer to fail to prevent segregation caused by the workers themselves. In this case, only Asian workers were employed in the paint shop, and it was alleged that this was segregation by the employer on racial grounds since the paint shop was considered 'dirty' work which no one else wanted to do. Only Asian people were put forward for these jobs, but, as it turned out, this was not because of any policy of the employer but because when vacancies arose in the shop they were filled by persons introduced by workers already working there, usually relatives. The failure of the employer to enforce a positive policy to remove any possibility of segregation was not unlawful discrimination. Such a recruitment practice, involving 'word of mouth' advertising of roles is, however, not to be recommended and may amount to unlawful indirect discrimination even if it does not amount to direct discrimination. This point was not considered in *Modgill*.

6.9   *Unfavourable and Less Favourable Treatment Distinguished*

The requirement in *RRA 1976, s 1(1)(a)* refers to *less* favourable treatment. This requires a comparative element. Thus showing unfavourable or unreasonable treatment will not be enough to satisfy the stage one test. The House of Lords has stated:

'[T]he conduct of a hypothetical reasonable employer is irrelevant. The alleged discriminator may or may not be a reasonable employer. If he is not a reasonable employer he might well have treated another employee in just the same unsatisfactory way as he treated the complainant, in which case he would not have treated the complainant "less favourably" (*Glasgow City Council v Zafar* [1998] ICR 120). In *Madarassy* (a sex discrimination case) the Court of Appeal held that the Claimant had failed to show discrimination at the first stage where there was no *less* favourable treatment as all employees were treated equally badly regardless of gender or level within the company. The Tribunal had found that there was "equality of shouting regardless of gender or level".'

The principle from *Zafar* was applied in *Marks & Spencer Plc v Martins* [1998] ICR 1005, where the Court of Appeal held that a tribunal had erred in law in asking whether there had been bias on the part of the employer instead of asking whether the complainant had been treated less favourably than a person of a different racial group (see also *Bradford Hospitals NHS Trust v Al-Shabib* [2003] IRLR 4).

Since *Zafar*, arguments have been raised that it is open to a tribunal to infer discrimination from unreasonable treatment if the alleged discriminator does not show that equally unreasonable treatment was or would have been applied to others (see the *obiter* comment of Lord Justice Sedley at p.857A of *Anya v University of Oxford* [2001] ICR 847). This argument was rejected by the Court of Appeal in *Bahl v The Law Society and others* [2004] IRLR 799. The Court applied *Zafar* and emphasised that showing unreasonable treatment of others is only one way of avoiding an inference of discrimination. However, their Lordships did state that the absence of an explanation for unreasonable treatment (rather than the unreasonable treatment itself) could lead a tribunal to infer racial discrimination which the respondent could then rebut through leading evidence of a genuine reason which is not discriminatory and was the ground of his conduct. In *Igen v Wong* [2005] ICR 931 (another sex discrimination case) the Court of Appeal cautioned tribunals from too readily inferring unlawful sex discrimination from unreasonable conduct where there is no evidence of other discriminatory behaviour on such ground, but held that 'it was open to a tribunal to make such an inference'.

6.10   Comparators

The test in *RRA 1976, s 1(1)(a)* requires the tribunal to compare the treatment of the complainant to that to which other persons are or would be subjected.

This 'other person', commonly referred to as the 'comparator', has to be someone of a different racial group whose circumstances are the same, or not materially different to those of the complainant (*RRA 1976, s 3(4); Shamoon v Chief Constable of the Royal Ulster Constabulary* [2003] ICR 337).

It is for the complainant to choose the comparator(s) with whom he wishes to be compared. Where there is no appropriate actual comparator whose circumstances were the same or not materially different to the complainant, a hypothetical comparator can be used.

The courts have interpreted *s 3(4)* as requiring a comparison of 'like with like' (*Shamoon; Dhatt v McDonalds Hamburgers Ltd* [1991] ICR 238). This does not mean that the comparator has to be a clone of the complainant in every respect except race (*Madden v Preferred Technical Group CHA Ltd and another* [2005] IRLR 46), but the circumstances of the comparator must be the same as the complainant in all material respects apart from in respect of the protected category (*Shamoon*). The circumstances that are important will inevitably depend on the facts of each case. In *Shamoon*, the comparators identified by the tribunal were two male chief inspectors in other regions. They were regarded by the tribunal as suitable comparators because 'they were in the traffic branch, held the same rank and carried out similar responsibilities in their regions to the complainant'. However, the Court of Appeal ultimately held that the two Chief Inspectors were not proper comparators. It held that the tribunal had 'overlooked the fact that Shamoon's superintendent had no authority over [them]... and no complaints or representations had been made about them'. In other words, their circumstances were materially different to those of the claimant. The way in which the complainant carries out his/her role is likely to be a significant factor in deciding the suitability of comparators.

The following cases give examples of factors which have led to a finding that the circumstances of a comparator were materially different to those of the complainant. In *Wakeman and others v Quick Corporation* [1999] IRLR 424, a claim for race discrimination on the basis that secondees from Japan received higher pay than the claimants, who were employed through the UK company, failed as the circumstances of the comparators' terms and conditions (as secondees) were materially different to those of the claimants. As it happened, the secondees were all Japanese, but, in fact, there was no reason why they could not have been of a different race. In *Famy v Hilton UK Hotels Ltd* [2006] All ER (D) 112 (Oct) the supervisor of a bar, who was of Filipino ethnic origin, complained that he had been discriminated against on grounds of race in not being promoted to the position of bar manager over several years, the position having been given to external white job applicants. These external white applicants were found to be inappropriate comparators as, in having formally applied for the position, their circumstances were materially different to those of the claimant, who had not applied for the job. There was therefore no actual comparator. With regards to any hypothetical comparator, the EAT held that the tribunal had rightly concluded that he would have been treated the same as the claimant (ie anyone not applying would not be appointed).

Where a complainant has selected actual comparators whose circumstances the tribunal does not think are sufficiently similar, the Court of Appeal has said that in appropriate cases the tribunal itself should consider the construction of a hypothetical comparator in place of the actual comparator(s) (*Balamoody v United Kingdom Central Council for Nursing, Midwifery and Health Visiting* [2002] IRLR 288, CA; see also *Chief Constable of Cambridgeshire v McLachlan* EAT (14 February 2003, unreported)). The Court of Appeal was mindful of the counter argument (that it was for the claimant to make out his/her case) and Lord Justice Ward was at pains to say (at paragraph 61) 'I am far from saying that in ... every case the tribunal has to be robustly interventionist and do the task which the applicant is not doing for himself or herself. Every case is different'. The Court of Appeal went on to hold that there was some evidence in this particular case to support an inference that the refusal to restore the applicant to the nursing register was discriminatory on the grounds of race. In the circumstances, and based on the particular facts of this case, it held that it was incumbent on the tribunal chairman to construct a hypothetical comparator and test the case against that benchmark.

To construct a picture of how a hypothetical comparator would have been treated in comparable circumstances, inferences will need to be drawn. As such, it may be appropriate for the tribunal to consider how 'actual unidentical, but not wholly dissimilar, cases' were treated (*Chief Constable of West Yorkshire v Vento (No 1)* [2001] IRLR 124, approved by *Balamoody* (CA) (at paragraph 60)).

In *Sidhu v Aerospace Composite Technology Ltd* [2001] ICR 167, the Court of Appeal stated that in certain cases, where the conduct of the alleged discriminator was 'race-specific', there is no need to go through the process of comparing the treatment of the complainant with that of a comparator. The Court of Appeal gave the example of where 'a person is harassed or abused because of his race, that conduct is race-specific' and stated that in such circumstances 'it is not necessary to show that a person of another race would be treated more favourably'. This approach appears to be out of line with the general approach taken by the courts, including the Court of Appeal in *Balamoody*. In any event, this case will now only be of significance to cases of discrimination on the grounds of colour or nationality, as under *RRA 1976, s 3A* there is no strict need to identify a comparator in harassment claims on the grounds of race, or ethnic or national origins. See COMMON CONCEPTS (1) for further discussion on this point.

6.11 **On 'racial grounds'**

To be unlawful under the *RRA 1976*, the less favourable treatment must be on 'racial grounds'. 'Racial grounds' means colour, race, nationality or ethnic or national origins (*RRA 1976, s 3(1)*). 'Racial group' means a group of persons defined by reference to one of the racial grounds (*s 3(1)*). Unlike indirect race discrimination, the definition of direct race discrimination is the same, no matter which racial ground is relevant (cf indirect race discrimination, where different tests now exist depending upon whether the relevant racial ground is race, ethnic or national origin or, alternatively, colour or nationality). See 6.14ff.

Following the Court of Session decision in *British Airways Plc v Boyce* [2001] IRLR 157, it is likely that in most cases where a complainant fails in bringing a claim under one of the racial grounds, he will be precluded through the principle of *res judicata* from bringing a new claim on a different ground. The key question being 'what was litigated and what was decided?'. The Court of Session did acknowledge the possibility of exceptions to this for 'special circumstances of a wholly unforeseen nature or for a situation ...in which the tribunal has made it clear that no final decision was intended'. However, except in such exceptional circumstances, *res judicata* should apply. As Lord Nimmo Smith observed, 'any other approach would leave it open to an applicant to lodge up to five separate applications under each of the five meanings of racial groups ...' in *s 3(1)*.

The courts have distinguished the different elements that make up the definition of racial grounds and it is clear that each has its own scope and meaning and should be treated separately. See 6.3–6.6 above.

6.12 *Determining whether the treatment was on racial grounds*

The approach in cases determined prior to the implementation of *s 54A* in July 2003 was to use the 'but for' test, asking, for example, 'but for A's race, would he have been treated less favourably?' If not, then causation was established (see *James v Eastleigh Borough Council* [1990] ICR 554 – a sex discrimination case). However, the use of the 'but for' test under *RRA 1976, s 1(1)(a)* was rejected in *Chief Constable of West Yorkshire Police v Khan* [2001] UKHL 48, [2001] 1 WLR 1947, as the House of Lords favoured a factual approach of looking at the reason (whether conscious or subconscious) for the discriminator's acts. The House of Lords held that this factual approach is a subjective test, unlike causation which is a legal conclusion, not a question of fact. In light of the *Khan* decision, tribunals should not restrict themselves to the 'but for' test, but should consider the reasons why the alleged discriminator acted as he did. The reversal of the burden of proof by *s 54A* means that in most cases it will now be for the respondent to provide a non-discriminatory reason for the treatment.

Provided that the tribunal is satisfied that the reason for the less favourable treatment was racial grounds, it does not need to identify a discriminatory motive or intention on the part of the alleged discriminator (*Nagarajan v London Regional Transport* [2000] 1 AC 501, HL). While the motive of the alleged discriminator may be relevant, it is not the decisive factor and motives which are well-meaning in nature will not save an act of direct discrimination from being unlawful where less favourable treatment is on racial grounds (*Din v Carrington Viyella (Jersey Kapwood) Ltd* [1982] ICR 256). In *Din*, the employer refused an employee's application for re-employment after he resigned to visit his native Pakistan, despite reassurances that he would be given favourable consideration for re-employment when he returned. The tribunal had identified that the motive of the employer in not re-employing was to avoid any potential industrial unrest that would be caused. This followed earlier unrest amongst the workforce following the claimant's involvement in an alleged racially motivated dispute with a manager. The EAT held that the motive to avoid industrial unrest was not in itself sufficient to amount to discrimination, but it could amount to such if the *reason* for the original unrest was racially discriminatory conduct. As the tribunal had not given reasons to support its conclusion that the original dispute was racially motivated, the case was remitted to another tribunal for further consideration.

Lack of knowledge of the claimant's racial, ethnic or national origin will not conclusively negate a finding of discrimination, but a lack of such knowledge may support a finding that there has not been less favourable treatment on *racial* grounds (*Simon v Brimham Associates* [1987] IRLR 307).

Direct discrimination can be either 'conscious or subconscious on the part of the discriminator' (*Appiah v Bishop Douglass Roman Catholic High School* [2007] All ER 240 (Jan)). In *Appiah*, a fight at school between two white pupils and two pupils of black African ethnicity resulted in the two black pupils being excluded from school. On a claim of racial discrimination, the EAT had concluded that there was no direct, conscious discrimination, but the Court of Appeal acknowledged that 'racial motive' could be both conscious and subconscious. The complainant put forward arguments of a 'racist ethos' at the school, based on statistics that 'the school had a high level of exclusions, particularly among the ethnic minorities' and of teachers 'having problems with black students', but ultimately the court concluded this did not cause any subconscious discrimination.

The racial ground does not have to have been the only reason for the less favourable treatment for there to be unlawful discrimination. So long as racial grounds were a 'significant cause of [the] decision to treat the complainant less favourably', discrimination is made out (*Nagarajan*). Where there are a number of reasons for the less favourable treatment, it will be for the tribunal which has seen and heard the evidence to decide whether or not the reason for the treatment was racial grounds (*Owen & Briggs v James* [1982] ICR 618). In this case, the Court of Appeal held that where the tribunal had found that 'colour' was 'an important factor in [the employer's] failure to consider the applicant's application further ... the tribunal were right in deciding that there was a sufficient case of racial discrimination'.

Seide v Gillette Industries Ltd [1980] IRLR 427 is an example of a case where, although the complainant's race was a factor in the factual background to the complaint, the reason for the treatment was not found to be on racial grounds. Mr Seide, a Jewish toolmaker, had previously suffered race-related comments from one of his co-workers. Therefore, he was moved to a different shift, with a Mr Murray, who complained that Mr Seide was inciting him to join his side in the dispute. As a result, Mr Seide was transferred to a day-shift where he could be better supervised, but this meant that he was paid less. Mr Seide claimed he had been treated less favourably on racial grounds. The EAT found, however, that although the matter had begun as a result of racially offensive comments, the transfer of Mr Seide resulted from the difficulties he was causing in the workplace, not because he was Jewish. Thus, although race had been a factor in the overall circumstances, the treatment complained of was based on the second incident with Mr Murray, and therefore was not on racial grounds. The EAT held that 'it is not sufficient merely to consider whether the fact that the person is of a particular racial group … is any part of the background … of what happens'.

In considering whether the less favourable treatment was on racial grounds, the tribunal can consider evidence on conduct before and after the act complained of (*Rihal v Ealing London Borough Council* [2004] EWCA Civ 623, [2004] IRLR 642). A tribunal is also entitled to rely on words said after the less favourable treatment as casting light on the actions at the time (*Securicor Custodial Services Ltd v Williams* EAT/0042/02 (29 January 2003, unreported)).

In cases where subconscious discrimination is a possibility, it will be particularly important for the tribunal to look for 'indicators from a time before or after the [alleged discriminatory treatment] which might demonstrate that an ostensibly fair-minded decision was, or was not affected by racial bias' (*Anya v University of Oxford* [2001] EWCA Civ 405, [2001] ICR 847).

6.13 *Race of another*

In many cases, claims of direct discrimination will involve the complainant alleging that he has been less favourably treated on the grounds of his own race. However, this is not necessarily the case.

It is now well established that it is unlawful to discriminate against a person on the grounds of another's race. In *Showboat Entertainment Centre Ltd v Owens* [1984] 1 All ER 836, [1984] 1 WLR 384 the white manager of an amusement centre refused to carry out the instructions of his employer to exclude young black people from the centre and was dismissed as a result. The dismissal was held by the EAT to be 'on racial grounds' under *RRA 1976, s 1(1)(a)*, and Brown-Wilkinson P said in his judgment at paragraph 11, that 'the words 'on racial grounds' are perfectly capable in their ordinary sense of covering any reason for an action based on race, whether it be the race of the person affected by the action or of others'. Notably, *RRA 1976* refers to less favourable treatment being 'on racial grounds' and not 'on grounds of [the employee's/complainant's] race'. Accordingly, Brown-Wilkinson P continues at paragraph 15, 'We can, therefore see nothing in the wording of the Act which makes it clear that the words 'on racial grounds' cover only the race of the complainant'.

Similarly, in the earlier case of *Zarczynska v Levy* [1979] ICR 184, [1979] 1 WLR 125, a barmaid who was sacked for refusing to comply with instructions not to serve 'coloured people' was held to have been treated less favourably on racial grounds.

This approach was approved by the Court of Appeal in *Weathersfield Ltd (t/a Van & Truck Rentals) v Sargent* [1999] ICR 425, CA, where an employee working for a vehicle rental company was told to inform 'any coloureds or Asians' that no vehicles were available for rental. The Court of Appeal held that whilst concluding that 'requiring [Sargent] to operate a racially discriminatory policy was treatment on racial grounds involved giving the expression [on racial grounds] a broad interpretation, it was [an interpretation] which was justified in the circumstances of the case'.

The EAT tried to take the concept of 'race of another' even wider in *Redfearn v Serco Ltd (t/a West Yorkshire Transport Service)* [2005] IRLR 744, [2006] ICR 1367, where it held that it was discrimination on 'racial grounds' where an employee working in a predominantly Asian workforce became a member of the

BNP and was subsequently dismissed on 'health and safety grounds' in fear of the reaction of the other employees. The Court of Appeal curbed this wide interpretation and reversed the decision of the EAT. Although the court accepted the previous authorities which stated that an employer can be guilty of discriminating against an employee on the grounds of another person's race, this does not extend to a situation where an employer is simply trying to protect against racist abuse or tension in the workplace. The sole reason that the employer dismissed Mr Redfearn was to avoid any such adverse effects that his BNP membership might have; this was not discrimination 'on racial grounds'.

6.14   INDIRECT DISCRIMINATION

Introduction

The essence of indirect discrimination lies in three elements:

(i)   that an employer applies some provision, practice or requirement to his employees;

(ii)   that it operates to the disadvantage of proportionately greater numbers of the claimant's racial group than non-members of that group; and

(iii)   that the requirement or condition cannot be defended on a race-neutral basis.

For example, a rule which prohibits all employees from having beards will disproportionately disadvantage Sikhs whose religion requires them not to shave. However, such a rule may be justified on the grounds of hygiene in certain circumstances (*Singh v Rowntree Mackintosh Ltd* [1979] IRLR 199 and *Panesar v Nestlé Co Ltd* [1980] IRLR 64 (discussed at 6.17).

6.15   The tests for indirect discrimination

There are now two distinct tests for indirect race discrimination. The reason for this is that a new test (see below) was introduced in the *2003 Amendment Regulations* to comply with the UK's obligations under the *Race Directive* (see 6.1) which only apply to discrimination on grounds of race and ethnic or national origins. Article 2 of the *Race Directive* provides:

'indirect discrimination shall be taken to occur when an apparently neutral provision, criterion or practice would put persons of a racial or ethnic origin at a particular disadvantage compared to other persons, unless that provision, criterion or practice is objectively justified by a legitimate aim and the means of achieving that aim are appropriate and necessary'.

The most significant test is that contained in *RRA 1976, s 1(1A)* ('the new test') and provides that a person discriminates against another where he applies to that other:

(i)   a provision, criterion or practice which he applies or would apply equally to persons not of the same race or ethnic or national origins as that other; but which

(ii)   puts or would put persons of the same race or ethnic or national origins as that other at a particular disadvantage when compared with other persons;

(iii)   puts that other at a disadvantage; and

(iv)   he cannot show to be a proportionate means of achieving a legitimate aim.

This test replaces that in *s 1(1)(b)* ('the old test') in relation to cases covered by it (*s 1(1C)*), but does not replace it altogether. This is because *s 1(1A)* only applies to discrimination on the grounds of race and ethnic or national origins and not to discrimination on the grounds of colour or nationality. As such, allegations of discrimination based only on colour or nationality will continue to be governed by the old test (which is considered in more detail below). However, as most cases of discrimination based on colour can be rephrased as being based on race, the only cases likely to be governed by the old test are those based on nationality.

The old test in *s 1(1)(b)* provides that a person discriminates against another where he applies to that other:

(a)   a requirement or condition which he applies or would apply equally to persons not of the same racial group as that other; but which:

   (i)   is such that the proportion of persons of the same racial group as that other who can comply with it is considerably smaller than the proportion of persons not of that racial group who can comply with it; and

   (ii)   is to the detriment of that other because he cannot comply with it; and

   (iii) he cannot show to be justifiable irrespective of the colour, race, nationality or ethnic or national origins of the person to whom it is applied.

It can be seen that although the two tests have similarities and possess some common elements, the new test is substantially more beneficial to claimants. These benefits include that the provision, criterion or practice need not operate as a complete bar to access to the relevant benefit, there is no need to produce statistical proof that a considerably smaller group of one's own race can comply with the requirement or condition and there is no need to show that the worker cannot comply with the requirement or condition. Further, the old test's concepts of justification and detriment are replaced with proportionality and disadvantage respectively.

The old test also applies to all allegations of indirect race discrimination occurring before 19 July 2003 (when the *2003 Amendment Regulations* entered into force). This is unlikely to be significant given the short time limit for issuing race discrimination proceedings (see 1.23). Many of the cases arise under the old test and are set out below where they are likely to continue to provide guidance.

6.16   **Applying the new test**

(*i*) *Provision, criterion or practice*

The first element of the new test is that the employer should apply a 'provision, criterion or practice' to the worker. These terms are not defined in the *RRA 1976*. A provision may be in the individual contract or in a more general policy which does not have legal effect. A criterion is likely to apply to selection, promotion or dismissal. A practice is potentially very broad and will cover general policies and the manner in which they are in reality applied by the employer.

In contrast to the law under the old test, it is no longer necessary for an employee to demonstrate that a provision, criterion or practice operates as a complete bar to the worker obtaining a particular benefit (see below). It is now sufficient that the worker demonstrates that the provision, criterion or practice operates to the disadvantage of members of their racial group even if it is only a desirable, and not a mandatory, element.

(ii)   Particular disadvantage

Again, this concept is not defined in the *RRA 1976*. It is thought that the term particular disadvantage is intended to exclude merely trivial or technical disadvantages. As under the old test, this element requires the claimant and the tribunal to identify a pool of comparison for determining whether members of the relevant racial group are disadvantaged compared to other groups. Although the claimant will be required to identify some pool for comparison, the tribunal will not be bound to adopt the claimant's suggestion where it forms the view that it is arbitrary or artificial (*Abbott v Cheshire and Wirral Partnership NHS Trust* [2006] EWCA Civ 523, [2006] ICR 1267). In *Abbott* (a case about indirect sex discrimination), the Court of Appeal held that the claimants (a mostly female group of domestic hospital workers who did not receive a bonus) were not entitled to compare themselves only to hospital porters (an entirely male group who did receive a bonus) and to ignore a another group of catering workers (mostly female who did receive a bonus). The court also held that, although it was desirable to have as large a group for comparison as was consistent with them being similarly situated, the expanded comparator group in the present case (of 37 workers) was sufficient.

The next question is how great a disparity of treatment is required between the claimant's racial group and that of the comparison group before one can say that the claimant's group is particularly disadvantaged. There is no guidance in *RRA 1976* and little in the cases and the matter is discussed at 1.44.

(iii)   Personal disadvantage

The claimant must demonstrate that the application of the provision, criterion or practice has disadvantageous consequences for him. It is not sufficient to show that a disproportionate number of members of his racial group cannot comply if, in fact, he can.

(iv)   Proportionality

The final element of the new test is that the employer cannot show (the burden being on him) that the provision, criterion or practice is a proportionate means of achieving a legitimate aim. This test is familiar from other areas of EU law and that under the ECHR. It is a three-stage process.

The first stage is to identify a legitimate aim. This must be an aim which is not infected by any discriminatory purpose and equates most closely to the idea of the legitimate economic, administrative or other needs of the business. An example would be where an employer can demonstrate that there is a genuine risk to health in a food production business if workers are permitted to wear beards. For reasons outlined previously, such a provision, criterion or practice is potentially racially discriminatory against Sikhs, a racial group whose religion requires them not to shave. By contrast, although considerations of cost are not of themselves illegitimate, they will not generally provide adequate justification unless combined with other factors (*R (on the application of Elias) v Secretary of State for Defence* [2006] EWCA Civ 1293, [2006] 1 WLR 3213). This decision also held that although it is not necessary for the employer to demonstrate that it carried out a balancing exercise to determine the proportionality of any provision, criterion or practice at the time of its adoption, its failure to do so may make it more difficult to establish justification.

If the employer demonstrates a legitimate aim, he is still required to fulfil the second element of the test, that is, that the provision, criterion or practice is a proportionate means of achieving that aim. The requirement of proportionality contains two distinct elements. The ECJ has set out the classic formulation of the test as requiring that the measures in question 'correspond to a real need ... are appropriate with a view to achieving the objectives pursued and are necessary to that end (*Bilka-Kaufhaus GmbH v Weber Von Hartz (Case 170/84)* [1986] IRLR 317). In applying the test of proportionality, the tribunal will apply its own judgment and adopt an objective approach (*Redfearn v Serco Ltd* [2005] IRLR 744, EAT applying *Hardy & Hansons plc v Lax* [2005] EWCA Civ 846, [2005] IRLR 726 on the *SDA 1975* (see SEX DISCRIMINATION (8)). The tribunal will not apply a 'range of reasonable responses' or 'margin of appreciation' test. The tribunal's task has been described as one of 'critical evaluation' of the justification put forward by the employer (*Allonby v Accrington and Rossendale College* [2001] EWCA Civ 529, [2001] IRLR 364 under the *EPA 1970* and the *SDA 1975*).

First, the employer must demonstrate that the provision, criterion or practice actually advances the aim. If it does not do so, it cannot be proportionate. Secondly, there must be a reasonable relationship between the provision, criterion or practice and the aim, and the tribunal is entitled to consider whether the legitimate aim could be achieved in a way which has a lesser impact on the affected individuals. *Elias* (above) concerned the Government's compensation scheme for those interned by the Japanese in the Second World War. Under the scheme, civilian internees had to show that either they (or a parent or grandparent) were born in the UK. The Government's aim of ensuring that claimants had a strong link with this country was a legitimate one, but there had been no attempt to analyse the impact of the requirement in terms of indirect race discrimination and no assessment of what other criteria could have been devised to establish a link with the UK. As such, the Court of Appeal rejected the Secretary of State's plea of justification.

By contrast, in *Azmi v Kirklees Metropolitan Borough Council* [2007] IRLR 484 (a case on religious discrimination), the EAT affirmed the tribunal's conclusion that the school's decision to prohibit a teaching assistant from wearing a full-face veil when teaching was proportionate in light of the fact that the school had conducted assessments of the claimant's effectiveness as a teacher with and without the veil and permitted her to wear the veil at all other times except when teaching.

The tribunal will also consider how serious the impact of the provision, criterion or practice is on the individuals concerned. In certain cases (such as *Elias* above), the tribunal may conclude that the criterion chosen is so closely linked to the prohibited ground (in that case national origins) that it could not be justified. There is also a limited statutory restriction on the availability of the justification defence in relation to Sikhs and the wearing of turbans under the *Religion or Belief Regulations 2003* (see RELIGION OR BELIEF (7)).

6.17 Applying the old test

As stated at 6.15, the old test for indirect discrimination under *RRA 1976, s 1(1)(b)* will continue to apply to cases not covered by the *Race Directive*, that is, those based on colour or nationality or occurring before 19 July 2003. The old test is set out at 6.15 and its elements are analysed below.

(*i*) *Requirement or condition*

To fulfil *RRA 1976, s 1(1)(b)*, the requirement or condition must be a mandatory criterion and not merely one of a series of discretionary factors which the employer may take into account. For example, in *Meer v London Borough of Tower Hamlets* [1988] IRLR 399, the employer adopted a number of criteria when drawing up a long list for employment as head of its legal department. These included age, date of admission as a solicitor, senior management experience, length in present post and experience in Tower Hamlets. The claimant was of Indian origin and claimed that the final requirement was indirectly discriminatory against those who shared his national origin. The Court of Appeal confirmed that the tribunal had been correct to conclude that the requirement of Tower Hamlets experience could not constitute a requirement or condition under *s 1(1)(b)* since it was not an absolute bar to recruitment, but only one factor to be considered.

The tribunal will not permit an employer to avoid the application of *RRA 1976* by describing a requirement or condition as merely 'desirable'. The Scottish EAT upheld the decision of the tribunal that, despite its description by the employer, the criterion of management training and supervisory experience was in fact a 'must' and so could constitute indirect (in that case, sex) discrimination (*Falkirk Council v Whyte* [1997] IRLR 560). A requirement or condition need not be express (or even conscious) and may arise in the case of informal recruitment practices.

(*ii*) *The proportion of the group which can comply*

To make out this element of the old test, the proportion of the claimant's racial group who can comply must be considerably smaller. The tribunal is interested in proportions of the claimant's racial group and the comparison group and not with overall numbers or ratios. For a more detailed analysis of this point see (see COMMON CONCEPTS (1)) Appellate courts have been reluctant to lay down strict guidelines as to how great a disparity is required before it can be said that the proportion who can comply is considerably smaller. Most of the case law on this question has arisen on the context of sex discrimination. As described above, the tribunal is not required to accept the claimant's choice of comparison. The importance of correctly identifying the appropriate section of the population for comparison is demonstrated by *Hussain v Midland Cosmetic Sales plc* EAT (9 May 2002, unreported). At first instance, the tribunal rejected Miss Hussein's complaint that her employer's insistence that she should remove her headscarf at work constituted indirect race discrimination against women of Pakistani origin. The tribunal relied on the fact that there were eight other Pakistani women in Miss Hussein's workplace and the difference between this group (90% of whom (eight out of nine) could comply) and the 100% of the non-Pakistani comparator group who could comply was insufficient to be considerably smaller. The EAT overturned the decision on the basis that the other Pakistani employees were not similarly placed to (and therefore not proper comparators for) Miss Hussein since they had been offered a choice as to whether to wear the headscarf and protective clothing. By contrast, Miss Hussein was told that she had to remove her headscarf and wear protective clothing.

Most requirements or conditions in indirect race discrimination cases are ones with which the claimant can (at least in theory) comply. Thus, a Sikh *can* comply with a requirement not to wear a turban and an observant Jew *can* work on a

Friday evening or a Saturday. However, the Act's protection would be much reduced if this approach were adopted. Instead, the tribunal should ask whether the claimant can *in practice* comply, in accordance with the customs and traditions of the racial group to which he belongs (*Mandla* and *Dutton*; see 6.5).

(iii) Individual detriment

The claimant must demonstrate that the requirement or condition has operated to his detriment. It is not enough that the claimant may find the requirement offensive. However, the detriment does not always have to operate in relation to tangible conditions of employment such as status or pay so long as a reasonable employee would or might conclude that the treatment was to his detriment in all the circumstances (*Shamoon v Chief Constable of the Royal Ulster Constabulary* [2003] UKHL 11, [2003] ICR 337). *Shamoon* concerned the decision to remove responsibility for carrying out appraisals of other staff from the claimant and this was held to be capable of amounting to a detriment under the *SD(NI) Order 1976*. Moreover, the claimant need not be aware at the time that a discriminatory requirement or condition had been imposed. In *Garry v Ealing London Borough Council* [2001] EWCA Civ 1282, [2001] IRLR 681, the claimant was selected for a fraud investigation because of her ethnic origins. This constituted an actionable detriment even if the claimant was not aware of it at the time.

(iv) Justification

In *Mandla* (above and 6.5), the House of Lords accepted that the issue of justification under the old test was a difficult one and the cases provide limited guidance. This is because justification was accepted to be a heavily fact-based issue and hence one which is left to the industrial good sense of the tribunal (with which the appellate court will be reluctant to interfere) (*Raval v Department of Health and Social Security and the Civil Service Commission* [1985] IRLR 370). In *Raval*, the Court of Appeal upheld the tribunal's decision that the Civil Service's requirement of GCE English Language for employment in clerical grades was justified despite the fact that the claimant was amply capable of demonstrating her proficiency in English by other means. The tribunal had accurately fulfilled its role of reflecting the attitudes of society as a whole in the degree of justification required and the fact that another tribunal might have reached a different view was not a ground of appeal.

The Court of Appeal has emphasised that the employer must at least demonstrate that the requirement is justified on an objective basis and that his own belief that the reasons were adequate will not suffice (*Hampson v Department of Education and Science* [1990] 2 All ER 25, [1989] ICR 179). However, such guidance as does exist reveals that the test for justification is not very stringent. For example in *Ojutiku and Oburoni v Manpower Services Commission* [1982] IRLR 418, the Court of Appeal approved the MSC's practice of requiring management experience before providing funding for a Diploma in Management Studies even though this disadvantaged West African immigrants such as the claimants. The MSC justified the practice on the basis that the Diploma would not enhance the student's employment prospects unless they possessed such experience. The court asked whether there were 'sound and tolerable' or 'good and adequate' reasons for the practice and regarded the MSC's requirement as justified.

The decisions in *Singh* and *Panesar* (see 6.14) concerning Sikhs with beards provide further illustrations of the requirement of justification in practice. In *Singh*, the Court of Appeal held that it could not interfere with the tribunal's decision that the ban on beards was justified even though the employer enforced it at only two of its eight factories. In *Panesar*, the Court of Appeal again declined to intervene with the finding of justification, notwithstanding the fact that the employer permitted moustaches and sideburns and had refused to accept that the beard could be covered with a snood. A further example of how appearance and clothing requirements can have indirectly discriminatory effect is provided by *Kingston and Richmond Area Health Authority v Kaur* [1981] IRLR 337. In *Kaur*, the tribunal found that the Health Authority had failed to justify a requirement that female trainee nurses should wear a standard uniform, which excluded Miss Kaur since her religion required her to wear trousers. The EAT overturned this decision on the basis that a statutory instrument specified the form of any uniform to be worn. It is highly unlikely that these requirements would pass the new test of proportionality.

6.18   VICTIMISATION

Introduction

The aim of the law of victimisation is to protect an employee from being subjected to a detriment by his employer because the employee has sought to rely on *RRA 1976* or has assisted another in doing so. The law on victimisation therefore represents a substantial extension of the scope of *RRA 1976* since the detriment suffered is not related to the race of the claimant. The elements of the cause of action are: that the employee has performed a protected act; that he has been treated less favourably by his employer than other employees; and that the reason for the less favourable treatment was that the employee had performed the protected act (*Lindsay v Alliance & Leicester plc* [2000] ICR 1234). These elements are considered below.

6.19   *Protected act*

The protected acts under *RRA 1976, s 2(1)* are:

(a)   bringing proceedings against the discriminator or any other person under the *RRA 1976*; or

(b)   giving evidence or information in connection with proceedings brought by any other person against the discriminator or any other person under *RRA 1976*; or

(c)   otherwise doing anything under or by reference to *RRA 1976* in relation to the discriminator or any other person; or

(d)   alleging that the discriminator or any other person has committed an act which would amount to a contravention of *RRA 1976*.

The section goes on to extend the protection of *RRA 1976* to situations where the discriminator knows that the employee intends to do any of the above acts or suspects that he has done, or intends to do so.

An illustration of the breadth of this definition is *National Probation Service for England and Wales v Kirby* [2006] IRLR 508. Mrs Kirby was interviewed in relation to an allegation of race-based bullying involving two other employees which was raised by way of internal grievance. Mrs Kirby was found to have performed a protected act under (c) above (and therefore 'by reference to' *RRA 1976*) by giving information in connection with an internal complaint of race discrimination. This was the case even though Mrs Kirby's information was to the effect that there had been no discrimination.

However, the tribunal does not always apply such a broad definition. In *Kirby v Manpower Services Commission* [1980] 3 All ER 334, [1980] 1 WLR 725, Mr Kirby worked as a clerk at a job centre and suspected three employers of discriminating on the grounds of race against potential employees. He reported his suspicions to the CRE and procedures were instituted against one of the employers. The MSC transferred Mr Kirby to less congenial work after discovering his actions. The EAT upheld the MSC's contention that it acted because of Mr Kirby's breach of confidentiality and not because of the substance of the allegations. The EAT held that Mr Kirby's conduct did not qualify under (b) since no proceedings had been brought at the time of the allegations. Equally, his conduct did not fall within (c) since he was not acting pursuant to any duty. Finally, Mr Kirby could not rely on (d) since he did not allege that the employers *had* breached *RRA 1976*, but merely that they *might have* done so.

If the employee complains of actions which would not be unlawful under *RRA 1976*, there is no basis for a claim of victimisation (*Waters v Metropolitan Police Commissioner* [1997] IRLR 589). See also (see COMMON CONCEPTS (1)).

6.20   *Less favourable treatment*

The claimant must identify a comparator by reference to whom it is claimed that he has suffered less favourable treatment. The cases demonstrate that the tribunal should not approach this question in an unduly technical manner. In *Chief Constable of West Yorkshire v Khan* [2001] UKHL 48, [2001] IRLR 830, Lord Nicholls held that the *RRA 1976* calls for a simple comparison between the treatment afforded to the claimant and that which would be afforded to other employees who have not done a protected act. *Khan* concerned a police officer who complained that he had been victimised by the Chief Constable's refusal to provide him with a reference. The Chief Constable stated that his refusal was based on his reluctance to prejudice the pending case for race discrimination which the officer had brought before the tribunal. The House of Lords held that the proper comparator was not another officer who had instituted legal proceedings against the Chief Constable under another enactment, but any other officer who requested a reference. In the end, Mr Khan's claim failed because the House found that the reason for the refusal was not that *RRA 1976* proceedings had been issued, but because legal proceedings were still pending.

6.21   *By reason that*

The claimant must also establish that the less favourable treatment was caused by ('by reason that') he had performed a protected act. The House of Lords in *Khan* held that this required the tribunal to consider the state of mind (both conscious and unconscious) of the employer rather than to ask whether 'but for' the protected act the less favourable treatment would not have taken place. Further guidance is provided by *Nagarajan v London Regional Transport* [2000] 1 AC 501, [1999] 4 All ER 65, in which the claimant alleged that the potential employer had victimised him by denying that they had received a job application from him. The tribunal inferred that the employer had treated Mr Nagarajan less favourably by reason of his protected act as they did not request him to re-apply and this was found to demonstrate a reluctance on their part to employ him. The House of Lords upheld this view. There was no need to show bad faith or consciously racist motivation on the part of the employer: it was enough to show that the reason for the less favourable treatment was the protected act.

Where the employer may have been influenced by a number of factors (including the protected act), it is sufficient for victimisation to be made out that the protected act was a significant (in the sense of not being trivial) part of the employer's reasons for their action (*Wong v Igen Ltd* [2005] EWCA Civ 142, [2005] IRLR 258).

The claimant failed to establish the causal connection between his protected act and the less favourable treatment he received in *Aziz v Trinity Street Taxis Ltd* [1989] QB 463, [1988] 2 All ER 860. Mr Aziz made allegations of race discrimination against the respondent (an association which protected the interests of taxi drivers) in tribunal proceedings. In the course of the hearing, it emerged that Mr Aziz had made covert tape recordings of his conversations with a number of members of the association. As a result, Mr Aziz was expelled from the association. There was no doubt that he had suffered less favourable treatment and making the recordings was 'by reference to' *RRA 1976* under *s 2(1)(c)*. However, the Court of Appeal found that the expulsion did not take place by reason of the protected act, but because Mr Aziz had behaved in an underhand manner and in breach of trust.

As stated above, in *Khan*, the House of Lords held that an employee may still protect his position in pending *RRA 1976* proceedings without being found to have victimised the claimant. However, *St Helens Metropolitan Borough Council v Derbyshire* [2007] UKHL 16, [2007] IRLR 540, the House of Lords set clear limits to how far the employer can go. In *Derbyshire*, the employer's solicitor wrote to the claimants before their equal pay tribunal proceedings explaining the severe impact on all staff that the proceedings would be likely to have. This letter was also sent to other staff in the claimants' department. The House of Lords was not prepared to interfere with the tribunal's conclusion that the employer here had crossed the line and had not conducted itself like an 'honest and reasonable' employer. The House emphasised that less favourable treatment required more than the ordinary incidents of all litigation. See COMMON CONCEPTS (1) for further consideration of this point.

6.22   HARASSMENT

Before the *2003 Amendment Regulations* came into force in July 2003, an employee who had suffered racial harassment had to bring a claim of direct discrimination under *RRA 1976, s 1(1)(a)*, showing that they had been treated less favourably and that this had caused them a detriment under *RRA 1976, s 4(2)(c)*.

The *2003 Amendment Regulations* implemented the *Council Directive 2000/43/EC* of 29 June 2000 implementing the principle of equal treatment between persons irrespective of racial or ethnic origin (*'Race Directive'*). *Article 2(3)* of the *Race Directive* defines harassment as being deemed to be discrimination when 'unwanted conduct related to racial or ethnic origin takes place with the purpose or effect of violating the dignity of a person and of creating an intimidating, hostile, degrading, humiliating or offensive environment'.

RRA 1976, s 78, as amended by the *2003 Amendment Regulations*, now defines 'detriment' as not including harassment falling within *RRA 1976, s 3A* and introduced a statutory definition of harassment resulting in a free-standing cause of action. *S 3A* prohibits harassment on the grounds of race, or ethnic or national origin. The new definition does not apply to harassment on the grounds of colour or nationality, which will continue to be actionable under the head of direct discrimination.

Although there is now a separate, free-standing claim for certain types of racial harassment, case law that considered the pre-2003 test for harassment will still be relevant to claims for harassment on the grounds of colour or nationality, and may also continue to have some relevance in the other cases. Although tribunals will not be bound by these earlier cases in relation to the grounds covered by the statutory definition, they are likely to refer to them for guidance.

In addition to the civil remedies under *RRA 1976*, harassment on racial grounds (or indeed on other prohibited grounds may amount to a criminal offence or be actionable in the civil courts under other legislation (see 6.33ff).

6.23   **Harassment under RRA 1976, s 3A**

Under *RRA 1976, s 3A* (as inserted by the *2003 Amendment Regulations*) a person unlawfully harasses another person where, on the grounds of race or ethnic or national origin he engages in unwanted conduct, which has the purpose or effect of:

(a)   violating that other person's dignity; or

(b)   creating an intimidating, hostile, degrading, humiliating or offensive environment for that other person.

Conduct will be regarded as having the effect in (a) or (b) if, having regard to all the circumstances, including in particular the perception of that other person, it should reasonably be considered as having that effect.

RRA 1976, s 4(2A) makes harassment by employers of a person whom he employs or who has applied to him for employment unlawful. It therefore expressly applies to job applicants. Job applicants are, however, less likely to be able to avail themselves of protection from harassment on grounds of their colour or nationality, given the more restrictive definition which applies by virtue of *s 4(1)* (see below for further details).

Harassment also applies to acts outside the employment relationship (see COMMON CONCEPTS (1)).

6.24   *On grounds of race or ethnic or national origins*

Article 2(3) of the *Race Directive* refers to unwanted conduct 'related to' racial or ethnic origin. The UK legislation may be narrower in scope in its use of the words 'on grounds of', although the practical effect (if any) of this distinction has not been tested.

Tribunals and courts must interpret UK law to give full effect to the EU Directive, which will require them to apply a broader meaning to 'on grounds of' and it is likely that tribunals will take the same approach to 'on grounds of racial or ethnic origin' as they have been taking to 'on racial grounds' under the direct discrimination test (see 6.11).

Under the direct discrimination provisions, harassment was made out where abuse was on the ground of someone else's race and directed at another person (but overheard by the complainant): *Chin v Post Office* (12 December 1996, unreported), upheld by the EAT in *Post Office and Another v Chin* EAT/162/97 (24 February 1998, unreported) (although see 6.27).

In a harassment claim under *RRA 1976, s 3A*, there is no requirement for the complainant to point to a real or hypothetical comparator as it is unnecessary to show that someone of a different racial, ethnic or national origin would have been treated differently. Harassment is deemed to be discrimination on the grounds of race   (*Wandsworth   NHS   Primary   Care   Trust   v   Obonyo   (No   1)*

UKEAT/0237/05/SM (8 February 2006, unreported) and *Gravell v London Borough of Bexley*, UKEAT/0587/06/CEA (2 March 2007, unreported). The complainant must still prove that there was a discriminatory reason for the conduct in question. Where the conduct is race-specific (such as racist language), it is likely that the complainant will be able to show that the conduct is on the particular protected ground. Stereotypical assumptions will also be indicative of the particular ground.

Where the conduct does not relate specifically to a protected ground (for example, isolating someone or swearing at someone) it will be difficult for a tribunal to conclude that the conduct is on the ground of race unless the complainant can show that he was targeted because of his race – a comparative exercise – which would lead to a similar approach to that under the direct discrimination route.

6.25 *Unwanted conduct*

The complainant must show that the conduct was unwanted. There are no reported cases that consider in detail when conduct is 'unwanted' in the context of racial harassment. However, guidance can be sought from sexual harassment cases (see 1.51).

There is no requirement for the complainant to have previously made it clear that the conduct is unwanted. Although there will often be a course of conduct or number of incidents, a one-off incident (e g racist joke) can constitute harassment (both under the statutory definition and direct discrimination) if sufficiently serious (*Insitu Cleaning Co Ltd v Heads* [1995] IRLR 4). Failure to complain at the time of the conduct or soon after does not automatically preclude a finding that it was unwanted but may have evidential weight. The complainant may feel unable to object because of fear for his job (*Driskel v Peninsula Business Services Ltd* [2000] IRLR 151).

6.26 *Having the purpose or effect of*

Where it is a person's 'purpose' to violate another's dignity or create an intimating, hostile, degrading or offensive environment for that person, there is no 'reasonableness' requirement. An oversensitive complainant could therefore succeed with a harassment claim where a person deliberately harasses him. However, an alleged harasser will not readily admit to the conduct. A tribunal will therefore have to consider the surrounding circumstances.

For the second limb (*RRA 1976, s 3A(1)(b)*), there is an objective reasonableness test. Conduct will be regarded as having the necessary effect only if it should 'reasonably be considered as having that effect', having regard to all the circumstances (*s 3A(2)*). There is a subjective element, however, in that the complainant's perception, in particular, must be taken into account. Nonetheless the conduct must still be such that it could reasonably be considered as having that effect. A claim for harassment will fail if the complainant is being hypersensitive (*Driskel*) (as long as there was no intention to cause offence, in which case the claim would come within the first limb).

It is clear that when considering 'effect', the harasser does not have to have intended to violate the complainant's dignity or cause offence, but a bad motive will make the complainant's case stronger (*Chief Constable of the Kent Constabulary v Kufeji*, EAT 1135/00 (4 May 2001, unreported)).

6.27 *Dignity and working environments*

This part of the statutory definition is wider than *Article 2(3)* of the *Race Directive* in that it covers conduct that has the purpose or effect of violating dignity *or* creating an intimidating, hostile, degrading, humiliating or offensive environment, whereas the *Race Directive* requires the conduct to satisfy both elements. On this basis, it should be easier for complainants in the UK to make out a harassment claim than if the wording of the *Race Directive* had been tracked. The reason for this broader definition was existing case law which had already established this greater protection for UK employees.

As to what could constitute a violation of dignity or an offensive environment, there have been few cases under the new provision. Cases pre-dating the statutory definition are illustrative.

Often the two elements will overlap. For example, a derogatory or abusive comment, whether directed at the complainant or at a third party, could violate the complainant's dignity at the same time as creating an intolerable environment in which to work.

In *Chin*, a tribunal held that Mr Chin, who witnessed the taunting of a black colleague (including his being called names such as 'black bastard', 'Zulu warrior' and 'tribes Mandela') could claim harassment on the basis that the abuse of his fellow worker could amount to a detriment to Mr Chin, even though it was not directed at him or on the ground of *his* race.

Overhearing a one-off racially abusive comment about oneself, however, was held not to be harassment on the basis that it did not amount to a detriment (*De Souza* – see below), although as considered below, there is some doubt as to whether this case would be decided in the same way if it were to be heard now.

In a more recent tribunal case, an employee (a Maltese national) who overheard her supervisor saying 'I hate foreigners' and 'I am against immigration' was awarded compensation against the supervisor and her employer, even though the comment was not directed at her (*Ruby Schembri v HSBC*, ET/330/361/05 (14 July 2006, unreported). The chairman commented that *RRA 1976, s 3A* does not require the alleged harasser to have used racist language or other overtly race-specific behaviour. The comments made by her supervisor were 'specific unwarranted and by any objective assessment signalling at the very least she disliked immigrants coming to Britain and being employed and at worst a racist comment intended for or directed at the Claimant'.

A one-off incident may be sufficient to violate dignity if it is sufficiently serious, but a series of acts, which individually would be insufficient by themselves to amount to harassment, could create an offensive environment (see 6.31).

A case on the statutory definition held that racist text messages sent by a colleague could amount to harassment by creating an offensive environment for an employee *Gravell v London Borough of Bexley* UKEAT/0587/06/CEA (2 March 2007, unreported). The fact that the text messages were sent to the claimant outside the ordinary scope of employment did not prevent the employer being fixed with responsibility for the act of harassment (see 1.109ff) for more detail on liability of employer for acts of employee). Further, although the comments made were not on grounds of Ms Gravell's race, they were on grounds of someone else's race and created an offensive environment for Ms Gravell.

Gravell also established that an employer's practice or policy of not challenging racist comments or behaviour by clients is capable itself of having the effect of creating an offensive environment for an employee under *RRA 1976, s 3A(b)*. This appears to be a move away from the findings in *Macdonald v Advocate for Scotland*; *Pearce v the Governing Body of Mayfield School* [2003] UKHL 34 which disapproved the decision in *Burton* (see 6.29). In *Gravell*, the EAT expressed the view that there was scope for argument as to whether the findings in *Pearce* would apply to a claim under *RRA 1976, s 3A* as they were based on the law before the statutory tort of harassment was introduced into the *RRA 1976*. Notably, *Gravell* was an appeal against a strike out by the tribunal on the basis that the claims would not have a reasonable prospect of success. A policy of not challenging racist behaviour by clients also arguably goes further than a one-off failure to protect employees from such behaviour as had been the case in *Burton*.

The cases above give some guidance on what could amount to a violation of dignity or an offensive environment. The position remains unclear in relation to overheard comments. The insertion of *s 3A* and the proposed amendments for this statutory tort also to apply to nationality and colour through the enactment of a Single Equality Act suggest that tribunals should be finding that overheard comments are capable of having the effect of creating an offensive environment.

6.28   Harassment as direct discrimination

Nationality and colour were not covered by the *2003 Amendment Regulations* (or the *Race Directive*). An employee wishing to claim harassment on the grounds of nationality and/or colour must therefore bring a claim for direct discrimination. This requires him to establish that he has been treated less favourably on racial grounds under *RRA 1976, s 1(1)(a)* and that this is unlawful under *s 4(2)*. Harassment is most likely to made out where the employee can show that he has been 'subjected to any other detriment' under *s 4(2)(c)*.

The test for job applicants is different from that for employees. Under *s 4(1)*, it is unlawful to discriminate against a job applicant:

(a)   in the arrangements made to determine who should be offered employment;

(b)   in the terms on which employment is offered; or

(c)   by refusing or deliberately omitting to offer him employment.

An applicant cannot therefore rely on the 'any other detriment' test and is therefore unlikely to be able to bring a claim for harassment itself; a claim that he has not been offered a job on grounds of his colour or nationality is the more likely route.

6.29   *Less favourable treatment on the prohibited ground*

To bring a harassment claim under the direct discrimination provisions, the complainant must identify a suitable comparator and show that he was treated less favourably on the grounds of nationality or colour.

Race-specific language does not remove the requirement to point to a comparator. In *Burton v De Vere Hotels Ltd* [1996] IRLR 596, harassment which was race-specific in form was held to be less favourable treatment on racial grounds, where two black waitresses were the subject of racist (and sexist) jibes by a third party, a comedian. However, *Pearce* (see 6.27) disproved *Burton*, holding that there is a requirement under *RRA 1976, s 1(1)(a)* to show that a white person would have been treated differently. In *Pearce*, it was commented that in *Burton*, the employer would not have taken any different steps if the waitresses had been white and had been the 'butts of the entertainer's offensive humour'. According to the judge's comments on *Burton* in *Pearce*, the racist comments had been made by a third party and the employer's failure to protect the employees was not on racial grounds.

Although race-specific language does not remove the requirement to point to a comparator, in some cases the language used will be so specific to the complainant's race and will be used by someone who is racially motivated that it will be obvious that the complainant was treated less favourably than a person of another race would have been treated. The comparison must still be made but is *res ipsa loquitur* (ie the treatment speaks for itself) (*Smith v Gardner Merchant Ltd* [1998] 3 All ER 852, [1999] ICR 134, and *Pearce*).

The EAT in *Hussain v Elonex Plc* UKEAT/80/95 (25 April 1996, unreported) (subsequently upheld by the Court of Appeal ([1999] IRLR 420)) reluctantly held that calling the complainant (a Pakistani by birth and ethnic origin) a 'slave' or 'servant' was not racially motivated in the relevant circumstances. It accepted that 'there may well be circumstances where the use of the words 'slave' or 'servant' may have a racist connotation, particularly here where they were uttered by a white man against a black man. But equally, they may not.' The employer treated everybody equally badly; there was no evidence that his treatment of the complainant was racially motivated.

6.30   *Requirement for a comparator*

The requirement for a comparator has been removed in respect of harassment on the grounds of race, ethnic or national origin with the implementation of *RRA 1976, s 3A*. However, language that is colour or nationality related will not of itself amount to harassment unless it can be shown than a person of a different colour or nationality would not have been treated in the same way. There is no requirement for there to be an actual comparator – a hypothetical comparator can be used.

6.31   *Requirement to show 'detriment'*

In the context of a claim under *RRA 1976, s 4*, the employee must show that his employer has 'subjected him to any other detriment'. There has been a considerable amount of case law on what amounts to a 'detriment' as well as when the employer will be liable for harassment. The employer's liability is considered in more detail in COMMON CONCEPTS (1).

Overhearing a racial insult about oneself may not by itself amount to a detriment, even where this has caused distress (*De Souza v Automobile Association* [1986] ICR 514). In this case, the complainant had overheard one of her managers refer to her as a 'wog'. The Court of Appeal held that the complainant could not properly be said to have been 'treated' less favourably by whoever used the word, unless that person intended her to overhear the conversation in which it was used, or knew or ought reasonably to have anticipated that the person he was talking to would pass the insult on or that the complainant would become aware of it in some other way. A reasonable worker must have felt disadvantaged in the circumstances and conditions in which he had thereafter to work. Lord Justice May said:

> 'If the discrimination was such that the putative reasonable employee could justifiably complain about his or her working conditions or environment, then whether or not these were so bad as to be able to amount to constructive

dismissal, or even if the employee was prepared to work on and put up with the harassment, I think this too could contravene the subsections [*RRA 1976, s 4(2)(c)* and *SDA 1975, s 6(2)(b)*]'.

The sexual harassment case of *Shamoon v Chief Constable of the Royal Ulster Constabulary* [2003] ICR 337 confirmed the reasonable person test, but Lord Scott also commented that the test must be applied 'by considering the issue from the point of view of the victim. If the victim's opinion that the treatment was to his or her detriment is a reasonable one to hold, that ought, in my opinion, to suffice'. (see COMMON CONCEPTS (1)).

De Souza was followed in *Youri v Glaxo Wellcome Operations UK Ltd (1) and Smith (2)*, EAT/448/99, (3 August 1999, unreported). In this case, the tribunal did not regard a comment to the effect of 'imagine Louis in his car with tinted windows – no one would be able to see him, he would have to keep smiling' as racial discrimination because the employee had not suffered a 'detriment'. The comment was considered by the tribunal to be a joke (albeit insensitive) in an environment where such jokes were not unusual. Mr Youri's appeal to the EAT was dismissed, the EAT concluding that the tribunal had correctly followed *De Souza*. The EAT commented that what constitutes detriment is a question of fact and degree but normally more than hurt feelings would be required, especially in relation to a one-off incident.

The objective test in *De Souza* was also considered in *Thomas v London Borough of Hackney*, UKEAT 461/95 (13 March 1996, unreported). The EAT in this case overturned a finding by the tribunal that there had been no racial discrimination where a West Indian employee of African origin had called another West Indian employee of Indian origin a 'coolie' and had also physically abused him. The tribunal accepted the word 'coolie' was racially abusive, but considered it in isolation of the physical abuse (which it held not to be on racial grounds) and therefore concluded that it had not amounted to a detriment. The EAT disagreed, concluding that the two were interlinked and that the tribunal had departed from the objective approach (established in *De Souza*) and introduced a subjective element, namely the motivation of the harasser. The complainant was concerned that he might be assaulted again, and in the circumstances, a reasonable worker would take the view that he had been disadvantaged in the conditions in which he had thereafter to work.

In *Chin* (see 6.24), the tribunal held that racist taunts made openly in the complainant's presence but directed at his colleague amounted to racial abuse and a detriment. Although the tribunal did not refer to *De Souza,* it made the comment that, 'This was not merely a case of someone overhearing a remark which was not intended to be heard'.

The decision in *De Souza,* however, should be treated with some caution.

In *Thomas v Robinson* [2003] IRLR 7 the EAT considered *De Souza* and held that the effect on the person must be considered and some levels of distress will be regarded as detriment. It further held that requiring someone to work in an environment where racist remarks are tolerated may itself be a detriment. Referring to the sexual harassment case, *Insitu Cleaning Co Ltd v Heads* [1995] IRLR 4, which held that a single act of verbal sexual harassment could amount to a detriment, it considered that this principle could apply to racial harassment, but a single instance of racial abuse will not necessarily amount to harassment. The two elements of harassment must be made out. The first is the targeting of the person being harassed and the second is causing distress to the target. In many cases, it will not be difficult for the employee to establish detriment, but a tribunal cannot decide that, once it has established that particular words were used, there is an irrebuttable presumption of detriment. In this case, the EAT held that there may be some work environments, regrettably, where racial abuse is given and taken in good part by members of different ethnic groups. In these circumstances, making a racist remark would not amount to detriment.

In *Kufeji* (see 6.26) the EAT upheld the tribunal's decision that the sending of a postcard to the complainant (black and of Nigerian origin) with a picture of bare-breasted black African women with a message on the reverse that read: 'To all the lads. South Africans answer to Mayfair ... [sic]' amounted to racial harassment. The complainant was genuinely distressed (whereas the white officers were laughing) and was seriously offended as the only black officer in receipt of the card. The tribunal had considered the motivation of the perpetrator and the complainant's perception to reach 'an overall objective assessment of the facts so as to arrive at a conclusion'.

Under the free-standing claim for harassment on grounds of race or ethnic or national origin, this objective test, with a subjective element, is set out in *RRA 1976, s 3A(2)*.

Where there is a series of incidents, they should not be considered individually, but as a whole. A tribunal should look at the totality of the facts, keeping in mind that each successive episode has its predecessors, that the impact of the separate incidents may accumulate and that the working environment may exceed the sum of the incidents (*Qureshi v Victoria University of Manchester*, [2001] ICR 863; *Reed v Stedman* [1999] IRLR 299 and *Driskel* (see 6.25)).

A series of acts, including being subjected to racist name-calling, whipped with a leather belt and branded with a red-hot screwdriver amounted to harassment. The employer was liable for the discrimination by employees because the acts were committed during the course of employment (*Jones v Tower Boot Co Ltd* [1997] 2 All ER 406, [1997] ICR 254).

In *Bayliss v Hounslow London Borough Council* [2002] EWCA Civ 354, [2002] All ER (D) 332 (Mar) the Court of Appeal dismissed an appeal by an employee, holding that two questions asked by another employee that had arisen out of and related to earlier incidents of 'explicit racial remarks', but which did not contain any racial language or racial content themselves, could not constitute racial discrimination subjecting the complainant to a detriment. The earlier acts were out of time and the two questions were a 'distinct and separate act' and the tribunal could therefore consider that they did not form part of any continuous act.

6.32   **Stand-alone claim of harassment or direct discrimination?**

RRA 1976, s 78 expressly excludes harassment under *s 3A* from the definition of 'detriment'. Therefore, a claim for harassment on grounds of race, ethnic or national origin *must* be brought under *s 3A* and cannot be pleaded as a detriment in a direct discrimination claim (although the set of facts may, of course, give rise to more than one cause of action).

In practice, it is likely that a complainant will set out both a cause of action for harassment under *RRA 1976, s 3A* on grounds of race, ethnic or national origin and for detriment for direct discrimination on grounds of colour or nationality in any claim and plead them in the alternative.

There will often be overlap between the prohibited grounds. Evidence of harassment on grounds of colour or nationality may also indicate that the conduct was related to 'race', 'ethnic origin' or 'national origin'. A complainant's nationality will often be the same as his national origin and, depending on the nature of the conduct, it could be on grounds of both nationality and national origin. For example, making Irish jokes could constitute harassment on both grounds. Harassing someone by using derogatory language related to skin colour may in fact be on the grounds of race or ethnic or national origin. It is also arguable that 'race' encompasses 'colour'. Applying the broader test under the *Race Directive*, it is difficult to see how a tribunal could not find that colour was 'related' to race. 'Nationality', however, is excluded from the ambit of the protection under the *Race Directive, Article 3(2)*. (For a more detailed discussion of the meaning of these terms, see 6.3ff.)

6.33   Other legal remedies

Racial harassment may also be actionable under other legislation. In addition to the victim being able to take action in the civil courts, some statutes make it a criminal offence to harass another person.

6.34   *Protection from Harassment Act 1997*

The *Protection from Harassment Act 1997* ('*PHA 1997*') makes harassment both a civil tort and a criminal offence. Initially introduced to protect victims from stalking, it has been used by complainants in harassment claims. Employers can also be found vicariously liable where the harassment occurs in the course of employment (*Majrowski v Guy's and St Thomas's NHS Trust* [2006] UKHL 34, [2006] 4 All ER 395). See COMMON CONCEPTS (1) for further discussion of the impact of *PHA 1997* in the employment field.

6.35   *Public Order Act 1986*

The *Criminal Justice and Public Order Act 1994* amended the *Public Order Act 1986* so as to include a new *s 4A* which created an offence of causing intentional harassment, alarm or distress, where a person uses threatening, abusive or insulting language or behaviour, or disorderly behaviour, or displays any writing, sign or other visible representation which is threatening abusive or insulting, which causes that or another person harassment, alarm or distress. As specified in the preamble to the Act, the offence was originally introduced to deal with racial harassment cases and to control the 'stirring up of racial hatred'.

The maximum penalties under this section are six months imprisonment and/or a fine of £5,000.

6.36   *Crime and Disorder Act 1998*

The *Crime and Disorder Act 1998* ('*CDA 1998*') created 'racially aggravated offences' which cover serious offences such as assault, grievous bodily harm and criminal damages and also include harassment. These carry significantly higher penalties with imprisonment of up to two years when convicted on indictment. If a person is convicted on indictment of putting a victim in fear of violence and the offence was racially aggravated (under *CDA 1998, s 32(1)(b)*), the maximum penalty is imprisonment for up to seven years, and/or a fine.

6.37   OTHER UNLAWFUL ACTS

Discriminatory practices

The Commission for Racial Equality ('CRE') had the right to issue an enforcement notice against any person operating a discriminatory practice which amounts or could amount to indirect discrimination under *RRA 1976, s 1(1)b* or *s1(1A)* (*RRA 1976, s 28*). *S 28* is broad enough to cover practices the application of which has not, as a matter of fact, caused detriment to any particular individual and in respect of which not claim could therefore be brought in the employment tribunal. So, for example, a strict requirement that all applicants have five GCSEs, grade A–C (which requirement would exclude those who were schooled outside the UK) might be the subject of an enforcement notice even if, in practice, all interested candidates have to date been able to satisfy that requirement.

6.38 **Discriminatory advertisements**

It is unlawful to publish (or cause to be published) an advertisement which indicates, or might reasonably be understood to indicate, an intention by a person to do an act of discrimination (*RRA 1976, s 29(1)*).

A number of acts which are rendered lawful by the provisions of *RRA 1976* are excepted from this general prohibition (see *RRA 1976, s 29(2)(a)*). Specific exceptions also exist where the advertisement relates to the services of an employment agency (*RRA 1976, s 29(2)(b)*), or employment outside Great Britain (*s 29(3)*).

The CRE was empowered to bring proceedings in respect of a contravention of *s 29(1)*. Where such proceedings are brought against a publisher of an advertisement, it is a defence for that person to show that it was published in reasonable reliance upon a statement made to him by the person causing the advertisement to be published that it was not unlawful by virtue of one of the exceptions (*s 29(4)*). It is an offence to knowingly or recklessly make a false or misleading statement to this effect to a publisher (*s 29(5)*).

The Equality and Human Rights Commission (EHRC) now has an equivalent power to bring proceedings for breach of *s 29* (see COMMON CONCEPTS (1) for further information). This power is provided by *EA 2006, s 25*.

6.39 **Instructions to commit unlawful acts**

It is unlawful for a person who has authority over another person, or in accordance with whose wishes that other person is accustomed to act, to instruct that other person to do any act which is unlawful under *RRA 1976, s 30*.

Once again, the CRE had the right to bring proceedings against the guilty party. However, this does not serve to prevent individual employees from seeking redress. An individual employee who is dismissed for failing to comply with such an instruction, or who resigns and claims constructive dismissal, will be entitled to bring proceedings in the employment tribunal for direct discrimination contrary to *RRA 1976, s 1(1)(a)* and *s 4(2)(c)*. The reason for this is that, in accordance with the line of authority dating back to *Showboat Entertainment Centre Ltd v Owens* [1984] IRLR 7, 'on racial grounds' in *s 1(1)(a)* has been held to include action based upon the race of someone other than the affected employee. So, for example, white bar staff who were dismissed for refusing to obey an instruction not to serve 'coloured' customers had been discriminated against (*Zarczynska v Levy* [1979] 1 All ER 814, [1979] ICR 184). Similarly, a receptionist who resigned after having been told by a car rental company not to hire vehicles to 'coloureds or Asians' was entitled to claim direct discrimination in respect of her constructive dismissal (*Weathersfield Ltd v Sargent (t/a Van & Truck Rentals)* [1999] ICR 425). See 6.11 for further details regarding the meaning of 'on racial grounds'.

Individual employees will also be protected from victimisation and harassment (by virtue of *RRA 1976, s 2* and *s 3A* respectively).

The EHCR now has an equivalent power to bring proceedings for breach of *s 30* (see COMMON CONCEPTS (1) for further information). This power is provided by *EA 2006, s 25*.

6.40 Pressure to commit unlawful acts

It is unlawful to induce, or attempt to induce, a person to do any act which is unlawful by virtue of *RRA 1976, s 31(1)*. An attempted inducement is not prevented from being unlawful because it is not made to the person to be induced, if it is made in such a way that he is likely to hear of it (*s 31(2)*). In this context, 'to induce' has been held to mean 'to persuade' or 'to prevail upon' (See *Commission for Racial Equality v Imperial Society of Teachers of Dancing* [1983] ICR 473 in which the society was found to be in contravention of *s 31* when it sought applicants for a filing clerk role from a local school, but informed the head of careers at the school that it would rather not be sent any 'coloured' candidates as they were likely to feel out of place).

The EHCR now has an equivalent power to bring proceedings for breach of *s 31* (see COMMON CONCEPTS (1) for further information). This power is provided by *EA 2006, s 25*.

6.41 Employer's liability for unlawful acts of employees

In common with the other discrimination legislation, anything done by an employee in the course of his employment is treated for the purposes of *RRA 1976* as done by his employer as well as by him. This will be the case whether or not the unlawful act was done with the employer's knowledge or approval (*RRA 1976, s 32(1)*).

It is a defence for an employer to show it took such steps as were reasonably practicable to prevent the employee from doing that act, or from doing during the course of his employment acts of that description (*s 32(3)*). This is commonly known as the 'employer's defence' or the 'statutory defence'. Note, however, that the employment tribunal will rarely accept the mere existence of an equal opportunities policy prohibiting discrimination on grounds of race to be sufficient for an employer to successfully rely upon the employer's defence. Employers will need to be able to demonstrate that the employee(s) in question have themselves received equal opportunities training (including, where relevant, updates/refreshers) and that the employer has taken active steps to prohibit discrimination in the workplace and to stamp out race discrimination whenever it has arisen. Evidence of steps taken to comply with the CRE's Code of Practice may also be required. Where *s 32(3)* is pleaded in defence of a claim, employees will often seek to have individual employees named as co-respondents to prevent that section from depriving them of a remedy (see 6.44).

For further information on the vicarious liability of employers, see 1.109ff.

6.42 Liability for unlawful acts of agents

Anything done by a person as agent for another person (the principal) with that other person's express or implied authority is treated as done by the principal as well as by him (*RRA 1976, s 32(2)*). Note that, unlike for the other forms of discrimination, vicarious liability of principals does not extend to offences under *RRA 1976* (for example, under *s 33(4)*).

For the purposes of *s 32(2)* it is irrelevant whether the authority is given by the principal before or after the act is committed by the agent. Nor does the principal need to have given the agent specific authority to discriminate. It is sufficient if the agent has authority to do an act which is equally capable of being done in both a lawful and a discriminatory manner (see *Lana v Positive Action Training in Housing (London) Ltd* [2001] IRLR 501, a case considering the similar provisions in the *Sex Discrimination Act 1975, s 41(2)*). So, for example, an employer would potentially be liable for the actions of a recruitment consultant which operates a policy of not putting forward ethnic minority candidates. No employer's defence exists in relation to claims under *s 32(2)*. For this reason, employers should ensure that the terms upon which they engage agents contain appropriate drafting to prohibit unlawful discrimination and provide for an indemnity in the event of such discrimination in the performance of the agency.

6.43 Liability for acts of other third parties

Where an employee suffers race discrimination at the hands of a third party, an employer will not be liable unless the employer's failure to prevent that discrimination was, itself, an act of discrimination under *RRA 1976, s 1(1)(a)* (*Macdonald v Advocate for Scotland; Pearce v the Governing Body of Mayfield School* [2003] UKHL 34 in which the House of Lords disapproved the broader approach taken by the EAT in *Burton v De Vere Hotels Ltd* [1996] IRLR 596) Note that in *Gravell v London Borough of Bexley*, UKEAT/0587/06/CEA (2 March 2007, unreported) the EAT questioned whether the decision in *Pearce* would now apply to harassment under *RRA 1976, s 3A*.

For further discussion on this point, also see 6.29 and COMMON CONCEPTS (1).

6.44 Aiding an unlawful act

By virtue of *RRA 1976, s 33(1)*, aiding an unlawful act of discrimination is, itself, a separate act of discrimination of the same description. Employees bear personal liability for their discriminatory conduct by virtue of *s 33(2)*. This personal liability exists even if the employer has a defence to a claim against it under *s 32(3)* (see 6.41). It is a defence for a person accused of aiding an unlawful act to show that:

(a)   he acted in reliance upon a statement made to him by another person that, by reason of any provision of *RRA 1976*, that act would not be unlawful; and

(b)   it was reasonable for him to rely on that statement (*s 33(3)*).

An employee acting with his employer's assurance that his act will not amount to race discrimination will not therefore be personally liable, unless his reliance upon the employer's statement was unreasonable.

It is an offence to knowingly or recklessly make a false or misleading statement of the type described at (a) above (*s 33(4)*).

See also 1.26 on aiding an unlawful act.

6.45 Liability of Chief Police Officer

Members of the police force are, strictly speaking, office holders rather than employees working under a contract of employment. This obviously would have a knock-on effect upon the protection afforded to police officers and the ambit of the vicarious liability provisions contained in *RRA 1976, s 32* (see 6.41) which applies only to acts done in the course of employment. *RRA 1976* therefore makes specific provision for this by providing that police officers are to be treated as employees for all material purposes(*s 76A*). The Chief Officer will therefore be liable for any acts of discrimination by his police officers under *s 32*. *S 76A* was introduced by the *2003 Amendment Regulations* as a result of the Court of Appeal's decision in *Chief Constable of Bedfordshire Police v Liversidge* [2002] ICR 1135.

6.46 **EXCEPTIONS, DEFENCES AND NON-EMPLOYEES COVERED BY THE EMPLOYMENT PROVISIONS**

This section sets out the miscellaneous exceptions and defences to discrimination claims in the employment sphere brought under *RRA 1976*. A number of these exceptions are common to the other forms of discrimination. However, the impact of the *2003 Amendment Regulations* is that in many cases the exception has different application depending upon the racial ground under consideration – i e whether discrimination is on grounds of race, ethnic or national origins or alternatively on grounds of colour or nationality. As already noted, in practice, many cases of discrimination on one ground (e g colour) may also constitute discrimination on another (e g ethnic origins) and employers should exercise caution before placing reliance upon some of the more limited exemptions discussed below.

6.47 **Genuine occupational requirement or qualification**

The general differences between genuine occupational requirements and genuine occupational qualifications are set out in 1.95ff.

For the purposes of *RRA 1976 s 4A(2)*, a genuine occupational requirement (GOR) only applies to discrimination on grounds of race or ethnic or national origin and where, having regard to the nature of the employment or the context in which it is carried out:

(a)   being of a particular race, or of particular national or ethnic origins is a genuine and determining occupational requirement;

(b)   it is proportionate to apply that requirement to the particular case; and

(c)   either:

(i)   the person to whom that requirement is applied does not meet it; or

(ii)   the employer is not satisfied (and in all the circumstances, it is reasonable for him not to be satisfied) that the person meets it.

Where these requirements are met, the existence of a GOR creates an exception to those parts of *RRA 1976, s 4* which make it unlawful to discriminate in relation to: the arrangements made to determine to whom employment should be offered; the refusal or deliberate omission to offer that employment; the way access to opportunities for promotion, transfer or training are offered; and dismissal from employment (*s 4(1)*). It follows that the existence of a GOR is no defence to a claim brought in relation to discrimination in the terms on which employment is offered, access to other benefits, services and facilities and subjecting an individual to any other detriment.

In cases involving discrimination on grounds of colour or nationality, or which occurred before 19 July 2003 (when *s 4A* entered into force), the defence of genuine occupational qualification (GOQ) may be available (*s 5*). A GOQ arises in limited circumstances where:

(a) the job involves participation in a dramatic performance or other entertainment where authenticity demands a person of that racial group;

(b) the job involves being an artist's or photographic model in the production of a work of art, visual image or sequence of visual images where a person of that racial group is required for authenticity;

(c) the job is in a public restaurant, bar or similar establishment where the setting is such that authenticity demands that that particular job be filled by a person of a particular racial group; or

(d) the job involves providing personal welfare services which can be most effectively provided by someone of a particular racial group (s 5(2)).

A GOQ may arise where only some of the employee's duties fall within (a)–(d) (s 5(3)). However, an employer cannot make out a GOQ in relation to filling a vacancy where, at the relevant time, the employer has a sufficient number of employees of the appropriate racial group who can fulfil his requirements (s 5(4)). The existence of a GOQ will provide a defence to liability to the same extent as a GOR, except that it will not protect a discriminatory dismissal (s 5(1)).

The EAT has held that the requirements to make out a GOQ under category (d) should not be applied too stringently in relation to a responsible employer (*Tottenham Green Under-Fives' Centre v Marshall* [1989] ICR 214, [1989] IRLR 147). In that case, a day care centre catering for an ethnically diverse group of children was entitled to advertise for an Afro-Caribbean worker to replace an employee of the same ethnic origin. The personal welfare services in question were found to be maintaining the children's cultural links, dealing with parents, reading and speaking in dialect and looking after the children's skin and hair. However, the EAT did emphasise in a related decision that the personal services concerned must not be trivial and must not be inserted in the job description as a sham (*Tottenham Green Under-Fives' Centre v Marshall (No 2)* [1991] ICR 320, [1991] IRLR 162). In Lambeth London Borough Council v Commission of Racial Equality [1990] ICR 768, [1990] IRLR 231, the Court of Appeal adopted a narrower definition of personal services. As an exception to the general prohibition on discrimination, a GOQ for personal services would generally require that they were provided directly (often face-to-face) where knowledge and understanding of language and cultural or religious issues were material. Balcombe LJ also held that the use of the word 'personal' in category (d) referred to both the identity of the provider of the services and the recipient. As such, the defence was not made out in relation to an advertisement for managerial and supervisory posts in the Respondent's housing department.

6.48 **Exceptions**

Skills to be exercised outside Great Britain

Prior to the *2003 Amendment Regulations*, *RRA 1976* differentiated between training in skills to be exercised within Great Britain and those which it appeared to the employer were to be exercised by the employee wholly outside Great Britain, permitting discrimination on grounds of race in relation to the latter. Since 2003, this exception (*RRA 1976, s 6*) now applies only in respect of discrimination on grounds of colour or nationality.

6.49 *Private households*

RRA 1976 contains the only remaining vestige of a historical exemption applied across the discrimination legislation and relating to employment for the purposes of a private household: it remains lawful to discriminate on grounds of colour or nationality in respect of such employment (although this exception does not apply to victimisation).

This exception is likely to be of limited practical application. The meaning of the phrase 'for the purposes of a private household' will fall to be assessed on the facts of each case. It seems, however, that the primary purpose of the engagement is likely to be the determining factor. So, a chauffeur employed by a company for its chairman to use both for business and personal purposes was held not to be employed 'for the purposes of a private household' (see *Heron Corpn Ltd v Commis* [1980] ICR 713, in which the EAT held that the question is whether the employment is for the purposes of a private household to a 'substantial degree').

6.50 *Seamen recruited abroad*

Seamen recruited or engaged (whether as employees or contract workers) outside Great Britain may lawfully be discriminated against in relation to their employment on any ship, to the extent that the discrimination:

(a) relates to pay (which includes retirement and death benefits); and

(b) is on grounds of nationality only (*RRA 1976, ss 9(1), 9(2)*).

This exception does not apply to offshore work areas, for the time being designated under either the *Continental Shelf Act 1964* or specified under the *Petroleum Act 1998*, or to any part of the continental shelf to which the law of Northern Ireland applies (*s 9(3)*).

A person brought to Great Britain with a view to his entering into an agreement in Great Britain to be employed on a ship is covered by the exception (*s 9(4)*).

6.51 *Sports and competitions*

It is not unlawful to discriminate on grounds of nationality, place of birth or the length of time for which a person has been resident in a particular area or place, when selecting a person to represent a country, place or area, or any related association in any sport or game, or in pursuance of the rules of any competition relating to eligibility to compete in any sport or game (*RRA 1976, s 39*).

6.52 *Sikhs and safety helmets*

Under the *Employment Act 1989, s 11* (the '*1989 Act*'), a specific exemption was introduced for turban-wearing Sikhs working on construction sites. Such individuals are exempt from any provision which would otherwise require them to wear a safety helmet on that site. That section goes on to provide that where a Sikh who is wearing a turban on a construction site suffers injury, loss or damage, his recovery against any third party is limited to such sum as would have been recoverable had he been wearing a safety helmet.

The *1989 Act, s 12* provides that an employer who requires a Sikh to wear a safety helmet on a construction site is guilty of indirect race discrimination which is not capable of justification. An employer can escape liability for indirect discrimination if it has reasonable grounds for believing that the Sikh will not wear a turban at all times when on the construction site. The *1989 Act, s 12(2)* makes clear that any special treatment accorded to Sikhs by virtue of these provisions cannot be used by non-Sikhs to mount a claim of discrimination under *RRA 1976*.

The *Employment Equality (Religion or Belief) Regulations 2003, reg 26* incorporate a similar exception to their application (See RELIGION AND BELIEF (7)).

6.53 *Employment outside Great Britain*

RRA 1976 contains similar limits upon the scope of its jurisdiction as the other discrimination legislation (see COMMON CONCEPTS (1)). Note, however, that the jurisdiction test is more restrictive in respect of discrimination on grounds of colour or nationality. For an employee to be protected by the provisions of *RRA 1976* in respect of discrimination on grounds of his colour or nationality, that employee must work wholly or partly in Great Britain (*RRA 1976, s 8(1)*). Employees working abroad may be able to bring a claim for discrimination on grounds of colour or nationality if their employment when viewed as a whole is classed as partly in Great Britain. The tribunal is not entitled to limit its consideration to the time at which the discrimination took place (*Saggar v Ministry of Defence* [2005] EWCA Civ 413, [2005] ICR 1073).

EU nationals have the ability to bring a claim of discrimination under *RRA 1976* on grounds of nationality only if their job is within the EU and the act of discrimination (which occurs in the UK) restricts their freedom of movement as workers within the EU. See, in particular, *Van Duyn v Home Office* [1975] Ch 358 and *Bossa v Nordstress Ltd* [1998] IRLR 284. Where an employee is posted to another Member State temporarily, national non-discrimination laws will apply by virtue of the *Posted Workers Directive (96/71/EC)*.

RRA 1976 also differs from the other strands of discrimination in that it does not contain specific provision for employment on aircraft or hovercraft being covered by the provisions of the act in certain circumstances.

6.54 *Employment under an illegal contract*

In discrimination cases brought under *RRA 1976* the fact that an individual is employed pursuant to an illegal contract will not automatically exclude the tribunal's jurisdiction. So, in *Hall v Woolston Hall Leisure Ltd* [2001] ICR 99 (which approved the EAT's decision in *Leighton v Michael* [1995] ICR 1091) the Court of Appeal found that an employee's knowledge that her employer was paying her in cash, and thereby defrauding the Revenue, did not prevent her recovering damages (in that case under the *SDA 1975*). Jurisdiction may, however, be excluded where the employee's claim is so clearly connected or inextricably bound up or linked with their illegal conduct that the tribunal could not permit the employee to recover compensation without appearing to condone that conduct (*per* Peter Gibson LJ in *Hall*). Also see COMMON CONCEPTS (1).

6.55 *Benefits provided to the public*

In common with the other discrimination legislation, protection extended to employees under *RRA 1976* does not apply to benefits, facilities or services provided by their employer which they receive as a member of the public, rather than as an employee (for example, a current account provided to an employee of a high street bank). Where the benefits are materially different to those provided to members of the public, are regulated by the contract of employment or relate to training, the anti-discrimination provisions will have effect (*s 4(4)*).

6.56 *Discrimination in compliance with the law*

Special provision is made in *RRA 1976* for lawful discrimination on grounds of race in order to comply with certain legal requirements. Before the *2003 Amendment Regulations* were implemented, *RRA 1976* included a blanket exception where the discrimination was carried out pursuant to any enactment.

The current position is now set out in the amended *RRA 1976, s 41* and *s 69*. The exception does not apply to any form of discrimination on grounds of race, ethnic or national origins (*s 41(1A)*). The exception that remains is only, therefore, applicable to discrimination on grounds of colour or nationality, to the extent that such discrimination does not also amount to discrimination on one of the other racial grounds. Under *s 41(1)*, discrimination on grounds of colour or nationality shall not be unlawful if done:

(a)   in pursuance of any enactment or Order in Council; or

(b)   in pursuance of any instrument made under any enactment by a Minister of the Crown; or

(c)   in order to comply with any condition or requirement imposed by a Minister of the Crown by virtue of any enactment (*s 41(1)(a),(b),(c)*).

'Enactment' is specifically limited to those which post-date *RRA 1976*. The words 'in pursuance of' have been held by the House of Lords to be much more restrictive than 'by virtue of', such that the application of *s 41(1)* is limited to acts done in necessary performance of an express obligation contained in the act or other instrument (*Hampson v Department of Education and Science* [1990] ICR 511).

Note that *s 41(2)* also provides an exception for discrimination on the basis of nationality, place of ordinary residence or the length of time for which a person has been present or resident in or outside the UK, if that act is done for one of the reasons set out at (a) to (c) above, or:

(d)   in pursuance of any arrangements made by or with the approval of, or for the time being approved by, a Minister of the Crown; or

(e)   in order to comply with any condition imposed by a Minister of the Crown (*s 42(2)(d),(e)*).

See the case of *R (on the application of Mohammed) v Secretary of State for Defence* (2007) 104(20) LSG 32 for consideration of the application of *s 41(2)(d)* to a government scheme for the making of ex gratia payments to ex-servicemen who had been Japanese prisoners of war.

6.57 *National security*

Discriminatory acts (on any racial ground) done for the purpose of safeguarding national security are not unlawful, provided that those acts are justified by that purpose (*RRA 1976, s 42*).

6.58 *Employees working for those with State immunity*

The *State Immunity Act 1978* applies equally to claims of race discrimination as it does to the other forms of discrimination in the UK.

6.59 NON-EMPLOYEES AND NON-EMPLOYERS COVERED BY THE EMPLOYMENT PROVISIONS OF *RRA 1976*

RRA 1976, Part II sets out provisions relating to discrimination in the employment field. In certain circumstances the provisions of *Part II* are extended to apply to non-employees and non-employers. These circumstances are, for the most part, common to the other strands of discrimination law in the UK. The below sections identify where the provisions of *RRA 1976* differ from the norm. For further information on the generally applicable rules, see COMMON CONCEPTS (1).

6.60   Contract workers

It is not unlawful for a principal to act in a discriminatory manner (on grounds of colour or nationality only) for the benefit of a contract worker not ordinarily resident in Great Britain in, or in connection with, allowing that worker to do contract work, where the purpose of allowing him to do that work is to provide him with training in skills which it appears to the principal the contractor intends to exercise wholly outside Great Britain.

6.61   Office holders

In the public sector

Holders of public offices are protected from discrimination by virtue of *RRA 1976, s 76* as though they were employees and the Crown their employer. This provision remains narrower in scope that the provisions in the other discrimination legislation and applies only to appointments made by a Minister of the Crown, rather than the broader category of appointments provided for in *SDA 1975, RBR 2003, SOR 2003* and *AR 2006*. See COMMON CONCEPTS (1).

RRA 1976 also extends the protection against discrimination to recommendations and approvals by a Minister of the Crown or a government department in relation to the conferment of any dignity or honour.

Complaints of discrimination on grounds of race, ethnic or national origins may be made by holders of public offices both in the employment tribunal and by way of judicial review proceedings in the High Court. Complaints of discrimination on grounds of colour or nationality may only be brought by way of judicial review proceedings (*RRA 1976, s 76(12),(14)*).

6.62   *Other office holders*

Other office holders come within the ambit of the employment provisions set out in *RRA 1976, Part II* by virtue of *s 76ZA*. To be entitled to protection, the post must be one which is to be discharged personally by one person under the direction of another, and one in respect of which remuneration is payable (*s 76ZA(7)*). No further explanation is given as to what offices or posts are likely to be covered, but political offices and posts are excluded, as are posts to which an individual has been elected (*s 76ZA(9)*).

6.63   Crown Employees

Crown employees are protected under *RRA 1976* in broadly the same way as private sector employees by virtue of *ss 75, 75A* and *75B*. However, nothing in *RRA 1976* will invalidate any rules restricting employment in the service of the Crown, or by any prescribed public body, to persons of particular birth, nationality, descent or residence. A specific exception also exists in relation to the publication, display or implementation of such rules, or the publication of advertisements referring to them (*s 75(5)*).

6.64   *Armed Forces*

Members of the armed forces are specifically included within the ambit of *RRA 1976, s 75(2)(c)*. However, generally speaking, no complaint in respect of an act of discrimination under *RRA 1976, s 4* may be brought by a member of the armed forces where it relates to service in those forces and has not first been presented internally to the appropriate authorities (*s 75(9)*). Exceptions to *s 75(9)* are set out in the *Race Relations (Complaints to Employment Tribunals) (Armed Forces) Regulations 1997 (SI 1997/2161)*.

6.65 The police and barristers and advocates

The provisions of *RRA 1976* relating to police officers and barristers and advocates are common to those set out in the other discrimination legislation (see *s 26A* (barristers), *s 26B* (advocates), *s 75A* (police forces) and *s 76B* (other police bodies) and COMMON CONCEPTS (1).

6.66 Partnerships

The provisions relating to partnerships under *RRA 1976* are in common with the other discrimination legislation (see COMMON CONCEPTS (1)), save that:

(a) for discrimination on grounds of colour and nationality, *RRA 1976* only applies to firms with six or more partners (*s 10(1A)*); and

(b) under *RRA 1976,* the genuine occupation requirement/qualification provisions set out in *ss 4A* and *5* only apply to discrimination in the arrangements made for the purposes of determining who to offer a position as a partner or a refusal to offer a position as a partner.

6.67 Other categories

The employment provisions are extended in certain circumstances to trade organisations (*RRA 1976, s 11*), qualifications bodies (*s 12*), providers of vocational training (*s 13*), employment agencies (*s 14*) and employment-related services provided by the state (*s 15*). Each of these is for practical purposes dealt with in the same way as for all other forms of discrimination legislation (see COMMON CONCEPTS (1)).

6.68 THE CRE AND EHRC

The Commission for Racial Equality (CRE) was brought into being by *RRA 1976, s 43*. As discussed in COMMON CONCEPTS (1), the Equality and Human Rights Commission (EHRC) replaced the CRE in October 2007.

The CRE was granted authority to issue codes of practice in its field by *RRA 1976, s 47*. The EHRC is granted similar power (in respect of all forms of discrimination, not just race) under *Equality Act 2006 (EqA 2006), s 14(1)*. These statutory codes of practice do not have legal force, but are instead intended to provide practical guidance on the elimination of discrimination in the field of employment and the promotion of equal opportunity (amongst other things). Breach of the statutory codes of practice will not of itself amount to unlawful discrimination. However, *EqA 2006, s 15(4)* makes clear that the contents of any code of practice issued by the CRE or EHRC are admissible in evidence in an employment tribunal or court. Further, if any provision of a CRE code appears to the tribunal or court to be relevant to any question arising in the proceedings before it, it *must* take the code's provisions into account.

Although the EHRC may ultimately issue its own codes of practice or revise those already in place, until it does so the CRE code remains in full force. This code was extensively redrafted by the CRE in 2006 under the Chairmanship of Trevor

Phillips, now the first Chairman of the EHRC. With that in mind, it seems reasonably unlikely that revision of the race code will take place in the near future.

6.69   **INSTITUTIONAL RACISM AND THE POSITIVE DUTY**

The duty to promote race equality

Public authorities are under a general duty in carrying out their functions to have due regard to the need to: (a) eliminate unlawful racial discrimination; and (b) promote equality of opportunity and good relations between persons of different racial groups (*RRA 1976, s 71*, inserted by the *Race Relations (Amendment) Act 2000* with effect from 1 April 2001). Public authorities are listed in *RRA 1976, Sch 1A*, which has been supplemented at various stages and now covers most bodies which would be regarded as exercising public functions. The Security Service, the Intelligence Service and Government Communications Headquarters are expressly excluded (*Sch 1A, para 1(2)*). The House of Commons, House of Lords, Scottish Parliament and judicial bodies are not included in the list. This duty is without prejudice to the obligation of any person to comply with any other provision of the Act (*s 71(7)*). The duty may be enforced by means of judicial review in the High Court by any person or group with an interest in the matter or the CRE itself. The CRE also has the power to issue compliance notices where it is satisfied that an authority is failing to comply with its duties (*s 71D*).

The duty applies to all the activities of public authorities, including policy-making, service delivery, procurement and employment. The duty is at present explained and supplemented by Codes of Practice by the CRE (*s 71C*). The CRE's Code of Practice on the Duty to Promote Racial Equality (2002) requires public authorities to carry out ethnic monitoring of their workforce and to publish the results annually (para 5). The Code goes so far as to recommend that an authority in which certain racial groups are under-represented may consider positive action (para 5.12). 'Positive action' is defined to include providing facilities to meet the special needs of people from particular racial groups in relation to their training or welfare and targeting job training or the advertising of posts. However, the Code makes clear that permitted positive action does not go so far as allowing preference to be given to certain racial groups in the decision to appoint a candidate.

6.70   **Impact of the duty on private employers**

This Code makes clear that when a public authority contracts with a private company or voluntary organisation to carry out any of its functions, the duty applies to those functions and the authority remains responsible for them (para 2.9). Public authorities are also encouraged to enter into a voluntary framework with contractors to promote race equality (para 2.10).

These provisions are repealed by the *Equality Act 2006* from a date to be appointed and will be replaced with a single scheme for all discrimination. Additional duties to publish a race equality scheme and monitor employees are imposed on listed public bodies by the *RRA 1976 (Statutory Duties) Order 2006*.

7   Religion and Belief

7.1   INTRODUCTION

Protection from discrimination on the grounds of religion or belief in employment and related fields is found in the *Employment Equality (Religion or Belief) Regulations 2003 (SI 2003/1660)* ('*RBR 2003*'), made on 26 June 2003 and coming into force on 2 December 2003. These Regulations give effect to *Directive 2000/78/EC* ('the Framework Directive'), issued by the Council on 27 November 2000 and establishing a general framework for equal treatment in employment and occupation, insofar as it requires Member States to regulate discrimination in certain fields where it is connected to religion and belief. Accordingly, the general scheme of the *RBR 2003* is similar to that of the *Employment Equality (Sexual Orientation) Regulations 2003 (SI 2003/1661)* ('*SOR 2003*'), which also give effect to the provisions in the Framework Directive insofar as it requires Member States to regulate discrimination in the same fields where it is connected to sexual orientation. *RBR 2003* do not extend to Northern Ireland (*reg 1(2)*), which has its own legislation dealing with discrimination on the grounds of religion or belief and which is outside the scope of this book.

7.2   Pre-existing protection

Prior to *RBR 2003* coming into force, protection from discrimination on the grounds of religion or belief could be found under two legislative schemes.

The first was the *Race Relations Act 1976* ('*RRA 1976*'); however, only religious groups that could also claim to belong to a particular racial group as defined in *RRA 1976, s 3(1)* were protected from discrimination. The resulting protection was hugely unequal as between different faiths: Sikhs and Jews were protected, but Muslims were not (compare *Mandla v Dowell Lee* [1983] 2 AC 548, [1983] 2 WLR 620, [1983] 1 All ER 1062, [1983] ICR 385, [1983] IRLR 209, CA and *Seide v Gillette Industries Ltd* [1980] IRLR 427, EAT with *JH Walker v Hussain* [1996] ICR 291, [1996] IRLR 11, EAT). Even those faiths that were protected only found themselves so where the less favourable treatment in question was attributable to their membership of the ethnic group synonymous with their faith, and not to their adherence to the faith in question.

The second was the *European Convention on Human Rights* ('*ECHR*') and the *Human Rights Act 1998* ('*HRA 1998*'). *Article 9(1)* of the *ECHR* guarantees freedom of thought, conscience and religion, subject to the limitations set out in *Article 9(2)*; moreover, *Article 14* prohibits discrimination in the enjoyment of these rights. However, these provisions have been relied on with limited success by claimants in the United Kingdom, Strasbourg case law having placed considerable weight on *Article 9(2)* to balance the right to religious expression against the contractual and *Article 9(1)* rights of others (*Ahmad v United Kingdom* (1981) 4 EHRR 126; *Stedman v United Kingdom* (1997) 23 EHRR CD 168). The protections in the *ECHR* have been made somewhat more accessible by *HRA 1998*; but *s 6(1)* of the Act only imposes direct obligations on 'public authorities' so that the availability of protection remains dependent upon the status of the relevant employer. Even in cases where protection has been available, the rights protected by *Article 9(1)* have been interpreted narrowly, and the limitations provided by *Article 9(2)* broadly (see, for example, *R (Williamson) v Secretary of*

State for Education and Employment [2005] UKHL 15, [2005] 2 AC 246, [2005] 2 WLR 590, [2005] 2 All ER 1; *Pretty v United Kingdom* (2002) 35 EHRR 1 and *R v Taylor* [2001] EWCA Crim 2263, [2002] 1 Cr App R37 respectively).

7.3 Legislative history

The origins of *RBR 2003* lie in the consultation that was initiated by the Government on the implementation of the Framework Directive: *Towards Equality and Diversity, Implementing the Employment and Race Directives: Consultation Documents* (2001) Department of Trade and Industry and Cabinet Office ('the Consultation Paper'). There followed lengthy debates, particularly in the House of Lords, on the content of the draft Regulations and specifically the definition of 'religion and belief'. *RBR 2003* as enacted following those debates were soon amended, principally to provide for discrimination in respect of occupational pension schemes and in institutions of further and higher education (see *Employment Equality* (*Religion or Belief*) (*Amendment*) *Regulations 2003* (*SI 2003/2828*), *Employment Equality* (*Religion or Belief*) (*Amendment*) *Regulations 2004* (*SI 2004/437*), but also *Employment Equality* (*Religion or Belief*) *Regulations 2003* (*Amendment*) (*No 2*) *Regulations 2004* (*SI 2004/2520*)); they have since been amended again, in various respects, by the *Equality Act 2006* ('*EA 2006*') and the *Employment Equality* (*Sexual Orientation*) (*Religion or Belief*) (*Amendment*) *Regulations 2007* (*SI 2007/2269*).

EA 2006, aside from introducing new protection, makes a number of material changes to *RBR 2003*. These include amending the definition of 'religion and belief' provided by *RBR 2003, reg 2(1)*, amending the definition of 'direct discrimination' though a new *reg 3(1)(a)* and extending the protection found in *RBR 2003* to the provision of goods, facilities and services. The resulting legislative provisions are considered below.

7.4 Guidance

Given the relatively recent enactment of *RBR 2003*, case law on their interpretation is relatively sparse. However, there are two principal sources of guidance on interpretation. The Government itself has produced guidance on the Regulations as first enacted: *Explanation of the provisions of the Employment Equality* (*Sexual Orientation*) *Regulations 2003 and the Employment Equality* (*Religion or Belief*) *Regulations 2003* (DTI) (the 'DTI Guidance'), available at http://www.dti.gov.uk/files/file29350.pdf. There is also guidance from ACAS: *Religion or Belief in the Workplace: a Guide for Employers and Employees* (2003, ACAS) ('the ACAS Guidance'), updated in November 2005 and available at http://www.acas.org.uk/media/pdf/f/l/religion_1.pdf. In addition, under the provisions of the *EA 2006*, there is likely to be a Code of Practice forthcoming from the Commission for Equality and Human Rights at some future date (see *EA 2006, s 14(1)(h)*).

7.5 THE 2003 REGULATIONS

RBR 2003 follow a similar structure to *SOR 2003*, and both sets of regulations follow the same broad pattern as *SDA 1975* and *RRA 1976*, leading to significant overlap between ancillary provisions from *reg 8* onwards. Many of these provisions were explored in COMMON CONCEPTS (1). As a result, what follows focuses on provisions which are particular to *RBR 2003*.

7.6 Definition of 'religion or belief'

The terms 'religion' and 'belief' are defined in *RBR 2003, reg 2(1)*, as amended by *EA 2006, s 77(1)*. 'Religion' means any religion, 'belief' means any religious or philosophical belief, and references to both include references to a lack of religion or belief. There is no prescriptive list in respect of either of the terms; given the wide variety of different faiths and beliefs in the country, this was felt to be unduly restrictive and it has been left to courts and tribunals to decide how far protection extends (para 13.4, Consultation Paper; para 10, DTI guidance). However, both terms require the relevant opinions to be held as a matter of principle rather than logic or consideration of an evidence base (*McClintock v Department for Constitutional Affairs* [2008] IRLR 29, EAT at [45]).

The interpretive exercise of what is and what is not a religion or belief does not take place in a vacuum, but has regard to the jurisprudence of *Article 9* of the *ECHR*, given the references to that provision in recitals (1) and (4) of the Framework Directive and the requirements of *HRA 1998, s 3*. There may be interesting issues to resolve here, *Article 9(1)* being broader than *reg 2(1)* in protecting freedom of 'thought' and 'conscience' (rather than belief), together with religion and including within that protection the right to manifest religion or belief, subject to the limitations of *Article 9(2)*.

(a) meaning of 'religion'

The reference to 'religion' appears to be a broad one, and includes those religions widely accepted in this country, together with the branches and sects within them (para 11, DTI Guidance). In this regard, Appendix 2 to the ACAS Guidance helpfully lists 'some of the most commonly practiced religions and beliefs in Britain'. According to *Article 9* jurisprudence, the reference might include more controversial 'religions' such as Scientology (*X and Church of Scientology v Sweden* 16 DR 68 (1979)). It might also include what are commonly termed 'cults' (para 16, DTI Guidance). The main limitation is that the 'religion' must have a clear structure and belief system (*X v United Kingdom* 11 DR 55 (1977)).

(b) meaning of 'religious belief'

RBR 2003 distinguish between 'religion' and 'religious belief', potentially because religious beliefs go beyond a belief about a god or gods to include other beliefs founded in a religion. Such beliefs can vary, and their protection would therefore assist in cases where issues arise between members of the same faith in relation to particular tenets of that faith. Religious beliefs appear to warrant protection only where they attain a serious level of cogency, seriousness, cohesion and importance, and provided they are worthy of respect in a democratic society and are not incompatible with human dignity (*Campbell and Cosans v United Kingdom* (1982) 4 EHRR 293 at [36] and para 12, DTI Guidance). This is potentially concerning, *Article 9* jurisprudence making clear that it is not the role of the courts to assess the worthiness or otherwise of a particular belief (see, for example, *Williamson* at [22]). The explanation for the difference of approach may lie in the fact that *Article 9(2)* imports a requirement that beliefs be consistent with basic standards of human dignity and integrity (*Williamson* at [23]), such that a 'belief' under *Article 9(1)* can be interpreted broadly; conversely, since there is no filter equivalent to *Article 9(2)* under *RBR 2003*, the interpretation of 'religious belief' must be narrower.

(c) meaning of 'philosophical belief'

Prior to the amendments introduced by *EA 2006*, in order to be protected under *RBR 2003*, a philosophical belief had to be 'similar' to a religious belief. This requirement has been removed by the amendments. The change was not intended to be significant, only to remove a word which does not appear in *Article 1* of the

Framework Directive and was considered to be redundant, in the sense that a 'philosophical belief' in the context of *RBR 2003* must always be of a similar nature to religious belief (Hansard, HL, Vol 673, Col 1109–10 (13 July 2005)). Nevertheless, the change is to be welcomed, eliminating, as it does, doubt as to whether philosophical beliefs must be predicated on belief/absence of a belief in a supreme being. Like religious beliefs, and of similar concern, philosophical beliefs must attain a serious level of cogency, seriousness, cohesion and importance, be worthy of respect in a democratic society and must not be incompatible with human dignity (*Campbell and Cosans* at [36] and para 13, DTI Guidance). Examples are Rastafarianism (*Harris v NKL Automotive*, EAT/134/07/DM), and perhaps paganism and humanism (ACAS Guidance, para 1.1).

The remaining area of controversy over this provision relates to whether philosophical beliefs include political beliefs. It seems clear that *RBR 2003*, as originally enacted, were not intended to protect such beliefs, at least unless they are similar to a religious belief (para 13.4, Consultation Paper; para 13, DTI Guidance). Supporting the British National Party would not therefore qualify (*Baggs v Fudge* ET/1400114/05). But this leaves a grey area of ideologies which are akin to religious beliefs in terms of the coherence of their structure and belief system and the conviction with which they are held; and the area has arguably been widened by the removal of the word 'similar' following *EA 2006* amendments.

(d) lack of 'religion' or 'belief'

Although *RBR 2003* as originally enacted were intended to cover the absence of belief and belief in the absence of a god or gods or philosophies (para 14, DTI Guidance; Hansard, HL, Vol 649, Col 792 (17 June 2003) and *Article 9* jurisprudence such as *Kokkinakis v Greece* (1994) 17 EHRR 397), this has now been made express with the new *EA 2006, ss 2(1)(c)* and *(d)*.

(e) manifestation of a religion or belief

It remains unclear whether or not the definition of religion or belief includes the manifestation of, or conduct based on or expressing, a religion or belief. The point is significant because if the answer is in the affirmative, then the manifestation of religion or belief may give rise to direct discrimination under *reg 3(1)(a)*, which, unlike indirect discrimination, is not capable of justification under *RBR 2003*. The result is potentially broader than that provided for by the *ECHR*, in which *Article 9(2)* specifically qualifies freedom to manifest religion and belief.

Article 9 expressly protects the right to manifest religion and belief, albeit in a qualified fashion, and the jurisprudence on this topic indicates that freedom of religion implies freedom to manifest that religion and to bear witness in words and deeds (*Kokkinakis* at [31]). Moreover, direct discrimination under *SOR 2003* does not appear to distinguish sexual orientation and the manifestation of that orientation (*R (Amicus) v Secretary of State for Trade and Industry* EWHC 860 (Admin), [2007] ICR 1176, [2004] IRLR 430). However, the DTI guidance suggests that the *RBR 2003* definition of 'religion and belief' is not intended to go this far; and arguably manifesting a religion or belief is one step more removed from holding that religion or belief than manifesting a sexual orientation is from being of that orientation. To date, the EAT has declined to express a view on the issue (*Azmi v Kirklees Metropolitan Borough Council* [2007] ICR 1154, [2007] IRLR 484 at [75]).

7.7   **Definition of 'discrimination on the ground of religion or belief'**

RBR 2003, reg 3 as amended outlaws both direct (*reg 3(1(a)*)) and indirect (*reg 3(1)(b)*)) discrimination and specifies the characteristics of the relevant comparator for the purposes of establishing less favourable treatment (*reg 3(3)*). The key distinction between the two forms of discrimination, as elsewhere in anti-discrimination legislation, is that direct discrimination cannot be justified; although a 'genuine occupational requirement' can be applied to direct discrimination, it provides a much narrower defence to that available for indirect discrimination.

Prior to its amendment by *EA 2006*, the structure of *RBR 2003, reg 3(1)(a)* was materially identical to *SDA 1975, s 1(1)(a) or 1(2)(a)* and *RRA 1976, s1(1)(a)*, but since its amendment, the new *reg 3(1)(a)* states expressly that a person may be directly discriminated against on the grounds of a person's religion or belief *whether or not it is also the discriminator's religion or belief*. This clarifies the previous state of affairs which arose from the provision in *reg 3(2)* that A treating B less favourably than he would treat other persons, on grounds of religion or belief, did 'not include A's religion or belief'; it affirms the principle that the motivation of the discriminator is irrelevant to the question of whether discrimination has taken place (paras 28–29, DTI Guidance).). The discriminator must, however, be aware of interference with the religious or other similar philosophical belief in order for the less favourable treatment to be conferred *on grounds of religion or belief* (*McClintock* at [46]).

It is also significant that direct discrimination on the grounds of religion or belief includes:

●   discrimination against a person based on a religion or belief to which he is perceived to belong or subscribe;

●   discrimination against a person by reason of the religion or belief of someone with whom the person associates; and

●   discrimination against a person by reason of a refusal to follow an instruction to discriminate against another person on the grounds of religion or belief (paras 24–27, DTI Guidance).

The appropriate comparator for direct discrimination is an individual in the same or not materially different circumstances as A (see *reg 3(3)*); in the case of a complaint regarding a prohibition on the wearing of a veil while teaching young children in the company of a male teacher, this was a woman who, whether Muslim or not, wore a face-covering for a reason other than religious belief (*Azmi* at [55]).

Reg 3(1)(b) relating to indirect discrimination remains materially identical to *SDA 1975, s 1(2)(b)* and *RRA 1976, s1(1A)*. Examples of a 'provision, criterion or practice' (PCP) might be policies requiring holidays or breaks to be taken at certain times or regular informal socialising involving alcohol. In determining whether a PCP puts or would put persons of the same religion or belief as B at a particular disadvantage when compared with other persons, care must be taken in identifying the appropriate group of persons of the same religion or belief and otherwise in the same or not materially different relevant circumstances (see *reg 3(3)*). For example, for the purposes of a complaint by a Sabbath-observant Jew about a PCP requiring him to work a full-time week, including the Sabbath, the relevant group would be other Sabbath-observant Jews, notwithstanding that this may be only 5–10% of Jews overall (*Wetstein v Misprestige Management Services* EAT/523/91). It must also be shown that B, the individual, is put at a disadvantage. On the question of whether a PCP is a proportionate means of achieving a legitimate aim, likely legitimate aims might be business efficacy or health and safety, for example, in the context of work patterns and dress codes respectively; and a PCP will be proportionate where it strikes a balance between the importance of that aim and its otherwise discriminatory effect. On this reasoning, a prohibition on the wearing of a veil while teaching young children in the company of a male teacher has been held to be justified since it is intended to prevent the teacher's communication being obscured, and since alternative ways of accommodating the individual's belief were unduly onerous (*Azmi*). Similarly, it has been suggested that the requirement to abide by the judicial oath, requiring Justices of the Peace to apply the laws of the land 'without fear or favour, affection or ill-will', including placing children for adoption with same-sex couples when this conflicts with their religious or philosophical beliefs, would be justified by the need to uphold good administration of justice (*McClintock* at [49]–[57]).

7.8 Victimisation and harassment

RBR 2003, regs 4 and *5* govern victimisation and harassment and are similar to *SDA 1975, ss 4* and *4A* and *RRA 1976, s 2* and *3A* respectively. The definition of detriment in *reg 2(3)* ensures there is no overlap between the concepts of harassment and direct discrimination for the purposes of *RBR 2003*.

7.9 Discrimination in employment

RBR 2003, reg 6 prohibits employers from discriminating against applicants for employment 'at an establishment in Great Britain' (as defined in *reg 9*) in various circumstances. It is similar to *SDA 1975, s 6* and *RRA 1976, s 4*. The term 'employment' is defined in *reg 2(3)* as 'employment under a contract of service or apprenticeship or a contract personally to do any work'. A proposal for an artistic display which contains no specification of personal service, and which is made to a rolling open-tender programme, is not a response to an offer of employment; it is a response to an offer to listen to a proposal which may, or may not, lead to an offer of employment (*Padgett v Serota and the Board of Trustees of the Tate Gallery* EAT/97/07 and EAT/99/07).

Like in other areas of equality legislation, the definition of 'employment' is broader than that in *ERA 1996, s 230*. Discrimination against contract workers by those to whom their employer contracts to supply their services, rather than by the employer himself, is covered by *reg 8*.

7.10 Genuine occupational requirements

RBR 2003, reg 7 is an exception which allows an employer in certain circumstances (see *regs 6, 8, 10, 14, 17, 18, 20*), when recruiting for a post, to treat job applicants differently on the grounds of religion or belief if being of a particular religion or belief is one of two 'genuine occupational requirements' (GORs). It may also allow an employer in the same circumstances to dismiss an employee where an employee's religion or belief changes after taking up a post (paras 67–68, DTI Guidance). A GOR can only apply in relation to discrimination under *reg 3* (whether direct or indirect), and not to victimisation or harassment, and even then only in the circumstances defined in *reg 7(1)*.

The first GOR, in *reg 7(2)*, is identical to the GOR in *SOR 2003*. It is in general terms and applies where:

- being of a particular religion or belief is a genuine and determining occupational requirement (*reg 7(2)(a)*);

- it is proportionate to apply that requirement in the particular case (*reg 7(2)(b)*); and

- either the person to whom that requirement is applied does not meet it or the employer is reasonably not satisfied that he does not meet it (*reg 7(2)(c)*).

The phrase 'genuine and determining occupational requirement' sets a high test, suggesting something which is necessary or essential to the performance of a job (ACAS Guidance, Appendix 1, para 5; DTI Guidance, para 73). It is rarely likely to be satisfied. The further test of proportionality is equally stringent, meaning that the GOR must be an appropriate *and necessary* means of achieving the legitimate aim in question. This includes consideration of whether the aim could be achieved by other means which have lesser discriminatory effects (DTI Guidance, para 78). As to the final test, the legitimacy of the employer forming his own view of whether a GOR is satisfied has been unsuccessfully challenged as incompatible with the Directive; courts and tribunals are to be trusted to apply the test responsibly, not, for example, finding it satisfied upon mere suspicion by an employer that a GOR is not met (*Amicus*).

The second GOR, in *reg 7(3)*, is specific to *RBR 2003*. It is limited to situations where an employer has an ethos based on religion or belief and, having regard to that ethos and to the nature of the employment or the context in which it is carried out, substantially the same tests as in *reg 7(1)* are satisfied. The key difference here is that being of a particular religion or belief need only be a genuine, and not also determining, occupational requirement. The provision has the potential to apply to a significantly broader category of organisations than *SOR 2003, reg 7(3)*, such as faith schools or care homes with a religious ethos; but it seems it will not apply to local authorities that merely maintain such organisations (*Glasgow City Council v McNab* [2007] IRLR 476, EAT).

7.11 Discrimination outside employment

Like *SDA 1975* and *RRA 1976*, *RBR 2003* also prohibit discrimination in a variety of areas outside employment, such as within barristers' chambers (*reg 12*), trade organisations (*reg 15*), qualifications bodies (*reg 16*), providers of vocational training (*reg 17*), employment agencies (*reg 18*) and institutions of further and higher education (*reg 20*). *EA 2006, ss 46–47* extends this protection to a number of other areas, including the provision of goods, facilities and services and the disposal of premises.

7.12 Differences with other anti-discrimination legislation

It unlawful for trustees or managers of occupational pension schemes (as defined in the *Pensions Act 1995*) to discriminate against, or to subject to harassment, the members or prospective members of the scheme in carrying out any of their functions, or to subject a member or prospective member to harassment (*RBR 2003, reg 9A*, inserted by the *Employment Equality (Religion or Belief) (Amendment) Regulations 2003 (SI 2003/2828)*). This provision contrasts with the rules relating to sex discrimination by trustees and managers of pension schemes found in the *Pensions Act 1995*, and the absence of any such rules relating to racial discrimination. It does not apply retrospectively.

7.13 Religion and Belief

Both *RBR 2003* and *EA 2006* also contain particular protection or exemptions from protection for specific organisations and individuals. For example, *reg 26(1)* provides that a PCP that relates to a Sikh wearing a safety helmet while on a construction site, applied when the employer has no reasonable grounds for believing that the Sikh would not wear a turban at all times while on the site, shall be incapable of justification for the purposes of *reg 3(1)(b)(iii)*. This is akin to the protection found in the *Employment Act 1989, s 12(1)*, and like that provision, is restricted to employees on construction sites (*Dhanjal v British Steel plc, IT/50740/91*). Equally, it is not unlawful for organisations relating to religion or belief to restrict membership, participation in their activities, the provision of goods, facilities or services, or the use and disposal of premises (*EA 2006, s 57*); charities to restrict membership (*EA 2006, s 59*) or to provide benefits only to persons of a particular religion or belief (*EA 2006, s 58*); or faith schools to restrict the provision of goods facilities or services or the use and disposal of premises (*EA 2006, s 60*) in certain limited circumstances. Nor is it unlawful to meet the special needs for education, training or welfare of persons of a religion or belief or to provide them with care within the family (*EA 2006, s 61 and 62*).

7.13 PRACTICAL CONSIDERATIONS

Particular issues that are likely to arise under *RBR 2003* include complaints about recruitment, working time and dress codes. Guidance on these issues is set out below, together with advice on monitoring and drafting suitable policies. Although the existing case law under *RBR 2003,* and even more so under *EA 2006*, is limited, assistance can be found in UK and ECJ sex discrimination, and more particularly, race discrimination, law, as well as under the *ECHR* and *HRA 1998*; however, care should be taken in drawing analogies.

7.14 Recruitment

Advertising for positions should reach as diverse an audience as possible. Making use of religious press is acceptable provided that multiple faiths are targeted, unless a GOR applies. If a GOR does apply, this should be identified at the beginning of the recruitment process (bearing in mind the duties of the role and its profile within the organisation), made clear in any advertisements for the position and reiterated in the selection process.

Organisations should recruit based on merit, irrespective of religion or belief, and interview questions should be framed accordingly. However, some positive action is justifiable under *RBR 2003, reg 25* (similar in its provision to *RRA 1976, ss 37 and 38*). This may take the form of an advertisement to encourage applications from a minority religion, provided it makes clear that ultimate selection will be merit-based, or training existing employees for work which has historically been the preserve of individuals from a particular religion or belief (ACAS Guidance, para 1.7).

7.15 Working time

Employers are not legally obliged to provide time and facilities for religious or belief observance in the workplace or elsewhere. Employers should, however, try to accommodate requests for time off where possible by approving annual leave, time off in lieu, unpaid leave, use of flexi-time and/or flexible working arrangements.

Workers may request time off for prayer and access to a prayer or contemplation room. While employers are not legally obliged to provide a prayer room, the

ACAS Guidance notes that best practice will be 'in consultation with staff ... to designate an area for all staff for the specific purpose of prayer or contemplation rather than just a general rest room (para 4.6). However, employers will not be obliged to cause problems for other workers or the business to this end, or to enter into 'significant expenditure' and /or building alterations to make this provision (paras 4.6 and 4.7).

Where a worker seeks to opt out of regular working on a day which has religious significance for them, employers should consider whether working on that day can be justified as a legitimate business need and whether it is proportionate to apply that justification to the individual (ACAS Guidance, para 2.11). This excludes workers in the retail or betting trades who seek to opt out of Sunday working, specific provision for whom is made in the *Employment Rights Act 1996, ss 36–43*. Complaints of indirect discrimination by a Jew refused leave on the Sabbath (*Fugler v Macmillan-London Hair Studios Ltd* ET 2205090/04 (15 July 2005)) and a Christian given shift patterns that included Sundays (*Williams-Drabble v Pathway Care Solutions* ET 2601718/04 (10 January 2005)) have been upheld. In contrast, indirect discrimination has been found to be justified where a Muslim teacher was refused Friday afternoon leave because of the disruptive effect on students that would follow from granting the leave (*Mayuff v (1) The Governing Body of Bishop Challoner Catholic Collegiate School and (2) The Mayor and Burgesses of the London Borough of Tower Hamlets* ET 3202398/04 (21 December 2005)) and where Saturday working was accepted as standard practice in the tourism industry (*James v MSC Cruises Ltd* ET 2203173/05 (12 April 2006)). Working time claims made under human rights law have met with little success. The Commission has also held there to be no breach of *Article 9* where a Muslim teacher was refused Friday afternoon leave; the employee had entered freely into his contract of employment, which stipulated Friday working, and the employer had not, in relying on that contract, arbitrarily disregarded his freedom of religion (*Ahmad*).

Where workers request holiday in order to celebrate festival or spiritual observance periods, the ACAS Guidance recommends that employers 'should sympathetically consider such a request where it is reasonable and practical for the employee to be away from work, and they have sufficient holiday entitlement in hand' (para 4.2). Failure to consider requests can in itself be held to be discriminatory (*Khan v G and J Spencer Group t/a NIC Hygiene Limited* ET 1803250/04 (9 January 2005)).

Where a number of requests are made, 'employers should carefully consider whether their criteria for deciding who should and who should not be granted leave may indirectly discriminate' (ACAS Guidance, para 4.2). Refusals of religious holiday have been held to indirectly discriminate in the context of Eid (*JH Walker*).

Requests/representations from people with less well known religions or beliefs – and those with no religion or belief – should be treated in the same way as those from followers of better known religions or beliefs. The logical result of the extension of the definition of religion to include a reference to lack of religion and of belief (see 7.6(b)) is the possibility of direct and/or indirect discrimination claims from those who do not hold the same belief or share the same religion as the comparator and those who have no religion or belief. Such claims could arise in connection with leave arrangements if they are seen as disproportionately favourable to adherents of particular religions.

Employers that operate or alter shift patterns should:

- make work patterns clear at recruitment;

- when changing work patterns review whether religious issues might be an issue and include in any consultation process;

- offer alternative solutions where practicable; and

- give the business reasons for any refusal to work required shifts.

7.16 Dress codes and uniform requirements

Many employers impose uniform requirements and/or dress codes, whether contractual or non-contractual, precise/prescriptive or imprecise/descriptive, e g 'business dress', 'smart casual'. Those which conflict with the dress requirement of a particular religion or faith may constitute indirect discrimination unless they can be justified as a legitimate business need. Any which are targeted at particular religious practices and requirements may discriminate directly.

Dress codes may be easier to justify where there are health and safety concerns or where employees work directly with the public. For example, a complaint of indirect discrimination was upheld where a Muslim female shop assistant was required to wear an overall over a skirt for image purposes, because the detriment caused to her outweighed any benefit to the employer (*Malik v British Home Stores* (ET 29014/79); but a Sikh woman's complaint regarding her employer's prohibition on trousers, following the dress regulations laid down by the General Nursing Council, which led to the withdrawal of her training place, was dismissed on the basis of justification (*Kingston and Richmond Area Health Authority v Kaur* [1981] ICR 631, [1981] IRLR 337, EAT). Similarly, both refusals to employ and dismissals of Sikhs for failing to cut their hair or shave their beards have been held to be justified on the grounds of hygiene (*Singh v RHM Bakeries (Southern) Ltd* EAT 818/77 and *Singh v Rowntree Mackintosh Ltd* [1979] ICR 554, [1979] IRLR 199, EAT respectively). But where the grounds for justification, such as safety requirements, are implausible (*Bhakerd v Famous Names Ltd*, ET 19289/87, where a turban was not plausibly any less suitable than the prescribed company hat) or not enforced consistently, a provision, criterion or practice will be difficult to justify (*Hussain v Midland Cosmetic Sales Plc and ors*, EAT 915/00, where the employer did not allow Ms Hussain to wear a headscarf as well as protective headgear, but had permitted eight other Pakistani women employees to do so).

(Now see also *Eweida v British Airways plc* ET 2702689/06, where a tribunal considered whether refusing to allow an employee to wear a cross around her neck, in contravention of a policy which forbade the wearing of accessories that could not be concealed beneath uniform, constituted direct or indirect discrimination. The claim was ultimately dismissed. The decision was not available on 1 January 2008.)

As to the jurisprudence under *Article 9* of the *ECHR*, domestic courts have been slow to find interferences with the right to manifest religious beliefs in the context of uniform policies that perform valid functions. In *R (on the application of Begum) v Headteacher and Governors of Denbigh High School* [2006] UKHL 15, [2007] 1 AC 100, [2006] 2 WLR 719, [2006] 2 All ER 487 the House of Lords found that a school uniform policy, which was acceptable to mainstream Muslim opinion but did not permit the wearing of a jilbab, did not interfere with a Muslim schoolgirl's *Article 9* rights; the girl's parents had chosen the school with knowledge of its uniform requirements, and anyway her right to manifest her religion did not extend to any time and place of her choosing. Similarly, in *R (on the application of Playfoot) v Governing Body of Millais School* [2007] EWHC 1698 (Admin), [2007] 3 FCR 754, a school uniform policy which forbade the wearing of jewellery did not infringe *Article 9* by preventing a pupil from wearing a chastity ring; the girl had voluntarily accepted the school's uniform policy, which was both a legitimate and proportionate means of fostering the school identity and an atmosphere of allegiance, discipline, equality and cohesion which was conducive to learning.

When instituting dress codes, employers should consider whether:

- any part of an existing or proposed dress code is likely to conflict with religious or other genuinely held beliefs;

- any such elements are strictly necessary and, if not, whether they can be objectively justified;

- to seek workplace validation (by means of employee survey) of the code;

- to seek external expert advice from, say, representatives of a particular faith group.

It should be made clear to employees that if any elements of a dress code cause them personal difficulty, problems should first be discussed in confidence with HR/line managers.

Ideally, dress codes should be neutrally worded, flexible and minimal.

7.17   Special treatment

In policies which are as accommodating as possible for individuals from a variety of faiths, employers must also be careful not to accord special treatment to individuals from any one faith; even if this is intended to avoid discriminating directly or indirectly against them, it may constitute unlawful direct or indirect discrimination if it amounts to less favourable treatment of others on the grounds of their religion or belief (DTI Guidance, para 43). Examples might be giving a Jewish employee extra paid holiday to mark a religious festival or paying employees extra to work on Sundays, to the disadvantage of Christians who observe Sunday as a day of rest.

Exceptions to the general rule against special treatment are provided by *RBR 2003, regs 25* and *26* (see 7.12 and 7.14).

7.18   Monitoring and information-gathering

In the UK there is no legal obligation to include religion or belief in any equal opportunities monitoring processes, nor are job applicants or employees obliged to respond to any such enquiries. However, monitoring can assist employers in ensuring that their equality policy is working to the benefit of all concerned.

Before opting to monitor, employers should consider how information could be obtained, how accurate it might be and what should be done with it. Without a clear purpose and, in particular, the willingness and ability to act where appropriate, monitoring on this ground could be counter-productive. Thereafter, staff should be told why information is being collected, how it will be used and whether or not it will be kept confidential and anonymous. A named and trained individual should have responsibility for the collation and storage of such information, which will constitute sensitive personal data under the *Data Protection Act 1998*.

7.19   Religion and Belief

Some employers that monitor invite staff to classify themselves under the categories used in the 2001 census: Christian, Buddhist, Hindu, Jewish, Muslim, Sikh, any other religion, no religion or religion not stated. Given the breadth of the definition of 'religion or belief' in *RBR 2003*, however, it is unlikely that questions could be devised which would dovetail with the full range of potential claims or satisfy any genuine requests for such information.

In the face of potential difficulties with formal monitoring processes, anonymous surveys and information from other sources such as exit interviews or grievance meetings may provide useful information – but these can create difficulties if the information, supplied in confidence and/or anonymously, reveals specific problems which require resolution, eg complaints about specific people. Alternatively, information can be collated from the workforce by enquiring whether any changes are necessary or desirable to specific rules or practices to accommodate particular religions or beliefs. This approach may be better tailored towards ensuring compliance with *RBR 2003*, whilst also acknowledging that people manifest their religion or belief in a range of ways, even amongst those who affiliate themselves with a particular religious denomination. If from this data there appears to be a substantial number of people who consider a particular working practice such as shift arrangements, staff food facilities or the dress code to be disadvantageous on the grounds of religion or belief then consideration should be given to reviewing and adjusting those arrangements. However, it should be explained at the outset that it may not be reasonable, or possible, to remedy all perceived disadvantages.

7.19   Drafting suitable policies

Whilst employers do not have to have an equality policy in place, doing so is a commonplace means of demonstrating that an employer has taken reasonably practicable steps to prevent employees discriminating against or harassing other employees. Either the equality policy or other policies of the employer should provide guidance on how to resolve conflicts between either the equality policy and other policies on working time or dress codes, or between protection from discrimination on the grounds of religion and belief and discrimination on other grounds. An obvious example of the latter sort of conflict is where a fundamentalist Christian refuses to work with a gay colleague. Any such guidance should be formulated neutrally so as to give rise to claims of indirect, rather than direct, discrimination. Similarly, when considering whether adjustments need to be made to standard company rules or practices, care should be taken not to create specific formal exemptions only available to people of a particular religion or belief. The aim should be minimal procedures, maximum flexibility and regular review of all practices and procedures.

The *Azmi* case (see 7.6 and 7.7) indicates for the present that the tribunals consider that treating any consequent claims as indirect rather than direct discrimination, where that is possible, is the better approach (although not the only one) for, as a matter of principle in respect of provisions, conditions and practices which are genuinely neutral, the employer should have the opportunity of showing that the provision, etc is justifiable. This will not be possible where a rule or practice, even if well intentioned, is directed at adherents of a particular religion or a particular manifestation of that belief. For example, a policy which specifically permits (and/or delimits) time off for religious observance (particularly if it is especially beneficial) may conceivably give rise to claims of direct discrimination from atheists or agnostics, whereas the better course might be to refer instead to a general policy on the treatment of time off for purposes not expressly covered by the *Employment Rights Act 1996*.

7.20   **Further sources of information**

- The BBC website contains information on many religions or beliefs, including their history, beliefs, ethics and customs: http://www.bbc.co.uk/religion/religions.

- A five-year religious calendar can be found at http://www.interfaithcalendar.org.

- The ACAS Guidance, Appendix 2 contains information on 'commonly practised religions'. This covers food, clothing and bereavement requirements.

8 Sex Discrimination

8.1 INTRODUCTION

The *Sex Discrimination Act 1975* ('*SDA 1975*') makes gender discrimination unlawful in the field of employment (*Part II*) and in other fields such as education and the provision of goods, facilities and services (*Part III*). Much of this chapter focuses on pregnancy and maternity-related matters. Whilst this is of course not the only context in which sex discrimination can arise, it is an area on which a great deal of law – legislation and case law, domestic and European – has been generated. This, and other 'family friendly' rights which often arise in the context of sex discrimination claims, are therefore what the bulk of the chapter focuses on – but this does not detract from the importance of the general provisions of *SDA 1975*.

8.3 Who is protected?

8.2 It is unlawful for an employer to discriminate against employees (broadly defined to include those working under a contract for services), contract workers, or job applicants (*SDA 1975, s 6*). The *SDA 1975* also prohibits discrimination by bodies such as vocational training bodies and employment agencies. It makes specific provision for certain types of work, such as office holders and the police. See 1.7–1.26.

Unlawful discrimination

Types of discrimination

Unlawful discrimination takes four different forms. *SDA 1975* categorises the different types of discrimination as follows:

(a) direct discrimination (*s 1(2)(a)*);

(b) indirect discrimination(*s 1(2)(b)*);

(c) discrimination by way of victimisation (*s 4(1)*); and

(d) harassment, including sexual harassment (*ss 4A* and *6(2A)*).

See 1.27–1.82 for further information.

8.4 *Specific provisions*

There are specific provisions for certain types of gender discrimination:

(a) discrimination on the grounds of gender reassignment (see GENDER REASSIGNMENT (4));

(b) discrimination against married persons and civil partners (see MARITAL STATUS AND CIVIL PARTNERSHIPS (5)); and

(c) discrimination on the ground of pregnancy or maternity leave (see 8.68ff).

8.6 Sex Discrimination

8.6 Definitions

8.5 Although usually relied upon by women who experience discriminatory treatment, *SDA 1975* applies equally to discrimination against men (*s 2*) (although see 8.7). For the purposes of *SDA 1975*, the terms 'woman' and 'man' include young persons and children.

Limitations in scope

Scope of legislation

Discrimination is unlawful only in so far as it is prohibited by the terms of *SDA 1975* (subject to compliance with EU Directives: see 8.10ff). There is no residual common law rule against gender discrimination. Therefore, it is essential to identify at the outset of every case whether a claimant comes within the scope of one or more of the anti-discrimination provisions in *SDA 1975*. Those provisions relating to employment are primarily found in *SDA 1975, Part II*.

8.7 *Negative and positive discrimination*

The primary objective of *SDA 1975* is to prohibit less favourable treatment on grounds of gender. Positive discrimination is prohibited, even where it would compensate for historic inequalities. However, positive action is permitted in certain cases (see 8.63).

8.8 *Equal Pay Act 1970*

SDA 1975 complements the *Equal Pay Act 1970* (*EqPA 1970*), but the two statutes are mutually exclusive. Discrimination in relation to contractual terms relating to pay and other terms and conditions comes within the scope of *EqPA 1970* and cannot be pursued under *SDA 1975*. See EQUAL PAY (11).

8.9 Family-friendly provisions

In response to EU Directives and developing social policy in the UK, a raft of family-friendly provisions have been introduced in the last decade. They are considered in detail below at 8.10ff. In summary, they are:

(a) the right to be absent from work to care for young children (*Maternity and Parental Leave etc Regulations 1999 (SI 1999/3312)*);

(b) the right to take time off work to care for dependants in the event of family emergencies (*Employment Rights Act 1996 (ERA 1996), ss 57A* and *57B*);

(c) paternity and adoption leave and pay (*ERA 1996, ss 75A–75D, 80A–80E*; *Paternity and Adoption Leave Regulations 2002 (SI 2002/2788)*); and

(d) flexible working arrangements to care for children and adults (*ERA 1996, Part VIIIA*; *Flexible Working (Eligibility, Complaints and Remedies) Regulations 2002 (SI 2002/3236)*; *Flexible Working (Procedural Requirements) Regulations 2002 (SI 2002/3207)*).

8.10 EU law

EU law has had a significant impact on the development of gender discrimination law in the UK.

8.11   *Treaty of Rome*

Although the *Treaty of Rome 1957, Article 119* (now *Article 141* of the Treaty establishing the European Community 1992, (*'EC Treaty'*) initially only contained express provision in relation to the right to equal pay, not other forms of gender discrimination, it was subsequently amended to add an obligation on the Council to 'adopt measures to ensure the application of the principle of equal opportunities and equal treatment of men and women in matters of employment and occupation'. This falls short of a directly enforceable right under the *EC Treaty*.

8.12   *Equal Treatment Directive*

The *Equal Treatment Directive (76/207/EEC)* required Member States to put into effect the principle of equal treatment for men and women in respect of access to employment, training and working conditions. The *Equal Pay Directive (75/117/EEC)* and the *Equal Treatment (Social Security) Directive (79/7/EEC)* imposed similar requirements in those areas. In the seminal case of *Defrenne v Sabena Airways (No 3)* [1978] ECR 1365, the European Court of Justice (ECJ) at paras 26–27 held that:

'... respect for fundamental personal human rights is one of the general principles of community law ... There can be no doubt that the elimination of discrimination based on sex forms part of those fundamental rights.'

8.13   *Further Directives*

Important amendments were introduced by the *Equal Treatment Amendment Directive (2002/73/EC)*. In addition, directives on occupational social security *(86/378/EEC)*, pregnant workers *(92/85/EEC)*, parental leave *(96/34/EC)*, the burden of proof *(97/80/EC)*, part-time work *(97/81/EC)* and the *Framework Directive (2000/78/EC)* made further changes to UK law. *Directive 2006/54/EC* (*'2006 Directive'*), which consolidates and updates the major Directives on equal opportunities and equal treatment, must be implemented by Member States by 15 August 2008 (*2006 Directive, Article 33*).

Directives may be relied upon:

(a)   directly, in a claim against an 'emanation of the State' but not against a private individual or organisation;

(b)   to interpret the scope and meaning of domestic law in conformity with the directive e g *Webb v EMO Air Cargo (UK) Ltd (No 2)* [1995] 4 All ER 577, [1995] 1 WLR; and

(c)   to set aside conflicting domestic law where it derogates from a general principle of community law, e g *Mangold v Helm* [2006] All ER (EC) 383, [2006] IRLR 143.

Proceedings may be brought against a Member State for failure to implement a directive (for example, *Equal Opportunities Commission v Secretary of State for Trade and Industry* [2007] EWHC 483 (Admin), [2007] 2 CMLR 1351) and where appropriate, damages awarded for loss suffered (*Francovich v Italy* [1991] ECR I-5357).

8.14   *Charter of Fundamental Rights*

The preamble to the 2006 Directive has express regard to The Charter of Fundamental Rights of the European Union ('Charter'), which enshrines the right to equal treatment between men and women in all areas, including employ-ment, work and pay. Although the Charter is not yet legally binding on Member States, it is referred to in ECJ case law as an aid to interpretation.

8.15   *European Court of Justice*

Judgments of the ECJ have played an equally important part in shaping UK law, by identifying aspects of UK law which are incompatible with EU law. A notable example is *Marshall v Southampton and South West Hampshire Area Health Authority (No 2)* [1994] QB 126, [1993] 4 All ER 586 in which the ECJ held that the statutory cap on compensation for sex discrimination was in breach of the Equal Treatment Directive. As Miss Marshall's employer was an 'emanation of the State', the directive had direct effect, so enabling her to rely on it before the UK courts.

8.16   *Recommendations*

The Commission also has power to make recommendations to Member States. The Commission has made a recommendation regarding the protection of dignity of men and women at work, which includes a Code of Practice on sexual harassment. The Commission recommendations and code are not legally binding, but will be taken into account by courts and tribunals (Recommendation *92/131/EEC*).

8.18   Equal Opportunities Commission/ Equality and Human Rights Commission

8.17   *SDA 1975, Part VI* established the Equal Opportunities Commission (EOC), which had a wide range of powers in the field of sex discrimination. It has been replaced by a single equality body, the Equality and Human Rights Commission (EHRC), in the *Equality Act 2006*. *SDA 1975, Part VI* has now been repealed. The EHRC replaces the Commission for Racial Equality, the Disability Rights Commission and the EOC.

Codes of Practice and Guidance

EOC and EHRC

The EOC issued a Code of Practice for the elimination of discrimination on grounds of sex and marriage and for the promotion of equality of opportunity in employment (1985), and a Code of Practice on gender equality duty (2007). These will remain in force until amended or revoked by the ECHR (*Equality Act 2006, s 42*). Under the *Equality Act 2006, s 14*, the ECHR has power to issue further codes of practice. Failure by an employer to observe a code of practice is not in itself unlawful, but may be taken into account by a tribunal.

8.19   *DBERR and ACAS*

The Department of Business, Enterprise and Regulatory Reform's website is a useful source of guidance on employment discrimination. The guidance has no formal legal status, but may be referred to in legal submissions. ACAS has also published a guide for employers called 'Tackling discrimination and promoting equality' (January 2007).

8.20   **SEX DISCRIMINATION**

Discrimination under SDA 1975

Under *SDA 1975*, a man or woman may bring a claim of discrimination on the grounds of gender only if the discriminatory conduct falls within one or more of the types of discrimination which are prohibited under *SDA 1975*.

SDA 1975 is intended to implement the *Equal Treatment Directive 76/207/EEC*, as amended by *Directive* 2002/73/EC (the *Equal Treatment Amendment Directive*). The same concepts are used in other areas of discrimination, notably race, and therefore they are analysed fully in COMMON CONCEPTS (1). Below is a brief summary of the legislation. An act of discrimination may also amount to a breach of contract; see for example *Shaw v CCL Ltd* UKEAT/0512/06/DM (22 May 2007, unreported).

8.21   *Direct discrimination*

A person discriminates directly against a woman if:

'on the ground of her sex he treats her less favourably than he treats or would treat a man.'

This section (*SDA 1975, s 1(2)(a)*) applies equally to the treatment of men, but no account may be taken of special treatment afforded to women in connection with pregnancy or childbirth (*SDA 1975, s 2*).

Liability for direct discrimination only arises if the claim falls within the scope of *SDA 1975, Parts II, III* or *IV.*

There are various examples in case law of the ways in which direct discrimination can occur. Many of these relate to pregnancy, maternity or childcare-related matters (as do many claims of indirect discrimination or harassment), and these issues are dealt with below. Recently, there have been a number of relatively high-profile cases – not all successful – which relate to 'City' institutions, typically involving female employees who allege that they have not been paid bonuses or received promotions because they are women; see, for example, *Barton v Investec Henderson Crosthwaite Securities Ltd* [2003] IRLR 332.

8.22   *Indirect discrimination*

A person discriminates indirectly against a woman if:

'he applies to her a provision, criterion or practice which he applies or would apply equally to a man, but –

(i)   which puts or would put women at a particular disadvantage when compared with men,

(ii)   which puts her at that disadvantage, and

(iii)   which he cannot show to be a proportionate means of achieving a legitimate aim.'

This definition of indirect discrimination (set out in *SDA 1975, s 1(2)(b)*) was introduced to give effect to the *Equal Treatment Amendment Directive, Article 2(2)*. This definition applies to *SDA 1975, Part II* (field of employment), *ss 35A* and *35B* (barristers and advocates) and provisions of *SDA 1975, Part III* relating to vocational training. The section applies equally to men.

A different definition of indirect discrimination, contained in *SDA 1975, s 1(1)(b)*, is applied to the other fields of discrimination in *Part III*, such as the provision of goods and services.

Liability for indirect discrimination only arises if the claim falls within the scope of *SDA 1975, Parts II, III* or *IV.*

Where a person adopts a discriminatory practice, the EHRC may take proceedings against him under *SDA 1975, s 37.*

8.23   *Victimisation*

Under *SDA 1975, s 4(1)*, victimisation occurs when a person (the 'discriminator') discriminates against another person (the 'person victimised') by treating that person less favourably than he treats or would treat other persons, and does so because the person victimised has done or intends to do a protected act, namely:

(a)   brought proceedings against the discriminator or any other person under *SDA 1975, EqPA 1970*, or the *Pensions Act 1995, ss 62–65;*

(b)   given evidence or information in connection with proceedings brought by any person against the discriminator or any other person under *SDA 1975, EqPA 1970*, or the *Pensions Act 1995, ss 62–65;*

(c)   otherwise done anything under or by reference to *SDA 1975, EqPA 1970*, or the *Pensions Act 1995, ss 62–65* in relation to the discriminator or any other person; or

(d)   alleged that the discriminator or any other person has committed an act which would amount to a contravention of, or give rise to a claim under, *SDA 1975, EqPA 1970*, or the *Pensions Act 1995, ss 62–65.*

(The *Pensions Act 1995, ss 62–65* incorporates the *Social Security Act 1989, Sch 5, paras 5–6.*)

If the discriminator treats the person victimised less favourably because he suspects that the person victimised has done, or intends to do a protected act, this also amounts to victimisation under *SDA 1975, s 4(1)*. The section applies equally to men.

8.24   *Harassment and sexual harassment*

SDA 1975 was amended to give effect to the anti-harassment provisions in the *Equal Treatment Amendment Directive, Article 2(2)*. Under *SDA 1975, s 4A(1)*, a person subjects a woman to harassment if:

'(a)   on the ground of her sex, he engages in unwanted conduct that has the purpose or *effect–*

    (i)   of violating her dignity, or

    (ii)   of creating an intimidating, hostile, degrading, humiliating or offensive environment for her, or

'(b)   he engages in any form of unwanted verbal, non-verbal or physical conduct of a *sexual nature that has the purpose or effect –*

    (i)   of violating her dignity, or

    (ii)   of creating an intimidating, hostile, degrading, humiliating or offensive environment for her, or '(c)   on the ground of her rejection or submission to unwanted conduct of a kind mentioned in paragraph (a) or (b), he treats her less favourably than he would treat had she not rejected, or submitted to, the conduct.'

Conduct shall be regarded as having the effect mentioned in (a) or (b) above only if, having regard to all the circumstances, including in particular the perception of the woman, it should reasonably be considered as having that effect (*SDA 1975, s 4A(2)*). This section applies equally to men (*SDA 1975, s 4A(6)*).

Liability only arises where the claim falls within the scope of the prohibitions on harassment in *SDA 1975, Parts II, III or IV.*

In *Equal Opportunities Commission v Secretary of State for Trade and Industry* [2007] EWHC 483 (Admin), [2007] 2 CMLR 1351, the High Court held that *s 4A(1)(i)(a)* failed to implement the *Equal Treatment Directive* correctly by including the words 'on the ground of her sex' (implying that causation was required) and by omitting to provide for claims that an employer failed to protect an employee from repetitive harassment by a third party, such as a supplier or customer. DBERR confirmed that amending regulations will be implemented; however, no date has been given at the time of writing. See further on this case at 8.71, 8.73 and 8.108.

8.25   *Codes of practice and guidance*

There is helpful guidance on harassment in European Commission's 'Code of Practice on Sexual Harassment'; the EOC's 'Detailed Guidance, Sexual Harassment: Managers' Questions Answered' 2006; the EOC's 'Code of Practice on Gender Equality Duty' (2007); ACAS' 'Bullying and Harassment at Work: A Guide for Managers and Employers' (2006); and DBERR's 'Equality and Diversity: Updating the Sex Discrimination Act' (2005) and 'Changes to Sex Discrimination Legislation in Great Britain' (2005).

8.26   *Discrimination on the ground of pregnancy or maternity leave*

See below at 8.68ff and 8.79ff.

8.27   *Discrimination on the ground of gender reassignment*

See GENDER REASSIGNMENT (4).

8.28   *Discrimination on grounds of marital status and civil partnership*

See MARITAL STATUS AND CIVIL PARTNERSHIPS (5).

8.29   *Burden of proof*

The *Burden of Proof Directive 97/80/EC*, as amended by *Directive 98/52/EC*, was implemented into domestic law by the *Sex Discrimination (Indirect Discrimination and Burden of Proof) Regulations 2001 (SI 2001/2660)* and *SDA 1975, s 63A(2)*, which provides:

'Where, on the hearing of the complaint, the complainant proves facts from which the tribunal could, apart from this section, conclude in the absence of an adequate explanation that the respondent –

(a)   has committed an act of discrimination or harassment against the complainant which is unlawful by virtue of Part 2 [the employment field], or section 35A or 35B or

(b)   is by virtue of section 41 or section 42 [liability of employers and aiding unlawful acts] to be treated as having committed such an act of discrimination against the complainant,

the tribunal shall uphold the complaint unless the respondent proves that he did not commit, or, as the case may be, is not to be treated as having committed, that act.'

The effect of this provision is that a tribunal must uphold a complaint of sex discrimination where the claimant proves facts from which the tribunal could, in the absence of an adequate explanation, conclude that there has been discrimination and the respondent cannot prove that he or she did not discriminate. This shifting burden of proof has generated much case law, which is analysed in COMMON CONCEPTS (1).

8.30   **Who is protected by SDA 1975?**

Overseas workers

SDA 1975 only applies to employment at establishments in Great Britain. Employment is to be regarded as being at an establishment in Great Britain if (per *SDA 1975, s 10*):

(a)   the employee does her work wholly or partly in Great Britain; or

(b)   the employee does her work wholly or partly outside Great Britain but the employer has a place of business at an establishment in Great Britain, the employee's work is for the purpose of that business at that establishment, and the employee was ordinarily resident in Great Britain either when he applied for the job, or was offered it or at any time during the course of her employment.

There are specific provisions for ships, aircraft and oil rigs (see *s 10(2)–(6)*).

In applying *s 10*, the tribunal should consider the whole period of employment, not just the position at the date of the alleged discriminatory act (*Saggar v Ministry of Defence* [2005] EWCA Civ 413, [2005] ICR 1073).

This issue is discussed in more depth in COMMON CONCEPTS (1).

8.31   *Employment*

SDA 1975, s 82(1) defines 'employment' as 'employment under a contract of service or of apprenticeship or a contract personally to execute any work or labour, and related expressions shall be construed accordingly.' This extended definition is wider than the definition applied in unfair dismissal claims; see further COMMON CONCEPTS (1).

For the scope of the protection afforded by *SDA 1975*, see 8.39ff.

8.32   *Crown employment*

SDA 1975 applies to Crown employees (*s 85*). House of Commons and House of Lords employees are protected by *s 85A* and *85B* respectively, although ministers of the Crown (*s 85(10)*) are excluded.

8.33   *Police*

SDA 1975, s 17 provides that a police officer shall be treated as an employee of the relevant Chief Officer of the police, or in some cases, the police authority. A new *subsection 1A* was inserted in 2003 to confirm that Chief Officers of police are vicariously liable for the acts and omissions of police officers as employers under *s 41*, reversing the effect of *Chief Constable of Bedfordshire Police v Liversidge* [2002] EWCA Civ 894, [2002] ICR 1135. Proceedings should be brought against the Chief Constable and/or the police authority and the individual officers who have discriminated.

Chief Officers of the police may be directly liable for management decisions on matters such as recruitment and postings: see *Hendricks v Commissioner of Police of the Metropolis* [2002] EWCA Civ 1686, [2003] 1 All ER 654 endorsing *Chief Constable of Cumbria v McGlennon* [2002] ICR 1156, EAT.

Police cadets are also deemed to be employees (*SDA 1975, s 17(6)*).

See also 8.49.

8.34   *Armed forces*

SDA 1975, s 85(2)(c) as amended by the *Armed Forces Act 1996*, provides that *SDA 1975, Parts II* and *IV* apply to service in the armed forces. The *Sex Discrimination Act 1975 (Application to Armed Forces etc) Regulations 1994 (SI 1994/3276)* marked the successful culmination of a series of cases challenging the exclusion of members of the armed forces from the *SDA 1975*, as contrary to *Treaty of Rome, Article 119* and the *Equal Treatment Directive*. However, internal complaints procedures must be invoked before a claim to a tribunal is made (*SDA 1975, s 85(9B)–9(E)*).

However, an exception in *s 85(4)* provides, 'Nothing in this Act shall render unlawful an act done for the purpose of ensuring the combat effectiveness of the armed forces.'

In *Sirdar v Army Board and Secretary of State for Defence* [1999] IRLR 47, the ECJ rejected the submission that matters relating to national security fell outside EU anti-discrimination provisions, but held that exclusion of women from special combat units such as the Royal Marines may be justified under the *Equal Treatment Directive, Article 2(2)* which exempts occupational activities for which the sex of the worker is a determining factor. See also 8.61.

8.35   *Office-holders*

Office-holders are likely to fall outside the definition of employment in *SDA 1975, s 82(1)*.

SDA 1975, ss 10A–10B provide for private and public sector office-holders. Those appointed, recommended or approved by central government are included. Elected and appointed members of central or local government are expressly excluded. *S 10B* broadly mirrors *SDA 1975, s 6* in setting out how discrimination can occur.

S 10A limits the effect of *SDA 1975, s 85(2)(a)* and (*b*), which exclude holders of a statutory office from *Parts II* and IV. Cases decided prior to the amendment would therefore be differently decided now (for example, *Knight v AG* [1979] ICR 194, and *Department of the Environment v Fox* [1979] 1 All ER 58, [1979] ICR 736).

8.36   *Contract workers*

Under *SDA 1975, s 9*, acts of discrimination by an employer ('the principal') against contract workers, who are supplied to him by another employer, are also unlawful. Typical examples of contract workers are office temporary staff and building site workers. It is unlawful for the principal to discriminate:

(a)   in the terms on which he allows her to work;

(b)   by not allowing her to do or continue to do the work;

(c)   in the way he affords access to any benefits, facilities or services or refusing or deliberately omitting to afford her access to them; or

(d)   by subjecting her to any other detriment.

In *BP Chemicals v Gillick* [1995] IRLR 128, the EAT held that *s 9* applied where a principal had refused to allow an agency worker to return to her old job after maternity leave, even though at the date of the refusal she was no longer working for BP; see 8.118.

As in the case of employees, cases of genuine occupational qualification (*SDA 1975, s 9(3)*), and cases regarding benefits, facilities and services which are also being provided to the public (*s 9(4)*), are excepted from liability. See 8.50 and 8.55.

S 9 extends to discrimination between contract workers, and between employees and contract workers (*Allonby v Accrington and Rossendale College* [2001] EWCA Civ 529, [2001] 2 CMLR 559). In *Harrods Ltd v Remick* [1998] 1 All ER 52, [1998] ICR 156. A department store was held to be liable under *s 9* for discrimination against a worker employed by a concession operating within the store. See also *Abbey Life Assurance Co Ltd v Tansell* [2000] IRLR 387, CA.

8.37   *Partnerships*

SDA 1975, s 11 provides it is unlawful for a firm, in relation to a position as partner in the firm, or the formation of a new partnership, to discriminate against a woman in relation to:

(a)   arrangements for appointment;

(b)   the terms on which a position is offered;

(c)   refusing or deliberately omitting to offer her a position;

(d)   the way in which she is afforded access to any benefits, facilities or services, or by refusing or deliberately omitting to afford her access to them; or

(e)   expelling her from her position or subjecting her to any other detriment.

It is a defence to a claim of discrimination if being a man is a genuine occupational qualification for the position as partner (*s 11(3)*).

Harassment of partners or potential partners is also unlawful (*s 11(2A)*).

Expulsion from the position of partner includes, under *s 82(1A)*, non-renewal of fixed-term contract or constructive dismissal.

8.38   *Barristers and advocates*

SDA 1975, s 35A(1)(2) provides that it is unlawful for a barrister or a barrister's clerk to discriminate against a woman in relation to:

(a)   arrangements for offering pupillage or tenancy;

(b)   the terms on which it is offered;

(c)   refusing or deliberately omitting to offer it to her;

(d)   the terms applicable to her as a pupil or tenant;

(e)   opportunities for training or gaining experience, and benefits, facilities or services; or

(f)   termination or subjecting her to any other detriment.

S 35A(3) makes it unlawful for any person to discriminate against a barrister in the giving, withholding or acceptance of instructions. Harassment is made unlawful by *s 35A(2A)* and *(3)*.

There is similar provision for Advocates in Scotland in *SDA 1975, s 35B*.

Where a relationship under *s 35A* or *35B* has come to an end, it is unlawful to discriminate against or harass a woman by subjecting her to a detriment where the treatment of her arises out of and is closely connected to the relevant relationship (*s 35C*).

8.39   Unlawful discrimination in employment

Job applicants

Under *SDA 1975, s 6(1)* it is unlawful for an employer to discriminate against an applicant for employment:

(a)   in the arrangements he makes for the purpose of determining who should be offered that employment (e g recruitment procedures);

(b)   in the terms on which he offers her that employment (e g lower pay, fewer benefits); or

(c)   by refusing or deliberately omitting to offer her that employment.

Under *SDA 1975, s 6(2A)*, it is unlawful for an employer to harass a woman who has applied to him for employment.

Liability can be established under any one of the grounds set out above. Thus, it is sufficient to prove that the interview was conducted in a discriminatory manner, without showing that the interview arrangements were discriminatory (*Nagarajan v London Regional Transport* [2000] 1 AC 501, [1999] 4 All ER 65, approving *Brennan v JH Dewhurst Ltd* [1983] IRLR 357). If the employer has made discriminatory arrangements for recruitment, a claim may be made even if the post was not filled for other reasons (*Roadburg v Lothian Regional Council* [1976] IRLR 283).

Word of mouth advertisement may be indirectly discriminatory. In *Coker v The Lord Chancellor* [2001] EWCA Civ 1756, [2002] ICR 321, the claimants alleged that that the Lord Chancellor's decision to select an adviser from among people already known to him, and not to advertise, was discriminatory and in breach of *s 6(1)(a)*. The Court of Appeal held that informal recruitment, such as by word of mouth, may be indirectly discriminatory. But in this case the requirement that the appointee be known to the Lord Chancellor excluded almost the entirety of the pool of potential applicants and therefore did not constitute indirect discrimination. The fact that the claimants had not applied for the position was not a bar to the claim.

The terms on which a job is offered may be indirectly discriminatory. In *Meade-Hill and National Union of Civil and Public Servants v British Council* [1996] 1 All ER 79, [1995] ICR 84 a mobility clause requiring the employee to relocate to anywhere in the UK was held to discriminate on grounds of sex and marital status against a woman because a greater proportion of women are secondary earners and their husbands cannot move with them.

Under *SDA 1975, s 38(1)*, it is unlawful to publish an advertisement which indicates an intention to discriminate. Use of a job description with a sexual connotation, such as 'waiter' 'salesgirl' 'postman' or 'stewardess' shall be taken to indicate an intention to discriminate, unless the advertisement indicates to the contrary (*s 38(2)*). The publisher of an advertisement can rely, as a defence, on placing reasonable reliance on a statement by the author that the publication was not contrary to the *SDA* (*s 38(4)*). Breach of *s 38* is a criminal offence (*s 38(5)*). Proceedings can only be brought by the EHRC (*s 38(6)*).

The EOC's *Code of Practice* (1985) makes a number of useful recommendations as to advertising and selection, as does the more up-to-date *CRE Code of Practice* – which would apply equally to gender discrimination. Tribunals can take breach of the EOC *Code* into account by a tribunal *SDA 1975, s 56A(10)*. Note that unjustifiable age limits can discriminate indirectly against women who have taken a career break to have children, e g *Price v Civil Service Commission* [1978] IRLR 3, and see AGE DISCRIMINATION (2).

Questions about marriage plans or family intentions should not be asked (but see *Saunders v Richmond-upon-Thames London Borough Council* [1977] IRLR 362 where the EAT held it was not automatically unlawful to ask questions of a woman which would not be asked of a man; it depended on the purposes for which the questions were asked, and whether the woman had been treated less favourably).

ACAS' guide 'Tackling discrimination and promoting equality' (June 2006) also provides detailed guidance on advertising, application forms, shortlisting, interviewing, references and making a decision.

The *EqPA 1970* does not apply to job applicants and so the only remedy against discriminatory treatment is under the *SDA 1975*. If an offer of employment is made on terms which would enable the applicant, if she accepted the job, to claim modification of the terms as a remedy under *EqPA 1970*, the offer shall be taken to contravene *s 6(1)(b)* (*SDA 1975, s 8(3)*). This does not apply if the employer can show that the reason for the difference in terms was a genuine material factor (other than sex) within the meaning of *s 1(3)* (*EqPA 1970, s 8(5)*).

If the complaint relates to an offer of money, the claimant cannot succeed at all under *s 6(1)(b)* unless she would also succeed under *EqPA 1970*. But if the complaint relates to terms and conditions other than money, there is no such restriction. See *SDA 1975, s 6(5)*.

8.40   *Employees*

Under *SDA 1975, s 6(2)* it is unlawful for an employer to discriminate against an employee:

(a)   in the way he affords her access, or refuses or deliberately omits to afford her access to, opportunities for:

   (i)   promotion, transfer or training; or

   (ii)   to any other benefits facilities or services,

(b)   by dismissing her, or subjecting her to any other detriment.

8.41   Promotion, training or transfer

Again, the EOC's *Code of Practice* (1985) makes a number of recommendations.

Promotion decisions will be open to challenge where there is a failure to follow transparent and objective procedures and where opportunities are made known by 'word of mouth' or recommendation, rather than advertising. See *Watches of Switzerland v Savell* [1983] IRLR 141 where the EAT held that promotion procedures indirectly discriminated on grounds of sex.

Past practices may have a discriminatory impact on promotions and transfers. In *Steel v Post Office (No 2)* [1978] IRLR 198, transfers to popular delivery rounds were allocated on basis of seniority. Seniority was based on length of service as permanent employees but women were not eligible for permanent status prior to 1975. Mrs Steel had 16 years' service but only two years' seniority. The seniority condition was held to be discriminatory and unjustifiable.

Assumptions made on the basis of a person's sex are likely to be discriminatory. In *Horsey v Dyfed County Council* [1982] IRLR 395 the EAT held that the employer had discriminated against the female claimant by refusing her secondment to a two-year training course closer to where her husband was based. Her employer made the discriminatory assumption that married women normally move jobs to follow their husbands and therefore she would not return to her original job after completing the period of secondment.

Part-time workers and employees who are on a fixed-term contract have the right to be treated no less favourably than comparable full-time and permanent employees. See FIXED-TERM AND PART-TIME WORKERS (10). Discrimination against part-time and/or fixed-term workers may also amount to unlawful sex discrimination.

8.42   Benefits, facilities or services

The EOC's *Code of Practice* (1985) recommends (at para 28) that all terms of employment, benefits, facilities and services are reviewed to ensure that there is no unlawful discrimination on grounds of sex or marriage. For example, part-time work, domestic leave, company cars and benefits for dependants should be available to both male and female employees in the same or not materially different circumstances.

The EOC's *Code of Practice* (1985) also recommends (at para 29) that in an establishment where part-timers are solely or mainly women, unlawful indirect discrimination may arise if, as a group, they are treated less favourably than other employees without justification. It is therefore recommended that where part-time workers do not enjoy pro-rata pay or benefits with full-time workers, the arrangements should be reviewed to ensure that they are justified without regard to sex. See FIXED-TERM AND PART-TIME WORKERS (10) for the significant body of case law on discrimination against part-time employees.

EqPA 1970 prohibits discrimination in relation to any contractual terms, not just those relating to pay. *SDA 1975* applies in relation to any matter which is not included in the contractual terms, even if it is concerned with pay or financial benefits. No claim can be brought under the *SDA 1975* in cases where *EqPA 1970* applies. See *SDA 1975, ss 6(6), 8(5), Peake v Automotive Products Ltd* [1977] ICR 480, EAT and EQUAL PAY (11).

A woman cannot claim under *SDA 1975* about matters relating to the payment of money if this is regulated by her contract of employment (*SDA 1975, s 6(6)*). In

Hoyland v ASDA Stores Ltd [2006] IRLR 468, the Court of Session (Scotland) held that a claim about a discretionary bonus was 'regulated' by the contract of employment and therefore came within *EqPA 1970*, even though the entitlement was not part of the formal contract of employment (see also 8.112).

The *EC Treaty, Article 141(1)*, which confers a directly enforceable right to equal pay for equal work or work of equal value, applies to pay which is defined in *Article 141(2)* as 'the ordinary basic or minimum wage or salary and any other consideration, whether in cash or in kind, which the worker receives directly or indirectly, in respect of his employment, from his employer.' This definition is wide enough to include a claim in respect of non-contractual pay, and therefore may be relied upon in a claim under *SDA 1975*.

A claim may only be made in respect of benefits, facilities or services which are already in existence, but are being denied to a particular employee. In *Clymo v Wandsworth London Borough Council* [1989] IRLR 241, the EAT held that a refusal to allow a woman to job share was not a refusal to allow access to a 'facility' under *SDA 1975, s 6(2)(a)* since job sharing was not available to any workers in her grade; however, it is unlikely that this case would not decided the same way today because of different social and legal norms (see 8.145).

A trivial advantage in treatment, such as allowing women to leave five minutes early to avoid the peak hour 'crush', was held not to be a sufficient benefit to amount to discrimination against men in *Peak v Automotive Products Ltd* [1977] IRLR 365, CA, although it is questionable whether the case would be decided on the same basis today.

8.43   Dismissal or any other detriment

In many cases, a sex discrimination claim under *SDA 1975* will be combined with a claim for unfair dismissal. The absence of any cap on the award of compensation and the lack of any qualifying period of employment makes a discrimination claim the preferred choice for claimants.

The EOC's *Code of Practice* (1985) makes a number of recommendations (para 32) in relation to dismissal, discipline and working conditions.

The definition of 'dismissal' in *SDA 1975, s 82(1A)* includes non-renewal of a fixed-term or constructive dismissal.

Maternity and family leave dismissals are dealt with in 8.73–8.77.

It is not necessary to demonstrate physical disadvantage or financial loss if arguing that the employee has been subject to a detriment (see COMMON CONCEPTS (1)). An employee does not suffer a 'detriment' if she is denied a benefit which is not provided to others in the same grade of employment. In *Clymo v Wandsworth London Borough Council* [1989] 2 CMLR 577, [1989] ICR 250, the EAT held that Mrs Clymo was not subjected to a detriment when she was refused permission to job share, as no one else in her grade was entitled to do so. This case would probably not be decided the same way today.

Dress codes which impose different rules on male and female employees have generally been held not to be discriminatory on the grounds that, if the codes are different but equal, then less favourable treatment is not established. See COMMON CONCEPTS (1). However, a dress code which was less favourable to one sex could constitute a 'detriment'.

Under *SDA 1975, s 6(3)*, it is unlawful for an employer to harass an employee.

8.44 *Ex-employees*

SDA 1975, s 20A provides that where an employment relationship has come to an end, discrimination or harassment on grounds of sex is unlawful where it arises out of and is closely connected with the employment. The employment relationships include those covered by *SDA 1975, Part II.*

S 20A came into force in July 2003. In *Relaxion Group plc v Rhys-Harper* [2003] UKHL 33, [2003] 4 All ER 1113 (which pre-dated this section coming into force) the House of Lords held that *SDA 1975, s 6(2)* could not be extended to cover a complaint of sex discrimination made by a woman after she had been dismissed. However, in *Coote v Granada Hospitality Ltd* [1998] IRLR 656 the ECJ held that the *Equal Treatment Directive* required that protection be given to an ex-employee whose former employer was victimising her by refusing to provide references after she had brought proceedings against him to enforce her equality rights.

8.45 **Unlawful discrimination by other bodies**

Trade organisations

SDA 1975, s 12(1)–(3) prohibits organisations of workers, employers' organisations and other trade and professional bodies from discriminating against members and applicants for membership. It is unlawful to discriminate against an applicant in the terms on which membership is offered or by refusing to grant membership. See COMMON CONCEPTS (1).

Trade organisations may engage in positive action in relation to their members. See 8.63ff.

8.46 *Qualifying bodies*

SDA 1975, s 13 prohibits discrimination by bodies which confer qualifications for a profession or trade. *S 13(1)* provides that it is unlawful for an authority or body which can confer an authorisation or qualification which is needed for, or facilitates, engagement in a particular profession or trade to discriminate against a woman:

(a) in the terms on which it is prepared to confer on her that authorisation or qualification;

(b) by refusing or deliberately omitting to grant her application for it; or

(c) by withdrawing it from her or varying the terms on which she holds it.

It is unlawful for a qualifying body to harass a woman who holds or applies for an authorisation qualification.

In *British Judo Association v Petty* [1981] IRLR 484, the EAT rejected the respondent's argument that *s 13* only applied where the qualifying body's purpose in issuing a certificate (in that case, to referee judo) was to facilitate the certificate-holder's qualification or trade. The EAT held that *s 13* covered all cases where the qualification in fact facilitated the woman's employment whether or not it was so intended by the qualifying body. It was not necessary to show detriment or loss. See also *Hardwick v Football Association* UKEAT/1036/97.

'Authorisation' or 'qualification' includes recognition, registration, enrolment, approval and certification (*SDA 1975, s 13(3)(a)*); 'to 'confer' an authorisation' or qualification includes renewing or extending it (*s 13(3)(b)*).

Where there is a statutory right of appeal, or proceedings in the nature of an appeal, against a particular act, a complaint under *s 13* cannot be made to a tribunal first (*s 63(2)*).

S 13 does not apply to educational establishments or local education authorities (*s 13(4), (5)*).

S 19(2) permits a qualifying body to specify a person of one gender in relation to an authorisation or qualification for the purposes of an organised religion either:

(a)   so as to comply with the doctrines of the religion, or

(b)   to avoid conflicting with the strongly held religious convictions of a significant number of the religion's followers.

See below at 8.49ff.

Where a qualifying body is required by law to satisfy itself as to a person's good character before conferring on him an authorisation or qualification, it is required to have regard to any evidence tending to show that he or any of her employees or agents has practised unlawful discrimination in the carrying on of any profession or trade.

8.47   *Vocational training*

By *SDA 1975, s 14* it is unlawful for any person who provides, or makes arrangements for the provision of, facilities for vocational training to discriminate against a woman seeking or receiving vocational training:

(a)   in the arrangements for selection;

(b)   in the terms on which access is afforded;

(c)   by refusing or omitting to afford such access;

(d)   by terminating the training; or

(e)   by subjecting her to any detriment during the course of the training.

It is unlawful for a provider to harass a woman on vocational training or who seeks vocational training (*s 14(1A)*).

'Vocational training' is defined in *s 82(1)* as, 'all types and all levels of vocational training, advanced vocational training and retraining', 'vocational guidance' and 'practical work experience undertaken for a limited period for the purposes of a person's vocational training'. It also includes (if it would not otherwise do so) any training which would help fit a woman for employment (*s 14(1B)*).

In *Fletcher v Blackpool Fylde and Wyre Hospitals NHS Trust* [2005] IRLR 689, EAT, trainee midwives were entitled to claim under *s 14* when their bursaries were terminated during maternity absence from their course. The bursary was held to be a facility connected with training, falling within the scope of a 'working condition' under *Equal Treatment Directive, Article 3*.

In *Lana v Positive Action Training in Housing (London) Ltd* [2001] IRLR 501, EAT the respondents were liable for the termination of the claimant's work placement with a firm on grounds of her pregnancy. By authorising the unlawful termination, the respondents were liable under *s 41(2)*. See also 8.67 and COMMON CONCEPTS (1).

A 10-day unpaid internship for prospective trainees in the civil service was 'training' within the meaning of the equivalent provisions in *RRA 1976* (*Treasury Solicitor's Department v Chenge* [2007] IRLR 386).

S 14 does not apply to discrimination prohibited by *s 6* (job applicants and employees), nor to educational establishments covered by *ss 22–23* (see on jurisdiction, *Moyhing v Homerton University Hospitals NHS Trust* UKEAT/0851/04/MAA, [2005] All ER (D) and the second decision in *Moyhing* on detriment at [2006] IRLR 860).

S 16(1) provides that it is unlawful for the Secretary of State to discriminate, or subject a woman to harassment, in the provision of facilities or services under *Employment and Training Act 1973, s 2*. There is a similar provision in relation to Scottish Enterprise or Highlands and Islands Enterprise (see *s 16(1A)*).

SDA 1975 permits positive action in relation to vocational training. See 8.63ff.

8.48   *Employment agencies*

Under *SDA 1975, s 15(1)*, it is unlawful for an employment agency to discriminate against a woman:

(a)   in the terms on which the agency offers to provide any of its services; or

(b)   by refusing or deliberately omitting to provide any of its services; or

(c)   in the way it provides any of its services.

It is unlawful for an employment agency to harass a woman to whom it has provided services, or who has requested services (*s 15(1A)*).

Services provided by an employment agency include guidance on careers and any other services related to employment (*s 15(3)*). In *Silveira v Brocklebank* UKEAT/0571/05, [2006] All ER (D) 157 an employment agency which failed to carry out a risk assessment on a pregnant woman omitted to provide a service, in breach of *s 15(1)(b)*.

Discrimination by schools, colleges and local education authorities in the provision of services under *Employment and Training Act 1973, s 10* is unlawful (*s 15(2)*). This includes careers guidance.

The section does not apply if the discrimination relates to employment which an employer could lawfully refuse to offer the woman, eg where there is a genuine occupational qualification (*s 15(4)*). An employment agency or other body will not be liable if it proves that it acted reasonably in relying on a statement by the employer that he could lawfully refuse to offer the woman employment (*s 15(5)*).

The EOC's *Code of Practice* (1985) refers to employment agencies at para 9. There is more extensive guidance in the CRE's *Code of Practice* (2005) at paras 5.11–5.19, which although in the context of race, provides some useful analogies.

8.49   **Exceptions**

Acts of discrimination which would otherwise be unlawful are expressly excluded from the scope of *SDA 1975*. The exclusion may be by reason of:

(a)   the type of provision offered (see 8.50–8.54);

(b)   the nature of the position held (see 8.54–8.59); and

(c)   the nature of the activity (see 8.60–8.62).

8.50 Sex Discrimination

8.50 *Benefits, facilities or services*

Under *SDA 1975, s 6(7)*, benefits, facilities or services which the employer is concerned with the provision (for payment or not) to the public or to a section of the public comprising the woman in question are excluded unless:

(a) that provision differs in a material respect from the provision made by the employer to his employees;

(b) the provision to the woman in question is regulated by her contract of employment; and

(c) the benefits, facilities or services relate to training.

8.51 *Maternity leave*

Terms and conditions during maternity leave are excluded – see 8.108ff

8.52 *Occupational pensions*

Discrimination in relation to membership of, or rights under, an occupational pension scheme falls within the scope of *EC Treaty, Article 141* and *EqPA 1970* (see EQUAL PAY (11)). A discrimination claim would usually be made under *EqPA 1970*, not *SDA 1975*.

EC Treaty, Article 141 has been implemented in domestic law by the *Pensions Act 1995* and associated regulations, and the *Social Security Act 1989, Sch 5*, which treat occupational pension schemes as containing an 'equal treatment' rule, prohibiting sex discrimination, subject to certain exclusions and limitations.

SDA 1975, s 6(4) provides that it is not unlawful for an employer to discriminate against a job applicant or an employee in relation to membership of, or rights under, an occupational pension scheme if the *Pensions Act 1995* does not give effect to an equal treatment rule in relation to the relevant term of the scheme.

8.53 *Insurance*

SDA 1975, s 45 provides that discrimination in relation to insurance policies which involve an assessment of risk are not unlawful where the disparity in treatment is based on actuarial data on which it is reasonable to rely and the treatment is reasonable, having regard to that data and any other relevant factors.

8.54 *Communal accommodation and sport*

By *SDA 1975, ss 44* and *46* there are certain exemptions for communal accommodation and sport. The sports exception only applies to competitors, not officials (*British Judo Association v Petty* [1981] IRLR 484, where *s 44* was held not to apply to a referee).

8.55 *Genuine occupational qualifications*

The *Equal Treatment Directive, Article 2.6* provides that a difference in treatment based on a characteristic related to sex shall not constitute discrimination in access to employment and training where by reason of the particular activities or the context in which they are carried out, the characteristic constitutes a genuine and determining occupational requirement, providing that the objective is legitimate and the requirement is proportionate. The *2006 Directive, Article 14.2,* which consolidates and updates the major directives on equal treatment, is in the same terms. It is arguable that the provisions of *SDA 1975* do not give adequate effect to the principle of proportionality in this context.

SDA 1975, s 7(1) provides that where gender is a genuine occupational qualification (GOQ) for a job, it is not unlawful to discriminate:

(a)   in the arrangements made for determining who should be offered that job;

(b)   by refusing or deliberately omitting to offer the job to someone of the opposite gender; or

(c)   in affording opportunities for promotion, transfer to, or training for that job.

Employers are at liberty to appoint, say, a woman to a job for which being a man is a genuine occupational qualification. If they do, it is unlawful to discriminate against the woman once she is in a job, for example, in the provision of benefits or by dismissing her. See *Timex Corporation v Hodgson* [1981] IRLR 530.

There are specific provisions for contract workers (*s 9(3)–(3D)*) and for partnerships (*s 11(3)–(3D)*).

Although *SDA 1975* is silent on the point, the general view is that the employer must prove that a GOQ applies.

Qualifying and training bodies (*ss 13–14*) cannot rely on a GOQ (*Moyhing v Barts and London NHS Trust* [2006] IRLR 860).

The GOQ exception applies to direct and indirect discrimination, but not to victimisation.

The GOQ exception does not apply to discrimination on grounds of marital status.

S 7(2) sets out an exhaustive list of GOQs. Reasons which do not fit any of the statutory categories cannot be relied upon (*Greig v Community Industries* [1979] IRLR 158). *S 7(2)* refers to GOQ for men, but the list applies equally to GOQ for women. The list is set out below:

• Under *s 7(2)(a)*, a job where its essential nature of the job calls for a man for reasons of physiology (excluding physical strength or stamina) or, in dramatic performance or other entertainment, for reasons of authenticity, so that the essential nature of the job would be materially different if carried out by a woman.

• Under *s 7(2)(b)*, (*ba*), a job which needs to be held by a man to preserve decency or privacy because:

(a)   it is likely to involve physical contact with men in circumstances where they might reasonably object to its being carried out by a woman; or

(b)   the holder of the job is likely to do her work in circumstances where men might reasonably object to the presence of a woman because they are in a state of undress or are using sanitary facilities; or

(c)   the job is likely to involve work in a private home and objection might reasonably be taken to allowing a woman–

(i)   the degree of physical or social contact with a person living in the home; and

(ii)   the knowledge of intimate details of such a person's life.

Illustrations of the application of this GOQ may be found *in Wylie v Dee & Co. (Menswear) Ltd* [1978] IRLR 103; *Etam plc v Rowan* [1989] IRLR 150 (both sales assistants in clothing stores); *Timex Corporation v Hodgson* [1981] IRLR 530 (female first aid and toilet duties); *Lasertop Ltd v Webster* [1997] IRLR 498 (access to changing rooms and sauna in women-only leisure club); *Sisley v Britannia Security Systems Ltd* [1983] IRLR 404 (female security staff slept in underwear to avoid crumpling uniforms).

- Under *s 7(2)(c)*, where the nature of the job, or its location, makes it impracticable for the employees to live away from the employer's premises, the only premises available do not have separate sleeping accommodation and sanitary facilities for men and women, and it is not reasonable for the employer to provide them. See *Sisley v Britannia Security Systems Ltd* [1983] IRLR 404 (all female security staff in sleeping accommodation on premises, not practical to provide accommodation separately for one male employee).

- Under *s 7(2)(d)*, where the nature of the establishment requires the job to be held by a man because it is in a hospital, prison or other establishment giving special care, supervision or attention to only one sex and it is reasonable that the job should not be held by someone of the opposite sex.

- Under *s 7(2)(e)*, the holder of the job provides individuals with personal services promoting their welfare or education, or similar personal services, and those services can most effectively be provided by a man. The potential breadth of this exception is unclear. It could apply to social workers, probation officers, teachers etc. In *Roadburg v Lothian Regional Council* [1976] IRLR 283, the employer failed to establish a GOQ when he wished to appoint a man to the post of volunteer services officer which sometimes involved work with male clients. The case law under the analogous provision *Race Relations Act 1976, s 5* is useful. See RACE DISCRIMINATION (6), in particular, *Tottenham Green Under Five's Centre v Marshall* [1989] IRLR 147 (a nursery wanted to recruit an Afro-Caribbean worker to provide services for Afro-Caribbean children, the ET found the GOQ was not established, but the appeal was allowed because the ET had required employer to show it was 'essential' to have an Afro-Caribbean worker, which was too high a threshold); *London Borough of Lambeth v Commission for Racial Equality* [1990] IRLR 231, CA (management posts did not involve the provision of 'personal services').

- Under *s 7(2)(g)*, if the job needs to be held by a man because it is likely to involve the performance of duties outside the UK in a country whose laws or customs are such that the duties could not effectively be performed by a woman.

- Under *s 7(2)(h)*, where the job is one of two to be held by a married couple or civil partnership. See MARITAL STATUS AND CIVIL PARTNERSHIPS (5).

A GOQ may apply to a post even if only some of the duties fall within the statutory list (*s 7(3)*). The proportion of GOQ duties to non-GOQ duties is not a relevant consideration (*Lasertop Ltd v Webster* [1997] IRLR 498). The statutory GOQs do not apply in relation to the filling of a vacancy if at the time of filling the vacancy, the employer already has male employees who are capable of carrying out the duties within the statutory list, and it would be reasonable and not unduly inconvenient to expect them to do so (*s 7(4)*). See, for example, *Wylie v Dee & Co (Menswear) Ltd* [1978] IRLR 103 where there were seven other male shop assistants who could assist in measuring a male customer's inside leg and therefore this was not a valid reason to refuse the female claimant a job in menswear store.

8.56   *Ministers of religion*

SDA 1975, s 19(1), (2) permits gender discrimination in relation to employment, authorisation or qualification for an organised religion either:

(a)   so as to comply with the doctrines of the religion, or

(b)   to avoid conflicting with the strongly held religious convictions of a significant number of the religion's followers.

The permitted discrimination is where it is a requirement:

(a)   to be of a particular sex;

(b)   not to be undergoing or to have undergone a gender reassignment; or

(c)   in respect of marriage or civil partnership.

8.57   *Educational appointments*

The *Employment Act 1989, s 5(3)* exempts the application of *SDA 1975* to appointments of staff at women-only colleges which were established before *SDA 1975* came into force.

The *Employment Act 1989, s 5(1)* provides that, where any instrument relating to an educational establishment requires that its head teacher should be a member of a particular religious order, then an otherwise unlawful act done in relation to the appointment of the head teacher is not unlawful.

8.58   *Prison officers*

SDA 1975, s 18 permits discrimination in relation to height.

8.59   *Police*

SDA 1975, s 17(2) permits regulations made under the *Police Act 1996* to treat men and women differently with regard to:

(a)   requirements relating to height, uniform or equipment (or allowances in lieu);

(b)   special treatment afforded to women in connection with pregnancy or childbirth; and

(c)   pensions for special constables or police cadets.

See also 8.33.

8.60   *Acts authorised by statute*

Following criticism of UK domestic law by the ECJ in *Johnston v Chief Constable of the Royal Ulster Constabulary* [1986] IRLR 263, the *Employment Act 1989* limited the scope of statutory authority as a basis for exemption from *SDA 1975*. The exemption is confined to provisions for the protection of women, principally in the context of pregnancy and childbirth. This is intended to be consistent with the breadth of the exemption in *Equal Treatment Directive, Article 2(7)* for 'provisions concerning the protection of women, particularly pregnancy and maternity'.

The *Employment Act 1989, s 1* provides that any statutory provision passed before *SDA 1975* shall be of no effect in so far as it imposes a requirement to do an act now rendered unlawful by *SDA 1975, Parts II* and *III* in relation to vocational training and the application of *Part III* to those provisions. The *Employment Act 1989, s 1(3)* makes provision for indirectly discriminatory provisions, stating that it shall be for the respondent to show that the provision, criterion or practice in question is justifiable.

The amended *SDA 1975, s 51(1)* renders lawful any act done by a person which is necessary:

(a)   to comply with statutory provisions concerning the protection of women which pre-date the *SDA 1975* (including re-enactments); or

(b)   to comply with a requirement of a relevant statutory provision (within the meaning of the *Health and Safety at Work etc Act 1974, Part I*) if it was done by that person for the purpose of the protection of the woman in question (or of any class of women that included that woman).

In *Page v Freight Hire (Tank Haulage) Ltd* [1981] 1 All ER 394, [1981] ICR 299, a female tanker driver was prevented from driving tankers carrying chemicals which were dangerous to women of childbearing age. She told the company she did not want children and she was aware of the risks. Nonetheless, the EAT held that the employer had a defence to a claim of sex discrimination under *SDA 1975, s 51*, as it was obliged to ensure the health and safety of its employees under the *Health and Safety at Work etc Act 1974*. Although this case pre-dates the amendment to *s 51*, it would probably be decided in the same way today.

The *Employment Act 1989, s 4* supplements *SDA 1975, s 51* by providing that nothing shall render any act done by a person in relation to a woman unlawful if it was necessary to comply with the health and safety provisions listed in *SDA 1975, Sch 1*.

8.61   *National security*

SDA 1975, s 52 provides that nothing in *Parts II–IV* shall render unlawful an act done for the purpose of safeguarding national security. In *Johnston v The Chief Constable of the Royal Ulster Constabulary* [1987] QB 129, [1986] 3 All ER 135, a woman was prevented from taking on a full-time permanent post because this would require her to carry firearms. In considering equivalent Northern Ireland provisions, the ECJ rejected the submission that *EC Treaty, Article 224*, on public security, entitled the Government to disregard EU anti-discrimination measures. It also disapproved of the procedure under *SDA 1975, s 53(2)* entitling a Minister to certify that an act was done for the purpose of safeguarding national security (that provision has now been repealed in relation to *Part II* and vocational training in *Part III: Sex Discrimination (Amendment) Order 1988 (SI 1988/249)*). The ECJ held that the RUC was entitled to rely on *Equal Treatment Directive, Article 2(2)* (now replaced by *Article 2(6)*) permitting Member States to exclude occupational activities where the sex of the worker is a determining factor, provided that the principle of proportionality was observed. See also 8.55.

8.62   *Charities*

SDA 1975, s 43(2) renders it lawful for charities to confer benefits on persons of one sex provided it is pursuant to a provision contained in a charitable instrument, as defined in *s 43(3)*. This exception only applies to a charity's beneficiaries, not to its employees. In England and Wales, the charitable purposes must be exclusively charitable. This is not a requirement in Scotland. The charitable purposes recognised in law are the relief of poverty, advancement of education, advancement of religion, and other purposes beneficial to the community.

8.63 **Positive discrimination and positive action**

The principal purpose of *SDA 1975* is to prohibit discrimination between men and women. Positive discrimination (ie discrimination in favour of women to the detriment of men) is unlawful. However, positive action (ie action to overcome historical inequalities between men and women) is permitted and encouraged under EU law. The *EC Treaty* provides:

'The Community shall have as its task (by various means therein set out) to promote ... equality between men and women' (*Article 2*).

'In all the activities referred to in the Article, the Community shall aim to eliminate inequalities and to promote equality, between men and women' (*Article 3*).

'The principle of equal treatment shall not prevent any Member State from maintaining or adopting measures providing for specific advantages in order to make it easier for the under-represented sex to pursue a vocational activity or to prevent or compensate for disadvantages in professional careers' (*Article 141(4)*).

The *Equal Treatment Directive 76/207/EEC* provides:

'Member States shall actively take into account the objective of equality between men and women when formulating and implementing laws, regulations, administrative provisions, policies and activities in the areas referred to in paragraph 1' (*Article 1, para 1(2)*).

'Member States may maintain or adopt measures within the meaning of *Article 141(4)* of the *Treaty* with a view to ensuring full equality in practice between men and women' (*Article 2, para 8*).

The distinction between lawful positive action and unlawful positive discrimination has been considered by the ECJ in *Kalanke v Freie Hanestadt Bremen* [1995] ECR I–3051, [1996] All ER (EC) 66; *Marschall v Land Nordrhein-Westfalen* [1998] IRLR 39; *Re Georg Badeck and Ors* [2000] IRLR 432; *Abrahamsson and Anderson v Fogelgvist* [2000] IRLR 732; *Lommers v Minister Van Landbouw, Natuurbeheer en Visserij* [2002] ECR I-2891, [2004] 2 CMLR 1141. The case law was reviewed in *Briheche v Ministre for the Interior, Internal Security and Local Freedoms* [2004] ECR 1–8807, the ECJ stating (at paragraph 23):

'A measure which is intended to give priority in promotion to women in sectors of the public service must be regarded as compatible with Community law if it does not automatically and unconditionally give priority to women when women and men are equally qualified, and the candidatures are the subject of an objective assessment which takes account of the specific personal situations of all candidates.'

UK domestic law only permits positive action in very limited circumstances, set out below.

8.64 *Training*

SDA 1975, s 47 permits positive action to redress gender imbalance in certain industries. Where it reasonably appears that, at any time within the previous 12 months there were no persons of the gender in question doing a particular type of work, or the number was comparatively small, *s 47* permits provision of facilities for the training of the minority gender or encouragement to take up that work.

The comparison of the number of men and women carrying out the work in question must be in the whole of Great Britain or in an area of Great Britain. Where the comparison is confined to an area, the minority gender must appear likely to take up that work in that area.

A provider may be 'any person', such as a local authority or training organisation. *S 47* is not aimed at employers who take positive action under *s 48* (see below). Discrimination contrary to *s 6* (against job applicants and employees) is not permitted under *s 47* (see *s 47(4)*).

S 47(3) permits training for employment directed at those who have been out of work because they have been discharging family responsibilities, even though this may be discriminatory.

The Employment *Act 1989, s 8* contains a specific power for the Secretary of State to authorise training arrangements for lone parents, without breaching *SDA 1975, s 3* (discrimination on grounds of marital status). Two orders have been made providing for child care payments while participating in government training schemes.

SDA 1975, s 48(1) permits positive action by employers to redress gender imbalance among employees. Where at any time within the previous 12 months there were no persons of the gender in question doing particular work, or the number was comparatively small, *s 48(1)* permits provision of facilities for the training of the minority gender or encouragement to take up that work.

The EOC's 'Code of Practice for the Elimination of Discrimination' (1985) suggests positive measures for employers to adopt such as:

(a)   training their own employees for work which is traditionally the preserve of the other sex; encouraging women to apply for management posts;

(b)   advertisements which encourage application from the minority sex but make it clear that selection will be on merit without reference to sex; and

(c)   notifying job agencies, as part of a Positive Action Programme, that they wish to encourage members of the minority sex to apply for vacancies. In those circumstances, job agencies should tell both men and women about the posts but let the minority sex know that applications from them are particularly welcome.

S 48(2) permits positive action by trade organisations covered by *s 12 t*o redress gender imbalance within their organisations. Where at any time within the previous 12 months there were no persons of the gender in question holding particular posts in the organisation, or the number was comparatively small, *s 48(2)* permits provision of facilities for the training of the minority gender or encouragement to take up such posts. A similar provision applies to encouraging members of the organisation (*s 48(3)*).

Harvey on Industrial Relations and Employment Law, paragraph L464, suggests that *ss 47* and *48* may contravene the principles set out in *Kalanke v Greie Hanestadt Bremen* and other ECJ judgments (see 8.63), in so far as they entail applying a quota, and thus guaranteeing women a position, regardless of the individual merit of candidates of both sexes.

8.65   *Elections*

SDA 1975, s 42A excludes from the scope of *SDA 1975, Parts II–IV* arrangements made by registered political parties to regulate the selection of the party's candidates for the purpose of reducing inequality in the number of men and women elected as candidates in parliamentary, local government and European elections. This provision was added as an amendment to reverse the effect of *Jepson and Dyas-Elliott v Labour Party* [1996] IRLR 116, in which a tribunal held that all-women shortlists were unlawful.

In *McDonagh and Triesman v Ali* [2002] EWCA Civ 93, [2002] ICR 1026, the Court of Appeal held that *RRA 1976, s 12* – the equivalent provision to *SDA 1975, s 13* – did not apply to the Labour Party's procedures for selecting candidates since it was selecting individuals for its own purposes, not authorising them carry out a particular occupation. See 8.45.

Where a trade organisation covered by *SDA 1975, s 12* (for example, a trade union) has elected members, it may set a minimum number of males or females on its elected body, and may reserve seats or make extra seats available. See 8.45.

8.66   *Public authorities*

SDA 1975, s 76A imposes a general duty on public authorities:

> 'to have due regard to the need –
>
> (a)   to eliminate unlawful discrimination and harassment and
>
> (b)   to promote equality of opportunity between men and women.'

A 'public authority' is defined as any person who has 'functions of a public nature', utilising the same definition as the *Human Rights Act 1998, s 6*. This plainly includes local authorities and public sector bodies. In the human rights context, this definition has given rise to difficulties in the case of private bodies performing functions on behalf of public bodies (recently considered by the House of Lords in *YL v Birmingham County Council (Secretary of State for Constitutional Affairs intervening)* [2007] UKHL 27, [2007] 3 All ER 957). See the EOC's 'Code of Practice on Gender Equality Duty' (2007)', Appendix A on the definition of a public authority.

Bodies such as Parliament, the General Synod of the Church of England, the security and intelligence services, and other persons specified by the Secretary of State are expressly excluded from the duty by *s 76A(3)*.

Breach of the duty does not confer a cause of action at private law (*s 76A(6)*) but may be relied upon in a claim for judicial review (see *Equality Act 2006, s 32*). *SDA 1975* confers enforcement powers on the Commission in *s 76D*, enabling it to serve a notice requiring a body to comply and to make an application to a county court in the event of non-compliance.

The EOC has issued a 'Code of Practice on Gender Equality Duty' (2007) under *SDA 1975, s 76E*. The main focus of this Code is on public authorities as providers of services to the public, but the Code also addresses the duties of public authorities as employers to be proactive in eliminating discrimination and promoting equality of opportunity.

The Code provides guidance and illustrations of positive action which can be taken to:

(a)   ensure implementation through clear staff roles (paras 2.40–2.44);

(b)   build staff expertise (paras 2.45, 2.46);

(c)   meet the gender equality duty in policy development (paras 2.49–2.52);

(d)   meet the gender equality duty in employment (paras 2.62–2.64);

(e)   review practice and procedures in relation to transsexual employees and potential employees (paras 2.65, 2.66);

(f)   meet the gender equality duty for equal pay (paras 2.67, 2.68, 3.40–3.56);

(g)   meet the duty to eliminate harassment (paras 2.69–2.77).

The *Sex Discrimination Act 1975 (Public Authorities) (Statutory Duties) Order 2006 (SI 2006/2930)* imposes specific duties on those public authorities listed. Details are given in Chapter 3 of the Code and Appendices C and D. Public authorities are required to:

(a)   prepare and publish a Gender Equality Scheme;

(b)   ensure that the Scheme sets out the actions the authority has taken or intends to take to gather information on the effect of its policies and practices on men and women in employment, services, and the performance of its functions;

(c)   use the information to review the implementation of the scheme objectives;

(d)   assess the impact of its current and future policies and practices on gender equality;

(e)   consult relevant employees, services users and others (including trade unions);

(f)   implement the scheme and actions for gathering and using information within three years of publication of the scheme unless impracticable to do so;

(g)   review and revise the scheme at least every three years; and

(h)   report on progress annually.

8.67   **Liability of individuals and employers**

This issue, and the case law, is considered fully in COMMON CONCEPTS (1). The legislative framework is summarised below.

Anything done by a person in the course of his employment shall be treated as done by his employer, as well as by him, whether or not it was done with the employer's knowledge and approval (*SDA 1975, s 41(1)*). However, it is a defence to proceedings brought under *SDA 1975* for an employer to prove that he took such steps as were reasonably practicable to prevent the employee from doing that act, or from doing in the course of his employment acts of that description (*s 41(3)*).

Anything done by a person as agent for another person with the authority (express or implied, precedent or subsequent) of that other person shall be treated as done by that other person as well as by him (*s 41(2)*).

A person who knowingly aids another person to do an unlawful act under *SDA 1975* shall be treated as doing that unlawful act himself (*s 42(1)*). By *s 42(3)*, a person does not knowingly aid another if:

(a)   he acts in reliance on a statement made to him by that other person that the act which he aids would not be unlawful under the *SDA 1975*; and

(b)   it is reasonable for him to rely on the statement.

S 39 provides that it is unlawful for a person who has authority over another person, or in accordance with whose wishes that other person is accustomed to act, to instruct him to do any act which is unlawful under *SDA 1975, Parts II or III*, or procure or attempt to procure him to do such an act. Proceedings for contravention of *s 39* may only be brought by the EHRC.

Under *s 40*, it is unlawful to induce, or attempt to induce, a person to do any act which contravenes *Parts II or III* by providing or offering any benefit, or subjecting or threatening to subject him to any detriment. Proceedings for contravention of *s 40* may only be brought by the EHRC.

8.68   **DISCRIMINATION ON THE GROUNDS OF PREGNANCY AND MATERNITY**

An overview of the position prior to 1 October 2005

Prior to 1 October 2005, a female who claimed discrimination on the grounds of pregnancy or maternity brought her complaint under the general prohibition of sex discrimination under *SDA 1975, s 2*. Historically, this meant that she had to identify an appropriate male comparator (whether actual or hypothetical) to demonstrate that she has suffered less favourable treatment.

However, in the case of discrimination on the grounds of her pregnancy, the requirement for a comparator raised difficulties, since only women are capable of childbirth. The UK courts initially agreed that a pregnant employee should be compared to a male employee who was unavailable for work for medical reasons; however, the ECJ rejected this approach (see *Dekker v Stichting Vormingscentrum Voor Jong Volwassen (VJV – Centrum) Plus* [1990] ECR I-3941, [1992] ICR 325 and *Webb v EMO Air Cargo (UK) Ltd* [1995] IRLR 645). The ECJ made it clear that less favourable treatment on the grounds of pregnancy was gender-specific and so a male comparator was not required. In addition, in *Gillespie v Northern Health and Social Services Board* [1996] ECR I-475, [1996] All ER (EC) 284 the ECJ (at page 513) referred to pregnant women as being in a '... special position which requires them to be afforded special protection, but which is not comparable either with that of a man or that of a woman actually at work'. As a result of the ECJ jurisprudence, the UK courts disapplied the statutory requirement for a comparator in pregnancy and maternity cases.

8.69   **The position since 1 October 2005**

The Government sought to codify the position in respect of discrimination on the grounds of pregnancy and maternity by the insertion of *s 3A* into *SDA 1975* by the *Employment Equality (Sex Discrimination) Regulations 2005 (SI 2005/2467)*. *S 3A* came into force on 1 October 2005 and specifically prohibits discrimination on the grounds of pregnancy and maternity where:

(a)   at a time in a 'protected period' and on the grounds of the woman's pregnancy, she is treated less favourably than if she were not pregnant (*s 3A(1)(a)*); or

(b)   she exercises, or seeks to exercise, or has exercised, or sought to exercise a statutory right to maternity leave and she is treated less favourably than if she were not seeking to exercise that right (*s 3A(1)(b)*).

S 3A(2) also provides that a woman is discriminated against if she is treated less favourably on the grounds that she is not permitted to work during the compulsory maternity leave (CML) period than she would have been if the CML provision did not apply to her. *S 3A* applies to all those individuals protected by *SDA 1975, Part II.*

8.70   *Protected period*

For the purposes of *s 3A*, the protected period is defined as any time during which the woman is pregnant or on maternity leave. If the woman is not entitled to maternity leave, then the protected period ends two weeks after the end of the pregnancy (*s 3A(3)(1)*).

In addition, the provision makes it clear that a person's treatment of a woman on the grounds of her pregnancy-related illness is to be equated with treatment on the grounds of the pregnancy itself (*s 3A(3)(b)*).

The special protection for pregnancy-related discrimination ends at the end of the protected period. After this point, a woman must compare her unfavourable treatment with the treatment of a real or hypothetical man in similar circumstances.

8.71   **The position from 2007**

The EOC successfully brought an application for judicial review before the High Court in March 2007 in respect of *SDA 1975, s 3A* (see *Equal Opportunities Commission v Secretary of State for Trade and Industry* [2007] IRLR 327).

The EOC contended that *s 3A* did not comply with the UK's obligations under the *Equal Treatment Directive* as the wording of *s 3A* still required a comparator, albeit not a male comparator. This is because *s 3A* requires the woman to show that she had been treated less favourably than she would have been had she not been pregnant or not taken maternity leave. The High Court was persuaded by the argument that this was inconsistent with the ECJ's case law and held that *s 3A* should be recast so as to eliminate the statutory requirement for a comparator who is not pregnant or is not on maternity leave.

DBERR confirmed that amending regulations will be implemented. These regulations were due to come into force on 1 October 2007; however this date was not met and at the time of writing it is not clear when the draft regulations will become available or when they will come into force.

8.72   **Discrimination against men**

With regards to sex discrimination against men, no account shall be taken of special treatment afforded to women in connection with pregnancy or childbirth (*SDA 1975, s 2*).

8.73   **Pregnancy and maternity-related dismissals: discrimination claims**

Prior to the specific unfair dismissal and discrimination protection introduced by *ERA 1996, s 99* and *SDA 1975, s 3A*, it was well established that dismissing an employee because of her pregnancy amounted to direct discrimination on the grounds of sex (*Dekker* and *Webb v EMO*) and that no comparator was required; see 8.68.

In *Tele Danmark A/S v Handels-og Kontorfunktionærernes Forbund i Danmark* (HK) [2001] ECR I-6993, [2001] All ER (EC) 941, the ECJ confirmed that this was the case whether a woman was employed on an indefinite or fixed-term basis and notwithstanding any failure by the woman to inform the employer of her pregnancy. In this case, the employee was dismissed one month into a six-month contract when she told her employer she was pregnant and due to give birth almost two months prior to the expiry of the contract. The ECJ held, at paragraph 31, that:

> 'Since the dismissal of a worker on account of pregnancy constitutes direct discrimination on grounds of sex, whatever the nature and extent of the economic loss incurred by the employer as a result of her absence because of pregnancy, whether the contract of employment was concluded for a fixed or an indefinite period has no bearing on the discriminatory character of the dismissal. In either case, the employee's inability to perform her contract of employment is due to pregnancy.'

As set out at 8.69, *SDA 1975, s 3A* now provides that pregnancy and maternity leave are specific grounds on which to bring a discrimination claim under the *SDA 1975* and so are no longer merely facets of sex discrimination. In *Equal Opportunities Commission v Secretary of State for Trade and Industry*, it was submitted on behalf of the Secretary of State that it was intended that the introduction of the new *s 3A* would exclude the possibility of a pregnancy or maternity claim being brought under *s 1*. Although this submission was not challenged, it is likely that an employee who has been dismissed as a result of pregnancy or maternity will claim both that they have been discriminated against on these specific grounds under *s 3A* and also on the grounds of sex (under *s 1*) in the alternative (unless the anticipated amending regulations provide otherwise).

The following examples of pregnancy-related dismissals both amounted to sex discrimination under the old regime and would no doubt also amount to discrimination under *s 3A*:

(a)   In *O'Neill v (1) Governors of St Thomas More RCVA Upper School, (2) Bedfordshire County Council* [1997] ICR 33, Mrs O'Neill was a religious education teacher at a Roman Catholic school. She became pregnant as a result of a relationship with a Roman Catholic priest and was constructively dismissed. The EAT held that she had been discriminated against on the grounds of her sex, as the pregnancy precipitated and permeated the decision to dismiss her. The Respondents had sought to distinguish the case where an employee was dismissed for pregnancy per se (which they acknowledged would be discriminatory) and dismissal as a result of the pregnancy in these particular circumstances. The EAT did not accept this distinction and found the concept of pregnancy per se is misleading, because it suggests pregnancy as a sole ground of dismissal whereas, in fact, pregnancy always has surrounding circumstances which cannot be viewed in isolation from the pregnancy itself.

(b)   In *Abbey National plc v Formoso* [1999] IRLR 222, Ms Formoso was dismissed for gross misconduct but had been unable to attend the relevant disciplinary interview due a combination of her being 28 weeks' pregnant and suffering from anxiety. Ms Formoso's doctor certified that she was emotionally unfit to attend the disciplinary meeting and would remain so until after her pregnancy was over. The EAT upheld the employment tribunal's decision that the disadvantage she suffered as a result of her pregnancy amounted to direct sex discrimination. The EAT accepted that the pregnancy need not be the sole cause of the dismissal.

Pregnancy-related illness

SDA 1975, s 3A(1) also codifies the case law in relation to dismissal for maternity-related absence. The case law itself is now clear that an employer must ignore any absence caused by pregnancy or childbirth-related illness which occurs either during pregnancy or maternity leave (this period is referred to as the protected period). In *Brown v Rentokil Ltd* [1998] ECR I–4185, [1998] All ER (EC) 791, the ECJ held it was directly discriminatory on the grounds of sex to dismiss a woman during her pregnancy for pregnancy-related illness absence. The ECJ went on to state that illness relating to pregnancy or childbirth which occurs during pregnancy or the maternity leave period cannot be taken into account by an employer to justify a dismissal, but that absence arising after maternity leave can be taken into account in the same way as a man's absence.

The combined effect of the *Brown* decision and the requirement for a pregnancy discrimination claim to arise during the protected period (as well as the similar provision in the context of an automatically unfair dismissal connected to childbirth, see 8.74) means, however, that it would now be extremely unlikely that a woman could succeed in claiming either discrimination or automatically unfair dismissal if she was dismissed solely on the basis of absence occurring after the protected period but by reason of a maternity-related illness (as was the case in *Caledonia Bureau Investment Property v Caffrey* [1998] ICR 603).

8.74 Pregnancy and maternity-related dismissals: automatic unfair dismissal

Pursuant to *ERA 1996, s 99* and the *Maternity and Parental Leave Regulations 1999 (SI 1999/3312)* (*MPL Regulations*), *reg 20*, a woman will automatically be regarded as being unfairly dismissed in certain redundancy situations (see 8.75) or if the reason or principal reason for her dismissal is connected to:

(a)   her pregnancy;

(b)   the fact that she has given birth and the dismissal brings her ordinary maternity leave (OML) or additional maternity leave (AML) to an end;

(c)   her taking or seeking to take OML or AML;

(d)   her availing herself of the benefits of OML (as provided for by *ERA 1996, s 71* and *MPL Regulations, reg 9*).

(e)   her failure to return from OML or AML in circumstances where her employer did not give her the proper notice of when her maternity leave was to end and she reasonably believed her maternity leave had not ended;

(f)   her failure to return from OML or AML in circumstances where her employer gave her less than 28 days' notice of the date on which her maternity leave was to end and it was not reasonably practicable for her to return on that date; or

(g)   the fact that she undertook, considered undertaking or refused to work on a keeping in touch day (KIT days are dealt with at 8.115).

There is no qualifying period applicable to a claim of automatically unfair dismissal.

The employer must know of the employee's pregnancy, the fact that she has given birth or the other factors listed above; in *Ramdoolar v Bycity Ltd* [2005] ICR 368, the EAT held that it is generally not enough that the employer, for example, ought to have known that the employee was pregnant. It did, however, qualify this by recognising there may be an automatically unfair dismissal if an employer who merely suspects an employee may be pregnant dismisses her before his suspicion can be proved correct.

The words 'connected to' in *reg 20* should be interpreted widely to give full protection against the mischief envisaged by the legislation (*Clayton v Vigers* [1989] ICR 713, dealing with the precursor to the current provision).

In the case of *Paquay v Societe d'architectes Hoet & Minne SPRL C-460/06* [2007] All ER (D) 137 (Oct), the ECJ held that the protection against dismissal on the grounds of pregnancy and maternity contained in the *Pregnant Workers Directive* does extend beyond the protected period (ie pregnancy and maternity leave) to the extent that any preparatory steps relating to a dismissal took place during the protected period even though the dismissal itself was not notified to the employee until after the end of the protected period. It is likely that an employment tribunal would endeavour to give a purposive interpretation to the requirement in *reg 21(4)* that a dismissal connected to childbirth must bring OML or AML to an end in order to be automatically unfair in order to give effect to this judgement.

8.75   Pregnancy and maternity-related dismissals: redundancy

It is possible for an employer to make an employee redundant while she is on maternity leave. However, there are two situations when doing so may result in an automatically unfair dismissal.

First, there will be an automatically unfair dismissal if the reason or principal reason for selecting an employee for redundancy is one of the reasons set out at (a) to (g) of 8.74. This is the effect of *MPL Regulations, reg 20(2)*, which deals with a redundancy situation which applies equally to one or more employees in an undertaking holding similar positions to the employee in question but who has not been dismissed.

Secondly, there will also be an automatically unfair dismissal if a dismissal brings the maternity leave to an end, the reason or principal reason for the dismissal is redundancy and the *reg 10* requirements have not been complied with (*MPL Regulations, reg 20(1)(b)*). *Reg 20(1)(b)* does not apply where a woman either accepts or unreasonably refuses an offer by an associated employer of a suitable alternative job which is appropriate for her to do in the circumstances.

MPL Regulations, reg 10 gives a woman who is made redundant while on maternity leave the right to any suitable available job. It is generally accepted that this puts the woman in a better position than other potentially redundant employees; the employer cannot select a better qualified candidate if the work is a suitable alternative for the woman (see, for example, the employment tribunal's decision in *Bentley v Body Shop International plc* 3100348/00 (unreported)). This is the case notwithstanding the EAT's comment in *Bellamy v American Airlines* UKEAT/0542/05 (unreported)) that the policy behind the *MPL Regulations* is to ensure that women returning from maternity leave are not disadvantaged rather than providing them with a positive advantage over other employees.

Reg 10 stipulates that if it is not practicable for an employer to continue to employ a woman on maternity leave by reason of redundancy, then she must be offered any suitable available vacancy. The suitable alternative role may be with the employer, his successor or an associated employer and must:

(a)   be offered before the end of her employment;

(b)   start immediately on the ending of her employment;

(c)   be suitable in relation to the employee and appropriate for her in the circumstances; and

(d)   be not on substantially less favourable terms (including as to capacity and place of work) as her previous employment.

In a decision dealing with the precursor to *reg 10*, the EAT upheld an employment tribunal's decision that a vacancy was available even though the post was funded by a third party whose rules rendered the claimant ineligible for the post (*Community Task Force v Rimmer* [1986] ICR 491).

MPL Regulations, reg 10 has not been the subject of many appellate decisions. The EAT has, however, held that:

(a)   where a woman's position becomes redundant prior to her maternity leave, *reg 10* will still apply where the redundancy situation and matter of alternative roles is not resolved before the maternity leave starts (*The Secretary of State for Justice v Slee* UKEAT/10349/106 (20 July 2007, unreported));

(b)   redundancy in this context has the same meaning as under the ERA (*Slee*);

(c)   *Reg 10* does not mean that the consultation period must be extended until after maternity leave; the reference to the impracticability of continuing to employ a woman on maternity leave due to redundancy merely means that the employer must satisfy the employment tribunal that it needed to implement the redundancy during the period of maternity leave (*Calor Gas Ltd v Mrs D Bray* UKEAT/10633/04 (unreported)); and

(d)   where an employer has more than one suitable alternative vacancy, the employer can decide which one to offer to the employee in fulfilment of its *MPL Regulations, reg 10* obligation (*Bellamy v American Airlines*).

8.76   Pregnancy and maternity-related dismissals: notice of termination

As set out at 8.110, a woman's right to contractual notice of termination is preserved during both OML and AML. Once her entitlement to SMP or contractual maternity pay has expired, however, she is not entitled to be paid during any period of contractual notice, although she may be entitled to a payment in lieu of notice or to payment pursuant to *ERA 1996, ss 86–91*.

8.77   Pregnancy and maternity-related dismissals: written statement of reasons for dismissal

As a general rule, an employee with one year's service is entitled to a written statement of the reasons for his dismissal if he makes a request for this to his employer.

Article 10(2) of the *Pregnant Workers Directive* requires employers to 'cite duly substantiated grounds for her dismissal in writing' if they dismiss a woman during the protected period. *ERA 1996, s 92(4)* therefore amends the general position for women in this situation and provides that they are entitled to the written statement of reasons for dismissal whatever their length of service and whether or not they have requested it.

If the employer unreasonably fails to provide the statement or if the reasons are inadequate or untrue, the employee can seek a declaration of the reasons and an award of two weeks' pay. (A 'week's pay' is not subject to the statutory maximum for this purpose).

8.78 **Pregnancy or maternity-related detriment**

Women are protected from being subjected to a detriment as a result of pregnancy, childbirth and maternity leave by *ERA 1996, s 47(c)* and *MPL Regulations, reg 19*. The facts which give rise to a detriment claim are also likely to amount to discrimination under *SDA 1975, s 3A* and employees are likely to bring both claims in the alternative, as well as claiming discrimination on the grounds of sex – despite the submission in *Equal Opportunities Commission v Secretary of State for Trade and Industry* that these two causes of action were intended to be mutually exclusive, as explained in 8.73.

MPL Regulations, reg 19 provides that an employee is not to be subjected to any detriment by any act, or deliberate failure to act, by her employer for any of the following reasons:

(a) her pregnancy;

(b) the fact that she has given birth and the detriment takes place during OML or AML;

(c) her taking or seeking to take OML or AML;

(d) her availing herself of the benefit of OML provided for by *ERA 1996, s 71* and *MPL Regulations, reg 9*;

(e) her failure to return from OML or AML in circumstances where her employer did not give her the proper notice of when her maternity leave was to end and she reasonably believed her maternity leave had not ended;

(f) her failure to return from OML or AML in circumstances where her employer gave her less than 28 days' notice of the date on which her maternity leave was to end and it was not reasonably practicable for her to return on that date; or

(g) the application of a legislative requirement or recommendation under a Code of Practice that she be suspended from work on the grounds of her pregnancy, her having recently given birth or her breastfeeding (ie as defined in *ERA 1996, s 66(2)*).

If the detriment amounts to a dismissal, however, the employee must bring a claim of automatic unfair dismissal or discrimination and the detriment provisions do not apply.

An employee who has suffered a detriment is able to bring a complaint under *ERA 1996, s 48* within three months, beginning with the act or failure complained of or the last in a series of acts or failures. The time limit can be extended by a tribunal if it was not reasonably practicable for the claimant to bring a claim within the time limit.

If the tribunal finds that the complaint was well founded, it can make a declaration to that effect and make an award of compensation which it considers to be just and equitable in all the circumstances and will take into account the loss attributable to the act or omission, any reasonable expenses incurred in consequence of the act or omission and any benefit that the employee may have been expected to have but for the act or omission (*ERA 1996, s 49*).

The following are examples of situations where employees have succeeded in discrimination or detriment claims:

(a) An employee did not qualify for a performance assessment which was a pre-condition for a pay rise because of her absence of maternity leave. The

ECJ held that the denial of the assessment amounted to discrimination on the grounds of sex as, but for her maternity leave, the employee would automatically have had the assessment (*Caisse Nationale d'Assurance Vieillesse Des Travailleurs Salaries v Thibault* [1998] ECR I-2011, [1998] All ER (EC) 385).

(b)   An employee was not informed of a new role which arose during her pregnancy. She considered she was well suited to the new role (a view supported by one of her ex-colleagues), although the employment tribunal accepted that the employer was entitled to its view that she was not suitable for the job. The EAT upheld the employment tribunal's decision that the failure to inform the employee of the vacancy amounted to maternity-related detriment and discrimination on the grounds of sex (*Visa International Service Association v Mrs O L Paul* [2004] IRLR 42).

(c)   An employee on maternity leave was appointed to a new role with her employer and successfully argued that it would be discrimination on the grounds of sex for continuous service in the new job to run from the date she started working in that role as opposed to the date of her appointment (*Herrero v Instituto Madrileno de la Salud (Imsalud) C-294/04* [2006] IRLR 296).

(d)   Promotion to a higher salary grade was dependent on length of service. Only eight of the twenty weeks spent by Mrs Sass on maternity leave counted as qualifying service as these were equivalent to the then West German maternity leave; the other twelve weeks of the then East German statutory maternity leave entitlement did not count. The ECJ held that the failure to recognise this additional period of statutory maternity leave would amount to sex discrimination if its purpose was the same as the West German eight-week compulsory leave. They stated that taking such leave should interrupt neither the employment relationship nor the application of the rights derived from it. The ECJ left it to the national courts to decide whether the purpose of the additional leave was in fact the same, but made it clear that neither the compulsory nature of the West German maternity leave nor the question of whether the leave was paid could be decisive factors in this assessment (*Land Brandenburg v Sass Case C-284/02* [2005] IRLR 147). If an employer has a policy of promoting (or considering for promotion) employees purely on the basis of time served, the discounting of time spent both on OML and AML may well be held to be discriminatory.

Interestingly, in the case of *Ojinnaka v Sheffield College* UKEAT/0201/00 (2001, unreported), an employee failed in her claim that the failure of her maternity cover to keep her informed of what was going on while she was on maternity leave (and, in particular, potential changes to the course she taught) amounted to discrimination on the grounds of sex. The EAT accepted there was no detriment as there was nothing of sufficient importance to discuss with the employee and that she would have been consulted had any concrete changes been proposed to her course or otherwise to her status or job description.

8.79   PREGNANCY AND MATERNITY RIGHTS

Paid time off for ante-natal appointments

If a registered medical practitioner, registered midwife or registered nurse has advised a pregnant employee to attend ante-natal care, the employee is entitled to take time off during the employer's working hours to keep this appointment (*ERA*

1996, s 55(1)). The employee is also entitled to be paid for this period of absence at the appropriate hourly rate (*ERA 1996, s 56(1)*) and this includes any travel and waiting time.

8.80   *What is ante-natal care?*

Guidance from DBERR refers to ante-natal care as including medical examinations, tests for the likelihood of any genetic conditions or abnormalities, parentcraft classes and relaxation classes where medically advised (see also *Gregory v Tudsbury Ltd* [1982] IRLR 267).

8.81   *Eligibility requirements*

There is no length of service eligibility requirement and this right is available to both full-time and part-time employees. With the exception of the employee's first appointment, however, the employer can request:

(a)   a certificate from a registered medical practitioner, registered midwife or registered nurse stating the employee is pregnant; and

(b)   an appointment card or other document showing that the appointment has been made,

and if the employee does not provide this information to the employer, she is not entitled to take paid time off for that ante-natal appointment (*ERA 1996, s 55(2)*).

8.82   *Unreasonable refusal*

An employer cannot unreasonably refuse an employee to take such time off work; however, there may be circumstances where an employer could reasonably expect an employee to make appointments outside of working hours (*Gregory v Tudsbury Ltd* [1982] IRLR 267). This is more likely to arise in situations where the employee works relatively few hours each week, although the DBERR reminds employers in its guidance (which is not binding) that they should bear in mind that there is often little flexibility as to when appointments can be arranged.

8.83   *Appropriate hourly rate*

The employee is entitled to be paid for the period of absence at the appropriate hourly rate, calculated in accordance with *ERA 1996, s 56*.

The employee's statutory right to remuneration does not affect any contractual right that the employee may have to remuneration, although any contractual remuneration will discharge the relevant portion of statutory entitlement and vice versa (*s 56(6)*).

8.84   *Complaint*

An employee may present a complaint to an employment tribunal within three months from the date of the act complained of where:

(a)   the employer has unreasonably refused to permit the employee to take time off (*ERA 1996, s 57(1)(a)*); or

(b)   the employer has failed to pay (in whole or part) any amount to which the employee is entitled in respect of the period of absence for ante-natal care (*s 57(1)(b)*).

This time period can be extended by a tribunal if it was not reasonably practicable for the employee to bring the claim within time. If the complaint is upheld, a tribunal can make a declaration to that effect and where relevant, order the employer to pay the employee the remuneration she would have been entitled to and that is due (*s 57(3), (4)*).

8.85 *The expectant father's rights*

There is no right for the expectant father to take paid time off work to accompany the employee to the ante-natal appointments. However, the DBERR and EOC encourage employers to take a flexible approach where practicable and suggest that it is considered best practice to either allow the expectant father to take paid time off or make up this time.

8.86 Health and safety, suspension from work

The TUC states that every year there are around 1,500 potential tribunal cases involving pregnancy and maternity-related discrimination and of these the vast majority (over 90%) involved a breach of health and safety legislation.

The *Pregnant Workers Directive* (*Council Directive 92/85/EEC*) has been implemented into UK law under the *Management of Health and Safety at Work Regulations 1999* (*SI 1999/3242*) ('*HSW Regs*'). This legislation states that:

(a)   subject to certain requirements, an employer should conduct a risk assessment in respect of new and expectant mothers as part of its general risk assessment (see 8.87); and

(b)   subject to certain requirements, an employer should carry out a specific risk assessment in respect of an individual employee who has informed her employer that she is a new or expectant mother (see 8.88).

8.87 The general risk assessment

Where an employer has:

(a)   persons working in the undertaking of a childbearing age; and

(b)   the work is of a kind that could involve risk, by reason of her condition, to the health and safety of a new or expectant mother or to that of her baby, from any processes or working conditions, or physical, biological or chemical agents that are listed in *Annexes I* and *II* of the *Pregnant Workers Directive*,

an employer is required to undertake an assessment that considers that risk as part of its general risk assessment (*HSW Regs, reg 16(1)*). If the employer has more than five employees, this assessment must be recorded in writing. If risks are identified, the employer should inform both the concerned employees of the risk and their employee representatives.

As part of the risk assessment hazards such as physical, chemical and biological agents; industrial processes; movements and postures; mental and physical fatigue and other physical and mental burdens should be identified. Such hazards may arise in connection with work materials, equipment, methods and practices. The potential for harm and the possible extent of the harm should be assessed in terms of its nature, intensity and duration. In assessing this, the employer should take into account all relevant information, including information from new or expectant mothers and their advisors. For example, early shift work and nauseating smells may be likely to have an affect on sickness and headaches, or if the employee has to stand for long period of time this may increase the risk of varicose veins. The Health and Safety Executive gives useful guidance on these types of considerations.

8.88   **A risk assessment for an individual new or expectant mother**

Where an employee has notified the employer in writing that she is a new or expectant mother, an employer is subject to further health and safety obligations in respect of that individual employee (*HSW Regs, reg 18(1)*).

A 'new or expectant mother' is an employee who is either pregnant, has given birth in the past six months, or who is breastfeeding. 'Given birth' means a woman who has delivered a living child, or miscarried after at least 24 weeks of pregnancy. The protection of the *HSW Regs* only extends for six months after the birth if the employee is still breastfeeding. For these definitions and others, see *HSW Regs, reg 1(2)*.

8.89   *Notification*

There is no prescribed form of notification that the employee must give to her employer. The only requirement is that the notification must be in writing and indicate pregnancy. For example, the EAT found that a medical certificate stating an employee suffered from 'hyperemesis gravidarum' (severe sickness associated with pregnancy) constituted written notification of pregnancy and the employer was unable to show that this was an inadequate notification (*Day v T Pickles Farm Ltd* [1999] IRLR 217).

The employer is able to request that the employee produces for its inspection a certificate from a registered medical practitioner or midwife showing that she is pregnant (such as a form MAT B1). If the employee fails to provide such evidence within a reasonable time, the employer will not be required to 'maintain action in relation to the employee' such as undertake an individual risk assessment or implement its recommendation (*HSW Regs, reg 18(2)(a)(ii)*).

8.90   *The individual risk assessment*

The employer must identify the risks that are applicable to that specific new or expectant mother. These may be risks that it has identified in the general risk assessment and also risks that the employer has identified from taking into account all other relevant information, such as information from the new or expectant mother and her advisor, including any medical advice, reports and certificates. Any information provided should be dealt with in the strictest confidence.

A single individual risk assessment may not be sufficient since during the various stages of pregnancy and after birth, the risks affecting the mother and her unborn or newborn child may change and so should be continually monitored.

8.91   *Duty to take action to avoid the risks*

The employer has a duty to take action in respect of the risks that are applicable to that individual employee and the employer should consult with the employee and any health and safety representatives regarding this. The action taken by the employer should 'avoid' the risk; however, the EAT has stated that this does not mean that the employer must eliminate the risk entirely but instead should reduce the risks to 'its lowest acceptable level' (*New Southern Railway v Quinn* [2006]

IRLR 266) (see also the general obligations on employers in relation to health and safety set out in *Article 6* of the *Framework Directive* (*Directive 89/391EEC*)).

The employer must do the following:

(a)   take action to avoid the risk – for example, if a risk is connected with manual handling it may be reduced by providing physical aids (*HSW Regs, reg 16(2)*);

(b)   if taking action would not avoid the risk, if it is reasonable to do so and this would avoid such risks, the employee's working conditions or hours of work should be altered (*reg 16(2)*). For example, providing that the employee no longer has to work early shifts when she is suffering from morning sickness;

(c)   if it is not reasonable to alter the working conditions or hours of work, or if it would not avoid such risk, the employee has a right to be offered 'suitable alternative work' (*reg 16(3)* and *ERA 1996, s 67*) (see 8.92); and

(d)   if suitable alternative work cannot be offered, the employer must suspend the employee for so long as necessary to avoid such a risk (*reg 16(3)*). Such suspension would be paid (*ERA 1996, ss 66* and *68*) (see 8.92).

8.92   *'Suitable alternative work'*

Care must be taken by an employer that the work offered is 'suitable alternative work', being:

(a)   work of a kind which is both suitable in relation to her and appropriate for her to do in the circumstances; and

(b)   the terms and conditions applicable to her for performing the work, if they differ from the corresponding terms and conditions applicable to her for performing the work she normally performs under her contract of employ-ment, must not be substantially less favourable to her than those corre-sponding terms and conditions (*ERA 1996, s 67*).

In *New Southern Railway Ltd v Quinn* [2006] IRLR 266, an employee was demoted from her position as a railway station duty manager to a personal assistant, and her salary was reduced accordingly to reflect the lower rate of pay for that role. The EAT upheld complaints of sex discrimination, constructive dismissal and unlawful deductions from wages on the basis that the risks identified were small and it was not necessary for the employer to demote Mrs Quinn or reduce her salary in order to comply with the *HSW Regs*.

In *British Airways (European Operations at Gatwick) Ltd v Moore and Botterill* [2000] IRLR 296, an employee was removed from flying duties to ground duties. The loss of her cabin crew member's flying allowance meant that the alternate role was on terms substantially less favourable than her previous terms (regarding pay and benefits). This meant that the transfer to ground duties did not constitute suitable alternative work within the meaning of *ERA 1996, s 67*. The claimants were therefore entitled to receive the remuneration due to them calculated in accordance with *s 67* and the principles set out in *S and U Stores Ltd v Wilkes* [1974] 3 All ER 401.

8.93   *Suspension from work*

To justify the suspension of a pregnant employee an employer must first assess the risk; second, take appropriate measures to avoid the risk; and third, (if the risks cannot be avoided or it is unreasonable to alter her hours or conditions) offer suitable alternative work. Only once these three steps have been pursued can the employee be suspended (see *New Southern Railway Ltd v Quinn*).

In addition, where a new or expectant mother normally works at night and a certificate from a registered medical practitioner or midwife shows that it is necessary for her health and safety that she should not be at work for any period, then the employer must suspend the employee from work for as long as is necessary for her health and safety (*HSW Regs, reg 17*).

In either case, an employee is entitled to be paid during the period of suspension (*ERA 1996, s 68*).

8.94   Exemptions to pregnant worker's risk assessment

Whilst there are no exemptions in relation to the general risk assessment for employees of a childbearing age, an employer is not required to take any action in relation to a new or expectant mother until she has notified her employer in writing that she is pregnant, or has given birth during the past six months, or is breastfeeding (*HSW Regs, reg 18(1)*).

In addition, *reg 18* provides that an employer is not required to 'maintain action' in respect of an employee:

(a)   if, following a request by the employer, the employee fails to provide evidence of her pregnancy within a reasonable time; or

(b)   once the employer knows that the employee is no longer a new or expectant mother; or

(c)   if the employer cannot establish whether she remains a new or expectant mother.

8.95   Failure to carry out a specific risk assessment

In *Hardman v Mallon (t/a Orchard Lodge Nursing Home)* [2002] 2 CMLR 1467 a failure to carry out a risk assessment amounted to sex discrimination as the new or expectant mother's work involved heavy lifting. It was thereafter thought that any failure to carry out a risk assessment in respect of a new or expectant mother is capable of constituting sex discrimination. However, the Court of Appeal has confirmed that the duty to conduct a risk assessment under *HSW Regs, reg 16* only arises where the work is of a nature that could involve potential risk for a new or expectant mother. In *Madarassy v Nomura International plc* [2007] EWCA Civ 33, [2007] ICR 867, the employee had a desk-based role and although she complained of radiation from her computer, this was not enough to trigger the obligation to conduct a specific risk assessment.

Although the mere possibility of discrimination is not enough to shift the burden of proof onto the employer (see 8.29), it is considered safer and best practice to carry out a risk assessment rather than rely on the narrow interpretation of *reg 16* in *Madarassy v Nomura International plc*, given that damages for sex discrimination are unlimited and failure to carry out a risk assessment could result in a negligence claim in the event of the mother or the baby suffering a detriment (such as an injury which would have been identified had a risk assessment been carried out).

The Health and Safety Executive is able to serve an improvement notice on the employer to require it to carry out the risk assessment or a prohibition notice (prohibiting an activity until remedial action has been taken). In addition, the

Health and Safety at Work etc Act 1974, s 33(1)(a) provides that it is an offence for a person to contravene the general duties of employers to their employees (such as provide a safe system of work) and *s 33(1)(c)* provides it is an offence to contravene any health and safety regulations and can be liable to on conviction to a fine (depending on the various breaches and whether conviction is a summary conviction or on indictment, the fines may not capped). Any action that the Health and Safety Executive takes should be proportional, consistent and in the public interest (see the Health and Safety Commission's Enforcement Policy Statement published by the Health and Safety Executive (HSC15, reprinted 5/04)).

8.96 MATERNITY LEAVE AND PAY

Maternity leave

The majority of the law relating to maternity leave is set out in the *MPL Regulations* and *ERA 1996, ss 71–75* (provisions relating to pay are elsewhere).

8.97 *Eligibility*

Subject to the notification requirements set out below, all employees are entitled to 52 weeks of maternity leave, regardless of their length of service; but not all employees are entitled to maternity pay (see 8.102–8.103). Individuals who are not employees – such as contractors/consultants – are not entitled to maternity leave, but in many cases are entitled to protection from discrimination; see, for example, 8.117ff.

8.98 *EWC and notification*

Under the *MPL Regulations, reg 4(1)(a)*, to receive maternity leave, the employee must notify the employer no later than the end of the 15th week before the expected week of childbirth – known as the EWC, the week (beginning with midnight between Saturday and Sunday) when childbirth is expected to occur, and 'childbirth' includes still birth after 24 weeks of pregnancy (*MPL Regulations, reg 2(1)*) – of the following:

(a)   that she is pregnant;

(b)   the EWC;

(c)   the date she intends her leave to start. This date cannot be earlier than the start of the eleventh week before the EWC.

The notification does not have to be in writing unless the employer asks for it (*MPL Regulations, reg 4(2)(a)*). The employer may also ask for a medical certificate – a MAT B1 – confirming the EWC (*reg 4(1)(b)*), but this certificate cannot be signed before the 20th week before the EWC (*Statutory Maternity Pay (Medical Evidence) Regulations 1987 (SI 1987/235), reg 2*). Upon receiving this notice, the employer must, within 28 days, notify the employee of the date on which her maternity leave will end (*regs 7(6) and 7(7)(a)*). Where the notification is not made within 28 days, the employee is exempted from the obligation to notify her intention to return to work early (*reg 11(5)*), and is protected from detriment or dismissal arising out of her failure to return to work on time, provided it was not reasonably practicable for her to return at that time (*regs 19 and 20*). Where the employer gives no notice at all, the employee is protected from detriment/dismissal so long as she reasonably believed her maternity leave had not ended (*regs 19 and 20*).

8.99 *Starting maternity leave*

Under the *MPL Regulations, reg 6*, maternity leave will start on the earlier of:

(a) the date notified by the employee;

(b) automatically the day after birth;

(c) the day after absence due wholly or partly to a pregnancy-related reason after the beginning of the fourth week before the EWC.

An employee may change their notified start date, but must give at least 28 days' notice of the change – that is at least 28 days' notice before the original date if it is to be postponed, or 28 days before the new date if leave is being started earlier (*MPL Regulations, reg 4(1A)*).

8.100 *Duration of maternity leave*

Maternity leave is a maximum of 52 weeks. It is split into two periods of 26 weeks. The first is ordinary maternity leave (OML) (*ERA 1996, s 71*). The second is additional maternity leave (AML) (*ERA 1996, s 73*). Historically some employees were entitled to OML but not AML, but the length of service requirement for AML was removed by amendments to the *MPL Regulations* under the *Work and Families Act 2006* and now all employees are eligible for both OML and AML. It is up to the employee to decide how much maternity leave she takes, save that the first two weeks of OML – referred to as compulsory maternity leave (CML) – must be taken and the employee is not permitted to work (*ERA 1996, s 72* and *MPL Regulations, reg 8*). CML is extended to four weeks for women employed in factories; it is a criminal offence to allow an employee to work in a factory at such time, punishable by a fine of up to £200 (*Public Health Act 1936, ss 205* and *343* and *Factories Act 1961, s 175*). More generally, allowing an employee to work during any period of CML is a criminal offence under health and safety law, punishable by a fine not exceeding level 2 on the standard scale, currently up to £500 (*ERA 1996, s 72*).

8.101 **Statutory maternity pay**

The relevant legislation is mainly set out in the *Social Security Contributions and Benefits Act 1992* (*SSCBA 1992*), Part VII and the *Statutory Maternity Pay (General) Regulations 1986* (*SI 1986/1960*) ('*SMP Regulations*').

Key terms:

(a) As for maternity leave, the expected week of confinement (or childbirth) (EWC) is the week in which the child is expected to be born. More precisely, confinement is defined as labour resulting in the issue of a living child or labour after 24 weeks of pregnancy resulting in the issue of a child whether alive or dead (*SSCBA, s 171(1)*).

(b) The 'qualifying week' is the fifteenth week before the EWC.

(c) The reference or qualifying period for calculating eligibility for and the amount of statutory maternity pay (SMP) is, broadly speaking, the eight-week period ending with the qualifying week.

8.102 *Eligibility*

The eligibility criteria for SMP differ from those for maternity leave. Once she has qualified for SMP, a woman will be entitled to receive it notwithstanding any subsequent dismissal. (See (c) below if the dismissal is in order to avoid paying

SMP). If she is not eligible to receive SMP, a woman may be entitled to maternity allowance. A woman who is absent from work is entitled to SMP if:

(a)   she is pregnant at the beginning of the eleventh week before the EWC (or has given birth at this point);

(b)   she has been employed for a continuous period of 26 weeks ending with the 15th week before the EWC (*Part III* of the *SMP Regulations* sets out the rules on continuous employment and these are similar to the rules contained in *ERA 1996*);

(c)   her normal weekly earnings during the qualifying period are higher than or equivalent to the lower earnings limit at the rate applicable at the end of the qualifying week;

(d)   she has given the required notice to her employer (see 8.103).

In this context, 'employed' means a woman who is employed in Great Britain either under a contract of service or as an office-holder and whose earnings are subject to income tax under the *Income Tax (Earnings and Pensions) Act 2003, s 7* and *SSCBA 1992, s 17(1)*.

In addition:

(a)   *SSCBA 1992, s 17* provides that anyone who is treated as an employed earner for National Insurance purposes by virtue of the *Social Security (Categorisation of Earners) Regulations 1978* will also be entitled to SMP. The most significant of these are agency workers who will qualify for SMP if the agency retains an ongoing role in paying them.

(b)   The *Statutory Maternity Pay (Persons Abroad and Mariners) Regulations 1987* provide for an employee who is based abroad to be entitled to SMP if her employer is liable to pay secondary Class 1 NI contributions in respect of her, or if she is working in an EU Member State and deemed to be subject to UK social security legislation by virtue of *EC Council Regulation 1408/71*.

(c)   If an employer brings an employee's employment to an end solely or mainly for the purpose of avoiding liability for SMP, the employer will be liable to make SMP payments if the employee was employed by him for a continuous period of at least eight weeks. (*SMP Regulations, reg 3(1); reg 3(2)* sets out how such SMP is calculated.)

Employers who do not have a liability to pay secondary Class 1 NICs will not be required to pay SMP.

A woman will not be entitled to SMP in respect of any week that she works during maternity leave other than a keeping in touch day (KIT days are dealt with at 8.115). There is also no liability to pay SMP in respect of a week when a woman is in legal custody or imprisoned, or if she dies.

8.103 *Notice requirements*

A woman is required to give her employer at least 28 days' notice of the date that she wants her SMP to begin or, if that is not reasonably practicable, she must give notice as soon as is reasonably practicable. The notice only has to be in writing if the employee requests it (*SMP Regulations, reg 23*).

As for maternity leave, a woman must also give her employer evidence of when the EWC is (or evidence of the date of birth if it has already occurred). The evidence must be provided by the end of the third week of the maternity pay period or, if there is good cause for the evidence to be submitted later, by the end of the thirteenth week of the maternity pay period (*reg 22*). This evidence is usually provided by giving the employer the MATB1 certificate in accordance with the requirements of the *Statutory Maternity Pay (Medical Evidence) Regulations* (see 8.98).

8.104 *Period of SMP*

SMP is payable for a period of 39 consecutive weeks. In common with maternity leave itself, this period starts either on the date:

(a)   notified;

(b)   that the employee gives birth, if that is before the notified date;

(c)   after the first day of absence if the employee is absent from work partly or wholly due to pregnancy or confinement at any time after the beginning of the fourth week before the EWC;

In addition, the payment of SMP starts after the date the employee's employment terminates if it terminates at any time after the beginning of the 11th week before the EWC.

8.105 *Amount, calculation and payment of SMP*

SMP is paid at a higher rate of 90% of a woman's normal weekly earnings during the eight-week reference period for the first six weeks and at a lower flat rate for the remaining period of up to 33 weeks. The flat rate with effect from 1 April 2007 is £112.75 per week and £117.18 per week with effect from 7 April 2008 (or continues at the rate of 90% of normal weekly earnings if that amount is lower). The flat rate is typically increased by regulation in April of each year.

The eight-week reference period and the method of calculating normal weekly earnings for this purpose are governed by the *SMP Regulations, reg 21*. Normal weekly earnings include any remuneration or profit derived from a woman's employment and so in addition to wages and salary, payments such as overtime pay, holiday pay, commission and bonuses must be included in the calculation. It is therefore possible for the higher rate of SMP to exceed a woman's normal weekly pay if, for example, a significant annual bonus is paid during the eight-week reference period.

As a result of the ECJ's decision in *Alabaster v Woolwich plc* [2004] ECR I-3101, [2005] All ER (EC) 490, which is dealt with at 8.107, *reg 21(7)* provides that where a woman is awarded a pay increase (or would have been awarded such an increase had she not been absent on statutory maternity leave) and the pay increase applies to the whole or any part of the period between the beginning of the eight-week reference period and the end of her maternity leave, the normal weekly earnings must be calculated as if the pay increase applied in each week of the eight-week reference period. The period from the beginning of the reference period until the end of the statutory maternity leave could extend to 17 months if a woman takes her full entitlement to maternity leave and this provision can result in women on maternity leave being treated more favourably than their colleagues.

Reg 27 provides that SMP should be paid in a like manner to normal pay and so monthly paid employees are typically paid SMP on a monthly basis. SMP can also be paid in a lump sum which is an option often used in case of redundancy.

8.106 **Contractual or enhanced maternity pay**

Many employers provide maternity pay in excess of SMP. Payments of SMP can be set off against any such enhanced payments and vice versa. The ECJ judgment in *Alabaster* is couched in wide enough terms to apply to contractual or enhanced pay if the enhanced pay is based on pay received by the employee prior to her maternity (for example, if a contractual scheme used the same reference period as for SMP).

8.107 **Maternity pay and discrimination**

Various challenges have been made to the SMP scheme and to enhanced maternity pay schemes on the basis that they are discriminatory on the grounds of sex.

(a)   In *Gillespie v Northern Health and Social Services Board* [1996] ECR I-475, [1996] All ER (EC) 284, the employees were entitled to an enhanced maternity pay scheme and sought to argue that it was directly discriminatory on the grounds of sex for:

(i)   their pay to be reduced at all while on maternity leave; and

(ii)   for them not to receive the benefit of a backdated pay rise which was awarded after the rate of their maternity pay had been calculated.

The ECJ held that, while women on maternity leave require special protection, there was no requirement that they should continue to receive full pay during maternity leave. The only requirement is that the amount of maternity pay cannot be so low as to undermine the purpose of maternity leave, namely the protection of women before and after giving birth. Without much analysis, they also held that a woman on maternity leave should, however, receive a pay rise awarded before or during the maternity leave period. This is on the basis that the principle of non-discrimination requires that a woman on maternity leave must, like any other worker, benefit from any pay rise awarded between the beginning of the period covered by the reference pay and the end of the maternity leave. The ECJ held that to deny such an increase to a woman on maternity leave would discriminate against her purely in her capacity as a worker since, had she not been pregnant, she would have received a pay rise.

It was as a result of the *Gillespie* case that the Government amended the *SMP Regulations* to provide that if a woman receives a pay rise backdated to a time within the reference period, SMP must be recalculated to take the increase into account.

(b)   This change then led to the challenge in *Alabaster v Woolwich plc*, as it did not fully implement the ECJ's decision in *Gillespie*. Before going on maternity leave, Mrs Alabaster received a pay rise which, although backdated, still fell outside the reference period for calculating SMP. Under the *Gillespie* form of the Regulations, Mrs Alabaster's SMP was not affected by the pay rise and she brought a claim of sex discrimination. The ECJ held, following *Gillespie*, that any pay rise having effect during the reference period or the entire period of maternity leave should be included in the calculation for SMP.

(c)   In *Boyle and Others v Equal Opportunities Commission* [1999] ICR 360 the EOC provided enhanced maternity pay if the employee agreed to return to work after maternity leave and to repay the enhanced element if they did not return. The ECJ held that it was not discriminatory on the grounds of sex to provide enhanced rate of maternity pay on the basis that the women return to work after maternity leave. Nor did such a provision infringe the *Pregnant Workers Directive* (but see 8.114).

(d)   In *Banks v Tesco Stores* [1999] ICR 1141, an employee challenged the lower earnings limit eligibility requirement for SMP relying on the ECJ's statement in *Gillespie* that the level of maternity pay should not be so low as to undermine the purpose of maternity leave. The EAT held it was not discriminatory to impose eligibility requirements of this sort.

(e)   In *North Western Health Board v McKenna* [2006] All ER (EC) 455, [2006] ICR 477, the employee claimed that a sick pay scheme which went down to half pay after a set period and was subject to an overall maximum period of payment was discriminatory on the grounds of sex when applied to a pregnancy-related illness. The ECJ held that employers are not required to pay full pay to women absent from work because of pregnancy-related illness. The ECJ drew an important distinction between dismissals and pay, explaining that while the only way to accommodate 'the special nature of pregnancy-related illness' is to prevent employers from dismissing women for this reason, the situation is different as far as pay or sick pay is concerned as accommodations can be made in other ways, such as a reduced level of pay, provided that this is not so low as to undermine the objective of protecting pregnant workers. The ECJ also held that offsetting pregnancy-related absences against a maximum total of days of paid sick leave were not discriminatory. Again, as in relation to the level of pay, there was a twist to this; the rules as to the offsetting of absences cannot result in a women receiving less than this protective minimum level of pay in a subsequent period of illness. This minimum level should be satisfied as long as the employee is receiving statutory sick pay or incapacity benefit.

It is not always possible to reconcile the ECJ cases in this area. Women are accorded special protection in recognition of the fact that pregnancy and maternity are unique to them and so their position cannot be compared with that of someone at work. This special protection has extended to many non-monetary matters such as dismissals (*Webb, Dekker* and *Tele Danmark*), performance assessments (*Thibault*) and promotions (*Sass*), but not to full pay, sick pay or bonuses (*Gillespie, McKenna* and *Lewen v Denda*; see 8.112). The distinction drawn by the ECJ in *McKenna* in between dismissals and pay does help to reconcile these decisions to some extent but still does not account for the difference in the treatment of pay itself (which does not come within the special protection) and pay rises (which do: *Gillespie, Alabaster*).

8.108   Benefits during maternity leave

Ordinary and additional maternity leave

During OML, the employee is entitled to the benefit of all the terms and conditions of employment, other than those relating to 'remuneration' (*ERA 1996, s 71(4)–(5)* and *MPL Regulations, reg 9*). Remuneration is in turn defined as 'wages and salary' (*MPL Regulations, reg 9(3)*). (The meaning of 'wages and salary' is considered in the context of claims relating to bonus entitlement (see 8.112).) The employee also gets the benefit of 'matters connected with ... employment whether or not they arise under her contract of employment' (*ERA 1996, s 71(5)*) – so non-contractual, as well as contractual, benefits also continue.

During AML, however, although the contract of employment continues, the majority of its terms and conditions are suspended (*ERA 1996, s 73* and see 8.112*reg 17*). The employee is entitled to the benefit of (a) the implied term of mutual trust and confidence, and terms relating to (b) notice, (c) redundancy compensation, and (d) disciplinary or grievance procedures.

She is bound by (a) her implied obligation of good faith, and terms relating to (b) notice, (c) disclosure of confidential information,(d) acceptance of gifts or benefits, and (e) participation in other businesses (*MPL Regulations, reg 17*).

In addition, an employee is entitled to any contractual rights regarding maternity leave which are more favourable than the statutory right (*MPL Regulations, reg 21*).

If a woman is unlawfully deprived of these terms, she has a number of possible claims:

(a)   pregnancy detriment under *MPL Regulations, reg 19*;

(b)   sex discrimination (*SDA 1975, s 3A*; note the exception in *s 6A* for claims in respect of remuneration during OML or any terms and conditions during AML, save for the few which continue, or for pay rises (per *Alabaster*), although these provisions are to be revised by the Government in light of the EOC's challenge in *Equal Opportunities Commission v Secretary of State for Trade and Industry* [2007] EWHC 483 (Admin));

(c)   unlawful deduction from wages (*ERA 1996, s 13*).

The differences between an employee's entitlements during OML and AML were held not to be discriminatory by the ECJ in *Boyle and others v Equal Opportunities Commission, C-411/96* [1998] IRLR 717 ECJ. The later ECJ decision of *Land Brandenburg v Sass, C-284/02* [2005] IRLR 147, however, distinguished *Boyle* and suggests that the suspension of contractual terms during AML amounts to unlawful discrimination. The ECJ held that the purpose of the leave should be considered; if the purpose of it is the protection of women as regards pregnancy and maternity:

> 'Community law requires that taking such statutory protective leave should interrupt neither the employment relationship … nor the application of the rights derived from it and cannot lead to discrimination against that woman.' (paragraph 48)

Boyle was distinguished on the basis that it concerned benefits which exceeded the statutory leave period. Whilst not binding, the Government conceded in *Equal Opportunities Commission v Secretary of State for Trade and Industry* (at 57) that the purpose of AML is the same as that of OML. The High Court held that the Government must make amendments to the *SDA 1975* so as expressly to permit claims of the type referred to in a certain fact sheet (e g to give an appraisal or consult about a reorganisation). *Sass* also casts doubt over the validity of the distinction between OML and AML, and the ability of employers lawfully to withhold benefits during AML.

8.109 *Social Security Act 1989*

Beyond the entitlement to certain benefits during OML, there is a separate entitlement to certain specified benefits for any period of paid maternity absence (*Social Security Act 1989, Sch 5* ('*SSA 1989*').

Pursuant to this, an employer is obliged to provide 'employment-related benefits' during a 'period of paid maternity absence'. A 'paid maternity absence' is any maternity absence for which pay is received, whether that pay is contractual or statutory (*Sch 5, para 5(3)(a)*).

The definition of 'employment-related benefits' is very detailed, and yet ambiguous in parts, and there is no case law about it. The definition includes:

'benefits, in the form of pensions or otherwise, payable in money or money's worth in respect of (i) termination of service, (ii) retirement, old age or death, (iii) interruptions of service by reason of sickness or invalidity, (iv) accidents, injuries or diseases connected with employment, (v) unemployment, or (vi) expenses ... in connection with children or dependants ...' (*SSA 1989, Sch 5, para 7(e)*).

There are a few, limited, exceptions (e g for non-contributory benefits and certain contracts of insurance where the employer is not a party (*para 7(a)–(b)*)) which will not often apply. The authors consider that the definition will likely catch all of the following:

(a)   Pension contributions. Note that employer contributions must be made at the employee's *notional* 'normal' pay whereas employee contributions are only required at the *actual* rate of pay they receive (i e based on SMP or enhanced maternity pay) (*para 5(1)–(2)*).

(b)   Private medical cover.

(c)   Permanent Health Insurance.

(d)   Life insurance.

(e)   Enhanced redundancy pay/notice. Where *SSA 1995, Sch 5* applies (i e the employee is receiving maternity pay), employees are entitled to benefits relating to 'termination of service'. That clearly captures benefits such as enhanced redundancy pay. It may capture pay for notice (whether it is 'working' notice or pay in lieu of notice) at the employee's normal rate of pay, although there is an argument that notice/notice pay is not a benefit, and that it is therefore not within the ambit of the *SSA 1989, Sch 5*. If notice/notice pay is a benefit within the meaning of the *SSA 1989*, employees may only be entitled to notice in full for the same period as they would otherwise have received maternity pay; however, this argument is untested.

8.110   *Notice*

A woman's right to notice is preserved during OML and AML. This period of notice may be unpaid if she is not receiving pay at the relevant time. In addition to the possible entitlement to paid notice under the *SSA 1989* referred to in 8.109, employees on maternity leave would be entitled to paid notice periods or pay in lieu of notice in certain other circumstances, including:

(a)   Employees at work are paid in lieu of notice ('PILON'). A failure to make a PILON to the employee on maternity leave is because of her pregnancy/maternity leave, and therefore unlawful discrimination. If there is some other (non-discriminatory) reason for the failure to pay a PILON, that is a potential defence to the claim.

(b)   If the employee's contractual notice period is *not* one week or longer than their statutory notice period. *ERA 1996, ss 86–91* provide that where an employee's contractual notice is not one week or longer than statutory minimum notice, then if they are absent from work because of sickness or pregnancy or on adoption, parental or paternity leave, the employee is entitled to their usual pay in respect of their statutory notice period.

In all cases, there would be credit for maternity pay received. While there is no double recovery, there would be an obligation to top up notice pay in those circumstances.

8.111 *Holidays*

Contractual holiday accrues during OML, but AML does not. For statutory holiday, the starting point is that a woman on maternity leave is entitled to statutory holiday under the *Working Time Regulations 1998* ('*WTR 1998*') in the same way as any other worker. Holiday to which she is entitled, but does not take in the relevant year, would be lost (subject to any practice the employer has for other staff allowing holiday to be carried over) pursuant to *WTR 1998*. *Ainsworth v IRC* [2005] EWCA Civ 441, [2005] IRLR 465 is authority for the proposition that if an employee is off work for an entire leave year they are not entitled to *WTR 1998* holiday. This could not apply to a woman on maternity leave, however, who must be able to take the her paid annual *WTR 1998* leave during a period other than maternity leave (*Gómez v Continental Industrias del Caucho* SA [2004] ECR I-2605, [2004] 2 CMLR 38). The precise scope of the *Gomez* decision is not clear, and we suggest that a woman absent for an entire leave year simply does not accrue leave (following *Ainsworth*), bearing in mind the purpose of the underlying *Working Time Directive 93/104/EC* to protect health and safety. *Gomez* does, however, open the door to a possible argument that women on maternity leave who are not absent for the entire leave year have *WTR* holiday entitlement and that a failure to allow those women to carry over the holiday entitlement to the following year is discriminatory.

8.112 *Payment of bonuses*

As a preliminary point, bonuses which reflect performance or contribution to the business in any way must be awarded to women in respect of any time spent at work in the relevant bonus year. Employers must assess performance for women who are only at work for a part of the relevant bonus year and should, for example, make allowances in situations where targets cannot be met because of lead-in times etc; a failure to do so is likely contrary to *SDA 1975, ss 1* and *3A*. *S 3A* is a relatively new provision, which codifies existing case law to make clear that discrimination on the ground of pregnancy is a breach of *SDA 1975*.

(a) Compulsory maternity leave – employees are entitled to receive bonus payments (whatever the nature of the bonus scheme) in respect of the two-week period of compulsory maternity leave; see *Lewen v Denda* [1999] ECR I-7243, [2000] All ER (EC) 261, which was followed in the UK in *Hoyland v Asda Stores Ltd* [2006] CSIH 21, [2006] IRLR 468. This position is now enshrined in statute (*EqPA 1970, s 1(2)(e)(ii)*), at least as far as contractual bonuses are concerned. Claims for a non-contractual bonus in respect of compulsory maternity leave can be brought as an unlawful deduction from wages claim under the *ERA 1996* (this 'mechanism' was accepted in *Hoyland v Asda Stores Ltd*) or under *SDA 1975, s 3A* if the bonus is *not* a payment by way of wages or salary. Following the decision of *Equal Opportunities Commission v Secretary of State for Trade and Industry*, the Government has confirmed that *SDA 1975* will be amended to make clear that such a claim is permissible.

(b)   Ordinary maternity leave – under maternity legislation, employees are *not* entitled to bonuses in respect of the remainder of OML if the bonus is a payment by way of wages or salary (see 8.108). A bonus is more likely to be regarded as a payment by way of wages or salary if it is a reward for performance (whether individual or company), part and parcel of the salary system, contractual, a structured discretionary scheme or pensionable. A bonus is less likely to be treated as wages or salary if it is a one-off bonus unrelated to performance, designed to promote retention or future motivation or truly discretionary with employees having very little idea of whether they will get a bonus or even a rough idea of the size of their bonus (see *Connolly v HSBC Bank plc*, May 2004, Employment Tribunal Case No. 3202622/2001 and *Hoyland v Asda Stores Ltd*).

(c)   Additional maternity leave – under maternity legislation, employees are *not* entitled to bonuses in respect of AML – but see 8.113 as to the possibility that this is unlawful under European law (particularly *GUS Home Shopping Ltd v Green* [2001] IRLR 75 and *Sass*).

8.113 *Discrimination claims in relation to OML and AML*

Notwithstanding the position under the maternity legislation, there has always been the potential for an employee to bring a discrimination claim under *SDA 1975* or *EqPA 1970* for unpaid bonus in respect of both OML *and* AML. Such claims are now less likely to succeed in light of case law and changes to *SDA 1975* and *EqPA 1970*, which took effect on 1 October 2005; although see 8.24 and 8.71 in relation to amendments to these provisions.

The cases indicate that whilst it is discriminatory to withhold a *performance* bonus in respect of compulsory maternity leave, employers can withhold in respect of the remainder of OML and AML. According to the ECJ in *Lewen v Denda*, it will not be discriminatory to withhold a one-off bonus in respect of maternity leave if the bonus is subject to the sole condition that employees are in active employment at the time of payment. If the purpose of the bonus is to reward performance or contribution to the business, then employers must pay it in respect of any period of compulsory maternity leave, but it will not be discriminatory to withhold the bonus in relation to any other maternity or parental leave. In the UK, this aspect of *Lewen v Denda* has been followed by the EAT in *Hoyland v Asda*. (*Hoyland v Asda* was appealed to the Court of Session on a different and more limited point).

The case of *GUS Home Shopping Ltd v Green* [2001] IRLR 75 is not in line with this approach. Here it was held that a loyalty bonus which was not linked to performance or actual attendance at work could not be withheld from a woman on maternity leave. Such facts are relatively uncommon in practice. A discrimination claim is therefore most likely to succeed in the case of a non-contractual bonus which is not payable by way of wages or salary such as one which is designed to promote retention or future motivation. In addition, *Lewen v Denda* and *Hoyland v Asda* may need to be re-considered in light of *Sass*, which postdates *Lewen v Denda* and was not cited in *Hoyland v Asda*; the conclusion of the ECJ in *Sass* means that the non-payment of bonus in respect of any period of AML may be open to further argument. There is a greater prospect of a successful discrimination claim in relation to bonuses withheld during OML or AML.

8.114 *Repayment of enhanced maternity pay*

Some company schemes provide that if an employee does not return from maternity leave, or returns within a certain period of time, the employee must repay some or all of the enhanced maternity pay she received. The ECJ concluded that such provisions were not unlawfully discriminatory (*Boyle*). Requiring repayment may, however, depending on the circumstances, amount to victimisation or whistleblowing detriment (*Visa International Service Association v Paul* [2004] IRLR 42).

8.115 **Keeping in touch days and reasonable contact**

KIT days

An employee can now agree to work for her employer during her period of maternity (or adoption) leave on 'keeping in touch days' ('KIT days') without that work bringing the period of leave to an end and without losing entitlement to SMP (as it did previously) (*MPL Regulations, reg 12A(1)* and *Statutory Maternity Pay (General) Regulations 1986 (SI 1986/1960), reg 9A*). A maximum of ten days' or part-days' work for the employer during the leave period is permitted without impacting upon maternity entitlements (work done on any day counts as a whole KIT day; in other words, if an employee works one hour a day on ten days that would exhaust the ten KIT days in the same way as working eight hours a day on ten different days) (*MPL Regulations, reg 12A(2)*). This applies to all periods of maternity leave with the exception of the two-week compulsory leave period (*MPL Regulations, reg 12A(5)*) when she is prohibited from working. Any work carried out as a result of these provisions shall not have the effect of extending the total duration of the statutory maternity (or adoption) leave period (*reg 12A(7)*).

During consultation on the new KIT day provisions, activities such as training, attendance at conferences, appraisals and team meetings were suggested as occasions where employees and employers may wish to take advantage of the KIT days.

KIT days may be taken either as a single block or separately. This will be a matter for agreement between employer and employee. Neither can be forced to allow or take a KIT day (*reg 12A(6)*). The employee is protected from dismissal or detriment because she undertook, considered undertaking or refused to undertake work in respect of a KIT day (*regs 19(2)(eee)* and *20(3)(eee)*).

There may be National Minimum Wage issues – if an employee agrees to work for nothing on a KIT day, or a very low amount, and she has received little or no pay in the National Minimum Wage reference period (usually the preceding month), then that would be a breach of National Minimum Wage legislation.

Although it has not been addressed in legislation or case law, the authors believe that maternity pay paid to the employee should be offset against pay which she may be entitled to for a KIT day – in other words, the employer must 'top up' maternity pay for a KIT day, not pay both normal pay and maternity pay.

The same analysis applies to benefits – a failure to provide benefits to a woman on a KIT day would amount to unlawful discrimination, although in practice, the administrative burden of stopping and re-starting pension contributions and other benefits may outweigh the cost of any successful claims for not providing these benefits.

8.116 *Reasonable contact*

In addition to KIT days, 'reasonable contact from time to time' between employer and employee during both maternity and adoption leave is permitted (*MPL Regulations, reg 12A(4)*).

This is not a change to the law per se – such contact was almost certainly permitted before – but it is a useful clarification of the law.

According to the Government, this is designed to enhance communication and may include, for example, discussing plans regarding a return to work or keeping an employee updated with developments. DBERR has advised that the frequency and nature of 'reasonable contact' will depend on a number of factors, such as the nature of the work and the employee's post, any agreement that the employer and employee might have reached before maternity leave began as to contact, and whether either party needs to communicate important information to the other, for example news of changes at the workplace that might affect the employee on her return. We believe that this approach is likely to be adopted by tribunals; what is reasonable will vary between employees, and depending on what is happening at the workplace at any given time.

If an employer does not keep an employee on maternity leave up to date on important matters in the workplace such as vacancies and restructurings, there is a high risk of a successful claim for sex discrimination and/or pregnancy detriment (e g *Visa International v Paul*).

8.117 Return to work

Return after maternity or parental leave

An employee who returns to work after a period of OML only, or parental leave of four weeks or less, is entitled to return to the 'job in which she was employed before her absence'. An employee who returns to work after a period of AML or parental leave of more than four weeks is entitled to return to the 'job in which she was employed before her absence, or if it is not reasonably practicable for the employer to permit her to return to that job, to another job which is both suitable for her and appropriate for her to do in the circumstances' (*MPL Regulations, reg 18*). The job 'before her absence' is defined as that she was doing immediately before the leave (or before the first period of consecutive periods of statutory leave) (*reg 18(3)*).

Upon return, the employee is entitled to seniority, pension and similar rights as if she had not been absent, but effectively excluding any period of AML (subject to the equal treatment provisions of the *Social Security Act 1989, Sch 5* – see further 8.109 and on terms and conditions (under the wider *ERA 1996, s 71* definition, i e including non-contractual items) no less favourable than if she had not been absent (*reg 18A*).

The practical question is what 'job' she returns to. 'Job' is defined as 'the nature of the work which she is employed to do in accordance with her contract and the capacity and place in which she is so employed (*reg 1*). The only appellate decision on the meaning of this is *Blundell v Governing Body of St Andrew's Roman Catholic Primary School* [2007] IRLR 652. It is a question of fact for the tribunal, but in *Blundell* the teacher's job was held to be that of a teacher at the school generally and not that of the particular reception class she taught before she went on maternity leave, although the background to this was that the school reserved the right to – and frequently did – change the classes which teachers taught.

A refusal to allow an employee to return because her replacement is more efficient or preferable is direct sex discrimination (*Rees v Apollo Watch Repairs plc* [1996] ICR 466). Although the contract of employment is in large part suspended during maternity leave, the employer's conduct (or indications of actions at the time the employee returns) can still constitute a constructive dismissal through anticipatory repudiation (*Nelson v Kingston Cables Distributors Ltd* [2000] All ER (D) 606).

8.118 *Temporary workers: right to return*

The definition of 'employee' contained in the *MPL Regulations* limits the rights afforded by the *MPL Regulations* (including the right to return to work following maternity leave) to 'an individual who has entered into or works under ... a contract of employment.' This definition operates to exclude temporary workers. However, *SDA 1975, s 82* contains a broader definition of individuals protected from discrimination (see further COMMON CONCEPTS (1)). Under *s 82(1)*, employment means 'employment under a contract of service or apprenticeship or a contract personally to execute any work or labour', and related expressions (such as 'employee') are to be construed accordingly. Therefore, although the *MPL Regulations* do not afford temporary workers the right to return to work following a period of maternity leave, a failure to allow them to do so may be a breach of *SDA 1975, s 3A*.

The protection contained in *s 3A* against discrimination on the grounds of pregnancy or maternity leave is extended to contract (agency) workers by virtue of *s 9*, which affords protection to those doing 'work for a person (the 'principal') which is available for doing by individuals ('contract workers') who are employed not by the principal himself but by another person, who supplies them under a contract made with the principal' (see further COMMON CONCEPTS (1)).

The effect is that an employee 'employed' (within the meaning of *SDA 1975*) by an agency is protected against sex discrimination by both the agency itself, and the 'principal', (ie end-user) to whom the services are provided.

It has previously been held that an agency worker may be entitled to return to her original position after a period of maternity leave (*BP Chemicals Limited v Gillick and Roevin Management Services Limited* [1995] IRLR 128 and *Patefield v Belfast City Council* [2000] IRLR 664, a decision of the Northern Irish Court of Appeal); note that these cases were decided prior to the introduction of *s 3A* (and the equivalent legislation in Northern Ireland) and were therefore based on general principles of sex discrimination. As a result of the fact that both Ms Gillick and Ms Patefield were engaged through agencies, the *Gillick* decision was made in reliance on *SDA 1975, s 9*, (and in *Patefield,* the equivalent legislation, being *Article 12* of the *Sex Discrimination (Northern Ireland) Order 1976*).

Although the *SDA 1975* may afford some temporary workers a right to return following a period of maternity leave, it cannot be assumed that *all* temporary workers will possess such a right. Firstly, *s 9* only applies to contract workers that are employed (using the *SDA 1975* definition which, as explained, goes beyond employment in the strict legal sense; see above and COMMON CONCEPTS (1)) by an organisation other than the end-user organisation that they are working for. There are some categories of worker – such as where there is a right of substitution – which may not be caught by *s 9* or the definition of employee. Secondly, even if a temporary worker falls within the ambit of *SDA 1975* in order to claim a right to return to her old position, a worker must demonstrate that were it not for her pregnancy, she would have continued to work for the end-user. In *Patefield*, for example, at the time of commencing her maternity leave, Ms Patefield had three years' service, and was the longest serving member of staff in her office. This enabled the Court of Appeal to conclude that she would have remained in her post were it not for her taking maternity leave. This may not always be the case, for example in circumstances where the employee has a shorter length of service and/or the end-user is able to demonstrate that she would not have been retained in her role regardless of her pregnancy.

S 3A also affords temporary workers who fall within the *SDA 1975* definition of 'employee' or 'contract worker' the right not to be discriminated against on grounds of pregnancy during the recruitment process, even where the role for which they are applying is for a fixed-term, to cover a period of maternity leave being taken by an existing employee.

8.119 **Pregnancy or maternity-related dismissals**

A woman who is dismissed because of pregnancy, childbirth or maternity leave may be able to bring a claim of discrimination under *SDA 1975, s 3A* and of automatic unfair dismissal (*ERA 1996, s 99* and *MPL Regulations, reg 20*). It is not yet clear whether a claim under *SDA 1975, s 1* is still permissible (see 8.73).

8.120 **Remedy**

For a general discussion on remedies available in discrimination cases, see 1.115ff. The approach taken to assessing the remedy for sex discrimination is the same as that taken in relation to other types of discrimination.

Some specific issues have been raised, particularly in circumstances when a pregnant employee is dismissed in a discriminatory manner and the employment tribunal must assess the losses which flow from this. One such question is whether, had the employee not been unlawfully dismissed, she would have returned to work following her maternity leave, and, if so, for how long she would have continued to have been employed by the same employer. The key cases on this point appear to place a burden on the woman to demonstrate that she would have returned to work, and also encourage the use of statistics to assess the chances that she would have done so. These cases are now over ten years old and it may be that tribunals would now apply the usual principles relevant to the determination of compensation for discrimination without giving special consideration as to the likelihood of a female employee returning to the workplace after a period of maternity leave (unless the particular facts of the case meant that this was in issue). An analysis of these cases is set out below in any event.

According to *Ministry of Defence v Cannock* [1995] 2 All ER 449, [1994] ICR 918, the questions which the tribunal must ask itself in assessing a pregnant employee's loss of earnings suffered as a result of being unlawfully dismissed are:

(a)   What are the chances that, had she been given maternity leave and an opportunity to return to work, the employee would have returned?

(b)   What are the chances that the woman would have been in a position to return to work, had she been given the opportunity?

(c)   How long would she have remained employed by the employer for?

The EAT made it clear that a determination of these matters involves an assessment of chance, rather than fact. Usually, there will be different percentage chances at each of these stages. For example, there may be an 80% chance that the employee would have returned to work, had she been given the opportunity, but only a 60% chance that she would have worked until retirement (or some relevant earlier date, such as the end date of a fixed-term contract). The tribunal would then calculate her earnings until retirement (or the relevant date), deduct any amount actually earned (or to be earned) by the employee through alternative employment, then multiply this figure by 80%, and then multiply the resulting figure by 60% (see *Ministry of Defence v Hunt and Others* [1996] IRLR 139).

The starting point in the MOD cases were the statistics showing the percentage of servicewomen who, given the option, return to work after childbirth. What actually happened after the woman gave birth is also relevant. For example, a woman who has made little or no effort to find suitable employment with another employer will struggle to show that there was a high percentage chance that she would have returned to work following maternity leave, had she not been dismissed. The question of searching for alternative employment will also be relevant to the employee's obligation to mitigate loss (see below and 1.115ff for further detail on this).

In determining whether the woman would have been in a position to return to work, the tribunal will consider the demands placed on her by the job in question, as well as what the woman (and her partner, where relevant), actually did after the child was born. In *Cannock*, the point was made that if the woman's partner was also in the armed services and the couple had decided to remain together as a unit, the tribunal would have to consider the chances of him or her giving up work in order for them to remain together. If the chances were that she would have given up her work, the award would be reduced accordingly.

According to *Cannock,* the starting point for the third question of for how long the woman would have remained employed would again be statistics demonstrating how long, on average, employees would be likely to remain employed by the same employer in the industry in question. Having said this, a claimant is likely to argue that, regardless of these statistics, there is a good chance that she would have been employed by the same employer up until retirement, or some earlier relevant date. *Vento v Chief Constable of West Yorkshire Police (No 2)* [2002] IRLR 177, EAT provides an example of this argument succeeding. The respondent employer will likely suggest that intervening events subsequent to the employee's dismissal mean that the employee would not have remained employed until that date. For example, in *Brash-Hall v Getty Images Limited* [2006] EWCA Civ 531, [2006] All ER (D) 111 (May), it was held that although Mrs Brash-Hall would have returned to work had she not been unlawfully dismissed, her employment would have terminated shortly after her return, owing to a restructuring exercise which meant her role would have been redundant. On this basis, the Court of Appeal held that she was only entitled to recover her losses up until the date of the restructuring.

Similarly, a tribunal may find that an employee would only have remained employed by her original employer for a limited period before resigning to take up another job. In *Fletcher-Cooke v Board of Governors of Hampton School* [2007] WL 504753 (a disability discrimination case), the EAT upheld such a finding. In doing so, it referred to the fact that the employee in question had a history of short periods of employment, and the fact that, at the time of her dismissal, the employee was already looking for alternative employment. In most cases, such evidence of a probable/actual intervening event such as this will exist to refute a claimant's suggestion that had she not been dismissed, she would have remained employed by the same employer until retirement. The exceptions to this, such as in *Vento* and the Ministry of Defence cases (in which the relevant date was not retirement, but the expiry of the term of engagement) appear to occur in occupations where employees often expect to have a 'job for life' and are therefore able to argue that, had they not been unlawfully dismissed, their jobs would have remained in existence and that they would not have left to take up an alternative position. Even in these cases, the tribunal will still have to assess the percentage chance that the employee would have worked until retirement (in *Vento*, this was assessed at 75%).

Notwithstanding that the test is one of probabilities rather than a determination of the facts, a tribunal may conclude that there was a 100% chance that 'the chance that had she been given the opportunity, a woman would have returned to work following maternity leave and, in 'exceptional and unusual' circumstances, that she would have remained employed for an extended period. In *Hunt*, it was held that there was a 100% chance that the claimant would have remained employed for sixteen years were it not for her employment having been terminated unlawfully. The factors which justified such a conclusion included Mrs Hunt's achievements during her employment, the fact that her mother had also always worked outside the home and was regarded as a role model by Mrs Hunt, and the fact that Mrs Hunt had previously had an abortion in order to continue working for her employer. The EAT emphasised in this case that statistics as to the probability of women returning to work had their limitations and should be used as a starting point only. Despite its assertions to the contrary, it would appear that the EAT was actually making a finding of fact that, based on her personal circumstances, Mrs Hunt would have returned to work. Therefore, although the EAT claimed to be following the decision in *Cannock*, *Hunt* may indicate a move away from an objective assessment of a woman's percentage chances of returning to work (which, arguably, is based on discriminatory stereotypes) and towards a finding based on the facts of the case.

A tribunal will also consider the extent to which an employee has attempted to mitigate her loss by seeking alternative employment. In *Hunt*, it was said that the tribunal was entitled to consider the difficulties in finding employment encountered by women with young children, which arose out of 'gender-based assumptions' made by employers at the time. See 1.115ff for further detail on the duty to mitigate.

It is also noteworthy that once a tribunal has assessed the likelihood of a woman returning to work, and the period for which she would have remained employed by the employer in question, it will deduct childcare costs from the compensation payable, on the basis that had the woman remained employed, she would have had to pay these. The fact that a woman's partner would have paid for half of these costs is not relevant for these purposes (*Ministry of Defence v Cannock and Others*).

8.121 OTHER FAMILY RIGHTS

Adoption leave

Entitlement to adoption leave

The entitlement to adoption leave generally mirrors the entitlement to maternity leave. For discussion in relation to bonuses, annual leave and the applicability of terms and conditions during a period of leave, see 8.108ff.

Under the *Paternity and Adoption Leave Regulations 2002* (*SI 2002/2788*) ('*PAL Regulations*'), an employee is entitled to adoption leave in respect of a child if he:

(a)   is the child's adopter (ie has been matched with the child for adoption by a UK adoption agency;

(b)   has notified the agency that he has agreed that the child should be placed with him and agreed the date of placement;

(c)   has been continuously employed by the same employer for at least 26 weeks ending with the week in which he is notified of having been matched with the child; and

(d)   has notified the employer of when the employee would like to take his adoption leave, no more than seven days after he was notified that he has been matched with a child.

An employer may request the employee provides evidence of the adoption by way of a document issued by the agency matching the employee with the child, the name and address of the agency, the date on which the employee was notified he had been matched with the child and the date on which the agency expects to place the child.

Ordinary adoption leave (OAL) may commence on the date of placement or on an alternative date which is no earlier than 14 days prior to the date of placement, provided this has been notified to the employer.

An employee may take 52 weeks of adoption leave, comprising 26 weeks of OAL followed by 26 weeks of additional adoption leave (AAL). As with maternity leave, the further service requirement for AAL was removed further to the *Work and Families Act* (although the service requirement for OAL remains). The leave period is the same regardless of the number of children placed as part of the same arrangement.

As with AML, an employee who wishes to return to work earlier than the end of his AAL, must now give at least eight weeks' notice of the date he intends to return. Further, 'Keeping in Touch' days whereby an employee may attend to work up to ten days, by agreement with his employer, have been introduced; see 8.120.

The *PAL Regulations, regs 19–27* set out terms relating to the right to return from adoption leave and the application of terms and conditions during OAL and AAL. These mirror the provisions relating to employees on maternity leave; see 8.117 for details.

Employees retain their entitlement to statutory annual leave throughout OAL and AAL. If the employee is also entitled to contractual annual leave, this will accrue during OAL but not during AAL, unless agreed otherwise with the employer.

8.122 *Adoption pay*

To qualify for statutory adoption pay (SAP) an employee must:

(a)   be an 'employed earner' (ie someone who is liable to pay the employer's share of their Class 1 National Insurance Contributions, such as agency workers, as detailed in the *Social Security (Categorisation of Earners) Regulations 1978 (SI 1978/1689)*);

(b)   earn at least the lower earnings limit;

(c)   have been matched with a child to be placed with him by a UK adoption agency;

(d)   have notified the agency that he agrees that the child should be placed with him and agree on a date of placement;

(e)   have been in employed earner's employment with the same employer continuously for at least 26 weeks ending with the week in which he is notified of having been matched with the child.

(f)   notify the employer of when he wants to receive SAP at least 28 days before the date he wants it to begin or as soon as reasonably practicable.

(Social Security Contributions and Benefits Act 1992, s 171ZL; Statutory Paternity Pay and Adoption Pay (General) Regulations 2002 (SI 2002/2822) ('SPP Regulations'), regs 23–24).

If an employee meets these qualifying conditions, he is entitled to 39 weeks' SAP, which is paid by employers and mostly or completely refunded by the Government. Where one partner takes adoption leave and pay, the other may take paternity leave and pay *(PAL Regulations, reg 8* and *SPP Regulations, reg 11).*

The right to adoption leave and SAP only arises where a new child is adopted into the family. It does not cover instances where a step-parent or foster-carer adopts a child already under their care. The guidance from the Department for Business Enterprise and Regulatory Reform states that where foster carers are fostering a child that has not been matched and placed with them for adoption by an adoption agency, but they have applied to the court for an Adoption Order to be made, they will not be eligible for statutory adoption leave or pay. This is because adoption leave is intended to support the care of a child during the initial stages of the placement. Adoption leave and pay is similarly not available to special guardians, although they may take parental leave. A person becomes a special guardian when a court makes a special guardianship order (SGO). This gives them parental responsibility for the child to the exclusion of others, such as the birth parents. Unlike adoption, however, under a SGO, the parents remain the child's parents and retain parental responsibility, although their ability to exercise this responsibility is extremely limited.

Even where adoptive parents or special guardians do not qualify for adoption leave or pay, they may be entitled to parental leave because they will have 'parental responsibility' when they adopt. 'Parental responsibility' is defined in the *MPL Regulations, reg 2* and the *Children Act 1989, s 3,* as the rights, duties, powers, responsibilities and authority which, by law, a parent of a child has in relation to the child and his property.

8.123 *Protection from unfair dismissal/detriment*

The *PAL Regulations, regs 28* and *29* provide that an employee may not be subjected to any detriment or dismissed by reason of their taking adoption leave or seeking to take such leave. A dismissal is therefore automatically unfair if it is by reason of the employee's taking or seeking to take adoption leave.

The employment tribunal case of *Anna Coulombeau v Enterprise Rent-A-Car (UK) Ltd* ET 2600296/06 (19 February 2007, unreported) is one of the few cases concerning adoption leave. In this case, an employee brought a claim against her employer on various grounds, including automatic unfair dismissal, namely the reason or principal reason for her dismissal was connected with the fact she took, or sought to take, or the employer believed it was likely she would take, adoption leave. The tribunal explained that the burden of proof required Ms Coulombeau to produce evidence to create a presumption of law that the dismissal was for an inadmissible reason under *ERA 1996, s 99.* The respondent then had to show the real reason for the dismissal was by reason of the claimant's conduct.

Ms Coulombeau had learned she would not be able to bear children and undertook various meetings with social workers to gain approval for eligibility to adopt. The claimant was subsequently subject to disciplinary investigations regarding three separate allegations of misconduct. These matters were investigated and the claimant was subsequently dismissed. The tribunal established that the investigations were inadequate and the dismissal unfair. It considered the reason for the dismissal by looking simultaneously at the issues of sex discrimination and adoption leave. The two male comparators put forward by the claimant had committed the same or more serious offences but were only given written warnings. The tribunal held that there was clear evidence of less favourable treatment of women in comparison with men as, on the balance of probabilities, a man would not have been dismissed for similar offences. They found that the reason for the dismissal was that the respondent considered that, as a woman, the claimant would be likely to need time off for adoption purposes including, ultimately, adoption leave.

8.124 *Disrupted placement*

A period of adoption leave may be disrupted if the child dies or is returned to the agency, or if the employee is simply notified that the placement will not go ahead. In such circumstances, the adoption leave comes to an end eight weeks after the end of the relevant week. The relevant week is the week the employee is notified that the placement will not be made or the week the child dies or is returned to the agency. Where the employee's period of OAL comes to an end within those eight weeks, the employee may take the unexpired remainder of the eight weeks as AAL. However, where the employee's period of AAL comes to an end within those eight weeks, the employee must return to work at the end of the AAL as the eight weeks will not extend AAL beyond the date it would originally have expired.

8.125 *Overseas adoption*

The entitlement for employees who are adopting a child from outside the UK is essentially the same as for UK adoptions, save for some minor differences in relation to eligibility criteria, notice and evidential requirements and when leave and pay may begin. The relevant provisions are included in the *Paternity and Adoption Leave (Adoption from Overseas) Regulations 2003 (SI 2003/91), Statutory Paternity Pay (Adoption) and Statutory Adoption Pay (Adoptions from Overseas) (No 2) Regulations 2003 (SI 2003/1194)* and *Social Security Contributions and Benefits Act 1992 (application of Parts 12ZA and 12ZB to Adoptions from Overseas) Regulations 2003 (SI 2003/499)*.

Rather than receiving a notification of matching, for overseas adoptions, the employee will receive an 'official notification'. The service requirement for adoption pay is 26 weeks ending with the week in which the adopter is notified of the match for UK adoptions; whereas, for overseas adoptions, the period is 26 weeks either ending with the week in which the notification was received, or from the start of their employment.

For the purposes of assessing and calculating eligibility to adoption leave and SAP, the relevant date in overseas adoptions is the date of the child's entry into Great Britain, or a fixed date no later than 28 days after entry. This contrasts with UK adoptions where the critical date when an employee can commence adoption leave and receive SAP is on or up to 14 days prior to the date of the placement. There are additional notification requirements in overseas adoptions, which require the employee to give his employer notice of the date he received an official notification, the date the child is expected to enter Great Britain, the date his adoption leave should begin and the actual date the child enters Great Britain.

8.126 **Paternity leave**

The entitlement to paternity leave was introduced by the *Employment Act 2002* which sets out the basic rights and amends *ERA 1996* and the *Social Security Contributions and Benefits Act 1992*. The detail of this entitlement is in the *PAL Regulations* and the *SPP Regulations*. In May 2007, the DTI (Now DBERR) published a consultation document on the administration of additional paternity leave and pay for which responses are due by 3 August 2007. This proposed extension to paternity leave is explained at 8.130.

8.127 *Entitlement to paternity leave*

An employee is entitled to paternity leave if he or she will be caring for a child or supporting the child's mother. These concepts are not defined and there are no reported cases concerning them. This right is available to employees who have 26 weeks' continuous service ending with the 15th week before the EWC or ending with the week in which the adopter is notified of having been matched with the child. The employee must also be either the father of the child or married to, or the civil partner or partner of, the child's mother or adopter, and he or she must have or expect to have responsibility for the upbringing of the child.

The employee must give his or her employer notice of intention to take paternity leave in or before the 15th week before the EWC specifying the expected week of birth, the length of leave and the date when the employee expects the leave will begin. An employer is entitled to request the employee provides a signed declaration confirming the purpose of the absence and stating that he or she satisfies the conditions of entitlement. Where an employee is the husband, partner or civil partner of the child's adopter, he or she will be entitled to paternity leave provided he gives notice within seven days of receiving notification of the match, giving the date the adopter was notified of a match and the expected date of placement.

Length of leave

An employee may take either one week's leave or two consecutive weeks' leave and this leave must be taken within 56 days of the child's birth or placement. During paternity leave, an employee is entitled to the benefit of all of his or her terms and conditions of employment, including the accrual of holiday, but with the exception of remuneration. The employee is similarly bound by his obligations under those terms and conditions.

At the end of the period of paternity leave, the employee is entitled to return to the same job in which he was employed prior to the leave. However, if the paternity leave was not an isolated period of absence and followed another period of statutory leave, namely parental leave of more than four weeks or additional maternity or adoption leave, then the employee's right to return is to the same job or, if that is not reasonably practicable, to a similar job which is suitable and appropriate in the circumstances.

8.128 *Statutory paternity pay*

Statutory paternity pay (SPP) is available to employees who meet the following conditions: 26 weeks' continuous service with his employer ending with the end of the 15th week before the EWC or ending with the week in which the adopter is notified of having been matched with the child, and continuous service from that week up to the child's birth or placement; a defined relationship with the child and mother; has given appropriate notification (of the EWC, the date from which SPP will be payable and the duration of the period during which it will be payable); and whose average weekly earnings are equal to or above the lower earnings limit (£87 per week from July 2007).

Employees who satisfy these qualifying conditions are entitled to the lesser of £112.75 or 90% of the employee's average weekly earnings (from 1 April 2007).

Some employers may offer enhanced paternity pay. It is unlikely that a failure to provide benefits equivalent to enhanced maternity pay amounts to sex discrimination, given the provisions of *SDA 1975, s 2* and that ECJ case law emphasises the special protection of pregnant women (*Gillespie v Northern Health and Social Services Board* [1996] ECR I-475, [1996] All ER (EC) 284).

8.129 *Protection from unfair dismissal/detriment*

An employee entitled to paternity leave is protected against detriment or dismissal as a result of taking or seeking to take paternity leave. A dismissal is automatically unfair if it is by reason of the employee's taking or seeking to take paternity leave and extends to selection for redundancy on grounds associated with the taking of paternity leave. Despite the 26 weeks' eligibility requirement, an employee can bring a claim on such grounds, regardless of their length of service.

8.130 *Consultation on additional paternity leave*

On 14 May 2007, the Government published a consultation document proposing the option for employed fathers to take the balance of a mother's untaken maternity leave and SMP as up to 26 weeks' additional paternity leave, some of which may be paid, if the mother ends maternity leave during the second six months of the child's life. This consultation period lasted until 3 August 2007. The Government's goal is to introduce this at the same time as extending SMP and SAP from 39 weeks to 52 weeks. The earliest date for implementation will be for babies due on or after April 2010, although no firm timing decisions have yet been made.

8.131 **Parental leave**

Entitlement to parental leave

Employees are entitled to parental leave, provided they have at least one year's continuous employment and have or expect to have responsibility for a child. An employee has responsibility for a child if he has parental responsibility or has been registered as the child's parent. This right was introduced by the *MPL Regulations* and is included at *ERA 1996, ss 76–80*. 'Parental responsibility' is defined in the *Children Act 1989, s 3*, as the rights, duties, powers, responsibilities and authority which, by law, a parent of a child has in relation to the child and his property.

Pursuant to *ERA 1996, s 78(7)* and the *MPL Regulations, reg 16*, parties may make their own agreements about how parental leave is to be taken within a particular workplace. This can be done by a collective agreement, workforce agreement, or individual agreement with the employee. Where no such agreement has been reached, the default provisions in *Schedule 2* of the Regulations will apply. Where an employee has a contractual right to parental leave, he may not exercise both the statutory right and the contractual right but may take advantage of the more favourable of the two.

Employees may take up to 13 weeks' unpaid leave in respect of any individual child up until that child's fifth birthday or, in the case of an adopted child, the earlier of the fifth anniversary of the date of placement or the child's eighteenth birthday. Employees are entitled to 18 weeks' unpaid leave for a child who is entitled to a disability living allowance, up until the child's eighteenth birthday. This leave can be taken by both parents in relation to each child. As with the other family-friendly rights, one week's leave is calculated to be the amount an employee is normally required to work in a week and, where this is irregular, an average should be calculated using a twelve-week reference period.

Under the default scheme, leave must be taken in multiples of one week. The only exception to this is in relation to children who are entitled to a disability living allowance, when parents can take parental leave in multiples of one day. In *New Southern Railways Ltd (formerly South Central Trains) v Rodway* [2005] EWCA Civ 443, [2005] ICR 1162, where an employer refused an employee's request to take one day's parental leave to look after his son on the ground that his job could not be covered on that day, the employee went ahead and took the day off and was given a written warning for his unauthorised absence from work. The employee claimed that he had been subjected to a detriment for a reason relating to parental leave. The EAT and Court of Appeal, which allowed the employer's appeal, held that where no workplace agreement provides otherwise, the default position is that leave can only be taken in weekly blocks.

The employee must give his employer 21 days' notice, specifying the proposed dates of leave. The *MPL Regulations, Sch 2* sets out the conditions of entitlement and provides that an employer may request proof of an employee's entitlement to parental leave. Evidence of entitlement may include proof of the child's date of birth or placement for adoption, and evidence of a child's entitlement to a disability living allowance. An employer may also postpone the period of leave where the employer considers that the operation of the business would be unduly disrupted by that period of leave. Such a postponement is possible on condition that the employer allows the employee to take a period of leave of the same duration within the following six months and provides written notice to the employee of the reason for the postponement and the dates of the rescheduled leave. An employer may not postpone leave when the employee has requested to take it immediately after the birth or placement of a child.

The ECJ case of *Kiiski v Tempereen Kaupunki C-11606* [2007] All ER (D) 120 (Sep) is authority for the extent to which employers may be required to reschedule parental leave at the employee's request. In this case concerning an employee in Finland, the ECJ held that an employer's refusal to allow the employee to change the dates of her unpaid parental leave so as to enable her to take paid maternity leave constituted direct sex discrimination. The relevant collective agreement, which provided that a new pregnancy was not a good reason to change the dates of parental leave once agreed, was contrary to both the *Equal Treatment Directive* and the *Pregnant Workers Directive*.

During parental leave, an employee is entitled to the same benefits and bound by the same obligations which are owed during additional maternity leave (AML) (see 8.108).

8.132 *Protection from unfair dismissal/detriment*

The *Rodway* case is also authority for the proposition that treatment by an employer is only victimisation it if is 'done for a prescribed reason'. In this case, the employee could not lawfully take one day of parental leave and therefore the disciplinary warning was not for a prescribed reason and was therefore not victimisation.

8.133 *Right to return to work*

Pursuant to the *MPL Regulations, reg 18*, where an employee has taken parental leave of four weeks or less and the leave is not taken immediately after a period of AML or AAL, he will be entitled to return to the same job. Otherwise, the employee's right to return is the same as after AML, being the same job unless it is not reasonably practicable, in which case he is entitled to another job which is suitable and appropriate in the circumstances.

8.134 **Time off for dependants**

Entitlement to time off for dependants

Pursuant to *ERA 1996, s 57A*, an employee is entitled to take a reasonable amount of time off in order to take action which is necessary for one of the following events:

(a)   to provide assistance when a dependant falls ill, gives birth or is injured or assaulted;

(b)   to make arrangements for the provision of care for a dependant who is ill or injured;

(c)   in consequence of the death of a dependant;

(d)   because of the unexpected disruption or termination of arrangements for the care of a dependant; or

(e)   to deal with an incident which involves a child of the employee's and which occurs unexpectedly in a period during which an educational establishment which the child attends is responsible for him.

A 'dependant' is a spouse or civil partner, a child, parent or person who lives in the same household as the employee, other than by reason of being his employee, tenant, lodger or boarder. A dependant also includes any person who reasonably relies on the employee for assistance or to make arrangements for the provision of care.

In the case of *Qua v John Ford Morrison Solicitors* [2003] IRLR 184, the EAT gave guidance as to the scope of this entitlement. In this case Ms Qua had been dismissed because of a high level of absences to look after her child. Ms Qua claimed she had been unfairly dismissed for exercising her right to time off but this was dismissed by the tribunal on the basis that Ms Qua had failed to tell the employer the reason for and duration of her absences as soon as reasonably practicable.

The EAT held that the tribunal had erred in how it approached the duty to inform the employer and remitted the matter to the tribunal. The EAT also clarified the purpose and limitations of the right to time off. It explained that the right was to 'reasonable' time off to take action which is 'necessary', and explained that, in determining whether the action was necessary, the disruption and inconvenience to the employer are irrelevant. The factors to consider include the nature of the incident, the closeness of the relationship between employee and dependant, and the extent to which anyone else was available to assist.

The entitlement is conditional upon the employee telling the employer the reason and the expected duration for the absence. In *Truelove v Safeways Stores PLC* [2005] ICR 589, the EAT held that there must be:

'a communication that imparted an understanding into the employer's mind that something had happened to cause the breakdown of what would otherwise be a stable arrangement affecting, in the present case, a child and making it necessary, urgently, for the employee to be absent from work.'

Overturning the tribunal's decision, the EAT held that the employee telling his employer that he might need leave on the following day because his partner had to attend a meeting and he had to look after their young child was sufficient communication, even though the employee had not disclosed that there had been an unexpected disruption to the arrangements. This case is authority for the proposition that when considering the reasonableness of an employee's request, an employer should consider how often it has happened before, whether or not there is another way of solving the problem and the business needs of the employer.

The case of *Forster v Cartwright Black Solicitors* [2004] ICR 1728 clarified that this provision does not cover the right to compassionate leave as a result of a bereavement, but rather is triggered by the need to take action which is necessary in consequence of the death, including registering the death and, where necessary, applying for probate. In practice, therefore, it appears the leave is for practical rather than emotional needs.

8.135 *Complaint to a tribunal*

ERA 1996, s 57B provides that an employee is entitled to make a complaint to the tribunal that his employer has unreasonably refused him the right to take time off, within three months of the refusal or such further period as the tribunal decides is reasonable. Where such a complaint is found to be well-founded, an employee is entitled to compensation which is just and equitable in light of the employer's default in refusing to permit time off to be taken by the employees, and any loss sustained by the employee which is attributable to the matters complained of.

8.136 **In vitro fertilisation (IVF)**

A woman may only succeed in a sex discrimination claim related to fertility treatment if she can show that a man undergoing fertility treatment is or would be given more favourable treatment in similar circumstances, or that the employer has treated her less favourably because she might become pregnant.

In the case of *Joyce v Northern Microwave Distributors Ltd* ET 5564/93 (16 August 1993, unreported), the tribunal held that a woman who was dismissed because she was on a course of fertility treatment had suffered discrimination owing to her employer's stereotyped and discriminatory attitude. The tribunal rejected the respondent's case that she was dismissed because the treatment would necessitate significant absences from work. However, in *London Borough of Greenwich v Robinson* EAT 745/94, the EAT held that the employer's decision to select a female employee for redundancy because of her absence for IVF treatment was neither direct not indirect sex discrimination. IVF is not a pregnancy-related illness and in this case the condition imposed was that time taken off as sick leave other than for pregnancy or confinement would be one of the redundancy criteria. The EAT explained there was no need to look at particular forms of sickness to see whether they had a discriminatory effect on the grounds of sex.

This EAT decision was followed by the tribunal in *Hickman v Prest Ltd* ET 59236/95 (13 May 1996, unreported); however in *Kaveri v Birmingham Power Ltd* ET 08037/95 (27 March 1996, unreported), the tribunal held that the dismissal of a woman because she was absent to undergo fertility treatment was pregnancy-related and therefore unlawful sex discrimination.

8.137 Surrogacy

Surrogacy is the practice whereby one woman carries a child for another with the intention that the child be handed over at birth to the intended parents and raised as their child. In a surrogacy situation, there may be up to four parties. The surrogate mother who is carrying the child and her husband or civil partner, as well as the woman who intends to take maternal responsibility for the child after birth, and her spouse or civil partner who intends to take parental responsibility.

There are several ways surrogacy can occur, depending on whether or not the intended mother has donated an egg and also whether or not the sperm of the intended father is used.

If an embryo is created using gametes of two anonymous donors (ie from neither of the intended parents) this is not seen as surrogacy. Because neither of the intended parents would be genetically related to the child, they would have to adopt the child in any case.

8.138 *Taking responsibility for the child*

The surrogate mother is always registered on the birth certificate, even if she is not genetically related to the child (*Human Fertilisation and Embryology Act 1990* ('*HFEA 1990*'), s 27(1)). Therefore, the intended mother can take responsibility for the child by obtaining a Parental Order from the courts or by adopting the child. Adoption is necessary where the conditions for obtaining a Parental Order are not fulfilled.

Under *HFEA 1990, s 30* the conditions of obtaining a Parental Order are:

(a)   the child is genetically related to at least one of the intended parents;

(b)   the surrogate parents have consented to the making of the order (unless untraceable or incapable of giving consent) no earlier than six weeks after the birth of the child;

(c)   the intended parents are aged eighteen or over;

(d)   the intended parents are married;

(e)   the intended parents apply for the Parental Order within six months of the birth of the child;

(f)   no money, other than expenses, has been paid in respect of the surrogacy, unless authorised by a court;

(g)   the child is living with the intended parents; and

(h)   the intended parents are domiciled in a part of the United Kingdom or the Channel Islands or Isle of Man.

The default position is that the surrogate mother's husband will be named on the birth certificate as the father (*HFEA 1990, s 28(2)*). However, if the surrogate mother is unmarried, or if the surrogate mother's husband states that he has not given permission for the surrogacy, then the intended father can be registered on the birth certificate as the father if he is the genetic father (*s 28(2)* and common law presumption that genetic fathers are legal fathers). It will not then be necessary for the intended father to obtain a Parental Order or to adopt the child. It does not appear to be possible for an intended father who is not genetically related to the child to be named on the birth certificate – therefore he would need to obtain a Parental Order or to adopt the child.

8.139 *Leave available for the intended parents*

(a)   *Adoption leave.* The intended parents will not usually be eligible for adoption leave or pay, as they have not been matched with the child through an agency. It is unclear whether a Parental Order is equivalent to adoption for the purposes of adoption leave (and paternity leave, since this is available to the partner of the adopter). However, this will only be relevant where an adoption agency is used – an unlikely situation in surrogacy.

(b)   *Paternity leave.* In a surrogacy situation, the intended father may be entitled to paternity leave even where his partner does not qualify for adoption leave under *PAL Regulations, reg 2(a)(i)*, if he is the child's 'father'. This would seem to entitle the intended father who is genetically related to the child to paternity leave, whether or not he is named on the birth certificate – although it would be open to the tribunal to determine if an individual is the 'father' by reference to the birth certificate.

(c)   *Parental leave.* Where a Parental Order is made or adoption – through an agency or otherwise – occurs, the intended parents will be eligible for parental leave as they will have 'parental responsibility' for the child under the law (*MPL Regulations, reg 13*). A Parental Order cannot be made within six weeks of the child's birth (*HFEA 1990, s 30(6)*). However, parental leave will be available even before the Parental Order is made (or adoption occurs) since an employee who 'expects to have' responsibility for a child is eligible for such leave (*MPL Regulations, reg 13(1)(b)*).

8.140 FLEXIBLE WORKING

The *Employment Act 2002* (*'EA 2002'*) creates a new right for employees to make a flexible working request. This can be a request to a change in the number of working hours worked by the employee, when those hours are worked, and/or where he or she works (ie from home or at the employer's place of business). The legislation was originally targeted at those who are responsible for caring for a child, but in April 2007 the right was extended to carers of adults over the age of eighteen.

8.141 Who can apply?

Under the *Flexible Working* (*Eligibility, Complaints and Remedies*) *Regulations 2002* (*SI 2002/3236*), *reg 3*, in order to qualify for the right to make a flexible working request, an employee must:

(a)   have at least 26 weeks' continuous service; and be:

(i)   the mother, father, adopter, guardian, or foster parent of the child; or

(ii)   married to, the civil partner or the partner of the child's mother, father, adopter, guardian or foster parent; and

(b)   have, or expect to have, responsibility for the upbringing of a child under the age of six, or eighteen if the child is disabled; or

(c)   care or expect to be caring for a person over the age of eighteen who is either:

(i)   married to, the civil partner, or the partner of the employee;

(ii)   a relative of the employee; or

(iii)   living at the same address as the employee.

Under the *Flexible Working (Eligibility, Complaints and Remedies) Regulations 2002*, from 1 October 2007, private foster carers (and the spouse, partner or civil partner of such a person) and those in whose favour a residence order is in force in respect of a child (and the spouse, partner or civil partner of such a person) have been entitled to request flexible working. Additionally, the definition of 'adopter' has been extended to those who are adopting a child which has not been placed through a UK adoption agency.

The purpose of the application must be to enable the employee to care for the child or adult for whom he or she is responsible, although some employers have voluntarily extended the right to all staff. Agency workers and military personnel are not entitled to make statutory requests, nor are parents of non-disabled children over the age of six.

8.142   How a request is made

The *Flexible Working (Procedural Requirements) Regulations 2002 (SI 2002/3207)* and *ERA 1996, ss 80F–80I* create a very specific procedure that must be followed by employer and employee. Employees are entitled to make one request every twelve months. The request must be in writing and must state the following:

(a)   that the application is being made under the statutory right to request a flexible working pattern;

(b)   the basis of the employee's eligibility, for example that he is a parent of a child under six, or a carer of an adult (see 8.141);

(c)   what working arrangements the employee is requesting;

(d)   what effect the employee thinks the arrangements might have on the employer's business, and how this could be addressed;

(e)   when the employee would like the new arrangements to take effect;

(f)   whether any previous requests have been made, and if so, when; and

(g)   the date of the application.

8.143   What an employer must do on receipt of a request

The process

Upon receipt of an application, an employer should first check its content. If the request is missing any of the details set out in 8.142, or does not meet the eligibility criteria, it is not valid (although refusing to consider it may give rise to claims of sex discrimination (see 8.145ff), or perhaps breach of the implied term of mutual trust and confidence. If the request is valid, the employer must hold a meeting within 28 days of receipt at which the employee and employer can discuss the application. The employee is entitled to be accompanied to this meeting by a colleague. However, if the request is to be accepted in full, no meeting is necessary, provided that the employee is notified of the decision and the date upon which it will take effect in writing within the 28-day period.

Within 14 days after the date of the meeting, the employer must given written notification of its decision, including, if the application is refused, a 'sufficient explanation' of the reason(s). If the request is refused, the employer must notify the employee of his right to appeal, and explain that any request must be received within 14 days, as well as what the appeal procedure will be. Again, the employee should be given the right to be accompanied.

In the event that the employee appeals against the decision, the employer must hold an appeal meeting within 14 days of receiving the notice of appeal. (No meeting is necessary in the event that the employer upholds the appeal and notifies the employee of this within the 14-day period). The employer must then give its final decision within 14 days after the appeal meeting. As with the original decision, the appeal decision must give a 'sufficient explanation' in the event that the application is refused. If the request is approved, the resulting changes to the employee's working arrangement will constitute a permanent change to his terms and conditions of employment.

Employer and employee may agree to extend any of the above timescales. If such an agreement is reached, the employer should write to the employee confirming the new timescales.

8.144   *Considering a request*

Employers are under no obligation to agree to a request for a flexible working pattern. However, such a request may only be refused for certain prescribed business reasons (*ERA 1996, s 80G*). These are as follows:

(a)   burden of additional costs;

(b)   detrimental effect on ability to meet customer demand;

(c)   inability to reorganise work amongst existing staff;

(d)   inability to recruit additional staff;

(e)   detrimental impact upon quality or performance;

(f)   insufficiency of work during periods the employee proposes to work; or

(g)   planned structural changes.

In refusing a request, employers must explain why they consider that one or more of the above reasons applies.

An employee whose request is refused may subsequently bring a claim against the employer. The types of possible claim are discussed at 8.145. In considering a complaint that an employer has failed to comply with its obligations under the right to request legislation, a tribunal will not consider whether the reason given by the employer was fair or reasonable; however, it will assess whether the reason is 'factually correct'. For example, in *Commotion Ltd v Rutty* [2006] ICR 290, Mrs Rutty, a warehouse assistant, made an application to work three days a week, which was refused on the grounds that such an arrangement would have a detrimental impact on the performance of the warehouse, would affect staff morale, and would put a strain on resources. In a decision upheld by the EAT, the tribunal found, at paragraph 11 of its judgment, that these were:

> 'really outdated responses to requests for part-time working; they are off the cuff and made without research.'

On this basis, the tribunal held that there had been a breach of the (*ERA 1996, s 80G*). Employers should therefore be prepared to substantiate any reasons they give. Crucially, even if the reason given is found to be 'factually correct,' if the refusal is found to be indirectly discriminatory, the employer will have to go one step further and show that the discriminatory treatment is justified in order to successfully defend the claim. This involves balancing the commercial reasons behind the decision against its discriminatory effect. Indirect discrimination in the context of flexible working is discussed in more detail at 8.145.

8.145   Remedies available to an employee where a request is refused

In the event that an employee's request for flexible working is refused, there are number of claims potentially available to him.

8.146   *Complaint under the ERA 1996*

ERA 1996, s 80H confers a right of complaint to a tribunal in circumstances where an employee's flexible working request has been refused and the internal procedure has been exhausted. The grounds for the complaint are either that the employer has failed to follow the prescribed procedure, or that the rejection was based on incorrect facts. If the tribunal upholds the claim under *ERA 1996, s 80I*, it can make a declaration to that effect, and may make an award of up to eight weeks' pay (capped at the statutory maximum (see *ERA 1996, s 227(1)(za)*)) or order the employer to reconsider the request. It cannot, however, require the employer to implement a new flexible working arrangement. For this reason, the remedies available to an employee under *s 80I* are generally regarded as somewhat limited, resulting in frequent claims for indirect sex discrimination, and sometimes unfair dismissal.

8.147   *Indirect sex discrimination*

Many claims under *ERA 1996, s 80H* will be made in conjunction with a claim for indirect sex discrimination, and prior to the introduction of the right to request legislation, this was the main cause of action available to an employee whose flexible working application had been refused. As mentioned in 8.143ff, successfully defending a claim for indirect sex discrimination will be much more of a challenge for employers than defending a *s 80H* claim, and the stakes are higher.

In considering a discrimination claim, the tribunal will first consider whether the refusal of the flexible working request constitutes or forms part of a provision, criterion or practice which places women (or men) at a particular disadvantage. If it is held that it does, the tribunal will then consider the reasons for the refusal to allow flexible working and will balance these against the discriminatory effect, to decide whether the discrimination is justified. Demonstrating justification is manifestly more difficult than simply showing that the reasons given for the refusals are factually correct (which is all that is required by *s 80H*, assuming that the procedure is complied with).

An example of this principle in action is *Chief Constable of Avon and Somerset Constabulary v Chew* EAT/503/00. Ms Chew was a police officer who made an application to work part-time. This was refused because it did not comply with the department's part-time working policy, which required staff to work a shift pattern. The tribunal found that this rule constituted a provision, criterion or practice which had a disparate impact on women, who were less likely to be able to comply because of childcare obligations (the claimant had adduced evidence to this effect). The tribunal then went on to consider whether this discriminatory policy was justified. The reasons given by the Constabulary for the policy were that there would be operational problems were it not strictly enforced, staff morale would be affected were some officers to work atypical hours, and any change would lead to large numbers of applications from other officers to work different hours. These reasons were rejected by the tribunal, partly because of a lack of evidence to support them, and the tribunal noted that the argument about large numbers of new applications was 'double-edged', since it assumed that there were many other workers who were also having difficulty in working the required shift pattern. The claim of indirect discrimination was upheld by the tribunal and the EAT on appeal.

In *Sinclair Roche and Temperley v Heard* [2004] IRLR 763, the EAT rejected the assumption that, following *London Underground v Edwards (No 2)* [1998] IRLR 364, female partners in a law firm were disadvantaged by a policy of allowing only full-time working. It took into account the fact that these women were in high-powered and very well-paid positions (presumably because this would be relevant to their ability to make childcare arrangements), and held that evidence would have to be adduced to demonstrate that the women partners would in fact be disadvantaged. It should be noted, however, that this case was decided prior to the new definition of indirect sex discrimination being implemented, meaning that the female partners were required to show detriment to a 'considerably larger proportion' of women than men. Under the new test, they would only have to show that the requirement to work full-time would put women at a 'particular disadvantage' (*SDA 1975, s 1(2)(b)*, as inserted by the *Employment Equality (Sex Discrimination) Regulations 2005*. See also COMMON CONCEPTS (1)).

There have been a number of other cases in which tribunals have upheld indirect discrimination claims relating to flexible working requests. See, for example, *Clarke v Telewest Communications plc*, ET 1301034/2004 (June 2005, unreported); *Starmer v British Airways* [2005] IRLR 862 ; *Hardys & Hansons plc v Lax* [2005] IRLR 726; *Giles v Cornelia Care Homes*, ET 3100720 (August 2005, unreported). These cases were decided prior to introduction of the new definition of indirect sex discrimination. For more information on indirect sex discrimination, see 8.22.

8.148 *Other forms of discrimination*

Employers should also ensure that requests are considered equally seriously regardless of the applicant's personal circumstances. For example, in the Scottish case *Walkinshaw v The John Martin Group* S/401126/00 (15 November 2001), which was decided prior to the introduction of the right to make a flexible working request, Mr Walkinshaw applied to work part-time to look after his newborn son. His employer refused on the basis that it would be 'too complicated' to arrange a job share, but the tribunal found that the employer had always accepted requests by women to work part-time. On this basis, Mr Walkinshaw's claim of direct sex discrimination was upheld. One can also envisage circumstances in which an inconsistent and/or subjective approach to flexible working requests could lead to other claims of discrimination, eg on grounds of race or sexual orientation.

It should also be noted that in circumstances where a request has been made in order to allow an employee to care for a disabled relative, and that request is refused, the refusal could constitute indirect disability discrimination, even though the employee making the request is not disabled. The question of disability discrimination by association, and whether *DDA 1995* contains adequate protection against it (as required by the *Framework Directive*), has been referred to the ECJ in the case of *Coleman v Attridge Law* ET 2303745/2005 (23 May 2006).

8.149 *Unfair dismissal and detriment*

Employees who are sufficiently adversely affected by a refusal of their request may resign and claim constructive unfair dismissal (see *Commotion Ltd v Rutty*). The dismissal of an employee because he has made a flexible working application will also be automatically unfair (*ERA 1996, s 104C*). An employee may also claim that he has suffered detriment (other than dismissal) because he made/ proposed to make a request or exercised rights or brought or threatened proceedings (*ERA 1996, s 47E*).

As an alternative to litigation, there is a special ACAS arbitration scheme which employers and employees can use to resolve a dispute arising out of a flexible working request (see the *ACAS* (*Flexible Working*) *Arbitration Scheme* (*Great Britain*) *Order 2004* (*SI 2004/2333*)). However, it cannot be employed in the event that any other claims, apart from unfair dismissal, are being brought, which has limited its use.

For information on the rights of part-time workers not to be discriminated against, see FIXED-TERM AND PART-TIME WORKERS (10).

9   Sexual Orientation

9.1   OVERVIEW

Directive 2000/78/EC ('the *Framework Directive*') was implemented in the UK, in relation to sexual orientation discrimination, by the *Employment Equality* (*Sexual Orientation*) *Regulations 2003* (*SI 2003/1661*) ('*SOR 2003*'). *SOR 2003* came into force on 1 December 2003 and prohibit direct and indirect discrimination, as well as victimisation and harassment, on grounds of sexual orientation. The general scheme of *SOR 2003* is similar to that of the *Employment Equality* (*Religion or Belief*) *Regulations 2003* (*SI 2003/1660*) ('*RBR 2003*'), also deriving from the protective provisions of the Framework Directive.

9.2   Pre-existing protection

Before *SOR 2003* came into force, there was little protection for workers who were discriminated against because of their sexual orientation. The House of Lords rejected a claim brought by a member of the Royal Air Force who was dismissed for being gay, and by a teacher who was subject to harassment by pupils because she was a lesbian (*Macdonald v Advocate General for Scotland* and *Pearce v Governing Body of Mayfield School* [2003] UKHL 34, [2003] IRLR 512). Both employees argued that they had been discriminated against on grounds of their sex. However, the court decided that the prohibition of discrimination on grounds of sex under *SDA 1975* does not include discrimination on grounds of sexual orientation. The treatment complained of by both employees was treatment on grounds of sexual orientation, not sex, and the law only recognised the latter as actionable discrimination, not the former.

The other potential complaint was that of a violation of human rights. See, e g *Smith and Grady v United Kingdom* (1999) 29 EHRR 493. From 2 October 2000, claims could be brought under the *Human Rights Act 1998*, relying in particular upon the *European Convention on Human Rights* ('*ECHR*'), *Article 8*, which provides a (qualified) right to respect for private and family life, and *Article 14*, which prohibits discrimination in relation to other Convention rights. Such claims remain an option, although not a simple one, especially where the employer is not a public authority: see *XXX v YYY* [2004] IRLR 471.

9.3   Guidance on SOR 2003

Useful guidance on *SOR 2003* is provided by the Explanatory Notes issued by the DTI (now the DBERR), 'Explanation of the Provisions of the Employment Equality (Sexual Orientation) Regulations 2003 and Employment Equality (Religion or Belief) Regulations 2003', the ACAS Guide 'Sexual orientation and the workplace – a guide for employers and employees' (April 2004) and the TUC's 'Guide for Union Negotiators'. Whilst these documents do not have legal force, they are useful in practice, especially in light of the fact that there have so far been only a very few authorities from the higher courts about the correct interpretation of *SOR 2003*.

9.4   DEFINITION OF 'SEXUAL ORIENTATION'

SOR 2003, reg 2(1) defines 'sexual orientation' as a sexual orientation towards:

9.5 Sexual Orientation

(a)   persons of the same sex;

(b)   persons of the opposite sex; or

(c)   persons of the same sex and of the opposite sex.

This definition will clearly include protection for homosexual, heterosexual and bisexual people. It does not, however, cover the absence of an orientation, or celibacy, nor does it provide protection on grounds that a person actually engages in any particular sexual practice. The protection given is in respect of a sexual orientation, expressly defined, rather than by reference to a looser concept of, say sexual activities or preferences. Transsexuals are not covered, although separate protection for them is governed by *SDA 1975* (see GENDER REASSIGNMENT (4)).

9.5 DIRECT DISCRIMINATION

SOR 2003, reg (3)(1)(a) provides that discrimination on the grounds of sexual orientation occurs where, 'on the grounds of sexual orientation, A treats B less favourably than he treats or would treat other persons'. This is direct discrimination, similar to the concept found in *SDA 1975* and *RRA 1976*. Direct discrimination, unlike indirect discrimination, cannot be justified.

9.6 What will constitute direct discrimination?

Direct discrimination will occur, in this context, whenever there is less favourable treatment of a person, on the grounds of that person's sexual orientation. For example, and in relation to offers of employment, a refusal to employ a homosexual person to work in a pub because of his sexuality will constitute direct discrimination, and the employer will not be able to attempt to justify such refusal (for example) by reference to an asserted adverse impact on his business. In relation to terms of employment, the provision of less favourable pay or conditions to an employee on grounds of sexual orientation will constitute direct discrimination. A refusal to provide equivalent training to an employee on grounds of sexual orientation will also be covered. Dismissing a person on grounds of their sexual orientation will be an act of direct discrimination under *SOR 2003*.

Failure to prevent sexual orientation harassment on the grounds of sexual orientation could constitute direct discrimination.

9.7 The appropriate comparator

A complainant must typically show that he has been treated less favourably than another person in the same relevant circumstances, or circumstances which are not materially different (*SOR 2003, reg 3(2)*). So, for example, an unsuccessful homosexual applicant for a post cannot simply point to a successful heterosexual applicant for the same post and thereby demonstrate discrimination. He must also demonstrate that, apart from sexual orientation, his case was materially the same as the person who was treated more favourably.

The concept of the actual comparator has proved complex in other strands of discrimination law, and can arguably be seen as a legalistic mechanism whereby the court reaches the desired conclusion on direct discrimination: see eg the analysis under *RBR 2003* in *Azmi v Kirklees Metropolitan Borough Council* [2007] IRLR 484. There may be further difficulties in basing claims of sexual orientation discrimination on actual comparators, because people do not always know each other's sexual orientation.

However, the use of the words 'would treat' in *SOR 2003, reg 3(1)(a)* means (as in *RRA 1976* and *SDA 1975*) that the use of a hypothetical comparator is also permitted. In the example set out above, the unsuccessful homosexual applicant for a post could therefore seek to demonstrate that, had his sexual orientation been heterosexual, he would have been successful. He does not necessarily need to prove that an actual comparator was in fact treated more favourably.

9.8   'On the grounds of sexual orientation'

It is important that *SOR 2003, reg 3(1)(a)* refers to 'on the grounds of sexual orientation', rather than to 'on the grounds of *that person's* sexual orientation'. In many cases, the complainant will have the sexual orientation which the discriminator imputes to him. But that is not always the case.

In particular, and as has been recognised in other discrimination claims, less favourable treatment will potentially be 'on grounds of' sexual orientation where the reason for that treatment is, for example, the sexual orientation of the complainant's friends or relatives rather than of the complainant himself. Dismissing a person for having homosexual friends is almost certainly direct discrimination under *SOR 2003*. Similarly, the dismissal of a person in the (mistaken) belief that that person is himself homosexual will be covered. See by analogy the principle explained in *Showboat Entertainment Centre Ltd v Owens* [1984] IRLR 7; although see now *Redfearn v Serco Ltd (t/a West Yorkshire Transport Service)* [2006] EWCA Civ 659, [2006] ICR 1367 (stressing the importance of the need to show that the relevant treatment is truly on the prohibited 'grounds').

For discussion of the concept of direct discrimination in more detail, see COMMON CONCEPTS (1).

9.9   INDIRECT DISCRIMINATION

Indirect discrimination (described in *SOR 2003, reg 3(1)(b)*) occurs where a person (A) applies to a person (B) a provision, criterion or practice which applies or would apply equally to persons not of the same sexual orientation as B, but which:

(a)   puts or would put persons of the same sexual orientation as B at a particular disadvantage when compared with other persons;

(b)   puts B at that disadvantage; and

(c)   A cannot show to be a proportionate means of achieving a legitimate aim.

An example of indirect discrimination in the sexual orientation context is where a childless, and homosexual, man or woman wishes to apply for a teaching job at a nursery whose recruitment policy expressly promotes applicants who are themselves biological parents over all other applicants. The nursery would in that situation be applying a criterion or practice, ie a preference for employees who are biological parents, which would put homosexual applicants at a particular disadvantage when compared with heterosexual applicants. This would constitute discrimination unless the nursery could show the discriminatory policy to be a proportionate means of achieving a legitimate aim.

9.10   The concept of 'disadvantage'

DTI Guidance recognises that the question whether persons of the same sexual orientation as the claimant are put at a particular disadvantage is likely to apply to smaller groups than in comparable discrimination legislation. It is therefore likely to be the case that statistical evidence will not always be required to show particular disadvantage, and reliance may instead be placed on expert evidence to show that a requirement disadvantages a particular group.

9.11   A proportionate means of achieving a legitimate aim

In determining what constitutes 'proportionate means' it is for the courts to balance the needs of the employer in applying the provision, criterion or practice against its discriminatory effect. This will involve a careful consideration of the facts in each case.

In order for a practice to be proportionate it must be an appropriate and necessary means of achieving a legitimate aim (see *Bilka-Kaufhaus GmbH v Weber von Hartz* [1986] IRLR 317) (see COMMON CONCEPTS (1)). A legitimate aim cannot itself be discriminatory. 'Necessary' means something that is more than merely convenient. ACAS guidance goes one step further and indicates that it must be necessary with no alternative means available. The measure taken must be a proportionate means of achieving the objective in question: if it can be shown that there is some other way of achieving the stated objective, in a manner that has a significantly less discriminatory effect, then this requirement is unlikely to be satisfied.

An employer's legitimate aims will also depend on the circumstances. They typically include business efficacy, or health and safety objectives, but cost considerations alone will rarely, if ever, amount to a legitimate aim capable of justifying discrimination.

9.12   VICTIMISATION

The concept of discrimination under *SOR 2003* includes discrimination by way of victimisation. The reasoning underlying all prohibitions on victimisation is that a person who complains (or who is about to complain) of being discriminated against should be protected from suffering the imposition of detriments in consequence. Otherwise the protection provided by the law against discrimination on prohibited grounds would be devalued.

Discrimination by way of victimisation in the context of sexual orientation will occur where a person (A) treats another (B) less favourably than he treats or would treat other persons in the same circumstances, and does so 'by reason that' B has done one of the four protected acts set out in *SOR 2003, reg 4(1)*, or by reason that A knows that B intends to do any of those protected acts, suspects that he has done any of those acts, or suspects that B intends to do one of those acts.

The protected acts set out in *reg 4(1)* are described very broadly. They are that:

(a)   B has brought proceedings against A (or any other person), under *SOR 2003*; or

(b)   B has given evidence or information in connection with proceedings brought by any person against A (or any other person) under *SOR 2003*; or

(c)   B has done something under or by reference to *SOR 2003* in relation to A or any other person; or

(d)   B has alleged that A (or any other person) has contravened *SOR 2003*. Note that the relevant allegation made by B does not have to state in terms that the conduct was a contravention of *SOR 2003*.

So, for example, if an employee is dismissed by his employer because his employer suspects that he is about to complain that a colleague, on grounds of sexual orientation, was demoted, the dismissal would potentially be an act of victimisation, with the protected (imminent) act falling within *reg 4(1)(c)* or *(d)*. Similarly, if an employer rejected an application for employment because he knew that the applicant had sued a former employer under *SOR 2003*, that would also amount to victimisation, with the protected act falling within *reg 4(1)(a)*.

Individuals will not gain protection against victimisation where the evidence, information or allegations that they make are both false *and* not given in good faith *(reg 4(2))*. The wording of this provision is potentially important, because it means that a person who alleges a contravention of the *SOR 2003*, honestly believing such allegation to be correct, is protected from suffering detriments at the hands of his employer as a result, even if the alleged contravention turns out to be false.

The prohibition on discrimination by way of victimisation under *SOR 2003* is similarly worded to that contained in other equality legislation (see *RRA 1976, s 2(1)*, *SDA 1975, s 5(1)(a)* and *DDA 1995, s 55(1)*). It is likely that any case law relating to those sections will also be of relevance in this context. See COMMON CONCEPTS (1).

9.13 HARASSMENT

SOR 2003 expressly protect employees (and applicants for employment) from being subjected to harassment *(reg 6(3))*. Harassment under *reg 6(3)* is an unlawful act which is discrete from the concept of unlawful 'discrimination' as separately defined. Thus, it is not necessary, for example, for a person complaining of harassment to show less favourable treatment. It follows that it is not a defence to a claim of harassment on grounds of sexual orientation for a person to say that he would have treated a person of a different sexual orientation equally badly – as long as the harassment complained of is in fact on grounds of sexual orientation.

The concept of 'harassment' is defined in *SOR 2003, reg 5(1)*. A person (A) will subject another (B) to harassment where, on grounds of sexual orientation, A engages in unwanted conduct which has the purpose or effect of either (a) violating B's dignity or (b) creating an intimidating, hostile, degrading, humiliating or offensive environment for B.

The wording of *reg 5(1)* ('purpose or effect') demonstrates that a person cannot escape liability for harassment merely because he did not intend to violate a person's dignity (where his conduct in fact had that effect). As in other strands of discrimination law, this is likely to be significant. The fact that one person believes he is engaging in what he might see as light-hearted banter with another does not necessarily mean that he is not harassing the other person. Nor will the alleged harasser have a defence where his purpose was violating a person's dignity but, in fact, his conduct did not have that effect, even though it was unwanted.

As to the 'effect' on B, the conduct shall only be regarded as having the effect specified in *reg 5(1)(a)* or *(b)* if, having regard to all the circumstances, including in particular the perception of B, it should reasonably be considered as having that effect *(reg 5(2))*. This means that the subjective impact on B is on the one hand highly relevant, but on the other not determinative. B must show that the conduct of A and of which he complains was (subjectively) 'unwanted', otherwise he will fail to satisfy *reg 5(1)*. But an assertion that A violated B's dignity, or created an intimidating, hostile, degrading, humiliating or offensive environment for B, must also be one that (objectively) could reasonably be considered as having such effect, otherwise B will fail to satisfy *reg 5(2)*.

The word 'unwanted' describes the conduct, and makes no logical requirement about the previous behaviour of the victim. It does not follow that simply because the victim has not previously objected to a particular type of conduct, such conduct is not unwanted (*Reed v Stedman* [1999] IRLR 299). If a single act is sufficiently serious it can amount to harassment even though notice that it is unwanted has not been given.

9.14   UNLAWFUL DISCRIMINATION

As with other discrimination legislation, having defined (in *regs 2–5*) the nature and meaning of 'discrimination' in this context, *SOR 2003* then proceeds to specify, in *Part II*, exactly what type of sexual orientation discrimination will be unlawful in the employment field.

The wording of *SOR 2003, Part II* closely resembles that contained in other equality legislation, and the case law relating to race and sex discrimination is likely to be followed in interpreting it. It is unlawful, in relation to employment at an establishment in Great Britain, for an employer to discriminate against a person in relation, broadly, to applications for employment (*reg 6(1)*), employees' terms and conditions, access to promotion and other benefits (*reg 6(2)(a)–(c)*), and dismissals or other detriments (*reg 6(3)(c)*). Harassment, as defined (see 9.13), is also unlawful (*reg 6(3)*).

Dismissal in this context includes constructive dismissal (*reg 6(5)(b)*). So, for example, where an employee resigns because of acts of harassment (or a failure to prevent them), and it is shown that those acts (or omissions) constitute a constructive dismissal, the dismissal may itself be an unlawful act within *reg 6(2)(d)*.

It is not only employees that are protected. The *SOR 2003, reg 2(3)* defines employment as 'employment under a contract of service or of apprenticeship or a contract personally to do any work'. See COMMON CONCEPTS (1).

Note that ex-employees may have recourse under *reg 21*, which makes it unlawful for one party to a 'relevant relationship' (A) to discriminate against another (B) by subjecting him to a detriment or harassing him, where the discrimination or harassment arises out of and is closely connected to the relationship. But the concept of the 'relevant relationship' here is not as wide as it could have been: it is a relationship during which A has already committed an act of unlawful discrimination against B under *SOR 2003, reg 21(1)*.

Where employees commit acts of discrimination against fellow employees, *reg 22* will be relevant to the question of the potential liability of the employer. The question here is not whether the employer knew or approved of the conduct in question (although express or implied authorisation of unlawful acts would lead to liability under the principles of agency: *reg 22(2)*). Rather, it is whether the conduct was in the course of employment of the employee carrying it out: *reg 22(1)*. The meaning of 'in the course of his employment' will probably follow the interpretation of that phrase in the context of other discrimination legislation: see e g *Jones v Tower Boot Co Ltd* [1997] ICR 254. If the employer is caught by *reg 22(1)*, he will be liable unless he can establish a defence under *reg 22(3)*: he will have to show that he took such steps as were reasonably practicable to prevent the employee from doing the act in question or from doing in the course of his employment acts of that description.

A person who knowingly aids another to do an act which is unlawful under *SOR 2003* will be liable under *reg 23(1)*. Slightly confusingly, this will include the guilty employee who by his conduct brought the employer within *reg 22(1)* (whether or not the employer had a defence under *reg 22(3)*) (*reg 23(2)*). So where an employee subjects a fellow employee to discrimination in the course of his employment, he may be sued as a person who is knowingly aiding another to do an unlawful act. He will have his own defence if acting reasonably on a statement by the employer that the act is not unlawful (*reg 23(3)*).

9.15   GENUINE OCCUPATIONAL REQUIREMENT

The concept of the genuine occupational requirement (GOR) is a familiar one to those who have considered the sex and race equality legislation (see COMMON CONCEPTS (1), RACE DISCRIMINATION (6) and SEX DISCRIMINATION (8), but it is perhaps particularly controversial in its application to religious belief and sexual orientation discrimination. Under what circumstances might it be acceptable to discriminate against people at work on the basis of their sexual orientation?

SOR 2003 provides one answer in the general employment context (*reg 7(2)*) and another answer in the specific context of employment for purposes of an organised religion (*reg 7(3)*). In both cases the defence can only potentially arise where a 'requirement' is being applied to a person, and the person does not meet that requirement, or the employer is reasonably not satisfied that he meets it (*regs 7(2)(c)* and *7(3)(c)*).

In relation to the general context (ie employment, other than in the context of organised religion), two further conditions will need to be satisfied. First, it will have to be shown that being of a particular sexual orientation is a 'genuine and determining occupational requirement' (*reg 7(2)(a)*). Secondly, it must be 'proportionate' to apply that requirement in the particular case (*reg 7(2)(b)*). These conditions constitute a demanding test. It will not be satisfied, for example, where a bar which is popular with homosexuals subjects its heterosexual employees to detriments, or is only interested in employing homosexual people. That is because being homosexual is not a 'requirement' for the occupation of serving drinks. Nor will it necessarily be satisfied even in the rare situation where an employer reasonably needs an employee who will desist from homosexual conduct (e g sending a representative to a country where all non-heterosexual activity is criminalised). That is because an employer should not assume that simply because a person has a sexual orientation, he will necessarily engage in a particular sexual activity.

In relation to employment for the purposes of an organised religion, there is only one further condition. It is that the employer is applying a requirement related to sexual orientation so as to comply with the doctrines of the religion (or so as to avoid conflicting with the strongly held religious convictions of a significant number of the religion's followers) (*reg 7(3)(b)*). This might have appeared on a literal analysis to be a significantly less demanding test and might have suggested that however outrageous or extensive the discriminatory tenets of a religion, they might in principle provide a complete defence to many claims of sexual orientation discrimination.

However, in *R (on the application of Amicus – MSF section) v Secretary of State for Trade and Industry* [2004] EWHC 860 (Admin), [2004] IRLR 430 various unions challenged the lawfulness of the genuine occupational requirement provisions contained in *SOR 2003*. It was said that they were insufficiently reflective of the right to be protected against discrimination on the grounds of sexual orientation, and therefore incompatible with both the *Framework Directive* and with *Articles 8* and/or *14* of *ECHR*. The challenge failed. The Administrative Court held that the Regulations needed to be construed purposively, and having done so, they survived scrutiny. In relation to *reg 7(2)(b)*, for example, a requirement would have to pursue a 'legitimate objective' in order to qualify as proportionate. In relation to *reg 7(2)(c)(ii)*, the concept of reasonableness would prevent an employer from stereotyping or making unjustified assumptions. And the exception set out in *reg 7(3)* was intended, and was to be treated, as a very narrow one (and narrower than the corresponding provision in *RBR 2003*), importing a demanding objective test. Employment as a teacher in a faith school, for example, would be unlikely to fall within it.

Where the GOR exception does apply, it will permit discrimination in the circumstances set out in *reg 7(1)*. Those circumstances include refusing to appoint, promote or transfer a person to a position, and dismissing him; but they do not include employing him on less favourable terms, harassing him, or victimising him. That reflects both the nature of the GOR defence (conceptually it applies to a position, rather than to an individual) and its limited scope as a defence to discrimination claims.

9.16   OTHER EXCEPTIONS

National security

Discriminatory acts done 'for the purpose of safeguarding national security' will not be unlawful, if the doing of the act was justified for that purpose (*reg 24*). This reflects a specific provision in the *Framework Directive* providing that the non-discrimination measures shall be 'without prejudice' to measures laid down by national law, relating to (among other things) national security.

9.17   Positive action

It may in certain circumstances be lawful to discriminate 'in favour of' persons with a particular sexual orientation (which is effectively a euphemism for discriminating against persons on the grounds of their – different – sexual orientation).

The exception will potentially apply where the act is done in connection with affording persons of a particular sexual orientation access to facilities for training which would help fit them for particular work, or encouraging them to take advantage of opportunities for doing particular work. In order for the exception to apply, the person doing the act in question must reasonably think that it prevents, or compensates for, disadvantages linked to sexual orientation suffered by persons of that sexual orientation doing that work or likely to take up that work (*reg 26(1)*).

Here the wording is different to that contained in other equality legislation. The race and sex discrimination laws provide for a narrower notion of positive action; the disability discrimination laws, through the concept of the reasonable adjustment, provide for a much wider one. Hence, it will eventually fall to the employment tribunals and appellate courts, largely unassisted by case law, to determine the difficult social and ethical questions about what might be reasonable for an employer to regard as 'compensating' for past discrimination against persons of a particular sexual orientation.

The concept of reasonableness in *reg 26* probably imports the concept of proportionality: see the approach of the ECJ in *Abrahamsson v Fogelqvist* [2002] ICR 932 (a sex discrimination case). So, where an employer is considering how to compensate for the fact that homosexual persons are significantly underrepresented in a particular job, he must be careful: whilst it might be proportionate for him to afford homosexual candidates somewhat greater access than others to training and support, it does not follow that he can rely on *reg 26* to go further than is necessary, in relation to the availability of training for others, or to close off the vacancy to heterosexual applicants so as to ensure the success of the homosexual applicants.

9.18 **Marital status**

It is not unlawful discrimination on the basis of sexual orientation to prevent or restrict access to a benefit by reference to marital status where the right to the benefit accrued or the benefit is payable in respect of periods of service prior to the coming into force of the *Civil Partnership Act 2004* (*reg 25*). This provision (in its original form) was one of those unsuccessfully challenged in the *Amicus* judicial review (see 9.15).

9.19 **MISCELLANEOUS**

One interesting question is whether there might appear to be tension or conflict between *SOR 2003* and *RBR 2003*. After all, *RBR 2003* exists in order to prevent discrimination on the grounds of religion or belief. Some of the beliefs protected, especially traditional religious beliefs, will themselves be inconsistent with the principles of equality upon which *SOR 2003* is based. Take, for example, an employer (A) who employs one employee (B). B, who is heterosexual, believes that, pursuant to very strict religious views, homosexuality is a serious moral evil (he also believes that heterosexual sex is morally virtuous because procreation is 'natural'). The business has expanded and A needs to employ an additional person. The new employee would have to work in close proximity with B. The employer interviews a candidate, C. C is openly homosexual and says that he believes that religious views are foolish delusions and the source of all evil in the world. Should A disregard the views of B and/or C, or just hope that neither harasses the other, or is he allowed to take a more 'realistic' or pessimistic view and reject C's application? By employing C, might he be at risk of breaching B's rights under *RBR 2003*, because C might harass B because of B's religious views? Might he even breach B's rights under *SOR 2003*, because B's views on sexual morality (although extreme) might be seen as a sexual 'orientation'? On the other hand, by not employing C, he is surely at risk of breaching C's rights under *SOR 2003* because he is refusing to offer employment because of C's sexuality, ie on grounds of sexual orientation, and possibly also under *RBR 2003*.

The question that might need to be answered is whether *SOR 2003* trumps *RBR 2003* in the event of any apparent conflict, because discrimination on the grounds of sexual orientation is recognised as one of the inherently suspect categories (see *R (on the application of Carson) v Secretary of State for Work and Pensions* [2005] UKHL 37, [2006] 1 AC 173 at para 17). There might need to be consideration of cases from other jurisdictions which touch on similar issues (see eg the USA case of *Peterson v Hewlett-Packard*, USA Court of Appeals, 9th Circuit, January 2004). Alternatively, the tribunals and the courts might strain to find a more subtle question to ask. But the wider conceptual problem – the tension between respect for equality and respect for beliefs – is one that arises out of constitutional values based on liberalism and individual rights, and is already one that is exercising the courts, outside of the employment context.

9.20 **ENFORCEMENT AND REMEDIES**

Questionnaire procedure

SOR 2003, reg 33 permits a person who believes that he has been discriminated against (or subject to harassment) to seek information from the employer by serving a questionnaire. (This is a similar format and process to questionnaires used in sex and race discrimination claims; see COMMON CONCEPTS (1))

9.21 **GOODS AND SERVICES**

The *Equality Act (Sexual Orientation) Regulations 2007 (SI 2007/1263)* contain prohibitions on discrimination related to sexual orientation which fall outside of the employment context. Unlike *SOR 2003*, which was enacted under powers conferred by the *European Communities Act 1972, s 2(2)* (ie by transposing the *Framework Directive*, which relates to employment, into domestic law), the 2007 Regulations required primary domestic legislation: see the *Equality Act 2006, Part 3*.

The provisions of the 2007 Regulations go beyond the scope of this book and are not considered in any detail here. Briefly, they prohibit discrimination on grounds of sexual orientation in the provision of goods, facilities and services to the public, in education, the use and disposal of premises, the exercise of public functions and in other areas. For example, it is no longer lawful for a hotel to refuse a double room to a gay couple. Enforcement is typically by way of a claim in the county court. Victimisation is also dealt with. Advertisements may be unlawful, if they can reasonably be understood to indicate an intention to act in a way which is unlawfully discriminatory (eg the hotel contemplated above, advertising that it is for 'straight people only').

10   Fixed-term and Part-time Workers

10.1   FIXED-TERM EMPLOYEES

Introduction

The *Fixed-term Employees* (*Prevention of Less Favourable Treatment*) *Regulations 2002* (*FTR 2002*) came into force on 1 October 2002.

They were made pursuant to the *Employment Act 2002* ('*EA 2002*'), *s 45* to give effect to *Directive 99/70/EC* ('the Directive') concerning the framework agreement on fixed-term work.

FTR 2002 gives fixed-term employees the right in principle not to be treated less favourably than permanent employees of the same employer doing similar work. The right, exercisable by complaint to an employment tribunal, applies where the less favourable treatment is on the ground that the employee is working under a fixed-term contract and the less favourable treatment in question is not justified on objective grounds.

10.2   *The Directive*

Article 1 of the Directive states that its purpose is to put into effect the framework agreement on fixed-term contracts concluded on 18 March 1999 between general cross-industry organisations.

Article 2 states that Member States should bring into force the laws, regulations and administrative provisions necessary to comply with the Directive.

The framework agreement, to which the Directive gives effect, is intended (as stated in *clause 1*) to:

(a)   improve the quality of fixed-term work by ensuring the application of the principle of non-discrimination;

(b)   establish a framework to prevent abuse arising from the use of successive fixed-term contracts or relationships.

To this end, *clause 4* sets out the principle of non-discrimination: that is, that fixed-term workers should not be treated in a less favourable manner than comparable permanent workers solely because they have a fixed-term contract, unless justified on objective grounds.

Further, under *clause 5*, Member States shall introduce one or more measures to prevent abuse of successive fixed-term contracts, such measures being the need for an objective reason to justify such renewals, the maximum total duration of successive fixed-term contracts and/or the number of renewals of such contracts.

10.3   *Pre-existing protection*

Prior to the coming into force of *FTR 2002*, there was protection for fixed-term employees only in certain situations.

For example, a claim of indirect sex discrimination (see 8.22) could be brought under the *Sex Discrimination Act 1975, s 1(1)(b)* (prior to the amendments made pursuant to the *Burden of Proof Directive* (*/97/80/EC*) if the facts supported a claim that a requirement or condition, when applied equally to both men and women had a disproportionate impact on one gender. So in *Whiffen v Milham Ford Girls' School* [2001] EWCA Civ 385, [2001] LGR 309, a teacher working under repeated fixed-term contracts was successful in showing that the failure to renew her final fixed-term contract was indirect discrimination since the proportion of the women who could comply with the requirement to work under a permanent contract (for the purpose of being included in a model redundancy process) was considerably smaller than the proportion of men, and the school had failed to put forward any relevant justification.

Alternatively, a complainant could bring a claim under the *Equal Pay Act 1970* ('*EqPA 1970*') on the basis that she was paid less than a man for like work (or work of equal value). There remain some advantages to an equal pay claim, compared with a claim under *FTR 2002*:

(a)   *FTR 2002* applies only to employees whereas *EqPA 1970* includes self-employed workers (as long as they work under a contract);

(b)   the range of comparators is wider (it not being possible to compare with a predecessor or successor under *FTR 2002*);

(c)   the *EqPA 1970* limits the comparison to a term by term approach, whereas *FTR 2002* allows for a less favourable term to be balanced by a more favourable term.

However, there are advantages to a claim under *FTR 2002*:

(i)   a comparison can be made with a worker of the same sex;

(ii)   *FTR 2002* applies to contractual and non-contractual terms;

(iii)   *FTR 2002* gives an employment tribunal the power to make a recommendation.

10.4   *Introduction of FTR 2002*

FTR 2002 was brought into force to give effect to the Directive in exercise of the powers granted to the Secretary of State under *EA 2002, ss 45* and *51(1)*.

According to the Explanatory Note to *FTR 2002*, in addition to giving positive rights, they:

'... make a number of amendments to primary legislation to remove discrimination in statutory rights between fixed-term employees (or certain types of fixed-term employees) and permanent employees.'

Guidance, which does not have statutory force, is available from the Department for Business, Enterprise and Regulatory Reform website (URN No 06/535). Its stated purpose is 'to explain the requirements of the new Regulations to employers, managers, union representatives and employees who may be affected by them and to let people know about their ... rights'. This Guidance is referred to in this chapter where relevant.

10.5   *Impact of FTR 2002*

It must be assumed that *FTR 2002* has had only limited impact since the Employment Tribunal statistics for 1 April 2006 to 31 March 2007 (and for the previous two years) have not included cases based on *FTR 2002* as a separate category. (The 'others' heading included 5,072 cases in 2006 to 2007, but no further information as to what constitutes 'others' is given.) This is in contrast to the *Part-Time Workers Regulations* (see 10.22), which are recorded as a separate category.

At the time of writing there have been several cases concerning fixed-term contracts in the Employment Appeal Tribunal (eg *Allen v National Australia Group Europe Ltd* [2004] IRLR 847 and *Coutts & Co Plc v Cure* [2005] ICR 298); one in the Court of Appeal (*Webley v Department for Work and Pensions* [2004] EWCA Civ 1745, [2005] ICR 577), and one in the European Court of Justice (*Adeneler v Ellinikos Organismos Galaktos* [2006] IRLR 716, concerning the Directive).

10.6   **What is a fixed-term contract?**

FTR 2002, reg 1(2) states that a fixed-term contract means a contract of employment that, under its provisions determining how it will terminate in the normal course, will terminate:

(a)   on the expiry of a specific term;

(b)   on completion of a particular task; or

(c)   on the occurrence or non-occurrence of any other specific event (other than the attainment by an employee of any normal and bona-fide retiring age).

These definitions would cover employees doing seasonal or casual work; cover for maternity, paternity, parental or sick leave, and those undertaking a specific task like painting a house.

A contract is for a fixed-term even when it includes a notice provision (*Allen v National Australia Group Europe Ltd* [2004] IRLR 847). The ability of the parties to bring the contract to an end at an earlier date does not make a contract anything other than one for a fixed-term. What is envisaged by the *FTR 2002* is a provision relating to the termination of the relationship 'in the normal course'. Provision for earlier notice does not destroy the original intention of such a contract that the parties would see out the fixed-term, unless and until some event which was not in the normal course occurs.

10.7   *Who is covered?*

Under *reg 2(1)*, a fixed-term employee can compare himself to a comparable permanent employee if, at the time when the treatment that is alleged to be less favourable takes place, both employees are:

(a)   employed by the same employer; and

(b)   engaged in the same or broadly similar work having regard, where relevant, to whether they have a similar level of qualification and skills.

The permanent employee must work or be based at the same establishment as the fixed-term employee or, where there is no such comparable permanent employee, must work or be based at a different establishment (while still satisfying the requirements above).

As the Guidance makes clear, a fixed-term employee cannot compare conditions with an employee at an associated employer's establishment.

Special classes of people included under *FTR 2002* are set out in *regs 13–17*. They are:

(a)   those employed by the Crown (*reg 13*);

(b)   those employed by an establishment for the purposes of the *Reserve Forces Act 1996, Part 11* (but not members of the naval, military or air forces) (*reg 14*);

(c)   House of Lords staff (*reg 15*);

(d)   House of Commons staff (*reg 16*); and

(e)   police officers and cadets (*reg 17*).

Those who are excluded from *FTR 2002* are set out in *regs 18–20*. They are:

(a)   those employed on schemes designed to provide training or work experience where the schemes are provided under arrangements made by the Government or are funded in whole or in part by an institution of the European Community (*reg 18(1)*);

(b)   fixed-term employees whose employment consists in a period of work experience not exceeding one year as part of a higher education course (*reg 18(2)*);

(c)   agency workers (*reg 19*); and

(d)   apprentices (*reg 20*).

10.8   *Comparator*

A fixed-term employee can compare his treatment to the treatment of a comparable permanent employee.

Where a fixed-term employee does the same work as several permanent employees whose contractual terms are different, the fixed-term employee may select a comparator.

Although the comparator may be of the same sex, a comparison cannot be made with:

(a)   a hypothetical comparator;

(b)   a comparator employed by an associated employer;

(c)   a comparator whose employment has ceased (*reg 2(2)*).

As stated above, only if there is no comparator in the establishment can a comparison be made with a similar permanent employee working for the same employer in a different establishment.

In *Hart v Secretary of State for Education and Skills*, Employment Tribunal, 2304973/2004, 8 September 2005, it was necessary to consider whether the claimant education advisers could compare themselves with a particular individual in order to show that they were excluded from redundancy and early retirement benefits payable under the Civil Service Compensation Scheme because of their status as fixed-term employees.

In order to determine this, the employment tribunal fastened on the word 'broadly' in *reg 2(1)(a)(ii)*, which suggested a 'reasonably ample approach' to any comparison. Further, a claimant must 'establish not only broad similarity in the nature and subject matter of the work but also approximate equivalence in the level of expertise and responsibility at which it is undertaken.

The employment tribunal considered that this approach was fortified by the Court of Appeal in *Matthews v Kent and Medway Towns Fire Authority* [2004] EWCA Civ 844, [2004] 3 All ER 620, [2005] ICR 84, which took a similar view in a case concerning the *Part-time Workers Regulations* (see 10.25), which are in almost identical terms to *reg 2(1)*. Following the Court of Appeal decision, the *Matthews* case did progress to the House of Lords (see 10.25) where Lord Hope, who was in a majority on this issue, cautioned that the question as to whether two kinds of workers had similar levels of skill and experience was relevant only so far as it bore on the exercise of assessing whether the work engaged in was the same or broadly similar.

In *Hart*, the particular individual was considered to be an appropriate comparator, the tribunal stating:

> 'We are quite satisfied that the Claimants are entitled to succeed on the Comparator Issue. Their essential function, to advise, was the same. The broad subject matter on which they were required to advise was the same and the fund of experience on which they were expected to call, while diverse, was similarly rooted in long experience in the education sector. The categories of individuals and bodies to whom their advice was directed were the same although there were minor differences in balance as between the recipients of the advice. The fact that [the particular individual's] work tended to focus on a particular problem (failing schools) whereas the Claimants' responsibilities tended to be arranged on a regional basis does not, to our minds, detract from the proposition that the work being undertaken was broadly similar. Nor does the modest difference in balance between the amount of time committed to 'policy' and 'field work' ... it seems to us self-evident that two jobs may be broadly similar despite the fact that one is somewhat more "operational" and the other has a rather higher "policy" content.'

It was not disputed that the claimants and the particular individual had similar levels of qualification and skills and, accordingly, the rider to *reg 2(1)(a)(ii)* was satisfied.

10.9   Less favourable treatment

Less favourable treatment is defined by *reg 3*. A fixed-term employee has the right not to be treated less favourably by his employer as regards the terms of his contract (*reg 3(1)(a)*) or by being subjected to any other detriment by any act, or deliberate failure to act (*reg 3(1)(b)*).

The right conferred by *reg 3(1)* includes, in particular, the right of the fixed-term employee not to be treated less favourably than a permanent employee (*reg 3(2)*) in relation to:

(a)   any period of service qualification relating to any particular condition of service;

(b)   the opportunity to receive training; or

(c)   the opportunity to secure any permanent position in the establishment.

However, the right conferred by *reg 3(1)* applies only if the treatment is on the ground that the employee is a fixed-term employee (*reg 3(a)*) and the treatment is not justified on objective grounds (*reg 3(b)*) (as defined in *reg 4*; see 10.11).

Further, in determining whether a fixed-term employee has been treated less favourably than a comparable permanent employee, the pro rata principles 'shall be applied unless it is inappropriate' (*reg 3(4)*).

The Guidance sets out examples of less favourable treatment including:

(a)   permanent employees being given free membership of a gym whereas fixed-term employees are not;

(b)   fixed-term employees being offered less paid holiday, or not being paid for bank holidays;

(c)   fixed-term employees being excluded from non-contractual bonuses, or training; and

(d)   fixed-term employees being selected for redundancy purely because they are fixed-term. (See, for example, *Whiffen v Milham Ford Girls' School*.)

When considering whether there is less favourable treatment a term-by-term approach is required (*Hart v Secretary of State for Education and Skills*). That approach was also adopted in *Matthews v Kent and Medway Towns Fire Authority*, in the EAT in the context of the *Part-time Workers Regulations* (reported at [2003] IRLR 732, and not appealed to the Court of Appeal). His Honour Judge Birtles said:

> 'In our view it will be practically impossible to achieve proper and effective equality between part-time and full-time workers if a broad brush approach is adopted ... Furthermore [cases concerning equal pay] ... provide strong judicial support from the House of Lords and the European Court of Justice for the specific term by term analysis contended for by [Counsel for the Claimants] and agreed by the Employment Tribunal to be the correct approach.'

There is no less favourable treatment if an employer simply fails to renew a fixed-term contract: *Webley v Department for Work and Pensions* [2004] EWCA Civ 1745, [2005] ICR 577, [2005] IRLR 288. Lord Justice Wall stated (paragraph 36):

> '... it seems to me inexorably to follow that the termination of such a contract by the simple effluxion of time cannot, of itself, constitute less favourable treatment by comparison with a permanent employee. It is of the essence of a fixed-term contract that it comes to an end at the expiry of the fixed-term. Thus unless it can be said that ... entering into a fixed-term contract is of itself less favourable treatment, the expiry of a fixed-term contract resulting in the dismissal of the fixed-term employee cannot, in my judgment, be said to fall within *regulation 3(1)*.

> '37. Similarly, the fact that the termination of the contract by effluxion of time results in the dismissal of the fixed-term employee cannot, of itself, represent a detriment within *regulation 3(1)(b)*. The same argument applies. The termination of the contract is an inevitable consequence of it being for a fixed term.'

10.10 *'On the ground that'*

Reg 3(3) states that the less favourable treatment must be 'on the ground that' an employee is a fixed-term employee.

It is interesting to note that this is a more favourable test for the employee than the principle as stated in the Directive (*clause 4*) which is that:

> '... fixed-term workers shall not be treated in a less favourable manner than comparative permanent workers *solely* because they have a fixed-term contract or relation unless justified on objective grounds.' (emphasis added)

In *Chief Constable of West Yorkshire Police v Khan* [2001] UKHL 48, [2001] 1 WLR 1947, [2001] ICR 1065, a case involving direct race discrimination and victimisation, the House of Lords stated that phrases such as 'on racial grounds' and 'by reason that' require an investigation as to why the discriminator did what he did. Lord Scott of Foscote put it in this way (paragraph 77):

> 'The words "by reason that" suggest, to my mind, that it is the real reason, the core reason, the causa causans, the motive, for the treatment complained of that must be identified.'

(For further detail see COMMON CONCEPTS (1)). In *Coutts & Co Plc v Cure*, it was contended that the employees were not treated less favourably on the grounds of being on fixed-term contracts, for the exclusion from the bonus applied to all non-permanent staff (paragraph 18). Although being a fixed-term employee may have been a contributory cause to their exclusion, it was only one of the causes. However, it was accepted in argument that the proper approach to 'on the ground that' in *FTR 2002* was that outlined in *Khan* (paragraph 34). On the facts, the EAT rejected the contention that the less favourable treatment was not 'on the ground that the employee is a fixed-term employee' (paragraph 50):

> '... the reason why the Respondents decided to provide no bonus to the [employees] was because they were members of an employee group which consisted of fixed-term contractors. The fact that the Respondent excluded other employee groups, or other business groups, is not relevant ... Once an employee is within scope of a relevant anti-discrimination measure, and suffers a detriment because he is in that category, it is not relevant to know whether the Respondent discriminates against other employees who may or may not be within the scope of that or another anti-discrimination measure. The Tribunal did not err when it found that the reason for the exclusion of the [employees] from the bonus was that they were in the group of fixed-term employees. As such they were protected by the Regulations, subject to any defence of justification.'

10.11 *Justification*

Under *reg 4(1)*, less favourable treatment of a fixed-term worker shall be treated as justified on objective grounds if the terms of the fixed-term employee's contract of employment, taken as a whole, are at least as favourable as the terms of the comparable permanent contract of employment.

This justification is in addition to the justification specified in *reg 3(3)(b)*.

Hence, there are two ways of justifying under the Regulations:

(a)   on a term by term basis (*reg 3(3)(b)*);

(b)   a 'package approach' peculiar to the Regulations (*reg 4*) (for example, such an approach in not available in *EqPA 1970* or in relation to cases of part-time discrimination).

The Guidance indicates that employers should ask themselves the question: 'Is there a good reason for treating this employee less favourably?' They should give due regard to the needs and rights of individual employees and try to balance those against business objectives.

The normal test of justification, available under *reg 3(3)(b)* (and *reg 4*, but by reference to the package approach rather than term by term) is explained in the Guidance as follows:

(a)   Does the measure achieve a legitimate objective, for example a genuine business objective?

(b)   Is the measure necessary to achieve that objective?

(c)   Is the measure an appropriate way to achieve that objective?

See, for example, *Bilka-Kaufhaus GmbH v Webber Von Hartz* [1986] IRLR 317, paragraph 36 (see 11.12). A shorter definition is more commonly used: Is the measure a proportionate means of achieving a legitimate aim?

The Guidance continues:

> 'Objective justification may be a matter of degree. Employers should therefore consider whether it is possible to offer fixed-term employees certain benefits, such as annual subscriptions, loans, clothing allowances and insurance policies, on a pro rata basis.

> 'Sometimes, the cost to the employer of offering a particular benefit to an employee may be disproportionate when compared to the benefit the employee would receive, and this may objectively justify different treatment. An example of this may be where a fixed-term employee is on a contract of three months and a comparator has a company car. The employer may decide not to offer the car if the cost of doing so is high and the need for the business for the employer to travel can be met in some other way.'

Applying the test of justification to a term-by-term approach is straightforward. The only question is whether the less favourable treatment in relation to the term in question can be justified.

Applying the test of justification to the package approach is a novel concept (since it is not available elsewhere in discrimination law). The Guidance suggests that, in determining the success of any trade-off in terms, the value of benefits should be assessed on the basis of their objective monetary worth, rather than the value that the employer or employee perceives them to have.

It gives the example of an employer paying a fixed-term employee the same as a comparable permanent employee, but with three days fewer paid holiday a year. To ensure this is not less favourable (or, more accurately, that the less favourable treatment is justified) the employer should pay the fixed-term employee extra for the three days' holiday.

In *Hart v Secretary of State for Education and Skills*, the tribunal described the alternative routes to justification as follows:

> 'It seems to us that [Regulation] 3(3)(*b*) read in conjunction with [Regulation] 4 provides the employer with two alternative routes to proving justification. The first … requires a narrow focus on the specific treatment complained of by the Claimant and any justification argument directed specifically to that treatment. The second … deems the justification defence under [Regulation] 3(3)(*b*) to be made out if the employer can establish, on a "compendious" approach, overall comparability between the terms of the claimant's contract and that of his comparator.'

10.12 Written statements

FTR 2002, reg 5. Reg 5 provides that, if an employee considers his employer may have treated him in a manner which infringes a right conferred on him by *reg 3*, he may request a written statement giving particulars of the reasons for the treatment. The employee is entitled to be provided with such a statement within 21 days of his request.

Such a written statement is admissible as evidence in any proceedings under *FTR 2002*. Further, if it appears to the employment tribunal in such proceedings that an employer deliberately, and without reasonable excuse, omitted to provide such a statement, or that the statement was evasive or equivocal, it may draw inferences (including that the employer has infringed the right in question).

However, *reg 5* does not apply where the treatment complained of is dismissal, the employee then being entitled to a written statement of reasons under *Employment Rights Act 1996, s 92 (ERA 1996)*.

FTR 2002, reg 9. Reg 9 provides that an employee who considers himself to be a permanent employee by virtue of *reg 8* is able to request in writing from his employer a written statement confirming that his contract is no longer fixed-term. Such a statement must, again, be provided within 21 days. Alternatively, the employer should give a statement giving reasons why the contract remains fixed-term (*reg 9(1)(b)*). With regard to the latter, this should include any assertion that there were objective grounds for engagement under a fixed-term contract, or the renewal of such a contract.

Such statements are admissible as evidence in any proceedings before a court, an employment tribunal and the Commissioners of the HM Revenue and Customs. Inferences may be drawn if the employer deliberately, and without reasonable excuse, omits to provide a statement or if the statement is evasive or equivocal.

If an employer fails to provide a statement, or has given a statement of reasons under *reg 9(1)(b)* (above), and the employee is still employed, the employee may present an application to an employment tribunal under *reg 9(5)* for a declaration that he is, in fact, a permanent employee.

10.13 Right to be informed of vacancies

Reg 3(6) provides that, in order to ensure that an employee is able to exercise the right conferred by *reg 3(1)*, the employee also has the right to be informed by his employer of available vacancies in the establishment.

Reg 3(7) makes it clear that an employee is so informed only if the vacancy is contained in an advertisement which the employee has a reasonable opportunity of reading in the course of his employment, or if the employee is given reasonable notification of the vacancy in some other way.

10.14 Unfair dismissal or other detriment

Reg 6(1) states that an employee who is dismissed shall be regarded as unfairly dismissed for the purposes of *ERA 1996, Part 10* if the reason – or, if more than one, the principal reason – is a reason specified in *reg 6(3)*.

Further, under *reg 6(2)* an employee has the right not to be subjected to any detriment by any act, or deliberate failure to act, of his employer done on a ground specified in *reg 6(3)*.

The reasons, or grounds, in *reg 6(3)* are that the employee:

(a)   brought proceedings against the employer under *FTR 2002*;

(b)   requested from his employer a written statement under *reg 5* or *9*;

(c)   gave evidence or information in connection with such proceedings brought by any employee;

(d)   otherwise did anything under *FTR 2002* in relation to the employer or any other person;

(e)   alleged that the employer had infringed *FTR 2002*;

(f)   refused (or proposed to refuse) to forgo a right conferred on him by *FTR 2002*.

(g)   declined to sign a workforce agreement under *FTR 2002*;

(h)   was a representative of members of the workforce of *Sch 1* to *FTR 2002* (concerning workforce agreements), or was a candidate to become such a representative.

Similarly, an employee is protected by *reg 6(3)* if the employer believes or suspects that the employee has done or intends to do any of these things.

As is usual with such provisions, there will be no unfair dismissal or detriment if any allegation made by the employee is false and not made in good faith (*reg 6(4)*).

Of course, by *ERA 1996, s 95(1)(b)* (substituted by *FTR 2002* as from 1 October 2002) an employee is dismissed by his employer if he is employed under a limited-term contract and that contract terminates because of the limiting event and is not renewed. (See also *ERA 1996, s 136(1)(b)*, in relation to dismissal by reason of redundancy.)

Hence any fixed-term contract which comes to an end requires an employer to follow the statutory dismissal procedure and, if relevant, to pay a statutory redundancy payment; the provisions enabling fixed-term employees to waive their rights have been removed by *FTR 2002*. Hence, fixed-term employees on task contracts of two years or more will now have a right to statutory redundancy payments if they are made redundant at the end of their contracts. They cannot be excluded from the statutory payments scheme, even where it may appear objectively justified. However, they may be excluded from contractual schemes if this may be objectively justified.

It should be noted, too, that even if it would have been futile to consult with employees who have completed a task (assuming there were sufficient numbers of employees to bring the *Trade Union and Labour Relations (Consolidation) Act 1992, s 188* into play) such consultation is still necessary (*Susie Radin Ltd v GMB* [2004] IRLR 400).

10.15 Complaint to an employment tribunal

Under *reg 7*, an employee may present a complaint to an employment tribunal that his employer has infringed a right conferred on him by *reg 3*.

Reg 7(2) provides that the employment tribunal shall not consider a complaint unless it is presented before the end of the period of three months beginning with the date of the less favourable treatment or detriment or, where an act or failure to act is part of a series of similar acts or failures, the last of them. If the alleged infringement relates to the right under *reg 3(6)* to be informed of a vacancy, then the three months runs from the date, or if more than one the last date, on which other individuals (whether or not employees of the employer) were informed of the vacancy.

In *Coutts & Co Plc v Cure* the date of the act complained of (being the non-payment of a contractual bonus) was not the date on which an intention in principle was enunciated, but when the employer decided on the date, detail and application to relevant employees of the bonus.

A complaint may be considered out of time if, in all the circumstances of the case, the employment tribunal considers that it is just and equitable to do so.

The remedies available to an employment tribunal are specified in *reg 7(7)*. If an employment tribunal considers that a case is well founded it can:

(a)   make a declaration as to the rights of the complainant and the employer;

(b)   order the employer to pay compensation to the complainant; and/or

(c)   recommend that the employer take, within a specified period, reasonable action to reduce the adverse effect on the complainant.

10.16   Fixed-term to permanent

Reg 8 provides that, where an employee is employed under a purported fixed-term contract, and such contract has previously been renewed (or the employee has previously been employed on a fixed-term contract), the employee shall be a permanent employee if he has have been continuously employed for a period of four years or more and the use of a fixed-term contract was not justified on objective grounds. The justification must be judged as at the time when the contract was last renewed, or if it has not been renewed, at the time of entering into the contract.

However, this rule can be modified by a collective or workforce agreement which specifies a maximum total period for fixed-term work, or a maximum number of fixed-term contracts, or objective grounds for such contracts.

The Guidance states that objective justification in a collective or workforce agreement might be acceptable in sport, for example, or in relation to actors, where it is the traditional practice to work on fixed-term contracts because of the nature of the work.

It should be noted that there is no limit on the duration of a first fixed-term contract. However, if a first fixed-term contract for four years or more is renewed, the second will be regarded as permanent (unless the second contract is objectively justified).

The limitation on successive fixed-term contracts will apply only where the employee has been continuously employed for the whole period. An employee may be continuously employed even where there is a gap between successive contracts. The relevant test for continuity is that in *ERA 1996, Part 14, Chapter 1, ss 210–219*.

10.17   Minimum notice

Employees on task contracts expected to last three months or less now have the right to a minimum notice period of one week if their contracts are terminated (other than by completion) after they have one month or more of continuous service. (This change is a result of the Regulations amending *ERA 1996, s 86*.) This means employees must also give their employers one week's notice of the termination of their contracts if they have one month or more of continuous service.

10.18   Liability of employers and principals

Reg 12 provides that anything done by a person in the course of his employment shall be treated for the purpose of the Regulations as also done by his employer, whether or not it is done with the employer's knowledge or approval.

10.19 Fixed-term and Part-time Workers

Similarly, under *reg 12(2)*, anything done by a person as agent for the employer with the authority of the employer shall be treated as done with the employer's knowledge or approval.

It shall be a defence for an employer to prove that he took reasonably practicable steps to prevent his employee from doing any act of which complaint is made.

10.19 Redundancy

Employers will now have to justify making staff on fixed-term contracts redundant before any permanent employee (although, insofar as such a claim constitutes indirect sex discrimination (see COMMON CONCEPTS (1)), justification in such circumstances has always been necessary (*Whiffen v Milham Ford Girls' School* (see 10.3)).

Justification will equally be necessary where a fixed-term employee is precluded from obtaining an enhanced redundancy payment (*Hart v Secretary of State for Education and Skills*).

It is impermissible for national legislation to exclude fixed-term employees for the purpose of calculating thresholds for collective redundancies (*Confederation Generale du Travail v Prime Minister, Case C-385/05*, 18 January 2007).

10.20 PART-TIME WORKERS

Derivation of UK Legislation

The *Part-time Workers* (*Prevention of Less Favourable*) *Treatment Regulations 2000* (*SI 2000/1551*) ('*PTWR 2000*') came into force on 1 July 2000, provision having been made for their introduction by *ERA 1999, ss 18–20*. They were introduced to implement *Directive 1997/81/EC* (the '*Part-Time Directive*'), which was adopted on 15 December 1997 (and which applied to the UK as a result of the provisions of *Directive 1998/23/EC*) concerning the Framework Agreement on Part-Time Work, which was concluded by cross-industry organisations in June 1997. *PTWR 2000* were subsequently amended by the *Part-time Workers* (*Prevention of Less Favourable Treatment*) *Regulations 2000* (*Amendment*) *Regulations 2002* (*SI 2002/2035*) (the '*PTWR* (*Amendment*) *2002*'), in relation to comparators and access to pension schemes.

10.21 Pre-existing protection

Part-time workers could run an indirect sex discrimination claim or equal pay claim (see SEX DISCRIMINATION (8)) in appropriate circumstances, prior to the implementation of the *PTWR 2000*. The *PTWR 2000* give rights to part-timers because of their status as part-timers and so provide a remedy for male part-timers who have been disadvantaged because of their part-time status.

In practice, many women will continue to bring a sex discrimination or an equal pay claim in addition to a claim under *PTWR 2000* (see SEX DISCRIMINATION (8) and EQUAL PAY (11)).

10.22 Why were the PTWR 2000 introduced and what has been their impact?

Part-time working is a very common form of atypical work in the UK. In 2006, there were approximately 7.5 million part-timers (5.5 million of whom were women) (*Labour Force Survey 2006*). The stated aim of the *Part-Time Directive* was to end the less favourable treatment of part-timers and support the development of a flexible labour market. This would be done, the *Part-Time Directive* envisaged, by encouraging the greater use of part-time employment, and increasing the quality and range of jobs that are considered suitable for part-time working or job-sharing. *PTWR 2000* were introduced in order to implement the Directive. The more aspirational aims of the *Part-Time Directive* are not directly addressed in *PTWR 2000*, but are to be found in the DTI Best Practice Guide, eg in respect of widening access to part-time work at the recruitment stage or maximising opportunities, career progression and mobility for part-timers.

PTWR 2000 create no right to work part-time.

Relatively few cases have been brought under *PTWR 2000*. For example, only 776 claims were brought in the year from April 2006 to March 2007 which compares with 44,491 unfair dismissal claims and 28,153 sex discrimination claims in the same period (*Employment Tribunal Service (ETS) Annual Report and Accounts 2006–2007*). In guidance that was published in 2002, ACAS expressed the view that 'less-favourable treatment of part-time workers is not widespread in the UK' ('Part-time Workers. The law and best practice – a detailed guide for employers and part-timers' URN No: 02/1710).

10.23 Guidance on the PTWR 2000

The *Employment Relations Act 1999, ss 20–21* anticipates publication of a Code of Practice. This has not been produced, but the EOC's Code of Practice on Sex Discrimination includes guidance on part-timers (recommending that employers consider whether certain jobs can be carried out on a part-time basis). (The Code will remain in force until/unless the Commission for Equality and Human Rights (EHRC) replaces it. The DTI has also produced a useful guide for employers entitled 'Part-time Workers. The law and best practice'. This is broken down into 'Compliance Guidance' and 'Best Practice Guidance'. The Best Practice Guidance provides examples of the ways in which employers can widen the access to part-time work, for example, by making a wider range of jobs available part-time, by operating job-sharing arrangements and by improving the flow of information to workers.

The ACAS guide 'Flexible working and work-life balance' also deals with issues concerning part-time working.

10.24 Who is covered?

The legislation protects 'part-time workers'. A part-time worker is defined as a person who is 'paid wholly or in part by reference to the time he works and, having regard to the custom and practice of the employer in relation to workers employed by the worker's employer under the same type of contract is not identifiable as a full-time worker' (*reg 2(2)*). This definition affords some flexibility: any worker who works and is paid in respect of less than full time work may qualify.

A worker is defined as 'an individual who has entered into or works under or (except where a provision of these Regulations otherwise requires) where the employment has ceased, worked under:

(a)   a contract of employment; or

(b)   any other contract, whether express or implied and (if it is express) whether oral or in writing, whereby the individual undertakes to do or perform personally any work or services for another party to the contract whose status is not by virtue of the contract that of a client or customer of any profession or business undertaking carried on by the individual.'

PTWR 2000 cover those in Crown employment, as well as House of Lords and House of Commons staff, together with members of police forces, special constables and those police cadets who are treated as being employed under a contract of employment. They also apply to members of the armed forces, but not necessarily to members of the reserve forces (*R (on the application of Manson) v Ministry of Defence* [2005] EWHC 427 (Admin), [2005] All ER (D) 270 (Feb)) and do not apply to any holder of a judicial office if paid on a daily-fee basis.

Unlike, for example, in the case of sex discrimination, job applicants are not protected. This means that an employer may advertise for a full-time position and reject any candidate who is only prepared to work part-time (although the rejected candidate may nevertheless have a valid indirect sex discrimination claim (see SEX DISCRIMINATION (8)).

There is no minimum qualifying period.

Under the *EA 2002* employees have a separate statutory right to request flexible working, which can include part-time working (see SEX DISCRIMINATION (8)).

In a slightly unusual case, *Hudson v University of Oxford* [2007] EWCA Civ 336, [2007] All ER (D) 356 (Feb), the Court of Appeal decided that an employee who worked full-time hours but under two separate part-time contracts might be able to contend that he is a part-timer in respect of each contract. (This case should, however, be treated with some caution because the decision was made in the context of an appeal against a strike out of the worker's claim, where the employee had only to show that he had a reasonable prospect of success. It was remitted back to the employment tribunal.)

10.25 Comparator

An actual comparator

PTWR 2000 set out the conditions that must be met by the part-timer and the full-time comparator.

PTWR 2000 require that (with the exception of circumstances explained in 10.26) the worker must choose an appropriate full-time worker with whom to compare himself. The option of using a hypothetical comparator is not permitted. The *Part-time Directive* is not as restrictive as it provides that where there is no comparable full-time worker at the same establishment, a comparison can be made by reference to national law, a collective agreement or 'practice'. This arguably provides scope for the use of a hypothetical comparator in certain circumstances. The question has arisen in various cases, but to date has not been definitively decided (*Tyson v Concurrent Systems Incorporated Ltd* UKEAT/0028/03 and *Royal Mail Group plc v Lynch* UKEAT/0426/03). The ECJ did not, however, construct a hypothetical comparator in *Wippel v Peek & Cloppenburg GmbH & Co KG C-313/02* [2005] IRLR 211.

PTWR 2000, reg 2 requires that:

● both the part-time worker and the full-time comparator must be employed by the same employer (reg 2(4)(a)(i)).

There is no provision for a part-timer to compare his treatment with that of a full-timer at an associated company. In theory, it appears that a business could set up a separate company to employ all its part-timers. However, if this were to be done solely to avoid claims under *PTWR 2000*, it is possible that a tribunal may take a purposive approach to the legislation and look beyond the corporate structure.

- both workers must be employed under the same type of contract (reg 2(4)(a)(i)).

Reg 2(3) identifies four categories of contract under which both workers must be engaged. These are: employees working under a non-apprenticeship contract (*reg 2(3)(a)*); employees working under an apprenticeship contract (*reg 2(3)(b)*); workers who are not employees (*reg 2(3)(c)*); and 'any other description of worker that it is reasonable for the employer to treat differently from other workers, on the ground that workers of that description have a different type of contract' (*reg 2(3)(d)*).

The previous requirement that a permanent part-timer had to compare himself with a permanent full-timer (and a fixed-term part-timer had to compare himself with a fixed-term full-timer) was removed by the *PTWR (Amendment) 2002*.

In *Matthews v Kent and Medway Towns Fire Authority* [2004] EWCA Civ 844, [2004] 3 All ER 620, [2005] ICR 84, it was acknowledged that although there were structural differences between the contracts that both part- and full-time firefighters worked under, for example in relation to the calculation of pay and working patterns, these did not mean that the types of contract were different. The House of Lords decided that both part-time and full-time firefighters were employed under a contract that, in the language of *PTWR 2000*, was not a contract of apprenticeship. Although the tribunal and the EAT decided that the part-time firefighters were employed on contracts that fell within the 'any other description of worker' type of contract, this was viewed by the House of Lords as a residual category that was only included in *PTWR 2000* in case an employer adopted an unusual contract that was not covered by any of the other three categories. The House of Lords said it could not envisage any such contract being agreed.

A more restrictive approach was taken by the ECJ in *Wippel v Peek & Cloppenburg GmbH and Co KG*. An employee working under a part-time 'zero hours' contract could refuse work and had no fixed hours. The ECJ held that she could not compare herself with either full-time or part-time workers working for the same employer whose contracts identified working hours.

- both workers must be engaged in the same or broadly similar work (*reg 2(4)(a)(ii)*), having regard to whether they have similar levels of qualification, skill and experience.

In *Matthews*, the House of Lords held (by a 4:1 majority on this issue) that the main purpose of both the part-time and full-time fighters jobs was the same (putting out fires) and that most of their duties and responsibilities were the same. The House of Lords decided that more weight should be given to the extent that both jobs are the same, rather than emphasising their differences, as it will commonly be the case that part-timers will be given different work than full-timers.

If a worker who has two part-time contracts can bring a claim under *PTWR 2000* in relation to either contract (see *Hudson*), his employer may argue that only a full-timer doing two comparable jobs can be considered to do broadly similar work – an impossibility. However, tribunals may be reluctant to uphold such a narrow approach and might conceivably permit the employee to compare himself with a full-timer doing only one of the jobs.

- both workers must be based at the same establishment. If, however, no full-time worker works or is based at the same establishment as the part-timer, the comparator can be based at a different establishment operated by the same employer (*reg 2(4)(b)*).

- both workers must be paid by reference to the time that they work (*reg 2(1), (2)*).

- the part-time worker must be identifiable as a part-time worker, and the full-time worker must be identifiable as a full-time worker. In each case, regard should be had to the employer's custom and practice in relation to workers employed by the employer under the same type of contract (*reg 2(1), (2)*).

A part-time employee at a school was unable to compare herself with two workers in the same department who worked 35 hours per week during term time only. This was because the employer's contractual documents stipulated that full-timers work 37 hours per week and the applicant had produced no evidence that the school had treated the workers who worked 35 hours as full-timers. It was noted, though, that if the employer, by custom and practice, had treated these workers as full-timers then a comparison could be made (*Mrs F England v The Governing Body of Turnford School* [2003] All ER (D) 105 (May)).

10.26 *Comparison with a worker's previous contract*

Using another worker as a comparator is not necessary in certain limited circumstances, where a comparison can be made with the same worker's previous contract. *Reg 3* permits a worker who switches from full-time to part-time work to compare his terms with those that he enjoyed immediately before the change, even if the new contract is of a different type from the previous one.

Reg 4 provides that this comparison can be made even if there is a break in employment, provided that this break lasts for less than 12 months and the worker returns either to the same job, or to a job at the same level. This means that, for example, a woman who meets these conditions after taking maternity leave or workers who take a career break, can compare themselves with the treatment or the terms that applied prior to the break. If the employer can show that the worker's original contract would have been varied during the period of absence, then the comparison must be made with that varied contract.

10.27 **Less favourable treatment**

A part-time worker has the right not to be treated less favourably by his employer than a comparable full-time worker (*reg 5(1)*). The right covers the terms of a worker's contract, which the DTI Guide explains includes:

(a)   the reorganisation of working hours;

(b)   seeking promotion;

(c)   rates of pay, including enhanced pay, overtime, profit-sharing, share option schemes and contractual sick and maternity pay;

(d)   access to occupational pensions;

(e)   access to training;

(f)   benefits, such as health insurance;

(g)   annual leave, maternity and parental leave and career breaks; and

(h)   public and bank holidays.

The right to protection from less favourable treatment in the *Part-time Directive* relates to employment conditions and other detriment arising from any act, or deliberate failure to act, by the employer. In this regard, the DTI Guide refers specifically to selection for redundancy of part-time workers before full-time workers. It is likely that 'detriment' will be construed as in other discrimination legislation (see COMMON CONCEPTS (1)). In *Hendrickson Europe Ltd v Christine Pipe* [2003] All ER (D) 280 (Apr) it was accepted that dismissal amounted to a detriment under *reg 5(1)(b)*. (The employer abandoned the contrary argument which seems to have been based on the premise that dismissals were only caught by the Regulations to the extent they came within the automatically unfair dismissal provision of *reg 7*.

Whilst lower remuneration and benefits are often straightforward to identify, some less favourable treatment may be less so. For example, will promotion of a comparable full-time worker be less favourable treatment where the full-timer is promoted to manage a team of full-time workers? Arguably yes, but there may be good counter-arguments to say that it is objectively justifiable. Would it make any difference if the employer were to interview the part-timer, to confirm his/her suitability and willingness to work full-time? The DTI Guidance says that employers should be open to workers' willingness to work full-time. In practice there may be other considerations and it may not be possible for an employer to justify preferring a full-timer – e g where no absolute requirement for the manager to manage full-time can be made out.

The question whether less favourable treatment may be counterbalanced by more favourable treatment in relation to other terms and conditions such that there would be a finding of no less favourable treatment overall was considered in *Matthews*. Baroness Hale (with whom Lord Hope and Lord Nicholls agreed), while considering this as a 'subsidiary question', did not wish to rule out the possibility. The DTI Guide, however, does not anticipate that an off-setting exercise will take place. The approach is one of a term-by-term analysis of less favourable treatment. For example, it states that part-time workers must receive the same basic rate of pay as comparable full-time workers, unless objectively justifiable. Subject to the pro rata principle, the same goes for other remuneration and benefits. There may be greater scope to argue that a package approach may be taken when considering justification (see 10.32). (*FTR 2002*, on the other hand, provide expressly that less favourable treatment is justified where the fixed-term employee's overall package is no less favourable (*reg 4(1)*).

10.28 *Pro rata principle*

Reg 5(3) introduces the pro rata principle to be used when determining whether there has been less favourable treatment, unless it is inappropriate. The pro rata principle derives from the *Part-time Directive, clause 4(2)* and is defined at *reg 1(2)*. It is limited to pay or any other benefits. The definition read in isolation provides that part-timers are entitled to receive proportionate pay and benefits. This was raised in *McMenemy v Capita Business Services Limited* [2007] IRLR 400, and the court confirmed that *PTWR 2000* do not provide a free-standing right to pro rata pay and benefits. The pro rata principle acts as a tool to enable a valid comparison to be made between part-time and full-time remuneration.

If it is appropriate to use the pro rata principle, it will be necessary to consider how it should be applied. For example, where a monthly wage is made up of component parts, should each part be analysed separately or should the wages as a whole be pro-rated? The DTI Guide suggests a term-by-term approach; however, this may not always produce a valid comparison. For example, in order to avoid a 'completely unreal and impractical' outcome, whereby part-time workers would be paid at a higher hourly rate than their full-time counterparts, *James and others v Great North Eastern Railways* [2005] All ER (D) 15 (Mar) held that the pro rata principle should be applied to the employees' average hourly wage. In this way, the composite hourly rate of full-timers who received an additional hourly allowance could be compared against the hourly rate of part-timers who did not.

Matthews is an example of where the pro rata principle may not be appropriate. The tribunal held that it was inappropriate to apply the pro rata principle to the entire financial package claimed by the fire fighters, which included pension benefit, sick pay and pay for additional duties. This was not challenged in the EAT.

Benefits such as health care or a company car are further examples of where applying the pro rata principle may not be appropriate. To provide no benefit would, however, be likely to be difficult to justify. It may therefore be that a pro rated car allowance, based on the cost of the car, or a contribution to health care cover, should be provided.

10.29 *Overtime*

Overtime is dealt with specifically in the *PTWR 2000*. *Reg 5(4)* reflects the principle laid down in *Stadt Lengerich v Helmig* [1995] IRLR 216, that part-timers are not entitled to pro-rata overtime payments until they have worked the same number of hours as their comparators.

This principle was tested in *James*. The case turned on the pay structure for GNER staff. The EAT held that the 'additional hours allowance', which formed part of contractual, rostered hours, did not amount to overtime in the *reg 5(4)* sense. The EAT's application of the pro rata principle, however, reflected its concern that part-timers should not benefit disproportionately from a pay structure originally implemented for full-time staff. In assessing the less favourable treatment, the EAT considered that the comparison should be between the average hourly rate of basic pay and additional hours allowance earned by full-timers, as against the basic pay (but no 'additional hours allowance') earned by part-timers.

The ECJ has also decided, in *Voß v Land Berlin Case C-300/06*, ECJ, that a female part-timer suffered a detriment compared with a male full-time employee where she was paid overtime at a lesser rate than that which applied during her normal working hours. This was the case even though the full-timer would also be paid for overtime at the same lesser rate. The decision was based on the fact that the part-timer's rate of pay for overtime would be less than the full-timer's rate of pay for normal work. The ECJ decided that this difference in treatment would be contrary to *Article 141(3)* of the *EC Treaty* where a considerably higher percentage of women would be affected as compared with the percentage of men so affected, and the difference in treatment could not be objectively justified (see SEX DISCRIMINATION (8)). In the absence of justification, any disparate impact could be remedied by paying the part-timer for overtime, for the period until the part-timer has worked the equivalent of the full-timer's normal working hours, at the same rate as a full-timer's normal working hours. The case emphasises that employers should carefully assess the impact on part-time workers when making and implementing their arrangements for overtime.

10.30 *Statutory holidays*

The risk of less favourable treatment arising for part-time workers in respect of Monday public holidays is identified in the DTI Guidance. It provides, '... because most bank and public holidays fall on Monday, those who do not work Mondays will be entitled to proportionately fewer days off. In many workplaces, these workers will predominantly be part-timers. In such cases, it may be necessary to remove the disadvantage suffered ... for example by giving all workers a pro rata entitlement of days off in lieu according to the number of hours they work.'

The Government has now taken steps to reduce the risk of less favourable treatment for part-timers in respect of statutory holidays. Minimum annual holiday entitlement for full-time workers under the *Working Time Regulations 1998* increased from 20 days to 24 days on 1 October 2007, and will increase to 28 days from 1 April 2009. This is said to benefit 2.5 million men and 3.5 million women, equating to 31% of part-time workers, and 14% of full-time workers. Where employers' holiday entitlement exactly mirrors the new statutory entitlements, the question of less favourable treatment under the *PTWR 2000* will reduce because there will be a requirement under the amended *Working Time Regulations 1998* to provide 5.6 weeks' per year holiday to all workers regardless of the days on which workers may be required to work. There is still scope for inequality, for example if employers offer bank and public holidays in addition to the 5.6 weeks minimum, or indeed for part-time workers required to take bank or public holidays, leaving them with less relative flexibility as to when they may take holiday.

For those workers who remain disadvantaged until the amended *Working Time Regulations 1998* come into force in full, there have been two Scottish decisions on statutory holidays, *Gibson v Scottish Ambulance Service* UKEATS/0052/04 and *McMenemy* (see 10.28). Both hinged on the reason for the less favourable treatment, and both found in favour of the employer, that the reason was not part-time status, rather that the employees did not work on Mondays. However, in both cases it was accepted that there had been less favourable treatment.

10.31 **Less favourable treatment on the ground that the worker is a part-time worker**

Reg 5(2)(a) limits the scope of *PTWR 2000* to less favourable treatment 'on the grounds that' the worker is a part-time worker. This reflects, but does not precisely mirror the *Part-Time Directive 1997/81/EC, clause 4,* which prohibits less favourable treatment 'solely' because of working part-time.

Case law has clarified the way in which 'on the ground that' should be interpreted under *PTWR 2000*.

(a) Unlike the test in other direct discrimination claims, (see, eg *Nagarajan v London Regional Transport* [2000] 1 AC 501, [1999] 4 All ER 65, [1999] 3 WLR 425, [1999] ICR 877), under the *PTWR 2000*, construed in accordance with the *Part-Time Directive, clause 4.1*, part-time status must be the only reason for the less favourable treatment (*Wippel, Gibson, McMenemy*).

(b)   The test is a subjective, factual one, looking at the motive operating in the mind of the employer, rather than a causative, 'but for' test (*Chief Constable of West Yorkshire Police v Khan* [2001] IRLR 830, [2001] UKHL 48; *Gibson, McMenemy*).

(c)   Dismissal will be on the grounds of part-time work and not redundancy where business needs require full-time, rather than part-time staff (*Hendrickson*).

(d)   A tribunal may consider a hypothetical full-time comparator when deciding on the motive of the employer (*McMenemy*).

(e)   Pressure to work full-time for employment to continue will be less favourable treatment on the grounds of part-time status (*Hendrickson*).

(f)   A tribunal may conclude that the less favourable treatment has not been on the ground of part-time status, despite the fact that no full-time worker has been so disadvantaged (*McMenemy*).

The analysis of the reason why the treatment occurred provides the tribunal with a broad discretion to make its decision based on the evidence in each particular case. Guidance on this analysis may be drawn from other areas of discrimination law (see COMMON CONCEPTS (1)).

Where less favourable treatment is a likely outcome of a particular practice, it follows that it may assist employers to put in place clear contractual and policy wording indicating the reasons for the practice. The disparate impact of the practice should be monitored, to avoid any adverse impact on part-timers. An example of this is access to training for part-time workers who do not work particular days. Whilst, on the *McMenemy* reasoning, the reason for the less favourable treatment would not be part-time status, but the fact that part-timers do not work on a particular day, the DTI Guidance recommends that steps be taken to minimise the less favourable treatment, for example, by paying part-timers for the extra hours worked to attend training, or by offering other training methods such as distance learning courses.

10.32 Justification

Neither *PTWR 2000* nor the *Part-Time Directive* give any guidance on objective justification. However, it is expected that this will be assessed in the same way as in other discrimination legislation (see COMMON CONCEPTS (1)), ie it can only be justified if the treatment aims to achieve a legitimate business objective and it is necessary and appropriate to achieve that objective.

Baroness Hale's judgment in *Matthews* considered whether less favourable elements contained in a part-timer's pay and benefits may be justified by other, more favourable elements contained elsewhere in the package. Baroness Hale said that it may be an appropriate route to take in certain cases; however, the House of Lords upheld the tribunal's conclusion that it was difficult for the employer objectively to justify the differences. Baroness Hale believed that it would be difficult to see how the differently configured pay package could justify part-timers' exclusion from the employer's pension or sick pay schemes.

It is significant, however, that the *PTWR 2000* do not contain the equivalent of *FTR 2002, reg 4(1)*, which require the terms of the employment contract as a whole, to be at least as favourable. The analogy, therefore, would more naturally be with the term-by-term analysis under *EqPA 1970*. The status of fixed-term employees, where more favourable terms may, in practice, be agreed, lends itself more naturally to a consideration of the 'package' approach (see 10.11). However, in appropriate circumstances, there should not be any reason why such an argument objectively to justify less favourable treatment should not succeed.

The pro-rata principle, whilst not a free-standing right, limits the scope of the justification defence. There is a presumption that proportionate remuneration or benefits will be provided, and a failure to do so will need to be justified on objective grounds which do not include financial constraints (*Hill v Revenue Comrs C-243/95* [1998] ECR I-3739, [1998] All ER (EC) 722, [1998] 3 CMLR 81, [1999] ICR 48), but which may include demand (*Gibson*).

10.33 Right to a written statement

Pursuant to a provision designed to reduce the number of tribunal claims, a part-timer who believes that he has been treated less favourably than a comparable full-timer, can write to his employer and ask for written reasons for the different treatment (*reg 6(1)*). The employer must respond in writing within 21 days, and the statement can be used in evidence in proceedings under *PTWR 2000*. The tribunal can infer that the worker was discriminated against on the ground of his part-time status if the employer does not provide a written statement, or if the reasons given are evasive or equivocal.

If an employee is dismissed, this specific right to receive a written statement under *PTWR 2000* will not apply. However, the employee will be entitled to receive a written statement of the reasons for his dismissal in accordance with *ERA 1996, s 92(1)*, within 14 days of making a written request. This statement can then be used in evidence in any proceedings (*ERA 1996, s 92(5)*). The tribunal can award two weeks' pay should the employer unreasonably refuse to provide the statement, or if it is inadequate or untrue.

10.34 Unfair dismissal or other detriment

Reg 7(1) provides that dismissing an employee will be automatically unfair if the reason or principle reason for the dismissal is that the employee has done (or the employer believes or suspects that he has done or intends to do) one of a number of protected acts. Workers also have the right not to be subjected to any detriment by any act, or any failure to act, on the same protected grounds (*reg 7(2)*). Protected status arises where a worker has:

● brought proceedings against the employer under *PTWR 2000*;

● requested from his employer a written statement of reasons (under *PTWR 2000, reg 6*);

● given evidence or information in connection with such proceedings brought by any worker;

● otherwise done anything under *PTWR 2000* in relation to the employer or any other person;

● alleged that the employer has infringed *PTWR 2000* (but if such an allegation is false and not made in good faith there is no protection);

● refused (or proposed to refuse) to forgo a right conferred on him by *PTWR 2000*.

An automatic unfair dismissal claim means that the employee will not need a minimum qualifying period of employment as is usual for unfair dismissal claims (*ERA 1996, s 108*).

10.35 Fixed-term and Part-time Workers

In addition to a *reg 5* claim, following general unfair dismissal protection, if the sole or principal reason for the dismissal is that the employee is a part-time worker, this will not be a fair reason in accordance with *ERA 1996, s 98(1),*.

10.35 Tribunal claims

Claims of less favourable treatment or unfair dismissal must ordinarily be presented to an employment tribunal within three months from the date of the less favourable treatment or detriment, or where an act or failure to act is part of a series, the last of them.

Perhaps erroneously, *PTWR 2000* are not included in the list of claims for which a worker is required to raise a grievance (*EA 2002, Sch 4*), nor in that to which tribunals can increase or reduce compensation for failing to follow an appropriate procedure (*EA 2002, Sch 3*). There does not appear to be any reason for omitting *PTWR 2000* from the schedules but, if it is an oversight, it has not yet been corrected. This omission means that a part-timer need not raise a statutory grievance before bringing a tribunal claim under *PTWR 2000*, but neither can he benefit from the three-month extension of time that would otherwise result from raising a grievance. The worker must still raise a grievance if wishing to bring some other complaint, for example sex discrimination.

10.36 Tribunal remedies

10.37 *Less favourable treatment*

Where the tribunal finds less favourable treatment or detriment, it can make a declaration, order the employer to pay compensation and make a recommendation that the employer, within a specified period, takes specified measures and/or reduces the adverse effect on the worker (see COMMON CONCEPTS (1)).

Unfair dismissal

Reg 8(11) expressly precludes a part-timer from obtaining an injury to feelings award if he is treated less favourably than a full-timer, and *Dunnachie v Kingston-Upon-Hull City Council* [2004] EWCA Civ 84, [2004] 2 All ER 501 established that such an award cannot be made in unfair dismissal cases. However, following *Virgo Fidelis Senior School v Kevin Boyle* [2004] ICR 1210, where an injury to feelings award was made for subjecting a worker to a detriment for making a protected disclosure, it is possible that a worker may obtain such an award if he is subjected to a *reg 7(2)* detriment, since this is not expressly excluded by *reg 8(11)*.

10.38 Employer's liability

Liability for employers and agents under *PTWR 2000* follows that in other discrimination legislation (see COMMON CONCEPTS (1)).

11   Equal Pay

11.1   INTRODUCTION

There is no separate legislative regime to address pay-related discrimination on prohibited grounds other than sex. Claims must be brought under the general legislation which applies to the relevant ground. However, a different approach is taken as regards differences in pay between men and women. Those differences are thought to be systemic and structural rather than resulting from individual acts of irrationality, and thus to require a very different regime to deal with them.

The present government proposes to bring the right to equal pay for men and women within a Single Equality Bill. However, it does not intend to apply the general anti-discrimination model to that right. It considers it to be inappropriate to expose employers to potential liability for aggravated or exemplary damages, damages for injury to feelings and any other injury suffered by the claimant as a result of the discrimination, since '[i]n many cases, structural differences in pay may have evolved over a long period, with no deliberate discriminatory intent' ('Discrimination Law Review: A Framework for Fairness: Proposals for a Single Equality Bill for Great Britain – A Consultation Paper' (Department for Communities and Local Government, June 2007), Chapter 3).

The gender pay gap remains deeply entrenched in the United Kingdom. Based on median hourly earnings, women in full-time work earn 13% less than men; based on mean hourly earnings, they earn 17% less. Women who work part-time earn 38% less per hour than the median hourly pay of women who work full-time and 41% less per hour than men who work full-time ('Shaping a Fairer Future' (Women and Work Commission, February 2006)). The underlying causes of the gender pay gap are thought to be 'related to differences between men and women in their experience of education, training and the workplace, and also in the roles men and women play in the family' ('Towards a Fairer Future: Implementing the Women and Work Commission recommendations' (Department for Communities and Local Government, April 2007)).

However, the limitations inherent in the present legislative regime may also be partly to blame. The absence of any positive obligation on employers to introduce or maintain non-discriminatory pay systems is thought by many to be most significant in this regard. Reliance is instead placed on individual complaints and litigation, which is frequently expensive, time-consuming and unpredictable in outcome. Positive duties to make pay systems transparent or to audit pay have been imposed in other jurisdictions, notably Ontario and Quebec. Despite the recommendation in 2001 of an Equal Pay Task Force set up by the Equal Opportunities Commission (EOC), the Government has to date resisted the introduction of similar statutory duties in this country.

11.2   OVERVIEW OF THE STATUTORY FRAMEWORK

There are two separate but overlapping legal regimes which regulate equal pay in the United Kingdom.

First, in domestic law, there is the *Equal Pay Act 1970* (*EqPA 1970*). Overlap with the *Sex Discrimination Act 1975* (*SDA 1975*) is avoided since the latter has no application to 'benefits consisting of the payment of money when the provision of those benefits is regulated by the [employee's] contract of employment' (*SDA 1975, s 6(6)*). The rights conferred by the two statutes are mutually exclusive and lead to different remedies (*Peake v Automotive Products Ltd* [1977] QB 780, EAT). However, they are complementary and should be construed as far as possible 'so as to form a harmonious code' (*Steel v Union of Post Office Workers and the General Post Office* [1978] 1 WLR 64, EAT at 69). Indeed, several provisions of *SDA 1975* apply to claims under *EqPA 1970*, such as *s 4* on discrimination by way of victimisation (see COMMON CONCEPTS (1)) and *s 10* on the meaning of employment at an establishment in Great Britain.

Secondly, *Article 141* of the EC Treaty (formerly *Article 119*) is directly effective. Accordingly, individuals can rely upon their rights under *Article 141* in domestic employment tribunals and courts (*Defrenne v Sabena (No 2) (Case 43/75)* [1976] ECR 455). A claim under *Article 141* is not 'free-standing' insofar as, absent detailed EC law rules, the procedural rules of *EqPA 1970* (concerning such matters as time limits) apply. However, EC law can be relied upon to disapply barriers to a claim which are incompatible with EC law (*Biggs v Somerset County Council* [1996] 2 All ER 734, [1996] 2 CMLR 292, [1996] ICR 364; *Barber v Staffordshire County Council* [1996] ICR 379).

In effect, claimants can choose to pursue claims under whichever regime is more advantageous to them. Although domestic law and EC law seek to give effect to the same basic principle, they sometimes produce different results. The extent to which this occurs has diminished since, where possible, *EqPA 1970* has been construed in a way that accords with *Article 141*. Nevertheless, it remains the case that the domestic and EC equal pay regimes approach the same task in quite different ways, which must be outlined before a detailed examination of each regime can be conducted.

11.3 EqPA 1970

EqPA 1970 is a highly technical piece of legislation, whose complexity has attracted criticism since its enactment. However, its essential mechanism can be summarised thus. *S 1(1)* implies into every contract of employment an 'equality clause', whose operation is set out in *s 1(2)*. The clause takes effect where the claimant and an individual of the opposite sex (the 'comparator') are employed in the same employment on like work, work rated as equivalent under a job evaluation scheme, or work of equal value. If any term of the claimant's contract (whether or not it is concerned with pay) is less favourable than a term of a similar kind in her comparator's contract, the claimant's contractual term shall be modified so that it is no less favourable, unless the employer can establish that the difference in pay is genuinely due to a material factor which is not the difference of sex (*s 1(3)*). If the claimant's contract does not contain a term corresponding to a beneficial term in the comparator's contract, the claimant's contract is treated as including such a term.

11.4 Article 141 EC

In contrast to the narrow, contractual approach of *EqPA 1970*, *Article 141* sets out the basic principle in general terms, while leaving it to the EC legislature and the European Court of Justice (ECJ) to provide a detailed scheme for implementing the principle. *Article 141* provides:

'1. Each Member State shall ensure that the principle of equal pay for male and female workers for equal work or work of equal value is applied.

'2. For the purpose of this article, 'pay' means the ordinary basic or minimum wage or salary and any other consideration, whether in cash or in kind, which the worker receives directly or indirectly, in respect of his employment, from his employer.

'Equal pay without discrimination based on sex means:

(a)   that pay for the same work at piece rates shall be calculated on the basis of the same unit of measurement;

(b)   that pay for work at time rates shall be the same for the same job.'

The express reference in *Article 141(1)* to the principle of 'equal pay for work of equal value' was inserted by the *Treaty of Amsterdam*. However, that principle had previously been referred to in *Article 1* of *Directive 75/117/EEC* on equal pay for male and female workers ('the Equal Pay Directive') and the ECJ has held that it was implicit in the original *Article 119* in any event (*Brunnhofer v Bank der Österreichischen Postsparkasse AG (Case C-381–99)* [2001] ECR I-4961). Other amendments effected by the *Treaty of Amsterdam* were the additions of *Article 141(3)*, which gives the Council an express legal basis for equal pay legislation, and *Article 141(4)*, which enables Member States to adopt or maintain positive-action measures for the under-represented sex in respect of professional careers.

11.5   EOC Code of Practice on Equal Pay

The EOC was empowered by *SDA 1975, s 56A* to produce Codes of Practice giving practical guidance on discrimination issues, which employment tribunals must take into account where they are relevant to matters in issue. The current Code of Practice on Equal Pay summarises the law on equal pay in non-technical language and provides guidance on good practice in matters of pay equality and the drawing up of an equal pay policy. It will remain in force until amended or revoked by the EHRC (see COMMON CONCEPTS (1)). The EOC has also produced a guide to good practice in job evaluation schemes, entitled 'Good Practice Guide – Job Evaluation Schemes Free of Sex Bias'. This does not have statutory force, but contains information on the risks of sex-related bias in job evaluation schemes, and how this may be minimised.

11.6   THE KEY ISSUES

Six key issues arise under both domestic law and EC law, all of which have been the subject of important recent decisions by the courts:

1   Who can bring an equal pay claim?

2   With whom may a claimant compare herself?

3   What can be compared?

4   How is the comparison conducted?

5   When can a difference in pay be justified?

6   What remedies are available?

A further issue concerns the mechanics of bringing an equal pay claim (see 11.41ff).

11.7 WHO CAN BRING AN EQUAL PAY CLAIM?

Categories of workers

EqPA 1970 gives rights to individuals who are 'employed', which is defined as meaning 'employed under a contract of service or of apprenticeship or a contract personally to execute any work or labour' (*s 1(6)(a)*). This is wider than the definition of 'employee' used in relation to many employment law rights, such as the right to claim unfair dismissal. Even the self-employed are covered if they work under a contract personally to execute work (*Quinnen v Hovells* [1984] ICR 525, EAT).

EqPA 1970 also makes express provision concerning specific categories of potential claimants. Thus, those employed by or for the purposes of the Crown are covered, with any reference to a contract of employment being construed as a reference to the terms of service (*s 1(8)*). There are two excluded sub-categories: those holding a 'statutory office' (meaning an office set up by or in pursuance of any enactment: *s 1(10)*) and government ministers listed in the *House of Commons Disqualification Act 1975, Sch 2* (*s 1(10)*). However, ss *1(6A)* and *1(6B)*, inserted by the *Employment Equality (Sex Discrimination) Regulations 2005 (SI 2005/ 2467)*, extend *EqPA 1970* to those appointed (as opposed to elected) to statutory office other than political office. Specific provision is made for the application of the Act to House of Commons staff (*s 1(10A)*) and House of Lords staff (*s 1(10B)*). The Act also applies to members of the armed forces (*s 7A*), although they must make a service complaint under the *Armed Forces Act 2006, s 334* before they can pursue a tribunal claim (*s 7A(5)*).

An issue of increasing importance is whether an agency worker (whose contractual relationship is with the agency, not the end user of her services) can bring an equal pay claim. This issue arose in *Allonby v Accrington & Rosendale College* [2001] ICR 1189. The claimants were teachers formerly employed directly by the college on fixed-term contracts, but who were subsequently engaged by an agency, ELS. The claimants worked on specific assignments at the college agreed by them with ELS. The college agreed the fee they were to receive for each assignment and set the conditions under which they were to work. The Court of Appeal held that the claimants' contracts with the agency qualified under *s 1(6)(a)*.

Unlike *EqPA 1970*, *Article 141* does not expressly address the question of what type of individual can bring a claim. The ECJ has for some time referred in this regard to 'workers', but until recently had not provided a detailed definition of that term. However, when the agency worker question was referred to the ECJ in *Allonby (Case C-256/01)* [2004] ECR I-873, it ruled that the concept of 'worker' cannot be defined by reference to national legislation but instead has an EC law meaning, namely 'a person who, for a certain period of time, performs services for and under the direction of another person in return for which he receives remuneration' (para 67). The Court justified this broad definition by reference to the fact that *Article 141* 'constitutes a specific expression of the principle of equality for men and women, which forms part of the fundamental principles protected by the Community legal order' (para 65). However, the Court went on to observe that, given the definition of 'pay' in *Article 141(2)*, the term 'worker' cannot cover 'independent providers of services who are not in a relationship of subordination with the person who receives the services' (para 68).

The question of whether such a relationship exists is one of substance rather than form, and is inevitably highly fact-sensitive. As regards the claimants in *Allonby* itself, the Court observed that 'it is necessary in particular to consider the extent of any limitation on their freedom to choose their timetable, and the place and content of their work' and that '[t]he fact that no obligation is imposed on them to accept an assignment is of no consequence in that context' (para 72).

11.8   Geographical scope

EqPA 1970 gives rights to individuals who are employed 'at an establishment in Great Britain'. 'Establishment' is not defined in the Act and there is little authority on its meaning. In *Dolphin v Hartlepool BC* (2006) 150 SJLB 1290, the EAT favoured a definition based on the unit to which the worker is assigned to carry out his or her duties, following the ECJ's approach in *Rockfon A/S v Specialarbeidsforbundet i Danmark (Case C-449/93)* [1995] ECR I-4291. Although the ECJ was addressing the meaning of 'establishment' in the *Collective Redundancies Directive (75/129/EEC)*, the EAT saw no reason to conclude that a different meaning applies in *EqPA 1970, s 1(6)*. *Rockfon* also establishes that it is not essential for there to be an 'establishment', that the unit in question should have managerial autonomy in relation to decision-making.

Comparison can also be made with the courts' interpretation of the term 'establishment' in the *Selective Employment Payments Act 1966* (now repealed). Whether a particular location is to be treated as a separate establishment is a question of fact and degree, with relevant factors including the exclusive occupation of premises, some degree of permanence, and some organisation of people working there (*Secretary of State for Employment and Productivity v Vic Hallam Ltd* (1969) 5 ITR 108; *Advocate (Lord) v Babcock and Wilcox (Operations) Ltd* [1972] 1 All ER 1130, [1972] 1 WLR 448).

An employee who is not actually employed *at* an establishment is deemed to be employed at the establishment *from* which he works; if he does not even work from an establishment, he is deemed to be employed at the establishment with which his work has the closest connection (*SDA 1975, s 10(4)*). 'Great Britain' is defined in *s 1(12)* as including 'such of the territorial waters of the United Kingdom as are adjacent to Great Britain'. *SDA 1975, s 10* makes further provision on this issue:

'(1) For the purposes of this Part and section 1 of the Equal Pay Act 1970 ("the relevant purposes"), employment is to be regarded as being at an establishment in Great Britain if–

(a)   the employee does his work wholly or partly in Great Britain, or

(b)   the employee does his work wholly outside Great Britain and subsection (1A) applies.

'(1A) This subsection applies if–

(a)   the employer has a place of business at an establishment in Great Britain,

(b)   the work is for the purposes of the business carried on at that establishment, and

(c)   the employee is ordinarily resident in Great Britain–

(i)   at the time when he applies for or is offered the employment, or

(ii)   at any time during the course of the employment.'

Subsections (2) and *(3)* address employment on ships, aircraft and hovercraft. Their effect is to exclude 'claims by those whose work is wholly or mainly done outside Great Britain, unless it is done on a British registered ship, or on a British registered aircraft or hovercraft operated by a person who has his principal place of business, or is ordinarily resident, in Great Britain, when only employees whose work is done wholly outside Great Britain are excluded' (*Haughton v Olau Line (UK) Ltd* [1986] 1 WLR 504, CA at 509). *Subsection (5)* provides for the extension of *EqPA 1970* to Great Britain's areas of continental shelf: see further the *Sex Discrimination and Equal Pay (Offshore Employment) Order 1987*.

11.9 THE COMPARATOR

By definition, the concept of 'equal pay' requires a claimant to allege his or her pay to be unequal to that received by another individual of the opposite sex. There is often protracted litigation on the question of whether the claimant's chosen comparator is a legitimate one. A number of sub-issues arise under this head.

11.10 Hypothetical comparators

Most domestic anti-discrimination legislation permits the use of hypothetical comparators, by prohibiting an employer from treating an employee less favourably, on discriminatory grounds, than it 'treats or would treat' other persons. *EqPA 1970* does not: a real comparator must be identified. The Government has indicated that it does not favour permitting hypothetical comparators, on the basis that this would create undue uncertainty as to whether pay arrangements were lawful or not, while at the same time claimants would in practice find it difficult to prove that a hypothetical comparator would have been employed under more favourable contractual terms. See 'Discrimination Law Review' (above), paras 3.25–3.29.

In *Macarthys Ltd v Smith (Case 129/79)* [1980] ECR 1275, the ECJ held that hypothetical comparators are not permitted under *Article 141* either. However, this is arguably no longer the case following the amendment of the *Equal Treatment Directive* (*Directive 76/207/EEC*, amended by *Directive 2002/73/EC*), which extends the general definition of discrimination to equal pay. Moreover, there is some indication that the ECJ may be becoming more amenable to hypothetical comparators. As noted above, in *Allonby* the Court held that agency workers in principle have rights under *Article 141*. The claimant's remaining problem was identifying an available comparator (because of the 'single source' test, examined below). However, the Court held that because she sought to challenge the discriminatory effect of a pension scheme rule derived from national law, she did not need to identify a comparator, but could simply rely upon statistical evidence to show that the rule had a disproportionate impact on female workers.

Nevertheless, it remains to be seen whether EC law will take a similar approach in cases where the claim does not concern the impact of discriminatory legislation. In *Shaikh v Department for Constitutional Affairs* UKEAT/0234/05 (31 August 2005), the EAT indicated that it will not. It further held that a rule embodied in statute must 'apply across the whole of the labour force' in order to trigger the *Allonby* principle, and that the principle requires a finding or a concession that there are workers of the opposite sex engaged in like work or work of equal value (para 25). *Shaikh* thus treats *Allonby* not as sanctioning the use of hypothetical comparators, but as merely relieving claimants of the need to point to a specific actual comparator where it is obvious that many actual comparators do exist.

11.11 **The temporal nexus**

Although an actual comparator must be identified, he need not still be employed at the time of the claim. If there was a point in time when the claimant met the conditions of *EqPA 1970*, then the equality clause will have operated to vary her contract, and the contract as varied remains in force notwithstanding the comparator's subsequent departure (*Sorbie v Trust House Forte Ltd* [1977] QB 931).

Under *Article 141*, the comparator need not ever have been employed at the same time as the claimant herself: he can be a predecessor or a successor of the claimant (*Macarthys Ltd v Smith*, above; *Diocese of Hallam Trustee v Connaughton* [1996] ICR 860, EAT). EC law was until recently thought to be more generous than domestic law in this regard. However, in *Kells v Pilkington plc* [2002] IRLR 693, the EAT cast doubt on whether, in light of EC law developments, *EqPA 1970* requires contemporaneous employment. This contradicts the decision of the Court of Appeal in *Macarthys Ltd v Smith* [1979] 1 WLR 1189. That the ECJ's decision in that case could lead to a new interpretation of the *EqPA 1970* itself (as distinct from permitting a non-contemporaneous comparator in a direct *Article 141* claim) illustrates the interplay between domestic and EC law.

11.12 **The work nexus**

Having selected a comparator, how does a claimant show that the two of them do work which should be equally well remunerated? There are three routes under *EqPA 1970*, the first and third of which are mirrored in *Article 141*.

11.13 *'Like work'*

The 'like work' route under *EqPA 1970, s 1(2)(a)* requires the claimant to show two things. First, her work must be 'of the same or a broadly similar nature' to the comparator's. Secondly, any differences in the duties they undertake must 'not [be] of practical importance in relation to terms and conditions of employment', having regard to 'the frequency or otherwise with which any such differences occur in practice as well as to the nature and extent of the differences' (*s 1(4)*).

Tribunals should consider these two questions of fact separately, but are not required 'to undertake too minute an examination' (*Capper Pass Ltd v Lawton* [1977] QB 852, EAT at 857). The first question 'can be answered by a general consideration of the type of work involved, and of the skill and knowledge required to do it'. As to the second question, 'trivial differences, or differences not likely in the real world to be reflected in the terms and conditions of employment, ought to be disregarded' (*ibid*).

As Lord Denning noted, '[t]he employer should not be able to avoid the principle by introducing comparatively small differences in "job content" between men and women: nor by giving the work a different "job description" ' (*Shields v E Coomes Holdings Ltd* [1978] 1 WLR 1408 at 1417). However, substantial differences in the duties undertaken cannot be ignored, save perhaps in extreme cases where 'part of the work, although subsumed under the general description of the tasks of the employee, is in effect a separate and distinct job' (*Maidment v Cooper & Co (Birmingham) Ltd* [1978] ICR 1094 at 1098, giving the example that if two cleaners, one male and one female, do identical work during the week, 'it might be right to ignore work of a quite different kind done by the man coming in, say on Saturdays, in order to cut the grass').

The key consideration is the work actually done as opposed to the work that might be done under the claimant's and comparator's particular contractual terms, although it is only work done *pursuant to those terms* that is relevant. Thus, an employer who prays in aid the comparator's additional contractual obligations may fail to defeat the claimant's assertion that she does like work if those obligations are rarely enforced (*Electrolux v Hutchinson* [1977] ICR 252; *Redland Roof Tiles Ltd v Harper* [1977] ICR 349; *Dorothy Perkins Ltd v Dance* [1978] ICR 760). Equally, a like work claim should not be defeated on the basis that the comparator is particularly diligent or talented and does more than he is contractually required to do. As Lord Denning put it, *s 1(4)* 'involves a comparison of the two jobs – the woman's job and the man's job – and making an evaluation of each job as a job irrespective of the sex of the worker and of any special personal skill or merit that he or she may have' (*Shields*, above, at p 1417).

While the focus is on the physical acts done by the claimant and the comparator, regard may also be had to the circumstances in which each does the work, and in particular to the degree of responsibility upon each of them. This might be decisive 'where it can be seen to put one into a different grade from the other' (*Eaton Ltd v Nuttall* [1977] 3 All ER 1131, [1977] 1 WLR 549, [1977] ICR 2; see also *Waddington v Leicester Council for Voluntary Service* [1977] 1 WLR 544, EAT).

The fact that the claimant and the comparator do the same work at different times of the day cannot justify a difference in their basic rates of pay: '[t]he only legitimate way of dealing with night work or work for longer hours is by paying a night shift premium or overtime rate assessed at a reasonable figure' (*Shields*, above, at p 1418). The same principle applies to work done on Sundays. However, difference of practical importance may exist as between the duties of those working at different times, such as the added responsibility of working alone and unsupervised at night, which may defeat a 'like work' claim (*/Thomas v National Coal Board* [1987] ICR 757).

The ECJ has interpreted the equivalent concept in *Article 141* – 'same work' – in broadly the same way as the domestic courts. Thus, it has said that the terms 'the same work', 'the same job' and 'work of equal value' in *Article 141* and the *Equal Pay Directive* 'are entirely qualitative in character in that they are exclusively concerned with the nature of the work actually performed' and that 'in order to determine whether employees perform the same work or work to which equal value can be attributed, it is necessary to ascertain whether, taking account of a number of factors such as the nature of the work, the training requirements and the working conditions, those persons can be considered to be in a comparable situation' (*Brunnhofer v Bank der Österreichischen Postsparkasse AG* (Case C-381/99) [2001] ECR I-4961 at 42–43).

11.14 *'Work rated as equivalent'*

The 'work rated as equivalent' route under *EqPA 1970, s 1(2)(b)* can only be used where an analytical, non-discriminatory job evaluation study (JES) has already been undertaken by the employer and has attributed equal value to the jobs of the claimant and her comparator (*s 1(5)*). Where such a scheme has given different values to the two jobs, the claim will fail unless the JES is no longer suitable to be relied upon, for example if the work of one of them has changed since the date of the evaluation (*s 2A(2), (2A)*). There is no obligation on an employer to undertake a JES, although an employer who sets pay levels without first conducting some form of job evaluation leaves itself vulnerable to 'equal value' claims (see below).

The key issues are whether any particular JES is analytical and non-discriminatory.

An *analytical* JES is one which assesses the content of jobs in terms of objective criteria which reflect the demands placed upon employees, such as skill, effort and decision-making (factors specific to individual employees, such as productivity and length of service, are irrelevant). Points are awarded for each criterion according to a predetermined scale and the total points determine a job's place in the overall ranking order. If the jobs of the claimant and the comparator obtain the same total scores, or having obtained similar scores are placed in the same 'band' or 'grade' (*Springboard Sunderland Trust v Robson* [1992] ICR 554), their work is rated as equivalent.

However, the EAT recently held in *Home Office v Bailey* [2005] IRLR 757 that if a claimant's job scores slightly lower than the comparator's and they are not then banded together, it is not open to the tribunal to hear evidence as to what would be regarded as a significant difference or to find that the jobs are of equal value. The EAT stressed that the formula used is 'if, but only if' the jobs have been given equal value in the JES and stated that 'the *s 1(2)(b)* gateway is precise when read with *s 1(5)*' (para 33). The difficulty with this approach is that *s 1(5)* refers to 'equal value', not 'equal scores', and JESs will usually treat different scores as indicating equal value where the difference is not regarded as significant. The EAT's decision may have been influenced by a desire to preclude claimants from attempting to unpick JESs and thereby lengthen tribunal proceedings. However, given that an 'equal value' claim under *s 1(2)(c)* is not open to a claimant where a JES is already in place, this ruling could produce unjust results.

The importance of a JES being *non-discriminatory* is that decisions as to how many points should be awarded to particular factors may themselves be influenced by discriminatory attitudes. In particular, there is a danger that qualities traditionally viewed as 'female' or as pertaining to 'women's work' will be undervalued. Consequently, it is only a JES which avoids such discrimination which can be invoked for the purposes of *s 1(2)(b)*. There is one exception: *s 1(5)* provides that a woman's job will be rated as equivalent to her comparator's if they have been accorded equal value by a JES or 'would have been given an equal value but for the evaluation being made on a system setting different values for men and women on the same demand under any heading'. An evaluation in a JES will be regarded as discriminatory where a difference, or coincidence, between values set by the JES on different demands under the same or different headings is not justifiable irrespective of the sex of the person on whom those demands are made (*s 2A(3)*).

A JES which has been completed but not yet implemented may be relied upon (*O'Brien v Sim-Chem Ltd* [1980] 3 All ER 132, [1980] 1 WLR 1011). However, it is not possible to 'backdate' a JES. In *Bainbridge v Redcar and Cleveland BC* [2007] IRLR 494, the claimants argued that, having had their jobs rated under a JES, they could rely upon that JES to pursue claims under *s 1(2)(b)* in respect of a period up to six years preceding its implementation. The EAT rejected this argument, primarily on the basis that '[i]t is simply wrong to say that somebody in the period prior to the job evaluation study coming into effect has had their job rated as equivalent under a job evaluation study' (para 36). Significantly, the EAT further rejected the argument that when jobs are related as equivalent under *s 1(2)(b)*, that is the same as jobs being of equal value under *s 1(2)(c)*, since '[i]t is not uncommon for jobs to be fitted into grades where there may be real distinctions in the value of the jobs' (para 41).

Finally, it should be noted that changes in job content occurring after a JES has rated two jobs as equivalent may support an argument that the jobs should no longer be regarded as rated as equivalent.

11.15 *'Work of equal value'*

The 'work of equal value' route under *s 1(2)(c)* was inserted into *EqPA 1970* in order to ensure compliance with the UK's obligations under the *Equal Pay Directive*. The importance of this route is that it can remedy pay discrimination even where there is gender segregation as between different jobs. Thus, a woman who is performing what might traditionally be viewed as 'women's work', such as a cleaner, might succeed in claiming pay parity with a man whose job sounds more valuable but on analysis is not.

The 'work of equal value' route is only available where the 'like work' and 'work rated as equivalent' routes are not (*s 1(2)(c)*). However, this limitation only applies in respect of any given comparator; it does not have the effect that a woman is bound to treat as the proper comparator a man who happens to be employed on like work or work rated as equivalent, in preference to any other man. As Lord Keith observed in *Pickstone v Freemans* [1989] AC 66 at 111, such a rule 'would leave a large gap in the equal work provision, enabling an employer to evade it by employing one token man on the same work as a group of potential women claimants who were deliberately paid less than a group of men employed on work of equal value with that of the women'. This case illustrates the purposive approach which the courts have generally adopted when construing *EqPA 1970*.

An analytical and non-discriminatory JES which rates the claimant's job as less valuable than that of the chosen comparator will defeat an equal value claim regardless of when the JES was carried out, provided that it evaluated the jobs done on the date when proceedings were issued (*Dibro v Hore* [1990] ICR 370). However, the JES must have properly evaluated the jobs in terms of demand made on the worker under various headings, as opposed to merely slotting those jobs into a ranking order produced using duly-evaluated 'benchmark' jobs (*Bromley v Quick* [1988] ICR 623).

The burden of proving that the work is of equal value is on the claimant. Equal value claims are notorious for giving rise to extremely complex factual investigation and argument, resulting in lengthy litigation. This has led to a specific set of procedural rules being created, the Employment Tribunals (Equal Value) Rules of Procedure (see 11.41ff).

11.16 **Beyond equal pay?**

Can a claimant claim pay proportionate to that of an individual who does unlike work or work of unequal value? This may seem right as a matter of principle, but it is not permitted at all under *EqPA 1970*. Thus, a woman cannot allege that, because her work is worth 70% of a man's, she should receive 70% of his pay rather than 60%. Nor can she claim to do work worth 120% of the man's and therefore demand 120% of his pay. For example, in *Pointon v University of Sussex* [1979] IRLR 119, a claimant who was paid more than her comparator but thought she should be paid yet more failed in her claim since she had not shown that her contract was less favourable than his.

Nor can a woman whose work is of equal value to that of her comparator claim higher pay by reason of her greater seniority. As Roch LJ stated in *Evesham v*

North Hertfordshire Health Authority [2000] ICR 612 at 628, 'neither the obligation to modify terms in the applicant's contract nor the obligation to include a term found in the comparator's contract in the applicant's contract require the employer to modify a term or to include a term so that the term in the applicant's contract becomes more favourable than the term in the comparator's contract'. As he observed, '[t]he title to the Act of 1970 is "Equal Pay Act" '.

The ECJ has also shied away from moving beyond equal pay to fair pay. However, it has held that a woman doing work of greater value than a man but being paid less than him may claim equal pay (e g she does work worth 120% of his work and is allowed to claim 100% of his pay) (*Murphy v An Bord Telecom Eireann (Case 157/86)* [1988] ECR 673). The English courts have held that this analysis applies not only to claims under *EqPA 1970, s 1(2)(c)*, but also to those under *s 1(2)(a)* (*SITA UK Ltd v Hope* UKEAT/0787/04 (8 March 2005) and *s 1(2)(b)* (*Redcar & Cleveland Borough Council v Bainbridge* [2007] IRLR 984).

11.17 The institutional nexus

What link must there be between claimant and comparator aside from the fact that they do work which should be equally well remunerated? This issue has been of importance in recent years, as organisational structures and working patterns have become increasing diversified.

Under *EqPA 1970, s 1(2)*, claimant and comparator must be in 'the same employment'. As set out in *s 1(6)*, this requires not simply that they do the same type of work, but that they be employed by the same employer (or associated employers), either at the same establishment or at different establishments belonging to that employer (or those associated employers) where common terms and conditions of employment are laid down for the two establishments.

The 'same employment' test is inherently somewhat restrictive. The courts have generally resisted attempts to narrow it further still, in particular on the question of what terms and conditions are 'common'. In *Leverton v Clwyd County Council* [1989] AC 706, the House of Lords overruled the EAT and Court of Appeal in holding that 'the concept of common terms and conditions of employment observed generally at different establishments necessarily contemplates terms and conditions applicable to a wide range of employees whose individual terms will vary greatly inter se' (Lord Bridge at p 745). Accordingly, the claimant could use a comparator at a different establishment, even though there were significant differences between her terms and his in relation to the actual number of hours worked and holiday entitlements. A similarly broad and purposive approach to construing *EqPA 1970* was taken in *British Coal Corpn v Smith* [1996] 3 All ER 97, [1996] ICR 515. The House of Lords held that to require terms that are 'common in the sense of identical' would be 'far too restrictive a test'; instead, only 'broadly similar terms' are required (Lord Slynn at p 527). Whether terms are sufficiently similar for a broad comparison to be made 'is a matter of factual judgment for the employment tribunal' (*South Tyneside Metropolitan Borough Council v Anderson* [2007] ICR 1581 at [21], per Sedley LJ). Moreover, at first instance in *Villalba v Merrill Lynch & Co Inc* [2007] ICR 469, the tribunal held that the territorial restriction in *s 1(6)* to employment at two different establishments 'in Great Britain' was 'an artificial bar to the elimination of sex discrimination in pay' (para 270) which should be disapplied and *Article 141* relied on directly, allowing the claimant to use a comparator based abroad.

The restrictive nature of the 'same employment' test under *EqPA 1970* has prompted many claimants to bring claims under *Article 141* instead. The parameters of permissible comparison under *Article 141* were previously somewhat unclear, but the ECJ recently set out its preferred approach in the leading case of *Lawrence v Regent Office Care (Case C-320/00)* [2002] ECR I-7325. It held that, although the applicability of *Article 141* is not limited to situations in which claimant and comparator work for the same employer, the differences in their pay must be attributable to a single source. Otherwise, there would be no body which was responsible for the inequality and which could restore equal treatment.

The single source test has not proved an unqualified victory for claimants. It was interpreted in *Allonby v Accrington and Rossendale College (Case C-256/01)* [2004] ECR I-873 to prevent the agency worker from using one of the end user's employees as a comparator. This was despite the fact that they worked in the same establishment and were both ultimately paid by the end user. The fact that the claimant's level of pay was influenced by the amount which the end user paid the agency was held not to be a sufficient basis for concluding that the end user and the agency constituted a single source to which the differences in pay could be attributed. Nor did it matter that the claimant had originally been employed by the end user directly and that the contracting out of her services was openly designed to reduce the end user's costs (see paras 41–50).

Concerns have been expressed that employers can now manipulate employment arrangements to deprive workers of equal pay rights by effecting changes of form rather than substance. This concern is enhanced by a recent Court of Appeal decision. In *Robertson v Department for Environment, Food and Rural Affairs* [2005] ICR 750, the single source test was held to preclude the use of a comparator who has the same employer as the claimant (in both the legal and factual sense) where they work in different departments which are individually responsible for negotiating and setting staff pay levels.

This interpretation arguably goes beyond what the ECJ envisaged in *Lawrence* and gives rise to serious questions as to whether employers are now able to avoid the application of *Article 141* by departmentalising the negotiating and setting of pay levels. Such departmentalisation is institutionally less disruptive than contracting out of the type found in *Allonby* and is therefore even more likely to be used as a cost-cutting measure. On the other hand, judicial acknowledgement that any large, complex organisation which delegates responsibility for setting pay levels to lower tiers of management will inevitably have numerous 'sources' of differences in pay will be viewed by some as a sensible recognition of industrial relations reality.

The Court of Appeal applied *Robertson* in *Armstrong v Newcastle upon Tyne NHS Hospital Trust* [2006] IRLR 124, holding that female hospital ancillary staff could not use male porters as comparators even though at the time of the claim they were all employed by the same hospital trust, on the basis that the porters had previously been employed by a different trust which was responsible for introducing the bonus pay which was the subject of the claim. The Court of Appeal has, however, proved willing to pursue this line of reasoning only so far. In *South Tyneside MBC v Anderson* (above), the council argued that the claimants (cooks and cleaners at local authority schools) and their comparators (who included drivers, street cleaners and refuse collectors) were not in the same employment because it was open to each school governing body to decide what an individual worker's terms and conditions of employment should be. The Court found that this discretion was 'largely illusory', and that it would be both unrealistic and arguably perverse for the governors to try to depart from the collectively agreed terms. The claimants and the comparators were, therefore, working under common terms and conditions of employment.

Ironically, it may prove more difficult to avoid domestic equal pay law. Had the claimants in *Robertson* and their comparators of choice been employed at the same establishment, comparison would have been permitted under *EqPA 1970* despite departmentalisation. There may therefore now be some situations in which domestic law is more generous to claimants than EC law, yet others where it is less so.

11.18 **Pregnancy**

As in sex discrimination law generally, *EqPA 1970* disapplies the equal treatment principle where special treatment is accorded to pregnant women. *S 6(1)(b)* provides that the equality clause will not operate in relation to terms affording special treatment to women in connection with pregnancy or childbirth.

Under *s 6(1AA)*, *s 6(1)(b)* does not affect the operation of an equality clause falling within *s 1(2)(d)*, (*e*) or (*f*), which makes specific provision addressing discrimination in pay related to pregnancy and maternity leave. These provisions were inserted into *EqPA 1970* in order to give effect to the ECJ's decisions in *Gillespie v Northern Health and Social Services Board (Case C-342/93)* [1996] ECR I-475 and *Alabaster v Woolwich Plc (Case C-147/02)* [2004] ECR I-3101.

The overall effect of *s 1(2)(d)*, (*e*) and (*f*) is that, where a woman is arguing that she receives lower pay or less favourable contractual terms on grounds of her pregnancy or maternity leave, she need not rely on a comparator. Thus, a pay increase which a woman would have received but for pregnancy or maternity leave must be taken into account when calculating any earnings-related maternity pay and pay on her return to work. Further, the equality clause guarantees the right to the benefit of any pay increase or bonus referable to periods before or after maternity leave and during the two weeks of compulsory leave (under the *Employment Rights Act 1996, s 72(1)*) at the time they would ordinarily fall due for payment.

11.19 **WHAT CAN BE COMPARED?**

The equality clause inserted into every employment contract by *EqPA 1970* affects *all* contractual terms, not merely those governing pay. *EqPA 1970* thus regulates contractual terms such as those governing sick leave, holiday entitlement and health insurance. However, where a claimant seeks to allege discrimination in the provision of payments or benefits which are not regulated by the contract, the claim must be brought under *SDA 1975* (see 8.112). In principle this should include discretionary bonuses, although there is Scottish authority to the effect that even where a bonus scheme is described as 'discretionary', a claim should be brought under *EqPA 1970* where the bonus is regulated by the contract of employment and depends on the satisfaction of (unchanging) qualifying requirements (*Hoyland v Asda Stores Ltd* [2006] IRLR 468 (Court of Session)). *EqPA 1970* does not cover state pensions, while equal treatment in occupational pensions is addressed by the *Pensions Act 1995*, which adapts the provisions of *EqPA 1970* for pension claims.

In contrast, *Article 141* focuses more clearly on 'pay' but is not restricted to contractual entitlements. Despite the extensive definition now provided in *Article 141(2)*, the ECJ has continued to produce a voluminous case law on the meaning of 'pay'. Much of the underlying litigation has been prompted by claimants' desire to bring their claims within *Article 141* as opposed to the separate social security Directives (*79/7/EEC* and *86/378/EEC*), which contain additional limitations on the equal treatment principle.

The trend has been for the definition of 'pay' to be extended beyond the core meaning of wages and salary. 'Pay' includes benefits which employers provide voluntarily or are required by legislation to provide. It can be 'immediate or future' provided that the employee receives it, albeit indirectly, in respect of his employment from his employer. Thus, the definition includes sick pay, redundancy pay, unfair dismissal compensation, occupational pensions, survivors' benefits, bridging pensions, maternity benefits paid under legislation or collective agreements, and concessionary travel facilities granted voluntarily to ex-employees (see, respectively, *Rinner-Kuhn (Case 171/88)* [1989] ECR 2743; *Barber (Case C-262/88)* [1990] ECR I-1889; *Seymour-Smith (Case C-167/97)* [1999] ECR I-623; *Bilka-Kaufhaus (Case 170/84)* [1986] ECR 1607; *Ten Oever (Case C-109/91)* [1993] ECR I-4879; *Roberts (Case C-132/92)* [1993] ECR I-5579; *Gillespie (Case C-342/93)* [1996] ECR I-475; *Garland v British Railways Board (Case 12/81)* [1982] ECR 359).

However, 'pay' does not include social security schemes or retirement pensions which are directly governed by legislation without any element of agreement and which are obligatorily applicable to general categories of workers (*Defrenne v Belgium (Case 80/70)* [1971] ECR 445). Moreover, not every employment-related benefit is caught by *Article 141*. The ECJ stressed in *Lommers v Minister van Landbouw, Natuurbeheer en Visserji (Case C-476/99)* [2002] ECR I-2891 that '[t]he fact that the fixing of certain working conditions may have pecuniary consequences is not sufficient to bring such conditions within the scope of *Article 141*, which is a provision based on the close connection existing between the nature of the work done and the amount of pay' (para 28). The Court held that a scheme under which an employer made nursery places available on advantageous terms to employees was not governed by *Article 141*. Sex discrimination claims concerning working conditions which fall outside *Article 141* must be brought under the *Equal Treatment Directive (76/207/EEC)*.

11.20 HOW IS THE COMPARISON CONDUCTED?

Once it has been established that the claimant has selected an appropriate comparator, each term of the claimant's contract (in domestic law) or each element of his or her 'pay' (in EC law) must be compared separately with the equivalent aspect of the comparator's contract or pay. Equality is required in respect of each individual element of the consideration received by the two employees in return for working. It is therefore no defence for an employer to argue that, when looked at as a whole, the claimant's contract or pay is no less favourable than the comparator's because the claimant is entitled to certain benefits (e g free meals, car allowance, etc) to which the comparator is not entitled.

In the leading domestic case of *Hayward v Cammell Laird Shipbuilders Ltd* [1988] AC 894, the House of Lords justified this rule by reference to the wording of *EqPA 1970*. In contrast, in the leading EC case of *Barber v Guardian Royal Exchange Assurance Group (Case C-262/88)* [1990] ECR I-1889, the ECJ – which does not have a detailed legislative scheme to interpret and apply – referred to the underlying policy reasons. Without such a rule, the courts would have to ascribe a monetary value to every element of the consideration received by claimant and comparator in order that overall figures could be calculated and compared. This would render judicial review difficult and thereby diminish the effectiveness of *Article 141* (paras 33–34).

Although the rule requiring term-by-term comparison is established by authority of the highest standing, it has recently come under a degree of pressure in the context of high-profile equal pay claims by local government employees in the

North East of England. In *Redcar and Cleveland Borough Council v Degnan* [2005] IRLR 179, EAT), the female claimants were respectively employed by the council as a cleaner, a supervisory cleaner and a supervisory assistant in schools and a home help in social services. Their male comparators (who the council accepted were employed on work rated as equivalent) were employed as gardeners, refuse workers and drivers and road workers. The claimants and their comparators were all paid at the same basic hourly rate. However, there were differences in relation to the rates for attendance allowances and bonuses. The gardeners received a fixed bonus of 40%. The refuse workers and drivers received a 36% bonus and an attendance allowance of between £33.81 and £34.88 per week. The road workers received a fixed bonus of 33% and an attendance allowance of between £13.91 and £14.61 per week.

Each claimant sought to compare herself with the male comparator most advantageous to her for the purpose of the bonus element of his pay and with the most advantageous comparator for the purpose of the attendance allowance element. The tribunal held that this was permissible, but the EAT disagreed, holding that the attendance allowance related to the same subject matter as basic hourly pay and the bonus and was an *element* of a distinct part of the contract rather than itself being a distinct part. As such, the contractual 'terms' that fell to be compared were the provisions for monetary payment for performance of the contracts, by attending at work and working during normal working hours. The Court of Appeal upheld this approach ([2005] IRLR 615).

The EAT was evidently influenced by the grave financial consequences of allowing the claimants to cherry-pick the best contractual benefits from a range of comparators. It felt that to allow this would 'impose an inequitable burden, surely not intended by Parliament, on the current generation of council tax payers and general tax payers' (para 30). However, it must be doubted whether the decision truly accords with *Hayward*, where Lord Goff expressly stated at p 907 that a construction of the word 'term' which collectively embraced basic pay, benefits in kind such as the use of a car, cash bonuses and sickness benefits would do 'unacceptable violence to the words of the statute'.

Whereas the Court of Appeal has sanctioned an apparent departure from the strictness of the term-by-term rule, the ECJ recently reaffirmed that rule in its full rigour in *Elsner-Lakeberg v Land Nordrhein-Westfalen (Case C-285/02)* [2004] ECR I-5861, stressing the need for a separate comparison in respect of the pay for regular hours and the pay for additional hours.

11.21 WHEN CAN A DIFFERENCE IN PAY BE JUSTIFIED?

Even if a woman establishes that she is engaged on like work, work rated as equivalent, or work of equal value to her better paid comparator, the equality clause will not operate in her favour if the employer proves that the difference in pay is genuinely due to a material factor which is not the difference of sex (*EqPA 1970, s 1(3)*). In a case involving like work or work rated as equivalent, the factor *must* be a material difference between the woman's case and the man's, whereas in a work of equal value case, it is sufficient that the factor *may* be a material difference. A similar justification defence is present under *Article 141*. The defence emphasises that equal pay legislation is concerned not with unfair pay differences *per se*, but only with those which involve sex discrimination.

11.22 Burden of proof

Once a woman establishes that she is engaged on like work, work rated as equivalent, or work of equal value to her comparator, the burden of proof is on the employer to make out its 'genuine material factor' (GMF) defence on the balance of probabilities (*National Vulcan Engineering Insurance Group Ltd v Wade* [1979] QB 132). As the EAT put it in *Villalba v Merrill Lynch & Co Inc* [2007] ICR 469, 'the principle is that once a woman demonstrates that her job is either like work or work of equal value to that of her male chosen comparator, there is a presumption of discrimination on grounds of sex [and it] is then for the employer to rebut that presumption' (para 104).

If, as is often the case, the employer's pay system is not transparent, the burden of proof may be difficult to discharge, since the tribunal will be entitled to draw inferences from the lack of transparency (*Barton v Investec Henderson Crosthwaite Securities Ltd* [2003] ICR 1205). For that reason, employers should exercise caution when responding to questions from an employee or their representative regarding the rates of pay of other employees. There is a careful balance to be struck between protecting the comparator employee's confidentiality, and disclosing sufficient detail to ensure that there is no prejudice to any subsequent defence put forward by the employer (see 11.41ff).

11.23   Material difference

How, then, does an employer establish a material difference between the claimant and her comparator? In *Rainey v Greater Glasgow Health Board* [1987] AC 224 the House of Lords provided the following guidance on the matters that may be taken into account in determining whether the employer has made out a 'material difference' for the purpose of *s 1(3)*:

> 'The difference must be "material", which I would construe as meaning "significant and relevant", and it must be between "her case and his". Consideration of a person's case must necessarily involve consideration of all the circumstances of that case. These may well go beyond what is not very happily described as "the personal equation", ie the personal qualities by way of skill, experience or training which the individual brings to the job. Some circumstances may on examination prove to be not significant or not relevant, but others may do so, though not relating to the personal qualities of the employee. In particular, where there is no question of intentional sex discrimination whether direct or indirect (and there is none here) a difference which is connected with economic factors affecting the efficient carrying on of the employer's business or other activity may well be relevant.' (Lord Keith at p 235)

Lord Keith also approved the view expressed by Browne-Wilkinson J. in *Jenkins v Kingsgate (Clothing Productions) Ltd* [1981] 1 WLR 1485 that the defence afforded to employers under *s 1(3)* is equivalent in scope to the justification defence available under *Article 141*, as set out by the ECJ in *Bilka-Kaufhaus GmbH v Weber Von Hartz (Case 170/84)* [1986] ECR 1607.

11.24   Genuine material factor – multiple uses?

Employers may rely on the same factor both:

(i)   in seeking to demonstrate a difference between the woman's work and the man's work in denying that work is like work or work of equal value; and

(ii)   in support of a *s 1(3)* defence if that similarity is made out (*Davies v McCartneys* [1989] ICR 705).

In fact, even where the factor has been taken into account by the tribunal in its determination that the work is like work or work of equal value, that same factor may be relied on under *s 1(3)* (*Christie v John E Haith Ltd* [2003] IRLR 670). This gives rise to the possibility of a difference in, say, the level of skill not being sufficiently important to make two jobs of unequal value, yet being treated as sufficient to defeat the equal pay claims of a claimant in one job vis-à-vis a comparator in the other.

11.25 **Objective justification**

Is the employer required objectively to justify the material difference relied on? That issue has caused the UK courts some difficulty. The controversy stems from an alleged conflict between the approach of the domestic courts and that of the ECJ as regards whether the employer must objectively justify *any* GMF relied on, or only those tainted with sex discrimination.

The starting point for most tribunals has been the ECJ's decision in *Bilka-Kaufhaus* (see 11.23). That case considered a potential infringement of *Article 141* in the form of indirect discrimination stemming from the exclusion of part-time employees from certain occupational pension scheme benefits. The ECJ was asked to address whether *Article 141* extended to indirect discrimination, and if so, whether such discrimination was capable of objective justification. It was held that *Article 141* did extend to indirect discrimination (which is now expressly provided in the *Equal Treatment Directive (2006/54/EC)*) and that the employer could potentially justify indirect discrimination where the means chosen for achieving a legitimate objective:

(a)   correspond to a real need on the part of the undertaking;

(b)   are appropriate with a view to achieving the objective in question; and

(c)   are necessary to achieve that end. Note that, in establishing whether the means are 'necessary', the focus is on proportionality; there is no require-ment to demonstrate absolute necessity (see *Hardys & Hansons Plc v Lax* [2005] ICR 1565 at [32], per Pill LJ) (and see 1.40ff).

The application of a requirement objectively to justify indirect discrimination in this way is fairly uncontroversial. More controversial, however, is the potential application of the objective justification requirement to cases where indirect discrimination is not in issue.

In *Enderby v Frenchay Health Authority (Case C-127/92)* [1993] ECR I-5535, the ECJ held that, when a measure has an adverse impact on substantially more members of one sex, it must be objectively justified (para 14). It was argued in *Tyldesley v TML Plastics Ltd* [1996] ICR 356 that, following *Enderby*, any GMF relied on by the employer must be objectively justified, even if there was no suggestion that the application of that GMF defence gave rise to indirect discrimination. The EAT (Mummery P) disagreed, holding that it was not necessary objectively to justify the GMF unless it was 'tainted by gender', either on the basis that it was indirectly discriminatory, or because it adversely impacted on one sex as in *Enderby* (insofar as such adverse impact does not itself constitute indirect discrimination). In that case, the comparator's commitment to 'total quality management' was a GMF untainted by gender, and so it was not necessary for the employer to justify its reliance on that factor.

Tyldesley was approved by the House of Lords in *Strathclyde Regional Council v Wallace* [1998] 1 WLR 259 and *Glasgow City Council v Marshall* [2000] 1 WLR 333. In *Marshall* at p 339, Lord Nicholls set out the following guidance on the application of *s 1(3)*:

'The scheme of the Act is that a rebuttable presumption of sex discrimination arises once the gender-based comparison shows that a woman, doing like work or work rated as equivalent or work of equal value to that of a man, is being paid or treated less favourably than the man. The variation between her contract and the man's contract is presumed to be due to the difference of sex. The burden passes to the employer to show that the explanation for the variation is not tainted with sex. In order to discharge this burden the employer must satisfy the tribunal on several matters. First, that the proffered explanation, or reason, is genuine, and not a sham or pretence. Second, that the less favourable treatment is due to this reason. The factor relied upon must be the cause of the disparity. In this regard, and in this sense, the factor must be a "material" factor, that is, a significant and relevant factor. Third, that the reason is not "the difference of sex"' This phrase is apt to embrace any form of sex discrimination, whether direct or indirect. Fourth, that the factor relied upon is or, in a case within *section 1(2)(c)*, may be a "material" difference, that is, a significant and relevant difference, between the woman's case and the man's case.

'When *section 1* is thus analysed, it is apparent that an employer who satisfies the third of these requirements is under no obligation to prove a "good" reason for the pay disparity. In order to fulfil the third requirement he must prove the absence of sex discrimination, direct or indirect. If there is any evidence of sex discrimination, such as evidence that the difference in pay has a disparately adverse impact on women, the employer will be called upon to satisfy the tribunal that the difference in pay is objectively justifiable. But if the employer proves the absence of sex discrimination he is not obliged to justify the pay disparity.'

However, the ECJ's subsequent decision in *Brunnhofer v Bank der Österreichischen Postsparkasse AG* [2001] ECR I-4961 cast some doubt on the correctness of that approach. The court emphasised that, whatever the mechanism that produced unequal pay as between men and women, unequal pay was prohibited by *Article 141* unless justified by objective factors unrelated to discrimination linked to the difference in sex (para 30). Further, 'an employer may validly explain the difference in pay ... in so far as they constitute objectively justified reasons unrelated to any discrimination based on sex and in conformity with the principle of proportionality' (para 68). There was no suggestion that the requirement to have an objectively justified and proportionate reason is restricted to cases of indirect discrimination.

In reliance on *Brunnhofer*, the claimant in *Parliamentary Commissioner for Administration v Fernandez* [2004] ICR 123 submitted that *Marshall* was no longer good law and that, following *Brunnhofer*, *Article 141* requires an employer to justify the difference in pay between a woman and her comparator even where there is no prima facie discrimination. The EAT (HHJ Peter Clark) had little hesitation in rejecting that argument, stating that it did not understand the ECJ in *Brunnhofer* to be laying down a requirement to objectively justify the factor relied on where there is no suggestion of discrimination (para 33).

A differently constituted EAT (HHJ Ansell) in *Sharp v Caledonia Group Services Ltd* [2006] ICR 218 declined to follow *Fernandez*, suggesting instead that *Brunnhofer* provides clear guidelines as to the need for objective justification in *all* cases. However, the *Marshall* approach was reaffirmed by the Court of Appeal in *Armstrong v Newcastle Upon Tyne NHS Hospital Trust* [2006] IRLR 124. Buxton LJ noted that, once the House of Lords has determined the meaning of EC law, it is not open to lower domestic courts to resort to the decisions of the ECJ on which the House of Lords based its analysis in order to find a different or wider meaning. Therefore, the proper approach to cases of indirect discrimination 'not only starts but also finishes' with Lord Nicholls' speech in *Marshall* (para 101).

In *Villalba* (see 11.22), the EAT (Elias P) again followed *Wallace* and *Marshall* in holding that there is no obligation objectively to justify the difference in pay in the absence of any evidence that the difference in pay is anything to do with sex, observing that 'it is only in the language of Lewis Carroll that such a pay differential not tainted in any way by sex could be rendered unlawful *under provisions which outlaw sex discrimination*' (para 183). The EAT (Elias P) has since taken the same approach in *Redcar & Cleveland Borough Council v Bainbridge* [2007] IRLR 91 and *Middlesbrough Borough Council v Surtees* [2007] ICR 1644. It emphasised in both cases that it runs contrary to logic to require objective justification even where there is no hint of sex discrimination. The equal pay legislation is designed to remove sex-related discrimination in pay, not to achieve fair wages.

Meanwhile, however, the ECJ in *Cadman v Health and Safety Executive (Case C-17/05)* [2006] ICR 1623 has repeated the statement relied on by the claimants in *Fernandez* and *Sharp*, that the principle of equal pay for equal work or work of equal value enshrined in *Article 141* prohibits comparable situations from being treated differently unless the difference is objectively justified (para 28), apparently without limiting that requirement to cases where there is a prima facie case of indirect discrimination (although *Cadman* was itself a case involving indirect discrimination).

It remains to be determined whether the view taken in the recent domestic court decisions (*Sharp* excluded) is shared by the ECJ. Its decisions in *Enderby*, *Brunnhofer* and *Cadman* arguably suggest not. There is certainly scope for further domestic appeal court decisions, since *Surtees* is, at the time of writing, on appeal to the Court of Appeal, where it will be heard with the appeal in *Redcar & Cleveland Borough Council v Bainbridge*.

The case of *Chief Constable of West Midlands Police v Blackburn & Manley* EAT/0007/07 (11 December 2007, unreported) provides a stark example of a tribunal's failure properly to consider the issue of objective justification. In that case, police officers were paid a shift premium for working a shift pattern that involved some night shifts. The claimant (female) police officers had been excused that shift pattern because of their childcare responsibilities, and so did not receive the relevant shift premium. They claimed equal pay with men who worked that shift pattern. The tribunal concluded that, although the police force's objective of rewarding those working 24/7 was legitimate, the difference in pay could not be justified because the respondent police force could afford to pay the shift premium to those excused night shifts on grounds of their childcare responsibilities. As the EAT noted, nothing in *EqPA 1970* requires an employer to deem that women have done that which they have not done. To say that the employer can afford to eliminate the difference in pay (ie there is no need for the difference in pay in the first place) does not engage with the *s 1(3)* defence at all.

11.26 **Establishing indirect sex discrimination**

If it is necessary for there to be some 'taint' of discrimination before justification is required, how does the tribunal establish whether such a 'taint' exists? The EAT in *Tyldesley v TML Plastics Ltd* [1996] ICR 356 stated that a 'taint' of gender meant evidence or a suggestion that the factor relied on was indirectly discriminatory. (And see 1.40ff.)

Following the Court of Appeal's decision in *Nelson v Carillion Services Ltd* [2003] ICR 1256, the burden appears to lie with the claimant to demonstrate a prima facie case of indirect discrimination. This is consistent with the requirements of the *Burden of Proof Directive (97/80/EC)*, which applies to equal pay claims. Note, however, Waller LJ's suggestion in *Home Office v Bailey* [2005] ICR 1057 that the claimant should not bear such a burden of proof (paras 37–38).

In *Middlesbrough Borough Council v Surtees* [2007] ICR 1644, the EAT (Elias P) suggested that there were three general types of situation where there is prima facie evidence of sex tainting:

(i)   where the criterion the employer chooses to differentiate pay scales will adversely affect workers of one sex because of the position of that sex in society (for example where full-timers are paid more than part-timers);

(ii)   where workers of one sex claim that pay arrangements adversely affect them as a group, and the disadvantage (typically gleaned from statistics) is sufficiently striking that it should be inferred that the difference in pay reflects traditional attitudes about what is appropriate male and female work and pay; and

(iii) where the employer identifies some factor which it says causes the difference in pay, but that factor is applied only to a group predominantly made up of one sex.

However, although this shorthand approach to establishing prima facie sex discrimination has been followed by the EAT (Elias P) in *Cumbria County Council v Dow & Others* EAT/0148/06 (12 November 2007, unreported), it has yet to be followed by another judge at the EAT, or to be approved by the Court of Appeal.

11.27 *Provision, criterion or practice*

The traditional method of establishing indirect discrimination is to identify a seemingly gender-neutral provision, criterion or practice that puts persons of one sex at a disadvantage compared with persons of the other sex. That will constitute indirect discrimination unless objectively justified by a legitimate aim, and the means of achieving that aim are proportionate and necessary. See, for example, the *Equal Treatment Directive (2006/54/EC), Article 2(1)(b)*. The classic example of this type of indirect discrimination is the less favourable treatment of part-time workers (see, for example, *Voss v Land Berlin (Case C-300/06)* [2007] ECR 00 in which, for an equal number of hours worked, part-time teachers were paid less than full-time teachers). It is to be noted that, in circumstances where disparate impact can be discerned from the tribunal's knowledge of the prevailing social or industrial climate (for example where the relevant criterion adversely affects those with childcare responsibilities), it may not be necessary to refer to statistical evidence to demonstrate disparate impact (see *London Underground Ltd v Edwards (No 2)* [1999] ICR 494, at para 24 and *Chief Constable of West Midlands Police v Blackburn & Manley* EAT/0007/07 (11 December 2007, unreported) at para 26)).

The difficult question concerns how stark the disadvantage must be in order to demonstrate a prima facie case of indirect discrimination. In *R v Secretary of State for Employment, ex p Seymour-Smith and Perez (Case C-167/97)* [1999] 2 AC 554, the issue arose in the context of the then two-year qualifying period of service at 16 hours or more per week before an individual was entitled to claim unfair dismissal. The claimants argued that that qualifying period of service constituted prima facie indirect sex discrimination against women. When the two-year qualifying requirement was introduced in 1985, 77.4% of men met the requirement, compared with 68.9% of women. The Divisional Court held that the claimants had failed to demonstrate prima facie discrimination, because the proportion of women who could qualify was not 'considerably smaller' than the proportion of men who could qualify. The House of Lords referred to the ECJ the question of what degree of disparate effect is sufficient to amount to indirect discrimination unless objectively justified.

The ECJ suggested (para 60) that the national court should determine whether the statistics suggested that a 'considerably smaller' percentage of women than men could satisfy the impugned requirement. It suggested that the figures in that case did not suggest that a sufficient disparity existed in 1985 to establish prima facie indirect discrimination. However, it also suggested (para 61) that a small but persistent disparity may be sufficient to establish discrimination. Applying that latter test, the House of Lords held ([2000] 1 WLR 435) by a 3:2 majority that a prima facie case of indirect discrimination had been established, on the basis of a persistent difference between 1985 and 1991 (as opposed to a sufficient disparity in 1985).

Perhaps unsurprisingly, there is commonly dispute as to how statistical evidence should be interpreted. Much of the debate centres around whether the tribunal should focus on the proportion of men and women who *can* comply with the impugned requirement, or the proportion who *cannot* comply. In *Barry v Midland Bank* [1999] 1 WLR 1465, Lord Nicholls suggested that the correct approach was to compare the proportion of men who are not disadvantaged with the proportion who are, and to compare those proportions with the equivalent proportions of women who can and cannot comply. However, he also noted that such comparisons could be misleading, since they would be affected by the size of the comparator groups. It was suggested that expressing the proportions in the disadvantaged group as a ratio of each other (for example, nine disadvantaged women for every disadvantaged man) would provide a better guide.

In *Rutherford v Secretary of State for Trade and Industry* [2005] ICR 119, Mummery LJ suggested that reliance on the disadvantaged groups (ie those who could not comply) alone could produce 'seriously misleading' results. It was held that the tribunal had erred when focusing solely on the disadvantaged group, and should instead have considered the respective proportions of men and women who could comply with the relevant requirement (namely the prohibition then in force on individuals aged 65 or over bringing unfair dismissal claims).

On appeal ([2006] ICR 785), a majority of the House of Lords considered that a statistical analysis was unnecessary, since the age limit of 65 applied equally as between men and women. However, Lords Nicholls and Walker did apply a statistical approach, and unlike the Court of Appeal reviewed both the proportions of advantaged and disadvantaged of each sex. Both of their Lordships emphasised the resulting proportions (1.4% of men versus 1% of women disadvantaged) were insufficient to demonstrate an adverse impact on a substantially higher proportion of men than women.

In *Grundy v British Airways plc be* [2008] IRLR 74, the tribunal had again focused on the smaller, disadvantaged group in concluding that there was disparate adverse impact. The EAT overturned that decision (prior to the decision of the House of Lords in *Rutherford*), but it was later reinstated by the Court of Appeal, which noted Lord Nicholls' statement in *Marshall* that the tribunal's choice of pool was primarily a finding of fact. It concluded that there is no single suitable pool for every case. The key determinant is the nature of the issue that the claimant has elected to pose. The tribunal's task is simply to find a pool which suitably tests the discrimination complained of. Provided it does so, the tribunal cannot be said to have erred if a different pool, with a different outcome, could equally legitimately have been chosen.

Following *Rutherford*, it seems that the proportions of both advantaged and disadvantaged groups may be relevant. However, it appears from *Grundy* that the tribunal is relatively unburdened (or unassisted, depending on your point of view) by legal principle in choosing the comparator group on which it wishes to focus, irrespective of the fact that a different choice may result in a wholly different finding on the issue of disparate impact. Unfortunately, that approach necessarily results in significant uncertainty for claimants and respondents alike.

11.28 *Statistical differences – the Enderby approach*

Following the ECJ's decision in *Enderby* (see 11.25), an employer may be required to provide objective justification if the claimant is able to show 'significant statistics [which] disclose an appreciable difference in pay between two jobs of equal value, one of which is carried out almost exclusively by women and the other predominantly by men' (para 19). That approach does not require the identification of some provision, criterion or practice. It simply requires 'cogent, relevant and sufficiently compelling statistics' to demonstrate that one sex suffers a disparate impact, even if it is not possible to identify from where that disparate impact derives: *Villalba* (see 11.22; para 117).

Attempts have been made to limit the effect of *Enderby* to only those cases where the disadvantaged group are almost exclusively of one sex. However, the Court of Appeal in *Home Office v Bailey* [2005] EWCA Civ 327, [2005] ICR 1057 suggested that there was no difference between the statistical analysis in *Enderby* cases and those where some provision, criterion or practice is relied on, although that decision was doubted by the EAT in *Villalba* (para 123).

Some doubt remains as to whether the presumption of sex discrimination established in an *Enderby* scenario (ie without reference to a provision, criterion or practice) can ever be rebutted. The Court of Appeal in *Armstrong* (see 11.25) suggested that, even where there is adverse disparate impact, the employer can avoid liability without requiring objective justification by demonstrating that the difference is caused by a reason other than sex. However, it did not expressly consider *Enderby*. The EAT (Elias P) in *Villalba* questioned whether the decision of the Court of Appeal in *Armstrong* was correct in the light of *Enderby* (para 131). However, in *Middlesbrough Borough Council v Surtees* [2007] ICR 1644, the EAT (Elias P) accepted that it had gone too far in *Villalba* and that, even where the claimant has demonstrated disparate adverse impact by reference to sufficiently cogent statistics, it is still open to the employer to demonstrate that that disparate impact is in no way attributed to any sex-tainted act, and thereby avoid the need to provide objective justification (para 46). Of course, in practice, it may be very difficult for the employer to prove that negative, since, in contrast to the employee, it will need to explain from where the disparate impact derives.

11.29 *Direct discrimination and EqPA 1970, s 1(3)*

In *Ratcliffe v North Yorkshire County Council* [1995] ICR 833, Lord Slynn cast doubt as to whether the distinction between direct and indirect discrimination is relevant in the field of equal pay. However, in *Wallace* (see 11.25) the House of

Lords referred to the need to construe *EqPA 1970* so far as possible to work harmoniously with *SDA 1975* and *Article 141*, both of which address direct and indirect discrimination. It therefore held that an employer will not be able to demonstrate that a factor is 'not the difference of sex' under *s 1(3)* if the factor relied upon is sexually discriminatory whether directly or indirectly. Recent decisions, both domestic (e g *Fernandez, Armstrong* and *Surtees*; see 12.25) and European (e g *Cadman*; see 12.25), have accordingly adopted the distinction.

At first reading, it would appear that direct discrimination cannot be justified under *s 1(3)*, since it is impossible to succeed in a GMF defence where the difference in pay is due to the difference in sex. This proposition accords with the view of Mummery LJ in *Clark v TDG Ltd (t/a Novacold Ltd)* [1999] ICR 951 at 963 that direct discrimination cannot be justified 'in any of the discrimination statutes' (although note that those comments have been superseded following the introduction of the *Employment Equality (Age) Regulations 2006 (SI 2006/1031)*, under which direct discrimination may be objectively justified) (see AGE DIS-CRIMINATION (2)) and was accepted as a matter of logic by the EAT in *Parliamentary Commissioner for Administration v Fernandez* [2004] ICR 123.

However, in *Wallace*, Lord Browne-Wilkinson suggested that, although there was no case to date in which the employer had been able to justify direct discrimination on grounds of sex, such a position could not be ruled out. The EAT (Elias P) has also recently suggested that direct discrimination arguably could be justified in very exceptional cases (see *Villalba v Merrill Lynch & Co Inc* [2007] ICR 469; *Middlesbrough Borough Council v Surtees* [2007] ICR 1644, *Cumbria County Council v Dow & Others* EAT/0148/06 & others (12 November 2007, unreported), and *Chief Constable of West Midlands Police v Blackburn & Manley* EAT/0007/07 (11 December 2007, unreported)).

11.30 **Example GMFs**

Length of service

Employers may commonly have pay scales related to length of service, perhaps simply to reward loyalty, but perhaps also to reward better performance on the basis that there is often a correlation between length of service and ability to do the job well. That latter defence would seem to be flawed, since the two do not necessarily go hand in hand. However, in *Handels-OG Kontorfunktionaerernes Forbund I Danmark v Dansk Arbejdsgiverforening (acting for Danfoss) (Case 109/88)* [1989] ECR 3199, the ECJ was happy to base its decision on that assumption. It stated that the criterion of seniority did not require specific justification, since it generally placed the worker in a better position to carry out his duties and was therefore justified as a means of achieving that legitimate objective.

That decision was called into question by subsequent ECJ decisions in *Nimz v Freie und Hansestadt Hamburg (Case C-184/89)* [1991] ECR I-297, *Gerster Freistaat v Bayern (Case C-1/95)* [1997] ECR I-5253, and *Hill v Revenue Commissioners and Department of Finance (Case C-243/95)* [1998] ECR I-3739. In all three cases, the ECJ stated that the national courts should determine whether there was sufficient proof of a link between length of service and acquisition of a certain level of knowledge or ability objectively to justify the lesser pay received by part-timers.

In light of the apparent contradiction, the Court of Appeal referred the case of *Cadman v Health and Safety Executive (Case C-17/05)* [2006] ECR I-9583 to the ECJ. In that case, the claimant female employee was paid less than four male comparators of the same grade, each of whom had longer service with the HSE than she did. The employers relied on the claimant's length of service as their GMF defence under *s 1(3)*. The Court of Appeal asked the ECJ whether, where the use of length of service had a disparate impact as between men and women, *Article 141* required the employer to provide special justification for the use of that criterion as its defence to an equal pay claim.

The ECJ clarified its previous decisions by stating that, as a general rule, the criterion of length of service is appropriate to attain the legitimate objective of enabling the employee to perform his duties better. However, where the employee provides evidence capable of giving rise to 'serious doubts' as to whether there is a link between that objective and the criterion of length of service, it will be for the employer to prove that, in the case in question, better performance does go hand in hand with length of service.

11.31 *Market forces/financial considerations*

Market forces may constitute a potential GMF defence (*Rainey v Greater Glasgow Health Board* [1987] AC 224). However, this defence is certain to fail where, as in *Ratcliffe v North Yorkshire County Council* [1995] ICR 833, the wider market forces were themselves tainted by discrimination. In that case, the claimants were dinner ladies who claimed equal pay with road sweepers and gardeners. The council argued that it had had to reduce its labour costs because of its need to tender for work at a commercially competitive rate following the introduction of compulsory competitive tendering. However, the tribunal (subsequently upheld by the House of Lords) found that that was insufficient to establish a defence under *s 1(3)*. It held that the need to compete with competitors employing women on less favourable terms was a factor which was due to the difference of sex, because it arose out of the general perception that women should stay at home to look after the children and any work must fit in with that domestic responsibility. In effect, therefore, where the market is so tainted by sex discrimination, reliance on the market cannot justify the difference in pay. However, as the Court of Appeal pointed out in *Armstrong v Newcastle Upon Tyne NHS Hospital Trust* [2006] IRLR 124 (para 121) and, more recently, the EAT noted in *Cumbria County Council v Dow & Others* EAT/0148/06 & others) (12 November 2007, unreported) (para 160), Ratcliffe is an exceptional case that turns on the findings of the employment tribunal in that case. It is not authority for the proposition that the adjustment of wages in order to compete in a predominantly female labour market is necessarily discriminatory.

The ECJ has suggested in *Schönheit v Stadt Frankfurt Am Main (Case C-4/02)* [2003] ECR I-12575 that an employer's budgetary considerations cannot be used as justification for treatment that would otherwise constitute indirect discrimination (paras 84–85). However, the EAT (Burton P) clarified in *Cross v British Airways Plc* [2005] IRLR 423 that, although indirect discrimination cannot be justified *solely* on the basis of the employer's budgetary considerations, such considerations can constitute a justification if combined with other reasons. The exception to this principle, according to the EAT, is where the party attempting to rely on financial considerations is an emanation of the state, in which case the fact that it effectively has a 'bottomless purse' precludes it from relying on budgetary considerations as providing any element of its objective justification – although query whether this has been undermined by the EAT's subsequent comments in a different context in *O'Hanlon v Commissioners for HM Revenue and Customs* [2006] ICR 1579 (upheld [2007] IRLR 404).

In order to evidence the importance of the relevant market forces or other financial considerations, the employer may refer to the fact that pay arrangements were collectively agreed. In *Specialarbejderforbundet I Danmark v Dansk Industri, acting for Royal Copenhagen A/S Case C-400/93* [1995] ECR I-1275, the ECJ noted that, although the principle of equal pay applies where elements of pay are determined by collective bargaining, the national court may take that fact into account in assessing whether the difference in pay is objectively justified (para 46). In *Cumbria County Council v Dow & Others* EAT/0148/06 & others (12 November 2007, unreported), the EAT noted that the tribunal was wrong not to attach any significance to the fact that the relevant union was a party to an agreed deterioration in terms, particularly given that the tribunal had stated that there was no connivance by the trade unions in any deliberate discrimination (para 157).

11.32 *Performance*

A difference in the levels of performance of two comparable employees clearly constitutes a potential material factor. A good example would be a bonus based on an employee's performance during the preceding year of her employment (as in *Villalba v Merrill Lynch & Co Inc* [2007] ICR 469). However, a difference in performance levels that becomes clear during the employee's employment will not constitute a valid GMF defence for differences in pay which existed from the commencement of the employee's employment, or which otherwise pre-date the difference in performance levels (*Brunnhofer v Bank der Österreichischen Postspar-kasse AG* [2001] ECR I-4961 at 76).

11.33 *Red circling*

'Red circling' often occurs following restructuring or a redundancy exercise. If an employee loses his job but obtains another within the employer's business, the employer will sometimes guarantee that additional payments will be made (often for a fixed period of time) in order to cushion the blow of a reduction in salary. This can raise difficulties in the context of equal pay where a woman carrying out like work, work rated as equivalent or work of equal value is paid less than a man as a result of his being red circled.

Red circling is also sometimes used in the context of job evaluation schemes. The natural result of a JES is that the pay of some employees will go down, and the pay of others will go up. In such scenarios, this type of pay protection arrangement effectively prolongs at least some element of the unequal pay.

In appropriate circumstances, red circling will constitute a valid GMF defence (*Farthing v Ministry of Defence* [1980] ICR 705). However, it is advisable to phase out the red circle as soon as possible, not only as a matter of good industrial relations practice, but also because a pay protection scheme which is justified on the date of inception may have ceased to be justified when the employer seeks to rely on it some years later (see 11.35 below).

The employer may also be able to defend a decision to exclude from the ambit of a pay protection scheme those employees who would have been included had the equality clause been applied to them at the correct time. This was the position in *Middlesbrough Borough Council v Surtees* [2007] ICR 1644. The EAT (Elias P) held that the employer's decision required justification, since it was tainted by sex. However, it also accepted that requiring the employer to extend the scheme to the claimants when the consequent liability was unquantifiable would have undermined its ability to implement a scheme that was crucial to the JES. The employer was entitled to take the view that it should limit the benefit of the pay protection to those actually in the group. Unless the pay was actually being received, there was nothing to protect. Therefore, the decision not to extend the scheme to the claimants had been justified.

Such a decision will not always be justified, however. If the employer knew when the scheme was implemented that it was underpaying the claimants in breach of the equality clause – and that, had it given them equal pay immediately upon accepting that it had been acting unlawfully, they would have had the benefit of pay protection – then the *s 1(3)* defence must inevitably fail. This was the position in *Redcar & Cleveland Borough Council v Bainbridge* [2007] IRLR 91, as explained in *Surtees* at paras 97–98. At the time of writing, both *Surtees* and *Bainbridge* are on appeal to the Court of Appeal, where they are due to be heard together.

11.34 *Mistake*

A GMF defence may be founded upon a genuine yet mistaken belief that there is some material factor which is not the difference in sex. In *King's College London v Clark* [2003] All ER (D) 118 (Oct), the EAT (HHJ Peter Clark) held that an employer who had genuinely but mistakenly concluded that the employee was correctly graded could rely on *s 1(3)*. Even a careless mistake, which could not possibly be objectively justified, can found a GMF defence (*Tyldesley v TML Plastics Ltd* [1996] ICR 356, EAT at 362).

11.35 *Historic differences*

In order to maintain a successful GMF defence the factor relied on must constitute a material difference in relation to the entire period for which the employer relies on it. For example, if an employer pays a premium to hire a member of staff at a time when such staff are scarce, that may constitute a valid material factor for the purposes of *s 1(3)* (see *Enderby*). However, should that factor cease to be relevant, for example because it is some years and many pay reviews since that pay premium was applied, the employer may not be able to rely on it (*Benveniste v University of Southampton* [1989] ICR 617).

A good example is *Bailey v Home Office* [2005] IRLR 757. A pension benefit for prison officers was discontinued for those who joined from 1987 onwards, but red circled for those whose service commenced prior to 1987. The EAT held that although the red circling would have amounted to a genuine material factor defence when it was introduced, that did not justify a continuing disparity in treatment in 1999 when the equal pay claim was brought.

11.36 *'After the event' justification*

Conversely, both the ECJ (in *Schönheit*; see 11.31) and the Court of Appeal (in *Cadman*; see 11.25) have recently stated that the employer may rely on a material difference which did not enter its mind at the time at which the impugned pay decision was made, or which is different from the difference relied on at that time. Although 'after the event' rationalisation may appear unattractive, the question is whether a justification in fact exists, not whether the employer appreciated this all along. However, as the EAT made clear in *Cumbria County Council v Dow & Others* EAT/0148/06 & others) (12 November 2007, unreported), the tribunal is entitled to take into account the fact that the justification relied on at tribunal was not a justification relied on at the time the pay decision was made in determining whether a *s 1(3)* defence is made out (para 105).

11.37 **REMEDIES**

Enforcing the equality clause

The primary remedy for a successful claimant who remains employed by the respondent is the enforcement of the equality clause. The tribunal will modify the less favourable term in the claimant's contract so that it becomes no less favourable than the term of a similar kind in the contract of the male comparator with whom she has been found to have been performing equal work. In future, they will have to be paid at the same rate.

As noted above, enforcement is on a clause-by-clause basis. It is no answer for an employer found to have been paying a woman a lower salary than an appropriate male comparator to say that she had more days of holiday, or better sick pay provisions. The tribunal will still increase the woman's salary to the man's level. From a practical point of view, it is then likely to be necessary for the employer to 'level up' the comparator's sick pay and holiday entitlements as well, or face possible claims from him.

11.38 **Arrears of pay**

Enforcement of the equality clause provides a forward-looking remedy for the claimant, but what of the historical disparity? Since the employer has been in breach of the contractual 'equality clause' since the difference in pay began or since any previous justification for it ceased, the obvious remedy is one in debt for arrears of wages.

The original *EqPA 1970, s 2(5)* limited claims to arrears or damages in respect of the two years immediately preceding the commencement of proceedings. However, in *Levez v TH Jennings (Harlow Pools) Ltd (Case C-326/96)* [1998] ECR I-7835, the ECJ held that that limitation was incompatible with Community law.

EqPA 1970 was therefore amended to provide that the period in respect of which arrears of pay may be recovered is six years prior to commencement of proceedings in England and Wales (*ss 2(5), 2ZB(3)*) and five years in Scotland (*s 2ZC*). This reflects the limitation period for actions for breach of contract in the two jurisdictions, thereby satisfying the EC law requirement that domestic law procedural and remedial rules for breach of *Article 141* must be no less favourable than those governing similar domestic law claims (the principle of 'equivalence').

Different rules apply in 'concealment' and 'disability' cases (see 11.42). In such cases, arrears can be claimed for the whole period since the date of the contravention to which the proceedings relate (*EqPA 1970, ss 2(5), 2ZB(4)*).

Where the equal pay claim includes a claim for non-monetary contractual benefits, the tribunal will award a sum equal to the monetary value of those benefits for the relevant period.

11.39 **Injury to feelings**

The EAT recently pursued the contractual nature of remedies under *EqPA 1970* to its logical conclusion in holding that an equal pay claimant cannot be awarded compensation for non-economic loss, such as for injury to feelings or aggravated or exemplary damages (*Newcastle upon Tyne City Council v Allan* [2005] ICR 1170). The EAT contrasted *EqPA 1970* with other domestic discrimination statutes, under which compensation claims are for a statutory tort and which specifically provide that damages may include compensation for injury to feelings.

However, it could be argued that since unequal pay is a species of sex discrimination, such compensation should in principle be available. Moreover, *EqPA 1970* itself, by its new reference (in *ss 2ZA, 2ZB, 7AA* and *7AB*) to cases where the employer has 'concealed' an inequality, acknowledges circumstances where an award of aggravated or exemplary damages would seem to be appropriate. In any event, an equal pay claim will often be combined with a sex discrimination claim, for which an injury to feelings award can be made.

11.40 Declaration

An employee may seek a declaration that they have been paid unequally, although in most cases this will be deemed unnecessary because of the automatic operation of the equality clause. An exception to this is where the claimant is a 'test case' for a class of employees, in which case a declaration may be considered desirable in order that it may be relied upon by other claimants.

11.41 PRACTICALITIES

Grievances and questionnaires

There is now a statutory procedure for an individual with cause for concern regarding equal pay to ask questions of her employer or former employer (*EqPA 1970 s 7B; Equal Pay (Questions and Replies) Order 2003 (SI 2003/722)*).

A claimant who submits an equal pay questionnaire before proceedings have commenced should ask for details of the pay and benefits of her proposed comparators. Unless the claimant already has verifiable information from some other source – unlikely, unless her employer has an unusually transparent pay system – she will need it both to form a view on whether a particular comparator is appropriate at all (anyone who has earned the same as, or less than, her throughout the relevant period will not be), and to assess, having regard to the extent of the disparity, how valuable the claim may be. This may determine whether she pursues the claim at all.

Receipt of such a request leaves the employer to perform a balancing act between, on the one hand, the desire to avoid adverse inferences being made against it through the absence of a response, or the provision of an evasive or equivocal response, and, on the other hand, the need to avoid breaching obligations it owes to the comparators under the *Data Protection Act 1998 ('DPA 1998')* and the law on trust and confidence. However, once litigation is underway, it is likely that the employer will have to disclose the pay details anyway – *DPA 1998, s 35* exempts disclosures of personal data that are required by law or made in connection with legal proceedings.

The employer may take the view that some comparators are so clearly not employed on like work/equal value work/work rated as equivalent, or that its GMF defence is so solid, that it is willing to accept the risk of not providing any pay details – the risk being that a tribunal will subsequently take a different view, and draw adverse inferences. This risk can be minimised to some extent by the employer stating clearly in the questionnaire response its explanation for not providing the information.

For comparators where the claimant has a more arguable case, the employer could simply state that the comparator is earning the same as, less or more than the claimant. The difficulty, however, with only stating that the comparator is earning 'more than' the claimant is that not only does this (arguably) fall into the 'evasive' category, but strategically it is unhelpful for all concerned. It gives the claimant no indication as to the value of pursuing a particular comparator, which in turn makes it more likely for both parties that litigation will be pursued at least for some period of time before a resolution can be reached.

An employer could consider, therefore, approaching each comparator and requesting their written consent to the disclosure of their remuneration details at the questionnaire stage. If the claimant is still employed, this should be accompanied by a clear statement that the claimant should not be victimised by any comparator as a result. The request will lead either to the details being provided, or to the employer being able to explain (supported by an appropriate paper trail) their non-provision for a reason that is unlikely to lead to adverse inferences being drawn.

The Government has indicated that the statutory dispute resolution procedures set out in *EA 2002, Sch 2* will be revoked. However, at the time of writing, those procedures require that a claimant must set out his or her grievance in writing before presenting a complaint to an employment tribunal under *EqPA 1970*. Claimants would be advised to take note of the decision of the EAT in *The Highland Council v TGWU/Unison, GMB & Others* EATS/0020/07 (18 December 2007, unreported) in this regard. In that case, the claimant had attempted to rely on comparators not referred to in her grievance. Noting that it is for the claimant to find her comparator and state her case, the tribunal found that, in order to constitute a valid grievance for the purposes of a claim under *EqPA 1970*, the grievance must specify the comparator relied on, at the very least by reference to a job or job type (para 31).

11.42 Time limits

An individual who is still employed can bring an equal pay claim against her employer at any time. The position once employment has terminated is less straightforward.

The original *EqPA 1970, s 2(4)* provided: 'No claim in respect of the operation of an equal pay clause relating to a woman's employment shall be referred to an [employment tribunal] if she has not been employed in the employment within the six months preceding the date of the reference'. In *Preston v Wolverhampton Healthcare NHS Trust* [1998] 1 WLR 280, the House of Lords held that, as far as domestic law was concerned, the time limit ran from the end of each contract under which an employee was employed – not from the end of any employment consisting of a succession of different contracts of employment with the same employer. However, the ECJ (*(Case C-78/98)* [2001] 2 AC 415) held that it was incompatible with EC law for a woman to have to make a claim in respect of each contract in these circumstances.

When the case returned to the House of Lords ([2001] 2 AC 455), Lord Slynn stated that 'it is clear that where there are intermittent contracts of service without a stable employment relationship, the period of six months runs from the end of each contract of service, but where such contracts are concluded at regular intervals in respect of the same employment regularly in a stable employment relationship, the period runs from the end of the last contract forming part of that relationship' (para 33). The effect was that the time limit would run from the end of the last contract forming part of that stable employment relationship, and not from the end of the stable employment relationship itself insofar as that might identify a different point in time (*Jeffery v Secretary of State for Education* [2006] ICR 1062).

However, *EqPA 1970* has since been amended to produce the latter result. The new *EqPA 1970, s 2(4)* provides that no determination may be made by a tribunal of an equal pay claim 'unless the proceedings are instituted on or before the qualifying date'. The 'qualifying date' in a standard case is the date falling six months after the last day on which the woman was employed in the employment. However, in a 'stable employment case' (defined as 'a case where the proceedings relate to a period during which a stable employment relationship subsists between the woman and the employer, notwithstanding that the period includes any time after the ending of a contract of employment when no further contract of employment is in force') it is the date falling six months after the day on which the stable employment relationship ended.

Unlike in other anti-discrimination legislation, there is no power for the tribunal to permit an equal pay claim to proceed out of time on the basis that it would be 'just and equitable' to allow this. However, *s 2ZA* extends the time limit in 'concealment' and 'disability' cases by specifying a different 'qualifying date' for such cases.

A 'concealment case' is a case where the employer deliberately concealed from the claimant any fact which is relevant to the contravention to which the proceedings relate, and without knowledge of which the claimant could not reasonably have been expected to institute the proceedings, and the claimant did not discover the fact (or could not with reasonable diligence have discovered it) until after either the last day on which she was employed in the employment or the day on which the stable employment relationship ended. The qualifying date is the date falling six months after the day on which the woman discovered the qualifying fact in question (or could with reasonable diligence have discovered it).

A 'disability case' is a case where the claimant was under a disability at any time during the six months after the last day on which she was employed in the employment, or the day on which the stable employment relationship ended, or (if it is later) the day on which she discovered (or could with reasonable diligence have discovered) a relevant concealed fact. The qualifying date is the date falling six months after the day on which the woman ceased to be under a disability or (if the case is also a concealment case) the later of that date and the 'concealment case' qualifying date.

The House of Lords held in *Powerhouse Retail Ltd v Burroughs* [2006] ICR 606 that an employee who transfers to a new employer under the *Transfer of Undertakings (Protection of Employment) Regulations 2006 (SI 2006/246)* must bring any equal pay claim against the transferor (eg a claim relating to occupational pensions) within six months of the date of the transfer. This is because *s 2(4)* requires a claim to be brought within six months of the end of the employment to which the claim relates, and that employment ends upon the transfer. The House rejected the employees' argument that time runs from the date on which her employment with the transferee ends. See further *Unison v Allen* [2007] IRLR 975).

The Government is currently considering whether to bring the time limit for equal pay claims, and the grounds on which that limit may be extended, into line with other anti-discrimination legislation. See 'Better Dispute Resolution: A review of employment dispute resolution in Great Britain' (Department of Trade and Industry, March 2007), Chapter 4, recommendation 13.

11.43 **Pleadings**

Key elements of an ET1 will include the following:

Choice of comparators

There is no limit on the number of comparators a claimant may name. It is desirable that she should identify all the comparators she wishes to pursue in her ET1. While the EAT held in *Bainbridge v Redcar and Cleveland Borough Council* [2007] IRLR 494 that a claimant is not estopped from bringing an equal pay claim in relation to one comparator when she has already failed in respect of the same period of time in relation to another comparator – on the basis that each claim is a separate and distinct cause of action for breach of contract – it did caution that such an approach may amount to an abuse of process, exposing the claimant to costs penalties.

Basis of comparison

For each comparator, the claimant should specify whether she considers that she is employed on like work, work rated as equivalent or work of equal value. It is common for claimants to plead like work or, in the alternative, work of equal value. A plea of equal value work will add significantly to the cost, length and complexity of proceedings. A claimant with a strong like-work claim will therefore need to consider carefully whether the benefits of adding an equal value claim are outweighed by these disadvantages.

Period compared

Particularly where more than one comparator is identified, the claimant should identify the time periods she is seeking to compare, for example 'Mr X for the period January 2003 to December 2005, then Mr Y who replaced Mr X for the period January 2006 to the present day'. Overlapping comparisons are permitted, although a claimant who makes such comparisons should be wary of the danger of losing focus.

Remedy

If it is intended that the claimant should stand as a 'test case' for a group of employees (which may even have been agreed with the employer), the ET1 should specify that a declaration is sought.

The employer should include the following in its ET3:

Are comparators employed on equal work?

The employer must consider whether to dispute the claimant's allegation that she is employed on like work/work rated as equivalent/work of equal value. While the employer's natural instinct may be to dispute it, concessions may be advantageous strategically if the employer has a strong genuine material factor defence. It can then focus on this defence and avoid becoming embroiled in a protracted and costly dispute about (in particular) whether two jobs are of equal value.

The GMF defence

Even if it does dispute that the claimant is employed on equal work with her comparators, the employer will normally argue in the alternative that there are one or more genuine material factors which are not the difference of sex which justify the difference in pay. Different GMFs may apply as between different comparators, and indeed for the same comparator in different time periods. An employer should nevertheless select its GMFs with care: any GMFs that are inconsistent with an earlier questionnaire response, or which are unsupported by contemporaneous evidence, could undermine an otherwise strong case. If there is, or may be, any suggestion that the GMF is tainted by discrimination, the employer should provide an explanation as to why this is objectively justified.

11.44 *Jurisdictional issues*

Depending on the circumstances, the employer may be able to raise jurisdictional points in its ET3, for example that the claimant has failed to submit a grievance and wait 28 days, that she is out of time, or that there has been a TUPE transfer and liability has not transferred, such that she is suing the wrong respondent.

Case management

In principle, the case management directions and orders that a tribunal may make regarding matters such as disclosure, witness statements, agreed statements of facts and chronologies are no different in an equal pay case than in any other discrimination proceedings. Where there is a plea of equal value, however, the tribunal must also grapple with the Employment Tribunals (Equal Value) Rules of Procedure (*'Equal Value Rules'*) found in the *Employment Tribunals (Constitution and Rules of Procedure) Regulations 2004 (SI 2004/1861)*, Sch 6.

The tribunal will often wish to consider the employer's GMF defence first, at a preliminary hearing. If the GMF succeeds, the claim fails; if the GMF fails, the claim proceeds to a full hearing on whether the claimant is employed on equal work, although the employer may come under pressure in the meantime to negotiate a settlement. The parties will have the opportunity to make submissions on whether the GMF should be dealt with first, which will be shaped by their respective views of its merits.

An issue which often arises at the interlocutory stage in equal pay cases is the extent of disclosure that an employer must provide about its pay processes. In *Villalba v Merrill Lynch & Co Inc* UKEAT/0461/04 (1 July 2004, unreported), the EAT upheld a tribunal decision to refuse an application by Ms Villalba for the disclosure of pay data for over 120 employees. The application was made on the basis that the employer's pay system was not transparent, that it was shown statistically that the average pay of a group of women was lower than the average pay of a group of men, and that this meant the employer was obliged to objectively justify that differential. The EAT found that the tribunal was entitled to bear in mind that there had been a lengthy equal pay questionnaire responded to at length by the respondent, that the disclosure which had been sought in relation to the claimant's pleadings had been given, and that the disclosure now sought was very wide ranging. The tribunal did, however, criticise the employer for refusing to provide pay data about the comparators until a very late stage in the proceedings.

11.45 Equal value claims and experts

As noted at 11.44, the *Equal Value Rules* apply to any proceedings 'involving' an equal value claim. This includes claims where like work or work rated as equivalent is pleaded in the alternative, as well as claims that involve entirely separate causes of action from equal pay.

The *Rules* require the tribunal to conduct a 'stage 1 equal value hearing' (*Rule 4*). At the hearing, and assuming the tribunal does not strike the claim out because the claimant and her comparators have been graded differently in an analytical and non-discriminatory JES (*Rule 4(3)(a)*), the tribunal must decide either to determine the equal value question itself, or to require a member of the panel of independent experts to prepare a report on the matter.

Details of the duties and powers of the independent expert are set out in *Rule 10*, and rules on the use of expert evidence generally in *Rule 11*. *Rule 11(1)* states that expert evidence is 'to be restricted to that which, in the opinion of the tribunal, is reasonably required to resolve the proceedings'. If the claim involves a comparison of jobs requiring easily comprehensible, and readily comparable, skills and responsibilities, the tribunal may decide to determine the equal value question on the basis of its own industrial relations experience. Conversely, if the jobs are highly specialised, or the comparators numerous, expert evidence is likely to be required.

Tribunals at stage 1 hearings (which are unlikely to have any great familiarity with the issues at this stage) generally give considerable weight to parties' submissions on the appropriate course to adopt. Each party should therefore decide in advance which approach they would prefer. This should include consideration of whether they wish to ask for permission to instruct their own experts (permission is required: *Rule 11(3)*). The tribunal is more likely to give permission if both parties are legally represented and each proposes to instruct an expert, and if the tribunal has decided to determine the equal value question itself without the assistance of an independent expert.

For a party, the advantage of its 'own' expert is that, while experts owe an overriding duty to the tribunal (*Rule 11(2)*), the party will nevertheless be able to make an informed choice of an expert with (say) knowledge of the relevant industry and/or the requirements of jobs within that industry. The degree of chance involved in relying on a member of the independent panel, or on the tribunal itself, is accordingly reduced. The disadvantages include cost – the parties must each pay for their own expert, whereas the costs of a member of the panel of independent experts are paid out of central funds – and the fact that the field of equal value experts is a relatively limited one, making selection decisions difficult.

Rule 5 sets out 'standard orders' that the tribunal must make at the stage 1 hearing unless it considers it inappropriate to do so. These essentially require each side to clarify its case. If the tribunal decides to appoint an independent expert, it must fix a date for a 'stage 2 equal value hearing'. *Rule 6(2)* allows the tribunal to order the independent expert to assist it in establishing the facts on which the expert may rely in preparing his report. The circumstances in which it may do so are specified in *Rule 6(3)*. The extent to which the tribunal makes use of these interventionist powers will normally depend on how successful the parties have been in complying with orders made under *Rule 5*.

At any stage 2 equal value hearing, the tribunal must make a determination of facts on which the parties cannot agree which relate to the equal value question, and require the independent expert to prepare his report on the basis of facts agreed between the parties or determined by the tribunal (*Rule 7(3)*). These facts then become the only facts relating to the equal value question on which the tribunal may rely at the full hearing (*Rule 7(5)*), unless the expert applies to the tribunal for some or all of the facts relating to the question to be amended, supplemented or omitted (*Rule 7(6)*). The tribunal must, unless it considers it inappropriate to do so, order the expert to prepare his report on the equal value question by a specified date and send copies to the parties and the tribunal (*Rule 8(1)(a)*). It must also fix a date for the full hearing (*Rule 7(4)(c)*).

Once an expert – independent or otherwise – has prepared a report, any party or other expert involved in the proceedings may write to her and ask her questions about the report (*Rule 12(1)*). This provides an opportunity for 'damage limitation' for whichever party's case has been adversely impacted by the expert report(s), although both parties are likely to have some points that they wish to clarify. The expert's answers are treated as part of their report.

The final stage is, of course, the full hearing. The *Equal Value Rules* include an 'indicative timetable' under which it is envisaged that claims not involving an independent expert will proceed to a full hearing within 25 weeks of a claim being filed, and claims involving an independent expert within 37 weeks. It is the authors' experience, however, that these timelines are more often honoured in the breach than the observance, given the complexity of the typical equal value claim.

11.46 Equal pay reviews and audits

Despite the best endeavours of the EOC, it remains comparatively rare for employers, at least in the private sector, to have undertaken an equal pay review/audit. The five step equal pay review model recommended by the EOC consists of the following:

Step 1: Deciding the scope of the review and identifying the data required. The EOC recommends that all employees in the same establishment or service should be included.

Step 2: Determining where men and women are doing equal work. This is, in essence, a process of job evaluation.

Step 3: Collecting pay data to identify equal pay gaps. This involves matching the job evaluation undertaken at step 2 to the pay data collected.

Step 4: Establishing the causes of any significant pay gaps and assessing the reasons for these. This involves the employer assessing the robustness of any prospective GMF defence.

Step 5: Developing an equal pay action plan and/or reviewing and monitoring. This involves taking steps – for example, awarding pay increases and paying back pay – to put right any issues that have been identified, and to keep the organisation's pay policies under review in the future.

At each stage the obstacles facing the employer can be daunting, particularly for large, decentralised organisations. In a company with thousands of employees based in numerous different locations, simply assembling accurate, up-to-date pay data broken down by gender can be a significant logistical challenge. As roles within the modern economy become ever more specialised, the process of evaluating and comparing jobs can be complex and open to challenge. Once the final stage is reached, the employer is not only likely to face a substantial bill to 'level up' those employees whom it is found are being underpaid (as 'levelling down' is rarely a palatable option), but also runs the risk of alerting those same employees to the fact that they may have a strong equal pay claim for arrears of pay for a period of up to six years.

Unless equal pay reviews are made compulsory, or a moratorium is imposed on equal pay claims for earlier periods where an employer has undertaken a review, or (as is increasingly becoming the case) having undertaken a review is made a requirement of undertaking work for public bodies, it seems likely that most employers will continue to abstain from the exercise.

Index

[*all references are to paragraph number*]

A

Ability to carry out normal day-to-day activities
day-to-day activities, 3.25
generally, 3.23
normal, 3.24

ACAS
disability discrimination, and, 3.124
sex discrimination, and, 8.19

Adoption-related discrimination
detriment, 8.123
disrupted placement, 8.124
leave, 8.121
overseas adoption, 8.125
pay, 8.122
unfair dismissal, 8.123

Advocates
age discrimination, and, 2.14
disability discrimination, and, 3.113
generally, 1.20
sex discrimination, and, 8.38

'After the event' justification
equal pay, and, 12.36

Age conditions
pay and benefits, and, 2.34

Age discrimination
advocates, 2.14
age conditions, 2.34
age group, 2.7
Age Regulations 2006
generally, 2.1
interpretation, 2.4
agency workers, 2.14
applicants, 2.13
assisting persons to obtain
employment, 2.14
barristers, 2.14
burden of proof
generally, 2.54
overview, 1.83–1.94
benefits based on length of service
business needs, 2.23
generally, 2.22
careers guidance, 2.14
Code of Practice, 2.3
common concepts
And see under individual headings

Age discrimination – *contd*
common concepts – *contd*
burden of proof, 1.83–1.94
comparators, 1.33–1.39
direct discrimination, 1.27–1.32
exceptions, 1.66–1.82
genuine occupational requirements
or qualifications, 1.95–1.100
harassment, 1.45–1.54
indirect discrimination, 1.40–1.44
introduction, 1.1
legislation, 1.2–1.6
particular parties, 1.7–1.26
positive action, 1.101–1.108
questionnaires, 1.126
sanctions, remedies and
enforcement, 1.115–1.125
vicarious liability, 1.109–1.114
victimisation, 1.55–1.65
comparators
generally, 2.6
overview, 1.33–1.39
compliance with statutory authority,
2.17
context, 2.5
contract workers, 2.14
direct discrimination
comparators, 2.6
introduction, 2.6
justification, 2.6
less favourable treatment, 2.6
'on grounds of B's age', 2.6
overview, 1.27–1.32
educational institutions, 2.14
'employees', 2.13
employment, during
age conditions, 2.34
insured benefits, 2.36
length of service, 2.35
pay and benefits, 2.33
employment agencies, 2.14
end of employment,, after, 2.52
enforcement
burden of proof, 2.54
jurisdiction of tribunals, 2.52
overview, 1.115–1.125
questionnaires, 2.55

Index

Age discrimination – *contd*
enforcement – *contd*
  remedies, 2.56
  time limits, 2.57
enhanced redundancy benefits
  generally, 2.49
  introduction, 2.24
exceptions and defences
  employment, in, 2.15–2.26
  generally, 1.79
  overview, 1.66–1.82
exceptions and defences
  benefits based on length of
    service, 2.22–2.23
  enhanced redundancy benefits,
    2.24
  genuine occupational
    requirements, 2.16
  introduction, 2.15
  life assurance cover to retired
    workers, 2.25
  national minimum wage, 2.21
  national security, 2.18
  pensions, 2.26
  positive action, 2.19
  retirement, 2.20
  statutory authority, 2.17
experience, and, 2.35
former employees, 2.13
Framework Directive, 2.2
genuine occupational requirements
  generally, 2.16
  overview, 1.95–1.100
harassment
  generally, 2.11
  overview, 1.45–1.54
indirect discrimination
  age group, 2.7
  generally, 2.7
  overview, 1.40–1.44
  provision criterion or practice, 2.7
instructions to discriminate, 2.10
insured benefits, 2.36
introduction, 1.1
job advertisements, 2.28
job application forms, 2.307
job interviews, 2.31
job specifications, 2.28
job titles, 2.29
jurisdiction of tribunals, 2.52
justification
  direct discrimination, and, 2.6
  generally, 2.8
  legitimate aims, 2.8

Age discrimination – *contd*
justification – *contd*
  proportionality, 2.8
legislative background
  Age Regulations, 2.1
  Framework Directive, 2.2
  interpretation of Regulations, 2.4
  overview, 1.2–1.6
  pre-200 Code of Practice, 2.3
legitimate aims, 2.8
length of service, 2.35
less favourable treatment, 2.6
life assurance cover to retired
  workers, 2.25
loyalty, and, 2.35
meaning, 2.5
national minimum wage, 2.21
national security, 2.18
notice periods, 2.50
objective justification
  direct discrimination, and, 2.6
  generally, 2.8
  legitimate aims, 2.8
  proportionality, 2.8
office-holders, 2.14
'on grounds of B's age', 2.6
particular parties, 1.7–1.26
partnership, 2.14
pay and benefits
  age conditions, 2.34
  generally, 2.33
  insured benefits, 2.36
  length of service, 2.35
  pension schemes, 2.36
pension schemes, 2.14, 2.26, 2.36
police, 2.14
positive action
  generally, 2.19
  overview, 1.105
proportionality, 2.8
'provision criterion or practice', 2.7
qualifications bodies, 2.14
questionnaires
  generally, 2.55
  overview, 1.126
recruitment, in
  advertisements, 2.28
  application forms, 2.30
  interviews, 2.31
  introduction, 2.27
  job specifications, 2.28
  job titles, 2.29
  methods, 2.32

Age discrimination – *contd*
redundancy
  criteria, 2.49
  enhanced schemes, 2.49
  statutory pay, 2.49
remedies, 2.56
retirement
  appeals, 2.44
  default retirement age, 2.39
  definitions, 2.44
  disciplinary and grievance
    procedures, and, 2.44
  duty of employer to consider request
    not to retire, 2.44
  duty of employer to notify of
    intended retirement, 2.44
  failure to comply with duties, 2.44
  introduction, 2.38
  justification, 2.40
  legal challenge to default age, 2.41
  meaning, 2.42
  meeting to discuss request not to
    retire, 2.44
  other circumstances, in, 2.40
  overview, 2.20
  procedure, 2.43–2.44
  right of employee to request not to
    retire, 2.44
  right o be accompanied, 2.44
sanctions, remedies and enforcement
  burden of proof, 2.54
  jurisdiction of tribunals, 2.52
  overview, 1.115–1.125
  questionnaires, 2.55
  remedies, 2.56
  time limits, 2.57
scope of employment concept, 2.13
SOCA, 2.14
statutory authority, 2.17
statutory disciplinary and grievance
  procedures, and, 2.44
termination of employment, on
  notice periods, 2.50
  redundancy, 2.49
  retirement, 2.38–2.44
  unfair dismissal, 2.45–2.49
time limits for claims, 2.57
trade organisations, 2.14
unfair dismissal
  fairness, 2.48
  introduction, 2.45
  normal retirement age, 2.46
  reason for dismissal, 2.47
validity of discriminatory terms, 2.52

Age discrimination – *contd*
vicarious liability, 1.109–1.114
victimisation
  generally, 2.9
  overview, 1.55–1.65
vocational training providers
  generally, 2.9
  overview, 1.14
Age group
age discrimination, and, 2.7
Agency workers
age discrimination, and, 2.14
generally, 1.22
Aggravated damages
compensation, and, 1.121
Aiding unlawful acts
disability discrimination, and, 3.93
race discrimination, and, 6.44
Ante-natal care
appropriate hourly rate, 8.83
complaint to tribunal, 8.84
eligibility, 8.81
expectant father's rights, 8.85
generally, 8.79–8.85
relevant care, 8.80
unreasonable refusal of time off, 8.82
Applicants
age discrimination, and, 2.13
equal pay, and
  'at an establishment in GB', 12.8
  employed persons, 12.7
Application forms
age discrimination, and, 2.30
disability discrimination, and, 3.98
Aptitude tests
disability discrimination, and, 3.98
Armed forces
disability discrimination, and, 3.110
exceptions and defences, and, 1.73
generally, 1.18
race discrimination, and, 6.64
sex discrimination, and, 8.34
Arrears of pay
equal pay, and, 12.38
Assisting persons to obtain employment
age discrimination, and, 2.14
Association or perception
direct discrimination, and, 1.31
Asymptomatic progressive conditions
disability discrimination, and, 3.31

B

Barristers
age discrimination, and, 2.14
disability discrimination, and, 3.113
generally, 1.20
sex discrimination, and, 8.38
Benefits
See also Pay and benefits
based on length of service
business needs, 2.23
generally, 2.22
disability discrimination, and, 3.105
Benefits, facilities and services
sex discrimination, and, 8.42
Benefits to the public
exceptions and defences, and, 1.68
race discrimination, and, 6.55
Burden of proof
age discrimination, and, 2.54
common law, 1.84
county courts, in, 1.90
disability discrimination, and
disability, 3.17
EC law
Directive, 1.85
equal treatment, 1.86
Framework Directive, 1.88
race discrimination, 1.87
employment tribunals, in, 1.89
equal pay, and
genuine material factors, 12.22
interpretation of statutory provisions
direct discrimination, 1.92
duty to make reasonable
adjustments, 1.93
general principles, 1.91
indirect discrimination, 1.93
victimisation, 1.94
introduction, 1.83
sex discrimination, and, 8.29
victimisation, and, 1.64
'But for' test
less favourable treatment, and, 1.30
'By reason that'
race discrimination, and, 6.21
victimisation, and, 1.59

C

Careers guidance
age discrimination, and, 2.14
Case management
equal pay, and, 12.44

Charities
disability discrimination, and, 3.114
exceptions and defences, and, 1.74
sex discrimination, and, 8.62
Civil partnerships
civil partners, 5.3
comparative jurisprudence, 5.9
direct discrimination, 5.4
exceptions and defences, 5.8
harassment, 5.7
indirect discrimination, 5.5
introduction, 5.1
less favourable treatment, 5.4
sex discrimination, and, 8.28
stereotyping, 5.6
Codes of practice
age discrimination, and, 2.3
disability discrimination, and, 3.6
equal pay, and, 12.5
generally, 1.4
sex discrimination, and
ACAS, 8.19
Departmental guidance, 8.19
generally, 8.25
EHRC, 8.18
Commission for Equality and Human Rights
disability discrimination, and, 3.5
sanctions, and, 1.125
Commission for Racial Equality (CRE)
sanctions, and, 1.125
Comparators
age discrimination, and, 2.6
comparable terms and conditions, 12.19
disability discrimination, and
disability-related discrimination, and, 3.60
generally, 3.50
'on the ground of', 3.50
practical examples, 3.51
reasonable adjustments, and, 3.77
equal pay, and
comparable terms and conditions, 12.19
hypothetical comparators, 12.10
institutional nexus, 12.17
introduction, 12.9
'like work', 12.13
overview, 1.33–1.39
pleadings, and, 12.43
pregnancy, 12.18
process of comparison, 12.20
proportionate pay, 12.16

Comparators – *contd*
equal pay, and – *contd*
temporal nexus, 12.11
work nexus, 12.12–12.16
'work of equal value', 12.15
'work rated as equivalent', 12.14
evidential, 1.38
fixed-term employees, and, 10.8
gender reassignment, and, 4.5
hypothetical comparators
equal pay, 12.10
generally, 1.38
illegitimate hypotheses, 1.39
indirect discrimination, and, 1.44
introduction, 1.33
own membership of protected class not
relied on, 1.37
part-time employees, and, 10.25–
10.26
pregnancy-related discrimination,
and, 8.71
race discrimination, and
generally, 6.10
harassment, and, 6.30
'relevant circumstances'
discriminatory circumstances, 1.36
generally, 1.35
sexual orientation discrimination,
and, 9.7
statutory requirement, 1.34
victimisation, and, 1.59
Compensation
aggravated damages, 1.121
exemplary damages, 1.121
indirect discrimination, 1.118
injury to feelings, 1.119
interest, 1.122
pecuniary loss, 1.117
personal injury, 1.120
Complaints to tribunal
disability discrimination, and
generally, 3.116
injury to feelings, 3.121
questionnaire process, 3.122
remedies, 3.120
restricted reporting orders, 3.119
statutory grievance procedure,
3.117
time limits for claims, 3.118
fixed-term employees, and, 10.15
flexible working, and, 8.146
part-time employees, and
generally, 10.35
remedies, 10.36–10.37

Complaints to tribunal – *contd*
time-off for dependants, and, 8.135
Compliance with statutory provision
age discrimination, and, 2.17
generally, 1.69
race discrimination, and 6.56
Compound claims
disability discrimination, and, 3.87
Conscious motivation
victimisation, and, 1.60
'Contract of service or apprenticeship'
employees, and, 1.7–1.9
Contract workers
age discrimination, and, 2.14
disability discrimination, and, 3.112
generally, 1.10
race discrimination, and 6.60
sex discrimination, and, 8.36
Contracting out
disability discrimination, and, 3.125
County courts
burden of proof, and, 1.90
Crown employment
armed forces, 1.18
disability discrimination, and, 3.113
generally, 1.16
police, 1.17
race discrimination, and 6.63
sex discrimination, and, 8.32

D
Declaration of rights
generally, 1.123
Declarations
equal pay, and, 12.40
Defences and exceptions
age discrimination, and
benefits based on length of
service, 2.22–2.23
enhanced redundancy benefits,
2.24
genuine occupational
requirements, 2.16
introduction, 2.15
life assurance cover to retired
workers, 2.25
national minimum wage, 2.21
national security, 2.18
overview, 1.79
pensions, 2.26
positive action, 2.19
retirement, 2.20
statutory authority, 2.17

Index

Defences and exceptions – *contd*
armed forces, 1.73
benefits to the public, 1.68
charities, 1.74
compliance with statutory provision,
1.69
disability discrimination, and
generally, 1.66–1.82
introduction, 3.109
national security, 3.111
overview, 1.77
particular individuals, 3.110
statutory authority, 3.111
equal pay, and
genuine material factors, 12.21–12.
overview, 1.66–1.82
excluded persons, 1.80
genuine occupational reason, 1.70
illegal contracts/conduct, 1.82
introduction, 1.66
national security, 1.67
positive action, 1.71
race discrimination, and
benefits provided to the public,
6.55
compliance with the law, 6.56
employment outside GB, 6.53
generally, 1.78
genuine occupational requirements
or qualifications, 6.47
illegal contracts, 6.54
introduction, 6.46
national security, 6.57
overview, 1.76
private households, 6.49
seamen recruited abroad, 6.50
Sikhs and safety helmets, 6.52
skills to be exercised outside GB,
6.48
sports and competitions, 6.51
state immunity, 6.58
religion and belief discrimination,
1.78
sex discrimination, and
communal accommodation, 8.54
benefits, facilities or services, 8.50
genuine occupational
qualifications, 8.55
insurance, 8.53
introduction, 8.49
maternity leave, 8.51
occupational pensions, 8.52
overview, 1.75
sport, 8.54

Defences and exceptions – *contd*
specific exceptions, 1.75–1.79
sport, 1.72
state immunity, 1.81
statutory exceptions, 1.67–1.74
Detriment
adoption-related discrimination, and,
8.123
employees, and, 1.9
flexible working, and, 8.149
parental leave-related discrimination,
and, 8.132
part-time employees, and, 10.34
paternity-related discrimination, and,
8.129
pregnancy-related discrimination,
and, 8.78
sex discrimination, and, 8.43
Direct discrimination
age discrimination, and
comparators, 2.6
introduction, 2.6
justification, 2.6
less favourable treatment, 2.6
'on grounds of B's age', 2.6
association or perception, 1.31
burden of proof, and, 1.92
'but for' test, 1.30
civil partnership, and, 5.4
definition, 1.27
disability discrimination, and
comparators, 3.50–3.51
disability-related discrimination,
and, 3.61
Framework Directive, under, 3.42
generalised assumptions, 3.52
generally, 3.45
justification, and, 3.46
knowledge of disability, 3.53
non-disabled persons, and, 3.47
'on the ground of', 3.50
problem areas, 3.56
reasonable adjustments, and, 3.55
relevance of other discrimination
legislation, 3.48
uniqueness, 3.49
wheelchair users, 3.54
equal pay, and, 12.29
gender reassignment, and, 4.5
introduction, 1.27
less favourable treatment
'but for' test, 1.30
comparison with other forms of
treatment, 1.29

Direct discrimination – *contd*
less favourable treatment – *contd*
generally, 1.28
motivation or intent, 1.30
reason, 1.30
marital status, and, 5.4
poor treatment, 1.29
race discrimination, and
generally, 6.7
harassment, and, 6.28–6.31
less favourable treatment, 6.8–6.13
sex discrimination, and
generally, 8.21
overview, 1.27–1.32
sexual orientation discrimination, and
comparators, 9.7
generally, 9.5
meaning, 9.6
'on the grounds of', 9.8
stereotypical assumptions, 1.32
unreasonable treatment, 1.29

Disability discrimination
ability to carry out normal day-to-day
activities
day-to-day activities, 3.25
generally, 3.23
normal, 3.24
ACAS, 3.124
advocates, 3.113
aiding unlawful acts, 3.93
application forms, 3.98
aptitude tests, 3.98
armed forces, 3.110
asymptomatic progressive
conditions, 3.31
barristers, 3.113
benefits, 3.105
burden of proof
disability, 3.17
overview, 1.83–1.94
charities, 3.114
code of practice, 3.6
collection of evidence, 3.39
Commission for Equality and Human
Rights, 3.5
common concepts
And see under individual headings
burden of proof, 1.83–1.94
comparators, 1.33–1.39
direct discrimination, 1.27–1.32
exceptions, 1.66–1.82
genuine occupational requirements
or qualifications, 1.95–1.100
harassment, 1.45–1.54

Disability discrimination – *contd*
common concepts – *contd*
indirect discrimination, 1.40–1.44
introduction, 1.1
legislation, 1.2–1.6
particular parties, 1.7–1.26
positive action, 1.101–1.108
questionnaires, 1.126
sanctions, remedies and
enforcement, 1.115–1.125
vicarious liability, 1.109–1.114
victimisation, 1.55–1.65
comparators
disability-related discrimination,
and, 3.60
generally, 3.50
'on the ground of', 3.50
overview, 1.33–1.39
practical examples, 3.51
reasonable adjustments, and, 3.77
complaints to tribunal
generally, 3.116
injury to feelings, 3.121
questionnaire process, 3.122
remedies, 3.120
restricted reporting orders, 3.119
statutory grievance procedure,
3.117
time limits for claims, 3.118
compound claims, 3.87
contract workers, 3.112
contracting out, 3.125
coping strategies, 3.28
Crown employment, 3.113
day-to-day activities, 3.23
deemed disability, 3.32
direct discrimination
comparators, 3.50–3.51
disability-related discrimination,
and, 3.61
Framework Directive, under, 3.42
generalised assumptions, 3.52
generally, 3.45
justification, and, 3.46
knowledge of disability, 3.53
non-disabled persons, and, 3.47
'on the ground of', 3.50
overview, 1.27–1.32
problem areas, 3.56
reasonable adjustments, and, 3.55
relevance of other discrimination
legislation, 3.48
uniqueness, 3.49
wheelchair users, 3.54

Index

Disability discrimination – *contd*
"disability"
  ability to carry out normal
    day-to-day activities, 3.23–3.25
  asymptomatic progressive
    conditions, 3.31
  burden of proof, 3.17
  collection of evidence, 3.39
  coping strategies, 3.28
  day-to-day activities, 3.23
  deemed disability, 3.32
  expert evidence, 3.37–3.39
  Framework Directive, under, 3.13
  'impairment', 3.17–3.32
  introduction, 3.11
  long term, 3.33–3.36
  material time, 3.36
  medical evidence, 3.37
  medical model, 3.14
  medical treatment, 3.27
  mental impairment, 3.22
  non-medical evidence, 3.38
  normal day-to-day activities, 3.23–3.25
  other legislation, under, 3.16
  past disabilities, 3.34
  physical impairment, 3.21
  practical issues, 3.37–3.39
  present and past disabilities, 3.12
  progressive conditions, 3.30–3.31
  psychologists' evidence, 3.38
  recurring effects, 3.35
  severe disfigurements, 3.29
  social model, 3.15
  substantial adverse effect, 3.26–3.32
disability-related discrimination
  comparators, 3.60
  direct discrimination, and, 3.61
  employer's state of mind, 3.64
  Framework Directive, and, 3.58
  indirect discrimination, and, 3.59
  introduction, 3.57
  knowledge of disability, 3.64
  less favourable treatment, 3.63
  meaning, 3.62
  reason 'which relates to', 3.62
Disability Rights Commission, 3.4
discriminatory advertisements, 3.89
enforcement
  ACAS, 3.124
  complaints to tribunal, 3.116–3.122
  Equality and Human Rights
    Commission, 3.123

Disability discrimination – *contd*
enforcement – *contd*
  injury to feelings, 3.121
  questionnaire process, 3.122
  remedies, 3.120
  restricted reporting orders, 3.119
  statutory grievance procedure, 3.117
  time limits for claims, 3.118
Equality and Human Rights
  Commission, 3.123
exceptions and defences, and
  generally, 1.66–1.82
  introduction, 3.109
  national security, 3.111
  overview, 1.77
  particular individuals, 3.110
  statutory authority, 3.111
expert evidence
  collection, 3.39
  medical evidence, 3.37
  non-medical evidence, 3.38
facilities provided to the public, 3.115
false statements, 3.94
former employees, 3.108
Framework Directive, under
  direct discrimination, 3.42
  "disability", 3.13
  disability-related discrimination,
    and, 3.58
  less favourable treatment, 3.42
  meaning of discrimination, 3.42
general prohibition, 3.9
genuine occupational requirements or
  qualifications, 1.95–1.100
harassment
  generally, 3.86
  overview, 1.48
health requirements, 3.98
impairment
  ability to carry out normal
    day-to-day activities, 3.23–3.25
  asymptomatic progressive
    conditions, 3.31
  burden of proof, 3.17
  coping strategies, 3.28
  day-to-day activities, 3.23
  deemed disability, 3.32
  medical treatment, 3.27
  mental impairment, 3.22
  normal day-to-day activities, 3.23–3.25
  physical impairment, 3.21
  progressive conditions, 3.30–3.31

Disability discrimination – *contd*
impairment – *contd*
severe disfigurements, 3.29
substantial adverse effect, 3.26–
3.32
indirect discrimination
disability-related discrimination,
and, 3.59
generally, 3.42
overview, 1.40–1.44
induction training, 3.103
injury to feelings, 3.121
introduction, 3.1–3.6
job advertisements, 3.98
job descriptions, 3.98
job interviews, 3.98
job specifications, 3.98
justification, and
direct discrimination, and, 3.46
generally, 3.65
'material and substantial' test, 3.66
practice, in, 3.68
reasonable adjustments, and, 3.67,
3.84
legislative background
code of practice, 3.6
comparison with other
discrimination legislation, 3.7
development, 3.2
overview, 1.2–1.6
post-1 December 1996 position, 3.3
pre-2 December 1996 position, 3.1
less favourable treatment
disability-related discrimination,
and, 3.63
Framework Directive, under, 3.42
generally, 3.44
pre-1 October 2004 position, 3.41
long term, 3.33–3.36
management of disability, 3.106
material time, 3.36
meaning
aiding unlawful acts, 3.93
compound claims, 3.87
direct discrimination, 3.45–3.56
disability-related discrimination,
3.57–3.68
discriminatory advertisements, 3.89
false statements, 3.94
Framework Directive, under, 3.42
harassment, 3.86
instructions to discriminate, 3.90
introduction, 3.40
less favourable treatment, 3.44

Disability discrimination – *contd*
meaning – *contd*
misleading statements, 3.94
post-30 September 2004 position,
3.43
pre-1 October 2004 position, 3.41
pressure to discriminate, 3.90
reasonable adjustments, 3.69–3.85
vicarious liability, 3.91–3.92
victimisation, 3.88
medical evidence, 3.37
medical model, 3.14
medical treatment, 3.27
mental impairment, 3.22
misleading statements, 3.94
national security, 3.111
non-medical evidence, 3.38
normal day-to-day activities, 3.23–
3.25
office-holders, 3.113
particular parties, 1.7–1.26
partnerships, 3.113
past disabilities, 3.34
pay and benefits, 3.105
pension schemes, 3.113
physical impairment, 3.21
police, 3.113
positive action, 1.106
practical issues
applicants for employment, 3.97–
3.100
avoiding discrimination, 3.96
general, 3.95
pre-2 December 1996 position, 3.1
present and past disabilities, 3.12
pressure to discriminate, 3.90
progressive conditions, 3.30–3.31
prohibited acts, 3.7
promotion, 3.104
protected categories of person, 3.8
'provision, criterion or practice', 3.74
psychologists' evidence, 3.38
qualifications, 3.98
qualifications bodies, 3.113
questionnaires, 1.126
reasonable adjustments
anticipatory duty, and, 3.72
comparators, 3.77
'core' requirements of job, 3.80
direct discrimination, and, 3.55
examples, 3.78
factors to be taken into account,
3.83
failure to assess or consult, 3.81

Index

Disability discrimination – *contd*
  reasonable adjustments – *contd*
    features of premises occupied by
      employer, 3.75
    generally, 3.69
    justification, and, 3.67, 3.84
    knowledge by employer, 3.73
    persons to whom duty owed, 3.71
    polices and procedures, to, 3.79
    pre-1 October 2004 position, 3.41
    preliminary considerations, 3.70
    problem areas, 3.85
    'provision, criterion or practice',
      3.74
    reasonableness, 3.82
    substantial disadvantage, 3.76
  recurring effects, 3.35
  refusal to offer employment, 3.100
  restricted reporting orders, 3.119
  sanctions, remedies and enforcement
    ACAS, 3.124
    complaints to tribunal, 3.116–3.122
    Equality and Human Rights
      Commission, 3.123
    injury to feelings, 3.121
    overview, 1.115–1.125
    questionnaire process, 3.122
    remedies, 3.120
    restricted reporting orders, 3.119
    statutory grievance procedure,
      3.117
    time limits for claims, 3.118
  severe disfigurements, 3.29
  social model, 3.15
  statutory authority, 3.111
  statutory grievance procedure, 3.117
  substantial adverse effect
    asymptomatic progressive
      conditions, 3.31
    coping strategies, 3.28
    deemed disability, 3.32
    medical treatment, 3.27
    progressive conditions, 3.30–3.31
    severe disfigurements, 3.29
  termination of employment, 3.107
  terms and conditions of employment
    generally, 3.102
    offers, 3.99
  time limits for claims, 3.118
  trade organisations, 3.113
  training and development, 3.103
  vicarious liability
    generally, 3.91–3.92
    overview, 1.109–1.114

Disability discrimination – *contd*
  victimisation
    generally, 3.88
    overview, 1.55–1.65
  vocational training providers, and,
    1.14
  wheelchair users, 3.54
  work experience, 3.113
Disability-related discrimination
  comparators, 3.60
  direct discrimination, and, 3.61
  employer's state of mind, 3.64
  Framework Directive, and, 3.58
  indirect discrimination, and, 3.59
  introduction, 3.57
  knowledge of disability, 3.64
  less favourable treatment, 3.63
  meaning, 3.62
  reason 'which relates to', 3.62
Disability Rights Commission (DRC)
  generally,
  sanctions, and, 1.125
Discriminatory advertisements
  disability discrimination, and, 3.89
  race discrimination, and, 6.38
Discriminatory practices
  race discrimination, and, 6.37
Dismissal
  sex discrimination, and, 8.43
Disparate impact
  indirect discrimination, and, 1.44
Dispute resolution procedures
  harassment, and, 1.53
  burden of proof, and, 1.92
Dress codes
  gender reassignment, and, 4.11
Duty to make reasonable adjustments
  burden of proof, and, 1.93

E
EC law
  burden of proof, and
    Directive, 1.85
    equal treatment, 1.86
    Framework Directive, 1.88
    race discrimination, 1.87
  equal pay, and 12.4
  harassment, and
    Commission Code, 1.46
    Directive, 1.45
  fixed-term employees, and, 10.2

EC law – *contd*
sex discrimination, and
Charter of Fundamental Rights,
8.14
ECJ judgments, 8.15
Equal Treatment Directive, 8.12
introduction, 8.10
other Directives, 8.13
Recommendations, 8.16
Treaty of Rome, 8.11
victimisation, and, 1.57
Educational appointments
sex discrimination, and, 8.57
Educational institutions
age discrimination, and, 2.14
Elections
sex discrimination, and, 8.65
Employees
generally, 1.7–1.9
Employer's liability
And see Vicarious liability
fixed-term employees, and, 10.18
part-time employees, and, 10.38
race discrimination, and
agents' acts, 6.42
employees' acts, 6.41
third party acts, 6.43
Employment agencies
age discrimination, and, 2.14
generally, 1.22
sex discrimination, and, 8.48
Employment outside GB
race discrimination, and, 6.53
Employment tribunals
burden of proof, and, 1.89
Enforcement
age discrimination, and
burden of proof, 2.54
jurisdiction of tribunals, 2.52
questionnaires, 2.55
remedies, 2.56
time limits, 2.57
compensation
aggravated damages, 1.121
exemplary damages, 1.121
indirect discrimination, 1.118
injury to feelings, 1.119
interest, 1.122
pecuniary loss, 1.117
personal injury, 1.120
declaration of rights, 1.123
disability discrimination, and
ACAS, 3.124
complaints to tribunal, 3.116–3.122

Enforcement – *contd*
disability discrimination, and – *contd*
Equality and Human Rights
Commission, 3.123
injury to feelings, 3.121
questionnaire process, 3.122
remedies, 3.120
restricted reporting orders, 3.119
statutory grievance procedure,
3.117
time limits for claims, 3.118
equal pay, and
arrears of pay, 12.38
declaration of unequal pay, 12.40
generally, 12.37
injury to feelings, 12.39
Equality and Human Rights
Commission, 1.125
gender reassignment, and, 4.8
procedure, 1.116
recommendation for action, 1.124
sexual orientation discrimination,
and, 9.20
summary, 1.115
Enhanced redundancy benefits
generally, 2.49
introduction, 2.24
Equal Opportunities Commission (EOC)
sanctions, and, 1.125
Equal pay
'after the event' justification, 12.36
applicants
'at an establishment in GB', 12.8
employed persons, 12.7
arrears of pay, 12.38
burden of proof
genuine material factors, 12.22
overview, 1.83–1.94
case management, 12.44
code of practice, 12.5
common concepts
And see under individual headings
burden of proof, 1.83–1.94
comparators, 1.33–1.39
direct discrimination, 1.27–1.32
exceptions, 1.66–1.82
genuine occupational requirements
or qualifications, 1.95–1.100
harassment, 1.45–1.54
indirect discrimination, 1.40–1.44
introduction, 1.1
legislation, 1.2–1.6
particular parties, 1.7–1.26
positive action, 1.101–1.108

Index

Equal pay – *contd*
  common concepts – *contd*
    questionnaires,   1.126
    sanctions, remedies and
        enforcement,   1.115–1.125
    vicarious liability,   1.109–1.114
    victimisation,   1.55–1.65
  comparators
    comparable terms and conditions,
        12.19
    hypothetical comparators,   12.10
    institutional nexus,   12.17
    introduction,   12.9
    'like work',   12.13
    overview,   1.33–1.39
    pleadings, and,   12.43
    pregnancy,   12.18
    process of comparison,   12.20
    proportionate pay,   12.16
    temporal nexus,   12.11
    work nexus,   12.12–12.16
    'work of equal value',   12.15
    'work rated as equivalent',   12.14
  declaration of unequal pay,   12.40
  direct discrimination
    generally,   12.29
    overview,   1.27–1.32
  EC law,   12.4
  enforcement
    arrears of pay,   12.38
    declaration of unequal pay,   12.40
    generally,   12.37
    injury to feelings,   12.39
  exceptions and defences
    genuine material factors,   12.21–12.
    overview,   1.66–1.82
  expert evidence,   12.45
  financial considerations,   12.31
  gender reassignment, and,   4.5
  genuine material factors
    'after the event' justification,   12.36
    burden of proof,   12.22
    establishing 'taint' of
        discrimination,   12.26–12.29
    financial considerations,   12.31
    historic differences,   12.35
    introduction,   12.21
    length of service,   12.30
    market forces,   12.31
    material difference,   12.23–12.24
    mistake,   12.34
    objective justification,   12.25
    performance,   12.32
    pleadings, and,   12.43

Equal pay – *contd*
  genuine material factors – *contd*
    red circling,   12.33
  genuine occupational requirements or
        qualifications,   1.95–1.100
  harassment,   1.45–1.54
  historic differences,   12.35
  hypothetical comparators,   12.10
  indirect discrimination
    generally,   12.26
    overview,   1.40–1.44
    'provision, criterion or practice',
        12.27
    statistical differences,   12.28
  injury to feelings,   12.39
  institutional nexus,   12.17
  introduction,   12.1
  justification for inequality
    'after the event' justification,   12.36
    burden of proof,   12.22
    establishing 'taint' of
        discrimination,   12.26–12.29
    financial considerations,   12.31
    historic differences,   12.35
    introduction,   12.21
    length of service,   12.30
    market forces,   12.31
    material difference,   12.23–12.24
    mistake,   12.34
    objective justification,   12.25
    performance,   12.32
    red circiling,   12.33
  key issues,   12.6
  legislative framework
    code of practice,   12.5
    EC Treaty,   12.4
    Equal Pay Act,   12.3
    introduction,   12.2
    overview,   1.2–1.6
  length of service,   12.30
  'like work',   12.13
  market forces,   12.31
  material difference,   12.23–12.24
  mistake,   12.34
  objective justification,   12.25
  particular parties,   1.7–1.26
  performance,   12.32
  pleadings,   12.43
  positive action,   1.101–1.108
  pregnancy,   12.18
  procedure
    case management,   12.44
    expert evidence,   12.45
    pleadings,   12.43

Equal pay – *contd*
proportionate pay, 12.16
questionnaires
generally, 12.41
overview, 1.126
red circling, 12.33
reviews and audits, 12.46
sanctions, remedies and enforcement
arrears of pay, 12.38
declaration of unequal pay, 12.40
generally, 12.37
injury to feelings, 12.39
overview, 1.115–1.125
sex discrimination, and, 8.8
statutory grievance and dispute
procedure, 12.41
temporal nexus, 12.11
time limits for claims, 12.42
vicarious liability, 1.109–1.114
victimisation, 1.55–1.65
work nexus, 12.12–12.16
'work of equal value', 12.15
'work rated as equivalent', 12.14
**Equality and Human Rights Commission
(EHRC)**
disability discrimination, and, 3.5
race discrimination, and, 6.68
sanctions, and, 1.125
sex discrimination, and
code of practice, 8.18
generally, 8.17
European law
harassment, and
Commission Code, 1.46
Directive, 1.45
victimisation, and, 1.57
Evidential comparators
generally, 1.38
Exceptions and defences
age discrimination, and
benefits based on length of
service, 2.22–2.23
enhanced redundancy benefits,
2.24
genuine occupational
requirements, 2.16
introduction, 2.15
life assurance cover to retired
workers, 2.25
national minimum wage, 2.21
national security, 2.18
overview, 1.79
pensions, 2.26
positive action, 2.19

Exceptions and defences – *contd*
age discrimination, and – *contd*
retirement, 2.20
statutory authority, 2.17
armed forces, 1.73
benefits to the public, 1.68
charities, 1.74
civil partnership, and, 5.8
compliance with statutory provision,
1.69
disability discrimination, and
generally, 1.66–1.82
introduction, 3.109
national security, 3.111
overview, 1.77
particular individuals, 3.110
statutory authority, 3.111
equal pay, and
genuine material factors, 12.21–
12.36
overview, 1.66–1.82
excluded persons, 1.80
genuine occupational reason, 1.70
illegal contracts/conduct, 1.82
introduction, 1.66
marital status, and, 5.8
national security, 1.67
positive action, 1.71
race discrimination, and
benefits provided to the public,
6.55
compliance with the law, 6.56
employment outside GB, 6.53
generally, 1.78
genuine occupational requirements
or qualifications, 6.47
illegal contracts, 6.54
introduction, 6.46
national security, 6.57
overview, 1.76
private households, 6.49
seamen recruited abroad, 6.50
Sikhs and safety helmets, 6.52
skills to be exercised outside GB,
6.48
sports and competitions, 6.51
state immunity, 6.58
religion and belief discrimination,
1.78
sex discrimination, and
communal accommodation, 8.54
benefits, facilities or services, 8.50
generally, 1.66–1.82

Index

Exceptions and defences – *contd*
  sex discrimination, and – *contd*
    genuine occupational
        qualifications, 8.55
    insurance, 8.53
    introduction, 8.49
    maternity leave, 8.51
    occupational pensions, 8.52
    overview, 1.75
    sport, 8.54
  sexual orientation discrimination, and
    genuine occupational
        requirements, 9.15
    marital status, 9.18
    national security, 9.16
    overview, 1.66–1.82
    positive action, 9.17
  specific exceptions, 1.75–1.79
  sport, 1.72
  state immunity, 1.81
  statutory exceptions, 1.67–1.74
Excluded persons
  exceptions and defences, and, 1.80
Exemplary damages
  compensation, and, 1.121
Experience
  age discrimination, and, 2.35
Expert evidence
  disability discrimination, and
    collection, 3.39
    medical evidence, 3.37
    non-medical evidence, 3.38
  equal pay, and 12.45

F
Facilities provided to the public
  disability discrimination, and, 3.115
  sex discrimination, and, 8.42
False statements
  disability discrimination, and, 3.94
Family-friendly provisions
  sex discrimination, and, 8.9
Financial considerations
  equal pay, and, 12.31
Fixed-term employees
  comparators, 10.8
  complaints to tribunals, 10.15
  EC Directive, 10.2
  employees covered, 10.7
  employers' liability, 10.18
  fixed-term contracts, 10.6
  introduction, 10.1
  justification, 10.11

Fixed-term employees – *contd*
  less favourable treatment
    generally, 10.9
    justification, 10.11
    'on the ground that', 10.10
  minimum notice, 10.17
  pre-existing protection, 10.3
  redundancy, 10.19
  Regulations
    generally, 10.1
    impact, 10.5
    implementation, 10.4
  unfair dismissal, 10.14
  vacancies, and, 10.13
  written statements, 10.12
Flexible working
  applicants, 8.141
  complaints to tribunal, 8.146–8.149
  consideration of request, 8.144
  detriment, 8.149
  employer's response to request, 8.143
  generally, 8.140
  indirect discrimination, 8.147
  remedies where request refused, 8.145
  request, 8.142
  unfair dismissal, 8.149
Former employees
  age discrimination, and, 2.13
  disability discrimination, and, 3.108
  generally, 1.25
  sex discrimination, and, 8.44
Framework Directive
  age discrimination, and, 2.2
  disability discrimination, and
    direct discrimination, 3.42
    "disability", 3.13
    disability-related discrimination,
        and, 3.58
    less favourable treatment, 3.42
    meaning of discrimination, 3.42

G
Gender reassignment
  application of provisions, 4.5
  case law background, 4.2–4.3
  common concepts
    And see under individual headings
    burden of proof, 1.83–1.94
    comparators, 1.33–1.39
    direct discrimination, 1.27–1.32
    exceptions, 1.66–1.82
    genuine occupational requirements
        or qualifications, 1.95–1.100

436

Gender reassignment – *contd*
common concepts – *contd*
harassment, 1.45–1.54
indirect discrimination, 1.40–1.44
introduction, 1.1
legislation, 1.2–1.6
particular parties, 1.7–1.26
positive action, 1.101–1.108
questionnaires, 1.126
sanctions, remedies and
enforcement, 1.115–1.125
vicarious liability, 1.109–1.114
victimisation, 1.55–1.65
common law, 4.2–4.3
comparators, 4.5
direct discrimination, 4.5
dress codes, 4.11
enforcement, 4.8
equal pay, 4.5
genuine occupational qualifications,
4.7
guidance for employers
checklist, 4.12
general guidance, 4.10
introduction, 4.9
specific guidance, 4.11
harassment, 4.5
introduction, 4.1
key concepts, 4.4
legislative background
Chessington decision, 4.3
introduction, 4.1
P v S decision, 4.2
Regulations, 4.4
less favourable treatment, 4.5
media interest, 4.11
policies, 4.10
problem areas, 4.6
promotion, 4.10
records and personnel file, 4.11
recruitment, 4.10
relocation, 4.11
remedies, 4.8
selection, 4.10
sex discrimination, and, 8.27
single sex facilities, 4.11
time off for medical treatment, 4.11
training, 4.10
Genuine occupational qualifications
age discrimination, and, 2.16
application, 1.96
differences from requirements, 1.97
exceptions and defences, and, 1.70
introduction, 1.95

Genuine occupational qualifications –
contd
job-specific qualifications, 1.100
race discrimination, and
generally, 6.47
overview, 1.95–1.100
Genuine material factors
'after the event' justification, 12.36
burden of proof, 12.22
establishing 'taint' of discrimination,
12.26–12.29
financial considerations, 12.31
historic differences, 12.35
introduction, 12.21
length of service, 12.30
market forces, 12.31
material difference, 12.23–12.24
mistake, 12.34
objective justification, 12.25
performance, 12.32
pleadings, and, 12.43
red circling, 12.33
Genuine occupational requirements
application, 1.96
differences from qualifications, 1.97
exceptions and defences, and, 1.70
gender reassignment, and, 4.7
general requirements, 1.98
introduction, 1.95
race discrimination, and
generally, 6.47
overview, 1.95–1.99
religion and belief discrimination, and
generally, 7.10
overview, 1.95–1.100
sexual orientation discrimination, and
generally, 9.15
overview, 1.95–1.100
specific requirements, 1.99
Good faith
victimisation, and, 1.63
Goods and services
sexual orientation discrimination,
and, 9.21

H
Harassment
age discrimination, and, 2.11
civil partnership, and, 5.7
common elements, 1.49
common law, 1.47
current UK law, 1.48
definitions, 1.50

Index

Harassment – *contd*
  disability discrimination, and, 3.86
  dispute resolution procedures, 1.53
  EC law
    Commission Code, 1.46
    Directive, 1.45
  gender reassignment, and, 4.5
  marital status, and, 5.7
  old UK law, 1.47
  other relevant legislation, 1.53
  purpose, 1.52
  race discrimination, and
    comparators, 6.30
    Crime and Disorder Act 1998,
      and, 6.36
    detriment, 6.31
    dignity, 6.27
    direct discrimination, as, 6.28–6.31
    generally, 6.22
    'having the purpose of effect of',
      6.26
    less favourable treatment, 6.29
    'on grounds of', 6.24
    other remedies, and, 6.33–6.36
    Protection from Harassment
      Act 1997, under, 6.34
    Public Order Act 1986, under, 6.35
    Race Relations Act 1976, s 3A,
      under, 6.23–6.28
    stand-alone claim, as, 6.32
    unwanted conduct, 6.25
    working environments, 6.27
  religion and belief discrimination,
    and, 7.8
  sex discrimination, and, 8.27
    generally, 8.24
    overview, 1.48
  sexual orientation discrimination,
    and, 9.13
  sources of further information, 1.54
  statutory definitions, 1.50
  statutory dispute resolution
    procedures, 1.53
  statutory harassment, 1.45
  unwanted conduct, 1.51
  vicarious liability, and, 1.113

Health and safety
  duty to act to avoid risks, 8.91
  exemptions to risk assessment, 8.94
  expectant mother risk assessment,
    8.88
  failure to carry out risk assessment,
    8.95
  general risk assessment, 8.87

Health and safety – *contd*
  individual risk assessment, 8.90
  introduction, 8.86
  notification of pregnancy, 8.89
  suitable alternative work, 8.92
  suspension from work, 8.93
Health requirements
  disability discrimination, and, 3.98
Historic differences
  equal pay, and, 12.35
'Honest and reasonable' exception
  victimisation, and, 1.61
Human Rights Act 1998
  generally, 1.3
Hypothetical comparators
  equal pay, and, 12.10
  generally, 1.38

I
Illegal contracts/conduct
  exceptions and defences, and, 1.82
  race discrimination, and, 6.54
Illegitimate hypotheses
  generally, 1.39
Illness
  pregnancy-related discrimination,
    and, 8.73
Impairment
  And see Disability discrimination
  ability to carry out normal day-to-day
    activities
    day-to-day activities, 3.25
    generally, 3.23
    normal, 3.24
  asymptomatic progressive
    conditions, 3.31
  burden of proof, 3.17
  coping strategies, 3.28
  day-to-day activities, 3.23
  deemed disability, 3.32
  medical treatment, 3.27
  mental impairment, 3.22
  normal day-to-day activities
    day-to-day activities, 3.25
    generally, 3.23
    normal, 3.24
  physical impairment, 3.21
  progressive conditions, 3.30–3.31
  severe disfigurements, 3.29
  substantial adverse effect, 3.26–3.32
In vitro fertilisation
  sex discrimination, and, 8.136

Indirect discrimination
age discrimination, and
  age group, 2.7
  generally, 2.7
  'provision criterion or practice', 2.7
burden of proof, and, 1.93
civil partnership, and, 5.5
colour, 1.43
compensation, and, 1.118
disability discrimination, and, 3.42
disability-related discrimination, and, 3.59
equal pay, and
  generally, 12.26
  'provision, criterion or practice', 12.27
  statistical differences, 12.28
introduction, 1.40
justification, 1.44
marital status, and, 5.5
nationality, 1.43
'particular disadvantage', 1.44
'personal disadvatnage', 1.44
'provision, criterion or practice'
  age discrimination, and, 2.7
  equal pay, and, 12.27
  generally, 1.44
  race discrimination, and, 6.16
race discrimination, and
  application of tests, 6.16–6.17
  disadvantage, 6.16
  introduction, 6.14
  justification, 6.17
  overview, 1.43
  proportionality, 6.16
  'provision, criterion or practice', 6.16
  tests, 6.15
sex discrimination, and
  generally, 8.22
  overview, 1.42
sexual orientation discrimination, and
  disadvantage, 9.10
  generally, 9.9
  proportionate means, 9.11
statistics, 1.44
statutory definition, 1.41
Induction training
disability discrimination, and 3.103
Information-gathering
religion and belief discrimination, and, 7.18
Injury to feelings
compensation, and, 1.119

Injury to feelings – *contd*
disability discrimination, and, 3.121
equal pay, and, 12.39
Institutional racism
race discrimination, and, 6.69–6.70
Instructions to discriminate
age discrimination, and, 2.10
race discrimination, and, 6.39
Insured benefits
age discrimination, and, 2.36
Interest
compensation, and, 1.122
Interpretation of statutory provisions
direct discrimination, 1.92
duty to make reasonable adjustments, 1.93
general principles, 1.91
indirect discrimination, 1.93
victimisation, 1.94
IVF
sex discrimination, and, 8.136

J
Job advertisements
age discrimination, and, 2.28
disability discrimination, and, 3.98
Job applicants
generally, 1.11
sex discrimination, and, 8.39
Job application forms
age discrimination, and, 2.30
disability discrimination, and, 3.98
Job descriptions
disability discrimination, and, 3.98
Job interviews
age discrimination, and, 2.31
disability discrimination, and, 3.98
Job specifications
age discrimination, and, 2.28
disability discrimination, and, 3.98
Job titles
age discrimination, and, 2.29
Jurisdiction of tribunals
age discrimination, and, 2.52
limitation period, 1.23
territorial scope, 1.24
Justification
age discrimination, and
  direct discrimination, and, 2.6
  generally, 2.8
  legitimate aims, 2.8
  proportionality, 2.8

Justification – *contd*
  disability discrimination, and
    direct discrimination, and, 3.46
    generally, 3.65
    'material and substantial' test, 3.66
    practice, in, 3.68
    reasonable adjustments, and, 3.67,
      3.84
  equal pay, and
    'after the event' justification, 12.36
    burden of proof, 12.22
    establishing 'taint' of
      discrimination, 12.26–12.29
    financial considerations, 12.31
    historic differences, 12.35
    introduction, 12.21
    length of service, 12.30
    market forces, 12.31
    material difference, 12.23–12.24
    mistake, 12.34
    objective justification, 12.25
    performance, 12.32
    red circling, 12.33
  fixed-term employees, and, 10.11
  indirect discrimination, and, 1.44
  part-time employees, and, 10.32
  race discrimination, and, 6.17

K
Keeping in touch days
  pregnancy-related discrimination,
    and, 8.115

L
Legislation
  codes of practice, 1.4
  general, 1.2
  Human Rights Act, 1.3
  Northern Ireland, 1.5
Legitimate aims
  age discrimination, and, 2.8
Length of service
  age discrimination, and, 2.35
  equal pay, and, 12.30
Less favourable treatment
  age discrimination, and, 2.6
  'but for' test, 1.30
  civil partnership, and, 5.4
  comparison with other forms of
    treatment, 1.29

Less favourable treatment – *contd*
  disability discrimination, and
    disability-related discrimination,
      and, 3.63
    Framework Directive, under, 3.42
    generally, 3.44
    pre-1 October 2004 position, 3.41
  fixed-term employees, and
    generally, 10.9
    justification, 10.11
    'on the ground that', 10.10
  gender reassignment, and, 4.5
  generally, 1.28
  marital status, and, 5.4
  motivation or intent, 1.30
  part-time employees, and
    generally, 10.27
    ground that worker is part-time
      worker, 10.31
    overtime, 10.29
    pro rate principle, 10.28
    statutory holidays, 10.30
  race discrimination, and
    comparators, 6.10
    distinction from unfavourable
      treatment, 6.9
    harassment, and, 6.29
    'on racial grounds', 6.11–6.13
    treatment, 6.8
    victimisation, and, 6.20
  reason, 1.30
  victimisation, and
    correct comparator, 1.59
    introduction, 1.58
Life assurance cover to retired workers
  age discrimination, and, 2.25
'Like work'
  equal pay, and, 12.13
Limitation period
  jurisdiction, and, 1.23
Loyalty
  age discrimination, and, 2.35

M
Marital status
  comparative jurisprudence, 5.9
  direct discrimination, 5.4
  exceptions and defences, 5.8
  harassment, 5.7
  indirect discrimination, 5.5
  introduction, 5.1
  less favourable treatment, 5.4
  married persons, 5.2

Marital status – *contd*
  sex discrimination, and, 8.28
  sexual orientation discrimination,
    and, 9.18
  stereotyping, 5.6
Market forces
  equal pay, and, 12.31
Material difference
  equal pay, and, 12.23–12.24
Maternity leave
  duration, 8.100
  eligibility, 8.97
  expected week of confinement, 8.98
  introduction, 8.96
  notice requirements, 8.98
  starting date, 8.99
Maternity pay
  amount, 8.105
  benefits during leave, 8.108–8.114
  bonuses, 8.112
  calculation, 8.105
  case law, 8.107
  claims, 8.113
  contractual, 8.106
  duration, 8.104
  eligibility, 8.102
  enhanced, 8.106
  holidays, 8.111
  introduction, 8.101
  notice requirements, 8.103
  notice of termination of
    employment, 8.110
  payment, 8.105
  period, 8.104
  repayment of enhancements, 8.114
Maternity-related discrimination
  ante-natal care
    appropriate hourly rate, 8.83
    complaint to tribunal, 8.84
    eligibility, 8.81
    expectant father's rights, 8.85
    generally, 8.79–8.85
    relevant care, 8.80
    unreasonable refusal of time off,
      8.82
  benefits during maternity leave,
    8.108–8.114
  claims, 8.119
  comparators, and, 8.71
  dismissal, and, 8.73
  equal pay, and, 12.18
  generally, 8.69
  health and safety
    duty to act to avoid risks, 8.91

Maternity-related discrimination – *contd*
  health and safety – *contd*
    exemptions to risk assessment, 8.94
    expectant mother risk assessment,
      8.88
    failure to carry out risk
      assessment, 8.95
    general risk assessment, 8.87
    individual risk assessment, 8.90
    introduction, 8.86
    notification of pregnancy, 8.89
    suitable alternative work, 8.92
    suspension from work, 8.93
  illness, 8.73
  keeping in touch days, 8.115
  maternity leave
    duration, 8.100
    eligibility, 8.97
    expected week of confinement,
      8.98
    introduction, 8.96
    notice requirements, 8.98
    starting date, 8.99
  maternity pay
    amount, 8.105
    benefits during leave, 8.108–8.114
    bonuses, 8.112
    calculation, 8.105
    case law, 8.107
    claims, 8.113
    contractual, 8.106
    duration, 8.104
    eligibility, 8.102
    enhanced, 8.106
    holidays, 8.111
    introduction, 8.101
    notice requirements, 8.103
    notice of termination of
      employment, 8.110
    payment, 8.105
    period, 8.104
    repayment of enhancements, 8.114
  overview, 8.26
  position of men, and, 8.72
  positive action, and, 1.107
  pre-1 October 2005 position, 8.68
  protected period, 8.70
  reasonable contact, 8.116
  remedies, 8.120
  return to work
    generally, 8.117
    temporary workers, 8.118
  time off for ante-natal care
    appropriate hourly rate, 8.83

Maternity-related discrimination – *contd*
  time off for ante-natal care – *contd*
    complaint to tribunal, 8.84
    eligibility, 8.81
    expectant father's rights, 8.85
    generally, 8.79–8.85
    relevant care, 8.80
    unreasonable refusal, 8.82
Medical evidence
  disability discrimination, and, 3.37
Medical model
  disability discrimination, and, 3.14
Medical treatment
  disability discrimination, and, 3.27
Mental impairment
  disability discrimination, and, 3.22
Minimum notice
  fixed-term employees, and, 10.17
Ministers of religion
  sex discrimination, and, 8.56
Misleading statements
  disability discrimination, and, 3.94
Mistake
  equal pay, and, 12.34
Monitoring
  religion and belief discrimination,
    and, 7.18

N
National minimum wage
  age discrimination, and, 2.21
National security
  age discrimination, and, 2.18
  disability discrimination, and, 3.111
  generally, 1.67
  race discrimination, and, 6.57
  sex discrimination, and, 8.61
  sexual orientation discrimination,
    and, 9.16
Negative discrimination
  sex discrimination, and, 8.7
Non-medical evidence
  disability discrimination, and, 3.38
Normal day-to-day activities
  disability discrimination, and, 3.23–
    3.25
Northern Ireland
  generally, 1.5
Notice periods
  age discrimination, and, 2.50

O
Objective justification
  And see Justification
  age discrimination, and
    direct discrimination, and, 2.6
    generally, 2.8
    legitimate aims, 2.8
    proportionality, 2.8
  equal pay, and, 12.25
Office-holders
  age discrimination, and, 2.14
  disability discrimination, and, 3.113
  generally, 1.19
  race discrimination, and, 6.61–6.62
  sex discrimination, and, 8.35
Overseas workers
  sex discrimination, and, 8.30
Overtime
  part-time employees, and, 10.29

P
Parental leave
  detriment, 8.132
  entitlement, 8.131
  return to work, 8.133
  unfair dismissal, 8.132
'Particular disadvantage'
  indirect discrimination, and, 1.44
Partnerships
  age discrimination, and, 2.14
  disability discrimination, and, 3.113
  generally, 1.12
  race discrimination, and, 6.66
  sex discrimination, and, 8.37
Part-time employees
  comparators, 10.25–10.26
  complaints to tribunals
    generally, 10.35
    remedies, 10.36–10.37
  detriment, 10.34
  employer's liability, 10.38
  guidance, 10.23
  impact of regulations, 10.22
  justification, 10.32
  legislative background, 10.20
  less favourable treatment
    generally, 10.27
    ground that worker is part-time
      worker, 10.31
    overtime, 10.29
    pro rate principle, 10.28
    statutory holidays, 10.30
  overtime, 10.29

Part-time employees – *contd*
persons covered, 10.24
pre-existing protection, 10.21
pro rata principle, 10.28
statutory holidays, 10.30
unfair dismissal, 10.34
victimisation, 10.34
written statements, 10.33
Paternity leave
additional leave, 8.140
detriment, 8.129
duration, 8.127
entitlement, 8.127
introduction, 8.126
pay, 8.128
unfair dismissal, 8.129
Pay and benefits
age discrimination, and
age conditions, 2.34
generally, 2.33
insured benefits, 2.36
length of service, 2.35
pension schemes, 2.36
disability discrimination, and, 3.105
Pecuniary loss
compensation, and, 1.117
Pension schemes
age discrimination, and, 2.14, 2.26,
2.36
disability discrimination, and, 3.113
Performance
equal pay, and, 12.32
Personal disadvantage
indirect discrimination, and, 1.44
Personal injury
compensation, and, 1.120
Personal liability
generally, 1.21
Personal work or services
employees, and, 1.8
Philosophical belief
religion and belief discrimination,
and, 7.4
Physical impairment
disability discrimination, and, 3.21
Police
age discrimination, and, 2.14
disability discrimination, and, 3.113
generally, 1.17
race discrimination, and
generally, 6.65
liability of Chief Police Officer,
6.45

Police – *contd*
sex discrimination, and
exceptions, 8.59
protected employees, 8.33
Poor treatment
direct discrimination, and, 1.29
Positive action
age discrimination, and
generally, 2.19
introduction, 1.105
disability discrimination, and, 1.106
exceptions and defences, and, 1.71
indirect discrimination, and, 1.108
introduction, 1.101
maternity, 1.107
pregnancy, 1.107
race discrimination
employees not ordinarily resident in
GB, 1.103
employees ordinarily resident in
GB, 1.102
religion or belief discrimination
employees not ordinarily resident in
GB, 1.103
employees ordinarily resident in
GB, 1.102
generally, 1.104
sex discrimination, and
elections, 8.65
generally, 8.63
introduction, 8.7
overview, 1.107
public authorities, 8.66
training, 8.64
sexual orientation discrimination, and
generally, 9.17
overview, 1.104
Predominant purpose of contract
employees, and, 1.8
Pregnancy
detriment, 8.78
dismissals
automatic unfair dismissal, 8.74
claims, 8.119
discrimination, 8.73
notice of termination, 8.76
redundancy, 8.75
written statement of reasons for
dismissal, 8.77
equal pay, and, 12.18
Pregnancy-related discrimination
ante-natal care
appropriate hourly rate, 8.83
complaint to tribunal, 8.84

Index

Pregnancy-related discrimination – *contd*
  ante-natal care – *contd*
    eligibility, 8.81
    expectant father's rights, 8.85
    generally, 8.79–8.85
    relevant care, 8.80
    unreasonable refusal of time off,
      8.82
  benefits during maternity leave,
    8.108–8.114
  claims, 8.119
  comparators, and, 8.71
  dismissal, and, 8.73
  equal pay, and, 12.18
  generally, 8.69
  health and safety
    duty to act to avoid risks, 8.91
    exemptions to risk assessment, 8.94
    expectant mother risk assessment,
      8.88
    failure to carry out risk
      assessment, 8.95
    general risk assessment, 8.87
    individual risk assessment, 8.90
    introduction, 8.86
    notification of pregnancy, 8.89
    suitable alternative work, 8.92
    suspension from work, 8.93
  illness, 8.73
  keeping in touch days, 8.115
  maternity leave
    duration, 8.100
    eligibility, 8.97
    expected week of confinement,
      8.98
    introduction, 8.96
    notice requirements, 8.98
    starting date, 8.99
  maternity pay
    amount, 8.105
    benefits during leave, 8.108–8.114
    bonuses, 8.112
    calculation, 8.105
    case law, 8.107
    claims, 8.113
    contractual, 8.106
    duration, 8.104
    eligibility, 8.102
    enhanced, 8.106
    holidays, 8.111
    introduction, 8.101
    notice requirements, 8.103
    notice of termination of
      employment, 8.110

Pregnancy-related discrimination – *contd*
  maternity pay – *contd*
    payment, 8.105
    period, 8.104
    repayment of enhancements, 8.114
  overview, 8.26
  position of men, and, 8.72
  positive action, and, 1.107
  pre-1 October 2005 position, 8.68
  protected period, 8.70
  reasonable contact, 8.116
  remedies, 8.120
  return to work
    generally, 8.117
    temporary workers, 8.118
  time off for ante-natal care
    appropriate hourly rate, 8.83
    complaint to tribunal, 8.84
    eligibility, 8.81
    expectant father's rights, 8.85
    generally, 8.79–8.85
    relevant care, 8.80
    unreasonable refusal, 8.82
Pressure to discriminate
  disability discrimination, and, 3.90
  race discrimination, and, 6.40
Principals
  generally, 1.10
Prison officers
  sex discrimination, and, 8.58
Pro rata principle
  part-time employees, and, 10.28
Progressive conditions
  disability discrimination, and, 3.30–
    3.31
Promotion
  disability discrimination, and, 3.104
  gender reassignment, and, 4.10
  sex discrimination, and, 8.41
Proportionate pay
  equal pay, and, 12.16
Proportionality
  age discrimination, and, 2.8
  race discrimination, and, 6.16
'Provision, criterion or practice
  disability discrimination, and, 3.74
  indirect discrimination, and', 1.44
  race discrimination, and, 6.16

Q
Qualifications
  disability discrimination, and, 3.98

Qualifications bodies
age discrimination, and,   2.14
disability discrimination, and,   3.113
generally,   1.15
race discrimination, and,   6.67
sex discrimination, and,   8.46
Questionnaires
age discrimination, and,   2.55
disability discrimination, and,   1.126
generally,   1.126
sexual orientation discrimination, and
generally,   9.20
overview,   1.126

R
Race discrimination
aiding an unlawful act,   6.44
armed forces,   6.64
benefits provided to the public,   6.55
burden of proof,   1.83–1.94
'by reason that',   6.21
common concepts
And see under individual headings
burden of proof,   1.83–1.94
comparators,   1.33–1.39
direct discrimination,   1.27–1.32
exceptions,   1.66–1.82
genuine occupational requirements
or qualifications,   1.95–1.100
harassment,   1.45–1.54
indirect discrimination,   1.40–1.44
introduction,   1.1
legislation,   1.2–1.6
particular parties,   1.7–1.26
positive action,   1.101–1.108
questionnaires,   1.126
sanctions, remedies and
enforcement,   1.115–1.125
vicarious liability,   1.109–1.114
victimisation,   1.55–1.65
comparators
generally,   6.10
harassment, and,   6.30
overview,   1.33–1.39
compliance with the law,   6.56
contract workers,   6.60
Crown employees,   6.63
direct discrimination
generally,   6.7
harassment, and,   6.28–6.31
less favourable treatment,   6.8–6.13
overview,   1.27–1.32
discriminatory advertisements,   6.38

Race discrimination – *contd*
discriminatory practices,   6.37
duty to promote race equality
generally,   6.69
impact on private employers,   6.70
employer's liability
agents' acts,   6.42
employees' acts,   6.41
third party acts,   6.43
employment agencies,   6.67
employment outside GB,   6.53
Equality and Human Rights
Commission,   6.68
exceptions and defences
benefits provided to the public,
6.55
compliance with the law,   6.56
employment outside GB,   6.53
generally,   1.78
genuine occupational requirements
or qualifications,   6.47
illegal contracts,   6.54
introduction,   6.46
national security,   6.57
overview,   1.76
private households,   6.49
seamen recruited abroad,   6.50
Sikhs and safety helmets,   6.52
skills to be exercised outside GB,
6.48
sports and competitions,   6.51
state immunity,   6.58
genuine occupational requirements or
qualifications
generally,   6.47
overview,   1.95–1.100
guidance,   6.2
harassment
comparators,   6.30
Crime and Disorder Act 1998,
and,   6.36
detriment,   6.31
dignity,   6.27
direct discrimination, as,   6.28–6.31
generally,   6.22
'having the purpose of effect of',
6.26
less favourable treatment,   6.29
'on grounds of',   6.24
other remedies, and,   6.33–6.36
overview,   1.48
Protection from Harassment
Act 1997, under,   6.34
Public Order Act 1986, under,   6.35

Race discrimination – *contd*
  harassment – *contd*
    Race Relations Act 1976, s 3A,
      under, 6.23–6.28
    stand-alone claim, as, 6.32
    unwanted conduct, 6.25
    working environments, 6.27
  illegal contracts, 6.54
  indirect discrimination
    application of tests, 6.16–6.17
    disadvantage, 6.16
    introduction, 6.14
    justification, 6.17
    overview, 1.43
    proportionality, 6.16
    'provision, criterion or practice',
      6.16
    tests, 6.15
  institutional racism, 6.69–6.70
  instructions to commit unlawful acts,
    6.39
  introduction, 1.1
  justification, 6.17
  legislative background
    generally, 6.1
    guidance, 6.2
    overview, 1.2–1.6
  less favourable treatment
    comparators, 6.10
    distinction from unfavourable
      treatment, 6.9
    harassment, and, 6.29
    'on racial grounds', 6.11–6.13
    treatment, 6.8
    victimisation, and, 6.20
  national security, 6.57
  non-employees, 6.59
  office holders, 6.61–6.62
  particular parties, 1.7–1.26
  partnerships, and
    generally, 6.66
    overview, 1.12
  police, and
    generally, 6.65
    liability of Chief Police Officer,
      6.45
  positive action
    employees not ordinarily resident in
      GB, 1.103
    employees ordinarily resident in
      GB, 1.102
  pressure to commit unlawful acts,
    6.40
  private households, 6.49

Race discrimination – *contd*
  proportionality, 6.16
  'provision, criterion or practice', 6.16
  qualifications bodies, 6.67
  questionnaires, 1.126
  race and racial grounds
    colour, 6.4
    ethnic origins, 6.5
    introduction, 6.3
    national origins, 6.6
    nationality, 6.6
    race, 6.5
  sanctions, remedies and enforcement,
    1.115–1.125
  seamen recruited abroad, 6.50
  Sikhs and safety helmets, 6.52
  skills to be exercised outside GB, 6.48
  sports and competitions, 6.51
  state immunity, 6.58
  trade organisations, 6.67
  types
    aiding an unlawful act, 6.44
    direct discrimination, 6.7
    discriminatory advertisements, 6.38
    discriminatory practices, 6.37
    employer's liability, 6.41–6.43
    harassment, 6.22–6.36
    indirect discrimination, 6.14–6.17
    instructions to commit unlawful
      acts, 6.39
    less favourable treatment, 6.8–6.13
    pressure to commit unlawful acts,
      6.40
    victimisation, 6.18–6.21
  vicarious liability, 1.109–1.114
  victimisation
    'by reason that', 6.21
    introduction, 6.18
    less favourable treatment, 6.20
    overview, 1.55–1.65
    protected act, 6.19
  vocational training providers, and
    generally, 6.67
    overview, 1.14

Reasonable adjustments
  anticipatory duty, and, 3.72
  comparators, 3.77
  'core' requirements of job, 3.80
  direct discrimination, and, 3.55
  examples, 3.78
  factors to be taken into account, 3.83
  failure to assess or consult, 3.81
  features of premises occupied by
    employer, 3.75

Reasonable adjustments – *contd*
generally, 3.69
justification, and, 3.67, 3.84
knowledge by employer, 3.73
persons to whom duty owed, 3.71
polices and procedures, to, 3.79
pre-1 October 2004 position, 3.41
preliminary considerations, 3.70
problem areas, 3.85
'provision, criterion or practice', 3.74
reasonableness, 3.82
substantial disadvantage, 3.76
Recommendation for action
generally, 1.124
Recruitment
age discrimination, and
advertisements, 2.28
application forms, 2.30
interviews, 2.31
introduction, 2.27
job specifications, 2.28
job titles, 2.29
methods, 2.32
employment agencies, and, 1.26
gender reassignment, and, 4.10
religion and belief discrimination,
and, 7.14
Recurring effects
disability discrimination, and, 3.35
Red circling
equal pay, and, 12.33
Redundancy
age discrimination, and
criteria, 2.49
enhanced schemes, 2.49
statutory pay, 2.49
fixed-term employees, and, 10.19
pregnancy-related discrimination,
and, 8.75
Religion and belief discrimination
burden of proof, 1.83–1.94
common concepts
And see under individual headings
burden of proof, 1.83–1.94
comparators, 1.33–1.39
direct discrimination, 1.27–1.32
exceptions, 1.66–1.82
genuine occupational requirements
or qualifications, 1.95–1.100
harassment, 1.45–1.54
indirect discrimination, 1.40–1.44
introduction, 1.1
legislation, 1.2–1.6
particular parties, 1.7–1.26

Religion and belief discrimination – *contd*
common concepts – *contd*
positive action, 1.101–1.108
questionnaires, 1.126
sanctions, remedies and
enforcement, 1.115–1.125
vicarious liability, 1.109–1.114
victimisation, 1.55–1.65
comparators, 1.33–1.39
direct discrimination, 1.27–1.32
employment, in, 7.9
exceptions, 1.66–1.82
genuine occupational requirements
generally, 7.10
overview, 1.95–1.100
harassment
generally, 7.8
overview, 1.45–1.54
indirect discrimination, 1.40–1.44
information-gathering, 7.18
introduction, 7.1
legislative background
generally, 7.3
overview, 1.2–1.6
monitoring, 7.18
particular parties, 1.7–1.26
"philosophical belief", 7.4
positive action,
employees not ordinarily resident in
GB, 1.103
employees ordinarily resident in
GB, 1.102
generally, 1.104
practical considerations, 7.13–7.18
pre-existing protection, 7.2
questionnaires, 1.126
recruitment, 7.14
"religion", 7.3
"religious belief", 7.3
sanctions, remedies and enforcement,
1.115–1.125
sexual orientation discrimination,
and, 9.19
special treatment, 7.17
vicarious liability, 1.109–1.114
victimisation
generally, 7.8
overview, 1.55–1.65
vocational training providers, and,
1.14
working time, 7.15
Relocation
gender reassignment, and, 4.11

Index

Restricted reporting orders
disability discrimination, and,   3.119
Retirement
appeals,   2.44
default retirement age,   2.39
definitions,   2.44
disciplinary and grievance procedures,
   and,   2.44
duty of employer to consider request
   not to retire,   2.44
duty of employer to notify of intended
   retirement,   2.44
failure to comply with duties,   2.44
introduction,   2.38
justification,   2.40
legal challenge to default age,   2.41
meaning,   2.42
meeting to discuss request not to
   retire,   2.44
other circumstances, in,   2.40
overview,   2.20
procedure,   2.43–2.44
right of employee to request not to
   retire,   2.44
right to be accompanied,   2.44
Return to work
generally,   8.117
parental leave, and,   8.133
temporary workers,   8.118

S
Sanctions, remedies and enforcement
age discrimination, and
   burden of proof,   2.54
   jurisdiction of tribunals,   2.52
   questionnaires,   2.55
   remedies,   2.56
   time limits,   2.57
compensation
   aggravated damages,   1.121
   exemplary damages,   1.121
   indirect discrimination,   1.118
   injury to feelings,   1.119
   interest,   1.122
   pecuniary loss,   1.117
   personal injury,   1.120
declaration of rights,   1.123
disability discrimination, and
   ACAS,   3.124
   complaints to tribunal,   3.116–3.122
   Equality and Human Rights
      Commission,   3.123
   injury to feelings,   3.121

Sanctions, remedies and enforcement –
   contd
disability discrimination, and – *contd*
   questionnaire process,   3.122
   remedies,   3.120
   restricted reporting orders,   3.119
   statutory grievance procedure,
      3.117
   time limits for claims,   3.118
equal pay, and
   arrears of pay,   12.38
   declaration of unequal pay,   12.40
   generally,   12.37
   injury to feelings,   12.39
   overview,   1.115–1.125
   Equality and Human Rights
      Commission,   1.125
gender reassignment, and,   4.8
procedure,   1.116
recommendation for action,   1.124
sexual orientation discrimination,
   and,   9.20
summary,   1.115
Seamen recruited abroad
race discrimination, and,   6.50
Selection
employment agencies, and,   1.26
gender reassignment, and,   4.10
Serious Organised Crime Agency
age discrimination, and,   2.14
Severe disfigurements
disability discrimination, and,   3.29
Sex discrimination
ACAS guidance,   8.19
adoption, and
   detriment,   8.123
   disrupted placement,   8.124
   leave,   8.121
   overseas adoption,   8.125
   pay,   8.122
   unfair dismissal,   8.123
advocates,   8.38
armed forces,   8.34
barristers,   8.38
benefits, facilities and services,   8.42
burden of proof
   generally,   8.29
   overview,   1.83–1.94
charities,   8.62
civil partnerships, and,   8.28
codes of practice
   ACAS,   8.19
   Departmental guidance,   8.19
   generally,   8.25

Sex discrimination – *contd*
  codes of practice – *contd*
    EHRC, 8.18
  common concepts
    And see under individual headings
    burden of proof, 1.83–1.94
    comparators, 1.33–1.39
    direct discrimination, 1.27–1.32
    exceptions, 1.66–1.82
    genuine occupational requirements
      or qualifications, 1.95–1.100
    harassment, 1.45–1.54
    indirect discrimination, 1.40–1.44
    introduction, 1.1
    legislation, 1.2–1.6
    particular parties, 1.7–1.26
    positive action, 1.101–1.108
    questionnaires, 1.126
    sanctions, remedies and
      enforcement, 1.115–1.125
    vicarious liability, 1.109–1.114
    victimisation, 1.55–1.65
  comparators, 1.33–1.39
  contract workers, 8.36
  Crown employment, 8.32
  definitions, 8.5
  detriment, 8.43
  direct discrimination
    generally, 8.21
    overview, 1.27–1.32
  dismissal, 8.43
  EC law
    Charter of Fundamental Rights,
      8.14
    ECJ judgments, 8.15
    Equal Treatment Directive, 8.12
    introduction, 8.10
    other Directives, 8.13
    Recommendations, 8.16
    Treaty of Rome, 8.11
  educational appointments, 8.57
  elections, 8.65
  employees, 8.30–8.31
  employment agencies, 8.48
  equal pay, and, 8.8
  Equality and Human Rights
    Commission, and
    code of practice, 8.18
    generally, 8.17
  exceptions and defences
    communal accommodation, 8.54
    benefits, facilities or services, 8.50
    generally, 1.66–1.82

Sex discrimination – *contd*
  exceptions and defences – *contd*
    genuine occupational
      qualifications, 8.55
    insurance, 8.53
    introduction, 8.49
    maternity leave, 8.51
    occupational pensions, 8.52
    overview, 1.75
    sport, 8.54
  facilities, 8.42
  family-friendly provisions, 8.9
  flexible working, and
    applicants, 8.141
    complaints to tribunal, 8.146–8.149
    consideration of request, 8.144
    detriment, 8.149
    employer's response to request,
      8.143
    generally, 8.140
    indirect discrimination, 8.147
    remedies where request refused,
      8.145
    request, 8.142
    unfair dismissal, 8.149
  former employees, 8.44
  gender reassignment, 8.27
  genuine occupational requirements or
    qualifications, 1.95–1.100
  harassment
    generally, 8.24
    overview, 1.48
  indirect discrimination
    generally, 8.22
    overview, 1.42
  introduction, 8.1
  IVF, and, 8.136
  job applicants, 8.39
  legislative framework
    generally, 8.20
    introduction, 8.1
    overview, 1.2–1.6
  limitations in scope
    equal pay, 8.8
    generally, 8.6
    negative discrimination, 8.7
    positive discrimination, 8.7
  marital status, 8.28
  maternity, and
    automatic unfair dismissal, 8.74
    benefits during maternity leave,
      8.108–8.114
    claims, 8.73, 8.119
    comparators, and, 8.71

Index

Sex discrimination – *contd*
  maternity, and – *contd*
    detriment, 8.78
    generally, 8.69
    health and safety, 8.86–8.95
    illness, 8.73
    keeping in touch days, 8.115
    maternity leave, 8.96–8.100
    maternity pay, 8.101–8.107
    notice of termination, 8.76
    overview, 8.26
    position of men, and, 8.72
    pre-1 October 2005 position, 8.68
    protected period, 8.70
    reasonable contact, 8.116
    redundancy, 8.75
    remedies, 8.120
    return to work, 8.117–8.118
    time off for ante-natal care, 8.79–8.85
    written statement of reasons for dismissal, 8.77
  ministers of religion, 8.56
  national security, 8.61
  negative discrimination, 8.7
  office-holders, 8.35
  overseas workers, 8.30
  parental leave, and
    detriment, 8.132
    entitlement, 8.131
    return to work, 8.133
    unfair dismissal, 8.132
  partnerships, 8.37
  paternity leave, and
    additional leave, 8.140
    detriment, 8.129
    duration, 8.127
    entitlement, 8.127
    introduction, 8.126
    pay, 8.128
    unfair dismissal, 8.129
  police
    exceptions, 8.59
    protected employees, 8.33
  positive action
    elections, 8.65
    generally, 8.63
    introduction, 8.7
    overview, 1.107
    public authorities, 8.66
    training, 8.64
  pregnancy, and
    automatic unfair dismissal, 8.74

Sex discrimination – *contd*
  pregnancy, and – *contd*
    benefits during maternity leave, 8.108–8.114
    claims, 8.73, 8.119
    comparators, and, 8.71
    detriment, 8.78
    generally, 8.69
    health and safety, 8.86–8.95
    illness, 8.73
    keeping in touch days, 8.115
    maternity leave, 8.96–8.100
    maternity pay, 8.101–8.107
    notice of termination, 8.76
    overview, 8.26
    position of men, and, 8.72
    pre-1 October 2005 position, 8.68
    protected period, 8.70
    reasonable contact, 8.116
    redundancy, 8.75
    remedies, 8.120
    return to work, 8.117–8.118
    time off for ante-natal care, 8.79–8.85
    written statement of reasons for dismissal, 8.77
  prison officers, 8.58
  promotion, 8.41
  protected persons
    advocates, 8.38
    armed forces, 8.34
    barristers, 8.38
    contract workers, 8.36
    Crown employment, 8.32
    employees, 8.30–8.31
    introduction, 8.2
    office-holders, 8.35
    overseas workers, 8.30
    partnerships, 8.37
    police, 8.33
  public authorities, 8.66
  qualifying bodies, 8.46
  questionnaires, 1.126
  sanctions, remedies and enforcement, 1.115–1.125
  services, 8.42
  sexual harassment, 8.24
  statutory authority, 8.60
  surrogacy, and
    generally, 8.137
    intended parents, 8.139
    taking responsibility for child, 8.138

Sex discrimination – *contd*
  time off for dependants
    complaints to tribunal, 8.135
    entitlement, 8.134
  trade organisations, 8.45
  training
    generally, 8.41
    positive action, 8.64
  transfer, 8.41
  types
    direct discrimination, 8.21
    harassment, 8.24
    indirect discrimination, 8.22
    introduction, 8.3
    sexual harassment, 8.24
    specific provisions, 8.4
    victimisation, 8.23
  vicarious liability
    generally, 8.67
    overview, 1.109–1.114
  victimisation
    generally, 8.23
    overview, 1.55–1.65
  vocational training providers, and
    generally, 8.47
    overview, 1.14

Sexual harassment
  generally, 8.24

Sexual orientation discrimination
  burden of proof, 1.83–1.94
  common concepts
    And see under individual headings
    burden of proof, 1.83–1.94
    comparators, 1.33–1.39
    direct discrimination, 1.27–1.32
    exceptions, 1.66–1.82
    genuine occupational requirements
      or qualifications, 1.95–1.100
    harassment, 1.45–1.54
    indirect discrimination, 1.40–1.44
    introduction, 1.1
    legislation, 1.2–1.6
    particular parties, 1.7–1.26
    positive action, 1.101–1.108
    questionnaires, 1.126
    sanctions, remedies and
      enforcement, 1.115–1.125
    vicarious liability, 1.109–1.114
    victimisation, 1.55–1.65
  comparators
    generally, 9.7
    overview, 1.33–1.39
  definition, 9.4

Sexual orientation discrimination – *contd*
  direct discrimination
    comparators, 9.7
    generally, 9.5
    meaning, 9.6
    'on the grounds of', 9.8
    overview, 1.27–1.32
  enforcement
    generally, 9.20
    overview, 1.115–1.125
  exceptions
    genuine occupational
      requirements, 9.15
    marital status, 9.18
    national security, 9.16
    overview, 1.66–1.82
    positive action, 9.17
  genuine occupational requirements
    generally, 9.15
    overview, 1.95–1.100
  goods and services, 9.21
  guidance, 9.3
  harassment
    generally, 9.13
    overview, 1.45–1.54
  indirect discrimination
    disadvantage, 9.10
    generally, 9.9
    overview, 1.40–1.44
    proportionate means, 9.11
  introduction, 9.1
  legislation, 1.2–1.6
  marital status, 9.18
  national security, 9.16
  'on the grounds of', 9.8
  particular parties, 1.7–1.26
  positive action
    generally, 9.17
    overview, 1.104
  pre-existing protection, 9.2
  questionnaires
    generally, 9.20
    overview, 1.126
  religion and belief discrimination,
    and, 9.19
  sanctions, remedies and enforcement
    generally, 9.20
    overview, 1.115–1.125
  'sexual orientation', 9.4
  unlawful discrimination, 9.14
  vicarious liability, 1.109–1.114
  victimisation
    generally, 9.12
    overview, 1.55–1.65

Index

Sexual orientation discrimination – *contd*
vocational training providers, and,
1.14

Sikhs
safety helmets, and,   6.52

Single sex facilities
gender reassignment, and,   4.11

Skills to be exercised outside GB
race discrimination, and,   6.48

Sport
exceptions and defences, and,   1.72

Sports and competitions
race discrimination, and,   6.51

State immunity
exceptions and defences, and,   1.81
race discrimination, and,   6.58

Statistics
indirect discrimination, and,   1.44

Statutory authority
age discrimination, and,   2.17
disability discrimination, and,   3.111
generally,   1.69
sex discrimination, and,   8.60

Statutory dispute and grievance resolution procedures
age discrimination, and,   2.44
disability discrimination, and,   3.117
equal pay, and,   12.41
harassment, and,   1.53

Stereotypical assumptions
civil partnership, and,   5.6
direct discrimination, and,   1.32
marital status, and,   5.6

Substantial adverse effect
asymptomatic progressive
conditions,   3.31
coping strategies,   3.28
deemed disability,   3.32
medical treatment,   3.27
progressive conditions,   3.30–3.31
severe disfigurements,   3.29

Surrogacy
generally,   8.137
intended parents,   8.139
taking responsibility for child,   8.138

T

Termination of employment
age discrimination, and
notice periods,   2.50
redundancy,   2.49
retirement,   2.38–2.44
unfair dismissal,   2.45–2.49

Termination of employment – *contd*
disability discrimination, and,   3.107

Terms and conditions of employment
disability discrimination, and
generally,   3.102
offers,   3.99
equal pay, and,   12.19

Terms of supply
employment agencies, and,   1.26

Territorial scope
jurisdiction, and,   1.24

Time off for ante-natal care
appropriate hourly rate,   8.83
complaint to tribunal,   8.84
eligibility,   8.81
expectant father's rights,   8.85
generally,   8.79–8.85
relevant care,   8.80
unreasonable refusal,   8.82

Time off for dependants
complaints to tribunal,   8.135
entitlement,   8.134

Time off for medical treatment
gender reassignment, and,   4.11

Trade organisations
age discrimination, and,   2.14
disability discrimination, and,   3.113
race discrimination, and,   6.67
sex discrimination, and,   8.45

Training
disability discrimination, and,   3.103
gender reassignment, and,   4.10
sex discrimination, and
generally,   8.41
positive action,   8.64

U

Unfair dismissal
adoption-related discrimination, and,
8.123
fixed-term employees, and,   10.14
flexible working, and,   8.149
parental leave-related discrimination,
and,   8.132
part-time employees, and,   10.34
paternity-related discrimination, and,
8.129
pregnancy-related dismissals, and,
8.74

Unlawful discrimination
sexual orientation discrimination,
and,   9.14

V

Vacancies
fixed-term employees, and, 10.13

Vicarious liability
disability discrimination, and, 3.91–3.92
employees, for
defence, 1.111
generally, 1.110
personal liability, 1.112
Protection from Harassment Act, under, 1.113
introduction, 1.109
sex discrimination, and, 8.67
third parties acts, for, 1.114

Victimisation
age discrimination, and, 2.9
burden of proof
generally, 1.64
interpretation of statutory provisions, 1.94
'by reason that', 1.59
comparators, 1.59
conscious motivation, 1.60
disability discrimination, and, 3.88
EC legislation, 1.57
good faith, 1.63
'honest and reasonable' exception, 1.61
introduction, 1.55
less favourable treatment
correct comparator, 1.59
introduction, 1.58
nature of claim, 1.65
overview, 1.55–1.65
part-time employees, and, 10.34

Victimisation – *contd*
protected acts, 1.62
race discrimination, and
'by reason that', 6.21
introduction, 6.18
less favourable treatment, 6.20
protected act, 6.19
religion and belief discrimination, and, 7.8
sex discrimination, and, 8.23
sexual orientation discrimination, and, 9.12
UK legislation, 1.56
unconscious motivation, 1.60

Vocational training providers
generally, 1.14
race discrimination, and, 6.67
sex discrimination, and, 8.47

W

Wheelchair users
disability discrimination, and, 3.54

Work experience
disability discrimination, and, 3.113
partnerships, and, 1.13

'Work of equal value'
equal pay, and, 12.15

'Work rated as equivalent'
equal pay, and, 12.14

Working time
religion and belief discrimination, and, 7.15

Written statements
fixed-term employees, and, 10.12
part-time employees, and, 10.33